Armageddon

ARMAGEDDON

The Battle for Germany 1944–1945

MAX HASTINGS

ALFRED A. KNOPF · NEW YORK · 2004

THIS IS A BORZOI BOOK
PUBLISHED BY ALFRED A. KNOPF

Copyright © 2004 by Max Hastings
All rights reserved under International and Pan-American Copyright Conventions.
Published in the United States by Alfred A. Knopf, a division of Random House, Inc.,
New York, and simultaneously in Canada by Random House of Canada Limited,
Toronto. Distributed by Random House, Inc., New York. Published in Great Britain by
Macmillan, an imprint of Pan Macmillan, London. Knopf, Borzoi Books, and the
colophon are registered trademarks of Random House, Inc.
www.aaknopf.com

Library of Congress Cataloging-in-Publication Data

Hastings, Max.
Armageddon : the battle for Germany, 1944–1945 / Max Hastings.—1st American ed.
p. cm.
Includes bibliographical references and index.
ISBN 0-375-41433-9
1. World War, 1939–1945—Campaigns—Europe.   I. Title
D743.H36 2004
940.54'21—dc22   2004046468

Printed in the United States of America
First American Edition

For Penny, who makes it all possible

*Tonight the sun goes down on more suffering
than ever before in the world.*

—Winston Churchill, 6 February 1945

*We were living an existence in which people's lives had absolutely no value.
All that seemed important was to stay alive oneself.*

—Lieutenant Gennady Ivanov, Red Army

CONTENTS

INTRODUCTION

A dictionary defines Armageddon: "The site of the decisive battle on the Day of Judgement; hence, a final contest on a grand scale." The last campaigns of the Second World War in Europe locked in bloody embrace more than a hundred million people within and without the frontiers of Hitler's Greater Reich. Their outcome drastically influenced the lives of many more. The Second World War was the most disastrous human experience in history. Its closing months provided an appropriately terrible climax.

Armageddon has its origins in my earlier book *Overlord*, which described the 1944 D-Day invasion of Europe and the campaign in Normandy. The narrative ended with the American and British breakthrough in August, followed by a triumphant dash across France. Many Allied soldiers believed that the collapse of Hitler's empire must swiftly follow. I concluded *Overlord*:

> The battles in Holland and along the German border so often seem to belong to a different age from those of Normandy that it is startling to reflect that Arnhem was fought less than a month after Falaise; that within weeks of suffering one of the greatest catastrophes of modern history, the Germans found the strength . . . to prolong the war until May 1945. If this phenomenon reveals the same staggering qualities in Hitler's armies which had caused the Allies such grief in Normandy, it is also another story.

The early part of this book is that story. The starting point was a desire to satisfy my own curiosity about why the German war did not end in 1944, given the Allies' overwhelming superiority. It is often asserted that in the west they had to overcome a succession of great rivers and difficult natural features to break into Hitler's heartland. Yet the Germans' 1940 blitzkrieg easily surmounted such obstacles. In 1944–45, the Allies were masters of armoured and air forces greater than the Nazis ever possessed.

Most works on the last months of the war address either the Eastern or Western Fronts. This one aspires to view the story as a whole. The Soviets were separated from the Anglo-Americans not only by Hitler's armies, but by a political, military and moral abyss. I have attempted to explore each side of this, to set in context the battles of Patton and Zhukov, Montgomery and Rokossovsky. I have, however, omitted the Italian campaign. It exercised a significant indirect influence upon the struggle for Germany, absorbing a tenth of the Wehrmacht's strength in 1944–45, but its inclusion would have overwhelmed my narrative. Beyond archival research, I have met some 170 contemporary witnesses in Russia, Germany, Britain, the United States and Holland. This is the last decade in which it will be possible usefully to conduct such interviews. Many people recall their experiences vividly, but they are growing very old. Those fresh, fit, vital, often brave and handsome young men, whose deeds decided the fate of Europe sixty years ago, are today stooped and frail, the destiny of us all.

It was helpful to me that a generation ago, when researching earlier books, I met American and British generals and airmen who held senior posts such as Air Chief Marshal Sir Arthur Harris, Generals "Pete" Quesada, James Gavin, J. Lawton Collins, and "Pip" Roberts. Today's surviving military witnesses rarely held ranks beyond that of major. For the perspective of senior officers, in this book I have drawn extensively upon unpublished manuscripts and oral-history interviews, of which rich collections exist in the United States, Britain and Germany. All historians are grateful for the recent flood of privately published veterans' memoirs. Because this book portrays a human tragedy, rather than a mere battlefield saga, I have also interviewed Russian and German women. Their wartime experiences deserve more attention than they have so far received, other than as victims of rape.

In *Overlord,* I argued that Hitler's army was the outstanding fighting force of the Second World War. There has since been a revisionist movement against such a view. Several writers, notably in the United States, have written books arguing that authors such as myself overrate the German performance. Some of the revisionists cannot be acquitted of nationalistic exuberance. An American military historian of my acquaintance observed justly, and without envy, that a best-selling colleague had "taken to raising monuments rather than writing history," by producing a series of volumes which pay homage to the American fighting man.

A U.S. veteran of the north-west Europe campaign praises the works of Stephen Ambrose, saying: "They make me and my kind feel really good about ourselves." There is absolutely nothing wrong with the creation of romantic records of military experience, which bring a glow to the hearts of many readers, as long as their limitations as history are understood. This book, too, tries to bring alive the experience of those who fought. Its chief purpose, however, is objective analysis. The defence of Germany against overwhelming odds reflected far more remarkable military skills than those displayed by the attackers, especially when all German operations had to be conducted under the dead hand of Hitler. Since I wrote *Overlord,* however, my own thinking has changed—not about the battlefield performance of the combatants, but about its significance. Moral and social issues are at stake, more important than any narrow military judgement.

A cultural collision took place in Germany in 1945, between societies whose experience of the Second World War was light years apart. What the Soviet and German peoples did, as well as what was done to them, bore scant resemblance to the war the American and British knew. There was a chasm between the world of the Western allies, populated by men still striving to act temperately, and the Eastern universe in which, on both sides, elemental passions dominated. Although some individuals in Eisenhower's armies suffered severely, the experience of most falls within a recognizable compass of what happens to people in wars. The battle of Arnhem, for instance, is perceived as an epic. Yet the entire combat experience of many British participants was compressed into a few days. Barely three thousand men died on the Allied side. Among British veterans of north-west Europe, Captain Lord Carrington remembers with considerable affection his service with the Grenadier Guards tank regiment: "We'd been together a long time. It may sound an odd thing to say, but it was a very happy period. We were young and adventurous. We were winning. One had all one's friends with one. We were a happy family." I do not extrapolate from this that British or American soldiers enjoyed themselves. Few sane people like war. But many found 1944–45 not unbearable, if they were fortunate enough to escape mutilation or death. Hardly any Americans felt the hatred for the Germans which Pearl Harbor, together with the Japanese cultural ethic expressed in the Bataan Death March, engendered towards the soldiers of Nippon.

It is a sombre experience, by contrast, to interview Russian and German veterans. They endured horrors of a different order of magnitude. It was not uncommon for them to serve with a fighting formation for years on end, wounds prompting the only interruptions. The lives of Stalin's subjects embraced unspeakable miseries, even before the Nazis entered the story. I have met many people whose families perished in the famines and purges of the pre-1941 era. One man described to me how his parents, illiterate peasants, were anonymously denounced by neighbours as counter-revolutionaries, and shot in 1938 at a prison outside Leningrad—the modern St. Petersburg. A woman listening to our conversation interjected: "My parents were shot at that prison too!" She employed the commonplace tones one might use in New York or London on discovering that an acquaintance had attended the same school.

After she spoke, another woman said darkly: "You shouldn't talk about things like that in front of a foreigner." In Russia, there is no tradition of pursuing objective historical truth. Even in the twenty-first century it remains difficult to persuade a fiercely nationalistic people to speak frankly about the bleaker aspects of their wartime history. Almost all important research on the wartime era is being done by foreigners rather than Russians who—led by their president—prefer to draw a veil across Stalin's years. Some twenty-seven million Soviet citizens died in the war,* while combined U.S., British and French combat fatalities amounted to less than one million. Yet respect for the achievement of the Red Army does nothing to diminish repugnance towards Stalin's tyranny, entirely as evil as that of Hitler, and towards the deeds that were done in Russia's name in eastern Europe. The Americans and British, God be thanked, inhabited a different universe from that of the Russian soldier.

As for the Germans, a few years ago I stood in front of a television camera on Hitler's rostrum at Nuremberg and said how much I admired the courage with which the post-war generation had confronted the Nazi legacy. After we finished filming our researcher, a young German woman who has worked on many documentaries about the period, intervened. "Excuse me," she said. "I think you are wrong. I believe our people are still in denial about the war." I have since thought a great deal about what she said, and concluded that she is partly right. Many young Germans are extraordinarily ignorant about the Nazi period. Some older ones seem less troubled by historic guilt today than when I first began meeting their generation, a quarter of a century ago. It is as if the horrors of the Nazi years were committed by people quite unrelated to the law-abiding pensioners who now occupy comfortable urban and suburban homes in Munich or Stuttgart, Nuremberg or Dresden, citizens in good standing of the European Union.

A woman described to me how, in May 1945, she stood with her terrified mother and siblings in a villa on the Baltic when two Russian officers burst in. One began to harangue them in fluent German about the crimes of their country in the Soviet Union. "It was so awful," she said, "having to listen to all this, when we knew that we had done nothing wrong." It was hardly surprising that she felt this, as a teenager back in 1945. It seems surprising that her view was unchanged in 2002. There is a growing assertiveness in Germany about the war crimes of the Allies. I share the view of German historians, such as Jorg Friedrich, that the British and Americans should more honestly confront their undoubted lapses, some of them serious. For instance, more than a few Germans were hanged in 1945 for killing prisoners. Such behaviour was not uncommon among Allied personnel, yet it seldom, if ever, provoked disciplinary action. New Zealanders massacred medical staff and wounded men at a Ger-

*Some modern estimates now place this figure as high as forty million, and it is unlikely that any conclusive total will be agreed.

man aid station in North Africa in June 1942. No one was ever called to account, though the episode is well documented. The British submarine commander "Skip" Miers systematically machine-gunned German survivors after sinking their ships in the Mediterranean in 1941. Any captured Nazi U-boat commander would have been executed in 1945 for such action. Miers, by contrast, received the Victoria Cross and became an admiral.

I suggested to Jorg Friedrich in a television debate, however, that it might be wise for a German to hesitate before saying anything which implies a moral equivalence between Allied excesses and the crimes of the Nazis. I admire the attitude of Helmut Schmidt, Germany's former chancellor, whom I interviewed about his wartime service as a Luftwaffe flak officer. Asked his opinion about the behaviour of the Red Army in East Prussia, he responded: "You will never hear me, as a German, say anything that suggests a comparison between what happened in East Prussia and the behaviour of Germany's army in the Soviet Union."

Some of Hitler's old adherents remain impenitent, of course. Interviewing a former Waffen SS captain at his home, I noticed on the wall of the lounge his medals and unit badges, which twenty years ago would have been discreetly closeted. After listening to his remarkable tale, I said, intending irony, that he seemed to have enjoyed his experience as a soldier. "*Ach*, they were great days!" he exclaimed. "The two biggest moments of my life were taking the oath to Hitler's bodyguard in 1934, and Nuremberg in 1936. You have seen the films—the searchlights, the crowds, the Führer? I was there! I was there!" Another proud veteran of Hitler's Leibstandarte inquired whether I might be interested in helping him to write his memoirs.

The vast majority of men and women who witness great events recall these solely in terms of personal experience. I met a German woman whose anger about the occupation of her house by GIs, the casual theft of cherished possessions, remained as great in 2002 as it had been in 1945. It would have been meaningless to suggest that she should set her grievances in the context of the mass murder of the Jews, the devastation of Europe, the destitution of millions. Only personal experience possessed real significance for her.

I have described the military campaign for Germany, but have made no attempt to embrace every action. This book is a portrait, not an official history. It concentrates on episodes which seem especially significant, and individual experiences which illustrate wider truths. My purpose is to consider how and why things happened, or did not happen, rather than to rehearse familiar narratives. I have dealt briefly with matters discussed in *Overlord*, such as the importance of the inferiority of many Allied weapons, and especially tanks, to those of the Germans. There is likewise little here about the Battle of Berlin. That story has been often told, most recently by the admirable Antony Beevor. For the Berlin battle, I have focused chiefly upon material hitherto unpublished, especially from Russian archives. Some episodes which must be discussed, such as Arnhem and the Battle of the Bulge, cannot fail to be familiar. Yet other sagas, such as those of East Prussia and the Dutch *Hongerwinter*, are amazingly little known. It seems fruitless to revisit the last days of Hitler and his fellow gangsters in the bunker, about which a huge popular pornography exists. This is a book chiefly about ordinary human beings, to whom extraordinary things happened. Although a few of the people I have interviewed are today famous men—Dr. Henry Kissinger, Chancellor Helmut Schmidt, Lord Carrington—most, by intent, are not.

I have devoted a chapter to prisoners of the Reich. Beyond the Jews who were explicitly destined for death, millions of other people were captives or slave labourers in Germany in 1945. It was a revelation to hear a survivor of several concentration camps observe: "In Auschwitz, you were either alive or you were dead. I have been in worse camps." Some soldiers ask: did it matter that the Allies took so long to liberate Germany? It was an issue of vital moment for hundreds of thousands of Hitler's subjects and captives who died in 1945, some of whom would have lived if their deliverers had been able to hasten just a very little more. Consider for instance Victor Klemperer, the Dresden Jew whose awesome diary records his fears and expectation of death, through almost every day of the war years. "Perhaps the annihilation of the English 'air landing division' at Arnhem is an unimportant, soon to be forgotten episode," he wrote on 21 September 1944, "but it is extremely important to me today."

I hope that readers of this book will find much that is new to them, as its discovery was new to me. Even after fifteen years' exposure to Western historians, Russian archives remain wonderful sources of new material. I feel no embarrassment about sometimes accepting conventional wisdom. After almost sixty years, it is unlikely that great secrets remain to be revealed about the conduct of the Second World War. The challenge is to improve our perspective upon it, and to reinterpret available evidence. Most new books which claim to have uncovered sensational revelations about the war prove to be rubbish. In the eighteenth century Oliver Goldsmith took a view noted by Boswell: "When Goldsmith began to write, he determined to commit to paper nothing but what was new; but he afterwards found that what was new was generally false, and from that time was no longer solicitous about novelty." I remain "solicitous about novelty," but follow Goldsmith's unwillingness to pursue innovation for its own sake. Many of the stories in this book are not state secrets—they simply represent the setting down of experiences which have been unremarked, and discussion of issues which seem neglected. One cautionary note is a commonplace for historians, yet bears rehearsing for readers. The statistics given in the text are the best available, yet many—especially those relating to casualties—are highly speculative. Error is inescapable when covering a huge canvas and addressing points which will never be conclusively resolved. All large numbers relating to the Second World War should be treated with caution.

I have been writing books about this period for twenty-five years. Familiarity does nothing, however, to diminish one's awe in the face of the summits of courage some men and women attained, the depths of baseness others plumbed. After listening for four hours to the story of a Hungarian Jewish survivor of the Holocaust who lives in New York's Queens, my wife and I waited for a taxi to take us to Kennedy Airport to catch a flight to London. It did not arrive. I grew visibly anxious. "Relax!" cried my hostess cheerfully. "It doesn't matter. When you have been in a death camp, you come to see that missing an aeroplane is not very important!" I blushed then, and I blush now, that I could have displayed before such a woman a preoccupation with trivia which is characteristic of the twenty-first century, and which our parents and grandparents perforce shed between 1939 and 1945. My own gratitude never diminishes, that our generation has been spared what theirs endured. I believe passionately in the truth of the words inscribed upon so many war memorials in the United States and Britain—"They died that we might live."

The first part of this book is chiefly about what uniformed combatants did to each other. Later, emphasis shifts to the human experience of all manner of people who found themselves in Germany in 1945. It should never be forgotten, however, that few of those wearing uniforms thought of themselves as soldiers. The tide of history had merely swept them into an unwelcome season's masquerade as warriors. They, too, were "ordinary people." It is sometimes suggested that too many books are written about the Second World War. Yet the stories still untold about the conflict's human sagas are so extraordinary that it seems a privilege to make a modest contribution to recording them, and to setting them in the context of the most significant event of the twentieth century.

Max Hastings
Hungerford, England
January 2004

THE PRINCIPAL COMMANDERS
AND THEIR FORCES

Although the names of many military commanders who feature in this story will be familiar, it seems helpful to offer a brief guide to the chief protagonists on both sides, and their responsibilities.

THE WESTERN ALLIES

General Dwight Eisenhower, as Supreme Commander, directed Anglo-American operations in north-west Europe from SHAEF—Supreme Headquarters, Allied Expeditionary Force—located at Granville in Brittany in September 1944; later moved to Versailles and thence to Rheims. His Chief of Staff was U.S. *General Walter Bedell-Smith*. His deputy was the British *Air Chief Marshal Sir Arthur Tedder*. The British *General Sir Bernard Montgomery* exercised operational control of the Allied armies for D-Day and the Normandy campaign, but surrendered this to Eisenhower on 1 September 1944, with the consolation from Churchill of promotion to field-marshal.

Under SHAEF's control were the following ground forces:

The U.S. 12th Army Group, led by *General Omar Bradley*. Under his command were the U.S. First Army (*General Courtney Hodges*); the U.S. Third Army (*General George Patton*); and U.S. Ninth Army (*General William Simpson*). The U.S. Fifteenth Army (*General Leonard Gerow*) was activated in February 1945. Command of American corps sometimes shifted within the armies. At various periods of the campaign, the following U.S. corps served in one or other of Bradley's armies: III (*Major-General John Millikin*, then *Major-General James van Fleet* from 16 March 1945); V (*Major-General Leonard Gerow*, then *Major-General Clarence Huebner* from 16 January 1945); VII (*Lieutenant-General J. Lawton Collins*); VIII

(*Major-General Troy Middleton*); XII (*Major-General Manton Eddy*, then *Major-General Stafford Le R. Irwin* from 20 April 1945); XIII (*Major-General Alvan Gillem*); XVI (*Major-General John Anderson*); XVIII Airborne (*Lieutenant-General Matthew Ridgway*); XIX (*Major-General Charles Corlett*, then *Major-General Raymond McLain* from 17 October 1944); XX (*Major-General Walton Walker*); XXII (*Major-General Ernest Harmon*); XXIII (*Major-General James Van Fleet*, then *Major-General Hugh Gaffey* from 17 March 1945).

The U.S. 6th Army Group in southern France and later southern Germany was commanded by *General Jacob Devers*. It comprised the U.S. Seventh Army (*General Alexander Patch*) and First French Army (*General Jean de Lattre de Tassigny*). For most of the north-west Europe campaign, 6th Army Group—much smaller than 12th—contained five corps: U.S. VI (*Major-General Lucian Truscott*, then *Major-General Edward Brooks* from 25 October 1944); XV (*Major-General Wade Haislip*); XXI (*Major-General Frank Milburn*), together with the French I (*Lieutenant-General Emile Bethouart*) and II (*Lieutenant-General Goislard de Montsabert*).

American corps normally contained three divisions. Each infantry division consisted of three fighting regiments plus support troops. A U.S. infantry regiment of 3,000 men was the equivalent of a British brigade. An American armoured division was normally divided for operational purposes into two "combat commands"—heavy brigades. Among all the combatants, field artillery was integrated into divisions, while heavier guns came under the orders of corps or armies.

The Anglo-Canadian 21st Army Group was led by *Field-Marshal Sir Bernard Montgomery*, whose chief of staff was *Major-General Frederick de Guingand*. Under its command was the British Second Army, commanded by *General Sir Miles Dempsey*. For most of the campaign, Second Army possessed four corps—I, VIII, XII and XXX, led respectively by *Lieutenant-General John Crocker, Lieutenant-General Sir Richard O'Connor, Lieutenant-General Neil Ritchie* and *Lieutenant-General Brian Horrocks*.

First Canadian Army was commanded by *Lieutenant-General Harry Crerar*, and comprised I Canadian Corps (*Lieutenant-General Charles Foulkes*) and II Canadian Corps (*Lieutenant-General Guy Simonds*). A Polish armoured division served under Canadian command.

A British or Canadian corps normally comprised two or three divisions, plus specialist troops—engineers, support and logistics personnel. Montgomery's two army commanders also possessed six independent armoured brigades, which were deployed according to operational requirements. A division—at full strength about 15,000 men, much less for an armoured division—normally fielded three brigades, each composed of three battalions or armoured regiments. The triangular pattern persisted down the hierarchy, so that a battalion comprised three fighting companies, and each company three fighting platoons or tank troops.

Eisenhower also possessed a strategic reserve, First Allied Airborne Army (*Lieutenant-General Lewis Brereton*), comprising I British (*Lieutenant-General Frederick Browning*) and XVIII U.S. Airborne Corps (*Lieutenant-General Matthew Ridgway*). In September 1944, Brereton's force contained two American and two British divisions. Two more American divisions were added in the spring of 1945, while the British 1st Airborne was removed from the order of battle after Arnhem. Brereton never exercised field command of his formations. These were placed under the orders of local commanders in north-west Europe as operational requirements demanded.

THE SOVIET UNION

Supreme Commander-in-Chief: *Marshal Joseph Stalin*

Each Soviet "front"—the equivalent of a Western Allied army group—comprised anything from three to ten armies of 100,000 men, up to a million men in all. The "fronts" in 1944–45 are listed here in north–south descending geographical order, from the Baltic to Yugoslavia:

Leningrad Front: *Marshal Leonid Govorov*

3rd Baltic Front: *Colonel-General Ivan Maslennikov* (terminated October 1944)

2nd Baltic Front: *General Andrei Eremenko* then *Govorov* from February 1945

1st Baltic Front: *Marshal I. Kh. Bagramyan* (merged into 3rd Belorussian 24 January 1945)

3rd Belorussian Front: *General I. Chernyakhovsky*, then *Marshal Alexandr Vasilevsky* from February 1945

2nd Belorussian Front: *Marshal Konstantin Rokossovsky* from September 1944

1st Belorussian Front: *Rokossovsky*, then *Marshal Georgi Zhukov* from November 1944

1st Ukrainian Front: *Marshal Ivan Konev*

4th Ukrainian Front: *General I. Ye. Petrov*, then *General A. I. Yeremenko* from March 1945

2nd Ukrainian Front: *Marshal Rodion Malinovsky*

3rd Ukrainian Front: *Marshal Fydor Tolbukhin*

The Soviet Union used the same nomenclature for its formations as the Western allies—armies, corps, divisions, brigades, regiments, battalions—but all were much smaller than their Anglo-American counterparts. A Soviet rifle division usually comprised between 3,000 and 7,000 men. Formations were granted the honorific title of "Guards" for distinguished conduct in action. "Shock" and "Tank" armies fulfilled the functions their titles suggest. Elite formations were trained and equipped to a much higher standard than the huge armed rabble which followed the spearheads, of whom little was expected save an ability to occupy ground and absorb enemy fire.

GERMANY

Army Commander-in-Chief: *Adolf Hitler*

Chief of Staff of the High Command of the Armed Forces (OKW): *Field-Marshal Wilhelm Keitel*

Chief of the Operations Staff of OKW: *Colonel-General Alfred Jodl*

Chief of the General Staff of OKH (Army High Command): *Colonel-General Heinz Guderian*, then *General Hans Krebs* from 28 March 1945

Commander-in-Chief of the Replacement Army: *Reichsführer-SS Heinrich Himmler*

If this structure sounds ambivalent and confusing, so it was to senior German officers at the time, reflecting rival centres of power within the Nazi military hierarchy. Hitler changed operational commanders so frequently that it would be wearisome to list all incumbents. The following were the principal holders of some major operational posts in the last months of the war:

GERMAN FORCES IN THE WEST

Commander-in-Chief West: *Field-Marshal Gerd von Rundstedt*, then *Field-Marshal Albert Kesselring* from 10 March 1945

Army Group B (*Field-Marshal Walter Model*) comprised Fifth Panzer Army (*Lieutenant-General Hasso von Manteuffel* to March 1945), Seventh Army (*General Erich Brandenburger*, then from 20 February 1945 *General Hans Felber*, then from 25 March 1945 *General Von Olstfelder*) and Fifteenth Army (*General von Zangen*). Sixth SS Panzer Army (*Colonel-General Sepp Dietrich*) was also under command until January 1945

Army Group G (*Colonel-General Paul Hausser*) comprised First Army (*General Otto von Knobelsdorff*, then *General Hermann Foertsch*) and Nineteenth Army (*General Wiese* to 16 February 1945, then *Foertsch*)

Army Group H (*Colonel-General Kurt Student* from November 1944 to January 1945, then *Colonel-General Johannes von Blaskowitz*) comprised First Parachute Army (*Student* then *General Alfred Schlemm*) and Twenty-fifth Army (*Günther Blumentritt* then from March 1945 *Philipp Kleffel*)

GERMAN FORCES IN ITALY

Army Group C (*Field-Marshal Albert Kesselring* to March 1945, then *General Heinrich von Vietinghoff*)

GERMAN FORCES IN THE EAST

Army Group Centre, which became AG North in January 1945 (*General Hans Reinhardt* to January 1945, then *Colonel-General Lothar Rendulic* to March 1945, then *Walter Weiss* to April 1945)

Army Group Vistula, organized in East Prussia in January 1945 (*Reichsführer Heinrich Himmler* then *Colonel-General Gotthard Heinrici*)

Army Group North Ukraine, which became AG Centre in January 1945 (*General Josef Harpe*, then from January 1945 *Field-Marshal Ferdinand Schörner*)

Army Group South Ukraine, which became AG Ostmark in April 1945 (*General Johannes Friessner* until December 1944, then *General Otto Wohler*, then from April 1945 *Rendulic*)

Army Group E (*Colonel-General Alexander Lohr*)

Army Group F, until disbanded in March 1945 (*Field-Marshal Maximilian von Weichs*)

Army Group Kurland (*Rendulic* in January 1945, *von Vietinghoff* to March 1945, then *Carl Hilpert*)

German forces were organized on roughly similar lines to those of the Allies but there was vastly more movement of corps and divisions between commands and fronts. The Waffen SS was responsible organizationally to Heinrich Himmler rather than to the Wehrmacht, but its formations were placed under the orders of local commanders as operational requirements and the whims of Hitler dictated. In this text, SS officers are described by their military, not SS ranks.

ARMAGEDDON

CHAPTER ONE

Time of Hope

ALLIES OF A KIND

THE FIRST OF September 1944 marked the fifth anniversary of the German invasion of Poland, outbreak of the Second World War. The struggle had already continued for nine months longer than the earlier conflict, once called the Great War. The 1914–18 conflict cost the lives of a mere nine million people. Its successor would account for at least five times that number, the overwhelming majority of whom died in the Soviet Union or in China (where their passing remained largely unremarked by Westerners, then or since).

The British people somewhat flattered themselves about their own role. France, Britain and the dominion were the only belligerents voluntarily to have entered the conflict against totalitarianism as a matter of principle in support of Polish freedom, rather than as victims of aggression or in hopes of booty. Churchill's brilliant defiance in 1940 mitigated Hitler's triumph in western Europe that year. Without his genius, it is likely that Britain would have sued for peace. At no time after June 1940 was there a possibility that British arms could defeat Germany, or even play the principal part in doing so. Yet it was characteristic of British self-indulgence that, when Hitler invaded in Russia in June 1941, some thoughtful people recoiled in disgust from the notion of fighting alongside the bloodstained Soviets, even though their participation opened up the first, perhaps only realistic, prospect of overcoming Hitler.

In Evelyn Waugh's great novel *Sword of Honour*, the British officer Guy Crouchback embraces war in 1939 as a crusade against the modern world in arms. His faith is lost, however, when he finds his country allied with the Russians. That was fiction, yet in cool reality the head of the British Army, Sir John Dill, said in 1941 that he considered the Russians "so foul that he hated the idea of any close association with them." Dill's successor as Chief of the Imperial General Staff, Sir Alan Brooke, initially regarded the Soviets with both moral and military contempt. Churchill's government embarked upon a huge propaganda campaign, to convince the British people that "Uncle Joe" Stalin and his nation were worthy friends of freedom. This was so successful that in 1945 it proved a painful task to shatter public delusions, to break the news that perhaps the Soviet Union was not quite such a good thing after all.

Yet if the accession of the Soviet Union as an ally prompted equivocal sentiments, that of the United States provided cause for unstinting celebration. "So we had won after all!" Winston Churchill exulted, on hearing news of Pearl Harbor in December 1941. Between that date and May 1945, the United States devoted 85 per cent of its entire war effort to the struggle against Germany. Yet, paradoxically, few Americans ever felt deep animosity towards the Germans, of the kind which they cherished towards the "yellow barbarians" who had attacked them at Pearl Harbor. "I didn't work up a great hate of the Germans," said Nicholas Kafkalas, a twenty-four-year-old captain commanding an armoured infantry company of 10th Armored Division in north-west Europe. "They were pretty good soldiers. A lot of Americans felt less engaged against the Germans than against the Japanese." By the autumn of 1944, largely armed and equipped by the industrial might of the United States, the Allies were in no doubt of victory. But the gratitude of the weary, battered, hungry British people was mingled with resentment as they watched Americans in their tens of thousands, brash and fresh, clean and rich, pour off the ships on their way to join Eisenhower's armies. The New World's soldiers came to harvest the fruits of victory without, as the British saw it, having endured their share of the Old World's pain.

A thirty-two-year-old academic serving as a combat historian with the U.S. Army in September 1944 read British newspapers. He noted the fears these expressed, that the Americans would claim to have won the war on their own. "Unfortunately [for the British], nothing can stop our people from claiming the victory," Forrest Pogue wrote presciently.

> They believe the British slow, they over-emphasize their [own] total contribution. The British will never get full credit for their part in winning the war, since their greatest glory was holding on in the 1939–42 period. This was negative type of fighting, and will fade ... Russia will be played down, perhaps, in later years at home ... Hers was the positive sacrifice that broke Germany and made the landing [in Normandy] possible. However, ours was the voice and the helping hand that encouraged England to keep fighting, that replaced the terrific loss of *matériel* suffered by the Russians.

All this was true.

Winston Churchill, whose irrational stubbornness in 1940 had averted Hitler's triumph, enjoyed the years of victory much less than he had expected.

THE ADVANCE TO BELGIUM AND THE MEUSE

North Sea

ENGLAND

Dover
Straits of Dover
Ostend (8 Sept.)
Dunkirk
Calais (30 Sept.)
Boulogne (22 Sept.)

Ghent
Brussels (3 Sept.)
Lille
Arras
Cambrai
R. Schelde
Mons   Namur
R. Sambre
Liège (8 Sept.)

NETHERLANDS
FIRST PARA ARMY (STUDENT)
Antwerp (4 Sept.)
ALBERT CANAL

English Channel

MULBERRY HARBOUR
Le Havre (12 Sept.)
BR. 1 CORPS
Arromanches
St Valery
Dieppe (1 Sept.)
Abbeville
Amiens
Rouen (30 Aug.)
Beauvais
BR. XII CORPS
BR. XXX CORPS
US XIX CORPS
R. Olse
Soissons
Compiègne
US V CORPS
St Quentin
Rethel   Sedan
Château Thierry
Rheims
R. Marne

Essen   Dortmund

Cologne
Aachen (21 Oct.)
R. Rhine

ARMY GROUP B (MODEL)

SEVENTH ARMY (BRANDENBURGER)
Coblenz
GERMANY
Trier
SIEGFRIED LINE WEST WALL

ARMY GROUP G (BLASKOWITZ)

BELGIUM

ARDENNES
LUXEMBOURG

Verdun   Metz

Caen (9 July)
FIRST CANADIAN ARMY (CRERAR)
Louviers
21st ARMY GROUP (MONTGOMERY)
BRITISH SECOND ARMY (DEMPSEY)
Dreux
US VII CORPS
Paris (25 Aug.)
US FIRST ARMY (HODGES)
Melun
Chartres   Fontainebleau
12th ARMY GROUP (BRADLEY)
US THIRD ARMY (PATTON)
R. Seine
US XX CORPS
Troyes
US XII CORPS
R. Marne
Epernay   Châlons
St Dizier
Chaumont

Nancy   Strasbourg
FIRST ARMY (KNOBELSDORFF)
Epinal   Colmar
FIFTH PANZER ARMY (VON MANTEUFFEL)
R. Moselle

THE ALLIED INVESTMENT OF EUROPE
FRONT LINE POSITIONS ON 1 SEPTEMBER 1944

North Sea

GREAT BRITAIN

London
Southampton
Portsmouth Dover

Kiel
Wilhelmshaven
Hamburg
Rostock
Peenemünde
Stettin
Bremen
R. Elbe

Amsterdam
The Hague
Arnhem
NETHERLANDS
Breda   Nijmegen
Ostend   Antwerp
Ghent
Dunkirk
R. Schelde
Brussels
Lille
Abbeville   Mons   Liège
Namur
Essen   Dortmund
Düsseldorf
Cologne
Aachen
Coblenz

Hanover
Berlin
Potsdam

GERMANY

Weimar
Leipzig
Dresden

Calais
Dieppe
Le Havre
St Valery
Caen
Cherbourg (27 June)
Rouen
Amiens
Soissons
Rheims
Verdun
Epernay
Melun
Châlons
Metz
Nancy
Strasbourg

R. Moselle
Mainz
Frankfurt
Ludwigshafen
R. Rhine
Nuremberg
Weimar
Stuttgart
R. Danube

CZECHO
Prague
Pilsen

Rennes (3 Aug.)
Le Mans (9 Aug.)
Paris
Troyes

FRANCE

R. Loire
Tours

R. Seine
Dijon
R. Rhine
Lyons (3 Sept.)

Mulhouse
Basle   Zurich
SWITZERLAND

Munich
Salzburg
Berchtesgaden
Innsbruck   AUSTRIA
Graz

THE POSITION IN NORTHERN ITALY
Trieste
R. Po
Venice
Bologna
Pisa
Florence
Rimini
Pesaro   Ancona
FIFTH ARMY   EIGHTH ARMY   POLISH CORPS

Grenoble
US 3, 39, 45 DIVNS
SEVENTH ARMY (PATCH)
7 FRENCH & 3 US DIVNS

Milan
Venice
Trieste
Genoa
ITALY
R. Po

Like his people he was weary, as well a man of sixty-nine might be. He suffered increasing ill-health. He was made wretched by consciousness of his shrinking power in the Grand Alliance of Britain, the United States and the Soviet Union. He was haunted by apprehension that Hitler's tyranny in eastern Europe would be supplanted by that of Stalin. In 1940, Britain's prime minister had been warlord of the sole bastion of resistance to the Nazis. In 1942, even if the Soviets treated him with the morbid suspicion due to an old imperialist and adversary of revolution, the Americans deferred to his greatness and to his nation's experience of war. From 1943 onwards, however, Churchill's influence upon the Grand Alliance dwindled almost to vanishing point. The Soviet Union displayed the icy arrogance it considered appropriate, as paymaster of the vast blood sacrifice necessary to bring Hitler's empire to bay. The United States made plain its intention to determine strategy in the west and invade Normandy in summer 1944—Operation Overlord—as its forces waxed in might while those of Britain waned.

"Up till Overlord," wrote Churchill's private secretary when it was all over, "he saw himself as the supreme authority to whom all military decisions were referred. Now, he is by force of circumstances little more than a spectator." Churchill himself acknowledged this: "Up to July 1944 England had a considerable say in things; after that I was conscious that it was America who made the big decisions." In 1944, the United States produced as many weapons as all the Axis powers together—40 per cent of the entire armaments employed by all the combatants on every front in the Second World War. Tensions grew between Britain's prime minister and America's president: "Roosevelt envied Churchill's genius, and Churchill increasingly envied Roosevelt's power," in the words of the historian John Grigg. The warmth of public exchanges between the two men masked a private coolness, and especially the consequences of Roosevelt's impatience with Churchill, which became ever more marked in the last months of the war.

While Roosevelt's life reflected the highest ideals, he was a much less sentimental and more ruthless man than Churchill. Roosevelt possessed, claims his most recent biographer, "a more perceptive and less romantic view of the world than Churchill." This proposition is justified insofar as Roosevelt recognized that the days of empires were done, while Churchill's heart refused to accept the signals of his brain that it was so. Yet any claim of Roosevelt's superior wisdom becomes hard to sustain convincingly in the light of the president's failure to perceive, as Churchill perceived, the depth of evil which Joseph Stalin and the Soviet Union represented. It may be true that the Western allies lacked the military power to prevent the Soviet rape of eastern Europe, but posterity is entitled to wish that Roosevelt had allowed himself to appear less indifferent to it.

The British considered that neither the president nor the U.S. Army Chief of Staff George Marshall, for all his greatness as lead manager of America's war effort, exercised the mastery of strategy that was needed to finish the war quickly. "As [Roosevelt's] grip slackened during the last year of his life," argues one of the best historians of Anglo-American relations at this period, "...the President became in some ways a liability in terms of the effective conduct of United States and Allied business...his refusal to face the facts concerning his own state of health...suggest, not so much heroism, as is usually argued, but irresponsibility and an undue belief in his own indispensability, if not a love of power." Even if this verdict is too harsh and ignores the likelihood that an elected replacement president in January 1945 would have been less impressive than Harry S. Truman, it is hard to dispute the assertion that Roosevelt's judgement was flawed, his grasp upon events visibly slipping, from his 1944 re-election campaign until his death in April the following year.

Yet American vision about the most important strategic decision of the western war, the assault on the continent, had proved superior to that of the British. As late as the winter of 1943–44, Churchill continued to fight a rear-guard action for his cherished Mediterranean strategy. He pursued the chimera of penetrating Germany through Italy and Yugoslavia. He remained instinctively anxious to defer an invasion of north-west Europe, which he feared could become a bloodbath reminiscent of the First World War. Painful experience of the limitations of Allied forces against those of the Wehrmacht, the greatest fighting machine the world had ever seen, dogged his consciousness. The prime minister always acknowledged that a confrontation in France must come sooner or later. But he remained uncharacteristically dilatory about its timing. General* Sir John Kennedy, Britain's Director of Military Operations, wrote after the war that he doubted whether the invasion of Normandy would have taken place before 1945 but for the insistence of the U.S. Chiefs of Staff: "American opinion on the landing in France in 1944 was, without a shadow of doubt, 'harder' than ours." Franklin Roosevelt could claim personal credit for insisting that D-Day should take place when it did. Marshall, likewise, declared with some justice that one of his own principal wartime achievements was to resist Churchill's follies.

In the summer of 1944, American confidence in Overlord was triumphantly vindicated on the battlefield. After ten weeks of bitter fighting in Normandy, German forces collapsed in rout. The broken remnants of Hitler's forces staggered away eastwards, leaving almost all their tanks and guns wrecked upon the battlefield. The Allies had expected to fight river by river and field by field across France. Instead, Paris fell without a fight. In the early days of September, British columns streamed into jubilant Brussels, where they received a far warmer welcome than they had encountered from the French, among whom political and psychological wounds ran deep. "One got the impression that the

*All military ranks given in the text are those held at the time of the events described.

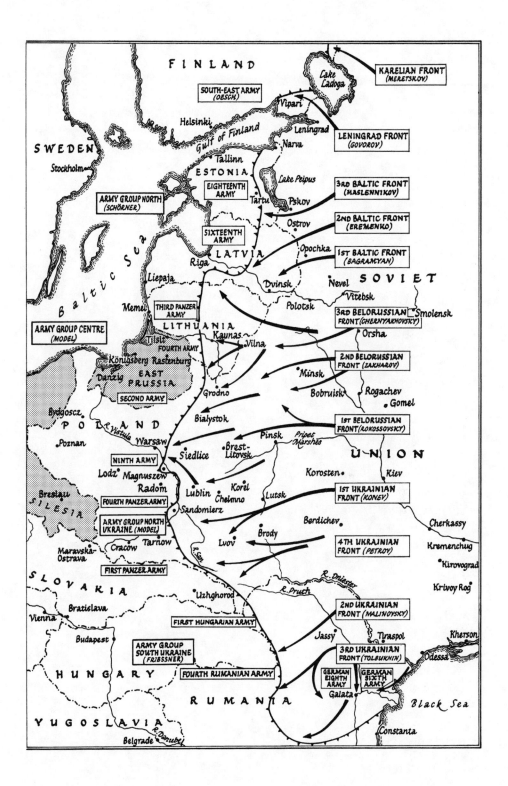

Belgians felt they had done their bit by eating their way through the war," said Captain Lord Carrington of the Guards Armoured Division, one of many Allied soldiers astonished by the plenty he found in Belgium, after years of privation at home in Britain. Courtney Hodges's U.S. First Army approached the frontiers of Germany. The vanguard of George Patton's U.S. Third Army reached the upper Moselle. Huge expanses of territory lay undefended by the Nazis. A few feeble divisions, supported by mere companies of tanks against the Anglo-American armoured legions, manned the enemy's line. For a few halcyon days, Allied exhilaration and optimism were unbounded.

Meanwhile in the east, the Soviet Operation Bagration boasted triumphs to match those of the Americans and British. Indeed, the Russians' achievement was much greater, since they faced three German divisions for each one deployed in France. Between 4 July and 29 August, the Red Army advanced more than 300 miles westwards from the start line of its northern summer offensive. The fervour of the Russians' loathing for their enemy was intensified by the desert they found in Belorussia as the Germans retreated—crops ploughed into the ground, all livestock gone, a million houses burned, most of the population dead or deported for slave labour. Private Vitold Kubashevsky of 3rd Belorussian Front had already lived through two years of war, but recoiled in horror from what he now saw in Belorussia. Once he and his platoon noticed a stench emerging from a shed beside a church, and entered to find it stacked with the rotting corpses of local peasants. When correspondents reported on a Nazi death camp found at Maidenek in Poland, where the ashes of 200,000 people were still piled in the crematorium, some Western media—including the BBC—refused to publish their dispatches, suspecting a Soviet propaganda ploy. The *New York Herald Tribune* said: "Maybe we should wait for further corroboration of the horror story ... Even on top of all we have been taught of the maniacal Nazi ruthlessness, this example sounds inconceivable ..."

By September, the Red Army had recovered all but a small fragment of the Soviet territories lost since 1941. Stalin's people, who had achieved their decisive victory over Germany at Kursk in July 1943, now stood at the borders of East Prussia, and on the Vistula within a few miles of Warsaw. The Germans clung to a mere foothold in Lithuania. Further south, the Russians had driven deep into Rumania, and held a line close to the capital, Bucharest. Only in the Carpathian Mountains did the Germans retain a narrow strip of Russian soil. German casualties were horrendous. Fifty-seven thousand captives from the Fourth Army were marched through the streets of Moscow on 17 July. Muscovite children jeered and threw stones. A watching six-year-old was so conditioned by propaganda images of the enemy that she noted her own astonishment on seeing that these Germans possessed human faces. She had expected to see the features of wild beasts. Most Russian adults looked on in grim silence. Yet a Western correspondent watching the shuffling parade of

Germans was surprised to hear an old Russian woman mutter: "Just like our poor boys...driven into the war." Between July and September, Hitler's forces lost 215,000 men killed and 627,000 missing or captured in the east. One hundred and six divisions were shattered. Total German losses on the Eastern Front that summer—more than two million men killed, wounded, captured and missing—dwarfed those of Stalingrad. It was little wonder that Stalin and his marshals were dismissive of Anglo-American successes in France. A recent American study has described Bagration as "the most impressive ground operation of the war." Yet if its gains were awesome, so was its human price. Russia's summer triumphs cost the Red Army 243,508 men killed and 811,603 wounded.

In the second week of August, Marshal Georgi Zhukov—who had brilliantly orchestrated the summer operations of the two Belorussian Fronts—together with Marshal Konstantin Rokossovsky, his subordinate at 1st Belorussian Front, considered with Stalin the possibilities of an early thrust west across Poland, on an axis which would lead finally to Berlin. This was rejected, chiefly because Rokossovsky's forces were exhausted by their long advance, and also because Stalin perceived opportunities elsewhere. Russia's warlord committed his forces, first, to new operations on the Baltic Front, where some thirty German divisions held out in coastal enclaves, some of which they retained until May 1945; and, second, to a series of major offensives in the Balkans, where several countries lay ripe for Moscow's taking.

Militarily, the Balkan campaign was rational but not essential. Politically, however, from Stalin's viewpoint the temptation was irresistible. On 20 August, the Red Army launched a million men into Rumania, whose people were known to be ready to abandon Hitler's cause. Allied bomber attacks were destroying the country's oil industry. For many months, the Rumanian government had been exploring the possibilities of a deal with Moscow to change sides. Now, the Soviets advanced twenty-five miles on their first day in sectors unconvincingly defended by Bucharest's forces. On 23 August, after a coup in the capital, Rumania announced its defection to the Allies. German intelligence, always the weakest arm of Hitler's war effort, was taken wholly by surprise. Rumania would now provide the Red Army's path to the Danube delta, Bulgaria, Yugoslavia, Hungary, Austria and Czechoslovakia. Some 70,000 German troops staged a fierce, brilliant breakout from Soviet encirclement, but many more found themselves cut off. The Red Army entered Bucharest on 31 August, having covered 250 miles in twelve days. The Rumanian Army had fought alongside the Germans, albeit ineffectually, throughout Hitler's campaigns in Russia. Now, when a Rumanian delegation arrived in Moscow and was shown into the office of Stalin's foreign minister, Molotov demanded contemptuously: "What were you looking for in Stalingrad?"

In Bucharest, the Rumanian Jewish writer Iosif Hechter described in his diary a mood of:

bewilderment, fear, doubt. Russian soldiers who rape women…Soldiers who stop cars in the street, order the driver and passengers out, then get behind the wheel and disappear. This afternoon three of them burst into Zaharia's, rummaged through the strongbox, and made off with some watches…I can't treat these incidents and accidents as too tragic. They strike me as normal—even just. It is not right that Rumania should get off too lightly. This opulent, carefree, frivolous Bucharest is a provocation for an army coming from a country laid waste.

When Hechter and his kind, delivered from the spectre of the death camps, clapped wildly as Soviet columns marched through the streets, other Rumanians "looked askance at the 'applauding yids'." Hechter gazed upon the weary, filthy, often ragged Red soldiers and reflected: "*Ils ne payent pas d'apparence*"— 'They don't look much'—but they are conquering the world."

Though the Soviets' pace slowed as difficulties of supply and maintenance overtook their armies, they maintained their push throughout September. The battle for Rumania cost the Germans some 230,000 men, and the Soviet Union 46,783 dead and 171,426 wounded, along with 2,200 tanks and 528 aircraft. To maintain a perspective between east and west, we should note that one of the least bloody Soviet operations of 1944–45 thus incurred greater casualties than those of the British and Canadians in the entire campaign for north-west Europe. Bulgaria, however, fell without a shot being fired. As soon as Russian troops crossed its border on 8 September, they were greeted by their supposed Bulgarian adversaries assembled in parade order with red banners unfurled and bands playing.

Hardly a single one of the Soviet soldiers now pouring into eastern Europe had ever before set foot outside his own country. They were fascinated, and sometimes repelled, by a host of novelties. "Russians had a stereotype of Poland as a bourgeois capitalist state hostile to the Soviet Union," writes a Russian historian. "I can't say we liked Poland much," wrote a Russian soldier. "We saw nothing noble there. Everything was bourgeois and commonplace. They looked at us in a very unfriendly way. They just wanted to rip off their liberators." Russian soldiers were ordered to respect Polish property, yet few took heed. When a man was reprimanded for stealing a sheep, his comrades protested. "Come on, we said," one of them remembered, "what's a sheep? This man has been fighting since Stalingrad."

Lieutenant Valentin Krulik could not understand why Rumanian peasant houses allowed cooking smoke to seep out through their front doors, until he learned that the state imposed a chimney tax. After the desperate poverty of the Rumanian countryside, he and his men were bewildered to find the capital, Bucharest, ablaze with lights, its shops open and full of goods. As Major Dmitry Kalafati led an artillery battery through the first Bulgarian villages in his Willys jeep, their vehicles were bombarded with water melons. The first Bulgarian troops they met said simply: "We're not going to fight you Russians." Kalafati drove unimpeded for miles across Bulgaria and into Yugoslavia in his cherished jeep with the commander of 3rd Ukrainian Front. The Russians liked Yugoslavia, but some found the Yugoslav people, and especially Tito's communist partisans, conceited and condescending: "They seemed to look down on us." Lieutenant Vladimir Gormin, one of the Russian gunners supporting the Yugoslavs, admired the partisans' spirit, but was doubtful about the tactical merits of their practice of advancing into action behind an accordionist singing nationalist songs. Yulia Pozdnyakova's signals unit was billeted for a time in the immense castle of a Polish count. Among the flowerbeds were stone reliefs of Poles who had fought with Napoleon's army in Russia in 1812. The young Russian girl felt very angry: "I was indignant that anybody could have lived like this count, waited upon hand and foot. I had never seen anything like it in Russia— the huge baths, the marble statues of naked women. It seemed all wrong."

It is the nature of every soldier in every war to focus overwhelmingly upon his own prospects of life and death, rather than to think much about distant battlefields. The men of the Red Army cared little for the doings of their allies, save that they were thankful for American trucks and canned meat. Among many other commodities, the United States supplied to the Soviet Union 500,000 vehicles, 35,000 radio sets, 380,000 field telephones and a million miles of signal wire. Few Russians were ever allowed to know that they marched to Berlin in boots manufactured by the U.S. under Lend–Lease, or that much of the Soviet Union's aircraft production was made possible by American aluminium supplies. Moscow never acknowledged that, from late 1943 onwards, only 20 per cent of the Luftwaffe was deployed on the Eastern Front, because the remainder was fighting the Western allies over Germany.

American ships which delivered vast consignments of equipment were rigidly quarantined in Russian ports. Every member of their crews was treated as a prospective spy and political seducer of Soviet citizens. "Three of our agents have been introduced into the dock unloading crews," the local NKVD chief reported to Lavrenti Beria, overlord of Stalin's security apparatus, when an American freighter docked at Sebastopol. "The main purpose is to prevent possible attempts to plant U.S. agents in the port, and to prevent possible provocation by hostile elements among the crew, and to prevent any contact between port staff and the crew. Female agents who have received most detailed briefings will be kept in close touch with officers who come ashore." Yet Roosevelt continued to believe that he could do business with Stalin in a way that Churchill could not. The U.S. ambassador in Moscow, Averell Harriman, who had become converted to a deeply sombre view of the Soviet Union, visited Roosevelt in November 1944 to urge the need for much greater American toughness towards Stalin. He emerged despondent: "I do not believe that I have convinced the

President of the importance of a vigilant, firm policy," he wrote. Many Americans were more troubled by the residual imperial ambitions of their British ally than by the designs of their Russian one upon eastern Europe. "The British would take land anywhere in the world, even if it were a rock or a sandbar," Roosevelt observed caustically to his secretary of state. A letter-writer to the *San Francisco Chronicle* complained that "American boys spilled their blood in Europe to protect the mighty Empire... Yesterday in her dark hour England whimpered for aid against the arrogant. Today, the winning of her battle made certain by the blood and wealth of America, England is arrogant." Washington strove manfully to sustain a working relationship with Moscow, despite relentless Soviet slights.

Russians nursed a contempt, not discouraged by Stalin, for the belated achievement of Overlord. "We spoke very little about the Second Front," said artillery officer Major Yury Ryakhovsky. "We never felt any weakening of German pressure because of what the Western allies were doing—indeed, we didn't feel they were doing much. Their campaign was merely a splinter in Germany's side." "It was a pity the Americans and British did not start fighting sooner," said Lieutenant Pavel Nikiforov sardonically, observing that he himself had been wounded in action three times before the first Allied soldier stepped ashore on D-Day.

Soviet behaviour towards the West throughout the Second World War conformed to an historic pattern identified by the historian Orlando Figes: "Complex feelings of insecurity, of envy and resentment towards Europe... define the Russian national consciousness." A Rumanian who visited Russia in September 1944 was awed by the hardships being endured by the population, and noted a mixture of arrogance and inferiority complex in Russian attitudes towards the world: "They are aware of their great victories but at the same time fear they are not being shown sufficient respect. This upsets them." The Russians scorned the political hypocrisy which they perceived in their Western allies. The Anglo-Americans exercised their consciences about the future governance of Bulgaria and Rumania while appearing wholly indifferent to Soviet expressions of concern about continuing fascist dictatorship in Spain. Here were characteristic bourgeois double standards. The Yugoslav partisan leader Milovan Djilas wrote after a meeting with Stalin in June 1944: "I was filled with admiration for the ruthless, inexhaustible will of the Soviet leaders. And with horror for the endlessness of the cunning and evil that surrounded Russia." John Erickson, British chronicler of the Red Army, speaks of a mood of "embattled isolation" among both Soviet soldiers and civilians.

The Russians revealed to the Western allies next to nothing about their operational plans. American pleas to deploy liaison officers at Soviet Army headquarters were summarily rejected. For all the public courtesies exchanged between Churchill, Roosevelt and Stalin, a spiritual divide separated Russia from its Western partners, which would become an abyss as the season approached to garner the spoils of victory. That majestic wartime phrase "the Grand Alliance" masked the reality that the Anglo-Americans and Russians were joined only by the purpose of destroying Hitler. Whatever Roosevelt's suspicions of Churchill, the war aims of the United States and Britain were largely unselfish. Those of the Soviet Union were not. Stalin's ambitions now embraced a lust for vengeance and conquest on a colossal scale. This was understood by every German who had participated in his nation's three-year rampage across the Soviet Union, or who was aware of what had taken place. It sometimes seemed that the Western allies were mere intruders, uncomprehending eavesdroppers, upon the death struggle taking place between the two rival tyrannies in eastern Europe.

At no time during the autumn and winter was the entire Eastern Front tranquil. But, for five months between mid-August 1944 and mid-January 1945, the line in Poland remained almost static. The Red Army could not have sustained simultaneous operations in Poland, on the Baltic Front and in the Balkans. The Russians needed hard ground to move tanks, and precious little was available in Europe before the turn of the year. It remains just plausible that Stalin could have pushed towards Berlin, and thus ended the war sooner, had the Soviet Union conducted strategy solely in accordance with military objectives. Instead, however, Stalin chose to secure the Balkans before amassing munitions for a new offensive on the Vistula river in central Poland, the decisive front against the Wehrmacht. Zhukov's armies began an autumn and winter of patient preparation, gathering their strength and extending their immense supply lines before launching Russia's mighty blow, towards the heart of Germany.

"EVERYTHING IS GOING SO WONDERFULLY WELL"

THE PEOPLES OF the democracies liked to suppose themselves better informed than those of the tyrannies concerning both the war and the world in which they lived. Yet in the autumn of 1944 many American and British soldiers fighting in the west shared an indifference and an ignorance about the misty struggle in the east which mirrored attitudes within the Red Army towards the Western allies. "In those days, we knew so little about the Russians," said Major William Deedes of 12th King's Royal Rifle Corps. "We were amazingly ignorant about what they were doing. We were much more interested in listening to Vera Lynn on the radio." Field-Marshal Montgomery, visiting the Polish division under his command, blithely inquired of its commander whether, at home, Poles communicated with each other in the Russian or German language. He would no doubt have been amazed to be informed that Poland had a longer independent history than Russia. American and British generals were aware of Soviet victories, but knew nothing of Soviet intentions. They were entirely pre-occupied with the next phase of their own war, the thrust towards the Rhine. They took for granted the pre-eminence of their own operations, because such is human nature.

American and British soldiers had fought battles in France through June and July which inflicted sufferings upon the infantry as grievous as any of the war, and which indeed matched the unit casualties of some 1916 actions. The British 4th Wiltshires, for instance, had been gravely depleted. In September the battalion's companies were reduced to eighty-odd men apiece, and many platoons were led by NCOs rather than officers. Captain "Dim" Robbins, a company commander, said: "Normandy had been a shattering experience for us. We hadn't realized the Germans were quite that good, even though they had nothing like what we had."

Many men of the British Army were very tired. A few had fought through France in 1940. More had served in Egypt, Libya and Tunisia in 1941 and 1942, through Sicily and Italy in 1943. Even those who remained in England without seeing combat had lived for years amid bombing and rationing, squalor and ruins and family separation. Most felt that they had "done their bit" and, in the case of the Mediterranean veterans, more than their bit. Before D-Day, in 3rd Royal Tanks a mutiny was only narrowly averted. Returning home after three years with the Eighth Army, they were told that they must fight another great battle, and were deeply distressed. Sixth Green Howards, who had campaigned through the desert, Sicily and Normandy, were so depleted by September that the unit was broken up. "We thought: that's it then. Some other buggers can carry on now," wrote one of the survivors, Private George Jackson. "But no, we were all split up and sent to reinforce other units that were desperately short of personnel. It seemed unfair, to say the least. Some of my mates were not really young, had wives and kids, while fit young men were still in England driving lorries or doing army accounts."

Meanwhile American sensitivity about the relative feebleness of the British contribution was growing. Senator Burton K. Wheeler of Montana complained in Congress: "It is hard for me to understand why we, with the biggest army in the world, should find it necessary to draft more men when we have four times as many in the war as the British." Some important Americans, their president foremost among them, were morbidly suspicious of what they perceived as Churchillian attempts to sacrifice American lives in support of the restoration of the British Empire. The United States had accepted in 1942 the policy urged upon it by the British of "Germany first." But many Americans, including a few at the summits of command, regarded the European war as regrettable business to be concluded before their country settled accounts with its principal enemy, Japan.

The divide between the Western allies and the Germans and Russians was most strikingly reflected in their attitude to casualties. Stalin's commanders looked forward to the last phase of the struggle for Europe with their customary indifference to death and suffering, save insofar as these influenced the Red Army's ability to fight its next battle. The leaders of Germany had conducted a romance with death for more than a decade. They still cherished hopes of final victory, though it was already plain that Hitler would settle almost equally willingly for a climactic bloodbath worthy of the Third Reich's place in history.

General Dwight Eisenhower's citizen soldiers, by contrast, were united in September 1944 by relief that after Normandy the end was in sight. Enough blood had been shed. It was good to believe that now it was a matter of mopping up. After the breakout in France, in Captain "Dim" Robbins's words: "we were told that the German Army was wrecked. It was just a question of crossing the Rhine." Men thanked their stars for approaching deliverance, and many resolved to take as few chances as possible in the last days. On 28 August, the British Air Ministry circulated a memorandum to all RAF commands about precautionary measures for celebrations of the end of the war. There should be no extravagant or destructive displays, it warned. Commanding officers should ensure that personnel had no unauthorized access to firearms, explosives or pyrotechnics. "Everything is going so wonderfully well," Colonel George Turner-Cain, commanding the British 1st Herefords, wrote in his diary on 1 September, "with the Huns showing little fight. Most seem content to give themselves up." Four days later, he recorded: "Rumours flying in streams. Swiss radio says Hitler has gone to Spain and peace has been declared."

Many Germans seemed eager to abandon the struggle. "A Jerry gives himself up to us in a cabbage field," Trooper John Thorpe of the 2nd Fife & Forfar Yeomanry wrote in his diary on 2 September. "The water is running out of his clothes, he's covered in mud and shaking with cold and fright. We give him a biscuit and hand him over to our infantry." "Dear Mum," Lieutenant Michael Gow of the Scots Guards wrote home on 1 September, "Isn't the news splendid? At last it seems that the German withdrawal, which in many respects was as masterly as our advance, has turned into a rout."

The weary remnants of I SS Panzer Corps found themselves approaching the little town of Troisvierges, just inside Luxembourg, on their retreat into Germany. "We could not believe our eyes," said Captain Herbert Rink, one of its battle-group commanders.

> Down in the town stood the entire population along the main street, flowers and drinks in hand. They were clearly waiting for the liberation forces...We did not have much time, if we wanted to beat the Americans to the town...We raced out of the forest...turned down the main street, keeping a watch to the south, and drove slowly past the waiting peo-

ple...Never in my life have I seen people so quiet and embarrassed. They did not know what to do with their flowers. They looked at the ground. Their hands sank in a helpless gesture.

Fortunately for the people of Troisvierges, the Americans were indeed close behind the SS half-tracks.

A Dutch doctor, Fritz van den Broek, was on holiday with his family near Maastricht. He gazed in wonder upon the spectacle of German occupation troops fleeing eastward on *dolle Dinsdag*—"Crazy Tuesday," as the Dutch christened 5 September—laden with the booty of half Europe—paintings, furniture, carpets, clocks, even pigs. The doctor thought, "Well, that's it then," and took the train complacently home to Dordrecht, untroubled even by the interruptions to his journey caused by strafing Spitfires, to wait out the few days that seemed likely to intervene before liberation. "It was a glorious feeling when we heard of the Allied breakout," said twenty-year-old Theodore Wempe, a Dutch Resistance worker in Appeldoorn. "The Germans seemed completely panic-stricken. We expected each day to be the last of the war."

"This period was made up of fruit," wrote Brigadier John Stone, chief engineer of the British Second Army. "Belgians stood by the roads with baskets of grapes, pears, apples, plums and peaches. If you stopped for a moment, presents were pressed on you, and a refusal hurt the offerer very much." "As we went across France with no resistance of any moment in front of us, we were racing towards Germany," recorded General Omar Bradley's aide Colonel Chester Hansen. "I thought they might quit." In the first week of September, 67 per cent of Americans questioned for a Gallup poll said that they expected the war to be over by Christmas. The British embassy in Washington reported to London on the national mood: "Early victory in the European campaign continues to be taken for granted." The Allied Control Commission for Germany was "called upon to make itself ready to operate in Berlin by 1st November." "Until mid-September," observed Sergeant Forrest Pogue, "the intelligence estimates all along the lines were marked by almost hysterical optimism."

On 4 September, for planning purposes the British Cabinet accepted 31 December as the likely date for the end of the war. The U.S. War Production Board in Washington cancelled some military contracts, on the assumption that the material would not be needed. On 8 September the Chief of the Imperial General Staff, Sir Alan Brooke, told the prime minister that, while the Chiefs of Staff did not ignore the possibility of continued German resistance, it seemed unlikely that the Nazis could survive the winter. Churchill, almost alone, dissented. He wrote to the Joint Intelligence Committee: "It is at least as likely that Hitler will be fighting on 1 January as it is that he will collapse before then. If he does collapse before then, the reasons will be political rather than military." More than any other man at the summit of Anglo-American power, the prime minister respected the fighting power of the German Army and had grown painfully familiar with the limitations of the armies of the democracies.

Yet what could the enemy fight with? Ultra, the wonderful fount of intelligence which poured forth to Allied commanders from Bletchley Park the daily riches of decoded German signals traffic, detailed the enemy's weakness. An intelligence estimate on 12 September suggested that the Germans could deploy only nineteen divisions for the defence of the West Wall—the frontier fortification of Germany also known as the Siegfried Line—reinforced with a further five or six by the end of the month: "The West Wall cannot be held with this amount, even when supplemented by enemy oddments and large amounts of flak." A jubilant intelligence summary by British Second Army on 5 September suggested that partisan activity against the Allies would henceforward pose a more serious threat to the Allied advance than the wreckage of the German Army:

> [It] is tolerably certain that the enemy has not kept at home a reserve which is well enough trained or equipped to hold an invading force at bay for long, particularly if the latter includes armour…But invasion of Germany is different to invasion of France. The population will not be friendly…pockets left may be more than a nuisance, and sniping, minor attacks on single vehicles, staff cars etc. may be prevalent. Even if a break-through proves relatively easy, the enemy left behind will have to be cleaned up. The population, which may be provided with small arms, will need to be disarmed.

American commanders shared this mood. Bradley's aide recorded on 5 September: "Brad believes the Germans may either fold up with our crossing of the Rhine, or…as long as the SS has its hold, we may be forced into a guerrilla clean-up of the entire country, a costly and troublesome process." Nor did the enemy seem to dissent. Field-Marshal Gerd von Rundstedt told Hitler on 7 September that it would be six weeks before the West Wall could be manned and made defensible. Meanwhile, Army Group B—the principal German force in the west—possessed just a hundred tanks with which to confront the Allies' 2,000. Ludwig Seyffert, a general commanding the German 348th Division, told interrogators after his capture on 6 September: "The Allies should be in the heart of Germany in less than two months." On 4 September, Corporal Joseph Kolb wrote home from the beleaguered German garrison at Calais: "I am still alive, but perhaps this will be my last letter of all to you. How we shall end up I don't know—either dead or in captivity." Likewise Private Fritz Gerber: "Our only hope is to be taken prisoner. Now, my dear ones, I send you my last greetings from the West, and should we not see each other again in this world, we must hope to be reunited in another one above." Sergeant Helmut Günther, serving with the ruins of 17th SS Panzergrenadiers on the Moselle, said: "We were amazed that it took the Allies so long to engage us. We were utterly exhausted. Yet we were given the chance to catch our breath and regroup at Metz. It seemed extraordinary."

Inside the Third Reich, among informed people with no connection to Hitler's regime, there was a desperate impatience for the end. Only peace could bring a halt to relentless death. Allied victory would mean a chance of life for millions of captives, not least those who had dared to oppose Nazi tyranny. "For the thousands locked up by the Gestapo and for those who were still waiting to be picked up," wrote Paul von Stemann, a Danish journalist who spent the war in Berlin, "it seemed to be a race with their lives at stake. 'If they can only hold on till October,' somebody said, 'the Allies will be here and they will be safe.' Somebody else said: 'The war cannot last till Christmas—it is only a matter of perseverance.'" Von Stemann was startled to hear Germany's official military spokesman, Major Sommerfeldt, observe casually one day in September that he expected the Allies to break through the Siegfried Line at any time, "and then the war will be over in 14 days." Off the record or not, Sommerfeldt's words seemed to the journalist a revelation of despair within the Wehrmacht.

Throughout Germany, by an order of 24 August Reich Propaganda Minister Joseph Goebbels closed theatres, cabarets and drama schools, and disbanded all orchestras except those essential for radio broadcasting. Only scientific and technical literature, school books and "certain standard political works" continued to be published. The working week was extended to sixty hours, and a "temporary" ban on holidays was imposed. Frau Keuchel of Betzdorf wrote to her husband: "It is dreadful to read the communiqués and realize that Tommy is progressing further, or rather coming nearer, every hour. Here, people are full of fears...No doubt you will have heard of the complete ban on holidays and now, to cap it all, the 60-hour working week. If I was to fulfil this, I would have to leave Betzdorf at four in the morning to get to the office!"

From Weichselstadt in Poland, Frau Kaiser wrote to her husband, a sergeant-major on the Western Front: "My nerves are bad...Your little girl is very sick—food poisoning and high fever. Even the doctor doesn't know what has caused it. I think it is the war. The food is bad and the bread is terrible. What will become of us? You are so far away and I am so alone. Day and night we hear the rumble in the distance. Everyone has to dig trenches, Poles and Germans alike. Couldn't you manage to get yourself captured in one of the encirclements?" Frau Strauch, a sergeant's wife, wrote in similar vein: "Today is Sunday, overcast and cold, and my state of mind matches the weather. I could cry. Yet I still cannot believe that God will permit that we Germans should be ruled by murderers like the Russians."

On 3 September, Field-Marshal Walter Model, "the Führer's fireman" who had succeeded as C-in-C of Army Group B after the suicide of the defeated

Günther von Kluge, issued an order of the day to his men: "We have lost a battle, but I tell you—we shall still win this war. I cannot say more now, although I know that there are many questions burning on the lips of every soldier. Despite everything that has happened, do not allow your confident faith in Germany's future to be shaken... This hour will separate the real men from the weaklings." Model's enigmatic words reflected only his hopes for Hitler's new rockets and jet fighters, none of which offered a realistic prospect of averting defeat. The Americans later computed that 24,000 conventional combat aircraft could have been built with the German resources squandered on "wonder weapons." Yet the short, stocky, frankly uncouth commander of Army Group B remained unswervingly loyal to Hitler. For all Model's competence as a commander, his behaviour, like that of many of his colleagues, reflected a refusal to confront reality. Rational military analysis led inexorably to despair.

Yet an astonishing number of German soldiers remained convinced that the war might be won. A straw poll was conducted among eighty-two prisoners of the Luftwaffe's 6th Parachute Division. Asked whether they still believed Germany would prevail, even in captivity thirty-two men replied "certainly"; fifteen "possibly"; nine "doubtful"; sixteen "impossible"; and ten refused to express an opinion. Captain Hans-Otto Polluhmer, former signals officer of 10th SS Panzer, nursed feelings of guilt, "a belief that I had let the side down," even as he languished at Camp Polk, Oklahoma, after being captured at the Falaise Gap. Many of Polluhmer's fellow prisoners still believed victory attainable, and some of them physically assaulted "weaklings" who revealed doubt. Eugen Ernst, a Wehrmacht reserve colonel captured in Holland, wrote to his family from prison camp in England, asserting boldly that he expected Germany's new wonder weapons would soon arrive and turn the tide of the war. An American survey of German PoWs showed that more than two-thirds still expressed belief in their Führer as late as November 1944. The Nazis' assiduous cultivation of the warrior ethos had created some young fanatics of the Waffen SS who simply liked fighting for its own sake, even now that they were losing the war. A captain of 1st SS Panzer said: "We reached a point where we were not concerned for ourselves or even for Germany, but lived entirely for the next clash, the next engagement with the enemy. There was a tremendous sense of 'being,' an exhilarating feeling that every nerve in the body was alive to the fight."

Private Bruno Bochum harboured no such sentiments. Like many of his comrades, the nineteen-year-old flak gun captain simply considered himself to be in the business of survival. Most of his battery's 20mm guns were lost during their retreat from Brussels. At one moment, they found themselves fleeing eastwards, while a column of British armoured cars raced them on a parallel road. By the time Bochum's group reached the Albert Canal, just one of their guns was left, together with a hundred gunners. The wreckage of the canal bridge was negotiable by men on foot, but impassable to vehicles. They pushed their truck and gun into the canal, and swarmed across the bridge girders under British fire. Then they walked day and night in search of their unit, constantly losing stragglers. Bochum somehow evaded the questing military police, who were rounding up fugitives like himself, made his way home to Mönchengladbach, broke into his family's empty apartment and sank gratefully into a bath: "We recognized that the war was lost, but there was nothing we could do to hasten its ending." After considering his predicament, he saw no choice save to quit Mönchengladbach and rejoin the remains of his unit, with which he then served to the end.

"Throughout August," wrote a British staff officer, "strategic policies remained confused... In the atmosphere of indecision combined with euphoria." The first of the errors which denied the Anglo-Americans a breakthrough into Germany in 1944 was made on 21st Army Group's front. On 4 September, the British 11th Armoured Division exulted as its men reported to Second Army that they had overrun the giant port of Antwerp in Belgium, with its facilities intact. This was a real stroke of fortune. Every officer in the Allied armies knew that supplies, and ports for unloading them, were now the vital factor in enabling the Allies to finish the war. At that moment, had they chosen to do so, the British could have driven onwards up the forty-mile coast of the Scheldt which linked Antwerp to the sea with nothing to stop them. The battered German Fifteenth Army, comprising 100,000 men who had lost most of their transport, would have been isolated if the British had advanced just a few miles further. For Fifteenth Army's commander, General Gustav von Zangen, the arrival of 11th Armoured in Antwerp was "a stunning surprise," which presaged doom for his forces.

Yet now the British made one of the gravest and most culpable errors of the campaign. They failed to perceive, as the Germans at once perceived, that Antwerp was useless as long as the Allies did not command its approaches. No ship could negotiate forty miles of German coastal artillery and minefields. The Royal Navy had repeatedly warned both SHAEF and 21st Army Group that it was essential to secure the banks of the Scheldt before the port could become operational. Admiral Sir Bertram Ramsay wrote to SHAEF, copied to Montgomery, on 3 September, the day before 11th Armoured Division reached the docks: "Both Antwerp and Rotterdam are highly vulnerable to mining and blocking. If the enemy succeeds in these operations, the time it will take to open ports cannot be estimated... It will be necessary for coastal batteries to be captured before approach channels to the river route can be established." Even as the tanks of 11th Armoured deployed in Antwerp, Belgian Resistance leaders warned of the vital importance of the Scheldt. Exhausted British officers, sated by the dash across Belgium they had just accomplished, brushed the civilians aside. Many of the liberators were so weary that they fell asleep in the tanks where they halted.

While the British celebrated, refuelled and rearmed, the Germans acted. Von Zangen was ordered at once to move his forces across the Scheldt, to occupy the island of Walcheren, commanding the river estuary from the north-east, and to secure an escape route northwards into Holland for the rest of his army. "Pip" Roberts, the slight, energetic thirty-eight-year-old commander of 11th Armoured Division which had occupied Antwerp, believed the British would thereafter be driving on eastwards, towards the Ruhr. The northern frag-ment of Holland seemed to him irrelevant. His division's post-war history observed apologetically: "Had any indication been given that a further advance north was envisaged, these bridges might have been seized within a few hours of our entry." As the Germans blew the Albert Canal bridge a few hours after the arrival of Roberts's men, "I realised that I had made a great error... This sort of situation is just like boxing; if your opponent seems a little groggy, you must keep up the pressure." Roberts was too self-critical. It seems wrong to place responsibility for British failure upon either himself or his corps commander, Horrocks. It was not their business to identify strategic objectives. Blame must be laid at the doors of Eisenhower, Montgomery and possibly Dempsey, com-manding Second Army. Each man had by this stage of this war enjoyed ample opportunities to recognize the importance of speed in all dealings with the Germans on the battlefield. Yet none made any attempt to galvanize Roberts's tired soldiers. Given Montgomery's contempt for his Supreme Commander's lack of strategic insight, the British field-marshal might have been expected to see for himself the pivotal importance of the Antwerp approaches.

Over the days that followed 11th Armoured's arrival at the port, the Germans used boats and ferries, chiefly by night, to carry out an operation as skilful and as important as their withdrawal from Sicily into Italy across the Straits of Messina a year before. In sixteen days, they moved 65,000 men, 225 guns, 750 trucks and 1,000 horses across the waterway north-west of Antwerp. While some men were left to hold the Scheldt approaches, the remainder escaped across the base of the Beveland Isthmus into Holland, to play a critical role in thwarting the British through the battles that followed. The German evacuation was com-prehensively monitored by British decoders at Bletchley Park. Every enemy movement was reported to SHAEF and 21st Army Group. Yet no effective action was taken to interdict the Scheldt. The area was heavily mined by the Germans, and thus Allied warships could not intervene from the North Sea. RAF aircraft of 84 Group repeatedly attacked the enemy's ferry crossings, and sank some ships. But the Germans were able to maintain an effective shuttle through the hours of darkness, when fighter-bombers could not interfere.

Only on 13 September, nine leisurely days after Antwerp was seized, was belated action begun to clear the Scheldt approaches. First Canadian Army was given the task. Its infantry divisions, however, were still committed to securing the French Channel ports. The only available formations were the Canadian

4th and 1st Polish Armoured Divisions. Tanks were wholly unsuitable for canal country, and the Canadians' infantry support was very weak. When the Algonquin Regiment set out in assault boats to cross the Leopold Canal and clear its north bank in advance of an armoured thrust, the unit met disaster. German counter-attacks battered its frail bridgehead into submission. On 14 September the survivors retired, having lost twenty-nine men killed, fifty-eight wounded and sixty-six taken prisoner—42 per cent of the battalion's already depleted strength. The retreating Canadians were ferried back across the canal under heavy fire by volunteers among their German prisoners, who seemed eager not to be deprived of the privilege of captivity.

Tactical responsibility for this débâcle was divided. General Harry Crerar, commander of First Canadian Army, was poorly regarded by his British colleagues—"quite unfit to command troops," in Montgomery's withering words. Montgomery lambasted Crerar on the evening of 3 September for having missed an army commanders' meeting earlier that day, because the Canadian was attending a memorial service for the victims of the disastrous 1942 raid on Dieppe. "The C-in-C intimated that...the Canadian aspect of the Dieppe ceremonial was of no importance compared to getting on with the war." Crerar's deputy, Lieutenant-General Guy Simonds, Canada's outstanding soldier of the campaign, from the outset identified the importance of seizing the Scheldt approaches. He urged this on Crerar, suggesting that the French ports were a far less urgent priority. But after the Canadian general's bruising encounter on 3 September he showed no appetite for renewed debate with his army-group commander: "Crerar refused to raise the issue with Monty." The consequence was that most of the Canadians persisted with the marginal task of clearing encircled French ports of Germans, while the Scheldt approaches received nothing like the urgent commitment they needed.

It was acknowledged that the Canadians' mission would require stronger forces. The operation was abandoned until men became available. Amazingly, for three weeks the Germans were left in peace to fortify their positions. This was the first of many instances of lethargy that would dog the Allied campaign. In the happy hangover that followed victory in France, 21st Army Group acted ineffectually. The contrast is extraordinary between the sluggishness of the victorious Allies and the energy of the shattered Wehrmacht. Whatever the requirements of rest and resupply, again and again the Allies paid with the lives of their men for an insouciant attitude to time. The Germans used each day of delay to reinforce their positions, and thus to increase their capacity to resist when an attack belatedly came.

Montgomery, never eager to acknowledge error, nonetheless admitted afterwards that the Antwerp–Scheldt disaster—and it was indeed a strategic disaster—was among his most serious blunders of the war: "a bad mistake—I underestimated the difficulties of opening up the approaches to Antwerp...I reckoned that the Canadian Army could do it *while* we were going for the Ruhr. I was wrong." The field-marshal's Chief of Staff, the highly respected Freddie de Guingand, was exhausted and in poor health. De Guingand "blamed himself specifically for the delay in gaining early use of…Antwerp." Yet Brigadier Charles Richardson, who was also serving on Montgomery's staff, detected in the field-marshal at this time a diminishing receptiveness to counsel, as he "grew steadily more aloof and remote." The fumbled handling of Antwerp was among the principal causes of Allied failure to break into Germany in 1944. It was not merely that the port was unavailable for the shipment of supplies; through two months that followed, a large part of Montgomery's forces had to be employed upon a task that could have been accomplished in days if the necessary energy and "grip" been exercised at the beginning of September, when the enemy was incapable of resistance.

All along the front, the Germans now began to improvise a defence with the energy and ingenuity which they invariably displayed in such circumstances. At the heart of Germany's extraordinary fighting performance in the last year of the Second World War was the *Kampfgruppe*, the "battle group," an ad-hoc assembly of infantry and armour, army and Luftwaffe, flak and service personnel, cooks and laundrymen, placed under the command of the most senior available officer. "Transport, signals and heavy equipment were almost non-existent," observed a British Second Army intelligence report. "…Battle groups were formed from regiments or from stragglers and were named after their commanding officers; they varied in strength from 100 to 3,000. Many went into battle so quickly that the men did not know the name of their battle group. Food and ammunition were short, but some of these groups fought with great and at times fanatical determination." No one pretended that such formations were satisfactory substitutes for the balanced divisions deployed by the Allies. Yet the achievements of the *Kampfgruppen* were considerable. Battle groups lacked the coherence, transport and artillery support to mount major attacks. But in defence—and defence was now the business of the German Army—their contribution was critical to Hitler's survival through the months ahead.

THE DASH ACROSS France and Belgium created a crisis for the supply of the Allied armies. In Patton's legendary phrase: "My men can eat their belts, but my tanks gotta have gas." An American heavy armoured division embraced 4,200 vehicles of all kinds, and required a combat load of 300,000 gallons of fuel, equivalent to 300 GMC trucks each carrying 1,000 gallons in five-gallon cans. By early September, American spearheads were operating more than 300 miles from their only source of supply, the beaches and small ports of Brittany and Normandy. Allied pre-invasion bombing had systematically devastated the French rail system. The British had passionately opposed the Americans'

August landing in the South of France. Yet Marseilles was to prove an invaluable asset, because the rail links of southern France were much less heavily damaged than those of the north. Supplies were soon moving more easily to the American armies from the Mediterranean than through the Channel ports.

In the short term, however, almost every shell, gallon of fuel and ration pack had to be shipped by road or—in dire circumstances and at huge cost—by air. The U.S. Transportation Corps in 1943 had demanded 240 truck companies for the campaign in Europe. Only 160 companies were allocated, of which most were equipped with light trucks, rather than the heavy vehicles the truckers had wanted. The British found themselves handicapped by an inexcusable technical failure. In September, 1,400 three-ton Austin trucks had to be withdrawn from service with Montgomery's armies because of faulty pistons. This deficiency was found to extend to every available replacement engine. Unlike the Americans, who equipped their armies with standard vehicle types using readily interchangeable spare parts, the British Army was dependent on contracts with a wide variety of civilian vehicle manufacturers. In consequence, the armed forces were obliged to service some 600 different models, which created chronic difficulties. Around Antwerp, Montgomery's armies were obliged for a time to commandeer thousands of horse-drawn wagons abandoned by the Wehrmacht, to make good its shortage of vehicles for the haulage of supplies.

Waste was prodigious, and contributed mightily to Allied logistical difficulties. Everywhere the armies went, in their wake lay great trails of discarded equipment and supplies. After coming upon a heap of 650 abandoned overcoats and 200 gas cans, the commanding general of the U.S. 36th Infantry Division lamented men's "utter disregard of property responsibility." Each day of the campaign, the U.S. Army lost 1,200 small arms and 5,000 tyres. The roads and fields of Europe were strewn with discarded American ration packs, and especially the detested powdered lemon juice. Of twenty-two million fuel jerrycans shipped to France since D-Day, half had vanished by September.

It was a remarkable feat to move some 89,939 tons of supplies by road to the armies between 25 August and 6 September, but the achievements of the "Red Ball Express" trucking columns have been much exaggerated. They consumed 300,000 gallons of gasoline a day on their own account, and reckless abuse of vehicles disabled them at a frightening pace—700 fifty-hundredweight trucks were written off for every week of the Red Ball's operation. Each "division slice" of the U.S. Army required 650 tons of supply a day—more than three times the German allocation—to keep it eating and fighting, which translated into a total of 18,600 tons of supply a day for the U.S. armies in the first half of October, rising to 20,750 by that month's end. An armoured division required 25,000 gallons of fuel a day to keep rolling, never mind fighting. Even an infantry division consumed 6,500 gallons. There were serious maintenance problems. By mid-September, the U.S. 3rd Armored Division possessed only some seventy-five "runners" out of its established tank strength of 232, a shortfall matched in most other formations. In the ten days ending 7 September, the British 7th Armoured Division lost twelve tanks to enemy action, and thirty-eight to mechanical breakdown; 11th Armoured Division lost six to the enemy and forty-four to breakdown.

Patton's tanks reached the Moselle after staging the longest and fastest drive across France made by Allied forces. On 2 September, however, their fuel supplies dried up. Third Army received just 25,390 gallons, when its divisions needed at least 450,000 gallons to resume their advance. Eisenhower's planners examined Patton's case for giving his formations overriding priority for fuel. If they did so, it seemed possible that he could get some ten or twelve divisions to the Rhine. But all the most vital strategic objectives were in northern Germany, rather than the south where Patton's path lay. A drive by Third Army would leave its flanks open across 300 miles of hostile territory. Even when Germany's forces were so desperately reduced, given the Wehrmacht's genius for counter-attack, there seemed an overwhelming likelihood that American hubris would be punished.

Third Army received sufficient fuel through mid-September to establish precarious bridgeheads across the Moselle. It was denied licence, however, to attempt any substantial strategic advance for the rest of that month. Patton fumed: "I am being attacked on both fronts, but not by the Germans." Here was weakness in the Allied Supreme Command. If Eisenhower did not intend Patton to drive on into Germany, he should have halted Third Army at the Meuse, and diverted its fuel supplies to Hodges's First Army, much of which was immobilized, yet which possessed a vastly better prospect of penetrating Hitler's West Wall. Patton was delighted when one of his formations hijacked a load of fuel destined for First Army, yet in truth such action was recklessly irresponsible. Patton said to Bradley on 14 September, "Don't call me till after dark," as he strove to entangle his Third Army so deeply on the Moselle front that Eisenhower would feel obliged to support its operations. Far from being matter for laughter, this was a grotesque way to allow any subordinate commander to drive strategy from the bottom. Montgomery was wrong about many things, but he was surely right that grip and discipline were essential at the summit of the Allied armies. Patton's crossings of the Moselle in early September were a waste of resources unless they conformed to a coherent SHAEF strategy. Third Army was allowed to parade the eagerness and egotism of its commander, at great cost to the interests of the other American armies. Likewise, Eisenhower allocated a million gallons of fuel to forces besieging Brest on the French Atlantic coast, a further dispersal of vital resources in favour of a marginal objective.

It has become a cliché of the north-west Europe campaign that the Allies' difficulties of supply were insuperable, given their lack of an operational big port in France. Yet for most of the war the United States displayed a genius for overcoming logistical obstacles, surmounting shortages that seemed intractable to the weary and impoverished British. Why did that genius fail in September 1944? The officer in overall charge of supply for the Allied armies was among the least impressive senior soldiers America sent to Europe in the Second World War. General John C. H. Lee was regarded even by his colleagues as vain, self-important, self-indulgent and undisciplined. Patton dismissed him as "a glib liar." Lee was colloquially known as "Jesus Christ," the only American general to wear stars on both the front and back of his helmet. There was immense anger within the fighting army when it was learned that Lee had descended upon Paris following its liberation and established himself and his sprawling empire of bureaucrats in sybaritic comfort, occupying no fewer than 167 of the French capital's hotels. There was a disease among the service units of the Allied armies, from which Lee was the most notorious sufferer, known as "Paris fever." At the most critical period of the Allied supply crisis, Lee allocated transport to ship to the city 11,000 men and 560,000 square feet of hutted accommodation for his own headquarters. "The movement naturally produced strong criticism from combat commanders," the U.S. official historian comments drily.

In late August and September, senior American officers believed that Lee, the man responsible for finding urgent means to carry the armies into Germany, was chiefly preoccupied with his own creature comfort. A U.S. Army report of 1 December condemned in withering terms the "lethargy and smugness" that had been displayed throughout the campaign by some ComZ—Communications Zone—personnel. "Lee...never ceased to be a controversial figure," in the understated words of the official historian.

It is a serious criticism of Eisenhower that he failed to focus upon Lee's shortcomings, and to replace him, when the Supreme Commander was foremost among those who recognized the tyrannical influence of logistics upon the battlefield. General Everett Hughes, ETO (European Theater of Operations) Chief of Staff, puzzled over Eisenhower's indulgence of Lee and observed sourly to his diary: "Alexander the Great loved *flatterers*." Even an administrator of genius might have been dismayed by the supply problems facing the Allied armies in September 1944. But Lee's failure to prepare contingency plans for a rapid Allied advance seemed deplorable to field commanders. Again and again, U.S. Army inspectors uncovered scandalous lapses and snarl-ups in the supply system. Bradley urged irritably: "Many of our ground forces have done the impossible; let [ComZ] try the impossible for a while. I am not convinced they are doing all they could." Likewise Patton: "Hell, have 'em get off their asses and work the way our troops have."

An energetic and imaginative officer occupying the post so indolently filled by Lee might have found ways to move fuel and supplies to the Allied spearheads in eastern France, to maintain the pace of their advance. This could have been decisive, in enabling Eisenhower's armies to exploit their summer successes before the Germans regrouped. In the event, the momentum triumphantly achieved in August was tragically lost in September. Hitler's armies used every day of grace they were granted, to create defensive lines on the borders of Germany against the Allied host.

MONTGOMERY TRIUMPHANT

IN THE EARLY days of September, there occurred one of the most notorious of many confrontations between Eisenhower and Montgomery. The fact that these did not end in a disastrous fracture of Allied relations reflected the self-control and political discipline of the Supreme Commander. For all Eisenhower's limitations as a strategist, his wisdom and generosity of spirit in the management of the Anglo-American alliance were worthy of the highest respect. He recognized the need to defer whenever possible to the sensitivities of the British, battered and wearied by five years of war, bleakly conscious of their shrinking power. Eisenhower would never jeopardize the vital interests of the United States, but he would go far to avoid trampling upon the fragile self-esteem of the British nation. As far as possible, he humoured the conceit of its most famous soldier.

The British commander was a highly gifted professional, "an efficient little shit," as one of his own generals confided to the Canadian Harry Crerar. Montgomery considered clearly and planned meticulously. "The difference between him and other commanders I had known was that he actually *thought*, as a scientist or a scholar thinks," wrote Goronwy Rees, an academic who served on Montgomery's wartime staff. Montgomery was acknowledged as a master of the setpiece operation. Whereas Eisenhower called for options from his planners, then made a choice, the British soldier believed that it was the business of generals to determine courses of action, and then invite staffs to execute them. If his vanity was a crippling weakness, it was balanced by a remarkable ability to inspire the confidence of his subordinates from top to bottom of the British Army. "We had total faith in Monty," said Lieutenant Roy Dixon of the South Staffordshire Yeomanry. "He achieved results, and he kept a lot of us alive." Montgomery retained the trust of his own soldiers until the end of the war, assisted by the fact that only a handful of British and American officers were aware of the depth of his egomania and the gravity of his wrangles with the Supreme Commander. Doubts persisted, however, about Montgomery's capacity for flexible thinking, for making a rapid response to evolving opportunities. He had battered several smaller German armies into defeat, but he had never managed a wholly successful envelopment, cutting off a retreating enemy. He possessed a shrewd understanding of what could, and could not, realistically be demanded of a British citizen army. But he had done nothing on the battlefield to suggest that his talents, or indeed those of his troops, deserved eulogy. The British had fought workmanlike campaigns in North Africa, Italy and France since their victory at El Alamein in November 1942. But their generals had nowhere shown the genius displayed by Germany's commanders in France in 1940, and in many battles since.

Montgomery himself was a strange man, respected by his subordinates yet often causing them bewilderment and dismay. Like many able soldiers of all nationalities, notably including Patton, MacArthur and the leading Germans, the field-marshal possessed an uncongenial personality. Monastically dedicated to the conduct of war, he seemed oblivious of the loathing he inspired among his peers. After the field-marshal relieved Eighth Army's armoured corps commander back in North African days, the victim declared in his London club: "I've just been sacked because there isn't enough room in the desert for two cads as big as me and Monty." A member of Montgomery's staff told a bizarre story from the north-west Europe campaign. One of the field-marshal's young liaison officers returned to duty after recovering from wounds, and found himself summoned to Montgomery's caravan. He was ordered to remove his clothes. The bemused young man stood naked at attention before his commander, who observed that he wished to ensure that he was fully fit for duty again. "Right!" said Montgomery after a few moments, in his usual clipped bark. "You can dress and go now!" According to one of his staff, that episode caused considerable surprise even at a headquarters well accustomed to "Master's" foibles.

Montgomery's most serious weakness, which he shared with other prominent British officers, stemmed from a refusal to acknowledge that in north-west Europe it was now essential for the British to defer to the overwhelming dominance of the United States. Sir Alan Brooke, senior British Chief of Staff and Montgomery's mentor, matched the disdain of 21st Army Group's commander for American military judgement, though he concealed his sentiments better. Sir Arthur Tedder, Eisenhower's deputy, quailed before the shameless nationalism of the British media, which he feared "was sowing the seeds of a grave split between the Allies." The absence of common courtesy, far less diplomacy, in Montgomery's dealings with the most senior American commanders was extraordinary. His status as a British national hero caused him to consider himself beyond any risk of dismissal. Whatever the doubts of others about his limitations, 21st Army Group's commander was confident that he possessed the stuff of genius, while the Americans remained rank amateurs in the conduct of war.

Still bitterly resentful that, after exercising overall command of Allied ground forces in Normandy, on 1 September he had been obliged to surrender this authority to Eisenhower, he urged that it was time for a big decision. Instead of merely allowing the Allied armies to advance on a broad front towards Germany, it would be vastly more effective, he said in a signal to SHAEF on 3 September, to throw the full weight of Allied logistics behind a single heavy punch: "I consider we have now reached a stage where one really powerful and full-blooded thrust towards BERLIN is likely to get there and thus end the German war." This would be commanded, of course, by himself, and involve a drive for Germany on an axis north of the Ruhr by some forty British and American divisions.

This proposal was certainly not politically viable, was probably also logistically impossible and militarily unsound. Characteristically, however, Eisenhower did not reject the field-marshal's proposal with the clarity which was essential if any message was to penetrate Monty's rhino-hide skin. "There was a confusion of purpose at the very moment when the Wehrmacht was desperately piecing together ad hoc divisions from the remnants of the old," wrote Brigadier Charles Richardson, one of Montgomery's senior staff officers. "It can be argued that in view of the prize at stake—victory in Europe in 1944—the attempt [to drive for Germany on a northern axis] should have been made in late August while the Wehrmacht was still reeling. That it was not made was due primarily to the formidable political obstacles barring the way to such a decision; these were brushed aside by Montgomery but fully appreciated by Freddie [de Guingand, 21st Army Group's Chief of Staff]."

Eisenhower never for a moment accepted the British view about a "single thrust" in the north. He made plain, in terms which everyone save Montgomery understood, that whatever advances the British made in the north, U.S. forces would meanwhile address the Siegfried Line further south, on the German frontier. At a big press conference in London on 31 August, he asserted that "General Montgomery's forces were expected to beat the Germans in the north; General Bradley's to defeat them in the centre; and the Mediterranean forces, under General Jacob Devers, to press from the south." Harry Butcher, Eisenhower's aide, described his master's plan as being "to hustle all our forces up to the Rhine." Nowhere in his career did the Supreme Commander reveal talent as a battlefield general. Few even among his biographers attempt to stake such a claim for him. Yet he displayed a greatness as chief manager of an alliance army for which he deserves the gratitude of posterity. No plausible candidate has ever been suggested who could have managed the personalities under his command with Eisenhower's patience and charm.

Montgomery was surely correct in supposing that a ground-force commander was needed, to provide the focus and impetus of which Eisenhower was incapable. But none of the available candidates, least of all himself, could credibly fill the role. To understand what took place in north-west Europe in 1944–45, it is important to note that no American or British general possessed the experience in manoeuvring great armies which was commonplace among their Russian and German counterparts. American and British staff colleges before the Second World War taught officers to fight battles involving tens of thousands of men, not millions. Many times Churchill was driven to despair by the difficulty of identifying British commanders capable of matching those of the Wehrmacht. "Have you not got a single general … who can win battles?" the prime minister cried out to Brooke early in 1942. The U.S. Army produced at least five outstanding corps commanders, whereas the British and Canadians boasted only two officers at corps level—Horrocks and Simonds—who could be considered competent. Lieutenant-General Sir Richard O'Connor, commanding VIII Corps, did nothing for his staff's confidence in him when he observed cheerfully in Holland one day: "Whatever balls-ups I make, chaps, I know you'll see me through." At divisional level too, the Americans were better served than the British, but it is hard to argue that either ally's general officers matched those of Germany. Exceptional professional skills coupled with absolute ruthlessness rendered many German—and Russian—generals repugnant human beings but formidable warriors. The democracies recruited their generals from societies in which military achievement was deemed a doubtful boon, if not an embarrassment. The American and British armies in the Second World War paid a high price for the privilege of the profoundly anti-militaristic ethos of their nations.

Montgomery was a superb planner and trainer, but he was always most comfortable directing a static battle, of the kind with which he had become familiar a world war earlier. He failed repeatedly in exploitation. Bradley was a steady, likeable officer who possessed solid virtues as commander of 12th Army Group, but showed no greater gifts than Eisenhower in the creation of grand strategy. In the last stages of the war, he became prey to jealousies and frustrations which caused him not infrequently, and almost literally, to sulk in his tent. Only Patton showed himself at ease in the imaginative direction of large forces. Had he not been disgraced for the notorious "slapping incidents" in Sicily*—behaviour curiously characteristic of a German or Soviet general rather than an American one—he might have commanded 12th Army Group in north-west Europe. Patton's critics point out that he suffered as many difficulties as other American generals, in persuading Third Army's infantry to show the determination against tough German opposition to match their commander's vaulting ambition. Patton's streak of recklessness and absolute lack of diplomatic skills disqualified him from the highest commands. Yet at 12th Army Group or at First Army, he might have provided an impetus that was to prove sorely lacking between September 1944 and May 1945.

---

*Patton had been dismissed from command of the U.S. Seventh Army after two episodes in which he lost patience with combat-fatigue cases whom he encountered in field hospitals. He slapped the men and abused them as cowards. The story eventually broke in the U.S. press, provoking outrage. Months later, when it was decided that Patton was indispensable for the north-west Europe campaign and re-employed, he became the subordinate of his former junior, Omar Bradley.

The management of alliances is very hard. Battlefield decisions must be constantly subordinated to national sensitivities. Marlborough suffered huge frustrations alongside the Dutch in the eighteenth century, echoed a hundred years later by those of Wellington among the Spanish, yet they were responsible for forces scarcely larger than a corps in the armies of the Second World War. It has sometimes been suggested that, if MacArthur had been transferred from the Pacific to north-west Europe in 1944, he could have provided the strategic vision which Eisenhower lacked. Yet MacArthur's ignorance of Europe and his loathing for the British rendered him an implausible candidate for alliance command. Some historians of the Second World War have underrated the animosity, jealousy and mistrust between senior American and British officers, which it required Eisenhower's rare diplomatic gifts to overcome. The cautious Kansan regarded the avoidance of disaster as his most vital responsibility. He sought to defeat the German armies in north-west Europe by a measured series of advances. He saw no virtue in excessive haste, and certainly none in excessive casualties. He had been given a mandate to accomplish the defeat of Germany which took no heed of political matters, foremost among these the shape of post-war Europe. Eisenhower handled himself throughout as a corporate chairman rather than a director of armies.

One of Patton's biographers has described how Third Army's commander felt "almost with a physical pain the absence of consistent direction from the top...trying to follow a conductor who did not quite know or failed to comprehend the delicate nuances of a score." Yet it remains debatable whether even the greatest of captains could have steered the citizen soldiers of the Anglo-American alliance into Germany in 1944 faster than the slowest ship in the convoy was capable of steaming. More will be said of this below. Just once in the entire campaign did Eisenhower endorse an imaginative, dramatic initiative to end the war quickly. In September 1944, he astonished his own staff, and deeply irked his American subordinates, by supporting a plan presented by Montgomery for a lightning British dash to the Rhine.

Despite Eisenhower's dislike for Montgomery, it is reasonable to surmise that somewhere in Ike's heart in the autumn of 1944 was a recognition that the British general knew more about the battlefield direction of armies than he did himself. Montgomery's behaviour in Normandy had been abrasive. Yet the British officer had managed that battle with notable competence, without losing his nerve amid savage fighting and some alarming setbacks. "I am no Montgomery-lover," wrote Bedell-Smith, Eisenhower's Chief of Staff, after the war, "but I give him his full due and believe that for certain types of operation he is without an equal...Normandy is such an operation." If this proverbially cautious British commander now believed that he could achieve a bold stroke against the Germans, it must be worth the gamble to let him try. The rewards of success could be immense.

The decision was made at a meeting on 10 September. Eisenhower accepted the British field-marshal's plan for a thrust through Holland to seize a bridge across the Rhine at Arnhem, opening a path to the Ruhr. For this purpose, the British would be reinforced by SHAEF's strategic reserve, the First Airborne Army awaiting orders around airfields in England. The British would also be granted a special allocation of fuel and supplies, diverted from the American armies. Eisenhower and his staff were bemused to hear from Montgomery soon after the 10 September meeting that, if the Rhine crossing at Arnhem could be secured, he now envisaged a northern drive through the Ruhr towards Berlin by some sixteen or eighteen divisions. SHAEF found it difficult to imagine that such a relatively small force could break the German front, any more than Patton's Third Army could make a war-winning advance on its own. The logisticians also doubted whether even sixteen divisions could be fuelled and supplied in Germany without the use of Antwerp.

Omar Bradley was among those who urged Eisenhower to forget the Arnhem plan and commit Montgomery to clearance of the Antwerp approaches. But SHAEF authorization for the airborne operation had been granted and was not rescinded. As late as 15 September, the Supreme Commander himself remained not merely optimistic but euphoric. He believed that within a week or two at most the Allied armies would have closed up on the Rhine. "The Germans will have stood in defense of the Ruhr and Frankfurt, and will have had a sharp defeat inflicted upon them... Clearly Berlin is the main prize," he wrote in a circular to his commanders. "There is no doubt whatever, in my mind, that we should concentrate all our energies on a rapid thrust." Bradley's aide likewise wrote on 15 September: "Brad and Patton agree neither will be too surprised if we are on the Rhine in a week... General anxious to slam on through to Berlin."

THE STRUGGLE TO destroy Hitler brought together in Europe an extraordinary mingling of humanity. World war had displaced tens of millions of people, some by choice and most by compulsion. Everywhere the shadow of conflict extended, there were men, women and sometimes children who had been arbitrarily removed from their natural abodes and relocated upon alien soil, among people they had never known before. Some in consequence found themselves in rags, others in uniform. The war created a host of temporary new loyalties and placed all manner of citizens of many nations in unfamiliar circumstances, united only by the demands of defeating the enemy and, if possible, surviving to go home. Within Eisenhower's huge command, there were men from every corner of the United States and the British Isles, as well as Frenchmen, Poles, Canadians, Belgians, Dutchmen and a smattering of representatives from scores of other nations. Consider one small unit, the RAF's 268 Squadron, flying

Typhoons on reconnaissance missions for First Canadian Army: in September 1944 this comprised seven Canadians, two Australians, three Trinidadians, one Maltese, one Scot and one Welshman. They were later joined by two Poles and an Indian. It is little wonder that such men emerged from their wartime experience as a very internationally minded generation.

Eisenhower's forces were now formed into three army groups, containing twenty-eight American divisions, eighteen British and Canadian, one Polish, and eight makeshift French formations, manned chiefly by undisciplined *maquisards*. The latter were included in the order of battle for their political rather than military value. The Germans in the west mustered forty-eight infantry and fifteen panzer and panzergrenadier divisions, but these possessed only 25 per cent of their proper strength and equipment. The Allies outnumbered the Germans by twenty to one in tanks. Against the Luftwaffe's western strength of 573 serviceable combat aircraft, the Allies could deploy some 14,000.

Yet the Allies' exhilaration about the inroads they had made upon their enemy's strength in Normandy might have been moderated had they paused to consider that Hitler still disposed of more than ten million uniformed men. The Wehrmacht's strength had peaked at 6.5 million in 1943, and now stood at 3.4 million, but that of the Waffen SS was still increasing, towards a summit of 830,000 at the beginning of 1945. Millions of foreigners from Hitler's empire had been armed and garbed in German uniform, and some fought with the desperation of the damned. It was true that many of the Germans being mobilized were untrained, poorly armed and not yet embodied in coherent formations. A million men wasted rations in the uniform of Göring's Luftwaffe, which in the air was almost moribund. A large proportion of German recruits would have been rejected for service in the American or British armies on grounds of age or physical infirmity. The Russians discovered that among their vast summer haul of captives was a Wehrmacht soldier who had spent two years in a British prison camp before being repatriated as unfit for military service. The Volkssturm, Germany's Home Guard, was a minimal asset. Yet granted the German genius for transforming the most unpromising human material into serviceable fighting units, the sheer mass of Germany's surviving men at arms demanded more respect than it received from Allied commanders in early September 1944. Even in the sixth year of the Second World War, some senior commanders experienced difficulty in grasping the titanic scale of the conflict, and the resources available to a ruthless and boundlessly ingenious enemy.

The Allies possessed overwhelming material advantages, above all in the might of the Red Army. But fighting soldiers were quicker to perceive the gravity of the task they still faced than those at rear headquarters. The optimism of Allied commanders was fed by a daily diet of intercepted signals between Germany's generals, proclaiming their desperation. At the sharp end, however, renewed fighting along the Allied front cooled optimism. On 14 September,

Colonel Turner-Cain wrote in his diary: "The national press is at last more sober in its estimate of when the war would end. They now talk of three months instead of next week. Their idiotic optimism had a peculiar effect on men's morale, and one could feel them saying to themselves: 'Why should I put myself at risk of being killed or wounded if the war is to end next week?' Hence they were a bit sticky about doing anything aggressive." The British forces' shortage of manpower, which was to dog their operations from Normandy to the Elbe, was already exercising its baleful influence. Most companies in Turner-Cain's battalion were reduced to two officers, and some to two platoons. Replacements proved to be a ragbag of men unwillingly transferred from the Service Corps, military police and disbanded units.

Eisenhower sustained hope in Montgomery's breast about a British charge into Germany by writing to him: "My own choice of routes for making the all-out offensive... is from the Ruhr to Berlin." Perhaps, after all, the Supreme Commander would grant 21st Army Group's commander his triumphal march on Hitler's capital. It would be time enough to review grand strategy, however, when it was seen whether Eisenhower's "choice" was attainable by way of a British bridge across the Rhine. While the commanders of America's armies fumed and fretted about the gasoline famine which Montgomery's grand play had forced upon them, in the third week of September 1944 Western Allied leaders' eyes focused upon a single road to the prim, neat Dutch town of Arnhem.

CHAPTER TWO

The Bridges to Arnhem

THE DROP

WINSTON CHURCHILL sent a note to the British Chiefs of Staff in August 1943, cautioning them against giving frivolous codenames to actions involving deadly peril. No wife or mother, he said, wanted to remember that her husband or son had died in an operation christened "Bunnyhug" or "Ballyhoo." Yet the planners of the assault on the Dutch bridges came close to breaching Churchill's injunction, by giving a codename of such notable banality as "Market Garden" to a battle that would have tragic consequences for many people of five nationalities.

In the last year of the war, Allied commanders often found themselves constrained by decisions made long before, in very different strategic circumstances. Ships and tanks were designed and committed to mass production before it became plain that other types of war machine could better serve navies and armies. Likewise, back in 1940 and 1941 the Germans had achieved spectacular successes with parachute troops. The imaginations of even such austere officers as Marshall and Brooke were seized by the possibilities of airborne assault. Both the British and Americans hastened to create parachute units, for which some of their boldest and best soldiers volunteered. British paratroopers carried out several notable small-scale raids. One British and two American airborne divisions achieved great success on D-Day in disorganizing the German defences. But sceptics drew attention to the fact that, wherever lightly armed, air-landed forces encountered serious opposition, they suffered heavily. The cost of paratroops in personnel and resources was enormous. U.S. and British airborne divisions showed outstanding fighting skills in Normandy. Critics asked why they could not simply be used as elite infantry rather than reserved for a parachute role, the relevance of which seemed increasingly doubtful. The Germans, indeed, never again deployed their *Fallschirmjäger* for massed drops after suffering terrible losses in Crete.

But the Allied Airborne Army had been created, and the apostles of the new art of envelopment from the sky were determined that it should be used. "Brereton [U.S. commander of First Airborne Army] seems determined to use paratroops, as is Browning," wrote Bradley's aide Colonel Chester Hansen on 1 September. "They have had any numbers of schemes... [Brad] had to remind [Brereton] of the parallel here with Patton's envelopment by sea [in Sicily], when it was not necessary." Major-General James Gavin of the 82nd Airborne, a passionate advocate of parachute war, voiced the impatience of many comrades about the failure to find them a role in what looked like the last act of the north-west Europe campaign. The brilliant thirty-seven-year-old "Slim Jim" Gavin, a former ranker who had reached West Point by way of a Brooklyn orphanage, wanted his division either thrown into action or transferred to Asia: "I am for the latter. This affair is practically wound up."

Although the Airborne were considered crack troops, they could not carry into battle the heavy weapons essential for sustained survival on the battlefield against enemy armour and artillery. Lacking significant transport, they could only occupy and hold ground below or close to their dropping points. But when the plan to seize the bridges to the Rhine was conceived in the first days of September, just a fortnight after the German Army in the west had suffered catastrophe in the Falaise Gap, it seemed unlikely that the airborne invaders would face much opposition. Many men felt as assured as Major Bill Deedes that "This is the end, this is it, we've beaten them." Deedes's unit took Lille with a squadron of tanks and a company of riflemen: "There seemed no limit to what we could achieve."

Release of the files of German signals intercepted by Bletchley Park has conclusively demonstrated Allied knowledge that 9th SS and 10th SS Panzer Divisions were refitting in the Arnhem area. Commanders had no need of the aerial photographs which were the focus of thirty-five years' post-war controversy. The German formations were, however, shadows of their old selves. They still possessed their reconnaissance battalions, together with a regiment apiece of armoured infantry, and an assortment of weak support elements. But they mustered only around twenty tanks between them, along with some 150 armoured cars and half-tracks. Allied commanders should have paused to consider that, while the latter posed no great threat to Allied armoured divisions, they still posed a formidable challenge to paratroopers, chiefly dependent on small arms. Yet when Bedell-Smith raised with Montgomery the issue of the panzers, the field-marshal ridiculed his doubts.

Lieutenant-General Frederick "Boy" Browning, the corps commander who would lead the airborne landing, was a forty-one-year-old Guardsman who aroused mixed feelings. His aristocratic mien received more respect than it deserved from some British colleagues. Although a junior officer of proven courage in the First World War, he had never seen action in Hitler's war. He possessed a certain celebrity as husband of the novelist Daphne du Maurier, yet Americans found him the sort of mannered Englishman they liked least. Gavin wrote in his diary on 6 September: "[Browning] unquestionably lacks the standing, influence and judgment that comes with a proper troop experience . . . His staff was superficial . . . Why the British units fumble along, 'flub the dub' as the boys say, becomes more and more apparent. Their tops lack the knowhow, never do they get down into the dirt and learn the hard way." But Browning's eagerness for Market Garden was plain. "We called it Operation KCB," a 1st Airborne Division intelligence officer, Captain John Killick, said sardonically, noting a belief among his comrades that its principal objective was to win Browning a knighthood. Killick described the airborne commander as "that popinjay," referring to the general's preoccupation with his own turn-out. Many even among the British would have been happier to see command of Market Garden in the hands of the able and combat-experienced American airborne commander Matthew Ridgway.

Gavin disliked the plan from the outset: "It looks very rough. If I get through this one, I will be very lucky. It will, I am afraid, do the airborne cause a lot of harm." The Polish Parachute Brigade commander, Stanislaw Sosabowski, whose men were scheduled to reinforce the British on the third day of the operation, also expressed fierce reservations. The British regarded the Pole as an absurd figure. Staff officers sometimes giggled like schoolboys when Sosabowski held forth emotionally at planning meetings. "But later," said John Killick, "we realized that some of the things he said, some of the difficulties he raised, were serious and valid."

If legend is correct, that "Boy" Browning suggested before the drop that Montgomery's plan represented an attempt to advance "a bridge too far," then the remark confirms his critics' views about the general's meagre intellect. Market Garden could not succeed partially, by winning some of the bridges northeast of the British front. To justify the whole operation, it was essential to seize the Rhine crossing at Arnhem. Anything less would be meaningless, an assault into a cul-de-sac.

The overwhelming flaw in the plan was that it required the British Second Army's tanks to relieve in turn the 101st Airborne at Eindhoven and Son, the 82nd at Nijmegen and the 1st Airborne at Arnhem along a single Dutch road. It was impossible for the vast armoured column to leave the tarmac, because the adjoining countryside was too soft to accommodate tanks, and in some places was heavily wooded. On the advance to Arnhem, the overwhelming superiority of the allied armies over the enfeebled Germans became irrelevant. The outcome would be determined by a contest between the defenders and the needle point of the British force—which effectively meant a single squadron of tanks and its supporting infantry. If the advance bogged down, 1st Airborne Division would be left unsupported to hold the most distant objective—the bridge at

Arnhem—for longer than any force in the short history of airborne warfare. The plan called for the tanks of XXX Corps to get there in forty-eight hours. Even that interval seemed perilously long if the Germans could deploy tanks against the paratroopers.

These hazards were known to the men who planned the operation, above all to Montgomery himself, normally the most cautious of commanders. His chief of staff, Freddie de Guingand, was ill in England. De Guingand telephoned from his sickbed to suggest that the airborne operation was being launched too late to exploit German disarray, and that XXX Corps's push to Arnhem was being made on too narrow a front. Montgomery dismissed these strictures, asserting that de Guingand was "out of touch." The field-marshal's enthusiasm for Market Garden was so uncharacteristic that it has puzzled some historians. Yet his motives do not seem hard to read. Bitterly chastened by his removal from the Allied ground command, he was determined to sustain the primacy of his own role in the battle for Germany. In consequence, he focused his entire attention on the issue of how the enemy's front might be broken in Holland, where the British stood. He displayed no interest in other opportunities further south, on the front of Bradley's U.S. 12th Army Group. David Fraser, a Grenadier officer in north-west Europe, later a general and biographer of Brooke, said: "Montgomery's jealousy of Eisenhower affected his decisions at every stage." This seems just.

The British field-marshal, like most of his fellow commanders, believed that the Germans in the west were broken and that the Allied task was now to exploit the victory achieved in Normandy only three weeks earlier. In the euphoria of September 1944, Montgomery and his colleagues concluded that the normal rules governing engagement with the German army could be suspended. The British planners persuaded themselves that the hard part was over, that they were now engaged in gathering the spoils of victory. They threw away all that they had learned since 1939 about the speed of reaction of Hitler's army, its brilliance at improvisation, its dogged skill in defence, its readiness always to punish allied mistakes. Market Garden was an operation that might have succeeded triumphantly, as several British African offensives succeeded triumphantly, if the defenders had been Italians of Mussolini's army. Instead, however, on the ground in Holland were soldiers of Hitler.

THE FIRST ELEMENTS of three airborne divisions landed by parachute and glider in the early afternoon of Sunday 17 September, ninety minutes before the tanks spearheading XXX Corps crossed their start line on the Meuse–Escaut Canal. Private Bob Peatling, a signaller with the British 2 Para, was thrilled to be seeing action at last. Although he had joined the army in 1942, he had never heard a shot fired in earnest: "We feared we'd never get into it unless we got cracking. I had no idea what battle would be like, but there was a wonderful feeling that Sunday." A keen boy scout in his childhood, Peatling packed in his kit for Arnhem two books on scouting, to read in his leisure hours on the battle-field. One was entitled *Rovering to Success.*

Jack Reynolds's mortar platoon of the South Staffordshires was part of the air-landing brigade of 1st Airborne. Lieutenant Reynolds, a former local govern-ment clerk from Chichester in Sussex, was a veteran of twenty-two. On his first parachute jump, he had seen a man in his "stick" plunge to the ground in a fatal "roman candle." Later he survived the bloodbath of the 1943 airborne landings in Sicily. Reynolds observed cheerfully that his platoon, who would have to carry into battle the terrific burden of three-inch mortars and ammunition, were "the biggest and thickest men in the battalion." He felt uncomfortably aware that the Staffords were not the unit they had been two years earlier: "The young recruits and officers seemed so innocent. In my platoon many blokes were fresh out of training. We had lost a lot of good chaps in Sicily and Italy. There wasn't the same spirit now. How could there be?" It is often asserted that 1st Airborne Division was an elite. Yet in truth even its own men had reserva-tions about the quality of several units, and especially of their commanders.

Captain Julius Neave was adjutant of the 13th/18th Royal Hussars, one of Montgomery's armoured units. Neave wrote in his diary: "There is no doubt in [our commanding officer's] mind that the war will be over this year, and this is undoubtedly the prevalent view everywhere . . . Yesterday we were told that the present operation 'Market Garden' would be the last Corps battle, and it is anticipated that now we shall be split into Battle Groups to liquidate isolated resistance."

Every man who parachutes into action faces a dramatic mental adjustment between the tranquillity of the world he quits on take-off and the white heat of battle which he encounters a few hours later. Captain John Killick found it unreal to sit among comrades reading the Sunday newspapers in their comfort-able mess in England until trucks arrived to take them to the airfield. He felt lit-tle apprehension: "We were young. We were light-hearted." Partly because so many transport aircraft were shifting fuel to the armies in France, the landings required three separate lifts, spread over three days. This badly weakened the fighting power of the Allied airborne divisions in the first vital hours. The short-age of capacity made it seem all the more grotesque that Browning used thirty-six aircraft to move his own headquarters in the first wave. He should have insisted that the Allied transport fleet make two trips, rather than one, on the first day. This would have been perfectly feasible, at the cost of some strain upon aircrew. The initial landings were overwhelmingly successful: 331 British aircraft and 319 gliders, together with 1,150 U.S. aircraft and 106 gliders, landed 20,000 men in good order between Eindhoven and Arnhem.

Lieutenant Jack Curtis Goldman was flying a Waco glider carrying a com-

munications jeep of the U.S. 504th Regiment. Like so many of his generation "Goldie," a twenty-one-year-old from San Angelo, Texas, had always yearned to fly: "More than life itself, I had wanted to be a fighter pilot." Imperfect eyesight caused him to be rejected for combat pilot training, but the recruiting sergeant said he would overlook the problem if Goldman would sign up for gliders. He found the experience "like trying to ride a brahman bull at a rodeo. Anyone who has ever experienced turbulence in an aircraft, just multiply it by ten and you will have some idea what a glider was like. Yet most of us... were eager to fly into combat, particularly those who were single and had no responsibilities. For me, the war was a big adventure, and September 17th, 1944, was to be one of the most fantastic adventures of my life."

Above Holland that Sunday, on tow at 120 m.p.h., the young Texan found an 82nd Airborne jeep driver squeezing into the cockpit behind him. "I'm praying for you," the soldier said. "Why?" "Because if you get hit, I don't know how to fly this glider." They cut the tow at 1,000 feet, and went into a steep, spiralling dive to avoid a stall. Goldman tried to align the glider with the plough lines he saw beneath him, but found the ground rushing up to meet him at right angles to the furrows. Bump, lurch, bump, they hurtled across the field in their flimsy vessel of plywood and canvas, already hearing explosions. Then they were down, just north of the Maas river, a mere six miles from the Dutch border with Germany. They flipped the nose hatches. The terrified jeep driver bore them full-tilt towards the shelter of a wood. Goldman met some fellow pilots. They exulted wildly in having done their job and survived: "We were really happy, happy campers at that moment." Unlike British glider pilots, their American counterparts were not expected to fight in the ground battle. Their job was over once they had landed their clumsy craft. Many disappeared on sprees in Holland and Belgium that lasted for days.

Bob Peatling of 2 Para was awed by the spectacle of 1st Airborne's drop: "It was a wonderful sight to see everybody coming down." At first, after he himself hit the ground amid the cloud of parachutes filling the sky and collapsing on the earth, he heard no firing. The British descended on to fields and open heathland some six miles north-west of Arnhem bridge, with the Rhine between themselves and XXX Corps. Everybody converged on the rendezvous where Colonel John Frost was blowing his hunting horn, and formed files for the advance into Arnhem. When they began to move, they made slow progress: "We kept meeting bits of opposition, and having to stop. It was a long, hot afternoon. But I thought: 'This is better than England!'" Peatling was not the only one dismayed by 2 Para's sluggish pace. The divisional commander, Major-General Roy Urquhart, expressed his concern in the first hours.

Corporal Harry Trinder's glider overshot the landing zone and crashed into a pine wood. He found himself trapped behind the cockpit bulkhead in the wreckage, and it was some time before he could be cut free. Before the battle even started, Trinder was out of it with a badly cut eye and a clutch of broken ribs. He was laid among the wounded who were already coming in, including some whose injuries were plainly mortal. Trinder noticed that "those whom the MO thought were completely beyond hope were given a massive injection of morphine, and put on one side to die." He thought himself lucky.

John Killick dumped his parachute and walked up to divisional headquarters on the Arnhem landing zone, to find a divisional signals officer reciting monotonously and vainly into a handset: "Hello, Sunray, are you receiving me?" This was the first evidence of the shameful, almost comprehensive failure of 1st Airborne Division's wireless communications, which was to dog every aspect of the battle which followed.* Killick set out to walk alone into Arnhem, in pursuit of Frost's men. A few yards down the road, he found an abandoned German BMW motorcycle. Commandeering this, he sped eastwards. A mile further on, he saw a string of German army signposts beside a house, and wandered in. This was the Tafelburg Hotel, Field-Marshal Walter Model's headquarters at Oosterbeek, hastily abandoned by Army Group B as they saw the first paratroopers descending. Not a soul was in sight. Killick switched on a radio set, and idly picked at some meatballs on the dining-room table. After starting his day reading the Sunday papers in England, "I felt in an absurd position, now to be listening to the BBC and eating the Germans' lunch."

Sergeant George Schwemmer, a panzergrenadier with 10th SS Panzer at Arnhem, had been drafted to the division as a replacement after its withdrawal from Normandy. Although Schwemmer was thirty-one, he had managed to stay out of the army until 1944, performing labour service. He would have been more than happy to continue his wartime career road-building and helping with the harvest. Now instead, however, he found himself reluctantly commanding a platoon of panzergrenadiers, most of them young replacements. More than a few of of 10th SS Panzer's soldiers were not eager Nazis, but "odds and sods" like Schwemmer, scraped together from the depots. He himself was billeted in a house on the edge of Arnhem, and ran out when he heard firing. His first glimpse of the attackers was a wrecked glider which had crashed in a field. He saw German soldiers gesturing to each other as they deployed. Dutch civilians were craning out of every house. Schwemmer shouted brusquely to them to get their heads in and close the windows. Then he ran to muster his unit, which was quickly plunged into street fighting for the town.

Field-Marshal Model, who received the surprise of his life when British

---

*One Arnhem wireless-operator suggested afterwards that the disastrous communications failure stemmed not from poor radio terrain, as apologists suggested, but laziness about recharging radio batteries after the many "stand-tos" for airborne operations that were subsequently aborted. This could not be a complete explanation for the disaster—it is known that many wireless sets were sent with the wrong crystals—but may have been a contributory factor.

paratroops began to land within two miles of his headquarters as he sat down to the lunch later sampled by John Killick, at first flattered himself that the attack was intended as a coup-de-main to seize his own person. He leaped into a car, papers spewing out of his briefcase as he ran down the steps of the Tafelburg, and shifted his command post six miles south-eastwards. Model was fifty-three, a music-master's son from Magdeburg whose undoubted military competence was less important in Hitler's eyes than his loyalty. Army Group B's commander was untainted by aristocratic connections, a blunt professional who still asserted that the war could be won. Model and his senior officers now urgently assessed the nature of the Allied threat, and began to assemble resources to meet it. The 9th SS and 10th SS Panzer Divisions possessed about 3,000 men apiece, together with a company of Mark IV tanks, and assorted support weapons. The strength of each division amounted, in total, to that of a weak Allied brigade.

At 1340* all units of the two divisions were ordered to stand to. General Walter Bittrich, commanding II SS Panzer Corps, quickly guessed that Allied intentions focused upon the bridges to the Rhine. He ordered 9th SS to address itself chiefly to dealing with the British at Arnhem. Tenth SS was to defend the Nijmegen bridge, ten miles southward. By 1540, 9th SS had assembled a force of thirty armoured cars and personnel carriers. "These soldiers were thinking about their families, as everything had virtually been packed for the move to [Germany]," said Captain Wilfried Schwartz. "The mood was a resigned: 'Here we go again!' They were inevitably disappointed at first, but the officers and NCOs were able to overcome this and get the soldiers quickly into action." At 1800, some two hours before British paratroopers reached the Arnhem bridge, Captain Viktor Graebner's 9th SS armoured column roared between the great sweeps of girders traversing the Rhine at Arnhem and headed for Nijmegen. Afterwards, there were recriminations among the Germans about a confusion of orders: Bittrich had intended 9th SS to secure both ends of the Arnhem bridge before proceeding to Nijmegen, and he had wanted Graebner on the south bank. Yet German success in reinforcing Nijmegen before the Americans got there was to prove even more important than events at Arnhem. Graebner's dash, along with the commitment of some 10th SS units, decided the outcome of the entire Market Garden battle, by pre-empting the Allies and attaining a vital objective on their road. We should note the timings. The British had begun to land five hours—*five hours*—before Graebner crossed Arnhem bridge. Frost's men were still not even in sight. This was a prodigious amount of leeway to allow German soldiers with motor vehicles to respond to a surprise assault. To have a chance of success, the Allies needed to seize the Dutch bridges within

---

*All times relating to military operations in the text are given in accordance with the twenty-four-hour clock, while those concerning civilian life are given on the twelve-hour clock—that is, 2 a.m. rather than 0200.

minutes of landing. The British and German timetables were already perilously out of step, to the detriment of the attackers.

General Maxwell Taylor's 101st Airborne Division was responsible for seizing the objectives closest to the Allied ground advance: the bridges at Eindhoven, thirteen miles from the XXX Corps start line; Son, five miles beyond; and the Willems Canal, five miles further. The moment the "Screaming Eagles" hit their drop zones, they moved with all the urgency that had been expected of them to secure four crossings over the River Aa and the Willems Canal. They gained the road bridge over the Dommel river and the canal bridge at Best. As they approached the bridge over the Wilhelmina Canal at Son, four miles north of Eindhoven, it exploded before their eyes. Paratroopers swam the canal to establish a bridgehead on the southern side. By midnight, though Taylor's men were facing heavy fighting, the 101st held a fifteen-mile corridor. And although Allied plans were optimistic, they had made ample provision for German demolitions. On 800 trucks and tank transporters, 5,000 British engineers and hundreds of tons of Bailey bridging stood in readiness to span the gap at Son and other river obstacles—granted only the hours necessary to get the equipment forward and to do the job.

The landing of Gavin's 82nd Airborne was an overwhelming success: 7,467 men reached their landing zones. One regiment, the 504th, dropped two miles east of its objective, the 1,500-foot Maas river bridge at Grave. They rushed the crossing, and seized it intact. The 505th and 508th had to cover six miles between their landing zone on the heights of Groesbeek and the town of Nijmegen. By 1930, they had secured intact a crossing over the Maas–Waal canal. This was a considerable achievement. Yet they faced the same problem as the British 1st Airborne. It took time for units to assemble on the ground and get into action. Given the decision to land the 82nd so far from its key objectives, no more could have been expected of the paratroopers. Yet once again a six- or seven-hour delay, against an enemy who could deploy in motor vehicles, was critical. Gavin's last objective, the 1,960-foot road bridge at Nijmegen, was the most important of all. Yet here his men were frustrated. As the 1/508th advanced through the streets into the town, they encountered heavy German fire. The Reconnaissance Battalion of 9th SS Panzer had got there before them. Though it had taken Graebner's men some hours to make their vehicles fit to travel, and to probe warily down the road south of Arnhem looking out for paratroopers, they had only fifteen miles to cover and suffered no interference. It remains a mystery why Allied fighter-bombers were not deployed to patrol this vital link, to deal with just such enemy movements as those of Graebner.

Gavin acknowledged long afterwards that he made a mistake by assigning Roy Lindquist, least impressive of his regimental commanders, to take Nijmegen. The 82nd's commander considered that Lindquist did not address the town and its vital bridge "either intelligently or aggressively," partly because the 508th had been given too many assignments, across too wide a front. American planning focused on the threat of German intervention from the Reichswald Forest north and east of Nijmegen, and laid much emphasis upon holding their dropping zone at Groesbeek, to frustrate such an enemy movement. Knowing the critical importance of Nijmegen, Gavin regretted not giving the job to Colonel Reuben Tucker's 504th, his best unit. Yet, for any airborne soldiers, the Waal was bound to be a tough assignment, once surprise had been lost and it became necessary to fight through urban streets to reach the bridge.

Some of the best troops in the German army were now deployed in readiness to fight the Americans for possession of Nijmegen bridge. Model had explicitly forbidden its demolition. He wanted to hold open the road to move reinforcements southwards for a counter-attack. Many accounts of Market Garden have concentrated on the "might-have-beens" of British failure at Arnhem. Yet it seems at least as relevant to examine those of Nijmegen. If elements of the 82nd Airborne had been landed closer to the bridge, and if the vast Allied force of fighter-bombers had been used to block German armoured vehicles dashing into battle along open Dutch roads, that crossing could have been taken on the first day. As it was, failure swiftly to secure Nijmegen was at least as damaging to the outcome of the battle as British inability to capture both sides of the bridge at Arnhem. If paratroopers were able quickly to seize objectives, they might realistically be expected to hold these against enemy counter-attacks. But if they were required to fight a long battle to capture their prizes, while the enemy was able to reinforce, then it was most unlikely that the airborne force could prevail.

The three British parachute battalions which set out to march into Arnhem on the first afternoon did not approach the town until evening. The Germans faced grievous problems in responding to the Allied assault. Many of their men, too, had to advance into battle on foot. Others travelled on bicycles and in commandeered civilian vehicles. But the defenders possessed just enough transport and were given just enough time for small forces to throw themselves across the paths of the paratroopers. It has often been suggested that the assault on Arnhem was frustrated by SS panzergrenadiers. This is a half-truth. In the first hours after the Allied landings, decisive delay was imposed by a miscellany of German sub-units. These created a thin screen east of the town where most of the available British soldiers expended hours, and suffered serious casualties, attempting to break through. By chance, SS Captain Sepp Krafft's 16th Training and Replacement Battalion, scarcely a crack force, was exercising that Sunday afternoon in woods less than two miles from the British landing zone—and between the paratroops and Arnhem. Krafft dispatched two patrols to investigate. He guessed immediately that Arnhem's bridge must be the British objective. He deployed his men to cover the two main roads into the town. By 1530, his force amounted to thirteen officers, seventy-three NCOs and 359 men, with some mortars and anti-tank guns. This was the force which first engaged the leading elements of 1 and 3 Para Battalions, to critical effect.

Through the three hours that followed, Krafft's men held the paratroopers in play. By the time the British at last found side roads by which they could out-flank Krafft's little force, it was too late. Other German units were converging on the battlefield. Meanwhile, a detachment of ninety Luftwaffe signallers attacked the British landing zone. They were ineffectual, but 1st Airborne's men had to expend more time and effort upon fending them off. An SS party consisting of eighty men with one 88mm flak gun and one 20mm cannon came under fire as they rolled through Arnhem. The Germans had no idea what was going on. They simply leaped out of their vehicles and engaged 1 Para. Four lorry-loads of passing assault pioneers were exasperated to see tracer flying across the road. " 'Idiots!' we thought, 'they are on exercise!' " said Corporal Wolfgang Dom-browski. "But then a Wehrmacht major called across: 'That's live ammunition—the Tommies have landed!' " The pioneers, too, were thrown into the battle.

"Head for the sound of gunfire! That's where the front is!" was the German motto that afternoon. Staff-Sergeant Erwin Heck, a twenty-four-year-old instructor at the SS NCO school in Arnhem, was at the Dutch coast with most of the school's trainees when they heard of the landings. Heck, an SS veteran since 1938, still limped from a leg wound he had received on the Eastern Front in June. But on 17 September he commandeered a motorcycle and reached the bat-tlefield around 1900, well ahead of his men, who were following on pedal cycles and even horses. One of Heck's comrades said afterwards that the unit's move-ment was such a chaos of improvisations that it looked more like the retreat from Moscow than an advance into battle.

Early in the evening of 17 September, 1 and 3 Para were at last able to out-flank Captain Krafft's men. But by now a new German line had been formed between themselves and the town, manned by another scratch force com-manded by thirty-four-year-old Colonel Ludwig Spindler, a much decorated veteran of Normandy and the Eastern Front. Before the battle was over, Spindler's force embraced elements of sixteen units. Most of them were gun-ners and dismounted tank men fighting as infantry. There were a hundred assault pioneers, and even a party of hastily armed civilian pioneers. There were also, importantly, some self-propelled anti-tank guns, armoured half-tracks and three tanks.

Not all the units of 1st Airborne Division won German respect for their per-formance. An SS dispatch rider was among a party which ambushed a British column of 1 Para marching towards Arnhem. The Germans killed most of the lead platoon and took more than thirty prisoners. "They were so beaten and submissive that it only needed one man to march them off to the rear," said Corporal Alfred Zeigler contemptuously. "We were not too impressed by this lot. They were completely surprised. I ask you, they came marching straight down the road in a company file! What a nonsense! We were so few! They should have taken a route through the trees…perhaps they were too arrogant or too cocksure." Neither 1 nor 3 Para ever reached the bridge at Arnhem. As early as Monday evening, 18 September, they had already suffered heavy attrition. Both battalions contained some brave men, but neither seems to have fought imaginatively or skilfully.

The outcome of the later stages of the Arnhem battle, when the Germans had time to deploy major units, was unsurprising. But it was an extraordinary achievement by low-grade troops, taken utterly by surprise, that in the first hours they were able to halt elite British units, thoroughly briefed and trained for the operation. Much of the credit lies with Colonel Spindler. Something is also due to the unidentified German sergeant who searched a crashed Waco glider, no doubt looking for loot. Instead, he found a copy of Market Garden's air plan, inexcusably carried into battle by an Allied officer. By the evening of 17 September, Model knew the Allied objectives and order of battle.

THE DÉBÂCLE

THE FIRST HOURS decided the fate of Market Garden. If the British ground advance had started better, if the Americans had gained Nijmegen bridge, if the British had been able to occupy Arnhem in force and create a defensive corridor along the river to their dropping zone, they might, just might, have been able to hold out until relieved by XXX Corps. Instead, only a mixed force of some 500 men, based on Colonel John Frost's 2 Para, was able to reach the north end of Arnhem bridge at 2000, having chanced upon the only road into town which was not blocked by Krafft's or Spindler's men.

Captain John Killick on his captured BMW motorbike joined the tail-end of 2 Para's long march column, snaking through the streets in failing light. The British soldiers saw the railway bridge over the Rhine suddenly explode, as the Germans detonated demolition charges. In the deepening darkness, one of Frost's men said crossly to Killick: "Take that fucking motorcycle away." Its exhaust had been punctured by a bullet and emitted vivid blue flames. Killick ditched the bike, together with his pack, an action which caused him lasting guilt, because it contained his notebook, listing names of Dutch Resistance contacts. The paras trudged on towards the road bridge, infantrymen mingled with assorted stray bodies such as himself. Eventually, Killick's group came to rest in a Dutch police building close to the pontoon below the road bridge. There, among men of 2 Para's A Company, the intelligence officer fell into uneasy sleep.

As Colonel Frost approached the bridge, he ordered Private Bob Peatling to go and look for his lost B Company. Peatling returned after an hour wandering empty streets, to report that he could find no sign of the missing men. There was desultory firing across the bridge, from the south end still held by the Germans. Peatling was ordered to escort Frost's second-in-command to inspect the pontoons, a little way downriver. As they approached, Germans began to fire tracer at them from the far bank. Peatling fired a few rounds back, then looked for his officer. "Major Wallis! Major Wallis!" he called in vain through the darkness of the town. Wallis was killed shortly afterwards, by a burst of "friendly fire" from a quick-fingered British Bren-gunner. The bewildered private soldier, now alone, walked the silent streets until he met some military police escorting twenty-two German prisoners. Peatling attached himself to the column. They arrived at the police station, where they put the Germans in the cells, and exchanged warm greetings with some Dutch policemen, who then left, saying cheerfully: "It's all yours now." The little group of British soldiers remained silent and watchful all night, listening to the firing in the town. At first light, to their dismay a column of German trucks drew up outside. Infantry descended and clattered along the street. Peatling said to the only British officer present: "I'm off back to the bridge." The lieutenant told him to stay put. The German prisoners began to demand food. Two German soldiers strode heedless into the police station. The British shot them, then waited in deep apprehension. Amazingly, nothing happened. The Germans outside appeared not to have noticed the firing. Then a paratrooper on the first floor loosed a Sten-gun burst into the street. There was a brief exchange of fire, before silence fell again. The enemy in Arnhem seemed as bewildered and uncertain as the British.

It was Tuesday afternoon before a large body of Germans approached the police station purposefully. Somebody said to a British NCO, Sergeant Galloway: "Are you going to take that lot on?" No, said Galloway, "XXX Corps are going to be here in forty-eight hours." He walked out of the door with his hands in the air, and was shot at once. Chaos followed. Peatling bolted to the attic at the top of the building. He heard uproar as bursts of fire disposed of his comrades. Then the Germans broke in to release the prisoners. At last, the shooting stopped, and the enemy moved on. No one searched the attic. The frightened soldier assuaged his thirst by slipping downstairs when he dared, to drink water from the toilet bowl. He settled down to wait for British tanks.

YET THE RELIEF column was a long, long way off. At Arnhem bridge, half-tracks of 10th SS Panzer were now deployed on the south bank. Their firepower enabled the Germans to halt every attempt by Frost's men, holding the north end, to cross over. In a clash between armies, lightly protected half-tracks and armoured cars were regarded merely as tools for reconnaissance and transporting men. In Arnhem, however, every German fighting vehicle capable of withstanding small-arms fire was a menace to the paratroopers, equipped with only hand-held PIATs—British counterparts of the American bazooka—and two six-pounder anti-tank guns. From now on, the Germans were able to reinforce steadily, while the British haemorrhaged irreplaceable men, weapons and ammunition. The whole of 1st Airborne Division save Frost's little band was engaged in a desperate, ill-coordinated series of battles to break through into Arnhem while retaining control of its landing zones north-westwards. In the days that followed, the British perimeter shrank under relentless pressure. Historians have devoted so much attention to the heroism of 1st Airborne's struggle outside Arnhem that some have lost sight of the essential reality: within twelve hours of their landing, the British were no longer engaged in an operation with any chance of securing Arnhem bridge, but were battling for personal survival. Frost's men did not hold the bridge at Arnhem, they merely possessed a toehold at one end of it, which enabled them to dispute passage with the Germans. Extraordinary success would have been required from the relieving ground force to undo the consequences of the paratroopers' initial failure.

On Monday morning, 18 September, Lieutenant Jack Reynolds of the South Staffordshires had just assembled his platoon on the landing zone outside Arnhem, when he heard the booming voice of his brigadier, forty-seven-year-old "Pip" Hicks: "Reynolds—I want you to go forward. You're my 'eyes'." The young officer thought his brigadier "a pompous old fool with a First World War mentality and no idea how to deploy troops." But he obediently hitched a lift on a motorbike down the tramline towards Arnhem. They saw a tram on fire and heard distant gunfire, but at first met no enemy. Like hundreds of men that morning, Reynolds passed the German *Stadtkommandant* of Arnhem, Kussin, still hanging dead from his staff car at Wolfheze where British fire had caught him the previous day. He noticed that the cigarette the general had been smoking was burned down to his fingers. Reynolds returned to report that the road was open. The rifle companies began to advance, the mortar platoon following with its weapons on clumsy trolleys. Soon, they began to take incoming fire from the far side of the river. They could not get off the road, because every Dutch house and garden they passed was solidly fenced. The mortarmen found themselves among D Company, pinned down and suffering a steady drain of casualties. "From then on, it was a muddle," said Reynolds. He sited his mortars and went forward with a signaller, though the unit's 18 sets had not worked since they landed. He met a few stragglers, whom he took with him. Suddenly, he was disheartened to observe German tanks on the road below, on the British bank of the river, moving towards Arnhem bridge: "They weren't just trying to get behind us—they were already there." From that moment, British infantrymen were playing a deadly local game of hide-and-seek with German armoured vehicles. Reynolds never saw his mortars again. He asked his radio-operator whether he could make any contact. The signaller tried a bleak little joke: "Message from Brigade HQ—the men may shave. No sir, sorry sir, the set's dead." "Fuck it," said his officer, "pick up a Sten gun."

At the bridge engagement was not continuous. There were long intervals of inactivity, even boredom, for the paratroopers of Frost's A Company, while the Germans prepared their next move. "In some ways, the silences were the worst," said John Killick. "There was the apprehension, and then the sound of engines starting around the corners, followed by the grinding, squealing clatter of tracks, and the sudden terrible sight of a tank coming round the corner, traversing its turret towards you." It is interesting to speculate whether the battle might have been transformed had the British possessed a hand-held anti-tank weapon as good as that of the Germans, whose Panzerfaust frustrated many Allied attacks in the last year of the war. As it was, the British soldiers holding the north end of Arnhem bridge found themselves being relentlessly bombarded towards destruction, without the means to do much about it. "Everything was on fire," said John Killick. "It was a hellish scene." British ammunition was running out fast. The paratroopers in and around Arnhem, some nine battalion groups strong, now faced fourteen equivalent German units, which also possessed an overwhelming superiority in armoured vehicles and support weapons. Hereafter, the balance of forces would continue to shift relentlessly in the Germans' favour.

THE BRITISH LAND dash for Arnhem was commanded by the much loved Brian Horrocks of XXX Corps. "A tall, lithe figure," according to Chester Wilmot, "with white hair, angular features, penetrating eyes and eloquent hands, Horrocks moved among his troops more like a prophet than a general." "At the time, we liked Horrocks's affability and effervescence," said Captain David Fraser of the Guards Armoured Division. "Later, I came to think that he was a superficial character." Horrocks had brought with him from the North African desert a reputation as a driving leader. Yet from the outset almost everything that could go wrong with XXX Corps's breakout from their bridgehead on the Meuse–Escaut canal did so.

The 17 September operation began with a bombardment at 1415, pounding the German defences on a front a mile wide and five miles deep. The Irish Guards, leading the British advance, enjoyed a few illusory moments of optimism. Their Sherman tanks, adorned with huge orange phosphorescent panels to identify them to circling RAF Typhoons, sped away up the road at 1435. Then the Germans opened fire with machine-guns and Panzerfausts from well-concealed positions in neighbouring trees and ditches. It became plain that XXX Corps's bombardment had failed to suppress the defences. Half the leading squadron of Shermans was destroyed within minutes. British infantry advanced towards the woods to winkle out the opposition. Heavy air strikes were called in. The Germans had deployed elements of five battalions, mostly SS and paratroopers, with the dubious assistance of a penal unit. Many of the Germans holding the road had escaped from Belgium with Fifteenth Army, through the gap so disastrously left open by the British beyond Antwerp a fortnight earlier.

Horrocks had hoped that his tanks would be in Eindhoven within two hours. Instead, by nightfall they had advanced only seven miles. Among the German dead, to their alarm they identified men from 9th SS and 10th SS Panzer, General Student's First Parachute Army and Fifteenth Army. The enemy units defending the road were under strength, sketchily organized and ill equipped, but they included some of the best German fighting soldiers in Holland. As darkness fell, the British halted. The commanding officer of the Irish Guards later quoted a remark of his divisional chief of staff, who said that evening: "Push on to Eindhoven tomorrow, old boy, but take your time. We've lost a bridge." This remark—obviously influenced by reports of the crossing demolished at Son—reflected very poorly upon the leadership of Guards Armoured. The blown crossing at Son made it more urgent, not less, to reach the town and start repairs. Here was the first evidence that the divisional commander Allan Adair and his staff took far too relaxed a view of their task.

Captain Karl Godau, commanding a 105mm battery of 10th SS, was astounded when he saw the British stop that night. Godau never forgot the first Market Garden battles, because they fell on his thirty-first birthday. He had been a Waffen SS officer since 1938, with long service on the Eastern Front. He joined the panzers in Holland after a spell with a reserve regiment while he convalesced from wounds. On 17 September, his unit received the Alarm message at 1400, and soon afterwards was strafed by fighter-bombers as it moved forward, losing some trucks. Godau's four guns were sited within yards of the Eindhoven road, as the first Shermans rolled towards them. He spoke to the headquarters of *Kampfgruppe Walther*, and urged that his battery should not open fire at close range. Once they did so, revealing their own positions, they would have no hope of withdrawing to fight again, even if they knocked out a few Shermans. Godau's commander agreed, and ordered the battery to relocate a thousand yards further back, as the battle raged in front. There they waited for the British that evening. But the British did not come. "Their attack could have worked," said Godau wonderingly. "We had so little. If they had kept going that night, there was nothing worth mentioning between their halting place and Eindhoven." But moving tanks at night on a single-road front was a hazardous business, which the rulebook for armoured operations strongly discouraged. XXX Corps stopped.

Although British attention focused upon the enemy's self-propelled guns and 88mms, Germans say that on the first day most of the damage was done to the British armoured column by infantry armed with fausts, firing at point-

blank range from ditches beside the road. It should be stressed that the defenders did not find these encounters agreeable; indeed they found them shocking
affairs, in which they suffered casualties of around 50 per cent, most from
fighter-bombers and artillery fire. German communications were shattered.
Small parties of men were fighting when they met British forces, then falling
back as best they could. Kurt Student's so-called First Fallschirmjäger Army, in
reality amounting scarcely to a division, was split down the middle by the Allied
advance, and despaired of its own position. But, in a battle in which speed was
vital, Student's men had already inflicted crippling delay on the British.

Next morning, 18 September, the Guards met little opposition until they
reached the village of Aalst, and thereafter at a bridge over the Dommel, where
four 88mm guns covered the road. The tankmen called for air strikes, and were
furious to discover that these were unavailable. Despite bright sunshine over
Holland, the RAF's airfields in Belgium were fogged in. After two hours of
fighting, however, British luck changed. A reconnaissance group found a track
by which it outflanked the defenders, then charged them from the rear and
cleared the road. An hour later, Guards tanks were crawling through hysterically cheering Dutch crowds in Eindhoven. Men of the American 101st said later
that the people of Holland gave them their warmest welcome of the war. They
loved it. One of Taylor's men observed that he found the Dutch a great deal
more sympathetic than the British.

At 1930 on Monday, Guards Armoured reached the bridge at Son. The Allies
now controlled twenty-eight miles of the sixty-five-mile corridor to Arnhem.
The tanks halted to wait for the bridge to be repaired.

JACK REYNOLDS and his unit, the South Staffs, were locked into the long, messy,
bloody battle in the suburbs of Arnhem. There was no continuous front, no
coherent plan, merely a series of uncoordinated collisions between rival forces
in woods, fields, gardens and streets. "If anything moved, you fired." A German
tank shell landed beside Reynolds as he smoked a bulldog pipe. A blasted clod
of earth drove the pipe down his throat, breaking half his front teeth. Dutch
civilians craned from their homes in terrible innocence to watch the battle. The
British kept imploring them to take cover. "Typically British—whenever we
went into a house, we knocked on the door." Reynolds possessed a low opinion
of his own colonel, which was not improved when he heard the battalion padre
demand anxiously, "Shouldn't we protect the right flank?," and the CO duly
deployed a platoon as his spiritual adviser suggested. The young officer felt a
mounting rage towards his commanders—"That was when it got home to me,
what a very bad operation this was. The scales dropped from my eyes when I
realized just how far from our objective, the bridge, we'd been landed. We knew
what even a handful of Germans could do—they were so damned efficient."

During one endless night, as Reynolds crept from one position to another, he glimpsed a dark shape, groped forward and touched it. It was a German tank. He ran his hand down one of its tracks, then tiptoed away into the darkness: "I realized that we were completely overrun." He and his little group were forced to surrender next morning.

Colonel John Frost's men of 2 Para, holding the north end of Arnhem bridge, always understood that they had a simple task, albeit a herculean one: to survive. But for the rest of 1st Airborne Division, amid a complete breakdown of command and communications, it is hard to overstate the chaos that persisted throughout the battle. Units struggled piecemeal to resist German pressure on their shrinking perimeters. From beginning to end, most men were bewildered. "There was a lot of toing and froing among the officers about what we should do," said Private Ron Graydon, a signaller with D Company of the Border Regiment. At one point, Graydon was detailed to accompany a platoon probing a wood beside the road. He was able to use the excuse of his signalling responsibilities to say, "I'm not going into that bloody wood." Instead, he walked along the road. The platoon which went into the trees was not seen again for three days. Runner after runner was sent to the rear to describe the company's plight, but none returned. Graydon once made contact with XXX Corps on his 18 set and provided a map reference of his own position. This was his only successful radio link-up throughout the battle. Eventually abandoning his useless wireless, the signaller became a rifleman and lay in a foxhole, watching his company hour by hour bleed to death. Suddenly one morning, he woke from an uneasy doze at dawn to find Germans all around them, amid silence. Firing had stopped. The Borderers' survivors surrendered. "It was a total shambles."

In his lonely attic in Arnhem police station, Bob Peatling was keeping a diary, to relieve the dreadful boredom. "I am getting fed up with hearing German voices," he wrote, "and hope to wake up in the morning and hear a British sergeant-major blaspheming at his children in the approved style. This should make quite a historic diary, but personally, I would rather stay the quiet stay-at-home lad. There is no noise of any firing whatever. I can't make it out. Field-Marshal Montgomery has dropped a clanger at Arnhem, but me a bigger one. I keep hoping for a sight of a Sherman tank."

Along the 82nd Airborne's stretch of the corridor more than ten miles southwards, Gavin's men were fighting off German counter-attacks. The enemy had thrown into the battle replacement battalions of untrained conscripts and elderly First World War veterans. As they lay on their start line, one of the Germans called to his commander: "Captain, we've already stormed the Craoneer Heights in 1914!" His officer answered: "Yes, can't you see that it's up to us old boys to run the whole show again, and we will do it exactly as we did then." Gavin himself took up a rifle as his men raked these wretched elderly Germans with fire. "I was amazed by their stupidity," he wrote later. "To cross an open field in the face of the enemy was foolish." The Americans contained and eventually pushed back these attacks from the south. But the 82nd was still unable to break through to the bridge at Nijmegen, where the SS were strongly dug in on both banks. The division was obliged to withdraw some men from the fighting in the town, in order to launch a counter-attack to recover the Groesbeek dropping zone, which German troops had temporarily overrun. First Sergeant Leonard Funk of the 508th and a handful of men from his company killed fifteen Germans and knocked out four 20mm guns and three 88mms, for which he was awarded a well-deserved DSC. Funk later became a Medal of Honor winner in the Ardennes battle. The 508th was just able to clear the American landing zone in time for the arrival of 450 gliders carrying the 325th Infantry and their artillery.

The 101st Airborne was resisting constant pressure on its precarious perimeter. The commanding officer of the 3/502nd, Lieutenant-Colonel Robert Cole, who had won the Medal of Honor for his leadership in Normandy, was killed approaching a canal bridge at Best. The Germans promptly blew the bridge, but one of Cole's platoon leaders set about securing the area with only fifteen men. A two-man bazooka team, Privates Mann and Hoyle, successfully knocked out an 88mm gun. Joe Mann was hit twice, but fought on through the day until he was hit twice more, in both arms. The Germans counter-attacked, throwing grenades as they came. An American NCO, Sergeant Betras, threw one "potato masher" back at the enemy before it exploded. Another exploded beside the platoon machine-gunner, Private Laino. His left eye was blown out, and he lost the sight of the other. He was holding together what remained of his face when he felt another grenade land in his foxhole. He groped with his blood-soaked hands, found the grenade, and threw it out before it exploded. Joe Mann was in a trench with six other men, his shattered arms taped to his body. He suddenly shouted "Grenade!" as yet another fell in among them, then threw himself on top of it. After the explosion, he murmured, "My back's gone," then died. He was later awarded a posthumous Medal of Honor. Very few soldiers of any army can be expected to display the capacity for sacrifice shown by Private Mann. But every army needs a handful of his kind, in order to prevail. The survivors of his platoon were obliged to surrender when their ammunition was exhausted, but were freed soon afterwards by another unit of the 502nd.

The first British tanks crossed the new Bailey bridge at Son at 0645 on the morning of 19 September. They were thirty-five miles from the Waal at Nijmegen. At 0830, they linked up with elements of Gavin's 82nd at Grave, amid more cheering Dutch crowds. By midday, they were in the suburbs of Nijmegen. Soon after, Generals Horrocks, Adair of Guards Armoured Division, Browning and Gavin stood together within sight of the bridge, watching Germans moving unconcernedly across it. The Anglo-American attack began at 1530. German 88mm guns "brewed up" the first British tanks, which caught fire with their usual facility. U.S. airborne troops fought vigorous battles with panzer-grenadiers through the streets and market square. At nightfall, the attack was broken off until daylight. The 82nd had by now lost over 200 dead and 700 wounded since its drop, with many more men missing. That evening, convinced that frontal assaults would continue to fail, Gavin proposed a desperate alternative. His men would cross the 400-yard-wide Waal in boats a mile downstream, and outflank Nijmegen bridge. "The attempt must be made," he told Browning, "if Market Garden is to succeed."

While they waited for three trucks carrying British collapsible canvas assault boats to reach the town, after two days of wireless silence from Arnhem Browning received the first grim news of 1st Airborne's predicament. Its signal said in part: "senior formation still in vicinity north end of main bridge but not in touch and unable resupply ... Arnhem entirely in enemy hands. Request all possible steps expedite relief. Fight intense and opposition extremely strong. Position not too good." It was plain that every hour now counted.

Gavin's assault boats were delayed everywhere along the jammed road to Nijmegen, not least by a Luftwaffe raid on Eindhoven. They finally arrived at the river bank at 1440 on the afternoon of 20 September, twenty minutes before the chosen H-hour. The preliminary Allied bombardment had already begun. Under intense machine-gun and mortar fire, the first wave of 260 men of twenty-seven-year-old Major Julian Cook's 3/504th plunged into the water, and began frantically to paddle across the Waal, in a boat race with death. Some of the clumsy craft were blown out of the water. Others floundered, holed and sinking. A brisk wind blew away a protective smokescreen laid by the tank gunners. As the first Americans struggled up the far bank, Browning said to Horrocks: "I have never seen a more gallant action." Germans who belatedly sought to surrender were cut down ruthlessly by paratroopers enraged by their terrible losses. Only half the twenty-six canvas boats that carried the first wave were fit to return and bring over the second.

By 1700, the Waal rail bridge was in American hands. On the south bank, a new Anglo-American assault at last cracked open the German defence and pressed forward to the highway bridge. Guards tanks began to cross, machine-gunning German engineers clinging to the girders and destroying an 88mm gun on the far side. As the leading Shermans rumbled on to the roadway on the north side, surviving U.S. paratroopers from the boat crossing emerged to greet them. A lone Royal Engineer officer ran after the tanks across the bridge, cutting demolition wires wherever he could see them. The mystery will never be resolved of whether the Germans failed to detonate the charges, or whether they lost the electrical means to do so. It was 1915 on 20 September. The Allies stood eleven miles from the bridge at Arnhem. The paratroopers who had paddled across the Waal had paid with losses of over 50 per cent—134 men killed, wounded or missing. The achievement of the 82nd and 101st Airborne was superb. They displayed a dash, initiative, skill and determination which, had it been repeated elsewhere in the Allied armies during the autumn and winter of 1944, would have finished the war by Christmas.

The Americans who paid so dearly for the bridge at Nijmegen were now bewildered and disgusted to behold the British armour halt on the north bank of the Waal, harbour for the night and begin to brew tea. The British said they had to wait for supporting infantry, that it was madness for tanks to advance into darkness. The Americans expostulated that after all the delays and sacrifices of the day it was time to throw away the rulebook and risk everything to reach 1st Airborne. Gavin wrote: "Had Ridgway been in command at that moment, we would have been ordered up the road in spite of all our difficulties, to save the men at Arnhem." Ridgway himself, that very afternoon, was in a towering rage after encountering a hold-up in his jeep between Son and the 101st CP. A young British Guards officer told the American that his unit had halted because of enemy fire. The general sat fuming for forty minutes without hearing a shot in the vicinity, nor any sign of energetic British activity. Finally, the corps commander abandoned his jeep and walked a mile and a half to Taylor's CP, without meeting fire. He later described himself as "much dissatisfied with the apathy and lack of aggressiveness of the British forces," a view shared by some British officers.

The vital infantry of 43rd (Wessex) Division, following up Guards Armoured, had not yet reached Grave, eight miles to the south. Fighting continued in the centre of Nijmegen against pockets of resistance. The Germans launched a new counter-attack against the Allied bridgehead on the north side of the Waal, supported by two tanks. Private John Towle of the 504th ran 200 yards alone across a field carrying his bazooka. He fired two rockets at the tanks, and forced them to withdraw. When a group of Germans ran into a nearby house, Towle put a rocket into that, too, for good measure. He then made another dash across 150 yards of open ground, to take another shot at a German half-track. As he raised the bazooka, he was caught by the explosion of a German mortar bomb, which killed him.

Far back down the road from Nijmegen to the start line, "Hell's Highway" as Americans had begun to call it, traffic jams held up progress for hours. An unfounded belief that the Germans had mined the road verges confined every British vehicle to the tarmac. Some stretches of the route lay silent and empty for long periods because of jams further back. A great column of smoke drifted across the highway near Son, where a lorryload of smoke grenades had caught fire. By now, every man committed to the battle was desperately tired. A British tank commander, Corporal Andy Cropper, was disconcerted to find that his Sherman driver had fallen asleep as they advanced. Fortunately the driver's hatch was open. Cropper was able to clamber down the hull and shake the man awake before they crashed.

The road that lay ahead from Nijmegen to Arnhem was straight and steeply embanked, enabling German defenders to fire upon advancing British tanks as if these were being presented to them on a rifle range. Yet bolder and more imaginative soldiers—Germans, for instance—in these circumstances would have pushed on towards Arnhem through the darkness, risking everything for a great coup. It reflected poorly upon the British Army that it was unable to mount the next phase of its advance from Nijmegen for eighteen hours after the Waal bridges were secured. By the time the Irish Guards resumed the advance at 1100 on 21 September, men of 10th SS Panzer were ready to give them a hot reception. The last stage of the Allied advance towards the Rhine, whose only purpose was now the rescue of 1st Airborne's survivors, was as messy and botched as everything else about Market Garden.

On the evening of 20 September, the organized defence of the north end of Arnhem bridge by 1st Airborne Division came to an end, when the survivors of Frost's force surrendered. Other British paratroopers endured six more days of savage fighting, clinging to their shrinking perimeter at Oosterbeek, three miles from Frost's lost positions. The hapless Polish Brigade was parachuted on to the Rhine shore amid devastating German fire, at a moment when all chance of success was gone. The Poles retained a lasting, justified bitterness about their sacrifice. After 20 September, the heroism of 1st Airborne's survivors had become strategically irrelevant. All chance of seizing and exploiting a Rhine crossing was gone. The Germans held Arnhem in strength, and would do so almost until the end of the war. The resistance sustained by 1st Airborne's survivors at Oosterbeek until 26 September was the stuff of legend, but offered only a chance of escape for the survivors, rather than serving any higher military purpose.

Throughout the Market Garden battle, American paratroopers and British soldiers of XXX Corps were fighting bitter little actions along the entire length of the corridor northwards. "One of the worst sights for me," said John Thorpe of the 2nd Fife and Forfar Yeomanry, "was coming upon Guards Armoured men hanging out of burning tanks, and a shell-blasted transport vehicle with its occupants all dead and lying about with their clothes stripped from their bodies except their boots."

The same day, George Turner-Cain wrote in his diary: "Very bitter fighting, and getting more so each time we meet. We never fail to defeat the Hun, and his casualties are out of all proportion to our own, but still he fights on fiercely and without hope." He added three days later:

> Each little battle with a rearguard or group of infantry with an anti-tank gun takes longer than ever to deal with. The trouble is the wetness of the ground. We cannot operate our armour off the few straight roads as they get bogged down immediately in the small and wet fields. The Germans blow a bridge or a culvert on the only road, and cover it with anti-tank and

small arms fire. Getting our infantry round to the back of the enemy party to flush it takes a long time, and is a cold and wet process, and all the time there are commanders at the back screaming at us to make more haste.

Some bizarre delusions persisted at XXX Corps about the possibilities of achieving success. As late as 22 September, the company commanders of an infantry unit of 43rd Division between Nijmegen and Arnhem were issued with orders for an assault to link up with 1st Airborne. "*Intention:* 12 KRRC [King's Royal Rifle Corps] will attack and seize the rd bridge at ARNHEIM," declared this alarming document, which went on to detail deployments once the south bank had been secured: "at least one [tank] tp over bridge...KRRC will hold open bridge." German strength in Arnhem was estimated at 300–500 infantry. The planned timetable for the British assault ended: "1730–1745 hrs—Leading Tp reaches bridge." It was a source of extravagant relief to the riflemen when this flight of fantasy was cancelled a few hours before its execution.

An unhappy fate befell the 4th Dorsets of 43rd (Wessex) Division. They marched forward through darkness to the bank of the Rhine on 25 September, hurried on by NCOs muttering repeatedly, "Keep up lads, close up lads," until they reached waiting boats. Then they were paddled across the Rhine in a belated, grossly misjudged attempt to reinforce 1st Airborne Division's perimeter at Oosterbeek. On the northern shore, in the face of fierce German fire, a young lieutenant called on his platoon to charge, and leaped forward himself. None of the men followed. He turned back and said: "Come on, lads—charge." Still no one moved. Finally, he said furiously: "If you don't charge, you bastards, I'll shoot you!" Reluctantly, his platoon advanced, hounded every step by their officer. By dawn, they were locked in fierce fighting with the Germans. Their ammunition ran low. At last, their colonel, Gerald Tilly, ordered them to cease fire. One eighteen-year-old private admitted only to relief: "Perhaps we were going to live after all." They were marched into captivity, singing "Green grow the rushes, O."

The Germans were pressing the British and Americans along the entire sixty-mile length of their salient from the start line of Market Garden to the most forward positions on the south bank of the Rhine. The Allies could hold their ground, but only by relentless exertion which left scant energy, resources or ammunition for pressing on further. Near Nijmegen, the adjutant of a tank regiment of 4th Armoured Brigade wrote in his diary: "Brigadier arrived in the p.m. and I gather the policy is now a decided sit-down till they can clear up this bloody corridor. It is cut again this evening, this time in three places...This is really pretty serious, and has ceased to be the joke we have considered it as for some time." For the whole of 21st Army Group, the "joke" was over. It was now merely a matter of stabilizing the front, and rescuing the victims of failure.

The British XXX Corps suffered 1,480 casualties in the Market Garden battle. The two American airborne divisions, together with U.S. aircrew, lost 3,974. The chronically querulous General Lewis Brereton, U.S. commander of First Airborne Army, wrote in his diary: "In the years to come, everyone will remember Arnhem, but no one will remember that two American divisions fought their hearts out in the Dutch canal country and whipped hell out of the Germans." For once, Brereton's sourness seemed justified. The Americans had done their part better than the British. The survivors of 1st Airborne Division were evacuated across the Rhine on the night of Tuesday 26 September, nine days after the first landings. Of the 10,005 men who had started the formation's battle, 2,163 now came out of it. Urquhart's division had lost 1,200 men killed and more than 6,000 captured, many of these wounded. Overall Allied casualties were trifling by Russian or German standards, in pursuit of such an ambitious strategic goal as a Rhine bridgehead. Arnhem was a small battle in the context of the Second World War. It was rendered famous by the glamour of the paratroopers; the British romantic weakness for "last stands"; and a belief, probably illusory, that a great opportunity had been lost. For a British army troubled by its shrinking strength in the sixth year of war, the losses seemed a heavy price for failure.

"The soldiers who beat back these first-rate British troops metre by metre," enthused a war correspondent for the German soldiers' newspaper *West-Kurier,* "were drawn from every branch of the service. Only 24 hours before, they had not known each other... Only a few were familiar with the principles of fighting in forest and hedgerow, or with street-fighting. In one infantry battalion, members of as many as 28 different units fought side by side, led by an officer with a wooden leg." For once, Nazi propaganda did not exaggerate. The German achievement was indeed remarkable. They were able to frustrate Market Garden with an assortment of available reinforcement units, without significantly disrupting their strategic deployments. For instance, excepting 9th and 10th SS Panzer around Arnhem, none of the formations already earmarked for Hitler's Ardennes offensive were distracted from their refits to meet the airborne assault.

Private Bob Peatling was rescued from his refuge in Arnhem police station by two Dutch policemen who found him there at the end of October, living off scraps of food scavenged from empty buildings. Like several hundred other 1st Airborne survivors, Peatling began a confinement of more than six months behind the German lines, hidden by brave Dutch people. His wife Joan was informed that she could draw a widow's pension, since her husband was "missing—believed killed." She refused to do so, convinced that he would return. So he did, after reaching the Allied lines at last on 18 April 1945.

MANY OF THE causes of the disaster at Arnhem were readily identified soon after it took place. Market Garden was a rotten plan, poorly executed. Although the paratroopers would have suffered substantial casualties by dropping on the bridges, such losses would have seemed trifling alongside those which they incurred in fighting their way into Arnhem and Nijmegen. At the very least, gliderborne coup-de-main parties should have been landed close to all the bridges at H-Hour, as had been done so successfully at the Orne on D-Day, and as some officers urged before the drop in Holland. Failure to do this reflected a fastidiousness about exposing soldiers to excessive risk which was characteristic of the north-west Europe campaign, but which almost always cost more Allied lives in the end. Much has been said about British failure quickly to seize Arnhem bridge, yet the German achievement in denying Nijmegen bridge to the American 82nd Airborne for three days was almost equally critical. It was a scandal—for which in the Russian or German armies some signals officers would have been shot—that the communications of 1st Airborne Division remained almost non-existent throughout the battle. The British paratroopers' command and control scarcely functioned from 17 September onwards. A lamentable lack of initiative caused British officers to ignore the local expertise of the Dutch Resistance and the potential of civilian telephone communications, both imaginatively exploited by the Americans.

Horrocks's XXX Corps faced a formidable task, reaching Arnhem up a single road against the clock. But its units displayed an embarrassing lack of urgency, and fought a tactically clumsy battle. One of the most persistent weaknesses of the British and American armies in north-west Europe was poor tank–infantry co-ordination, about which more will be said below. A British academic who has conducted a meticulous study of Guards Armoured's training before its deployment in north-west Europe paints an abysmal portrait of its officers' incomprehension of armoured tactics. Montgomery had tried to sack the division's commander, Allan Adair, early in 1944, but the social popularity of that amiable gentleman frustrated him. In short, the performance of Guards Armoured on the road to Nijmegen, admittedly in adverse circumstances, was what 21st Army Group's commander would have described as "a poor show."

American parachute units were much better commanded than most of their British counterparts. Browning, Urquhart, Hicks and several British battalion COs performed inadequately. After the operation, Browning received one of the least deserved knighthoods awarded to a wartime general, and spitefully insisted upon the sacking of Sosabowski, the Polish Parachute Brigade's commander. Given the indifferent British leadership, it is likely that the U.S. 82nd or 101st Airborne Divisions would have made a better showing if either had been given responsibility for Arnhem, though it is hard to see how any unilateral achievement on the north bank of the Rhine could have been decisive for the overall outcome. Chester Wilmot, who witnessed the battle as a war correspondent, as well as becoming one of the greatest post-war historians of the campaign, was contemptuous of the lame performance of 43rd (Wessex) Division beyond Nijmegen: "There was considerable truth in the criticism the Germans had made in Normandy that British infantry sought 'to occupy ground rather than to fight over it'." Yet 43rd Division's alleged poor showing, to which Wilmot alludes, took place on 22 September, by which time Market Garden had already irretrievably failed.

The drive to Arnhem was thwarted by the startling achievement of the Germans in mustering an assortment of depleted units into battle groups which held at bay the best of the British Army. The Allies possessed overwhelming superiority, yet were unable to exploit this in the flatlands of Holland. Lack of effective ground control, as well as indifferent weather, marginalized the value of air support. It is sometimes argued that the British would have fared better had they adopted the plan initially favoured by the army, but vetoed by airmen alarmed by the threat of flak, to seize a crossing higher up the Rhine towards Wesel. It is hard to see why a drive to Wesel should have succeeded when one to Arnhem failed.

There is a further question. Even if the Allies had been able to capture a Rhine bridge, would they have been able to use this effectively to launch a drive to the Ruhr? Given the energy displayed by the Germans, and the reinforcements rushing to the Western Front in late September 1944, it seems unlikely that the British could have exploited their narrow corridor to achieve a swift German collapse, even if they had got across the river. Hitler's commanders would have thrown everything into frustrating the Allied purpose. It is highly improbable that Montgomery's cherished forty-division thrust at the Ruhr, or even his more modest sixteen-division plan, could have been fuelled, ammunitioned and provisioned without the use of Antwerp.

A hero of the Arnhem battle, and one of its shrewdest post-war chroniclers, Major Geoffrey Powell of 156 Para, became a prominent critic of the "Airborne Army" concept. It made sense, he suggested, for the Allies to possess small parachute forces capable of coup-de-main operations, but "it is arguable that Eisenhower would have been better served in the autumn of 1944 by another half-dozen infantry or armoured divisions ... than by First Airborne Army ... It is not easy to justify the scarce resources which the Americans and British devoted to their fine airborne troops, and to the aircraft which flew them into battle." Here, from a parachute officer, was a fundamental criticism of the Arnhem fiasco. Paratroopers achieved a glamour in the Second World War which they have never lost, but nowhere did the airborne divisions justify their cost in men and equipment by changing the outcome of a big battle which would have been lost without a drop.

SERGEANT ERWIN HECK of the Arnhem SS NCO school was impressed by the disciplined bearing of British prisoners, who marched into the town singing "It's a long way to Tipperary." But the Germans were even more gratified by their own achievement. "We felt proud of ourselves," said Heck, "especially when we had achieved victory with so few resources." It has often been suggested that the Arnhem battle was distinguished by chivalry between the German and Allied combatants. It is true that there were local truces in the midst of the battle, to allow both sides to remove their wounded to a German hospital. Some British prisoners were treated with courtesy and consideration by the SS, as gallant warriors. But neither side gave much quarter during the battle, and there were ugly incidents when it was over. A British medical officer was shot in cold blood by a drunken German war correspondent. Captain John Killick said: "It was pretty dismaying that while the Germans were giving us food, water and cigarettes, on the other side of the square they were shooting out of hand Dutchmen whom they believed had helped us." The entire civilian population of Arnhem was summarily expelled from the town. On 24 September in heavy rain, almost 100,000 dispossessed people trudged like a defeated army from their homes, clutching such belongings as they could carry, the silence of the Dutch broken only by the sobs of children and the sounds of battle a few miles distant. In the months that followed, the sufferings of local people at the hands of the Germans were very great. Lieutenant Jack Reynolds was awarded a Military Cross for his own contribution at Arnhem, yet it was half a century before he could bring himself to go back to the town. "I felt so ashamed. When we left the Dutch people, they were far worse off than before we came."

Considerable bitterness towards Horrocks's XXX Corps persisted among the British paratroopers when the battle was over. One of 1st Airborne's survivors, arrived at last at Nijmegen, shouted at the 5th Wiltshires, who had come north up the road with 43rd Division: "It took you a bloody long time to get here!" A Wiltshireman shouted back with equal asperity: "Yeah, and quite a few poor bastards didn't get this far!" When Corporal Denis Thomas arrived as a prisoner at Stalag XIB in October, a paratrooper cried to the rest of the hut: "Here's another bloody tank man who's come to relieve us!"

Gavin of the U.S. 82nd urged that the U.S. Army should review its policy of ruthlessly relieving formation commanders who failed in a single battle. He argued that it might be wiser to allow general officers to gain experience, and to enjoy at least a second chance. He suggested that the U.S. might learn something from the British practice of distributing decorations after a disaster, to relieve the burden of guilt on those responsible. Lieutenant-General "Boy" Browning "lost three-quarters of his command and a battle. He returned home a hero and was personally decorated by the King. There is no doubt that in our system he would have been summarily relieved and sent home in disgrace." Decorations were awarded to other British senior officers, whom some of their subordinates would have preferred to see dismissed. Air Chief Marshal Sir Arthur Harris once remarked caustically upon the British habit of assuaging the pain of defeats with a deluge of "gongs." At Arnhem, the British fielded too many gentlemen and not enough players. After its failure, senior American officers were even less willing than before to accept lessons in the conduct of war from their allies.

A bitter sense of anticlimax followed Market Garden. The British would be leading no triumphant advance into Germany through Holland and the Ruhr. Second Army Intelligence recorded ruefully on 29 September: "The enemy has gained a respite, of which he has taken fuller advantage than it was supposed he might manage." De Guingand, Montgomery's Chief of Staff, always believed that, even if XXX Corps had broken through to Arnhem, "the Germans would have produced an answer to the single thrust into Westphalia favoured by Monty." The dash for Arnhem was the last occasion of the war when Eisenhower unequivocally accepted a strategic proposal advanced by Montgomery. There is little doubt that the resources employed upon Market Garden should instead have been devoted to the far less glamorous task of clearing the approaches to Antwerp, which thereafter occupied a large part of Montgomery's forces for two months. The true cost of the Rhine operation was not failure to secure the bridge, but the diversion of the army and its supplies at a vital moment when they should have been otherwise employed.

Arnhem was a British idea. Operational responsibility for its failure must rest chiefly with 21st Army Group's commander. Almost all his American peers revealed private satisfaction at the spectacle of Montgomery suffering such a rebuff. General Carl "Tooey" Spaatz, senior USAAF officer in Europe, drafted a scathing letter to a friend in which he said that "any deficiency in the operation was probably more the fault of the famous British General Montgomery than any other cause." Eisenhower cannot escape all blame, however. September saw the end of the first phase of the north-west Europe campaign. Thereafter, unusual opportunities presented themselves, if only the Allies had shown themselves able to exploit these more effectively, and if their forces had been led by a commander who displayed the grip to which Montgomery rightly attached such importance. Instead, however, Eisenhower's new headquarters at Granville in Brittany was, at a crucial period in early and mid-September, disastrously handicapped by poor communications. Signals sometimes took twenty-four hours or longer to reach the Supreme Commander's desk. His staff was shaking down in its new responsibilities. He himself was labouring under grave misapprehensions—albeit shared by his subordinates—about the terminal weakness of the enemy.

Yet, by his own choice, Eisenhower had assumed command of the Allied ground forces and was thus the man in charge. We shall explore below the possibilities available to the American armies in September. That month, there was a real chance of breaking into Germany in 1944—by opening Antwerp, and by breaking von Rundstedt's line on Bradley's front, rather than by adopting the ill-conceived British Arnhem plan. While the Supreme Commander was still gathering the reins of authority, as ever the Germans were labouring furiously. By October, the window of opportunity on the Western Front had slammed shut. It is ironic that Dwight Eisenhower's first serious error as ground commander was to allow Montgomery, the man who wanted his job, to have his own way over Market Garden. The Supreme Commander could have made a notable contribution to ending the war in 1944 by asserting other priorities, and preventing Montgomery's Arnhem adventure from taking place at all.

CHAPTER THREE

The Frontiers of Germany

FADING DREAMS

THERE WAS NEVER a specific moment in the late autumn of 1944 at which the Western allies resigned themselves to continuing the war into 1945. Arnhem loomed larger in the consciousness of the British than in that of a GI in a foxhole in Alsace-Lorraine. Rather, as each local offensive faltered, as German resistance stiffened, and above all as incessant rain and the movement of the armies ploughed the battlefield between Switzerland and the sea into a quagmire, commanders progressively diminished their expectations and moderated their ambitions. Each small disappointment or failure fed the next.

In the historiography of the Second World War, millions of words have been expended upon the British defeat at Arnhem, where prospects of success were always slight. Montgomery's failure to secure the approaches to Antwerp has been discussed. Yet the best chances of breaking through into Germany in 1944 lay many miles further south, around Aachen and in the hills and forests of the Ardennes. During their summer planning sessions, Eisenhower's staff eliminated the Ardennes from the list of prospective Allied routes into Germany. In considering options, they talked only of the northern and southern sectors of the front, with the Ardennes as a hinterland in between, unconsidered as a site for offensive operations. This was probably a mistake. Once already in the war, in 1940, the Germans had demonstrated what could be done by determined men among the Ardennes passes, and of course they would so again in December 1944. It became impossible to send large forces through the Ardennes once the Germans stiffened their line in October, but in September something important might have been achieved there. At that stage, however, the Allied planners believed that other and easier avenues lay open.

The principal American command in the west was held by the fifty-one-year-old Missourian Omar Bradley of 12th Army Group. This was already larger than Montgomery's 21st, and was destined to keep growing fast through the months that followed. Bradley was responsible for two armies, which would eventually become four, the greatest American force in history to be led by a single officer. It was a myth created by the correspondent Ernie Pyle that Bradley was beloved of his men as the "soldiers' general." Patton and Montgomery were the only two senior commanders familiar to their own men, because both took great pains to see that it was so. Bradley had risen to his role not because of any conspicuous feat of generalship, but because he inspired confidence among his peers and possessed a well-deserved reputation for efficiency and grasp of logistics—a science which Patton, for one, neglected. During their time together in the Mediterranean, Eisenhower had grown implicitly to trust and respect Bradley, who had commanded first a corps and then an army there: "the best rounded combat leader I have yet met in our service," Ike wrote to Marshall. "While he probably lacks some of the extraordinary and ruthless driving power that Patton can exercise at critical moments, he still has...force and determination...a jewel to have around." Amid the stresses to which Eisenhower was subjected by Montgomery and in some degree by Patton, it was a relief for him to turn instead to the plainspoken, reliable 12th Army Group commander, a keen bridge-player and expert rifle shot since his rural childhood.

In recent years, Bradley has incurred harsh censure from some critics, notably the American historian Carlo d'Este, who dismisses him as a plodder. In north-west Europe, to his own detriment the Missourian allowed exasperation with Montgomery to become an obsession. For all his customary steadiness, Bradley was prone to outbursts of savage temper. He showed himself far more ruthless than Montgomery in sacking corps and divisional commanders, while he was no more successful than the British commander in persuading his armies to hurry on the battlefield. In one important respect, however, Ernie Pyle's judgement on Bradley was correct: 12th Army Group's commander wanted to do the business of defeating the Germans with the maximum application of American firepower and industrial might, and the least possible expenditure of American lives. He had not come to Europe to prove himself a Rommel or von Manstein. He intended to take every possible American under his command home with him again. For this, indeed, he deserved the gratitude of his soldiers.

ON 13 SEPTEMBER, Bradley's forces—men of Hodges's First Army—were close to Aachen, and barely sixty miles from Cologne, on the Rhine. Yet it would be almost six months before they took the latter city and closed up to the greatest of Germany's rivers, a mere hour's road drive from their autumn front line. In August and early September, Patton's Third Army had pushed some 500 miles across France in twenty-six days. America's other armies had likewise advanced far and fast. From September until the early spring of 1945, however, most of the fighting along the entire front would take place within a belt of Dutch, Belgian, German and French territory ten to twenty miles deep. Before D-Day, Churchill feared that the Allied armies would become locked in a long battle of attrition in Normandy. In reality, they were able to break out of their D-Day beachhead and secure a critical victory in little more than two months. Yet in Holland, in the western hills of Germany and in the fields of Alsace-Lorraine, the liberators became stalemated for almost half a year, making small advances at painful cost. Once momentum had been lost, it was not regained until the Germans were ground down in battles etched painfully into the legend of the U.S. Army. American failures were less spectacular than those of the British in Holland, but they were at least as serious in delaying the end of the war.

Part of the German—and sometimes Russian—genius for war was a readiness to seize opportunities with both hands, swiftly to exploit weakness before the enemy could reinforce a threatened spot. At no time in the north-west Europe campaign before the Ruhr Pocket in April 1945 did Anglo-American forces achieve the kind of comprehensive envelopment of enemy forces which was commonplace on both sides of the Eastern Front. Even the undoubted disaster inflicted upon the Wehrmacht at the Falaise Gap in August 1944 was incomplete, and allowed the escape of just sufficient men to provide skeletons upon which broken formations could be clothed with the flesh of new men and equipment.

"The Allied drive lost its impetus with reaching of the Siegfried line in the north and the Moselle river in the south," recorded the U.S. Army's official post-war report on "Strategy in North-West Europe." "The prepared enemy positions, the extent of the area covered by the Allied troops over a short space of time, and the need for additional supplies at forward points to sustain the drive, made it apparent that no further large-scale offensive could be launched until additional forces could be concentrated and the logistical situation improved . . . A period of relative inactivity was essential."

This comfortable official declaration of the inevitability of what took place in the autumn of 1944—or rather did not take place—masks complex issues and possibilities. All the paper arguments about the Allies' logistical difficulties in early September are valid. But a greater field commander than Eisenhower, together with a more vigorous spirit of enterprise than that which prevailed in his armies, might have overcome the difficulties and found means to drive forward into Germany while the Wehrmacht was still reeling. No setback could alter the inevitable outcome of the war, but the Germans used every day of delay to greater advantage than did the Allies. It was unrealistic for Eisenhower to suppose in September that his armies could head straight for Berlin. The sheer mass of German forces still available to defend the Reich militated against a successful one-stop dash for Hitler's capital. But the Allies could and should have got to the Rhine, beyond which there were no further significant terrain features to assist the defence, before winter imposed its deadly grip upon military movement.

Patton's Third Army ran out of fuel in eastern France, well before reaching Hitler's West Wall, the Siegfried Line. Once his tanks were refuelled, they sped onwards to reach the ancient fortress city of Metz, on the Moselle, on 8 September. Patton expected an easy victory here. The planners were oblivious of the strength of the great chain of sunken forts created in a belt around Metz over a period of 200 years. They received a brutal shock. The Germans had garrisoned the forts strongly, and were reinforcing fast. Not only could the Americans not seize them, but enemy shellfire from Metz rained down on Third Army's bridgeheads thrown across the Moselle.

The U.S. 317th Infantry suffered much misery at the river, beginning on a warm, clear day, 5 September, when the regiment made its first attempt to cross. Rain over American airstrips precluded fighter-bomber support, and it was decided to attack without artillery preparation. The 1/317th jumped off at 0930, crossing a canal over a partly demolished footbridge. At 1000, the unit halted in the face of enemy machine-gun fire, soon afterwards followed by shelling. American counter-battery fire silenced the German artillery, and at 1030 B Company reached the river bank. Almost half an hour later, as the Americans launched their boats, five were destroyed by mortar fire. By 1500, C Company had withdrawn to its start line, while A and B had dug in along the nearby canal. That night, the 1/317th tried again. German concentrations of mortars and machine-gun fire destroyed most of the boats "and demoralized the troops," according to the corps' after-action report. Although the battalion had suffered few casualties, a regimental staff officer reported it "unfit for further immediate action." The 2/317th was late leaving the start line for its own crossing. As it launched its boats in tense silence, a German voice shouted from the far bank: "*Halt! Machinen gewehr!*" German guns began to fire across the water on fixed lines, and the crossing was abandoned. The regiment's third battalion got clear over the Moselle by 1500 on 5 September. But energetic German counter-attacks drove in its bridgehead. The Americans retired to the western shore.

The Germans generally fought well, but their weaker units sometimes surprised the Allies by lack of will and skill, while good American soldiers behaved with resolution. In one of the Moselle bridgeheads at Comy on 11 September, B Company of the 11th Infantry was established around a brick factory. In the early hours of the morning, Lieutenant Mitchell Hazam ran into company headquarters shouting "Tanks!" Sergeant Norris Boyer alerted a nearby 57mm anti-tank gun crew, and the company commander Captain Harry Anderson dashed upstairs. An approaching German tank fired at and missed Hazam as he ran across the street. German infantry were following. Anderson ordered everyone to keep absolutely quiet, and to withhold fire. The enemy made no attempt to clear the houses in which the Americans lay. Anderson called in a

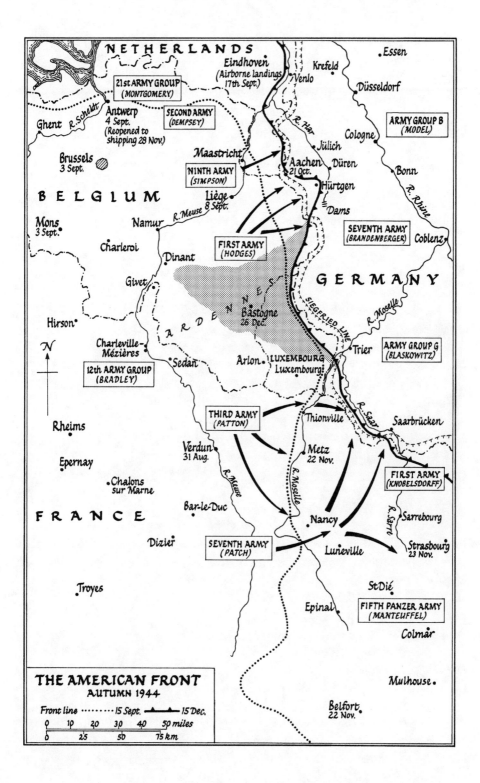

NETHERLANDS

Essen

Eindhoven
(Airborne landings
17th Sept.)

Krefeld

Venlo

Düsseldorf

21st ARMY GROUP
(MONTGOMERY)

R. Scheldt

Antwerp
4 Sept.
(Reopened to
shipping 28 Nov.)

SECOND ARMY
(DEMPSEY)

Ghent

R. Maas

Jülich

Cologne

ARMY GROUP B
(MODEL)

Brussels
3 Sept.

Maastricht

Aachen
21 Oct.

Düren

Bonn

R. Rhine

BELGIUM

Liège
8 Sept.

NINTH ARMY
(SIMPSON)

Hürtgen

Mons
3 Sept.

Namur

R. Meuse

Dams

Charleroi

Dinant

FIRST ARMY
(HODGES)

SEVENTH ARMY
(BRANDENBERGER)

Coblenz

Givet

GERMANY

Hirson

A R D E N N E S

Bastogne
26 Dec.

SIEGFRIED LINE

R. Moselle

N

Charleville-
Mézières

Sedan

Arlon

LUXEMBOURG
Luxembourg

Trier

ARMY GROUP G
(BLASKOWITZ)

12th ARMY GROUP
(BRADLEY)

Rheims

THIRD ARMY
(PATTON)

Thionville

Saarbrücken

Epernay

Verdun
31 Aug.

R. Meuse

Metz
22 Nov.

R. Moselle

R. Saar

FIRST ARMY
(KNOBELSDORFF)

Chalons
sur Marne

Bar-le-Duc

Nancy

R. Sarre

Sarrebourg

F R A N C E

Dizier

SEVENTH ARMY
(PATCH)

Lunéville

Strasbourg
23 Nov.

Troyes

StDié

Epinal

FIFTH PANZER ARMY
(MANTEUFFEL)

Colmar

THE AMERICAN FRONT
AUTUMN 1944

Mulhouse

Front line ········ 15 Sept. ▲——▲ 15 Dec.

0   10   20   30   40   50 miles

0   25   50   75 km

Belfort
22 Nov.

tank destroyer, which promptly knocked out one German tank. A 57mm gun hit another. Anderson shot one tank commander in his turret with a rifle. The tank destroyer finished off the tank as it tried to escape. Anderson's men then opened fire on the German infantry to devastating effect, inflicting some twenty-eight casualties, for the loss of only two Americans killed. Just as firing was dying away and the GIs were rounding up another twenty-eight of the attackers who had surrendered, a German officer suddenly appeared in the street with a machine pistol. Sergeant Boyer shot him. B Company's notable little success was marred by the loss of one nineteen-man platoon, which was presumed captured in its entirety, since no American bodies were found on its positions after the attack. But the action showed how richly determination could be rewarded on the battlefield.

The archives of the European campaign suggest that many American officers were more honest and self-critical about their units' weaknesses and failures than their counterparts in any other combatant army. It is impressive to observe the frankness of U.S. Army after-action analyses. Lieutenant-Colonel William Simpson, commanding the 2/10th Infantry, submitted a report in September arguing that the drive towards the German border was seriously hampered by excessive caution: "We lost time because of a lack of boldness and aggressiveness on the part of our scouts." Suggesting that infantry were much too ready to pull back if they met resistance, he highlighted an incident in his own battalion on the Moselle. He was dismayed to discover an entire rifle company preparing to withdraw on its own initiative, after American artillery rounds began to fall short in its sector. When two tank destroyers withdrew from the forward area, "some of the men of my reserve company, whose commander had been killed, started to withdraw. They were checked by a battalion liaison officer."

"Every day seems like the day before...with the rain pouring down," Lieutenant-Colonel D. K. Reimers of the 90th Division wrote gloomily in his diary on 23 September. After Third Army's early repulses at Metz, Patton shifted the focus of his advance thirty miles further south, to Nancy. Here his men made good headway east of the river, until they met substantial armoured forces of the German First Army. Thereafter, in the middle days of September, Patton's forces fought the fiercest tank battles the Allies had known since Normandy.

The Germans feared Patton above all his peers. More than any other Allied commander, his vision of war reflected their own driving urgency. Von Rundstedt's deployments on the Western Front flattered Patton's role in Eisenhower's plans, and reflected German respect for the explosive American's energies. In September 1944, Army Group B dispatched in haste to Alsace-Lorraine the best new tanks von Rundstedt could muster, and threw them into battle against the American Shermans. Chester Wilmot observed that in September this became the only sector of the entire Western Front where von Rundstedt's troops could meet the Allies on more or less equal terms. At heavy cost, above all in armour, the Germans checked Third Army. But the American performance showed what able commanders and determined troops could accomplish. Armoured units of von Manteuffel's Fifth Panzer Army attacked near Lunéville on 18 September. In the four days fighting that followed, General John S. Wood, one of the outstanding U.S. tank leaders in Europe, fought his 4th Armored Division to such effect that the Germans were not merely beaten but shattered. 111th Panzer Division, which had arrived in Lorraine with ninety-eight tanks, ended the battle reduced to seven tanks and eighty men. Unusually, American casualties were far smaller than those of the Germans. It is true that many of the Wehrmacht units were new formations, and that their tanks fresh from the factories suffered as severely from mechanical failure as from enemy fire. But these handicaps did not suffice to grant the Allies victory on many other occasions. When the Germans renewed their offensive on 25 September, they made a little ground, but by the end of the month they had run out of steam. The Americans were going nowhere in a hurry in Lorraine, but Third Army had destroyed some of the strongest forces von Rundstedt possessed on the Western Front.

Patton now began to launch a long, bloody series of assaults on the forts of Metz which cost Third Army a thousand casualties a day, a higher rate of loss than the Arnhem battle. Even Patton's admirers have nothing to say in praise of his Metz attack, which seemed simply to reflect stubborn determination to achieve a declared objective. Captain Jack Gerrie, a company commander in the 11th Infantry, submitted a withering after-action report on the folly of attempting such operations with depleted units made up to strength with raw replacements. "I took a dim view of trying to take Fort Driant with these men," he wrote.

> I knew they were not trained nor hardened...We took a crack at Driant, and as expected we couldn't make it. The three days we spent in the breach of the fort consisted in keeping the men in the line. All the leaders were lost exposing themselves at the wrong time in order to get this accomplished. The new men seemed to lose all sense of reasoning. They left their rifles, flamethrowers, satchel charges and what not laying right where it was. I was disgusted, and so damn mad that I couldn't see straight. If it had not been for preplanned defensive artillery fire, they [the Germans] would have shoved us clear out of the fort with the calibre of troops we had. Why? The men wouldn't fight.

In the eyes of Patton's critics such assaults demonstrated that, for all his brilliance as a pursuit commander, in a slogging match against the German Army he fared no better than any of his rivals. It has continued to bemuse history that he expended so much effort and so many lives on battering Metz once the strength of the German positions there had become plain. Bradley argued that "there was nothing to be gained by pecking away at those forts. It was too costly." Patton himself wrote to Henry Stimson, the U.S. secretary of war, late in October: "I hope that in the final settlement of the war, you insist that the Germans retain Lorraine because I can imagine no greater burden than to be the owner of this nasty country where it rains every day and where the whole wealth of the people consisted in assorted manure piles." That month, rainfall in Lorraine doubled the average for the season. For the men on the line, conditions were wretched. Mildew attacked leather, rust coated metal, and mud clogged every movement by men or vehicles. Condoms became a universal prophylactic not for sexual activity, but for protecting rifle barrels, gunsights and radio and telephone mouthpieces from the relentless precipitation. It required an effort of will for a man merely to exist through the days and nights in foxholes and ruins, and an even greater one to participate in operations against the enemy.

The Germans possessed some redoubtable formations to throw into the line. "We were still pretty good," said Sergeant Max Wind of 17th SS Panzergrenadiers, rebuilt after Normandy into a formation of 8,000 men, about half its established strength. "There were some young boys, but we also had some very experienced men. We respected Patton, because we knew that he respected Germany. But the American soldier was nothing like the Russian. Yes, of course, the U.S. had the material. But we never thought a lot of their soldiers. They lacked the motivation we had."

The U.S. Seventh Army under Patch, having driven north from the Mediterranean, together with the French First under de Lattre de Tassigny, closed up on Patton's right through the Vosges Mountains to the Swiss border. The French military contribution was small, and almost entirely symbolic. Their formations suffered chronic problems of indiscipline—indeed, French colonial units in Italy and later Germany were sometimes responsible for mass rapes on a Russian scale. The French left to the Americans the mundane tasks of providing supply and support for their fighting units. No one anyway had illusions about the scope for swift progress in the Vosges region, or about the significance of advances in south Lorraine. Harsh though this reality might seem to men obliged to fight and die there, every Allied planner knew that the vital organs of Germany lay in the north, not in the south of the country.

The most painful missed opportunities of the autumn, perhaps of the entire campaign, occurred 120 miles from Metz, in the U.S. First Army's sector on the German border south of Aachen. On Wednesday 13 September, four days before Market Garden was launched, the U.S. VII Corps made tentative penetrations of Hitler's West Wall. The attacking forces were commanded by Major-General J. Lawton Collins, "Lightning Joe," the ablest and most combative American corps commander in north-west Europe. For the first three days, Collins's men made good headway. The fortifications were not inherently strong, for Hitler had never expected to need them. They encompassed an interlocking network of pillboxes, for which the German Army Group B had to scrabble to find keys after the August retreat, to allow defenders to occupy them. Most were protected by a thicket of concrete "dragons' teeth," designed to arrest armoured vehicles. Early American VII Corps operations encountered only German Home Guard units. By the weekend, however, three days after the first American incursions, substantial regular forces were moving into the line. Even pillboxes became formidable obstacles if they were manned by men who knew what they were doing.

E Company of the American 28th Division's 109th Infantry fought a typical little action on the morning of 14 September near Harspelt, just inside the German border. The company was depleted by casualties from mortar fire even before it began its attack on the West Wall. It was commanded by a first lieutenant, because its commander had been wounded the previous day. Technical-Sergeant Tom Beers was told to take a twelve-strong platoon with a tank to seize a pillbox. While it was still dark, Beers walked back into Harspelt to show his accompanying tank the way forward. The soldiers crossed their start line at 1030, following the Sherman, and quickly came under mortar and artillery fire. The tank stopped. Its commander called down to Beers, demanding to know when he should stop firing and—by implication—advancing. "Use your head," said the sergeant irritably. One squad set out towards a pillbox 350 yards away. They were stopped by wire. Beers went forward himself and started cutting it. Then a machine-gun opened fire on the Americans, causing some men to scurry back down the road. One sergeant, Moulding, picked up a BAR light machine-gun and continued forward with three riflemen. Beers said: "It was getting to be quite a run, and the machine-gun fire wasn't anything to sneeze at." He shouted back at the men who lay prone fifty yards behind him: "Keep coming—these heinie bastards can't hit us!" He moved forward himself, and others followed. Nine Americans finally reached the pillbox. Beers fired his rifle into its embrasure, "I guess just for my morale's sake." He ran round the back, throwing two grenades to keep the Germans' heads down. Then they laid a 10-pound satchel charge by the door, which failed to explode. The rest of the company was now 200 yards behind. There was a brief pause before an NCO of another platoon arrived, carrying a new satchel charge. This exploded without doing much visible damage to the pillbox, but evidently shocked its inhabitants. Beers left two men to watch the entrance, and scouted warily around its surrounding fire trenches and sleeping quarters, throwing grenades in front of him, though the positions proved to be empty. Then one of the watchers by the entrance hollered: "They're coming out!" Twenty-one Germans led by a captain emerged from the pillbox with their hands up. One attempted to make a run for it and was shot. The rest were taken prisoner.

This little skirmish was typical of a hundred others up and down the West Wall, save that attackers elsewhere often met more determined resistance. To the men of the 109th who advanced up the road from Harspelt, the overwhelming superiority of the Allied armies and the strategic weakness of the Germans possessed no significance. They knew only that their depleted company was being asked to assault the vaunted Siegfried Line, with precious little help from anybody else. "I think that the propaganda on the strength of the Siegfried Line has created a feeling of timidity in attacking the defences," Lieutenant-Colonel H. G. McFealey wrote to Bradley on 22 September. "Once they have had some success, the feeling is gone."

As with many units in many battles, most of the men involved in the 109th's little action behaved cautiously and hesitantly. The outcome was decided by the persistence and courage of a handful of NCOs and riflemen. So much depended upon a small minority of such men. As the bold and experienced soldiers were wounded or killed through the weeks that followed, they proved ever harder to replace. The pace of the Allied advance became progressively more sluggish. Lieutenant Witt of the 109th was especially scornful about the behaviour of supporting tanks: "If one gets hit, they all turn tail and run, and it surely is hard to get your men up when that happens."

South of VII Corps, V Corps also made initial penetrations. But these were halted by German reinforcements. The Americans reported, correctly, that they faced 9th Panzer Division. Its armoured strength was reduced to just three tanks. But as usual the Germans' professionalism and energy made the most of tiny resources. They counter-attacked again and again, pushing at exposed flanks, about which they considered the Americans morbidly sensitive.

In the chaos of a battlefield on which his forces were widely scattered and short of supplies and ammunition, V Corps' commander, Gerow, decided that he must consolidate, which meant pulling back his frail bridgeheads across the Sauer river. On Sunday 17 September, attacking American troops of VII Corps likewise encountered counter-attacking Germans head on, and stopped. At the time, this seemed a mere momentary check rather than a momentous issue. Yet just as the champions of tennis tournaments are those who play every point as if it was a match-decider, so the commanders who achieve greatness are those who fight every battle as if their nation's fate hinged upon it. General Courtney Hodges, commander of First Army, to whom Collins and Gerow reported, was a weak, nervous and indecisive officer. At this moment, had Hodges gripped the battle, thrown everything into pushing Gerow's corps forward, great things might have been achieved. Supply difficulties were real enough. These could be blamed partly upon Montgomery's activities on the road to Arnhem, and partly upon Patton's impetuous advance further south, which deprived Hodges of the opportunity to commit XIX Corps to support the advance on the West Wall in the vital days of mid-September. First Army was obliged to send too many men to cover Patton's left flank, instead of throwing weight on its own left, towards the Ruhr. Yet, even with all these difficulties, American strength in the Aachen sector was vastly greater than that of the Germans in men, tanks, guns. On 10 September, Eisenhower was still sublimely confident that the Germans could not hold the West Wall, and that Hodges's forces should be able to get to the Ruhr without serious delay. Instead small groups of Germans, using their weapons aggressively, pinned down much larger American forces, a recurring condition castigated by such able U.S. generals as Gavin. A fatal absence of boldness and determination robbed First Army of a breakthrough. Ground which could have been easily seized in September had to be fought across yard by bloody yard through the months that followed.

Meanwhile, further south, along a front of almost sixty miles through the Ardennes along the Luxembourg border, no significant attempt was made to move forward throughout the next three months, until Hitler launched his great offensive in the forests. The region was almost undefended by the Germans for most of September. The Ardennes had been ruled out of contention by SHAEF, leaving tens of thousands of Americans to fight the terrible battles of Aachen, the Roer dams and Hürtgen Forest, in the narrow sector further north which, the planners had decided, offered the only plausible path east into Germany.

The American battles around the Siegfried Line in September and early October have attracted nothing like the historic attention lavished upon Normandy, Arnhem, the Bulge. Yet in those days, and in that area, perished the last realistic prospect that the Allies might achieve a breakthrough to the heart of Germany in 1944. Thereafter, while it may be suggested that the Allied armies could have performed better in the November battles, it is impossible to argue that a stronger showing would have altered the timetable of the war. The decisive delays were those suffered by Montgomery at Antwerp, and by Bradley and Hodges in cracking the Siegfried Line around Aachen. Once the Germans had been granted a respite to rebuild their forces, the combination of winter weather, supply difficulties and strengthening resistance was bound to be fatal to swift progress.

It is fascinating to speculate what might have happened had Patton and not Hodges commanded First Army, or even 12th Army Group. For all that has been said about the failures of Third Army in Alsace-Lorraine, Patton was the best driver and motivator of formation commanders in north-west Europe. It was his misfortune, and that of the Allies, that in consequence of his disgrace in Sicily he now commanded forces in a sector which could not plausibly be decisive. For all Patton's fame, his forces were doomed to play a subordinate strategic role. Many of Patton's actions, and much of his bombast, in the winter of 1944 represented an attempt to wrest strategic primacy for the army under his command, in the face of logic and the instincts of almost all the Allied planners. Patton's genius for self-promotion, together with such striking achievements as Third

Army's intervention in the Ardennes battle in December 1944, has retained for his soldiers the avid attention of history. Yet the critical battles were fought, and the gravest disappointments suffered, in First Army's sector further north. If Patton had commanded First Army, even granted his limitations in a tough battlefield slogging match, he might have provided the impetus which Hodges could not give. In Alsace-Lorraine, Patton faced substantial German forces, and it is unsurprising that Third Army failed to achieve a breakthrough. Even if they had done so, a salient driven into southern Germany would not have meant much. Had Patton been employed further north, however, he might have been able to secure a decisive penetration of the West Wall in the autumn of 1944, and changed the course of the north-west Europe campaign.

Three distinguished British officers who fought in Holland that winter and later became army commanders believed that the Allied cause could have profited immeasurably from giving a more important role to Patton. Lieutenant Edwin Bramall said: "I wonder if it would have taken so long if Patton or Rommel had been commanding." Captain David Fraser believed that the northern axis of advance was always hopeless, because the terrain made progress so difficult. He suggests: "We might have won in 1944 if Eisenhower had reinforced Patton. Patton was a real doer. There were bigger hills further south, but fewer rivers." Brigadier Michael Carver argued that Montgomery's single thrust could never have worked: "Patton's army should have been leading the U.S. 12th Army Group." Such speculations can never be tested, but it seems noteworthy that two British officers who later became field-marshals and another who became a senior general believed afterwards that the American front against Germany in the winter of 1944 offered far greater possibilities than that of the British in Holland, for which Montgomery continued to cherish such hopes.

STORM OF STEEL

FOR SOLDIERS WHO took part, the north-west Europe campaign seldom looked like a clash of mighty armies, after the fashion of Waterloo or Gettysburg. Rather, it was an interminable series of local collisions involving a few hundred men and a score or two of armoured vehicles, amid some village or hillside or patch of woodland between Switzerland and the North Sea. Only the generals grasped the big picture—or not, as the case might be. For the student of history, it is impossible to follow the course of events without some understanding of how the soldiers of the Second World War fought their battles.

All the combatants accepted some common tactical principles, but applied them in different ways and emphasized different skills. The Germans were frequently obliged to jettison all the rules in 1944–45, because they had to fight with whatever resources were at hand. Theory held good, however, whatever the lapses in practice. Infantry divisions—each 15,000 strong in the case of the Americans, often less for the British and much less for the Germans—supported by modest numbers of tanks, started an attack. The footsoldiers were expected to occupy enemy forward positions after these had been pounded by artillery. Preliminary bombardment sometimes continued for several hours before an assault, with the intention of paralysing those defenders who were not killed. Once the enemy's front was broken, it became the responsibility of armoured divisions to leapfrog the infantry and exploit success by dashing on across country.

If an advance was sustained through some days or even weeks, fresh troops were passed through the front to take over the attack, as spearheads became exhausted or depleted by casualties. Because some divisions were far more effective than others, all commanders overtaxed their best formations—for instance, the airborne on the Allied side, the Waffen SS on the German—by giving them the toughest jobs again and again. During periods of static fighting, armoured divisions were usually held in reserve behind the front, while infantrymen manned forward positions, supported in daylight by a few tanks or self-propelled guns. Tanks seldom moved at night, because their crews could not see or hear, and became vulnerable to surprise even by infantrymen with grenades. As darkness fell, armoured crews pulled back from the front to refuel and perform maintenance, leaving infantry to hold the line.

When an infantry battalion—800–1,000 strong, but usually under-strength—attacked an enemy position, two of its three rifle companies walked or ran forward in extended line on a frontage of perhaps 400 yards, followed by battalion headquarters, with the third rifle company bringing up the rear, in reserve. The attackers aspired to silence the enemy's defences by bombardment before the infantry left their start lines, but few units in few battles were lucky enough to be granted a walkover. An infantry commander's troubles started when the defenders opened fire with machine-guns and mortars, and enemy forward observers called down shellfire. A common cliché was seized upon by fighting soldiers of every nationality to describe their predicament: "all hell broke loose." The instinct of any normal human being when confronted by mortal peril is to take cover. Again and again in north-west Europe, attacking infantry "went to ground," sometimes within a few minutes of leaving their start line. The greatest challenge for an officer was to keep his men going forward. Major-General Gerald Templer expressed the issue well, lecturing to a British junior leaders' course. Imagine yourself leading a platoon up a quiet country lane, he said: "Suddenly, all hell is let loose. You look up, and your platoon sergeant's guts are hanging on a tree beside you. The platoon is turning to run—it is then, gentlemen, that you must grip those men." One of Templer's students recalled: "He paused in absolute silence and, holding out his arm, tightened his fist slowly to give graphic illustration to his words. It was superb theatre, and we sat enthralled."

In the U.S. Army, some gap between the capability of line infantry and that of elite formations such as the Rangers and paratroopers was inevitable, since the latter attracted the most enthusiastic soldiers. Yet, even allowing for this, there was a notable contrast between the energy of the U.S. airborne divisions, along with a few other outstanding formations, and the lassitude of less proficient units. The 82nd and 101st Airborne showed that the American fighting man at his best—no less an amateur than the rest of the armies—possessed no superior. Yet few other U.S. infantry units matched their determination, leadership and tactical skill. For those of us who consider General James Gavin among the finest fighting soldiers America produced in the twentieth century, it is sobering to study his lacerating diary criticisms of American infantry performance.

Captain William DuPuy, who ended the war commanding the 1/357th Infantry, observed sardonically that he would have been happy to lead a much smaller battalion, if it could have been made up of men who would fight. In every battle, a small proportion of soldiers did all the work. Likewise, Captain Willie Knowlton of the 7th Armored Division said: "A few guys carry your attack, and the rest of the people sort of participate and arrive on the objective shortly after everybody else." William DuPuy said that he would willingly lead an attack with just forty of a company's 200 men, if he could choose the forty: "The average man, like nine out of ten, does not have an instinct for the battlefield, doesn't relish it, and will not act independently except under direct orders." These wise words miss one brutal point: even if only forty men out of 200 fought effectively or even fired their weapons, the presence of others, the non-fighters, was necessary to divide the enemy's fire. In other words, while the contribution of forty men might be decisive in winning a battle, the other 160 served an essential, if unwelcome, purpose. They were, quite literally, "cannon fodder."

Skilled and experienced soldiers were inculcated with the understanding that, when making an attack under fire, it was vital to keep moving. First, this was the only way to win the war. Second—and a more persuasive argument for those at the sharp end—if men halted on open ground between the lines, they became highly vulnerable to mortar and artillery fire. Paradoxically, the closer the attackers came to their enemy, the safer they might become, because he was obliged to stop shelling them. Unfortunately, however, many infantrymen never grasped this, and lacked both effective training and determined leadership. Attacks were especially difficult to control and sustain in wooded country or at night. Where men were out of sight of higher authority, it became hard to prevent them from melting away into cover. German officers complained about this almost as often as Allied ones.

A post-campaign U.S. Army report echoed this view: "Too much cannot be said about the necessity for bold and aggressive action on the part of the infantry. The desire to stop and dig in when first fired upon must be discouraged…[Observers reported that] as soon as troops came under heavy mortar and artillery fire, they stopped their forward movement. Unless they moved forward promptly to come to close grips with the enemy, unnecessary casualties were sustained." Half a century earlier, the American writer Ambrose Bierce offered wry advice to the ambitious professional soldier: "Always try and get yourself killed." Few of the men in Eisenhower's armies, however, were ambitious professionals. "The colonel's the only real soldier here," Private Charles Felix wrote in his diary, "the rest of us are just civilians." These were citizens of democracies, imbued since birth with all the inhibitions and decencies of their societies, in profound contrast to the ethos cultivated within the armies of Hitler and Stalin.

"An infantry assault…in many instances can be described as mass confusion," observed a young U.S. platoon commander. It required high courage and determination by officers and NCOs to keep men moving, especially when every visible leader was a target. The first advice Private "Red" Thompson was given by his buddies when he joined the 346th Infantry as a replacement in the winter of 1944 was never to stand anywhere near the company commander in action. The captain invariably carried his map in front of him. The company reckoned that their officer must be conspicuous to every German for miles.

Although radio communications were vital, and the relatively powerful sets mounted in vehicles and at unit headquarters were effective, within infantry companies and platoons 1944 portable wireless technology was unreliable, and often useless, especially in woods or among buildings. Batteries were short lived. At night, an impediment known as "mush" was especially prevalent in the atmospheric conditions of north-west Europe. Troops in fixed positions depended overwhelmingly on field telephones, whose cables were severed with irksome frequency by incoming fire or merely by passing vehicles. Once an action began, it was hard for a local commander to discover what was happening to his forward platoons and companies. If a unit ran into trouble, it was often many minutes, even hours, before its predicament became known at regiment, division or corps level. Lieutenant Edwin Bramall carried a small megaphone on his belt, to communicate with his men above the relentless din of battle. Tank crews, through their access to the radio net, were always better informed than their accompanying infantry, who knew nothing beyond what they could see through the hedge in front of them, or above the parapet of a foxhole. Platoon and company communications in 1944–45 depended chiefly upon runners carrying written messages to the rear, no advance upon the method employed by Greek and Roman armies two millennia earlier.

It was often hard for a local commander to judge how he should handle himself. Conscientious junior officers instinctively wanted to go first. Yet, if they did so, they often fell, and the assault lost impetus. Experienced leaders placed themselves near the front, but not on point, though this sometimes prompted feelings of guilt. Lieutenant William Devitt of the U.S. 83rd Division once asked for volunteers to cross a road first, and got none. Eventually he persuaded some men to move, and followed them. "Why didn't I go first? Perhaps I should have. I don't think it was fear. I just felt it was better to lose a man than the leader." Devitt was absolutely right, but such everyday battlefield decisions were hard for inexperienced young officers.

Like most riflemen, "Red" Thompson never fired an aimed shot in the whole campaign—only "approach fire" from the hip, as his unit advanced upon an objective. He never threw a grenade, and indeed was mortally frightened of the thermite bomb he was obliged to carry. When he joined his battalion, "Nobody had time to teach you anything, you just had to pick it up for yourself. I learned to take care of myself; to be wary; to look, to listen; and to dig holes which you usually left before you finished them. I knew I was just cannon fodder." Proficient American leaders were critical of the failure of officers to keep their soldiers informed. "If the men can be told each day just where they are and what should take place the next day," wrote a Ranger company commander sourly, "they would do their jobs a great deal better." Infantry replacements, who not infrequently joined a unit hours before it was committed to an attack, in such circumstances found themselves utterly bewildered about what was expected of them. A U.S. officer described an action during the winter of 1944 in which newcomers were "naturally scared and actually had to be herded out of their holes to make the attack."

Two British divisions which analysed officer casualties—very similar to those in U.S. formations—found that platoon leaders accounted for 31.2 per cent; company commanders for 30 per cent; battalion COs for a remarkable 18 per cent. Of these losses, 69 per cent were incurred in attack, 23 per cent in defence, 8 per cent on patrols. Fifty-seven per cent were caused by shelling, 35 per cent by small arms, 6 per cent by mines. Accidents with weapons and men shot by their own sentries accounted for 4 per cent. Forty per cent of officers were hit in close-quarter fighting—within 400 yards of the enemy—18 per cent at longer ranges, 13 per cent while forming up for attacks. A British rifle company officer who landed on D-Day faced an almost 70 per cent probability of being hit at some time before May 1945, and nearly 20 per cent prospect of being killed. Among other ranks, there was a 62 per cent likelihood of being hit, a 14 per cent chance of being killed.

"I never failed to be impressed as I went from the rear to the front," said U.S. Major-General W. M. Robertson. "I would see this mass of artillery and tank destroyers and regimental and battalion headquarters. At the front lines, a small number of men were carrying the attack. There were about 1,100 men in the assault element [of an infantry regiment]. They took 90% of the casualties. In an infantry division, they carry your battle." There was considerable bitterness among fighting soldiers about the promiscuity with which decorations were awarded to officers who never faced enemy fire. "Enlisted personnel," reported a U.S. Corps Combat Observer, "being far from dumb or gullible, wonder why a divisional commander, assistant divisional commander, divisional G-2, G-3* and other rear echelon personnel can receive Silver Stars for 'gallantry in action'."

Riflemen, Patton told an officers' conference, made up 65.9 per cent of a U.S. infantry division—an over-generous estimate by the general—inflicted 37 per cent of casualties on the enemy, but took 92 per cent of the formation's losses. Artillery comprised 15 per cent of manpower, inflicted 47 per cent of casualties, but suffered only 2 per cent of losses. The infantry elements of an armoured division accepted 65 per cent of its casualties. Third Army's commander put his own flamboyant spin upon these statistics, arguing for the use of technology and high explosives to minimize casualties: "Americans as a race are the most adept in the use of machinery of any people on earth, and ... the most adept in the construction of machines on a mass-production basis. It costs about $40,000 for a man to get killed. If we can keep him from being killed by a few extra dollars, it is a cheap expenditure." Here, from the commander most avowedly committed to the virtue of personal courage, was a vivid statement of the doctrine of firepower which dominated American tactics in north-west Europe.

Many Allied commanders lamented the infantry's practice of halting to call down artillery fire when they encountered even two or three Germans, rather than themselves engaging the enemy at close quarters. Infantry dependence on artillery created the chronic shortages of ammunition which so retarded the campaign timetable, and imposed a monumental burden on the supply system. "Reliance on fire superiority to win our battles alone is extremely fallacious," wrote U.S. Major-General John Dahlquist in an irritable circular to all units of his 36th Division. "We cannot sit off at a distance, shell the enemy and wait for him to quit ... Indiscriminate firing of heavy weapons and artillery at long distances at unremunerative targets must stop." Exactly the same failures were identified in the British Army. Von Rundstedt asserted in his post-war interrogation that he considered the British even more cautious in action than the Americans. "That [British] infantry tactics ultimately advanced little from the standards of 1916 is disgraceful," observes one magisterial study. Its author, Dr. Timothy Harrison Place, acknowledges the argument, made by defenders of both Montgomery and the British Army, that "artillery-dominated tactics ...

---

*G-1 is a U.S. Army staff designation. It signifies the staff officer responsible for operations at a divisional or corps headquarters (at regimental level he was known as S-1). Likewise a G-2 was responsible for intelligence, a G-3 for supply. British and German staff organization was similar.

were the only practicable ones given the fragility of morale and dwindling reserves of manpower." Yet Harrison Place rejects this view, and concludes that failure to master infantry small-unit tactics appropriate to the conditions of 1944–45, and to break free from the tyranny of dependence upon artillery bombardment as a substitute for energetic ground attack, accounted more than anything else for the indifferent performance of the British Army in north-west Europe.

The director of military training at 15th Army Group in Italy wrote a paper about British shortcomings in 1943 which remained just as valid in 1944–45: "Our tactical methods are thorough and methodical but slow and cumbersome. In consequence our troops fight well in defence and our set-piece attacks are usually successful, but it is not unfair to say that through lack of enterprise in exploitation, we seldom reap the full benefit of them. We are too flank-conscious, we over-insure administratively, we are by nature too apprehensive of failure and our training makes us more so."

Hitler's and Stalin's armies were imbued with an insouciance, indeed brutality, about casualties. It might be argued that 1944–45 Wehrmacht and Red Army battlefield behaviour characterized as "fanatical" or "suicidal" by the Western allies was no more than had been routinely demanded of British and French infantry in the First World War: the dictators' soldiers were required to obey orders that were overwhelmingly likely to result in their deaths. Yet here was the point: British and American generals of the Second World War believed that their soldiers neither would nor should allow themselves to be sacrificed in the same fashion as their fathers had been on the Somme, at Passchendaele and in the Argonne. Allied commanders in north-west Europe sought to avoid making demands upon their men which they believed would be found unacceptable.

"The American soldier," Brigadier-General Pearson Menoher, Chief of Staff of the U.S. XV Corps, wrote after the campaign, "... has not, in general, been as effective as the German infantryman... The desire to close with the enemy and kill him to the extent displayed by the Russians... is, to a great degree, missing." Colonel Hervey Tribolet likewise observed: "There has been considerable comment about lack of aggressiveness on the part of the infantry at times... There is something wrong with our system... A soldier in a rifle company, when he is kept in [line] continuously, may anticipate only four things: to be killed; to be wounded or to get sick; to be captured; or to get combat fatigue." Such strictures display the frustrations of professional soldiers about the performance of amateurs under their command. The battlefield behaviour, and limitations, of the Western allies reflected the societies from which they were drawn. "The British army's reliance on overwhelming firepower did have the disadvantage that it led to a slow rate of advance," an academic analyst acknowledges. But he adds: "it had the great advantage that it enabled troops to reach their objectives without intolerable losses and with morale more or less intact."

By common consent, Allied artillery was very well handled. As an infantry-man, U.S. Captain William DuPuy made a critical tactical point after the campaign: "When I seriously considered what I had accomplished, I had moved the forward observers of the artillery across France and Germany. You need the infantry to do that, but the combat power comes from this other source." This is true and important. Yet one of the major causes of the Allies' difficulties in north-west Europe was that their soldiers—and often generals—were over-impressed by the spectacle of bombardment, and sometimes failed to grasp its limitations. A soldier of the 22nd Infantry described watching a firepower demonstration during his training in the U.S. in 1942. Artillery and machine-guns plastered the ground before rifle companies assaulted it: "We walked over the hill that had been fired on and nothing could have lived after that."

This was a delusion. It was remarkable how resistant were defenders in well-dug positions to anything save a direct hit. Every soldier suffered trauma from the experience of bombardment, yet a shell might land ten feet from a foxhole without killing its occupants. Lieutenant-Colonel Wally Aux commanded a battery of the Americans' most powerful artillery. His regiment, attached to VII Corps, possessed 155mm and 240mm guns, together with eight-inch how-itzers. The latter could throw their shells 35,000 yards. Every spectator was awed by the spectacle of these huge pieces firing on the German positions. Yet, very often, the long reach of Aux's guns was meaningless, because targets could not be accurately observed. When they were firing upon map references transmit-ted by circling fighter-bombers, Aux "was never really convinced that they knew what they were asking us to shoot at." He said: "We seldom knew what we were firing upon. Very often, it was interdiction and harassing fire on roads, a round or two an hour through the night. Much of our fire was unobserved, and of doubtful effect."

Watching distant shellbursts, it was easy to fantasize about the anguish suf-fered by enemy soldiers beneath. Yet there was an immense amount of empty real estate in Europe, upon which imprecisely directed explosives could fall. At a range of 16,500 yards, Aux's guns achieved a probable error of fifty-four yards. This may suggest remarkable exactitude, but it meant that a German tank or artillery piece could be quite undamaged, save for its crew's nerves and burst eardrums, even by meticulously aimed shells. Allied firepower was of vital importance in deciding the outcome of the campaign. The Germans regarded American and British gunners with a respect seldom extended to their armour and infantry. But only footsoldiers and tanks could make the advance into Ger-many. Just sufficient Germans seemed to survive even the most intense bom-bardments to sustain a vigorous defence.

American and British footsoldiers might have performed better in the flat polder of Holland and in the forests around the German frontier if they had mastered the Wehrmacht's skill at infiltration. Small groups of German attackers often worked their way by stealth between gaps in defensive positions, rather than making frontal attacks in open order. Infiltration required a high degree of initiative by junior NCOs and men. German enthusiasm for such tactics reflected their "mission-led" tactical doctrine. That is to say, leaders at every level were told what they were supposed to do, then left to decide for themselves how to do it, whereas Anglo-American doctrine was far more prescriptive about tactical method. "The great story used to be that the Germans wouldn't fight unless there was somebody there to give them orders," said Lieutenant Roy Dixon. "We soon realized that this was nonsense."

It would be absurd to pretend that all German units displayed Clausewitzian zeal and imagination, especially in the last year of the war. But infiltration was the most effective and least costly means of gaining ground on terrain where tanks and men walking or running upright presented easy targets. "I thought our tactics were very unimaginative," said Lieutenant Edwin Bramall. "I would have liked to see more skirmishing and more fire and movement." Captain David Fraser said: "The British Army was enormously road-bound, and it affected operations." An American unit commander summarized the weaknesses of U.S. infantry training as follows: failure to follow creeping artillery barrages closely enough; carelessness when exposed to fire—"men walk when they should creep or crawl"; lack of defensive training in armoured units; unreadiness to undertake night operations; failure to take advantage of fog and darkness to cross open ground. As the armies advanced into Germany, there were also many complaints from commanders about their men's lack of training for street fighting, a highly specialized art.

"The Americans seemed to us very green," said Captain Walter Schaefer-Kehnert, a veteran gunner officer with 9th Panzer Division.

They operated by the book. If you responded by doing something not in the book, they panicked. It usually took them three days after an attack to prepare for the next one. We became accustomed to leave only an outpost screen in front for them to bombard, with the main defences positioned further back, so that their initial attack hit thin air. It took the Allies a ridiculously long time to get into Germany. If they had used our blitzkrieg tactics, they could have been in Berlin in weeks.

"With the Allies it was always the same," said Lieutenant Rolf-Helmut Schröder, a twenty-four-year-old regular officer who was adjutant of the 18th Volksgrenadiers.

They attacked in daylight, starting with artillery, then the tanks. If we had just one or two machine-guns still operational, we could make them stop and wait until next day. There was a basic difference between the Allied approach and our own. The Allies would never move without reconnaissance and preparation. We often expected to have to do it on the run, off the cuff. The last time we attacked in Russia, we formed up on the start line straight off the train.

Yet Sergeant Helmut Günther of 17th SS Panzergrenadiers observed sensibly: "It wasn't that the Allies were cowardly—they just didn't need to take chances. Slow? They were careful."

The most vital and difficult tactical relationship was that between tanks and infantry. Advancing armour had to be protected by accompanying footsoldiers. It was the job of a tank to use its gun to deal with its enemy counterparts, preferably at a range of several hundred yards. But when, as constantly happened, armoured vehicles found themselves facing enemy infantry equipped with the deadly Panzerfaust, or meeting well-concealed anti-tank guns, then a tank crew could see little through the narrow vision slits of their steel box. They could not readily use their guns upon short-range targets. Yet "tank terror" was a phenomenon familiar to the Allied infantryman, who also convinced himself, usually fallaciously, that every enemy armoured vehicle was a giant Tiger. "The tank's inherent weaknesses scarcely featured in [the infantryman's] thinking," in the words of a British analyst of the problem. Unskilled footsoldiers failed to perceive that the monsters became chronically vulnerable at close quarters, if defenders kept their nerve. When Allied tanks encountered a German blocking position, they were obliged to stop or even pull back a few hundred yards, until supporting infantry could work their way forward and eliminate the enemy with small arms and grenades.

It was standard German practice to create blocking positions with a mix of one or two well-concealed tanks or assault guns—turretless tanks which profited from their low silhouette—protected by a ring of infantry with Panzerfausts. Which attackers should approach first—footsoldiers or armour? Throughout the north-west Europe campaign, again and again advancing Allied forces played out a black comic music-hall sketch: "After you, Claude— no, after *you*, Cecil." Soldiers argued under fire about who should do the business. "Teach the men to work with tanks and not be afraid of them," urged Lieutenant Jack M. Brown of the U.S. Army. Attacking infantry often huddled behind their own tanks for protection from small-arms fire, which was fair enough. But then, if a Sherman suddenly lurched backwards down the road after spotting Panzerfausts—or, more likely, after two or three of its consorts had been knocked out—the accompanying infantry were prone to scamper backwards too. It was physically difficult for infantry leaders to communicate with armoured crews, shut down in their steel boxes under fire, even when telephones were installed at the rear of tank hulls. In both American and British armies, there was constant reciprocal backbiting. Tank crews complained that their supporting infantry lagged behind, often wilfully. Corporal Patrick Hennessy's squadron commander said bluntly to his accompanying infantry officer: "If you won't get in front and clear the fausts, we're not going on." Hennessy said: "The infantry were always trying to crowd against the tank for protection, and we kept telling them to keep away. If we hit a mine, the tank would only throw a track, but they would all be blown to bits."

Infantrymen, in their turn, protested that their supporting tanks were too cautious. "During the advance to Metz the tanks...worked wonderfully with doughboys, [but after Metz] I began to notice the change," wrote Major William Sheehan, a staff officer of the 377th Infantry. "As we went on further the tanks became more and more cautious, and the doughs were asked to do more and more. Of course the tanks are going to suffer losses. Who doesn't? But the faith first established in the tanks is now lacking." There was an ugly incident during 30th Division's actions on the Siegfried Line in September, when Shermans of 2nd Armored Division supporting the infantry against a German counter-attack suddenly discovered that they were all in need of "urgent maintenance." Lieutenant Roy Dixon, a Sherman troop commander, said: "The infantry always thought: 'As soon as anything nasty happens, the tanks push off.'" Captain "Dim" Robbins, an infantryman, said: "One always felt that the tanks were having a rather cushy time. Co-operation between infantry and armour was pretty poor."

It should be remarked, however, that the Germans were not immune to the same problem. "The infantry commander sees in the tank a cure for all difficult battle situations," lamented a combat report of 1/24th Panzer Regiment on the Eastern Front in February 1945.

The infantry commander sees in the tank a powerful armoured monster with a huge gun, without recognising its limitations such as weak side armour, limited vision and manoeuvrability...Some infantrymen expect tanks only to move in one direction—forwards. Every necessary halt and pause for observation required by armoured tactics makes them impatient...On 14 February tanks were engaged in street fighting in the village of Croesz. Our own infantry didn't close up with them, even though our gunfire had pinned down the Russian positions. The tanks were obliged to pull back to the infantry positions. In addition, two tanks became total write-offs after hitting mines. Many absurdly extravagant proposals made by infantrymen are simply ignored by tank officers, otherwise the losses would be higher.

When an Allied advance was going well, a tank troop or company led the way until it met resistance or—most frequently—until its leading vehicles were knocked out. Many units rotated the dubious honour of heading a column, because in the course of a given day whoever fulfilled this role could expect to lose his tank if he was lucky, and his life if he was not. It was impossible to avoid heavy tank losses in an advance, whichever army was doing the attacking. But it was a source of constant dismay and frustration to Allied commanders that, after a couple of Shermans had been brewed up by a small German force on the edge of a wood or at the entrance to a village, it frequently required hours to organize and carry out the necessary infantry attack to clear the way for tanks to renew the advance. Armour–infantry co-operation worked best when footsoldiers worked with the same tank battalion for weeks at a stretch, officers getting to know each other. But this was often impossible. Every armoured commander complained that he lacked sufficient infantry support, a reflection of the chronic Allied shortage of riflemen. The British 21st Army Group was armour-heavy, because armoured formations required less manpower. Montgomery's forces suffered from their imbalance of infantry and tanks throughout the campaign.

The faust, vastly superior German counterpart of the American bazooka anti-tank rocket and British spring-loaded bomb-throwing PIAT, was the decisive weapon in enabling Hitler's armies to continue the war until May 1945, given the weakness of their artillery and almost complete absence of air support. German units were prodigally supplied with fausts. Even a poorly trained teenager with the courage to ambush a tank at a range of thirty to sixty yards could expect to cripple it with a faust in his hands, and many did so. The Germans also exploited the use of mortars, "poor man's artillery." Experienced German units equipped themselves with machine-guns—the excellent MG42, with an alarmingly higher rate of fire than its allied counterparts—on a scale far in excess of their paper entitlement. They knew that on the battlefield few men fired their rifles, and even fewer hit anything when they did so. MG42s gave a small number of troops the ability to generate formidably heavy fire, and enabled German units to "punch above their weight" to the end. Their ingenuity was remarkable. It was not uncommon for a German machine-gunner covering an important line—a road or rail track—at night deliberately to fire tracer well above head-height. This encouraged Allied soldiers who saw the streaks above them to suppose that it was safe to walk upright. Meanwhile, a second gunner without tracer would fire much closer to the ground, his bursts invisible until they caused men to fall.

As S-3 of the 357th Infantry, Captain William DuPuy analysed German tactical skills:

> In defence, they took pieces of terrain and knitted them together into positions from which they were able to fire in all directions . . . they used cover and concealment, and they used imagination . . . A handful of Germans could hold up a regiment by siting their weapons properly. If they had two

assault guns and 25 men, they put one assault gun up one side of the road, perhaps on a reverse slope firing through a saddle, and another one behind a stone house, firing across the road. They protected these with some infantry and had a couple of guys with Panzerfausts up on the road itself, or just off the road in pits or behind a house. An imaginative Allied commander could send a company round them in a wide encircling movement. But sometimes a unit would stay there and fight all day against 25 men and two assault guns. That happened all too often.

In attack, they were masters of suppression using machine-pistols. They'd spray our front, drive our soldiers to the ground, and then they'd come in on us. The more they shot, the less our people shot, and the more dangerous it got, until finally, when our people had stopped shooting, we knew the Germans were either going to overrun us, or capture some of our people, or kill our people by getting right on top of us.

DuPuy described his horror on finding that a company commander in his unit had positioned his men on a forward slope in full view of the enemy: "It was murder. Finally, after they killed and wounded maybe 20 men ... the rest just got up and bolted out of there and went over the reverse slope, which is where they should have been in the first place."

Every German soldier was taught the doctrine of so-called "active defence." This required a focus not upon holding forward positions to the last man, but rather upon launching fierce counter-attacks while attackers were still milling in disarray upon captured positions. Especially towards the end of the war, on both Eastern and Western Fronts the Germans would man their forward positions thinly, deploying their main forces further back, hopefully beyond the reach of artillery bombardment. When Allied attackers had made their initial advance, occupied German forward positions and given way to physical and mental weariness after a great surge of effort, the Germans counter-attacked, repeatedly evicting Allied troops from positions they had just won. Allied commanders sought to drum into every unit the importance of digging in quickly on an objective. But this was easier said than done. German will and energy for such aggressive tactics remained astonishing to the end, even if there was a decline in the skill of the soldiers available to carry them out. It was a precept of the entire war, that the German Army always detected and punished an enemy's mistakes.

The qualitative superiority of German tanks to American and British ones was another critical factor in the Wehrmacht's performance against the Allies. Allied planners, and especially the U.S. War Department, made a fundamental error in 1943. They recognized the weakness of American tank guns and protective armour against those of the enemy. But they concluded that the Allies' quantitative advantage was so great that the qualitative issue did not matter.

"Before we went into Normandy," wrote an American armoured officer, "we had been led to believe that the M4 Sherman was...thoroughly capable of dealing with German armor on an equal basis. We soon learned that the opposite was true." His own 3rd Armored Division took 232 Shermans into France, and lost 648 completely destroyed, together with another 700 crippled but repairable—a total loss of 580 per cent of strength. The fact that such losses were readily replaceable reflected the Allies' huge resources. But, for men obliged to contest the battlefield against panzers, awareness of the inadequacy of their own tanks against those of the enemy profoundly influenced their combat behaviour. After painful early experience, most U.S. armoured units gave orders for platoon commanders to ride third in a column, not first.

For a tank crew, it was irrelevant to know that their own army possessed an overall superiority of anything up to ten to one. They were confronted only with the immediate reality that if they fired at a German Tiger or even Panther, their shell was likely to bounce off, unless it struck a weak point below the gun mantle or on the flank. Meanwhile, if an enemy's shell hit a Sherman, the notorious "Ronson" or "Tommy cooker," it was likely not merely to stop, but to burn. "The Sherman was a very efficient workhorse, but as a fighting tank it was a disaster," said Captain David Fraser. The first time Corporal Patrick Hennessy fired his Sherman's gun at a Tiger tank, he watched the shell hit its hull, then ricochet straight up into the air. "I thought: 'To hell with this!,' and pulled back." Who could blame Allied armoured units for displaying caution amid such realities?

The Germans envied the quantity of U.S. weapons and equipment. But American soldiers complained about the poor quality of much of their own fighting matériel against that of the enemy. A deluge of field reports descended on the U.S. War Department almost to the end of the war demanding more infantry for armoured units, a better tank gun, fewer dud shells, a better-armoured tank destroyer, tent poles which did not snap, combat jackets without a sheen that glittered dangerously in sunshine, a less clumsy sub-machine gun than the Thompson, genuinely smokeless ammunition, an anti-tank gun more impressive than the feeble 57mm, better field glasses, stronger divisional artillery with a less extravagant allocation of transport. Commanders wanted an infantry anti-tank weapon of the quality of the faust: "Numerous cases have been reported where bazooka teams have succeeded in immobilizing tanks, but since they are unable to destroy them, they themselves have been killed by retaliating fire from the tank, and the tank retrieved by the enemy."

By contrast, every German was dismayed by the ubiquity and impact of Allied air power. Any German vehicle movement in daylight was likely to be rewarded by fighter-bomber attack, of an effectiveness unknown on the Eastern Front. The Russians never matched the sophistication of Allied wireless ground control. The Allies profited hugely, of course, from the fact that their own vehicles could move freely behind the front by day or night, with the Luftwaffe driven from the skies. Yet almost all Germany's soldiers found it less painful to fight in the west than the east, because the Americans seldom troubled them during the hours of darkness. When Corporal Henry Metelmann was transferred to the west after three years on the Eastern Front, he was amazed to discover that the enemy seemed to undertake no patrolling: "Had they been Russians, they would have given us no rest. Psychologically, I found the drastic change from Russia very confusing." Especially during the winter months, with only some eight hours of daylight, night respites were priceless to the Germans. They enabled units to rearm, resupply and redeploy without interference save from random artillery harassing fire. It is also important to remember that there were many, many days in the winter of 1944 when characteristic European overcast prevented the Allies from using their air power even in daylight.

On the Western Front, the war was conducted with much greater humanity than in the east. A man had a better chance of being taken prisoner alive and treated decently. Attitudes in the rival armies varied widely, however, according to the circumstances of the moment. An angry German officer emptied a Luger at "Dim" Robbins after the British captured his positions. Fortunately, Robbins was wearing a heavy tweed coat, which absorbed most of the bullets. Only one hit flesh, removing the end of a finger holding a Sten gun. Soon afterwards, the German was brought in, covered in blood. Robbins's sergeant-major said comfortingly: "I'll take him behind that hedge, sir, and finish him off." Robbins had to dissuade the NCO from doing so. Wehrmacht Sergeant Otto Cranz's father, who had been a PoW of the Russians in the First World War, always advised his son that if he was captured he should do his utmost to reach the enemy's rear areas as quickly as possible. Front-line troops were most likely to shoot a prisoner, not least out of envy that a man destined for a camp was being granted a ticket to survive the war, denied to those left behind to continue the struggle.

Captain John Regan of the 357th Infantry "considered it bad psychology to treat prisoners well when first captured... [It] would be like congratulating a loser of a football game. We are here to kill Germans, not to baby them." Lieutenant Tisch of the German 5th Infantry offered a mirror image of Regan's view: "Front line troops deplore the attitude towards prisoners displayed by the rear echelons, such as giving them cigarettes, candy bars and other familiarities. Our soldiers must be endowed with a hatred and distrust of the enemy in order to pursue the war successfully." During one of the bloody Moselle crossings Captain Jack Gerrie, a company commander in the 11th Infantry, was enraged to see the Germans shooting down American medics trying to retrieve wounded men after the action. Instead, his men forced German prisoners to go out and retrieve the casualties. When the enemy shot them too, "finally we said 'to hell with it' *and shot the whole damn bunch* [of prisoners]." The highlighted phrase has been deleted in pencil from the U.S. National Archive's copy of the divisional after-action report. Some sixty German PoWs were killed by the U.S. 11th Armored Division, new to combat, whose men believed for some hours that they were not supposed to take prisoners. Patton wrote in his diary of "some unfortunate incidents in the shooting of prisoners. (I hope we can conceal this)."

Almost every soldier on both sides shared a hatred of snipers, which frequently caused them to be shot out of hand if captured. There was no logic or provision in the Geneva Convention to justify such action. Sniping merely represented the highest refinement of the infantry soldier's art. Its exercise required courage and skill. Yet sniping made the random business of killing, in which they were all engaged, become somehow personal and thus unacceptable to ordinary footsoldiers. Snipers were readily identified by the bruise and sometimes cuts inflicted by the recoil of a rifle with a telescopic sight tightly affixed to a man's right eye. The CO of the U.S. 143rd Infantry reported that his men were most reluctant to use sniper rifles themselves, "because they think they will be shot if captured." This was not a delusion.

Local truces not infrequently took place between Germans and British or American troops, to allow wounded men to be removed from the battlefield. There was a notable incident in the Belgian village of Bure on 3 January 1945. During three days of bitter fighting between the British 13 Para and German panzergrenadiers supported by a tank, the battalion doctor David Tibbs was treating wounded men when his sergeant, Scott, reported that there were some badly wounded men in a house on the front line, and he was going to get them out. Tibbs, preoccupied with his work, acquiesced: "the Germans had a pretty good record of respecting the red cross in our sector." Accompanied by the battalion padre, Sergeant Scott slowly drove an ambulance with a large red-cross flag up the main street. Firing on both sides stopped. Stretcher-bearers had begun to bring out the wounded when they heard the roar of a tank engine. A Panther clattered up the street towards them. It stopped by the ambulance, and the hatch opened. A German appeared, and admonished them in perfect English: "This time I let you do it—next time, I shoot!" He closed the hatch. The tank lurched back to the German line. The ambulance finished its work and drove to the rear. The battle resumed. Even on the British front, this episode provoked lasting astonishment. "Why were the Germans so accommodating?" mused Dr. Tibbs. "They must have hoped that we would behave in the same way in similar circumstances, and by and large, we did." It was unthinkable that anything of the kind could have happened in the east.

Most men were less fearful of death than of being maimed. As Private Tony Carullo of the 2nd Infantry walked up a road, he heard a shell and leaped aside into a ditch. When he climbed out again, he found that four men carrying a casualty in a shelter half (or groundsheet) had been obliterated: "There were body parts all over the road, one guy's nerves were still reacting, everything was mangled. You weren't scared you were going to die—you were scared of getting mangled up like those guys." This fear was echoed on the other side of the hill: "You were not afraid of being killed—you feared being horribly wounded, or taken prisoner by the Soviets," observed Lieutenant Helmut Schmidt of the Luftwaffe flak.

Because battles are fought by men who wear uniforms and carry weapons, it is easy to forget that, in the Second World War, the vast majority of those who served in every army did not think of themselves as soldiers. They were civilians, who strove even upon the battlefield to secrete a part of themselves from their military superiors and soldierly functions, from all the horrors around them. Even as they saluted, fired weapons or sheltered from bombardment, in their innermost selves most cherished the conviction that these horrors did not represent reality, that real life remained the small town or great city from which they had come; their loved ones; the civilian jobs they prayed desperately to survive to return to. Corporal Iolo Lewis said: "The whole experience didn't seem real to me. It was something big going on, that I was just a tiny part of. We knew so little about what was happening—our field of vision was so small." Staff-Sergeant Henry Kissinger of the U.S. 84th Division observed drily: "I cannot say that digging foxholes or carrying a heavy pack was my idea of fun. It's not what you're brought up to do, as a nice middle-class Jewish boy. But, for me, it was the way I got to know America."

Some American soldiers enjoyed the chance granted to them by the war to see the world, especially if they were not required to earn their passage by service with infantry or armour. "For my generation," wrote the historian Arthur Schlesinger, who served in France with America's intelligence service the OSS, "the Second World War was the supreme experience. And for many not killed or maimed, it was a liberating experience, annulling routine expectations, providing new contexts and challenges, testing abilities, widening horizons and opportunities, nourishing honesty, individuality, complexity, irony, stoicism. Above all, war was a reminder of the savagery of life." Private Rueben Cohen came from the lower east side of New York. He enjoyed a much harsher and less glamorous war than Schlesinger, yet as he travelled from North Africa through Sicily into France as a field artilleryman with the 1st Division, his thoughts often veered along the same path as those of the historian, albeit expressed in less elegant language: "Gee, I'll have something to talk about if I get through the war." But Cohen was a mature man of thirty-one, whom the boys of his battery called "Pop." Most soldiers were at least a decade younger, naive and innocent.

Like millions of young Americans, twenty-year-old Corporal Roy Ferlazzo from Jersey City found Europe a bewildering place. He was disgusted by primitive French notions of hygiene, and by his first sight of a bidet. A teetotaller, he felt no urge to join off-duty drinking orgies, nor for that matter to chase girls: "Very few of us were sexually active." Where some men became ambitious looters of cameras, pistols, binoculars, Ferlazzo's simple tastes confined him to pipes—the smoking kind—of which he amassed an impressive collection by the end of the campaign. From being a confused, frightened, very homesick young soldier at the outset, he learned to accept the army, and the war, without deep commitment, but also without much complaint. He simply lived each day as it came, and did the job he was asked to do, in the manner of millions of other young Americans shipped to Europe. Even the ubiquitous destruction of villages and cities made little impact on him: "I guess it was the same in the Crusades with swords and shields." His unit was lucky. It suffered a few casualties from shrapnel, but lost not a single man killed. Like most soldiers in the Western allied armies who were spared the whitest heat of combat, he traversed Europe amid the grimmest events of the twentieth century without being significantly touched by them.

An American officer combing abandoned Belgian houses for furniture for the mess was embarrassed to come upon a girl of seven, living with her three-year-old sister and eighty-year-old grandmother "in indescribably cold and dirty conditions." He sought consoling words for them only to be cut short by a Belgian. "They are collaborationists," he said dismissively. Few soldiers engaged in any meaningful fashion with the local civilians who clung to their ruins in the middle of the battlefield. The passing warriors merely drove or fought their way past them, throwing occasional gum or candy. Most men regarded local people with little more interest than exhibits glimpsed through the bars of a foreign zoo, unless they were young, female and pretty.

The American and British armies contained a few eager warriors, from Patton downwards, who embraced the experience of combat. "I remember wondering what life after the war would be like," wrote Brigadier Michael Carver, a professional soldier commanding a British armoured brigade. "Would I miss the intensity of an active life, lived to the full close to nature, as life on the battlefield, for all its fears and frightfulness at times, undoubtedly was? I was afraid I might." By contrast, the vast majority of those who fought in infantry or tanks simply yearned desperately for the war, and their own exposure to risk, to be over. Most men who thought at all—and many did not—felt quietly conscious of the justice of the Allied cause. "We were absolutely certain we were right," said Captain Lord Carrington, a future British foreign secretary. "It made a lot of difference."

Yet a critical divide persisted between the Eastern and Western Fronts in the Second World War: most American and British soldiers did not share the bitter hatred for their enemy which prevailed among the Russians. GIs or Tommies were subject to flashes of passion and rage when they were frightened, or when their unit was suffering heavy losses. But, once the adrenaline rush of battle slowed even a little, it was striking how little ill-will Allied soldiers, and especially Americans, sustained towards the Germans. "Hate them?" said nineteen-year-old Private Tony Carullo. "No, no, we respected them. Even if you captured them, they'd look you in the face and ask: 'What are you people doing here?' It was the French we didn't care for." RAF Squadron Leader Tony Mann said: "I never hated the Germans as I hated the Japanese." Mann had flown Hurricanes in Burma before being transferred to north-west Europe.

This was a view shared by Corporal Roy Ferlazzo. "The Germans were just soldiers like us." He found it impossible to regard them with the same hostility as the perpetrators of Pearl Harbor. "I never hated the Germans—I just wanted to beat them," said "Dim" Robbins. "Once we'd won a battle, I never liked shooting Germans just for the hell of it." Over the sights of his Bren gun, Sergeant Reg Romain of the 5th Wiltshires watched a badly wounded German crawling away from the wreckage of a half-track near Westerbreek: "I let him go, because it was plain his fighting days were over." "Don't let's be beastly to the Germans," sang the great English actor and writer Noël Coward, master of the drawing-room comedy. With hindsight, it is interesting that Coward's words found favour even as satire, in the midst of a bloody contest of arms. Yet, until the revelation of the concentration camps, many Allied soldiers fought their battles with remarkably little passion, save the desire to survive.

American and British historians have expended immense energy in recent years arguing the issue of whether the German soldier was superior to his Allied counterpart. To all save the most dogged nationalists, it must be plain that Hitler's armies performed far more professionally and fought with much greater determination than Eisenhower's men. Allied generals were constantly hampered by the fact that, even when they advanced bold and imaginative plans, these were often incapable of execution by conscientious but never fanatical civilian soldiers, opposed by the most professionally skilful army of modern times. Yet it seems wrong to leave the matter there. There is a vital corollary. If American and British soldiers had been imbued with the ethos which enabled Hitler's soldiers to do what they did, the purpose for which the war was being fought would have been set at naught. All soldiers are in some measure brutalized by the experience of conflict. Some lapses and breaches of humanity on the part of Allied soldiers are recorded in these pages. To an impressive degree, however, the American and British armies preserved in battle the values and decencies, the civilized inhibitions of their societies. It seems appropriate for an historian to offer military judgements upon the failures and shortcomings of the Allies in 1944–45, which were many and various. But there is every reason to cherish and to respect the values that pervaded Eisenhower's armies.

Many individual German soldiers were likewise unwilling warriors, men born and raised with the same instinctive humanity as their Allied counterparts. But they fought within the framework of an army which was institutionally brutalized. Hitler and his generals demanded of Germany's soldiers, on pain of savage punishment, far more than the Western allies expected from their men.

American and British officers knew that their citizen soldiers were attempting to fulfil tasks which ran profoundly against the grain of their societies' culture. The Germans and Russians in the Second World War showed themselves better warriors, but worse human beings. This is not a cultural conceit, but a moral truth of the utmost importance to understanding what took place on the battle-field.

Such observations lead in turn, however, to a consideration which might dissuade the democracies from celebrating their own humanity too extravagantly. Western allied scruples made the Americans and British dependent upon the ferocity of their Soviet allies to do the main business of destroying Hitler's armies. If the Russians had not accepted the casualties necessary to inflict a war-winning level of attrition on the Wehrmacht, the Western allies would have had to pay a far higher price, and the struggle would have continued for much longer.

AACHEN, ON THE Belgian border just forty miles west of Cologne and the Rhine, became the first major German city to fall to the Allies. Hodges's First Army began its slow, methodical operations to encircle the town in heavy rain on 1 October, after four days' artillery bombardment of German positions, on a scale that echoed the barrages of the First World War. The first American objective was to breach the West Wall north of the city. Initial air strikes failed. Not merely did they inflict little damage upon the Germans, but a navigational error caused the bombers to kill thirty-four Belgian civilians in a town twenty-seven miles from the target area. The mud made movement tough for infantry and tougher still for tanks. By 7 October, however, the northern arm of the American operation had done its business, piercing the West Wall. 1st Division began to push up behind Aachen from the south. Yet, in the days that followed, repeated German counter-attacks on the American flanks caused grief and delay. Several exposed units of the attacking formation were cut off and destroyed piecemeal.

"Remember those happy days when you stepped out with your best girl 'going places'?" inquired a propaganda pamphlet of which thousands were fired into the American lines by German artillery. "What is left of all this? Nothing! Nothing but days and nights of the heaviest fighting and for many of you NOTHING BUT A PLAIN WOODEN CROSS IN FOREIGN SOIL!" The Germans daubed a painted message across a house front in one of the villages through which the Americans advanced: "MANY OF YOU WHO COME UP THIS ROAD WON'T BE COMING BACK."

Huebner, commander of 1st Division, the "Big Red One," visited one of his regimental colonels. He found this officer in near despair about losses from shellfire: "General," said the hapless infantryman, "if we don't get some help pretty soon, the 16th Infantry is just going to cease to exist." Huebner puffed a pipe with his usual unshakeable calm. "Freddy," he said finally, "if higher authority has decided that this is the place and the time that the 1st Division is going to cease to exist, then I guess this is where we cease to exist."

The advance ground painfully on. It was a familiar story: the enemy's forces were small, but their fierce energy convinced American units of the need for caution. Corlett's XIX Corps made slow progress. The 30th Division took nine days to advance the last three miles to link up with 1st Division on 16 October. The entire operation cost the 30th some 3,100 casualties, about 20 per cent of its strength. So irked were Bradley and Hodges by XIX Corps's sluggishness that they sacked Corlett. The emotional Leland Hobbs, commanding 30th Division, burst into tears on hearing the news. He felt that if his men had been able to move faster on the north axis Corlett would not have lost his job.

When the German garrison of Aachen rejected a demand for its surrender, the Americans launched an intense air and artillery bombardment, then committed infantry and tanks. On the evening of 21 October, resistance ended in the devastated city. The operation had exhausted the men of 1st and 30th Divisions. Bradley acknowledged that they would have to be reinforced and rested before they could do more. Allied intelligence estimated that German strength in the west had trebled in the seven weeks since the beginning of September. It is valid to speculate about what might have happened if 30th Division had pressed on eastwards towards the Roer river after piercing the West Wall, as Corlett had suggested to Hodges, instead of pivoting to encircle Aachen. The German garrison of the city presented no significant threat to the Allied advance. The enemy lacked mobility and could have been mopped up at leisure. Once again, vital momentum had been lost for the dogged and doubtful purpose of seizing a landmark.

Just as Montgomery was surely right to bypass the German garrisons of the Channel ports during his dash east in August, so Patton might have left Metz to rot, and Hodges might have driven on eastwards beyond Aachen. Allied operations reflected an unimaginative commitment to winning ground, tidying lines on the map, eliminating ugly bulges and pockets. Commanders sought to gain terrain yard by yard, rather than focus upon the aim of all great generals throughout history—the concentration of combat power for the breaking of the enemy's main front. On 22 October, Marshall in Washington urged Eisenhower to examine the chances of launching an all-out offensive to end the war by Christmas. Yet by that date realistic prospects of a swift victory had perished. They slipped away when First Army failed to make good its penetration of the West Wall before the enemy and the weather foreclosed the options. Now, Germans were dug deep into the wooded hills that zig-zagged across their frontier with Belgium and Luxembourg. While the Allies retained superiority, the overwhelming dominance of autumn had been lost. The pain that lay ahead for First Army in its winter battles caused many thoughtful officers to lament the opportunity that might have been seized in September, with more imaginative leadership and without the drain of fuel and supplies to Market Garden, Lorraine and Brest.

One further point is worth making. If Germany's generals had followed the logic of their own fears about what the Russians would do to Germany, they might have saved their own people untold misery by engineering a surrender or even a tactical collapse in the west, to give passage to the Western allies. Of course, they did not do so, and sustained fierce resistance on both fronts. Only in the last weeks of the war did the Wehrmacht in the west give way, while still fighting fiercely in the east. The autumn failure to break into Germany was a mere disappointment for the Americans and British. For the German people, however, it augured disaster. Their fate in 1945 was to prove infinitely more terrible than it would have been had they lost the war in the west in 1944.

CHAPTER FOUR

The Russians at the Vistula

SOVIET WARLORD

LONG BEFORE Hitler invaded the Soviet Union in 1941, Joseph Stalin had created within its borders the greatest edifice of repression, mass murder and human suffering the world has ever seen. Hitler possessed greater democratic legitimacy in Germany through the ballot box than did Stalin in the Soviet Union. "Is there still a Tsar?" Winston Churchill's father, half a century dead, demanded in one of his son's dreams. "Yes. But he is not a Romanoff," his son answered. "He is much more powerful, and much more despotic." Stalin was now sixty-five, visibly worn by the strain of more than three years of war. Yet he retained a prodigious capacity for work. His charm never lost its capacity to inspire terror in the hearts of all who knew how many of those whom "Koba" professed to love he had killed. "Don't worry, we'll find you another wife," Stalin observed laconically to Poskrebyshev, his long-serving *chef de cabinet*, when the wretched man's spouse was dispatched for execution in 1939. Poskrebyshev remained at his post until 1952.

If Stalin did not embark upon a systematic Holocaust, his anti-semitism was almost as profound as that of Hitler. He shared his German counterpart's sexual prurience, together with an energy in the hours of darkness which seemed wholly appropriate to the nature of his toils. This son of a cobbler and a washerwoman, his face deeply marked by smallpox, had never been a soldier, yet affected military garb from 1941 onwards, to reflect his role as Russia's supreme warlord. Portraits of Suvurov and Kutuzov, the nation's great military heroes, were accorded prominent places in his study. Zhukov, however, observed in retirement: "Stalin always somehow remained a civilian." Like Hitler and in contrast to Churchill, he never visited the fighting fronts—or at any rate never put himself within range of gunfire—not least because he was frightened of flying. He did, however, devote thirty minutes each evening to watching newsreels from the battlefields. "He was of small stature," wrote Milovan Djilas, "and disproportioned, his trunk too short, his arms too long. His face was pale and rough, ruddy around the cheekbones, his teeth black and irregular, his moustache and hair thin. An admirable head, though, like that of a mountain man, with lively and impish avid yellow eyes... One felt the intent, constant activity of the mind."

Stalin, self-educated, had read obsessively all his life. In the 1930s he and his circle shared an implausible enthusiasm for Galsworthy's *The Forsyte Saga,* as an exposition of the corruption of capitalism. Now, there was no circle, for Stalin had murdered them all. He stood alone, served only by lackeys: Beria—"our Himmler" as Stalin introduced him—Zhanadov, Voroshilov, Molotov and a handful of others. In contrast to Hitler, Stalin never excelled as a public performer. He broadcast only with reluctance, at moments of crisis. His genius lay in judgement of men, committee management, mastery of the dark recesses of power. He displayed a compulsion to liquidate perceived threats to his authority which was more draconian than that of Germany's Führer. If the German generals' attempt to overthrow Hitler in 1944 was feeble, no man ever dared to raise a hand against Stalin. All those who might have done so were dead. Hitler crippled his own war effort by maintaining in power such old Nazi loyalists as Göring, even when their incompetence was plain. Stalin never indulged in sentiment. Those who failed, and suffered mere dismissal, considered themselves fortunate. Most were shot.

In the eyes of the democracies, before 1939 the Soviet Union's only merit was that it did not practise external aggression in regions of interest to them. Hitler became the enemy of the Western powers not because of what he did within the frontiers of Germany—even to the Jews—but because he sought world dominance. The democracies indulged Stalin, by contrast, because the victims of his tyranny, far more numerous than those of Hitler, were his own people. That perception changed with the Nazi–Soviet Pact of 1939, and Stalin's annexation of eastern Poland and invasion of Finland. As war beckoned in 1941, Stalin embraced a new prototype. "Our benefactor thinks that we have been too sentimental," wrote Boris Pasternak bitterly. "Peter the Great is no longer an appropriate model. The new passion, openly confessed, is for Ivan the Terrible, the *oprichnina* [tsarist enforcers], and cruelty. This is the subject for new operas, plays and films." Beyond hundreds of thousands of Russians and inhabitants of the republics whom he killed as state enemies, Stalin's policies had driven millions more to starvation and even cannibalism. He had gone far towards stripping from the Russian people their heritage of impulsive passion and artistic genius, replacing it with an ice-age universe in which even absolute obedience offered no warranty of survival. Stalin had contrived the destruction of human trust in a society now ruled by terror, manic suspicion and arbitrary injustice. He himself liked to tell a story of Beria, most terrible of secret policemen. Stalin loses a favourite pipe. A few days later, Beria calls to inquire whether it has been recovered. "Yes," replies Stalin, "I found it under the sofa." "Impossible!" says Beria. "Three people have already confessed to this crime!"

The German invasion provoked the deportation of entire Soviet subject populations, such as the Chechens and Crimean Tartars, more than two million people whose loyalty to Moscow was deemed suspect. They died in the hundreds of thousands. Stalin's conduct of his own dominions, in which he had already presided over at least ten million deaths, perhaps twenty million, commanded the respect, even envy, of Hitler. The Georgian shared his German counterpart's appetite for self-pity in adversity. He was a much cleverer man, however, especially in one vital respect. War made Hitler a fantasist and Stalin a realist.

It is unlikely that any other Soviet leader could have wrung from his own people the sacrifices necessary to defeat the Nazis. "Who but us could have taken on the Germans?" mused a Soviet soldier, Konstantin Mamerdov. Who indeed? Victory demanded the commitment of a tyranny as ruthless as that of Germany, and ultimately more effective militarily and industrially. But for Stalin's massive pre-war programme to industrialize the Soviet Union, heedless of the cost in millions of peasant lives, it is unlikely that his nation could have manufactured the weapons to resist Hitler in 1941. Once at war, Stalin "was oblivious of the fundamental principle of the military art, that the objective should be gained at minimal cost in human life," observes one of his modern Russian biographers, General Dmitry Volkogonov. "He believed that both victories and defeats inevitably reaped a bitter harvest... It seemed to Stalin quite unnecessary to make the attainment of strategic objectives dependent on the scale of losses."

The most important "if" of the Second World War is to consider the consequences had Germany not invaded the Soviet Union. The Battle of Britain notwithstanding, Churchill's island could have been conquered had Hitler's ambitions not been overwhelmingly fixed upon the creation of an eastern empire. The three years of attrition which followed, before the Western allies invaded France, demanded a price from the Russian people which the democracies were quite incapable of paying. It seems wrong to take for granted the Soviet Union's passionate resistance to Hitler. It remains extraordinary that its people, who had suffered so terribly from Stalin's rule, nonetheless rallied to the standard of Mother Russia under his leadership, in a fashion that determined the course of history.

To grasp the nature of the war against Germany, a crude rule of thumb is useful. Every mile of front on which the Americans and British fought, every German soldier deployed in the west, was multiplied three- or four-fold in the east. The disparity in casualties both suffered and inflicted during the last year of the war, when the Western allies were fighting in north-west Europe, was even greater. Eisenhower's armies suffered some 700,000 casualties—killed,

wounded and taken prisoner—between D-Day and the end; the Russians suffered well over two million during the same period. Between June 1941 and
December 1944, Germany lost 2.4 million battlefield dead on the Eastern Front,
against 202,000 men killed fighting the Americans and British in North Africa,
Italy and north-west Europe together. The conflict between the Red Army and
the Wehrmacht dwarfed the western campaign in scale, intensity and savagery.

Most Russian civilians spent the war years on the brink of starvation, working a sixty-six-hour week with one rest-day a month, receiving half the rations
of Germans. Only vegetables grown in sixteen million urban gardens saved
many people from death. In the course of the war, some 29.5 million Soviet citizens were drafted for service of one kind or another. By the autumn of 1944,
more than 11.4 million men and women were serving in Stalin's forces, 6.7 million of these with the active army. All statistics are unreliable, but the best available suggest that Soviet forces suffered total losses of 8.7 million killed, together
with twenty-two million sick and wounded. These casualties were, of course,
additional to at least eighteen million Soviet civilians who died.

It is important to qualify Soviet casualty figures. They fail to differentiate
between those who were killed by the Nazis and those who died or were
allowed to die at Moscow's hands. Stalin's agents continued killing and impris-
oning "saboteurs" and "enemies of the state" in the hundreds of thousands. A
quarter of all deportees in Siberian labour camps died of starvation in 1942—
some 352,000 of them. Beria recorded the deaths of 114,481 in 1944, the year of
victories. Around 157,000 men were shot for alleged desertion, cowardice or
other military crimes in 1941–42 alone. Official Soviet rationing policy reflected
indifference to the deaths from hunger of many weak and elderly people, since
these were incapable of working or fighting. Throughout the territories now
occupied by the Red Army the NKVD, Stalin's all-powerful secret police and
enforcing militia, was rounding up German civilians and PoWs in vast numbers,
and dispatching them for labour service in the Soviet Union. Beria reported to
Stalin in November 1944, for instance, that 97,484 German men between the
ages of seventeen and forty-five and women between eighteen and thirty were
being shipped to the Ukrainian mines from Bulgaria and Yugoslavia. Some of
these could replace the German slaves who were dying in Soviet hands—6,017
during the first ten days of November alone, as Beria also recorded.

Stalin dominated Russia's war more absolutely than Hitler controlled Germany's. The Nazi empire was fatally weakened by the rivalry, self-indulgence,
strategic folly and administrative incompetence of its leaders. In the Soviet
Union, there was only one fount of power, from whom there was no escape or
appeal. Ismay, Churchill's personal Chief of Staff, recoiled from the cringing
subservience of Russia's generals when he first visited the Kremlin in 1941. "It
was nauseating," he wrote, "to see brave men reduced to such abject servility."

The Soviet Union's defeats in 1941–42 were chiefly attributable to Stalin's own blunders. In the years that followed, however, in striking contrast to Hitler, the master of Russia learned lessons. Without surrendering any fraction of his power over the state, he delegated the conduct of battles to able commanders, and reaped the rewards. He displayed an intellect and mastery of detail which impressed even foreign visitors who were repelled by his insane cruelty. He showed himself the most successful warlord of the Second World War, contriving means and pursuing ends with a single-mindedness unimaginable in the democracies. Terror was a more fundamental instrument of Russia's warmaking than of Germany's. Even Stalin's most celebrated marshals were never free from its spectre.

In the late summer of 1944, Soviet armies stood on the Vistula after accomplishing their most spectacular victories of the war. Yet, in the eyes of the West, admiration for Russia's military achievement was overshadowed by horror prompted by events in Poland, to which Stalin responded with indifference, or worse.

WARSAW'S AGONY

ON 1 AUGUST, on the orders of its commander, General Tadeusz Bor Komorowski, the Polish Resistance launched an uprising designed to wrest control of their nation's capital from the Germans before the Russians arrived. At 1700 that day, "Hour Vee," the red and white banner of Poland was hoisted above the Prudential building, Warsaw's highest. The Poles signalled en clair to London: "The struggle [for the capital] has begun." Among the first of many suicidally courageous actions, ninety-eight men of the "Stag" battalion sought to storm one German position armed only with revolvers. Just seven survived. Only one in seven of the 37,600 insurgents possessed weapons of any kind; 2,500 died on 1 August alone; 35,000 civilians were killed in the Vola suburb in the first week.

The "London Poles," whose underground forces were known as the Resistance Army Krajowa, were goaded to act by nationalist fervour and by a radio broadcast on 29 July from Stalin's communists, the "Lublin Poles." This called for a people's rising against the Nazis, and asserted that Russian help was at hand. Bor Komorowski believed that if the "London Poles" failed to mobilize, they would forfeit any claim to govern their own country. His intention was not to assist the approaching Russians and Lublin Poles, but to pre-empt their hegemony. He expected the Red Army to reach Warsaw within forty-eight hours, though he believed that his forces might maintain their struggle for five or six days if necessary. In the most spectacular and indeed reckless fashion, the Polish commander wanted it both ways: the success of his revolt hinged upon receiving Russian military support, while its explicit objective was to deny the Soviet Union political authority over his country.

The British Chiefs of Staff, recognizing their own inability to provide assistance, declined to offer the Poles any directive or guidance about their actions one way or the other. This, too, was extraordinarily irresponsible. Three months earlier the British Joint Intelligence Committee had concluded that, if the Poles carried out their long-planned uprising, it was doomed to failure in the absence of close co-operation with the Russians, which was unlikely to be forthcoming. It seems lamentable that, after making such an appreciation, the British failed to exert all possible pressure upon the Poles to abandon their fantasies. The Red Army made no move westward in support of the Rising. The scene was set for a tragedy.

On 31 July, the Japanese ambassador in Berlin had informed Tokyo that the Germans would not seek to hold Warsaw to the last. Withdrawal was indeed the Wehrmacht's intention in the face of an envelopment by the Red Army; when this later came, Warsaw was scarcely defended. In August, however, confronted instead by domestic insurgency, the Nazis' loathing and contempt for the Poles provoked them to exploit an opportunity to diminish the numbers of these troublesome people, and to reassert German authority. Military desirability and political inclination marched together. The Germans assumed that the Rising was orchestrated with the Soviets, and would soon be followed by a Russian link-up with the Resistance in Warsaw, which should be thwarted. Even in the last months of his empire, Hitler's zeal in fulfilment of ideological doctrine never flagged. His business with the Jews was almost complete. The Nazis' eagerness for innocent blood increased, rather than diminished, as their grasp upon power grew more precarious. German commanders, notably Heinrich Himmler, somehow scraped together forces to suppress the Rising. The Germans addressed their task with absolute ruthlessness. During the sixty-three days that followed, some 10,000 Resistance fighters died, along with 250,000 civilians—a quarter of Warsaw's population—many of these people massacred in cold blood.

Cossacks, paratroopers and SS units were thrown into the battle. They employed flamethrowers, siege mortars, gas, explosive-carrying robots and systematic flooding of the Poles' underground refuges. Much of Warsaw was reduced to rubble by bombardment. The surviving inhabitants were driven out into the countryside or shipped to concentration camps. The men of the SS, and especially the Dirlewanger Brigade, surpassed even their record in Russia of pillage, rape and mass murder, overlaid with sadism. The wounded were machine-gunned. Prisoners were hurled from the windows of apartment buildings. Polish women and children were used as human shields for the advance of German troops. On 5 August Hans Frank, the Nazi governor, reported to Berlin:

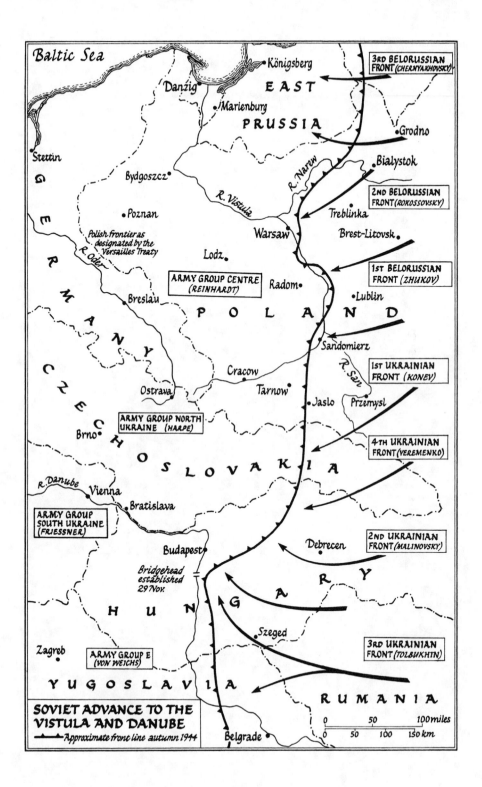

Baltic Sea

3RD BELORUSSIAN FRONT (CHERNYAKHOVSKY)

Königsberg

Danzig

EAST

Marienburg

PRUSSIA

Grodno

Stettin

Bydgoszcz

Bialystok

R. Narew

2ND BELORUSSIAN FRONT (ROKOSSOVSKY)

R. Vistula

Poznan

Treblinka

R. Oder

Polish frontier as
designated by the
Versailles Treaty

Warsaw

Brest-Litovsk

Lodz

1ST BELORUSSIAN FRONT (ZHUKOV)

G E R M A N Y

ARMY GROUP CENTRE (REINHARDT)

Radom

Breslau

Lublin

P O L A N D

Sandomierz

C Z E C H

Cracow

R. San

1ST UKRAINIAN FRONT (KONEV)

Ostrava

Tarnow

Jaslo

Przemysl

ARMY GROUP NORTH UKRAINE (HARPE)

Brno

O S L O V A K I A

4TH UKRAINIAN FRONT (VEREMENKO)

R. Danube

Vienna

Bratislava

ARMY GROUP SOUTH UKRAINE (FRIESSNER)

Budapest

2ND UKRAINIAN FRONT (MALINOVSKY)

Debrecen

Bridgehead
established
29 Nov.

H U N G A R Y

Szeged

Zagreb

ARMY GROUP E (VON WEICHS)

3RD UKRAINIAN FRONT (TOLBUKHIN)

Y U G O S L A V I A

R U M A N I A

SOVIET ADVANCE TO THE VISTULA AND DANUBE

Belgrade

Approximate front line autumn 1944

0   50   100 miles
0   50   100   150 km

"For the most part, Warsaw is in flames. Burning down the houses is the most reliable means of liquidating the insurgents' hide-outs." Hitler awarded Knight's Crosses to Erich von dem Bach-Zelewski and Oskar Dirlewanger for their roles in recapturing the Polish capital. It is a measure of the savagery of the forces suppressing the Rising that the Nazis themselves shot the commander of the RONA Brigade, a unit of Russians serving in German uniform. Its anarchic brutalities became an embarrassment even to Himmler. The Germans lost 9,000 dead in Warsaw in the first three weeks of the Rising, amid merciless street fighting. "Kamil" Baczynski, one of many Polish poets who flourished in those days, wrote before he was killed on 4 August:

O Lord of the apocalypse! Lord of the World's End!
Put a voice in our mouths, and punishment in our hand.

The horrors of Warsaw highlighted the futility of any attempt by guerrillas to engage regular troops equipped with heavy weapons, artillery and armour. Though the Polish resisters were plentifully supplied with courage, most lacked essential military training. They were armed only with weapons parachuted from Britain, for many of which they possessed only a few magazines of ammunition apiece, together with such small arms and armoured vehicles as they could capture from the Wehrmacht. Lieutenant-General Wladyslaw Anders, commanding the Polish II Corps in Italy, was among those bitterly critical of the Rising. He was privately convinced that it must end in tragedy. He recognized, as others should have done at the outset, that irregular forces could neither defeat the armies of Hitler nor expect aid to do so from the Russians.

The Germans shrewdly grasped these realities. Ninth Army observed that "Army Krajowa considers ourselves and the Russians equally its enemies." As early as 5 August, Ninth Army's intelligence department suggested that "many civilians who were enthusiastic about the uprising are now having second thoughts... They fear that the city of Warsaw will suffer the same fate as the former Warsaw ghetto... They fear German revenge." The insurgents' leaders sought to inspire their own people and dispirit the enemy by feeding them upon fantasies: that 300 Soviet tanks were already advancing on Warsaw from the south-east; that Russian aircraft were only awaiting better weather to launch attacks in support of the uprising. Sceptical civilians remarked that the weather was not preventing the Germans from flying.

It has often been suggested that Stalin incited the Rising in order to induce the bitterly anti-communist Army Krajowa to immolate itself. This seems mistaken. The Lublin Poles' appeals to their countrymen to revolt were of a piece with many other flights of radio propaganda rhetoric. The Soviet high command took them much less seriously than Bor Komorowski. A Western correspondent quizzed the Soviet Marshal Konstantin Rokossovsky, commanding

1st Belorussian Front opposite Warsaw, about the broadcast. Rokossovsky shrugged: "That was routine stuff." The Red Army's logistics were drastically stretched after its summer leap westwards. For the first ten days of August, Rokossovsky's armies were committed to stemming an energetic German counter-attack east of the Vistula. In the beginning, therefore, Moscow had good military reasons for refusing to make a dash upon the Polish capital. The Russians might also have pointed out that in the west Eisenhower resisted all appeals from the Dutch to change Allied military plans and drive north in the winter of 1944, to save occupied Holland from terrible sufferings. The political and military leaders of the U.S. and Britain insisted that the best service they could render to Holland was to maintain their strategy to defeat Germany as swiftly as possible. They refused to allow military operations to be deflected by short-term humanitarian considerations.

It might also be noticed that in Italy the Allied Commander-in-Chief General Sir Harold Alexander encouraged partisans to rise on the widest possible scale in the summer of 1944, when it was believed that liberation of the whole country was imminent. With the coming of winter, and the Allies bogged down in the mountains, the partisans suffered terribly from German counter-measures. In November, Alexander felt obliged to reverse his earlier policy and urge the partisans to abandon open military activity until spring. In some areas upon which German repression fell most heavily, there was deep and lasting bitterness about Allied incitement to premature action, followed by failure to relieve the partisans before the Germans fell upon them. Alexander could plead military necessity for his actions—and inaction. So did Stalin. All the Allies behaved with considerable cynicism in encouraging armed resistance in occupied Europe while possessing no means of preventing inevitable German retribution. The consequences for Warsaw were, however, vastly more terrible than anything which took place in the west.

Stalin, of course, went beyond mere passivity towards the uprising. He informed the Western allies, in response to their appeals for aid to the Poles, that he would not lift a finger to preserve these "criminals" from the consequences of their folly. He refused to provide refuelling facilities in Russian territory for British aircraft attempting arms drops to the insurgents. Late in the Rising, he allowed just one force of American aircraft to land at Poltava after dropping supplies, most of which fell into German hands. "We don't want British and American planes mucking about here at the moment," Rokossovsky told Alexander Werth. The RAF lost an aircraft for every ton of supplies dropped to the Poles on the perilous 780-mile trip from Italy. Forty-one Allied planes were destroyed out of 306 dispatched to aid the Warsaw resisters, while the nearest Russians were a mere fifteen miles away.

As we shall see later, when the Red Army occupied Poland its forces launched a ruthless second front against the survivors of Army Krajowa. This struggle continued long after Hitler fell, almost unnoticed by the world, with substantial casualties on both sides. Poland's destiny, to become a Soviet vassal state, was decided before the first shot of the Rising was fired. One of the German propaganda leaflets launched into the Allied lines in north-west Europe was directed at the Polish Armoured Division: "WHY DIE FOR STALIN?" it demanded; "... your soldiers are not dying for democracy or the preservation of the democratic form of government—they are dying for the establishment of Communism and a form of the Stalinist tyranny ... so that Poland shall be a Soviet state." From a Polish viewpoint, all this was perfectly true. "Within a very short space of time," a modern Russian historian writes, "the Poles were translated from Russia's enemies to its allies, and then once more into its enemies."

It is unlikely that the full facts about Stalin's actions in the autumn of 1944 will ever be known. Even the most distinguished Western historian of Poland, Norman Davies, writing in 2003 with access to considerable Soviet documentation, concludes that many aspects of Russian behaviour remain conjectural. There were real tensions between Moscow and its lackeys, the communist Lublin Poles, who seem to have shared the assumption of Bor Komorowski's men that the Red Army would move swiftly to liberate Warsaw. Soviet policy wavered through August and September. In the early stages of the Rising, Moscow seemed merely sceptical and indifferent about its outcome. In late August, however, Stalin went much further, making a considered decision to allow the Germans to eliminate the Army Krajowa in Warsaw. He shifted troops from the Vistula Front to the Baltic and the Balkans, even while the Army Krajowa was in the midst of its agony a few miles westward. To confuse matters further, he allowed Soviet forces to make some trifling gestures of support for the beleaguered Poles, to appease the Western allies. But, while Rokossovsky busied himself establishing bridgeheads on the western bank of the Vistula to secure start lines for further advances, the Red Army made no substantial moves to enter the Polish capital. "The Soviet government do not wish to associate themselves directly or indirectly with the adventure in Warsaw," the Soviet deputy commissar for foreign affairs, Andrei Vyshinsky, told Averell Harriman, U.S. ambassador in Moscow, on 18 August.

The story is rendered still uglier by the behaviour of some of those in the West. The socialist intelligentsia was still much enamoured of the Soviet Union. British media comment on the Rising was slight and massively ill informed. Some writers remained for weeks extravagantly sympathetic to Soviet passivity. The left-wing *New Statesman* dismissed the Polish resisters as "Macchiavellian *dilettanti*." *The Times* observed indulgently: "It is not difficult to understand Russian unwillingness to supply arms to people who are opposed to friendly relations with Russia." George Orwell, almost alone among his kind, denounced Russian behaviour towards Poland passionately and publicly, in a noble flight of prose in *Tribune:* "the 'Lublin regime' is not a victory for socialism ... It is the reduction of Poland to a vassal state... Woe to those in a vassal state who want to maintain their independent views and policies... If they happen to lead a heroic rising that embarrasses the protégés of the great 'Protecting' powers, they will be stigmatised as 'criminals'... Please do not ask us to show enthusiasm for such policies." Orwell castigated his compatriots who refused to consider whether a given Russian action was or was not defensible. Instead, they simply said to each other: " 'This is Russian policy; how can we make it appear right?... The Russians are powerful in Eastern Europe, we are not; therefore we must not oppose them.' This involves the principle, of its nature alien to Socialism, that you must not protest against an evil which you cannot prevent."

Far more serious than the behaviour of British communist fellow-travellers, however, was the refusal of President Roosevelt to exert wholehearted pressure on Moscow. The secretary of state, Edward Stettinius, argued that the U.S. should seek to send aid to Warsaw, if remotely feasible. Roosevelt appalled Churchill, however, by the cold-bloodedness of a note drafted by his Chief of Staff, Admiral Leahy, on 5 September: "I am informed by my officers of Military Intelligence that the fighting Poles have departed from Warsaw, and that the Germans are now in full control... The problem of relief for the Poles in Warsaw has therefore, unfortunately, been solved by delay and German action." In reality, of course, while the Poles had been driven out of Warsaw's Old Town, they were still fighting fiercely in the centre of the capital. But Warsaw was scarcely discussed at the Anglo-American Octagon conference in Quebec in mid-September. The Russians continued to treat the Poles' lunge for freedom with cold contempt. Rokossovsky likened the Rising to "the clown in the circus who pops up at the wrong moment and only gets wrapped up in the carpet." The marshal later asserted that, if the Poles had delayed their revolt until his forces had gained the Praga suburb of Warsaw east of the Vistula in September, the liberation of the city might have been achieved. This seems implausible.

Churchill described Soviet behaviour at this period as "strange and sinister." The prime minister recognized Stalin's determination to impose Soviet hegemony upon every state liberated by his armies. The Russian leader perceived this as natural justice. He also cherished a bizarre expectation that such a polity would be welcomed by the proletarians of eastern Europe. The absence of such sentiment fuelled his animosity towards the Poles. American attention was fixed upon the military defeat of the Nazis. Washington displayed a remarkable indifference to the political future of the eastern battlefields until it was too late. Roosevelt's most recent biographer seeks to acquit his hero of the charge of naivety towards the Soviet Union in 1945, pleading the inevitability of Soviet domination. This argument seems unconvincing. Too many of those closest to Roosevelt at this period have testified to their dismay about his behaviour towards Stalin, and about the president's conviction that he could do business with the Soviets if the British imperialists were circumvented. Yet it is unmistakably true that the Russians already stood on Polish soil, beyond any conceivable reach of Anglo-American forces. Even if the Red Army had hastened forward to relieve Warsaw in August or September, the fate of the insurgents would have been no different. Those who resisted Soviet mastery, as many later attempted to do, would merely have been killed by Russian bullets rather than German ones.

Polish behaviour was characterized from beginning to end by a heroic spirit of self-immolation. Even when the Poles recognized that the Soviets were disinclined to aid them, they rejected Stalin's demands. The Soviet leader indicated to the Polish prime minister, leader of the London Poles who visited Moscow early in August, that before he could expect anything from the Russians his government must resign; the Soviet seizure of eastern Poland must be recognized; and the London Poles must publicly accept Moscow's preposterous claim that the massacre of Polish officers at Katyn was the work of the Nazis, not the Soviets. When Bor Komorowski in Warsaw heard of all this, he signalled proudly on 26 August: "Poland has not been fighting the Germans for five years, bearing the greatest losses, just to capitulate to Russia. Our fight against the Germans has shown that…we love freedom more than life." Here, indeed, reality matched rhetoric in the most dreadful fashion.

There was a tragic romance about the mood in Warsaw, even as the city was battered into ruin. The Poles, determined to celebrate the resurrection of their national culture amid catastrophe, staged recitals, concerts, plays in the public buildings within their perimeter. A profusion of pamphlets, newspapers and political treatises was written and published. There was a plan to stage an opera, until the leading players were killed in action. An engaged couple, a lieutenant and a girl courier, asked to be married in the city's cathedral. One of the two witnesses could not walk, having been wounded by shrapnel. He was carried into the cathedral sacristy for the wedding on the back of his fellow witness. The twenty-three-year-old bride and groom were buried alive by a Stuka strike a few days later.

The Red Army observed the last thrashings of the Rising with detached contempt. "The British and Americans are supplying the Germans, not the insurgents," reported an officer of 1st Belorussian Front after watching an Allied parachute drop on 30 September. A Soviet agent codenamed Oleg who was sent to make contact with the Rising's leaders in the last days reported afterwards to Moscow: "The interview was not particularly friendly. I could sense their suspicion and hostility towards me, as a representative of the Red Army." The Russians had little enough compassion to spare for their own people. Why should they waste it on Poles?

The last shot of the Warsaw battle was fired on 2 October 1944, sixty-seven days after it began. Throughout September, while the Resisters in Warsaw were negotiating with the Germans through the Red Cross for a ceasefire, they rejected capitulation and insisted upon terms, notably the recognition of Poland's fighters as combatants, entitled to the protection of the Geneva Convention. In this they achieved some small measure of success. An officer of the Army Krajowa, Major Kazimierz Sztermal, confronted von dem Bach-Zelewski, Nazi high priest at Warsaw's sacrifice: "You, the nation which gave your Goethe and Schiller to the world, have tried through terror to take the rights of freedom and existence from us." The German shrugged: "This is war." So indeed it was, in Hitler's universe. The survivors—11,668 Polish combatants including 2,000 women, together with countless thousands of civilians—marched out in their columns of misery, to face imprisonment or mere destitution. Some shot themselves rather than accept captivity. After the insurgents had made their last broadcast from their own Radio Lightning, they smashed its transmitter with a sledgehammer. "We have been treated worse than Hitler's allies in Romania, Italy and Finland," declared the Polish Home Council of Ministers in its final statement on 3 October. "[Our] Rising is going under at a time when our armies abroad are helping to liberate France, Belgium and Holland...may the God of Justice pronounce a verdict on the terrible wrong, which the Polish nation has encountered, and may He punish the perpetrators."

The Germans claimed to have lost 17,000 dead. The Rising was the ultimate heroic folly of the European Resistance movement nurtured by Churchill since 1940. For all the succour which Resistance gave to the soul of occupied Europe both during and after the Second World War, except in Yugoslavia its military achievements were negligible, and purchased at a grim price in blood. The Allied Chiefs of Staff would have done well to recall an observation of Wellington, derived from his experience of guerrilla warfare in the Iberian peninsula 140 years earlier: "I always had a horror of revolutionizing any country...I always said, if they rise of themselves, well and good, but do not stir them up; it is a fearful responsibility."

There is just a grain of truth in Stalin's self-serving remark: "These people [the Home Army] have exploited the good faith of the inhabitants of Warsaw, throwing many almost unarmed people against the German guns, tanks, and aircraft. A situation has arisen in which each new day serves, not the Poles...but the Hitlerites who are inhumanly shooting down the inhabitants of Warsaw." The Warsaw Rising was of a piece with the Polish people's long history of acts of passion, courage, misjudgement, succeeded by repression at the hands of forces beyond their power to resist. When Rokossovsky's forces at last seized the eastern suburbs of Warsaw, the NKVD began rounding up the fighters of Army Krajowa with the same ruthlessness as the Germans. "Nazi and Soviet repressions were proceeding simultaneously in one and the same city," observes Norman Davies. For the Western allies, the conduct of the war was overwhelmingly a military matter. For the Soviet Union, it never ceased to be also a political one.

"WE WERE DIFFERENT PEOPLE IN 1944"

MILOVAN DJILAS met a Soviet soldier on a road in Yugoslavia one day in October 1944. The Russian was driving a horse-drawn cart loaded with sacks, pots and bedspreads. He hailed the Yugoslav partisan and asked: "Is this the road to Berlin?" This was the only destination the man recognized, or had thought of since Stalingrad. The soldiers of the Red Army had seen too much destruction and misery in their own country to be shocked by what they found in eastern Europe. For days after Lieutenant Vasily Filimonenko crossed the Polish border in August 1944 with troops of 1st Belorussian Front, he did not see a single civilian. All had fled, save those too old to move. There were only burning buildings, and abandoned German vehicles and equipment. A few Russians recognized that something especially shocking had happened. "We knew that Warsaw was once the most beautiful capital in Europe," said Alexandr Markov, a twenty-one-year-old Soviet bomber pilot. "Now, when we flew over it we saw huge palls of smoke, and even from the air we could smell burned flesh. My spine crawled, to see so much beauty transformed into ruins... all those golden bell towers gone." Yelena Kogan, serving as an interpreter with the NKVD, said long afterwards: "I felt terrible about what happened in Warsaw. I still don't know the truth about what happened politically." Yet few Russians harboured love or sympathy for Poles. Stalin had been shooting them in tens of thousands since the Purges of the late 1930s. His people regarded them with no greater pity after the horrors of the Rising than before. A Soviet girl soldier wrote to a friend about the Poles: "When you look at them, you feel such anger, such hatred. They're having fun, loving and living. And you are fighting to liberate them! They just laugh at us Russians. Bastards!"

The mood within the Red Army in the autumn of 1944 was incomparably different from that of earlier years. Many American and British soldiers had seen little or no action before D-Day. Most Soviet soldiers, by contrast, had fought without interruption or leave since June 1941. They were weary, but now they were also exultant. "It never looked easy on our front," said Corporal Anna Nikyunas, a veteran of the siege of Leningrad, "but in 1944 there was a totally different feeling: we knew that we would win." "It was a great thing to fight during this time when at last we were on top," said Major Yury Ryakhovsky. Lieutenant Pavel Nikiforov: "It was a wonderful life in reconnaissance in the last months of the war—lots of loot, vodka, brandy, girls *everywhere*. We wanted to get to Germany, to be there for the end." Corporal Anatoly

Osminov of 32nd Tank Army said: "It was good to be out of Russia, and fighting on enemy soil."

"We were different people in 1944," observed Sergeant Nikolai Timoshenko. "We had enough weapons. Our officers had learned how to plan operations. We knew our business." Yet he added: "We never thought about the end of the war. The only thing to do was to get through the tasks of one day at a time." Given the speed of the Russians' huge advances, many men had no idea where they were, or even what country they were in. "Sometimes somebody would ask: 'Where are we, by the way?'" said Lieutenant Gennady Klimenko, a staff officer with 2nd Ukrainian Front. "The answer would be: 'Oh, Poland maybe.' It was only when we reached a big city that the place name meant anything. Once, in Rumania, a division was ordered to advance on some town, and mistook another of similar name for its objective. There was an inquiry. People were shot for less." The Red Army was no longer much troubled by the Luftwaffe, cause of such grief in earlier years. It took time for men who had known the earlier campaigns, in which advances were measured in metres, to adjust to the vast movements of 1944. "We were so used to living in the earth," said Nikolai Timoshenko. "We felt positively disorientated out of trenches. It seemed an entirely different war."

Stalin's armies had progressed far in skills and equipment since the desperate days of 1941 and 1942. In attack, Russian commanders displayed much better understanding than their American counterparts of the importance of concentration—focusing a massive weight of men and armour on their main axis of advance. Soviet generals persisted with assaults after losses that would have caused any Anglo-American operation to be broken off. Even after receiving substantial shipments of American radio equipment, the Soviet armies were handicapped by poor communications. Higher commands were sometimes uncertain of what whole divisions were doing, and this remained a weakness until the end, deplored in a host of Red Army internal reports.

These were soldiers drawn from a society in which extreme harshness, the capacity both to endure and to inflict pain, had been inbred for centuries, and refined to the highest degree under Stalin. Shortly before Lieutenant Vasily Kudryashov's tank unit crossed the border from Russia into Poland, as they halted in a village just vacated by the Germans, a woman came out of a house and presented his crew with a cake. "I've been waiting four years to do this," she said. Kudryashov's orderly Semyon came from a village fifteen miles away. He begged leave to go home and see how his family had fared. Inevitably, this was refused. Semyon sulked, in an emotional mood. When he encountered a woman in the village who was said to have slept with German soldiers, he shot her. Asked to explain himself, he said: "I suddenly thought: maybe my wife also has been sleeping with German soldiers." Kudryashov reported the incident to his brigade commander, who said simply: "I quite understand." This small lapse of propriety was forgotten.

The war in the east was characterized by colossal cruelties. By 1944, these had become institutionalized on both sides of the front. Hitler and Stalin nurtured in their respective peoples a systemic inhumanity which found full play upon the battlefield. German soldiers had been conditioned for a decade to regard Slavic people as sub-humans. It was not only the SS who killed Russians of all ages and both sexes with casual indifference.

"Here in the east," wrote Colonel-General Hermann Hoth of the German Seventeenth Army in an order to his men, "spiritually unbridgeable conceptions are fighting each other: German sense of honour and race; and a soldierly tradition of many centuries, against an Asiatic mode of thinking and primitive instincts, whipped up by a small number of mostly Jewish intellectuals." The American historian Omer Bartov writes: "Increasingly during the last two years of the war, [German] troops at the front came to see themselves as the missionaries of the entire German nation, indeed of Western civilization as a whole. Rational evaluation and clear perception of events were replaced by intense terror from and rage against a faceless, monstrous enemy." Neither Germans nor Russians readily offered quarter, save when prisoners were required for intelligence purposes, or more slaves were needed for their respective mines and factories. At Dr. Nikolai Senkevich's field hospital, a group of captured Germans refused to answer questions from their interrogators: "We simply took them 100 metres off, and they were shot." Sergeant Nikolai Timoshenko said: "The rule of war is that you go into battle, you see the enemy, and that enemy is not a human being. Putting your hands up isn't going to save you." Only a minority of Germans who attempted to surrender reached PoW camps. "We killed prisoners just like that," said Captain Vasily Krylov, snapping his fingers. "If soldiers were told to escort them to the rear, more often than not they were 'shot while trying to escape'." Lieutenant Pavel Nikiforov: "There was no serious control over the treatment of prisoners. If they were sent back to regimental headquarters, they were usually shot on the way." Vitold Kubashevsky hated shooting prisoners, and found himself striving to avoid any eye contact with the doomed men, but like everyone else he fired when he was told to do so—which was invariably the case with Waffen SS captives.

It is interesting that such an attitude reflected the vision of Russia's greatest novelist a century earlier. Leo Tolstoy argued that the taking of prisoners maintained a sham of humanity amid the reality that war "is not a polite recreation, but the vilest thing in life. Our attitude towards the fearful necessity of war ought to be stern and serious. It boils down to this: we should have done with humbug, and let war be war, and not a game...If there were none of this magnanimity business in warfare, we should never go to war, except for something worth facing certain death for."

The history of German barbarity within the Soviet Union since 1941 was familiar to every Russian soldier. Many had experienced its manifestations at first hand. Russians were repelled by Germans' pretensions to represent a superior civilization. "They are completely shameless," a Russian war correspondent, Alexei Surkov, observed with disgust. "They strip naked in front of women to wash. They mount women like stallions. They fart at table when they eat. Do they behave in this way at home?" Stalin's soldiers were encouraged to keep "ledgers of revenge," recording German atrocities, and to match these with notes about their personal contributions to levelling the account. Political officers held "Revenge Meetings," fostering the same spirit.

The draconian retribution that fell upon those who flinched or failed was an important force in sustaining Russian will. Russians have always prided themselves upon the extravagance of their own emotions and behaviour. Nikolai Lvov, the nineteenth-century poet–engineer, applauded his people's spontaneity:

> In foreign lands all goes to a plan
> Words are weighed, steps measured.
> But among us Russians there is fiery life,
> Our speech is thunder and sparks fly.

The Red Army often displayed courage and determination far beyond anything that could have been asked of American or British troops. Yet its achievements on the battlefield seem all the more remarkable given its manic indiscipline. Even the relentless efforts of firing squads proved unable to deter excesses that often became suicidal. Huge injections of alcohol alone rendered service in the eastern war endurable to many of those who took part. Yet institutionalized alcoholism could be deadly to men in possession of weapons. Lieutenant Vasily Kudryashov's orderly started a drunken fight following an argument about—of all things—which tank possessed the thickest armour. A pilot shot him dead. In a cellar in the Hungarian town of Tokay, Kudryashov saw the bodies of three soldiers who had drowned. After piercing a vast vat of wine with tommy-gun fire, they drank themselves insensible, then lay collapsed upon the floor until a torrent submerged them. Recklessness with vehicles was a source of many Russian casualties. "Brake or die," proclaimed a Red Army sign posted on many roads in Yugoslavia, but scores of Russian truck drivers cheerfully ignored it—and died. Vladimir Gormin once saw three successive Dodges in a column surge over the same precipice. Such behaviour seems of a piece with Orlando Figes's description of the historic Russian experience: "long periods of humility and patience interspersed with bouts of joyous freedom and violent release."

A German doctor, Hans von Lehndorff, painted a vivid word portrait of the more primitive soldiers of the Red Army, when he observed them as a prisoner. "They are utterly insensitive to noise," he wrote.

Some of them stand the whole day in the garages, working all the available motor-horns. The radio blares without a stop in their quarters, until far into the night. Lighting circuits are installed at top speed, and where there is glass left in the windows, holes are shot in the panes so that the wires can be led through. One is repeatedly astonished at the rapidity with which they hit on the simplest way of attaining their purpose; the immediate moment is all that exists for them; everything must serve it, no matter whether what they ruin in the process is something they will be in dire need of the next minute. One is perpetually dumbfounded by their total lack of any relationship to things which, to us, are a part of life itself. One ends by giving up thinking of them as creatures of one's own kind, and gradually assumes the attitude of lion-tamer... To show fear is to fare worst of all with them, it provokes them visibly to attack. Audacity, on the other hand, can get one a surprisingly long way. The most hopeless policy of all is to try and make them like you... The Russians have no use for such arts; they use people of that sort for their own purposes and openly despise them... It never occurs to them to look upon us as anything resembling themselves, and our claims on their humanity find hardly any echo in them. The fact that they drive cars, fire rifles, listen to the radio, and are trained to many other of our tricks, still creates no living bridge from man to man.

Some writers have sought to argue that by 1944 the Red soldier was man for man a match for his counterpart of the Wehrmacht. The truth seems more complicated. At the highest level, Soviet generalship was much more imaginative than that of the Western armies. Zhukov was the outstanding Allied commander of the Second World War, more effective than his Anglo-American counterparts, master of the grand envelopment. Several other Soviet marshals—Vasilevsky, Konev, Chernyakhovsky, Rokossovsky—displayed the highest gifts.

On the ground, the Russians excelled at night fighting and patrolling. Every German soldier who moved from the Eastern Front to the west remarked upon the dramatic change he experienced, that he could move freely during the hours of darkness, when the Americans, especially, were content to leave the front in peace. The Russians harassed the enemy relentlessly. Night patrols sometimes slit the throats of German sentries and left the mutilated bodies to provide food for thought among their surviving comrades. Lieutenant Pavel Nikiforov, a Soviet reconnaissance officer, derived pride and pleasure from his hours watching the German lines through his periscope, observing the enemy eating, sleeping, washing, defecating. "I always felt that I knew the Germans better than most men, because I had spent so much time so close to them." The Germans respected Russian exploitation of well-camouflaged massed anti-tank guns in defence. Lacking any counterpart for the hand-held bazooka, PIAT or faust, Soviet infantry would drag anti-tank guns into attacks immediately behind their spearheads.

The Russians' command of artillery was superb, though it relied for effect upon weight rather than accuracy of fire. Their principal weapons, including the T-34 and Stalin tanks, together with their 1944–45 aircraft, were as good as or better than anything the Western allies possessed. They had developed one weapon unique to themselves, the Katyusha, which the Germans greatly feared. A battery of the rockets deployed on trucks could deliver in seconds a barrage of 192 projectiles, each weighing 120 pounds, which carpeted a front 400 yards wide, to a depth of 300 yards. Katyushas could be effective up to four miles, but they were dangerous to the firer as well as to the enemy, especially if he was careless with fusing. The rockets were not remotely as accurate as the German Nebelwerfer multiple mortar. Katyushas not infrequently savaged their own infantry if a launch rail became bent or a stabilizing fin fell off. Lieutenant Alexandr Vostrukhin took the precaution of crawling under his tank whenever outgoing rockets were flying overhead, "just in case." But their moral effect on the enemy was devastating. Just as British and American airmen would chalk rude messages on their bombs, so Russian crews scrawled on their rockets: "This is for my mother and sister." When Lieutenant Valentin Krulik first saw massed Katyushas in action, he was awed by "this incredible wall of fire, which the batteries kept up for most of the day." The batteries were seldom employed casually. They were almost always used to support a big attack or a desperate defence.

Yet, if the Red Army at last possessed hitting power and command skills as great as those of any combatant, its infantry and armoured assaults relied upon the sacrifice of lives rather than upon tactical ingenuity or even common prudence. To this day, Russian casualty figures are a source of perverse pride to many veterans. "Of course the Red Army was reckless with the lives of our men," said Vladimir Gormin of 3rd Ukrainian Front. "Nobody knew how many died, and who cared, anyway? It was typical that there was always some grand operation on the great revolutionary holidays—1 May, 7 November, 23 February. Men died, simply so that a few generals could collect another medal." By contrast with the Western armies, the Soviets adopted a cavalier attitude to the threat of encirclement. "The Shock Armies pushed on regardless of what was happening on their flanks," said a Russian officer. "They got cut off by the Germans, sometimes for weeks, sometimes running out of fuel, food, ammunition. But they were expected to break out again."

Lieutenant Tony Saurma, who fought the Red Army as a Tiger troop commander with the famous Grossdeutschland Panzergrenadier Division from 1942 to the end, admired the stoicism of the Russian soldier. His unit often fought opposite the Soviet "Red Flag" Guards Division. Each side collected the other's cap badges. But Saurma qualified his respect by saying: "The Russians didn't think much. They were usually being driven by their officers." The Germans feared the Soviet Stalin tank, but thought little of Soviet tank gunnery. In battle, Saurma sought to keep moving constantly. "It's much harder to hit a running hare," he told his own tank commanders. Like every German soldier, he was awed by the spectacle of the Red Army in attack. T-34s would approach six, twelve abreast. The Germans would knock out four or five, but there were always more. "You couldn't believe the way they kept coming—their infantry simply charging our tanks, running and shouting, even when the bodies were piled up in front of our positions. Sometimes our infantry seemed paralysed by the spectacle. One thought: 'How can we ever stop such people?' " Rolf-Helmut Schröder, a Wehrmacht officer who became a post-war Bundeswehr general, said: "The Russians were not good soldiers. But they had very good generals, and they had mass."

The Nazis acknowledged an unwilling but profound respect for the Russians as adversaries which they never extended to the Americans and British. Deriding the Western allies' lack of spirit, Hitler said at one of his military conferences: "The Russian—that pig—has managed it. If someone starts to whine among us, I can only say: take the Russian in his situation in Leningrad." General Heinz Guderian, the Army Chief of Staff, agreed that the Russians were "brilliantly" led. Hitler marvelled: "The way they have survived this crisis [Leningrad]!" Göring interjected: "They let a million die of starvation." Guderian said: "They lead very energetically, very quickly, and very decisively. It is a lot." Stalin returned the respect of his adversary, once describing Hitler to Roosevelt's aide Harry Hopkins as "a very able man."

The fastidiousness of the Americans and British about the lives of their men was admirable in humanitarian terms, and reflected the fact that the Western allies possessed strategic choices about where and when to confront the Germans. Delaying D-Day until June 1944 represented a prudent, even self-indulgent decision, of a kind that was denied to the Russians. They were forced to maintain an unbroken struggle from June 1941 to the end, because their armies were continuously in the presence of the enemy. It was necessary for somebody, somewhere, to pay a heavy price to break down the mass of the Wehrmacht. Who can imagine the democracies, in any circumstances, bearing a loss akin to that of the 900,000 citizens of Leningrad who starved to death to sustain its defence? Even if Britain had been invaded, the inhabitants of its cities would have chosen surrender rather than eat each other. American and British leaders and generals required a degree of consent from their soldiers and their peoples. It would be wrong to underrate the degree of consent even in Stalin's Russia, the real patriotic passion that impelled most of its people to resist the Germans. In decisive contrast to the Russians' military collapse before the 1917 Revolution, the national spirit of the Red Army grew with every day of war. But it would be foolish also to deny the compulsion which underpinned the Soviet war effort, reinforced by draconian and usually mortal sanctions against those who faltered.

In the autumn of 1944, Stalin's armies faced the Germans on fronts totalling almost 2,000 miles—though now shortening fast—and embracing the soil of eight foreign countries. For both sides, it was a stupendous undertaking to maintain supplies of men, food, weapons and ammunition to the millions doing the fighting. In 1944, the Soviet supply system delivered the equivalent of 1,164,000 railway wagon-loads of supplies to the fronts, of which ammunition alone accounted for 118,000. Stalin's armed forces consumed four million tons of fuel in 1944. Russia's factories in the last year of war produced almost 30,000 tanks and self-propelled guns, together with 40,000 aircraft. The Red Army had travelled an immeasurable distance since June 1941, from the days when men were expected to arm themselves by seizing the rifles of the dead on the battlefield, Soviet airmen fought in biplanes and there were no tank radios. Private Vitold Kubashevsky of 3rd Belorussian Front remembered fighting through the campaigns of 1942 wearing *lapti*—boots made for his unit by local peasants out of birch-bark—and patched or washed clothing stripped from dead or wounded men.

American supplies made a critical contribution. It was often suggested in Washington and London that the Soviets were ungrateful. Stalin might have given the contemptuous response he once gave to Zinoviev, who made the same charge: "Gratitude? Gratitude is a dog's disease!" Russians observed that America's contribution to the war cost mere money. Russia was paying for her victories with blood, torrents of blood. Woven into the entire Soviet vision of the Second World War from 1941 to the present day, transcending any issue of mere ideology or propaganda, has been the conviction that the Western allies were content to wage war against the Nazis at their leisure, husbanding the lives of their peoples with bourgeois parsimony. Churchill observed, with justice, that Britain entered the war in 1939 as a matter of principle, and fought alone for almost two years, while Russia was content to play vulture on the carcasses of Hitler's kills until Germany invaded the Soviet Union. It was impossible to dispute, however, that Stalin's people were overwhelmingly responsible for destroying Hitler's armies.

The remains of Germany's Army Group Centre now stood on the Vistula less than 400 miles from Berlin. Marshals Rokossovsky and Zhukov held several bridgeheads westwards across the river, which repeated German counter-attacks had failed to dislodge. On the great Polish plain, the River Oder was the only major natural obstacle which remained between Stalin's armies and Hitler's capital. Yet the price of the Russians' huge summer advances was that months of labour became necessary, to rearm and resupply Stalin's armies before they could strike anew. Their difficulties in the autumn of 1944 mirrored those of the Americans and British on a larger scale and over much greater distances. The Russians customarily required three months after a big offensive on a given front before they were ready to hurl themselves forward once more. From Poland southwards to the Czech border, between September and the turn of the year there were no significant advances. Men on both sides dug, patrolled, rested as best they could, and harassed each other's positions. Germans and Soviets alike recognized that this was a mere respite before a new and even more terrible battle.

Yet, even while the central front lay quiescent through the autumn months, bitter fighting continued in the Baltic states. The German Army Group North still possessed some powerful formations and commanders. Nine hundred thousand Soviet troops together with 1,328 tanks and self-propelled guns were deployed on a battlefront that sometimes extended to 750 miles. Advancing Soviet forces which broke through a German line repeatedly found the enemy retreating to new prepared positions a few miles back. The Wehrmacht's appetite for counter-attack seldom faltered. Between 14 September and 24 November 1944, Stalin's three Baltic Fronts suffered 103,946, 73,735 and 55,488 casualties respectively. The Leningrad Front added a further 28,776. The Germans were pushed back into Baltic enclaves at Courland and Memel, but the Russians failed to achieve the absolute destruction of the enemy's forces which they had sought. Any rational commander would have pulled back German forces from the Baltic states to East Prussia and Poland, to provide desperately needed reinforcements for the defence of the German homeland. But Hitler, obsessive in his rejection of retreat, insisted that he must maintain a foothold on the Baltic coastline, as a testing centre for the new generation of U-boats. Through October and November, the Wehrmacht did so at dreadful cost.

Every Russian with a spark of honesty acknowledged respect for the enemy's fighting power. "I was not surprised the Germans fought to the end," said Major Yury Ryakhovsky. "They did what we would have done. They were the only fighters in Europe who deserved our respect." "They were wonderful soldiers," said Sergeant Nikolai Timoshenko, a Cossack. "The Hungarians, Rumanians, were nothing to the Germans. The German nation has a marvellous discipline, and they were very well trained. Russian history has always been entwined with that of Germany. Russians are good soldiers, but our culture is different. We had to teach ourselves how to fight—our training was poor. When we advanced, we often found ourselves outrunning our supplies. The Germans were better organized." Yet none of this diminished his hatred for Hitler's nation. "A soldier who hates the enemy is a good soldier," said Timoshenko. Most of his schoolfriends were killed in the years of war—the rollcall of death was endless. Many of his old schoolteachers were slaughtered by the Germans during their occupation of his home district around Kuban. Like a host of Soviet soldiers, he entered the last phase of the war with the sense of a long, bloody score to pay off.

Through the autumn of 1944, the Soviets made dramatic advances in southern Europe. While the Western allies were closing up to the German frontier, in the east throughout September the 1st and 4th Ukrainian Fronts drove west, deep into Hungary, "a land so flat that you could have played golf on it," as Lieutenant Valentin Krulik of Sixth Guards Tank Army observed laconically. Bitter fighting persisted through November and December, with the Germans in Budapest encircled and cut off by the end of the year. Most of the Hungarian population fled before the Red Army. One report to Stalin at the end of November described how when Soviet forces entered Kethemet, a town once occupied by 87,000 people, only 7,000 remained. The NKVD claimed that Hungarians fired on Soviet troops when they were obliged to withdraw during a local German counter-attack: "a Hungarian fascist shot a Soviet lieutenant with a hunting rifle."

Such allegations were, of course, employed to justify savage retribution when Soviet forces secured an area. And as news of the Red Army's ruthlessness spread, so the great migration before the Soviet advance increased in scale and desperation. "[Russian] soldiers' conduct in this enemy country was influenced by the press, and by [political officers'] talks invoking hatred, and calling for revenge and retribution," wrote Gabriel Temkin, an interpreter with 78th Rifle Division of Twenty-seventh Army. "The simplest way to avenge was to prevail over the enemy's women, to satisfy a sexual need, while simultaneously retaliating for actual or perceived wrongs."

While the qualitative superiority of the German Army to its opponents should be acknowledged by every student of the Second World War, it would be mistaken to imagine the Wehrmacht fighting with skill and imagination on all occasions. The gun in Tony Saurma's Tiger of the Grossdeutschland once jammed in action, because his loader was drunk. Especially in the last months of the war, many German after-action reports contain cries of anguish about command follies and poor performance by untrained soldiers with inadequate support. A characteristic account from *Kampfgruppe Oelmer,* about an action at Tapiostentmarton on 11 November 1944, paints a sorry picture of incompetence. Oelmer violently protested orders from 13th Panzer Division to conduct a night attack with his Tiger battalion:

1. The wood was heavily occupied by the enemy...it was not possible, even in daylight, to push through it with Tigers without very strong infantry close support. 2. The terrain was very marshy, and it was impossible to leave the roads, especially at night. 3. Tigers on roads cannot even traverse their guns because of the trees, and if one tank was knocked out, it would become impossible for others to pass it. 4. Tigers cannot drive around at night five kilometres in front of our own main battle line on

ground impassable for armour. 5. Last night's forced march reduced the unit's strength to six fully operational tanks, and one conditionally operational.

Despite heavy rain and pitch-black conditions, 13th Panzer insisted that the attack should go ahead. One Tiger soon threw a track, and two others became bogged down. A Russian anti-tank gun disposed of another, killing its crew. The remainder were soon immobilized by the terrain. "Working with this division was extremely disagreeable," observed the German tank commander angrily. "Absolutely no attention was paid to the tactical principles for employing Tigers. When a vehicle carrying forward supplies broke down and a request was made for the loan of another for a few hours, the division's senior staff officer refused, saying: 'it's your problem to get your own fuel forward! I'm not here to lug fuel for you!' " In the east as in the west, therefore, immense frustrations and setbacks dogged the operations of the German Army in the last year of the war. Not every German commander was a von Manstein, not every soldier a young Waffen SS fanatic. Yet the achievement of the Wehrmacht in resisting the Red Army against overwhelming odds, and amid such follies as that described above, remained remarkable.

The Russians swiftly secured Bulgaria and began to move into Yugoslavia. Major Dmitry Kalafati, a thirty-year-old graduate student from the Ukraine who became a distinguished scientist after the war, was ordered to take four artillery regiments to provide support for infantry of the 6th People's Proletarian Division of Tito's army. He found this a disturbing experience, since the partisans were prone to decamp to local villages at night, leaving the Russian guns unprotected. Tito's men were also studiedly vague about where they might encounter the Germans. By the autumn of 1944, Russian ground forces were receiving highly effective tactical air support, but in Yugoslavia Kalafati was constantly frustrated by the refusal of Sixteenth Aviation Army to respond to his coded requests for Stormoviks. In desperation he sent a plain-language signal, "Fuck you—where are the planes?," which at last produced Soviet dive-bombers.

Just as the British failed to cut off the retreat of the German Fifteenth Army through Holland, so in the east the German Army Groups E and F retreated north and west from the Balkans, escaping entrapment by the Russians sweeping through Rumania. Once again, the Wehrmacht demonstrated its skill in postponing the inevitable. Although the Warsaw Rising is well known in the West, much less familiar is the Slovak revolt in the autumn of 1944. It began in eastern Slovakia in late August. Local partisans—who were, unlike those of Warsaw, overwhelmingly loyal to Moscow—perceived their Soviet liberators close at hand beyond the Carpathians. When the Slovaks rebelled against their

German occupiers, the Russians marched to their aid. Soviet troops pushed
west with the support of Moscow-trained Czech troops. But the Germans concentrated two SS and five Wehrmacht divisions to resist the Soviet advance, and
they were successful. "Because of the mountainous terrain, we would not use
tanks and cavalry effectively, so could not exploit our successes," Konev wrote
to Zhukov on 27 September. "Our infantry was also untrained in mountain warfare. We advanced so slowly that the enemy had time to move troops to threatened sectors." Konev reported that most of his infantry divisions were reduced
to barely 3,000 men apiece, and his tank corps to an average of sixty tanks, most
of which suffered constant mechanical breakdown in the mountains. Shortages
of ammunition and fuel made it impossible to use artillery effectively. Between
8 September and 28 October, Konev's 1st Ukrainian Front in the East Carpathians alone lost an average of 1,216 casualties a day, giving a total of 62,014. Then
the Germans turned on the Slovaks. The notorious Dirlewanger and Kaminski
Brigades, fresh from their triumphs in Warsaw, were deployed in eastern Slovakia. They wreaked a terrible vengeance upon all who failed to flee into the
mountains. Although the Germans had suffered defeat, substantial forces were
able to escape westwards from the battlefield.

Within a matter of months, Stalin's political hegemony had supplanted that
of Hitler across vast tracts of territory. With great difficulty and in defiance of
fierce American criticism, Churchill was able to save Greece from communist
domination, chiefly because British forces were able to land there from the
Mediterranean. Elsewhere in eastern Europe, however, a grim pattern was
emerging. The Western allies, and above all the Americans, still perceived the
war overwhelmingly as a military event. For Stalin, it was always a political one.
The days were over when Moscow confined its ambitions to dominance of its
own republics. Russia's reward for victory was to be an empire of buffer-states,
which would ensure that never again was the nation vulnerable to direct aggression. Stalin scarcely troubled to disguise from Russia's allies his determination
that political settlements determined by Soviet wishes would be imposed upon
territories liberated by Soviet arms. He argued, not unreasonably by his own
logic, that the Western allies likewise pleased themselves about the governance
of every nation their own armies liberated. "This war is not as in the past,"
Stalin told Milovan Djilas. "Whoever occupies a territory also imposes on it his
own social system. Everyone imposes his own system as far as his army can
reach. It cannot be otherwise."

As the Americans and British advanced across western Europe, although
some disorder persisted behind their front, there was no armed resistance to
their administration. They were presiding over a genuine process of liberation.
Across millions of square miles of Soviet-occupied territory, however, desperate fighting persisted for months. Far behind the front, whole Soviet divisions
were deployed to clear up the armed flotsam of many nations, men who knew

that they possessed no hope of survival if they fell into Russian hands. In addition to German stragglers, there were Ukrainians and representatives of Soviet minorities of every hue who had been rash enough to throw in their lot with the Nazis. Forming bands sometimes hundreds strong, they sallied from their eyries in forests and mountains to attack Soviet supply dumps and villages, in search of food or vengeance. "For some reason," Beria reported to Stalin on 25 November 1944, "there are a great many people who call themselves partisans, operating in groups of several hundreds, dressed in the ragged uniforms of several armies, or of Ukrainian police. They rob, rape women and shave their heads and otherwise provoke trouble in cunning ways. They make swift, sudden thrusts, using the forests for cover and infiltrating men into our positions to provoke unrest. They harry our forces, cut off units and establish road blocks. They know their areas very well."

The Soviet archives are filled with NKVD reports of partisan activity, both real and fictional. It will never be possible to determine how many of those hunted down and killed were indeed traitors to the Soviet cause or mere hapless innocents. Beria, the NKVD's overlord, was a killer at least as terrible as Himmler or Heydrich, and more effective than either. While generals measured their triumphs in the miles that their armies advanced, Beria reported his achievements to Stalin in a ghastly game bag of captured and slaughtered state enemies, submitted monthly to the Kremlin. On 31 December, he declared a total of 13,960 Ukrainians, 7,228 Belorussians, 9,688 Moldavians and 45,011 citizens of Leningrad returned to Russia from captured territories, along with similar flotsam from other minority groups. Of these, 38,428 had been sent to their homes; 5,827 conscripted for the armed forces; and 43,693 sent to NKVD camps. Among them 153 "spies and traitors" had already been identified, said Beria.

Alexandr Klein, a Red Army officer captured by the Germans, escaped back to the Russian lines, where he faced an interrogation characteristic of Soviet paranoia:

Suddenly the Major raised himself sharply, and asked, "Can you prove that you are Jewish?"

I smiled, embarrassed, and said that I could—by taking off my trousers.

"And you are saying that the Germans didn't know you were a Jew?"

"If they had known, believe me, I wouldn't be standing here."

"Ach, you *yid* mug!" exclaimed the dandy, and kicked me in the lower stomach so hard that I suddenly gasped for breath and fell.

"What are these lies? Tell us, you motherfucker, with what mission were you sent here? Who are you involved with? When did you sell yourself? For how much? How much did you give yourself for, you creature for sale? What is your code name?

Klein was sentenced to death, reprieved, and finally sent for twenty years to one of the worst camps in the Soviet Gulag. Alongside such people as his interrogators were the Western allies seeking to destroy Nazi tyranny.

Stalin issued an order giving high priority to mopping up rear areas behind the Red Army: "All agents, saboteurs and terrorists must be captured, [together with] all those who have served in German police units, as public prosecutors, leaders of local fascist organizations, editors of newspapers and magazines, members of the so-called 'Russian Liberation Army' as well as other suspicious elements." Already 31,089 NKVD troops were operating behind the Soviet front. A further four divisions and four independent regiments—27,900 men plus 1,050 "experienced NKVD specialists"—were sent to reinforce them.

To the very end of the war, German military intelligence continued to dispatch agents behind the Soviet lines. The Germans used Soviet renegades with absolute ruthlessness, parachuting them into Russian-occupied territory in full awareness that their prospects of survival were negligible. Two Armenians in German pay were arrested in the Crimea in July 1944. They were ex-Komsomol members who had been trained by the Germans and dropped into the area with a transmitter. The NKVD used them to play a "radio game" with their German controllers. The prisoners sent some forty signals, announcing the creation of fictitious sabotage groups and demanding more agents and supplies. The Germans swallowed all this, and asked for daily local weather reports. On 23 December, they parachuted another agent into Soviet hands, carrying 427,000 roubles in cash and new radio batteries. Such wretched men, shuttlecocks between such adversaries, could expect mercy from neither.

IN THE WINTER of 1944, Churchill felt isolated in his struggle against Stalin's ambitions in eastern Europe. After more than five years of strife in the name of freedom, tens of millions of people were merely to exchange one tyranny for another. Some historians highlight the notorious slip of paper which the prime minister handed to Stalin in Moscow in October, acknowledging Russia's hegemony in large parts of its conquests. The Soviet dictator casually ticked the note. This exchange represented, say Churchill's critics, an unworthy and indeed unprincipled acquiescence, which belies his claims as a crusader for east European freedom. Even those Americans who recognized the malevolence of Soviet intentions, such as Harriman, recoiled from Churchill's apparent willingness to concede much of eastern Europe as a Soviet sphere of influence. The United States deplored the very concept of spheres of influence, whether Russian or British. Its government argued that it was committed to the rights of all peoples everywhere to self-determination.

Yet Churchill perceived himself reluctantly to be accepting some faits accomplis, in order to throw everything into the struggle to save Poland and

Greece from Stalin's maw. Several leading members of the U.S. administration were by now thoroughly alarmed by Soviet behaviour. Their views counted for little, however, while the ailing Roosevelt nursed his delusions that he could forge an equable relationship with Stalin. The minds of Allied generals, even including Churchill's closest military partner, Sir Alan Brooke, were fixed solely upon the defeat of Germany and Japan. They were thinking little about the shape of post-war Europe, and, indeed, why should soldiers have been expected to do so? Britain's prime minister, with such assistance as the Foreign Office could give, continued to strive vainly to thwart Stalin's ambitions, while publicly asserting British support for the Soviet alliance. In particular, in the autumn of 1944 Churchill went further in risking Stalin's wrath than at any period of the war, to fight for Poland.

After the defeat of their Rising, the plight of the Poles was dreadful indeed. Since Stalin had seized eastern Poland in 1939, his minions had laboured to eliminate potential resistance to communist domination. It is now known that the 4,000 Poles whose bodies were found by the Nazis at Katyn in 1943 represented only a sample of at least 26,000 Polish officers murdered by Beria's NKVD. A single Soviet executioner achieved an unspeakable record, by killing 7,000 men personally, with a German Walther pistol. To this day, mass graves of Stalin's victims continue to be uncovered in eastern Poland. As the Soviet armies advanced into the country in 1944, the NKVD followed in their wake, killing Polish resisters who had survived the struggle for Warsaw. Russia waged war upon the Army Krajowa long after the last German had been driven from Polish soil. Moscow's policy was implacable. For all Churchill's passionate pleadings for the nation for whose freedom Britain had gone to war, he received no glint of comfort from Moscow, its determination fortified by confidence in Washington's acquiescence. Stalin liked Roosevelt personally, while disliking Churchill. The Soviet leader acknowledged after the war, however, that his attitudes were formed by the fact that the American president would humour his purposes, while the British prime minister would not. And nothing could alter the reality that Soviet troops stood upon Polish soil, while the American and British armies were immeasurably remote.

FEAR, LOVE AND THE PARTY

They were a strange mixture, the soldiers of the Red Army, the largest fighting force the world had ever seen, deployed from the Baltic to the Balkans. There were great masses of illiterate peasants from the Soviet republics, who performed the worst of the Red Army's brutalities, and from whom neither human thought processes nor tactical skills were demanded. In the better formations and technical arms, by contrast, many officers and some soldiers were

educated, sensitive men and women, cultured within the limits permitted to
Stalin's Russia. It was a paradox, that while the Red Army was capable of terrible brutalities, many of its soldiers were deeply puritanical. Captain Vasily
Krylov, twenty-two, had only once kissed a girl in his life before he went to the
war, though he made up for lost time when he encountered Red Army nurses.
Twenty-one-year-old Major Yury Ryakhovsky professed himself shocked to
discover pornographic pictures in a German bunker. When he was wounded
and in hospital, he formed a warm friendship with Klava, his nurse. They sometimes sang songs together, but never went to bed. "I was a very sensitive, innocent young man." Like so many of his generation of educated Russians,
Ryakhovsky read voraciously—never whodunits or romances, but Tolstoy,
Chekhov, Pushkin and endless poetry. Vasily Krylov carried a volume of Shakespeare in his pack beside his lucky teddy bear. Half the Red Army had read
Anna Akhmatova's patriotic poem "Courage," published in 1942:

> We know what lies in balance at this moment,
> And what is happening right now,
> The hour for courage strikes upon our clocks,
> And courage will not desert us.
> We're not frightened by the hail of lead,
> We're not bitter without a roof overhead –
> And we will preserve you, Russian speech,
> Mighty Russian word!
> We will transmit you to our grandchildren
> Free and pure and rescued from captivity
> Forever!

The men of the Red Army were drawn from every corner of the millions of
square miles of the Soviet Union. A T-34 commander, Anatoly Osminov, was an
eighteen-year-old Muscovite. His driver, Boris, was a Tartar. Andreyev, the
loader, was an Udmurt. Gospodimov, the gunner, was Ukrainian. "Nobody
cared about nationalities at that time," said Osminov, "any more than they cared
whether you were an officer, NCO or soldier. We were just all in it together."
The war proved an extraordinary unifying force for a society in which Russian
had supplanted French as the chosen language of its rulers barely a century earlier. For many Russians, wartime service offered fractionally greater freedom to
think and to speak than they had known in the worst years of Stalin's Purges.
"When war broke out its real dangers and its menace of death were a blessing
compared with the inhuman power of the lie," says one of Pasternak's characters in *Dr. Zhivago*. "It broke the spell of the dead letter." The vitality of the war
years remains for many veterans a memory which made its sufferings seem
endurable. Yet the poet Akhmatova herself was a suspect person in the eyes of

Moscow. Yury Ryakhovsky was shocked to find a fellow officer court-martialled for quoting poetry that was deemed "politically incorrect."

Sometimes, all the 150 girls of Lieutenant Gennady Klimenko's signals regiment would gather for an evening to sing folk songs. Long before they finished, tears were coursing down the cheeks of men and women alike. "It is when they sing that we realise most clearly that they come from another world. They form a community then, and include us as hearers, in some immeasurable expanse," wrote Hans von Lehndorff, observing the Russians as a prisoner. "They are living over there, for the moment at least, and everything here is as unreal to them as some circus they have been led into. When they return home later on, all their experience here will seem to them like a mad dream."

When they were not in foxholes, men slept under trucks, in the open under blankets, or in ruined houses. When Klimenko thought of wartime billets afterwards, his most vivid memory was of the shattered glass that crackled underfoot every yard of the road between Moscow and Berlin, in a world in which few windows survived a battle. They lived chiefly off bread, cabbage soup, canned meat, milk powder and the legendary "100 grams"—the official daily issue of vodka which fuelled the Red Army from 1941 to 1945. They rolled their own cigarettes using scraps of newspaper. Many men suffered from boils caused by the poor diet. There were frequent outbreaks of disease, especially typhoid—even an artillery general died of it. Colds and 'flu were endemic, as indeed they were in all the armies, as soldiers perforce lived a semi-animal existence for months on end, denied the shelter of heated buildings, and laying their heads each night on sodden or frozen earth. Among the Russians, poor hygiene contributed significantly to the prevalence of disease, when men could seldom bathe or change clothes. Their rations were prepared and cooked in conditions of unbridled squalor.

Despite all that has been said above about the Soviet capacity for sacrifice, it would be wrong to suppose that all Russian soldiers were fired by suicidal courage or that they never ran away. Vitold Kubashevsky remarked that his bowels and those of many of his colleagues customarily collapsed before an attack, while their officer was prone to uncontrollable attacks of hiccups. One night in Yugoslavia, German officers watching on a hill observed Soviet troops occupying a town below. They ordered their Cossack unit to mount. Then the long line of horsemen charged, shouting and firing flare pistols as they scrambled down the slope. The Russians ran, throwing away their weapons as they went. This was among the last instances in the history of warfare of modern infantry succumbing to a cavalry charge. Even in the last months of the war, "tank panic" could sometimes cause entire Soviet regiments to turn and fly. "If you saw the turret of a Tiger traverse towards you and stop, you bailed out fast," said Corporal Anatoly Osminov, commander of a T-34. The complaints of Soviet officers about the quality of young replacements reaching them in

1944–45 exactly mirrored those of their American, British and German counterparts: "One has to work and work at these men," lamented Captain Oleg
Samokhvalov. "They know absolutely nothing about fighting, military discipline, real soldiers' spirit. Most of them having been hanging about for the past
three years, hiding either from the Germans or to avoid being drafted."

The only man in Gabriel Temkin's division to become a Hero of the Soviet
Union received his award for staying to engage German armour with anti-tank
grenades after every soldier around him had run. Anatoly Osminov freely
admitted that in his own early battles he often soiled his trousers, as did many
men in all the armies. "But you got used to it, in the same way you got used to
killing people. I started off thinking: 'How can I kill a human being?' But then,
of course, I learned to understand that it was simply a matter of killing to save
oneself from being killed." During his first battle, Osminov found himself turning white-haired at the age of seventeen, amid the relentless clatter of small-
arms fire and shrapnel on his tank's hull. "I expected us to catch fire at any
minute." Anti-tank gun officer Vladimir Gormin never forgot seeing a German
standing up in his tank turret roaring with laughter at the spectacle of Russian
troops running for their lives during the retreat across the Don back in 1942. But,
little by little, Gormin himself learned to master fear. "My corporal often saved
me—he was a veteran of three encirclements and he would crouch beside me
muttering, 'Let them get closer, let them get closer,' as the Germans came on. I
learned to keep control of myself even when I was shaking all over."

It was never possible for a Russian soldier to report sick with trench foot or
battle fatigue, as was commonplace in the west, but there were other means of
escaping combat. A Soviet reconnaissance officer, Lieutenant Pavel Nikiforov,
said: "If you got the wrong sort of guys in your unit, they were quite capable of
shooting you in the back on your first patrol, and running off to the Germans."
By 1944, the army was receiving many young replacements born in 1926, who
were poorly trained. "Some of them were very scared—they took time to get
used to the business." Even in the years of victory, some Soviet soldiers found
their plight in Stalin's armies so intolerable that they preferred to accept the
mortal risk of deserting.

By 1944, while the Red Army was vastly better supplied with the essentials of
war than it had been in the desperate days of 1941 and 1942, there were still few
indulgences. Soviet tanks were superb war machines, but made scant compromise with human comfort. "The T-34 was not a luxury apartment," observed
Vasily Kudryashov, who commanded one. While German and Western tanks
ran on petrol, those of the Soviets used diesel, which emitted black exhaust
smoke that could be a deadly betrayer on the battlefield. Soviet armoured crews
had been greatly hampered in the early years of the war by lack of radio—they
could communicate only by hand signals both inside their tanks and between
units. By 1944, however, they possessed at least platoon communications. Some

Liberation: The euphoric moment at the beginning of September 1944, when the end of the war seemed at hand. Here, Allied vehicles enter Brussels.

Insurrection: Men of the Polish Home Army rise against the Nazis in Warsaw, with tragic consequences.

"MARKET GARDEN," SEPTEMBER 1944

The narrow road: American paratroopers watch a convoy facing German fire.

Nijmegen: The town is shattered by fierce fighting between German and American and British soldiers—but the bridge survives.

The toughest moment for every infantryman: Advancing down a road covered by fire. Note the papers scattered beside the dead Germans—almost certainly letters discarded during the usual hasty intelligence search for documents.

Defiance in defeat: Lt. Jack Reynolds, captured at Arnhem, makes a two-fingered gesture towards the German cameraman.

COMMANDERS

Montgomery

Eisenhower

Bradley

Patton

Hodges

Zhukov

Konev

Rokossovsky

Von Rundstedt

Guderian

WATER: Exploited by the Germans at every turn to impede the Allied advance.

U.S. infantrymen plough through floods created by enemy demolitions in western Germany.

Crossing one of the battlefield's innumerable rivers and canals in an assault boat. These frail wooden and canvas craft, chronically vulnerable to enemy fire, carried men into action from France to the Elbe.

THE SOVIET JUGGERNAUT:

These are classic propaganda images. Even if—like most Soviet war pictures—the scene of troops storming a Polish city street is staged, it vividly conveys the urgency of combat. But the shot of a tankman embracing a Pole amidst his family belies the reality of Soviet savagery towards the Poles, and of the two nations' historic hatred.

GERMANY BESIEGED

Joachim Peiper, archetype of the pitiless
SS officer

Paul von Stemann, the Danish journalist who wrote a vivid
narrative of Berlin life in the last months of the catastrophe.

(RIGHT) Joe Volmar
(FAR RIGHT) Captain Karl Godau
of 10th SS Panzer

(BELOW) Hans Moser
(BELOW RIGHT) Sergeant Otto Cranz

A haunting image of a doomed young German: Klaus Salzer, an eighteen-year-old East Prussian who yearned to become a photo-journalist, and instead became a reluctant paratrooper. He was killed in action within months.

Helmut Fromm

Michael Wieck

The former eager Nazi Maria Brauwers, who hid in the woods in the snow with her husband and young baby Hermann, as battle raged around them.

Vasily Kudrashov

Lt. Gennady Ivanov poses proudly beside his Stalin tank.

Alexandr Sergeev

Mikhail Devyataev, the Soviet fighter pilot who staged one of the most astounding escapes of the war by stealing the commandant's Heinkel from the slave-labour camp at Peenemünde.

Evsei Igolnik

Vladimir Gormin

*Zinaida Mikhailova, photographed
after the war in the prison garb
she wore in Ravensbrück.*

Scenes from the German battlefield. Almost every Allied soldier was awed by the scale of destruction.

David Tibbs, the doctor who served with 13 Para.

Lt. Tony Moody

Three guys from Tyler, Texas: U.S. glider pilot "Goldie" Goldman (right) with triumphant fellow flier after the Rhine crossing.

Lt. William Devitt, the young Minnesotan who vividly recorded the experience of leading an infantry platoon in the hell of the Hürtgen Forest.

Jack Ilfrey, the U.S. fighter pilot who scooped a comrade from his wrecked aircraft behind the German lines.

The brilliant, feisty Jim Gavin, commanding the 82nd Airborne Division.

THREE FUTURE STATESMEN

Major Peter Carrington   *Lt. Helmut Schmidt*   *Staff-Sergeant Henry Kissinger*

A scene in the streets of newly captured Aachen which vividly captures the shock, bewilderment and terror of many Germans.

THE PAIN OF DEFEAT

Peasants peer cautiously from behind their makeshift shelter, parading the white flag token of their surrender.

A fifteen-year-old, Hans-George Henke, collapses into childish tears after his capture by the U.S. Ninth Army.

T-34s were equipped with the superior 85mm gun in place of the earlier 76mm. Since the Red Army lacked tracked carriers to move infantry on the battlefield, a squad of tommy-gunners rode on every tank hull, to provide close support. Tommy-gunners could be formidably effective, leaping down to engage German infantry at close range. But they were appallingly vulnerable to enemy fire.

The Russians experienced the same problems as the British and Americans when tanks became separated from supporting infantry. Vasily Kudryashov's T-34 company once found itself alone in the narrow streets of a small town, and suffered badly at the hands of German infantry who closed in, throwing grenades and Molotov cocktails. Kudryashov was pulled out of his blazing tank by his crew, and escaped. He was lucky. The top hatches of T-34s often jammed in a crisis. Most of his company was destroyed.

Russian tank crews usually fought "closed down," with their hatches shut, which meant that those within the turret could see little of the battlefield. There were long, incomprehensible halts, the men dozing in their cramped seats, listening to the hiss of static from the radio until they were abruptly ordered to move again. Even experienced Russian tankers found their steel monsters claustrophobic. Ventilation was poor, and crews choked amid the lingering fumes when they had been firing their main armament continuously.

While American and German soldiers were given special leave as a reward for battlefield achievements, in Stalin's armies cash was offered as an incentive. An anti-tank gun crew received 2,000 roubles for every German tank it destroyed—500 to the gun commander, 500 to the gunlayer and 200 apiece for the rest. Much more useful, a crew which smashed a tank that did not burn were entitled to loot its contents. Lieutenant Vladimir Gormin and his men were thrilled to find a German Mark IV full of cognac and chocolate "and all sorts of other things we didn't have." They marvelled to see the leather-covered crew seats, and stripped them to make boots.

In an army in which fear played so large a part, many officers were reluctant to accept orders by telephone. They demanded written instructions, which could be preserved and produced if matters went awry. "Orders were never a matter for discussion," said Lieutenant Alexandr Sergeev. Even when German artillery was registering on Captain Vasily Krylov's Katyusha battery, it was unthinkable for him to shift position without a direct order. Individual initiative was discouraged. Savage penalties were introduced to stop drivers abandoning their vehicles under air attack, an almost universal practice in all the armies. When Lieutenant Vasily Filimonenko was recovering from shrapnel wounds in hospital a visiting marshal, Vasilevsky, gave him a cigarette. The young lieutenant was much too frightened of his commander to smoke it.

Except in the extremities of battle, all units assembled at least once a month for Communist Party gatherings, to be harangued by their commissars about current events. Political officers inspired the same mixed feeling as chaplains in the Western armies—some were very good, and notably brave; others were hated and despised for their hypocrisy, inciting men to do their duty to the motherland while themselves remaining at the safest possible distance from the front. Every man and woman in a key position, such as the cipher specialists in Gennady Klimenko's signals unit, was required to be a Party member: "Ninety per cent of people joined the Party because they knew they had no future unless they did," Klimenko said sardonically. Major Yury Ryakhovsky was telephoned in his artillery forward observation post on 23 February 1944 by an angry and bewildered divisional commander who demanded: was his regiment in serious trouble, since its batteries were throwing shells over open sights? Ryakhovsky reassured the colonel: the guns were merely firing a *feu de joie* on their political officer's orders, to celebrate Red Army Day.

It is remarkable that the Soviet command system functioned as well as it did, given the ideological resistance to truth which was fundamental to the Stalinist system. In war, telling the truth is essential not for moral reasons, but because no commander can direct a battle effectively unless his subordinates tell him what is happening: where they are, what resources they possess, whether they have attained or are likely to attain their objectives. Yet since 1917 the Soviet Union had created an edifice of self-deceit unrivalled in human history. The mythology of heroic tractor drivers, coal miners who fulfilled monthly production norms in days, collective farms which produced record harvests, was deemed essential to the self-belief of the state. On the battlefield, in some measure this perversion persisted. Propaganda wove tales of heroes who had performed fantastic and wholly fictitious feats against the fascists. Vladimir Gormin was reprimanded for reporting after an action that his anti-tank unit had failed to destroy any German tanks. A new return, citing two panzers destroyed, was duly composed and dispatched to higher command. "The statistics were always ridiculous. It was pretty hard to tell the truth," said Gormin.

Yet somehow, through a morass of commissar-driven rhetoric and fantasy, Stalin's armies hacked a path to victory. Most Soviet intelligence reports of the 1944–45 period are notable for their common sense and frankness. In 1941, the Russians sought to interpret the war in ideological terms. Interrogators addressed captured German soldiers about "the need for class solidarity." Gradually, these delusions fell away. Von Paulus, Hitler's vanquished commander at Stalingrad, observed acidly to his captors: "You should know that Germany's workers and peasants are among the most prominent supporters of Hitler." Though the enemy continued to be described as "the fascists," hatred became extended to the German nation: "Those who had recently been brothers in class struggle became beasts who could only be killed," in the words of a Russian historian. A Red Army nurse, Sofia Kuntsevich, wrote: "I had so much hatred stored up. I thought: what are we going to do to these people when we get to Germany? I wanted to see the mothers who had given birth to these monsters. I thought that they would never be able to look us in the eye."

The Red Army professed that the 125,000 women in its ranks were mere comrades in battle and in suffering. In reality, however, and despite earlier remarks about Russian puritanism, many girl soldiers found themselves employed off-duty as sexual playthings for their officers, "campaign wives." Some men as well as women resented this practice. "There shouldn't be any women at war," said Corporal Nikolai Ponomarev of the 374th Rifle Division. "I felt terribly sorry for girls at the front—they couldn't wash or change their clothes, they were exploited by officers: they had no choice." "War and women in trenches do not mix well," wrote Sergeant Gabriel Temkin. "I heard this many times, and I shared this view... A young, healthy woman, for months or even a couple of years without a furlough, always surrounded by so many equally young, healthy men did not have to be harassed or abused to become a willing sex partner... either because she fell in love, or just to satisfy sexual desire, or to improve her lot, or because she expected to find a husband, or she wanted to get pregnant and be released and go home." Sergeant Natalia Ivanova once had to summon Thirty-third Army's chief of operations to rescue her from his deputy, who became both drunk and predatory while giving her dictation. The brigade commander of Gennady Ivanov's tank unit kept the same mistress from 1943 to 1946, an extremely pretty blonde headquarters telephonist named Katya. The women's medal *Za Boyeuye Zaslugi,* "for military services," was often derisively called *Za Polovye Zaslugi,* "for sexual services." Abortions at the front were commonplace, acknowledged Nikolai Senkevich, a Red Army doctor. "Whole trainloads of girls were sent home pregnant," said Gennady Klimenko contemptuously. "Every senior officer had his girlfriend." "Hospitals were your best chance of getting lucky," said Captain Vasily Krylov. His girlfriend, a nurse named Nina, told him quite coolly one day: "I want to get pregnant so I can get sent home." She got her wish, but he never knew whether he himself was her benefactor.

Corporal Anna Nikyunas had suffered even more than most Russians of her generation. She was orphaned at fourteen in 1937 when her parents, Leningrad workers, were denounced and shot by the NKVD. She first went to the front in 1941 as a nurse. She neither wrote nor received any letters at the front, because she no longer had a family with which to correspond. The nurses carried submachine guns as well as medical bags, but found it very hard to grasp the reality of battle. "Tracer bullets looked like sparklers to us at first. They seemed too innocent and pretty to hurt anyone." Their commanding officer would shout at them furiously under fire: "Get your heads down, girls!" Anna was wounded in the epic Leningrad battle by a shell which killed the girl next to her, and removed the legs from another. She herself was hit by fragments in the neck: "I felt little pain, just the warmth of blood running down my back." After her recovery, she returned to the front. She, too, had a "field husband": "He was a very handsome surgeon. He was married, but even after the war he would phone me and say 'You are still my darling.'" For all its horrors, she always remembered the war with deep emotion. "That time was full of life," she said.

Yet it would be mistaken to exaggerate the sexual role of women soldiers. Many served with cool and courageous professionalism. Women often fulfilled an intensely hazardous role as telephone linesmen, repairing signal links under fire. Vasily Krylov was manning a forward observation post when he lost contact with his battery and thought that a German attack had started. He was running hard for a bunker when he met a girl soldier who asked matter-of-factly: "Where are you going?" "It's an attack!" he shouted. "The Germans are on the way!" The girl said: "Calm down. There's no problem." She set off under fire in pursuit of his telephone line, repaired the break caused by mortaring and cheerfully returned to reassure the troubled captain.

By the autumn of 1944, Sergeant Natalia Ivanova had seen more of war than most men. She was the twenty-three-year-old daughter of a Moscow dentist, herself a secretary at the Finance Ministry until she was called to the army in June 1941, and sent to Smolensk at twenty-four hours' notice. "At first, it all seemed rather romantic," she said. But before they even arrived at the front the truck carrying herself and other girls, still in civilian clothes and high heels, hit a mine. Several were killed. When she reached army headquarters, still shocked, a colonel told her to go and get some sleep, and pointed to a nearby shed. It proved to be already occupied by corpses. Soon afterwards, she was serving as a typist at Thirty-third Army when she and her section were ordered to attend small-arms practice in the woods. They returned to find the head-quarters a blazing shambles following a Luftwaffe raid. The staff was hastily evacuating, with German tanks a mile away. Natalia was roundly cursed by an officer for insisting on running into the wreckage to retrieve her clothes before boarding a cart. "Girls are girls," she shrugged. During the long retreat that followed, she found herself on a truck with two pilots and all Thirty-third Army's files when they ran out of petrol. "You go and ask for some," said the pilots. "Nobody will give it to a man." She went to a nearby unit, who were tending scores of wounded. The soldiers said they would give her some fuel if she would first help with the casualties. "It was the first time I had dressed a wound," she said. "My hands were shaking as I tried to deal with the stomach cases." She ended up walking for hours through a forest, "slightly drunk and very frightened and hungry." They picked potatoes from the gardens of houses they passed, and eventually escaped successfully, to reach Moscow.

She was reposted to the 222nd Rifle Division where, in her first battle, she and other girls were sent to recover wounded men under fire from German tanks. Because she was very small, the physical difficulties were very great: "It was hard to make oneself crawl out of cover, and then try to lift these big men. I was in shock." She was awarded the Red Star for her part in that action. One day in 1943, she found herself in the middle of the German Dnieper counter-attack, with the men of their division running for their lives, as the Chief of Staff vainly lashed out at the fleeing soldiers with a fence post to check their flight. She herself swam the river with two other girls and the divisional files. At the far bank, having lost most of their clothes, they loaded their burden on to a wounded horse, which immediately collapsed. German tank fire from across the river killed a girl signaller beside her. At last, she found another horse to carry the files, and rejoined the division's survivors, who were suitably amazed to see her arrive wearing only a bra and skirt. She was reposted to Thirty-third Army.

In 1944, she fell passionately in love with a gunner officer: "I met hundreds of nice men, but he was the best." Dmitry Kalafati first caught her attention when, in an idle moment, he told the fortunes of some of the girls with a pack of cards. She told him mischievously that, if he made a wish, it would be granted. He immediately leaned over and kissed her. They began a passionate affair. When the chief of staff heard about it, he said to her: "Well, you must have been the one who made the running, because Dmitry wouldn't have had the nerve." In battle or out of it, the couple found time together. She sometimes scrounged a jeep and driver, and followed him to the front. Once, she was forcefully reprimanded by the head of operations, Viktor Grinyushin, when Dmitry was roused in the night at the Hungarian castle where he was billeted, and Natalia was found with him. The couple didn't care, not least because the head of operations was in a weak position to complain, himself enjoying a passionate affair with another girl soldier named Lida, whom he married in 1945. But senior officers drew the line when Natalia was found to be sending cipher messages to Dmitry at his unit. This, they said not unreasonably, was an abuse of military communications. Natalia and Dmitry Kalafati were married after the war ended.

By September 1944, so desperate was the Red Army's demand for manpower that 1,030,494 prisoners from the Gulag had been released for military service. Most of these men were, however, mere thieves and minor malefactors. Serious political criminals remained ineligible even for the privilege of dying for their country. Among the most savage manifestations of Soviet ruthlessness were the Red Army's "penal battalions." These punishment units rendered all those assigned to them players in a deadly roulette game. A man possessed perhaps one chance in thirty or forty of escaping death. Men were customarily posted to penal battalions as an alternative to execution. "[These units] are intended," said Zhukov in his order No. 258 of 28 September 1942, "to enable senior officers and political officers to make use of men who are found guilty of cowardice, indiscipline, instability, to compound for their crimes towards the motherland by shedding their blood in the most difficult engagements with the enemy." They were employed to clear minefields under fire, to probe enemy positions and to spearhead desperate advances in the manner of a "forlorn hope" in the wars of Napoleon.

An officer unfortunate enough to be posted to lead such units was expected to serve with them for only one to three months, each month counting sixfold for pension purposes, in the unlikely event that he survived to enjoy old age. Officers sent to penal battalions because they were themselves being punished were stripped of rank and decorations. Any breach of discipline in these battalions was punished by summary execution. "A soldier who distinguishes himself in action can receive remission of sentence . . . All those released from penal battalions are assumed to have completed their sentences. Any man wounded is automatically deemed to have served his sentence."

"I once watched a penal battalion go into an attack," said Major Yury Ryakhovsky with uncomplicated respect. "I have never seen infantry so brave. They were wearing blue tunics and black caps, and boots made from tree bark. They advanced shoulder to shoulder, with a rifle between three men." The commander of Anatoly Osminov's T-34 in Thirty-second Tank Army was so desperate to escape combat that he drained the radiator, causing the engine to overheat. Osminov threw the culprit out of the tank at pistol-point. The man ran away, and was later found wounded. The NKVD placed the entire crew under arrest pending trial. Afterwards, the others were acquitted, while their former commander was sent to a penal battalion. He was lucky. Men found guilty of *samostrel*—self-inflicted wounding—were customarily shot in front of their units like deserters, after digging their own graves. The regiment formed three sides of a square, and the command was given to the firing squad: "For our motherland . . . At the enemy . . . Fire!" Offenders were buried with a sign on their graves declaring "eternal shame on the coward who has betrayed his comrades and his motherland." Vitold Kubashevsky, a survivor of a penal battalion who witnessed many such executions, found himself quite unmoved by them: "One felt no pity. At the front, all one's sensibilities were dulled." Notice of crime and punishment was sent to a man's former factory or collective farm. The official Soviet view of penal battalions was simple: men were needed to perform military tasks which were likely to result in their deaths. Was it not appropriate that such duties should fall upon those deserving of death?

The image of the Soviet soldier as an unfeeling brute was justified by the immense rabble of Mongols (that is, from Central Asia) and conscripts from the eastern republics who followed the spearheads. But many men in Russian uniform shared the same misgivings about the experiences of battle as their American, British or German counterparts. Gabriel Temkin was appalled to see his friend Grishin torn open by a shell splinter: "I saw him crouching and squeezing his bloodied guts as if trying to push them back into his open belly. Pale and sweating, his lips trembling as bloody foam came from his mouth, he was half-conscious when I bid him farewell. He died on the shaking horse-drawn cart, even before reaching hospital."

Although the Luftwaffe was a mere shadow of its former self by the winter of 1944, it still produced spasms of devastating activity. Twenty-two-year-old Vasily Kudryashov was conducting a fighting reconnaissance of a river crossing with two platoons of T-34s, tommy-gunners on their hulls, when German aircraft caught them in the open. Kudryashov ordered his crew to jump down and take cover beneath the hull, but he himself was still on the hatch when bomb fragments caught him in the leg and took off his foot. It was the eighth tank he had lost in action since 1942. Official notice was sent to his mother that he had been killed, but mercifully she had never received it when he returned home from hospital six months later. "I went away a boy and came back a man," he said, "but I also possessed the sadness of a cripple."

Even a surgeon, Nikolai Senkevich, never entirely reconciled himself to the sight of corpses that had been crushed beneath tank tracks, or of great sheets of white ice strewn with huddled dead. One day during an advance, he was appalled to come upon three abandoned German trucks, piled high with bandaged bodies—obviously wounded men who had died at a dressing station. His own field hospital handled almost 3,000 men in three days during an action in 1944. "It was a question of making very swift decisions about who had a chance of living, and concentrating on them. Some men already had gangrene. They were just left to die." The Russian doctors were too short of morphine even to end the agony of doomed men. Combat fatigue, Senkevich professed, was unknown to the Red Army, and certainly not officially acknowledged: "I never saw such a case. By that stage of the war, people were feeling quite cheerful." Yet Sergeant Nikolai Timoshenko described seeing men faint from fear. In the Red Army as in all armies, the real fighting in every battle was done by a small minority of men. Many others did little nor nothing save to attempt to stay alive. By the time it was all over, said Timoshenko drily, "one knew the difference between those who took part in a battle and those who were mere spectators." Soviet soldiers were as vulnerable to terror and panic as any others. The sanctions for succumbing to it were merely incomparably more severe.

AT THE BEGINNING of November 1944, the Soviets and the Western allies stood almost equidistant from Berlin. Stalin, passionately determined to ensure that the Soviet Union enjoyed its triumph in Hitler's capital, still harboured some thoughts of launching an early thrust across the Vistula. Zhukov dissuaded him. Soviet offensive operations in Poland were halted, to prepare for the next phase of the great assault on Germany, to be launched at some date between 15 and 20 January 1945.

Stalin's Stavka, the high command directing Russia's war, considered three alternative plans. There was a southern axis, through Budapest and Vienna. There was a northern route, through East Prussia, where Soviet forces already heavily outnumbered the Germans. Yet it always seemed inevitable that the Berlin assault would be staged from the centre, by 1st Belorussian Front through Poland. In October 1944, Rokossovsky was supplanted by Zhukov as 1st Belorussian's commander, and shifted northwards to direct 2nd Belorussian Front against East Prussia. Russian generals vied for primacy at least as eagerly as their Western counterparts. Rokossovsky, a commander of proven ability and with a willingness to delegate unusual among his peers, was furious at being moved to a subordinate role for no better reason than that he was half Polish. Stalin had no intention of allowing any sort of Pole to take Berlin. A lingering taint of the prison cell also hung over the marshal, who had been imprisoned during the 1937 army purges. "I know very well what Beria is capable of," Rokossovsky once observed bitterly to Zhukov. "I have been in his prisons." Here was one of the greatest Soviet generals of the war, who had emerged from confinement without his fingernails amid the miasma of suspicion and persecution during the purges just seven years earlier.

On Zhukov's left flank in Poland stood 1st Ukrainian Front, led by the swaggering, shaven-headed figure of forty-eight-year-old Marshal Ivan Konev. A former tsarist NCO, he was a man of little education, and found it difficult to express himself on paper. It was his fate always to be overshadowed by Zhukov, yet he had proved himself an almost equally effective commander, and enjoyed the additional merit in Stalin's eyes of being less celebrated by the Red Army. Zhukov had saved Konev from obscurity, or something worse, and secured his rehabilitation after he was summarily dismissed from his command by Stalin in February 1943, as so many able officers were likewise dismissed. Konev is sometimes described as "ruthless." This adjective seems superfluous in speaking of any Soviet commander. None could hold his rank or perform the tasks demanded of the Red Army without possessing a contempt for life unusual even in the ranks of the Waffen SS. Konev had come within a whisker of execution by Stalin, during the bloody torrent of recrimination that accompanied the 1941 battles for Moscow. There is no biographical evidence to suggest that Stalin's marshals possessed either cultural refinement or humanitarian scruple, that any was, in truth, much more than a militarily gifted brute.

Zhukov forcefully argued to Stalin, who needed little persuasion, that the principal drive into Germany must be made on Russia's central front, with its main weight deployed south of Warsaw. This view prevailed. It was obvious, however, that pressure must be maintained in East Prussia, Hungary and Yugoslavia, to ensure that the Germans could not shift forces to Poland from the Baltic area and south-east Europe. The broad principles of future operations were established. Zhukov would strike the main blow south of Warsaw, while Konev on his left sought to envelop the vast industrial areas of Silesia, rather than attack head-on against strong defences. Stalin was anxious to capture Silesia's mines and factories intact, and emphasized his wishes to Konev. In the north, Chernyakhovsky and Rokossovsky would address East Prussia.

The Germans were defending the west with seventy-four divisions and 1,600 tanks, against an Allied army of eighty-seven vastly stronger divisions and over 6,000 tanks. In the east, the Germans deployed some two million men, 4,000 tanks and 2,000 aircraft. Against these, by January 1945 the Red Army would be able to commit six million troops. Its order of battle boasted 500 rifle divisions—each half the size of its Western counterpart—13,000 tanks and self-propelled guns, 100,000 guns and heavy mortars, 15,000 aircraft. In the past, Russian armies had often attacked in the frozen winter months, when the ground and even the rivers could carry tanks. Traditionally, it was in the spring thaws that the Eastern Front became stagnant. But on the Vistula in November the logistical difficulties were immense. Eastern Europe lacked the road and rail network of the west. The Germans had demolished every possible communications link during their summer retreat. Though the Red Army was far better supplied with transport than it had been two or three years earlier, it possessed nothing like the resources of the Americans and British. Many of the new replacements reaching the Russian formations were ill trained. For the best part of three waterlogged and then snowbound months, therefore, while fierce fighting persisted to the north and south, the critical axis of the Eastern Front lay dormant, as Stalin's armies began the build-up for their decisive blow in the battle for Germany.

CHAPTER FIVE

Winter Quarters

THE SCHELDT

A
FTER THE FAILURE of Market Garden, Montgomery described its only
legacy—the long, thin salient to Nijmegen—as "a dagger pointed at
the heart of Germany." This was a characteristic piece of braggadocio
by 21st Army Group's commander. Privately, he cannot have believed it. The
point of that "dagger" drove nowhere until the spring of 1945. To hold the eastern "blade," a sixty-mile front, he was obliged to retain for weeks the services of
the two U.S. airborne divisions which had seized the corridor in September
1944. In October the most urgent objective for Montgomery's forces lay in the
opposite direction from Germany: the Antwerp approaches. Tedder wrote: "I
was never able to convince myself that at any stage until we held Antwerp,
Montgomery really believed that we could march a sizeable army to Berlin
with our existing resources of supply and maintenance."

First Canadian Army was committed to the unglamorous yet vital task of
clearing the Scheldt, and above all the defences of Walcheren Island, to open
the shipping path to the port. Operations began on 3 October, with a devastating
air attack against the Westkapelle Dyke by 247 Lancasters of Bomber Command. When the RAF aircraft turned for home, the great earth wall that had
held back the sea from Walcheren for 400 years was breached. Within a few
days, large parts of the island were under water, flooding some German positions, at the cost of 125 Dutch civilian lives. But during the first ten days of October the ground advance made slow progress. Throughout the campaign, the
Canadian Army suffered even more acutely than the British from a shortage of
men. Because many French-Canadians bitterly opposed participation in "England's war," Canada's prime minister Mackenzie King decreed in 1940 that
only volunteers would be sent overseas, and that even these men would fight
only in Europe. As a consequence, by 1944 some 70,000 fit Canadian soldiers—

the "zombies" as they were known—remained at home, doing nothing more useful than guarding prisoners of war. "We had five divisions, or the equivalent, of trained men sitting back there in Canada," lamented a Canadian officer bitterly, "and that s.o.b. Mackenzie King just wouldn't send them overseas." At the very end of the war, when 15,000 non-volunteers were drafted for overseas services, more than three-quarters of them deserted before embarkation.

Meanwhile in the field, Canada's fighting forces suffered constant manning difficulties. When the units which had trained for so long in England before D-Day were eroded by battle casualties, the quality and fighting power of the Canadian Army deteriorated, to the chagrin of those who commanded its units in battle. The Black Watch of Canada, for instance, had suffered heavily in Normandy, and by October possessed only some 379 men in its rifle companies, of whom 100 were recent replacements. Many of these proved wholly untrained, to the point of being unfamiliar with infantry small arms. When they met German paratroops in an attack on 13 October, they were heavily mauled, losing 183 casualties including fifty-six killed. That night, the survivors were given a hot meal and a movie show. When officers learned that the scheduled entertainment was entitled *We Die at Dawn,* a less provocative alternative was substituted.

On 16 October, the commander of the Royal Hamilton Light Infantry, Lieutenant-Colonel Denis Whitaker, was consolidating his battalion's positions after a successful assault when the German 6th Parachute Division counterattacked. Whitaker was appalled to see his A Company commander shamelessly about-turn and disappear towards the rear. "Unfortunately," wrote the colonel later, "when men see their own leaders turn away from battle, it becomes a very natural choice that they shall follow, and that is what happened on Woesdrecht Hill. I...had to watch this horrible sight, those wretched men running panic-stricken down the hill towards us. I pulled out my revolver and stopped some of them at gunpoint." Whitaker's battalion suffered 167 casualties, including twenty-one killed. One of his other company commanders checked the German assault by calling down artillery fire on his own positions.

On 31 October, the CO of the Black Watch of Canada, Lieutenant-Colonel Bruce Ritchie, wrote a note for his battalion's war diary: " 'Battle morale' is definitely not good, due to the fact that inadequately trained men are, of necessity, being sent into action ignorant of any idea of their own strength, and, after their first mortaring, overwhelmingly convinced of the enemy's. This feeling is no doubt increased by their ignorance of fieldcraft in its most elementary form." Individually, many Canadians made fine and brave contributions to the war. Lieutenant-General Guy Simonds was among the outstanding corps commanders in north-west Europe. Some Canadian officers who volunteered for service with British units showed themselves exceptional soldiers. But collectively, the Canadian Army was a weak and flawed instrument because of the chronic manning problems imposed by its nation's politics. Canada's soldiers paid the price of their prime minister's pusillanimity on the flooded battlefields of Holland in the winter of 1944.

Eisenhower told Montgomery, undoubtedly rightly, that he was unconvinced 21st Army Group was giving sufficient priority to Antwerp: "I believe the operations designed to clear up the entrance require your personal attention." The field-marshal grudgingly reinforced the Canadians with four British divisions, which pushed north towards the Waal. A painful struggle followed. Some 10,000 Germans in the so-called Breskens Pocket inflicted on the Canadian 3rd Division some of the most miserable fighting of its war, amid the October rains and floods. The Wehrmacht's 64th Division, core of the Breskens defence, was one of the most effective formations under Model's command. The Leopold Canal, which had caused such grief during the first Canadian crossing attempt in September, required a major assault operation three weeks later. A soldier of the Toronto Scottish recorded in the battalion's war diary for 9 October: "Living conditions at the front are not cosy. Water and soil make mud. Mud sticks to everything. Rifles and brens operate sluggishly. Ammunition becomes wet. Slit trenches allow one to get below the ground level, but also contain several inches of thick water. Matches and cigarettes are wet and unusable." A Canadian officer, Major Oliver Corbett of the North Shores, said: "The whole Scheldt battle was company attacks, day after day, sometimes two or three attacks in 24 hours...We were soaked all the time. Along the dyke was the only place a soldier could dig in."

Among the British formations further south, Private Kenneth Pollitt advanced into the old fortress town of 's-Hertogenbosch with 7th Royal Welsh Fusiliers on 26 October. A young Dutchman wearing the Orange armband of the Resistance dashed to meet Pollitt's platoon, and volunteered to show the way through the streets, because he desperately wanted to play some part in the liberation of his hometown. They reached the town hall, where even amid continued fighting local people were offering celebratory glasses of wine to every passing British soldier. They moved on towards the south bank of the canal, failing to notice a German tank tucked in beside a building on the far side, 150 yards away. Its gun fired. Most of Pollitt's section collapsed dead or wounded. His corporal was hit in the stomach, face and legs. The Dutch boy was dead. "That one shell cost our platoon more casualties than we had suffered since Normandy." Pollitt dashed into a nearby monastery, and tried to find a window from which he might get a shot with his PIAT. The Germans had disappeared. Next morning, he heard cheering, and ran out on a house balcony to see men of the East Lancashires making a dash across a canal bridge. Yet, even as they watched, a German sniper dropped one of the spectators stone dead. Carelessness on the battlefield was often cruelly punished. Shelling started, from both sides. Pollitt watched curiously as a dispatch rider, obviously very drunk, stood in full view

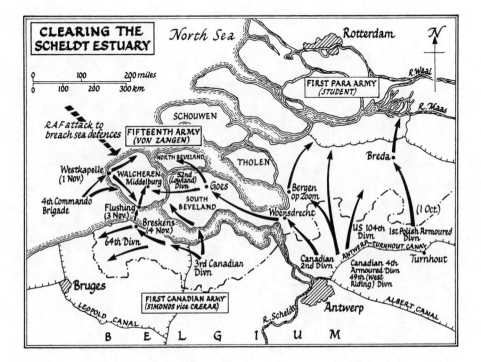

in the street and blazed wildly in the direction of the German positions with a tommy-gun. He was fortunate enough to survive, "the only man I saw drunk in action in the whole campaign." It took the British two days to secure 's-Herto-genbosch and its network of canals, just one among a hundred such bitter and destructive little actions.

Third Canadian Division finally completed the capture of the Breskens Pocket on 4 November, having lost 314 killed, 231 missing and 2,077 wounded. They took more than 12,000 German prisoners. On 1 November, British and Canadian troops staged three amphibious landings on Walcheren. They fought their way through the streets of Flushing to secure the town. On 3 November, after several Canadian attempts had been bloodily repulsed, 52nd (Lowland) Division finally forced the causeway to west Walcheren. On 5 November, Allied troops entered the town of Middelburg. In all, it took eight days of fighting and cost some 7,700 casualties to secure the island. Bitterness persisted within both Canadian and British units over the manner in which they had been driven again and again to assault the Walcheren causeway, at heavy cost, even as the island was being taken from the other side by amphibious assault. The Scheldt actions have been given scant attention by students of the north-west Europe campaign because they seemed inglorious and lay far from the direct path to Germany. Yet for all those who took part, including the Dutch people strug-gling to survive in the midst of a battlefield, they provided a dreadful experi-ence. Wilhelmina Helder, a twenty-year-old girl in Middelburg, spent two weeks among a hundred people in a cellar while bombs and shells thundered down above them. On 6 November, the trapdoor opened to reveal a very dirty Canadian soldier peering down at them. Her eighty-six-year-old grandmother said thankfully, almost euphorically: "I can go home." Yet she emerged to find her house submerged beneath the floodwaters which now covered huge areas of the Dutch battlefield. The old woman died that night.

The guns did not finally fall silent on Walcheren until 8 November. The opening of the Scheldt had cost 18,000 casualties. The Royal Navy was obliged to clear 267 sea-mines before the estuary was navigable. The first Allied ship unloaded at Antwerp only on 28 November, eighty-five days after "Pip" Roberts's 11th Armoured Division first seized the docks. Until that date, almost every ton of Allied supplies had to be trucked or carried across the devastated French rail net from the Normandy beaches or the Channel ports, most of which had now been cleared of their German garrisons. It is scarcely surprising that the Americans showed little patience with Montgomery's professions of eagerness for a rapid dash into Germany when he and his forces made such heavy weather of performing one of the most vital strategic tasks of the cam-paign. The operations to open Antwerp were the overwhelming preoccupa-tion of 21st Army Group between the failure of Market Garden and November 1944. By the time the job was done, it was plain that the British would make no important progress towards Germany until the wet, dismal winter was past its worst.

First Canadian Army was left to hold a long line east–west along the estuary of the Maas and up the Waal, then turning south down the Arnhem–Nijmegen salient. Northern Holland remained in German hands. The difficulties had now become apparent of attacking across the Dutch flatlands. The British focused their main forces upon the eastern axis towards Germany, and maintained only a holding front against the German forces occupying northern Holland.

Dempsey's Second Army began a long series of operations to make ground into Germany. The Siegfried Line ended some miles north of Aachen, so the British faced no major German fortifications. They were now fighting eighty miles from the heart of the Ruhr. But through October and November, in awful weather and on difficult terrain, they encountered disappointment after disappointment as they struggled to find a way through. An attack by VIII Corps into the Peel Marshes took five days to cover three miles, where the few roads were heavily mined and fiercely defended by Student's paratroopers.

That operation was broken off on 15 October. The Germans launched an impressive counter-attack of their own twelve days later, against the American 7th Armored Division on the British right. The Germans regained some ground, caused considerable mayhem and prompted Bradley to relieve the commander of 7th Armored. The British VIII and XII Corps spent the entire month of November clearing the Peel Marshes, closing up to the River Maas early in December. The neighbouring XXX Corps pushed painfully through Geilenkirchen, twelve miles north of Aachen, to touch the Roer in mid-December. The officer commanding 5th Royal Tanks, Lieutenant-Colonel Tony Leakey, reflected the mood of many British units at this time: "The regiment had seldom been out of the action throughout the war...and they had certainly had their bellyful. The 5th fought as hard as any...even so, I missed that 'urge to go.'" The CO of 1st Herefords, George Turner-Cain, found it painful to contrast the lack of enthusiasm among his own men with the dogged performance of the Germans:

> ...hard fighting and heavy casualties had a depressing effect on morale all round. Men became jumpy and unwilling to go forward in the face of fire or possible fire, unless led by their leaders. The Germans, who were highly disorganized, fighting in penny packets and not in formations, were showing splendid spirit and defiance, fighting until told to withdraw...

Major-General "Pip" Roberts wrote of the difficulties that winter: "Now, mistakes and failures could only delay the end. Of course we wanted to finish the war as quickly as possible, but at what cost? Unless morale was high, we would not achieve our objectives; heavy casualties in a fruitless battle will not help morale. We must try to win our battles without heavy casualties; not very easy." Montgomery once described his unhappiness when Churchill conveyed to him American reproaches that the British seemed unwilling to take their share of casualties. "It was you, Prime Minister," responded the field-marshal, "who told me that we must not suffer casualties on the scale of the Somme."

Familiar tensions resurfaced between British and Americans. "The *Sketch* had a big write-up for the Yanks about their attack at Overloon," George Turner-Cain wrote on 19 October. "We had to clear part of the wood for them. Rex took in a couple of platoons, killed about 20 Huns and brought back 17 prisoners. The Yanks had sat looking at the place with a battalion of infantry plus tanks. They appear to sit down opposite the enemy and wait for them to retire, rather than pushing continually. They use an abundance of artillery and air bombardment to break the enemy will to defend, then follow up on the ground." Yet throughout this period Montgomery continued to press for a reinforcement of U.S. divisions to strengthen the British axis of advance. It is hard to overstate the scepticism which these demands provoked among the Americans. "When you analyse how difficult it would have been for the British to accomplish anything, even in the beachhead or coming across France, except where we were pulling them along," said Bradley scathingly after the war, "why would he [Montgomery] think the British would step out and win the war while the Americans stood still? He wanted to take a bunch of Americans to do it with." Bradley's aide Hansen observed not without satisfaction: "The British have had tough going in attempting to clear out Antwerp. They have grabbed a tiger by the tail in attempting to flank the Siegfried line...they know now it cannot be done."

To put the matter bluntly, and in a fashion that would deeply dismay those British and Canadian soldiers who suffered so much "at the sharp end," 21st Army Group's only substantial strategic achievement since the great dash across France and Belgium in August was the clearance of the Antwerp approaches, a task that should have been accomplished at negligible cost early in September. Even if some American commanders such as Patton and Gavin expressed doubts about the determination and skill of their own soldiers, they saw nothing about the British performance in Holland in the winter of 1944 to persuade them that their allies possessed grit or military gifts greater than those of the U.S. Army. The Australian Chester Wilmot, generally an admirer of British rather than American military conduct in north-west Europe, nonetheless observed brutally "what was at this stage the gravest shortcoming of the British army: the reluctance of commanders at all levels to call upon their troops to press on regardless of losses, even in operations which were likely to shorten the war and thus save casualties in the long run."

Freddie de Guingand, Montgomery's Chief of Staff, confided to Admiral Sir Bertram Ramsay on 28 November (according to the admiral's diary) that he was "rather depressed at the state of the war in the west...the SHAEF plan had achieved nothing beyond killing and capturing a lot of Germans, and that we were no nearer to knocking out Germany... The higher direction of the war had been bad in the last 2 months... Ike's policy was only skin-deep and anyone could deflect it." Between the beginning of November and mid-December 1944, British Second Army advanced just ten miles.

LIVING AND DYING

THE WEATHER INFLICTED much misery upon the combatants before the compound of enemy action was added. It was the wettest winter in Holland since 1864. "Some people begin to believe that Our Dear Lord has become pro-Nazi," wrote a Dutch doctor. Incessant rain reduced the battlefield to a quagmire, on which the movement of men and supplies was a Sisyphean task. The concentration of millions of soldiers and hundreds of thousands of trucks and armoured vehicles among the waterlogged fields and woods of north-west Europe made a mockery of mobility. The simplest military operation became a movie translated into slow motion. The living conditions of infantry in the forward positions resembled those of Flanders thirty years earlier. British boots and serge battledress were notoriously pervious to damp. Sodden canvas web equipment stiffened. Mould and rust became endemic. Men snivelled relentlessly, with common colds and 'flu, even without more violent threats to their well-being.

The soldiers of the Western armies were products of modern industrial societies. It is hard to overstate the transition inflicted upon them by warfare. Young men possess remarkable powers of adjustment to new circumstances. British and American soldiers had been expensively trained to endure hardship. But few became wholly inured to battlefield life. They were required to become creatures of the wilderness, perpetual campers and boy scouts, living in foxholes which allowed their occupants to sleep sitting, but seldom to lie prone. Every soldier spent far more time digging than shooting. It required the labour of many weary hours to contrive a hole deep enough to shelter a man effectively from shellfire. Within days of creating such a refuge, he was required to move on and repeat the process. Soldiers performed every natural function in the open; ate clumsy alfresco picnics of nourishing but monotonous food; lived in filthy and often damp clothing that went unwashed for weeks, even months; and were subject to the arbitrary authority of those appointed to lead them. This allowed individuals negligible discretion over their own lives in small things or large, through the seven days of the week and the eleven months of the campaign. Intelligent men found that among the hardest parts of war was the need to accept orders from stupid ones.

Routine was interrupted only by injury, death, spasms of movement from one drab patch of countryside to another or brief periods of rest. Mysteriously, attacks always seemed to be scheduled for Sundays. It became a luxury to enjoy the occasional opportunity to occupy quarters in a ruined building, a few days billeted in a farmhouse or factory. This was a life stripped of privacy and culture, in which men struggled to retain self-respect. A few enjoyed the opportunity to use weapons and to kill people; rather more learned to take pride in soldiering well; but many remained uneasy prisoners of their uniforms. Each day, they were forcing themselves to do things which did not come naturally, and indeed it would have been a tragedy for their societies if it had been otherwise.

Then the enemy took a hand. Mines, booby traps and skilfully sited German guns inflicted a toll on each small advance. There was none of the exhilaration of dashing charges across great swathes of country. Men were permanently filthy and wet, and often frankly demoralized. "There was a change of mood after Arnhem," said Captain "Dim" Robbins. "One just didn't feel the same. We were getting rather tired." One of Lieutenant Roy Dixon's comrades warned him dourly when he joined his unit: "We don't want any Victoria Crosses in this troop." Everyone knew that there would now be no big breakthrough before spring. It seemed a sorry business to risk one's life to attack some battered Dutch hamlet or marshy map reference when the outcome of the war was no longer in doubt. Even when nothing important was being done, there was a relentless round of digging, patrolling and manning positions which could steal a man's life as irretrievably as a big attack.

George Turner-Cain commented ruefully on the aggressiveness of German patrolling, the manner in which the enemy often reoccupied ground which the British thought was cleared. "Dim" Robbins's CO rebuked him for walking upright when German tanks were firing airburst shells among the trees above them. Robbins said: "I'd simply got into a state of mind in which I didn't care any more." A shell fragment hit the officer beside Robbins, decapitating him. The man's head fell into Robbins's hands. He himself was hit in the eye by a splinter, which removed him to hospital almost until the war's end.

Two mornings in succession, Corporal Denis Thomas's Honey light tank dashed down a road to reconnoitre German infantry positions, hosed them with machine-gun fire and returned safely to the British lines. The third day, 6 October, proved once too often. The tank found its usual path blocked by felled trees. On turning right into a village, there was a heavy explosion against the hull, which stopped the engine and severed the electrics—a Panzerfaust impact. The crew bailed out, Thomas more slowly than the others because he was injured in the leg and side. He had to struggle to pull himself over the breech of the gun. Once on the ground, he ran clumsily into a nearby house. He regretted his choice of refuge as soon as he saw a rifle barrel protruding from a window. Then

several Germans clumped in, carrying rations and other booty they had taken
from his tank. At first, they did not see Thomas. He tapped the shoulder of one
man, whose startled hands instinctively shot up in surrender. The injured tank
gunner explained that he was the one who was giving up. An English-speaking
lieutenant appeared, who genially introduced Thomas to the huge soldier who
had fired the faust which crippled the Honey. Then the prisoner was led out of
the back of the house to a motorcycle sidecar which took him to a field hospital.
A German doctor who tended his wounds inquired how old Thomas was. Nineteen, said the Englishman. The doctor shook his head disbelievingly and muttered: "Sixteen." Of the tank's crew, the wireless-operator was also captured.
The lieutenant in command escaped up a drainage ditch. The driver was killed
by "friendly fire" as he sought to re-enter the British lines.

The crusade to liberate Europe, upon which many men of the allied nations
embarked with real idealism in June 1944, had degenerated into a series of sodden local manoeuvres. These roused few expectations among higher commanders, and cynical resignation among those who had to carry them out.
Many men remarked upon the changed mood in Belgium and Holland that
winter, the faltering of the commitment displayed by those who had landed on
the Norman beaches in high summer. "After the airborne operation failed, we
seemed to run out of ideas," remarked Bill Deedes. "We moved very slowly. We
did what Julius Caesar used to do two thousand years earlier—we went into
winter quarters." There was never any open admission by British commanders
that they had abandoned hopes of a breakthrough, but the facts speak for themselves: until the German assault in the Ardennes, 21st Army Group moved
nowhere far or fast.

For those occupying forward positions during the hours of daylight, posi-
tional warfare imposed immobility and boredom, while requiring constant vigilance. Beyond the enemy's line of sight, men laboured on the daily round
of fatigue duties—ration-carrying, washing and repairing vehicles, priming
grenades, filling magazines, cleaning weapons. Intense activity began when
darkness fell. During the hours when civilians slept, soldiers were obliged to
exploit their invisibility. There were trenches to be dug, mines to be laid, units
to be relieved, supplies to be brought forward. Even where there was no gunfire,
the night silence was broken by the muffled thud and clink of spades, subdued
voices and distantly moving vehicles. Patrols were sent out, often across a river
or canal, to probe the German lines and sometimes bring back a prisoner for
intelligence purposes. Each such small operation was a nerve-racking ordeal for
those required to creep in darkness across water-logged countryside, poised
every moment for the explosion of a mine or trip-flare, the rattle of enemy fire.
Men were always tired, because even when there was no great battle to be
fought, the simplest everyday tasks—cooking, finding a tolerable place in which
to sleep, wash, defecate—become major challenges on a battlefield.

Thoughtful men, reared on the tradition of British bungling in the First World War, were pleasantly surprised by the administrative competence of the 1944–45 army, in which mail and rations never failed to appear. It is hard to overstate the importance of letters from home to morale in every theatre of war, and commanders knew it. "I was terribly impressed by the sheer efficiency of everything," said Roy Dixon. "Everybody talks about the chaos of war, but to us it didn't seem that chaotic at all. All the ordinary worries of peacetime life were taken away from us. We simply had to drive our tanks, and fight." Above all, American and British soldiers could take for granted a privilege denied to the rest of Europe—a sufficiency of food.

One of the more squalid manifestations of the presence of more than three million men in open country beyond reach of sanitation and—not infrequently—even of properly dug latrines was the ubiquity of human waste, as well as every other form of garbage. Ammunition boxes, half-empty ration packs, tins, paper, shell cases, signal wire, burned-out vehicles, abandoned foxholes, decaying human body parts, bomb craters, discarded munitions polluted great tracts of Belgium, Holland, France and now also Germany. Most of the metalled roads of Europe were ravaged by the passage of tracked vehicles. Men learned to live in a world of drab camouflaged greens and browns, in which the only primary colours were those momentarily generated by explosives.

"There was something happening all the time," said Edwin Bramall, "but it was all small-scale stuff—patrol actions where you threw a few grenades, lost men on schu-mines, took one or two prisoners. We were advancing inch by inch." Before the chilly grey light of dawn, each side's snipers took up position in front of the lines, commencing motionless observation with binoculars and telescopic sights. It was a cold-blooded business, studying so closely the humdrum activities of men whom it was one's duty to kill. A British sniper watched "Fat Hans," as he christened a portly German private, for several days. The man's routine was always the same. At dawn, he lifted his MG42 machine-gun on to the parapet of his trench and fired a test burst—what Bill Deedes described as "the grim rasp of a spandau clearing its throat." Then Fat Hans stamped backwards and forwards, swinging his arms across his chest in search of warmth—and rashly exposing the top half of his body. One morning a single British rifle bullet terminated his appearances, to the mild regret of those of his enemies who had been diverted by his homeliness.

Even after years of war, some men retained scruples about licensed homicide. "It is believed that certain individuals are not suited for the business of killing," observed a U.S. Army report regretfully. A Swedish soldier of the U.S. 563rd Field Battery practised for months handling his .50 calibre machine-gun. Yet when a Luftwaffe fighter made a rare appearance, flying so low that its pilot's face was visible in the cockpit, the soldier's fingers froze impotent on the trigger of his gun. Lieutenant Peter Downward commanded the sniper platoon of 13 Para. He had never himself killed a man with a rifle, but one day he found himself peering at a German helmet just visible at the corner of an air-raid shelter—an enemy sniper.

> I had his head spot in the middle of my telescopic sight, my safety catch was off, but I simply couldn't press the trigger. I suddenly realised that I had a young man's life in my hands, and for the cost of one round, about twopence, I could wipe out eighteen or nineteen years of human life. My dithering deliberations were brought back to earth with a bump as Kirkbride suddenly shouted: "Go on, sir. Shoot the bastard! He's going to fire again." I pulled the trigger and saw the helmet jerk back. I had obviously got him, and felt completely drained . . . What had I done?

A British report on the autumn fighting showed overall casualty rates per thousand of 7.71 battle; 1.27 accident; 0.05 self-inflicted wounds; 2.06 battle exhaustion. Almost a third of all wounds were caused by shell splinters, 15 per cent by mortars, 30 per cent by gunshot. Blast, burns and mines each accounted for 10 per cent. Mishaps with weapons were a constant source of grief. Corporal Stan Proctor was proudly displaying a captured Luger when it went off, hitting a dispatch rider in the leg. The man fell to the ground moaning: "It hurts, it hurts." An angry sergeant-major said unsympathetically: "You don't expect it to tickle, do you?" Proctor felt deeply embarrassed, because it was his third accident with firearms.

Sometimes it seemed that something more than chance decided a man's fate. Dr. David Tibbs was driving up a snowclad hillside, recovering British dead. With him was a stretcher-bearer, Billy Roper, a pacifist like many of his kind. Roper suddenly cried out: "Please sir, stop, sir!" Tibbs did so. "Why, Billy?" he demanded. "Because the Lord tells me I should, sir," said the man earnestly. Next day, another officer who saw their jeep tracks in the snow reported that they had halted on the edge of a German minefield. God meant a lot to many men of that generation, especially Midwestern Americans. "I could worry every minute of every hour if it were not for my faith and trust in God," Staff-Sergeant Harold Fennema from Wisconsin wrote to his wife. "I know his presence is everywhere, and I have resigned myself to his will. Army life has been and always will be a shroud of uncertainty."

Most of Dr. David Tibbs's work consisted of patching up men for transfer to field hospitals, but he also found himself treating puncture wounds, for which he had little training, and even carrying out tracheotomies. One of the harshest tasks for every battlefield medic was to make an instant judgement about which men might survive and which were hopeless cases. Many doctors gave the latter swift and massive injections of morphine. Bullet wounds were usually clean, but mortar and shell fragments inflicted grotesque injuries. Tibbs was horrified to find himself confronted by one man whose shoulder had been pierced by a falling baulk of timber, which protruded from his chest. He was still alive and conscious, though plainly doomed. Men sometimes shouted aloud: "I'm not going to die! I'm not going to die!," despite having had all the flesh stripped from their lower limbs by blast. No normal soldier ever grows wholly inured to the spectacle of other young men hideously mangled by deliberate human intent.

Almost all soldiers found disposal of the dead a distasteful task. Corporal Iolo Lewis put his hand on a shrivelled body and felt the flesh hardened into carbon, which upset him deeply: "Nothing had prepared me for the smells of war, above all that of roasted flesh. It was very unnerving for a young lad." Corporal Andy Cropper, a tank commander in the Sherwood Rangers, was sent to identify some dead comrades:

> I saw a line of soldiers in uniform, feet towards me. Slowly I walked along searching. Sometimes, I had to step between them to get a better look at a face, half turned away, or a regimental insignia that was partly obscured. None of them appeared to be grossly mutilated. No separate messes here—officers rubbed shoulders with privates, a sergeant-major with a corporal. All had the same waxen pallor, some eyes were closed, some open, but all unseeing. At last, I had found one of the lads—old Harry, who was never on net. I touched him. He was icy cold, and somewhat rigid. Carefully I removed one of his identity discs. I did it as if he were asleep and I didn't want to awaken him. I stood before him for a few seconds. I didn't pray. I didn't think. It wasn't homage really, just a sort of "cheerio, Harry."

Recovering bodies often demanded the collection of mere human fragments, sometimes hanging on bushes and trees. David Tibbs, though a medical officer, recoiled in revulsion from the spectacle of pigs snuffling around the separated torso of a much respected sergeant, who had been leading his company into an attack. "When people ask me what war is like," Tibbs said afterwards, "I tell them to imagine that." Some commanders of fighting units refused to allow their own men to handle corpses, arguing that it damaged morale. The task then fell to Field Hygiene Sections. Sometimes it was impossible to reach the dead for days. Even veterans flinched at bloated corpses, the skin of their fingers swelling green over the nails. Some remains had to be sprayed with oil and creosote before they could be handled, especially if they had been badly burned in armoured brew-ups. During the Scheldt battle, 52nd (Lowland) Division's Reconnaissance Regiment found scores of German dead, who had been lying in the Leopold Canal for a fortnight. Their padre Captain Charles Bradley asked for volunteers to help bury them. Not a man came forward. "That's quite all right," said Bradley mildly, "I do understand."

Shortly afterwards, an astonished soldier reported that the padre was digging graves entirely alone. One by one, men sheepishly drifted over to assist him. When the awful job was done, the priest asked: "Do you mind if we have a little service? I know they are our enemy, and it's through them that we are here. But they all belong to someone. They are all somebody's son, husband or father. They have come and paid the price for their country, as we are paying the price for our country. Whoever they are, everyone deserves a proper burial." Padre Bradley held his service for the German dead.

It was an even worse task to clear human body parts from damaged tanks. In the U.S. 3rd Armored Division, the repair crews one day baulked at addressing a mess of twisted steel and charred flesh which had been towed into the depot. A tall, weedy soldier from the maintenance battalion stepped forward, and surprised his comrades by doing the job single-handed. He said afterwards: "I figured somebody had to do it. I have a younger brother who's a rifleman in 1st Infantry somewhere forward of us. If he was killed, I would like someone to recover his body so it could be given a decent Christian burial." It was hard to remove the lingering stench of death. Maintenance units did their best, by respraying the interior paintwork before handing over a repaired Sherman to a new crew.

Just as in the First World War, infantrymen cherished periods of quiet on their front, and were happy to pursue a policy of "live and let live" with the Germans opposite, especially at night. But most commanders considered it their duty to keep the enemy awake and to dislocate his activities. Thus, unless there was a friendly patrol out in front, in darkness flares were sent up at irregular intervals to illuminate no-man's-land. Machine-guns fired on fixed lines where German troops were likely to be moving. There were spasmodic mortar barrages. The business of attempting to kill your enemy was seldom adjourned for long.

Fear seized men in different ways. Corporal Patrick Hennessy's troops were embarrassed one day when their young officer burst into tears. One wireless-operator would never leave his tank in the forward area, even at night. A sergeant-major bringing up supplies to the tanks, who back in England had seemed a rock-like figure, turned and bolted for the rear in his jeep when German shelling started. In "Dim" Robbins's company, a sergeant-major and his own batman sought to escape action through self-inflicted wounds. He sent both men for court-martial. "All the ones who said before we landed in France 'Can't wait to get at 'em!' turned out to be useless," said Lieutenant Roy Dixon. "We had an ex-boxing blue who ran away." A squadron commander of 2nd Fife & Forfar Yeomanry was dismayed to find one of his men hiding in a barn to escape going into action. The trooper was persuaded to return to duty. Another soldier

narrowly escaped court-martial after leaping out of his tank in action and pelt-
ing towards the rear.

"The British soldier is a little slow-witted," suggested a German intelligence
report of November 1944. "The NCO is for the most part very good. Junior officers are full of theoretical knowledge, but in practice generally clumsy...not
really trained to be independent. The rising scale of casualties has led the
British Command recently to behave more and more cautiously. Favourable situations have not been exploited, since the leadership has not responded to the
new situation quickly enough." The Germans, however, praised British intelligence, reconnaissance, camouflage and ground control of air support. A report
from 10th SS Panzer Division suggested that some recent German attacks had
been compromised by noisy and visible preparations which had attracted
British attention. The most successful tactic in winning ground against Montgomery's men, it concluded, was "an inconspicuous infiltration into an enemy
sector weakly occupied by infantry." Propaganda loudspeakers were deployed
by both sides during static periods. In 15th (Scottish) Division's sector late in
September, a British officer broadcast a brutal running commentary to the German lines during an incoming Typhoon strike. This, he claimed, yielded a useful trickle of prisoners and deserters.

Given the overwhelming Allied superiority of resources, the Germans' psychological dominance of the battlefield was remarkable. A British intelligence
report on the morale of German prisoners, composed after the Scheldt battles,
concluded in some bewilderment: "Few thought that Germany had any hope of
final victory; most had had their fill of fighting and recognised the futility of
continuing the struggle. Nevertheless, they all fought hard. The deduction
would seem to be that no matter how poor the morale of the German soldier
may be, he will fight hard as long as he has leaders to give him orders and see
that they are obeyed." Patrick Hennessy said of the Germans: "We felt they
were more professional than we were." "Dim" Robbins, a career soldier, "always
felt conscious that German small arms were better than ours. And if you spotted a Tiger tank, you simply stopped. They handled those tanks with such dex-
terity and accomplishment, it was fascinating to watch. There was a marked
difference between their performance and ours."

Professor Sir Michael Howard, who possesses the unusual distinction of
being both a military historian and a veteran of combat against the Wehrmacht,
wrote frankly:

Until a very late stage of the war the commanders of British and American
ground forces knew all too well that, in a confrontation with the German
troops on anything approaching equal terms, their own men were likely to
be soundly defeated. They were better than we were: that cannot be
stressed too often. Every Allied soldier involved in fighting the Germans

knew that this was so, and did not regard it as in any way humiliating. We
were amateurs…drawn from peaceful industrial societies with a deep
cultural bias against all things military…fighting the best professionals in
the business…We blasted our way into Europe with a minimum of finesse
and a maximum of high explosive.

For even a modest local attack, the firepower deployed was awesome. Operation Clipper on 18 November involved four battalions of 43rd Division in an
attack on the town of Geilenkirchen. The outlying village of Bauchem was
bombed before 5th Dorsets began their assault. Then ten minutes of artillery
fire delivered forty-nine tons of explosives on to the objectives. Three hours of
mortaring provided a further forty-four tons, together with eighteen tons of
20mm, 40mm and 75mm tank ammunition. All this was followed by thirty minutes of medium artillery fire—73.5 tons of explosive. When the infantry
attacked, they met little resistance and suffered only seven casualties, four of
which were due to British shells falling short. The enemy's positions were found
to be held by 150 demoralized men of 183rd Volksgrenadier Division, mostly
Austrians occupying open trenches. Of these around 15 per cent had been killed
or wounded. Next day, a British battalion attempted a further advance without
a barrage, but halted after suffering eleven casualties and insisted upon waiting
for artillery support. In a subsidiary attack on Bauchem, the 4.2-inch heavy
mortars of 8th Middlesex fired 10,000 bombs in three hours.

Statistics for Clipper highlight the scale of fire support the Allies routinely
employed. They also demonstrate that, while mortar and artillery barrages
could be effective in demoralizing poor-quality enemy troops, they inflicted
remarkably few casualties against men occupying entrenched positions. Finally,
the aftermath of Clipper illustrates the lack of enthusiasm displayed by infantry
for pressing home an attack without massive "softening up." Their psychological dependence upon artillery and air power was very great. And given such
colossal expenditures of ammunition, it is scarcely surprising that there were
chronic shortages. Throughout November and December, British twenty-five-
pounder guns were restricted to forty-five rounds a day. Supplies of medium
artillery ammunition had to be diverted from the Mediterranean. The Americans were in no better case. Allied troops often considered themselves to be suffering heavy German artillery fire, but nowhere on the front in the winter of
1944 did the enemy possess either the guns or the ammunition to match the
weight of British and American fire.

It is sometimes supposed that Allied problems of supply disappeared once
Antwerp was opened. In reality, severe difficulties persisted until late January
1945. Though Antwerp possessed a discharge capacity of at least 80,000 tons a
day, for months stores moved from the dockside to the armies at a much slower

rate. Even in early January, only 10,500 tons a day were being cleared off the quays. The Germans maintained a ferocious V-weapon barrage—between September 1944 and May 1945 nearly 7,000 rockets and flying bombs landed in the city and port, inflicting more than 10,000 casualties, most of them civilian. There was a strike among Belgian dockworkers in January, in pursuit of more rations and better working conditions. As for the rail system, it was easy enough to replace track, but far more difficult and time-consuming to repair French bridges and tunnels systematically destroyed by the air forces before and after D-Day. The Allies burdened themselves with supply requirements which were wildly extravagant by German or Russian standards, but deemed essential to sustain the armies of the democracies. In the autumn and winter of 1944, some U.S. divisions were diverted on their transatlantic passage to holding camps in Britain because the means to support them on the continent were lacking. Vast logjams of rail cars persisted east of Paris, and supply-stock record-keeping remained deplorable. Confidence among the fighting commanders in General Lee's handling of the supply system, which was widely deemed a scandal, remained at rock-bottom. Still Eisenhower would not sack him.

There was a marked contrast in the outlook, background and behaviour of different British regiments. The old county infantry units did their business quietly and without fuss or illusions. They looked askance at aggressively smart cavalrymen like the 13th/18th Hussars, whose commanding officer Lord Feversham, a portly Yorkshire landowner, slept in blue silk pyjamas, and displayed an unaffected reluctance to wake up in the morning. As Feversham fought his way through Holland, he was considering an alternative offer of employment as governor of Madras. His officers' mess was famous for its addiction to high-stakes roulette and chemin-de-fer. General James Gavin remarked of some British units led by professional soldiers: "They seemed to be much more relaxed about the war than we were, and made themselves as comfortable as they could whenever they could ... At times, they seemed to enjoy the war." The attitude noted by Gavin partly reflected a familiar, studied British upper-class nonchalance in adverse circumstances. Yet it is perhaps true that some British soldiers resented the war less than their American counterparts. Brigadier Michael Carver of 4th Armoured Brigade observed: "I just accepted how long it took to finish the business—I was fairly cynical then. This was life for me—it was what I did."

Carver was a professional soldier wholly intolerant of amateurishness or inadequacy in others. He had risen to command an armoured brigade at the age of twenty-seven. He said later: "You couldn't afford to let a man remain in command if he had 'lost it.' I got rid of the CO of the Sharpshooters, who had a DSO and two MCs, when I found him cowering behind a tank, shaking under shell-fire. His regiment had become scruffy and idle." To some, it seemed remarkable that an officer as abrasive in addressing superiors and subordinates escaped dismissal. Carver said unapologetically: "I kept my job because I did it bloody well."

A FEW MILES behind the lines stood the thickets of camouflage-netted tents and vehicles which marked formation headquarters. Every Allied divisional HQ required the services of some 150 men, a corps slightly more, and their German counterparts significantly less. Those who served generals in the rear areas incurred little physical risk, save from the road accidents which took an appalling toll in the theatre of operations. Bradley's 12th Army Group HQ somehow found employment for 5,000 men, and Eisenhower's notoriously bloated staff was three times larger. There were many idle and useless mouths among the "pen-pushers." Yet, for the men at the heart of directing operations, the strain was daunting. There is a myth cherished by some front-line soldiers and amateur students of war that staff officers enjoyed a "cushy" life. Yet those doing the vital operational planning and organization of logistics worked far harder than any peacetime civilian. There were no weekends or holidays, only relentless labour until the small hours of morning, underpinned by awareness that the welfare and indeed survival of hundreds of thousands of men were in their hands.

More than a few senior staff officers succumbed to exhaustion or nervous collapse. Montgomery's Chief of Staff, the highly respected Freddie de Guingand, had to spend several weeks in an English hospital bed in the autumn of 1944. The health of General Sir John Kennedy, British Director of Military Operations, broke down after four years in his post. Most senior commanders worked punishing schedules. Guderian complained that he was sometimes unable to go to bed until 0500 if Hitler was in talkative mood. The German Chief of Staff, a man of fifty-six, had to be at his headquarters again three hours later. Sir Alan Brooke found Churchill's midnight monologues an acute strain. The CIGS was unable to take the afternoon naps favoured by the British prime minister. Most of the men making the vital decisions of the Second World War had been born in the nineteenth century. They were now in their fifties at least, yet obliged to work at a pitch of intensity few civilians of their age could tolerate. "Every day I feel older, more tired, less inclined to face difficulties," Brooke wrote gloomily in his diary. Montgomery, usually among commanders, adhered to a rigorous personal routine which allowed him to go to bed each night at 9:30 p.m. His immediate subordinates were not so fortunate. Chronic exhaustion was as normal a state for generals and staff officers as it was for the young soldiers who did their bidding in waterlogged foxholes.

The horizons of fighting soldiers of all nationalities became entirely bordered by their own company, the view discernible from the parapet of a foxhole.

Most knew the name of the unit's colonel, but few generals registered upon their consciousness. The thoughts of even intelligent and educated men were dominated by tiny matters such as whether the day's rations would contain canned stew, whether the unit might get to a mobile shower unit. "The outside world didn't seem to matter much," observed Bill Deedes. "Every soldier was overwhelmingly preoccupied with getting through the day, and avoiding being killed or wounded. I never remember being very frightened, because I was so preoccupied with doing whatever job I had been given—getting my company to wherever they were supposed to be on time." Opinion was divided over whether family ties at home were a help or an impediment in supporting the strains of battle. Some men believed that it was better to be unattached, but "Dim" Robbins thought that being married with a small daughter helped him a little as a soldier: "There was always someone who was interested in you— somebody you could feel that you were doing this for."

It was a curiosity of the campaign that British newspapers reached men in the front lines, often within forty-eight hours. Many fighting formations published their own modest newssheets, to provide a minimum of information about events outside their own sector, but most men scarcely bothered to read them. A proposal was put forward to produce a British Army newspaper, matching the Americans' *Stars & Stripes.* The British secretary of state for war, Sir James Grigg, commented scornfully to Montgomery on the two journalists who were suggested as its editors: "[Tom] Driberg—Austrian, Jew, Anglo-Catholic, churchwarden, homosexual, communist. Hannen Swaffer is Jew, unwashed near-communist, toady of Beaverbrook." Grigg's tone suggests that he could have enjoyed a congenial dinner-party conversation with the men whom the war was being fought to destroy.

Many British soldiers were both jealous of the Americans' vast resources and sceptical about their allies' manner of fighting a war. "The contrast with our own way of doing things was enormous," said Major John Denison. "They fought in a quite different way, approaching every operation like a gang of builders—very informal. We thought U.S. officers did not look after their men in the way we did. It was sacred in the British Army to ensure that your soldiers got a hot meal every 24 hours." Almost every British soldier resented the power of American wealth in his battered homeland. A private of the Duke of Cornwall's Light Infantry, passing a column of American troops newly arrived from Britain, shouted sourly at them: "How's my wife?"

"The Americans seemed very strange to us, and not terribly friendly," said Lord Carrington. "We asked some of their officers to dinner once, at the time of the Ardennes, and they never even bothered to reply." David Fraser shared his view: "We thought of the Americans without a great deal of respect, as unsoldierly and slovenly. Our views were ill-informed and unfair. The truth was that they had everything we would have liked and didn't have." Corporal Patrick

Hennessy said: "Funny lot the Americans—we felt they were roughly on our side, but we resented the way they lorded it in England." Edwin Bramall, who later became a field-marshal, greatly admired the U.S. Navy and air force, and the specialist arms of the U.S. Army. But he argued: "The Americans are least good at small-unit leadership." There may be some truth in this, but when David Fraser spent time as a liaison officer with the U.S. Airborne, his respect grew. "They did things in a different way from us, but it was impressive. At first I thought their planning left too much in the air, but then I decided that this was a plus. We were too precise about telling people how to do things." British criticisms and resentments were reciprocated, of course, by Americans, who often found the British snobbish, patronizing, slow and lazy. A USAAF pilot arriving to join a squadron in England late in 1944 recorded "a general feeling that the British were no longer pulling their weight in the war." It is less remarkable that these beliefs and tensions existed than that they were overcome to make the alliance work as well as it did.

Thanks to the chronic British shortage of manpower, rear units were combed to provide infantry replacements. Some of those who now found their way unwillingly to rifle companies would never have been accepted for frontline service earlier in the war, and were often poorly trained. "Many men are weak in handling their weapons," reported a company commander. "I know several who did not even know that a grenade had to be primed. Some NCOs cannot map-read, even on roads." While every week brought new American formations into the line, in the British Army battalions and even divisions were being broken up to maintain the strengths of others. This was a painful business for those concerned, given the strong loyalties bred into British soldiers by the regimental system. It was also worrying to those at the summit of command, who saw Britain's order of battle visibly shrinking. Churchill complained testily to Montgomery: "It is very difficult to understand this cutting-up of first-rate units." Platoon commanders, who bore the brunt of officer casualties, were desperately hard to replace. 21st Army Group sent a signal to the adjutant-general late in October: "Deficiencies in infantry officers now such as to seriously prejudice future operations." This provoked a blunt response, asserting that there was no possibility of finding more officers without cannibalizing existing units.

The gulf was almost unimaginably wide, between the life of the front-line soldier and that of hundreds of thousands of supporting troops, manning heavy gun batteries, maintenance depots, post offices, mobile laundries, rear headquarters, signal centres, field hospitals, who faced negligible peril and much lesser discomforts. Staff-Sergeant Harold Fennema from Wisconsin, serving with the U.S. 66th Signal Battalion, wrote to his wife: "I don't think this outfit will ever go anywhere that might be dangerous. I'm not at all sorry about it, because I want to come home in one piece." Stan Proctor, a brigade headquarters wireless-operator with 43rd (Wessex) Division, wrote in his diary, at a time when bitter fighting was taking place further forward: "A very pleasant day. Signals Office duty in the morning, and an afternoon relaxing with the Heynens girls...sold 250 cigarettes for 25 guilders...to see Bing Crosby in *Going My Way*." Proctor was disconcerted to be told that his services were required with an infantry battalion. He protested vociferously, pointing out that while he had already served time with a line unit, others had served continuously at headquarters since D-Day: "I had by this time lost the wish for the comradeship with the infantryman...My time at Brigade had been during some of the quieter spells. Now that things were going to hot up, I was to go back. I objected—to the extent of offering back my stripe, but it made no difference."

When front-line soldiers escaped from imminent peril for a few hours, their desires were usually pathetically simple. Soldiers talk much about women, but on the battlefield their private cravings are seldom sexual. A British officer described his men's priorities as "char, wad, flick and kip"—tea, food, a movie and sleep. "We thought about girls much less than about food and sleep in a bed," said Edwin Bramall. Once out of the line for a time, however, women and alcohol became obvious magnets for many men. Visiting a brothel offered the most realistic prospect of sexual congress. A post-war U.S. Army report on the disciplinary difficulties of controlling rape deplored the fact that brothels were officially off-limits to GIs. The same establishments which had serviced the German Army during its occupation now welcomed the Allies. Green crosses by day and green lights by night guided soldiers to condom-issuing stations, which did not prevent the U.S. Third Army from achieving an average monthly VD rate of 12.41 per 1,000, comfortably exceeded by the Canadian score of 54.6 per 1,000. In a nice exercise of official hypocrisy by the British Army, it was adjudged a moral bridge too far for medical officers to undertake inspections of prostitutes. The incidence of venereal disease among all troops rose sharply after the liberation of France and Belgium where, as a disciplinary report observed sardonically, "the civil population accorded the army a comprehensive welcome."

As the relentless rain of autumn gave way to winter ice and snow, it was hard for British officers, as well as their men, to escape despondency. Far from ending the war in 1944, there were now fears that the Germans might be capable of protracting their resistance through 1945, a shocking prospect. "There is a feeling of optimism at SHAEF," Montgomery wrote to Brooke on 21 November. "There are no grounds for such optimism." A gloomy 21st Army Group assessment on 24 November emphasized the steady arrival of German reinforcements, and the natural strength of many hostile terrain features: "Let us therefore face a situation in which the enemy gets stronger every day. His strategic reserve is very limited, and he is in doubt where to use it first." Two days later, Montgomery's staff estimated German strength in the west at seventy-one weak divisions, equivalent to thirty-five full-strength formations: "This is a larger total than we have had to face for many a long while." Most of the allied soldiers who landed in France on 6 June and in the weeks thereafter were imbued with a sense of mission, even crusade. Now, however, this had been displaced by mere acknowledgement of a bloody task to be completed, and if possible survived.

CHAPTER SIX

Germany Besieged

SHADOWS OF DEFEAT

MOST OF THE German people had not wanted war in 1939, but gained greater satisfaction than they expected from the early years of victory. Lieutenant Leopold Goesse, a young Austrian cavalry officer, thoroughly enjoyed the 1940 Norway campaign, in which finally he watched British soldiers fleeing to their boats. Heinz Knoke, a Luftwaffe fighter pilot, felt himself "enraptured" by an encounter with his triumphant Führer in December 1940. When Knoke heard rumours of the impending German invasion of Russia in June 1941, he wrote in his diary: "The idea appeals to me. Bolshevism is the arch-enemy of Europe and of European civilization." Eleonore Burgsdorf and her family filled the cellars of their home in East Prussia with Scotch whisky, French cognac and champagne brought to them as presents by the heroes of Germany's campaigns in the west. Many German soldiers revelled in Paris leaves, and rejoiced at their distant glimpse of Moscow.

All sensations of that kind perished, however, with Stalingrad. By the winter of 1944, the reality of war seeped into almost every corner of the Reich. Few households had been spared some personal sacrifice to the demented ambitions of Adolf Hitler. It was a custom in bereaved German families to distribute among friends a black-bordered memorial card, bearing a photograph and brief details of a lost son. Millions of such souvenirs of death now stood above fireplaces in millions of homes. Katharina Minniger, a twenty-two-year-old from the village of Hausach in the Schwartzwald, lost her brother Ludwig soon after Stalingrad. Her parents sent out the customary tokens of remembrance for him. Over the two years that followed, she was dismayed to see the neatly printed cards arrive again and again to mark the passing of old schoolfriends: "Joseph Mehrfeld—Stalingrad"; "Victor Mehrfeld—Stalingrad"; "Willi Enders—lost on a ship to Africa"; "Willi Webers—died Eastern Front aged 19.5," and likewise for many more. Lieutenant Helmut Schmidt, a Luftwaffe flak officer, now believed that when the Allies completed their triumph all Germans of working age would be deported to become slaves in Russia. Eighteen-year-old Klaus Salzer, a tall, serious, classically handsome middle-class Königsberger, was unwillingly conscripted to the paratroops in October 1944. As the boy left home, he lingered in the hall, gazing at its heavy, familiar furniture. "Why are you looking at everything like that?" demanded his mother. "Because I shall never see it all again," said Klaus sadly. Indeed he did not, for he was killed in action a few months later.

"The vain hope that the war would end before Christmas 1944 faded out as the autumn dragged along," wrote Paul von Stemann, a Danish correspondent in Berlin. Rationing tightened: "housewives counted potatoes as if they were gold nuggets." The fat porter at the city's grand Esplanade Hotel began to look like a circus clown, his uniform hanging in loose folds on his shrunken frame. Smart folk drank a lot, because there was little else to do—no books to buy, no films or theatres to visit, no sport or radio entertainment or social life. Privileged people seized opportunities to escape to the countryside for weekends. Yet even in great houses the small talk was bleak. When von Stemann went to stay with friends in Bavaria and asked his hostess how life was treating her, she responded tersely: "My uncle was hanged the other day." This was Berlin Police President Graf Wolf Heinrich von Helldorff, one of the July plotters against Hitler.* "Missie" Vassiltchikov, a young White Russian aristocrat who maintained a diary of wartime life in Berlin, shocked her old cook Martha by dossing down on one sofa in the drawing room one night, while a young man slept on another. *"In meiner Jugend kam so etwas nicht vor, aber dieser 20. Juli stellt alles aus den Kopf!"* sniffed Martha, "In my young days that couldn't have happened, but this 20 July has turned everything topsy-turvy." So it had for Missie Vassiltchikov, some of whose closest friends had already been executed.

Even in the face of looming catastrophe, most German civilians focused their minds upon the small details of their own daily lives, because that is human nature. Maria Hustreiter was troubled by the difficulty of getting shoes. She was a fourteen-year-old small farmer's daughter living at Landshut, thirty miles north-east of Munich. In the country, there was usually enough to eat. The household received a steady stream of city visitors, who walked miles to farmhouse doors hoping to barter their household goods for food. The people of Landshut were all conscious of the town's only Jew, a kettle-seller. Somehow, in that isolated rural community, the man was left alone to survive the war, which afterwards became a source of relief and even pride to his neighbours.

---

*On 20 July 1944, Colonel Claus von Stauffenberg planted a bomb in a briefcase during a meeting at Hitler's headquarters, before returning to Berlin to participate in a poorly organized military coup. Hitler suffered severe shock but only superficial injuries when the bomb exploded, while the coup was quickly and ruthlessly suppressed. Investigations, purges, trials and executions of actual and supposed plotters continued until the end of the war.

Maria's two elder brothers were in the army. Her mother prayed constantly to Our Lady for their deliverance, but one would never return.

There was church every Sunday and the inevitable Nazi school parades, but no parties, no dancing. In that simple community in those simple days, she was too young to think about boys. Two French prisoners, amiable young men, lived with them and helped to till their eighty acres. The family knew very little about events beyond their small world. "I understood that the war was not good, but life went on." Her immediate awareness of the conflict stemmed from watching the distant glow of Munich, Regensburg, Nuremberg, lit up by flames under bombing. Sometimes, the family found their fields littered with "window," the tinfoil strips dropped by Allied planes to baffle German radar. There was once a terrible time after a big raid, when the railway was cut. A train loaded with livestock en route to the slaughterhouse in Munich was obliged to halt for days on the track beside the Hustreiter farm. The sounds of pigs squealing and cattle lowing in despair haunted even a country girl like Maria, familiar with the traumas of animals.

The countryside was full of evacuees from the bombed cities. Ten-year-old Jutta Dietze from Leipzig lived on a farm in Saxony with her mother and three siblings for more than a year after their home was destroyed. They were expected to work hard in the fields, for the local farmers tolerated rather than welcomed their uninvited guests. They ate each day at a big table among a mixed gathering of French PoWs from a nearby camp and Russian labourers who slept above the stables. The bathroom of the farmhouse was crammed with every kind of household valuable from carpets to grandfather clocks, bartered for food by families who had trudged out from nearby Chemnitz. Unsurprisingly, the children adapted to their new circumstances more easily than the adults. Dietze family photographs of the period show the young ones grinning cheerfully as they posed among the animals in their rural idyll, even as Germany plunged towards final disaster.

Cities in the east of the country, hitherto immune from air attack, were now experiencing the devastating bombardments with which western Germany was already familiar. The tempo of destruction increased relentlessly. A Darmstadt housewife wrote to her husband at the front after a raid by the RAF's 5 Group on 12 September which precipitated a firestorm and killed 12,000 people: "This is now a dead town." Another woman reported from Wiesbaden: "13 full alerts and 18 warnings last week. We all broke down. 13 people were killed in one shelter." Emmy Suppanz wrote to her son from Marburg on 23 November: "Yesterday, against my will I had to go through one part of the town. Sepp, it was dreadful. Luckily I didn't have to go through the quarter where the station is, for it is said to be much worse there... Everyone is now talking such a lot about the new weapons, even Karl-Ludwig who is usually so discreet, so perhaps they really will come soon. Do you still believe in them?"

The first time Melany Borck, a sixteen-year-old evacuee in Schleswig-Holstein, saw British bombers' pyrotechnic markers drift down through the night sky towards Hamburg fifteen miles away, she merely watched curiously, without great emotion. When a burning British aircraft plunged into the sea nearby, she and her parents, watching, felt a shock of revulsion untinged by partisan satisfaction. "We simply said: 'Oh, my God.'" Yet with each month, their own circumstances worsened. They found that the experience of war made everyone abandon thought for the future. Like *Frontsoldaten*, they occupied themselves solely with demands of the moment: how to find food for the next meal, bandages for the next trainload of wounded arriving at the local hospital, electricity to cook with, space to sleep in a house crammed with twenty-two evacuees and refugees. As the horrors increased, everyone in Melany's small world became imbued, like the rest of Germany, with the same desperate yearning: "Please God, let it be over." There was one significant variation of this sentiment: some Germans yearned for peace on any terms; others still craved victory, and believed that this might be attained.

Every domestic radio set manufactured in Germany during the war bore a notice warning, "DO NOT TUNE TO FOREIGN STATIONS!," but many people did. Fourteen-year-old Eggert Stolten's mother was an ardent Nazi. She did not try to stop her son listening to the BBC and Radio Switzerland, but instead maintained a withering commentary on the statistics given by the British for the distances the Allies had supposedly advanced, and the prisoners they had captured. "It's lies, all lies!" said Frau Stolten. "Our numbers are the right ones!" She was immensely proud of having become a Party member before 1933. "We wanted to change things," she told her son. Eggert Stolten said: "Nobody's morale was broken by bombing. Everybody just thought: 'Those murdering bastards!'" Nonetheless, in their local shelter in Düsseldorf during the raids, when people were thinking rather more about God than about their Führer, some people objected to the big poster of Adolf Hitler on the wall, observing uneasily: "We don't like seeing him down here." One of the first big RAF raids on the Ruhr destroyed the Stoltens' new house and obliged them to go and live deep in the countryside of Thuringia. Yet being "de-housed"—as that apostle of area bombing Lord Cherwell categorized the German family's experience—did nothing to diminish Frau Stolten's unshakeable faith in victory.

What seems noteworthy is not how many people found the war terrible, but how many—especially at the humbler end of the social spectrum—still found life tolerable, almost until the end. Regina Krakowick lost everything when her Berlin flat was bombed in 1943, but she and her husband retained an impressive capacity to enjoy themselves. Johannes was a tailor, whom a bone-marrow deficiency rendered unfit for military service. The couple thought this a wonderful piece of good fortune, though because Johannes was tall and handsome and apparently healthy he incurred spiteful comment from people who did not know his medical history. The couple were regular play- and movie-goers as long as the theatres stayed open. They continued to entertain enthusiastically almost to the end. They saved up rations for weeks for their parties, at which Johannes's sister Louise played the accordion and the hosts produced their hoarded quota of schnapps. Until the first weeks of 1945, there always seemed to be just enough to eat, with some help from a family vegetable plot on the edge of the city. "We knew nothing about politics," said Regina, who was twenty-five, "but we went on hoping for final victory, because we could not conceive of what would happen to Germany if she lost the war."

Shortages of all kinds were endemic. There was no shoe polish, little to read. Clothes were scarce, both for civilians and soldiers. Over 300,000 volunteers worked in 60,000 collection centres around the country, receiving donations of clothing for soldiers and refugees. "The 'people's sacrifice' demands of us that we hand over everything we do not use every day," an official circular exhorted. "It is not enough to give up old clothing, or a few rags." Yet, even after Goebbels banned publication of almost all books as an economy measure, a torrent of Nazi propaganda material continued to flow. Men of the U.S. 9th Infantry Division were bemused to find in a German house a new children's book entitled *Mama, Tell Me About Hitler,* which dwelt enthusiastically upon the SS "and that beautiful black uniform which we love so well." "Faithful to the Führer, loyal to the death," Germans were urged to sing, "He will lead us one day, out of this distress." The record of Germany's churchmen throughout the Nazi era was indifferent, to say the least. Yet it seems remarkable that a priest of any kind could be found to deliver the German Army's prayer, that mockery of Christianity:

Your hand, O God, rules over all empires and nations on this earth
In your goodness and strength bless our German nation
And infuse in our hearts love of our Fatherland.
May we be a generation of heroes . . .
Especially bless our Führer and commander-in-chief in all the tasks
    which are laid upon him.

In the wake of the army's bomb plot against Hitler in July 1944, treachery real or suspected had become an obsession within the Third Reich. Most Germans, whether on the battlefield or at home, perceived no possibility of escaping their fate. But German diplomats stationed in neutral countries, often with their families, possessed exceptional opportunities to vote with their feet. In November 1944, Himmler sent a scornful memorandum to the foreign minister, von Ribbentrop, about "negative tendencies" within his ministry: "We are getting more and more reports of betrayals of the state." There was Dr. Zechlin of the Madrid embassy, a known anti-Nazi who had refused repeated orders for his recall, and was now apparently ensconced in a Spanish monastery. Germany's Madrid ambassador, Dr. von Deberlein, was married to a Spaniard and defiantly declined to return to Berlin. Consul Schwinner in Lausanne was reported as having declared publicly that the Soviet Union was a peaceful country, invaded by Germany. Schwinner had since vanished. Dr. Krauel, consul in Geneva, likewise acknowledged in a letter home that "he had no intention of returning to the lion's den." Krauel was summoned back to Berlin, but instead settled down at a Swiss sanatorium. Himmler quoted complaints from the Propaganda Ministry that Germany's foreign policy "seems moribund."

In the rhetoric of the Nazis that winter, it is striking to notice how often "fanatical"—a pejorative word in the eyes of Americans or Englishmen—was used as a term of approbation by everyone from Hitler downwards. "I have never before seen such a wholesale use of 'fanatical' and 'fanaticism'... the word is repeated in every article," noted Victor Klemperer as he read his Sunday paper in Dresden that October. A local gauleiter issued a proclamation to the people of one city threatened with imminent allied occupation:

> When the enemy reaches the German positions in the West, let him be met with our fanatical resistance... The eyes of our children, who want to see a future, plead for us to resist to the last breath... The voices of hundreds of thousands who have died on the battlefield for the honour and freedom of the Fatherland, or lost their lives through enemy terror attacks from the air, cry out to us. The spirit of fighters for freedom throughout our glorious history implore us not to weaken or to show cowardice at this decisive moment in our struggle for survival.

The order was given for every available man between sixteen and sixty to report for duty digging defences, while the remainder of the city's population was to be evacuated.

In addition to nightly air-raid duties, millions of boys and elderly men were now spending six hours a week training with their local Volkssturm home defence units, usually in icy huts or warehouses. They practised judging distances, deployment in open order and simple infantry tactics. All of this seemed worthless, however, when arms were chronically short. "What is lacking is familiarity with weapons," a disgruntled Volkssturm father wrote to his son at the front. This was a deficiency that would never be fully remedied. Among the elderly, there was no eagerness to die in the futile defence of one's town or village. The dangerous people were the children, whose entire conscious lives had been spent under Nazism. Goebbels had succeeded all too well with a generation of young Germans. A dreadful number were now ready to sacrifice themselves, ancient rifle or Panzerfaust in hand, in a rite of passage which they embraced with awful enthusiasm.

Helmut Fromm, who was serving as a teenage telephonist with a flak battery outside Heidelberg, once went to the cinema with some fellow gunners. They were in the midst of watching a movie entitled *Der Katzenstag* when the manager appeared at the end of their row, and ordered them out. "This film is not for young people," he said sternly. Back at the battery, the boys pinned up a notice beside their 88mm gun proclaiming "This is not for young people." Fromm, who had already been wounded by a near-miss from a British bomb, observed that it was typical of the Nazis to allow you to die for the fatherland at sixteen, but not to watch adult movies until you were eighteen. A friend of his old headmaster, a major on the General Staff, said to Fromm crossly: "You should be doing your exams, not going to the front." Yet the bespectacled boy soon afterwards found himself posted to an infantry regiment in Poland.

For the average German family, the cost of living had risen by some 13 per cent since 1939. Rural people seldom went hungry, but city-dwellers found it difficult to buy an increasing range of commodities, on or off ration. The bread allowance did not much diminish throughout the war, until April 1945. But a weekly allocation of 400 grams of meat in June 1941 had fallen to 362 grams in 1944, and would descend to 156 grams in February 1945. The fats ration, 269 grams a week in June 1941, fell to 156 grams by January 1945. "Well, my dear Hans," Julius Legmann of Zittau in Saxony wrote in October to an NCO friend at the front, "we were very glad to learn from your letter that you are well and fit, and also that all you good fellows in the army are well fed and not getting such dreary food as we do in the homeland ... Here it's a case of a lot of work and not much to eat ... We should like something with some fat in it for once in a way, instead of just potatoes with nothing to go with them."

Albert Speer, as armaments minister, was still accomplishing monthly miracles. In October 1944, Germany built more than five tanks and assault guns for each one that had been manufactured in January 1942. Production even increased towards the end of the year, as winter weather hampered Allied bombing. Yet after the war, amid Speer's orgy of self-abasement, he acknowledged the recklessness of his forecasts, especially those concerning future aircraft production. He perceived "something grotesque" about his efforts in the last months of the war to convince subordinates that new industrial exertions might yet arrest the Allied tide. As factories were destroyed by bombing and sources of raw materials were overrun by the Russians, production would inexorably shrink. It was one of the paradoxes of the Second World War that, while Speer directed industry to tremendous effect, Germany's war economy was incomparably less efficient than those of the Allies, including Russia's. The efforts of some brilliant managers and industrialists, the dogged achievements of their workforces, were set at naught by massive policy failures. Speer's performance was less remarkable in overcoming difficulties created by Allied bombing and raw-material shortages than in surmounting the follies of Hitler, Himmler and Göring. Contrary to widely accepted myth, the German war economy was a shambles. It is frightening to contemplate the consequences had it been otherwise.

The Greater German Reich created by Hitler embraced a population of 116 million people and an area of 344,000 square miles including much of Poland and Czechoslovakia, together with Alsace-Lorraine. Yet German industry had become heavily dependent upon foreign labour: 28.6 million German factory workers—14.1 million men, 14.5 million women—now required the support of 7.8 million foreigners, and still there were never enough hands at the lathes and assembly lines (not surprising, one might think, when to sustain morale the Nazis encouraged Germans to retain their domestic servants, of whom almost a million and a half were still butlering and maiding to the very end). Some of the foreign workers were volunteers, who had come to Germany in search of higher wages than they could hope to earn in their own occupied countries. Most, however, were forced labourers, rounded up in tens of thousands by German troops in France, Poland, Russia and every other nation under Nazi domination, for shipment under guard to Germany. The failure to exploit their individual skills, the policy of treating them merely as working animals—sending the biggest and fittest to the mines, for instance—was one of the most serious mistakes of Hitler's war economy.

Though all the labourers suffered hunger, the intensity of their sufferings varied immensely. The west Europeans were treated far better than the peoples from the east, whose plight will be examined below. In addition, German industry and agriculture were bolstered by 1.8 million prisoners of war. By 1945 imported workers of one kind or another made up a fifth of Germany's entire civilian labour force. Almost every community and farm in Germany possessed its quota of enemy aliens, some resigned to their lot, many treated as neither more nor less than slaves. Without them the German war economy would have collapsed long before it did. Since the Germans troubled themselves little about protecting PoWs and foreign workers from air raids, allied bombing killed thousands of such Nazi captives. A statistical breakdown of 8,000 victims of the catastrophic RAF raid on Darmstadt in September 1944 showed that 936 were military personnel; 1,766 were male civilians, 2,742 female; 2,129 children; 368 prisoners of war; and 492 foreign labourers. These proportions were approximately replicated in every German city which suffered bombardment. The RAF's legendary Dambusters' raid in 1943 killed 147 Germans, together with 712 prisoners of war and foreign labourers, 493 of these Ukrainian women. Among 720 victims of a typical RAF raid on Berlin, 249 were slave labourers permitted no access to shelters.

Above all, Germany faced a desperate shortage of fuel. The loss of eastern oilfields to the Soviets, together with American bombing, had imposed upon Hitler's empire a crisis that was strangling the training of pilots, the deployment of armies, even the movement of tanks on the battlefield. Charcoal-driven cars, trucks and buses, together with horses and carts, had replaced petrol-fuelled transport throughout Germany, for everyone save the armed forces and the Nazi bureaucracy. Allied assaults on communications imposed chronic delay on all train journeys. Astonishingly, however, so dense was the rail net that until the spring of 1945 it remained possible to travel by train across the country for anyone willing to endure interruptions, diversions and sometimes Allied strafing. German soldiers continued to receive rations and mail in the most desperate circumstances. "It was fantastic how well the logistical arrangements worked, almost to the end," observed Lieutenant Rolf-Helmut Schröder.

One of the few merits of Germany's vastly shortened lines of communication was that many soldiers now received mail from home a week after it was posted, rather than a month or more, as was commonplace in the days when Hitler's frontiers extended to the Balkans and the Crimea. Any benefit that correspondence may have rendered to men's morale was undone, however, by the nature of the tidings which Germany's defenders received from their loved ones. Corporal Rudolf Pauli was sent a letter by his fiancée in Hornsburg on 5 October: "Since last night, our Adelheid is pretty nervy. As soon as she hears the drone of a plane, she runs as fast as she can. Privately, I had always hoped the war would end this year, but I have now given up on that. It seems that the war will go on for ever. There will be no peace until everything is destroyed."

Many civilians, even in areas such as East Prussia and Silesia, which now lay close to the Red Army, found it difficult to comprehend the notion that their entire world was on the verge of extinction, that the streets in which they shopped, the farms on which they milked cows, the communities in which they had lived their lives, would forever be destroyed within a matter of months. It was hard for any ordinary person to discover the truth. And what was truth, anyway? An alarming number of German people retained some hope that the Führer's promised "wonder weapons" might yet avert defeat; that fissures among the Allies would undo Germany's oppressors. Many Germans found it unthinkable that the Western allies, fellow citizens of a civilized universe, would allow their country to be delivered into the clutches of Stalin's barbarian hordes. Few German civilians felt shame or guilt about what their nation had done to Europe. Instead, more than a decade of the most brilliantly orchestrated propaganda culture in history had imbued almost all, young and old, with a profound sense of grievance towards their country's enemies and invaders, a passionate resentment against the Allied armies and air forces. Germany's enemies were now destroying centuries of culture through bombing, while assisting the Red Army to reach the very frontiers of the Reich. As to such matters as concentration camps, Jews or even the plight of slave labourers who worked in factories within daily sight of the civilian workforce, most people shrugged that this was the regrettable order of things forced upon Germany by her persecutors.

"There was no guilt about what Germany had done in the world—or only a very little, at the very end," observed Gotz Bergander, a Dresden teenager who became a post-war historian. "They said: 'Who started this war? Germany was only defending itself.'" A collective self-pity underpinned German behaviour in the last phase of the conflict, embracing all from Adolf Hitler to the humblest civilian. Bergander, an uncommonly thoughtful young man, once observed to a friend that everywhere the Germans had gone in Europe they had been uninvited. His friend shrugged: "That's the way war is." Bergander said afterwards: "Everyone was convinced that we were surrounded by enemies." He and his family listened avidly, if perilously, to the BBC. He heard the famous "black propaganda" broadcasts of the British journalist Sefton Delmer, and—far more effectively from the Allied viewpoint—Glenn Miller and Benny Goodman. To young Bergander, American music possessed the status of holy writ. He thought: people who can make music like this must win the war. The cultural life which had meant so much to the Dresden teenager was being stifled month by month in the winter of 1944. Opera and ballet houses closed, as artistes were drafted for labour service. Most hotels abandoned their usual musical entertainments. Cafés still flourished, however. Piano and poetry recitals continued until a late stage.

On 3 December 1944, Hitler surprised his circle by leaving the Reich Chancellery to take tea with the Goebbels family in their home at 20 Hermann Göring Strasse. Goebbels, according to his aide Rudolf Semmler, "stood to attention with his arm stretched out as far as it would go." The children, dressed up for the occasion in long gowns made from curtain fabric, curtsied prettily. The Führer complimented their mother on how much they had grown. He presented Frau Goebbels with a small bunch of lily-of-the-valley, explaining apologetically that this was the best he could do, since her husband had closed all Berlin's flower shops. Semmler noticed a thermos protruding from the briefcase inscribed with a large painted white "F," and realized that Hitler, by now terrified of poison, had brought his own refreshments. But the occasion was a great social success, and delighted the hosts. "He wouldn't have gone to the Görings," observed Magda Goebbels smugly. It was one of the last events of her life which gave unmingled satisfaction to this doomed, unboundedly foolish woman.

SOLDIERS

AFTER THE FAILURE of the July bomb plot against Hitler few officers, far less ordinary soldiers, contemplated revolt. "Most Germans realized that it was necessary to end the war—but still they did not want to lose it," a German historian observes. "The July plot had made Hitler seem immortal. Ironically, it increased his authority rather than weakened it." Dr. Karl-Ludwig Mahlo, a twenty-nine-year-old Luftwaffe doctor, endorsed this view: "After 20 July," he said, "we felt that it must be Hitler's destiny to survive. We really believed in him. Hitler did a lot for me. I had a wonderful youth. We were young, we were so much indoctrinated by propaganda, by the years of victory reports. Afterwards, people said: 'How could you have believed in this man?' Yet we did—totally." Mahlo was disturbed, however, when some Luftwaffe comrades returned from a 1944 Berlin medal presentation by Hitler to report tersely: "He looks terrible."

In the smart Grossdeutschland Division, officers and men reflected a wide political spectrum. "There were some serious Nazis—especially those who had attended the Adolf Hitler schools," said Lieutenant Tony Saurma. But most thought little about politics, only about the survival of Germany—and of themselves. After the July plot, the commanding officer warned Saurma, son of a Silesian aristocratic family: "You blue-blooded types had better be careful now, or you'll find yourself in trouble." Saurma's uncle had already been imprisoned for his alleged role in the anti-Nazi Resistance. "I think you'd better write a letter to Dr. Goebbels," Colonel Willi Lankeit told Saurma thoughtfully. The young officer indeed wrote to the propaganda minister, who was known slightly to the Grossdeutschland's commander, assuring him of his loyalty to Germany's rulers.

"We retained some illusions," said Lieutenant Rolf-Helmut Schröder of the 18th Volksgrenadiers. "We thought it impossible that the Americans would allow the Russians to sweep Europe. We thought that, when the Americans had defeated us, they would turn on the Russians. And we believed that we must do everything possible to prevent Russia from overrunning our country." Schröder was the son of a prominent anti-Nazi retired officer, who had died in 1935. Yet he argued that even the Waffen SS were motivated by patriotism rather than ideology: "12th SS Panzer's men were always said to have been 'fanatical young Nazis,' but this was not so. I knew those people. They were fighting for Germany, not for Hitler." Luftwaffe ace Heinz Knoke was appalled by the July bomb plot: "The ordinary German fighting soldiers regard the unsuccessful revolt as treason of the most infamous kind." Major Karl-Günther von Hase was a scion of an old Pomeranian military family. He joined the army in 1936, "believing that I could pursue a military career without thinking of politics." He learned differently after the July plot. The Nazis hanged his father, military commandant of Berlin, as a leading participant. Yet, even after this horror, von Hase considered that it was his own duty to fight in defence of Germany to the end. He retained a deep professional respect for the Waffen SS: "We always liked to have them on our flanks, because we knew how good they were."

The condition of the nation's soldiers was worse than that of the civilians in one important sense. They knew more. From personal experience, the men fighting along almost 2,000 miles of front in the east, 700 miles in the west, had grown familiar with the overwhelming might of the Allied armies. All save the dedicated Nazis knew that their nation retained scant hope of military victory. Beyond this, every man who had served in the east knew what Germany had done to the Soviet Union, and what manner of enemies were the Russian people. German soldiers could anticipate the retribution that would fall upon their *Heimat,* or homeland, their own families and loved ones, if the Red Army reached them. The Allied commitment to accept nothing less than Germany's unconditional surrender, rejecting all negotiation of terms, together with the revelation of the American Morgenthau Plan for the post-war pastoralization of Germany—reducing Hitler's people to a nation of peasants, stripped of industrial capacity—had provided Goebbels with a propaganda feast. "The Jew Morgenthau sings the same tune as the Jews in the Kremlin," trumpeted Berlin Radio. A characteristic German fatalism about their nation's march to destruction persuaded most men of the Wehrmacht that there was no alternative save to fight on until they were released by death or the good fortune of Anglo-American captivity.

Wilhelm Pritz, an infantry sergeant, spent the autumn of 1944 in a military hospital in Germany, praying that he would not have to return to the Eastern Front. He had gone to Russia for the first time in April 1942, and was wounded by mortar fragments during the assault on Sebastopol. After some months in hospital, he rejoined his unit on the Volga in March 1943: "Almost everyone I knew was gone. They were very short of men." He contracted frostbite in the trenches, which cost him another two months in hospital, followed by a spell as an instructor at an infantry training centre. In the autumn of 1943, he was sent to the Ukraine. One of four sons of a Coblenz factory worker, he had by now lost one brother killed in Russia, while a second brother was missing and would never return: "my parents prayed that I would not have to go east again." In October 1943, he was among German forces encircled and cut off in their bridgehead on the Dnieper Bend. Pritz was manning an anti-tank gun when a Russian grenade exploded against the shield. A fragment knocked out two of his teeth. As he fled towards the river, grenade splinters wounded him in the back. His colonel, a ferocious fighter, stood raging among the carnage: "Why are you running, you miserable cowards? Where are your rifles?" The Russians clubbed the colonel to death when they overran his position.

Pritz and hundreds of others swam the Dnieper amid Russian fire, the water red with blood. On the western bank, he walked for three hours under Russian shelling among hundreds of men in similar condition, before reaching a field hospital. His wounds were not serious, and he was soon returned to duty. On 1 November, however, a Russian sniper inflicted a scalp wound which kept him in hospital until January. Then he was sent to southern Poland, for several terrible months of hand-to-hand fighting and headlong retreats, serving among men of whom he knew nothing and whose morale was at rock-bottom. On 19 August 1944, in the midst of an enemy attack Pritz raised his hand above the lip of a foxhole to seize his rifle at exactly the moment a Soviet grenade exploded near by, tearing open his arm.

A comrade used his neck scarf to make a tourniquet. Bleeding heavily, Pritz crawled away through an immense field of sunflowers, enemy machine-gun fire slashing through the blooms above his head. He hitched a ride on an ammunition truck to the battalion mess area, where some men were sitting eating goulash. He sat down shakily, and himself began to eat. Then came a storm of mortar and small-arms fire, and the Russians were upon them again. The dazed Pritz was helped on to a cart with the cooks. He preserved only shadowy memories of the hours that followed, as a great column of refugees and retreating soldiers trudged east under constant fire. At one point, German Nebelwerfers systematically blew a path through the refugees for the troops. The wounded soldier finally lost consciousness, and awoke in hospital.

When Pritz was discharged, his prayers to escape the east were answered. In October 1944, he was drafted to a heavy mortar unit confronting the Americans in the Saarland. After Russia, he found the posting "a vacation." His experience is not unrepresentative of that of the German soldier of the period, save that he survived. He possessed no pretensions to heroism. He simply continued to obey orders, as he had learned to do since his childhood in the Hitler Youth. In the autumn of 1944, the frontiers of Germany were being defended by a few hundred thousand genuine Nazi zealots, and millions of men like Wilhelm Pritz. A veteran of twenty-two who had known horrors no man should have to see, he now yearned only for survival.

For all its ferocious discipline and draconian punishments, however, the German Army was increasingly troubled by the problem of desertion. An order of 20 November issued by 708th Division in Alsace warned that any unit which posted "missing" figures in excess of 25 per cent after a battle would be subjected to special investigation. Many Alsatians serving in the Wehrmacht seized the opportunity granted by proximity to their homes to slip away. There was a row when it was discovered that a company commander in 352nd Volksgrenadier Division had written to the families of six of his men who were missing, believed to be Allied prisoners, saying: "The Americans opposite us have been fighting fairly, they have treated German prisoners well and fed them. If your husband is a PoW, you will probably receive news of him through the Red Cross." The division's National Socialist political officer exploded in fury at the suggestion that captivity might prove a tolerable fate for a German soldier. "The contents of this letter will have a demoralising effect," wrote the NSPO, "because people at home may influence soldiers in this direction. Unit commanders are held responsible for ensuring that biased information of this kind is suppressed." An American intelligence report recorded on 5 December: "A PW of 353rd Division captured in GROSSHAU had been sentenced to death for cowardice before the enemy and ... thought this entitled him to gratitude from our side." In the last months of the war, there was a drastic increase in court-martial sentences on delinquent German soldiers. Beyond 15,000 recorded executions—and many more unrecorded—tens of thousands of men were dispatched to penal battalions, where the possibility of survival was no higher than in their Soviet equivalents. A total of 44,955 men were sent for trial in October 1944 alone, and many of these received long sentences at hard labour. Desertion became a very serious problem for Hitler's forces in the last months of the war.

Dispirited Wehrmacht soldiers, hastening to the rear amid a Russian attack, shouted angrily at men of the Grossdeutschland Division, waiting patiently for the Soviets in their positions: "You silly sods are just keeping the war going!" Yet even as late as the winter of 1944 Germany possessed some outstanding fighting formations. "We knew we were still pretty good," said Sergeant Max Wind of 17th SS Panzergrenadiers with pride. "The important thing in war is not the equipment, but the man behind it. The allies' biggest mistake was 'unconditional surrender.' If there had been a chance of a deal, we would have taken it. Hitler did not play the role people think. He was simply our leader. The issue was Germany. It was common knowledge what the enemy would do if they won—and what indeed they did. Knowing that, we only wanted to fight."

Twenty-six-year-old Captain Walter Schaefer-Kuhnert of 9th Panzer Division had endured many hardships in the course of the war. His father, a proud First World War veteran and estate owner, had urged him to volunteer for military service, "because that is how a man grows up." Schaefer-Kuhnert was wounded once in France in 1940, then twice again in Russia, where he also survived typhus. He had known the exhilaration of marching towards apparent victory, "cheering like schoolboys" as his battery lobbed shells at the Kremlin in 1941. He had experienced the bitterness of retreat in the years that followed. Kursk, the vast tank battle of 1943, had been a turning point for Schaefer-Kuhnert, as for many thousands of other German soldiers. Before the battle began, his commanding officer said one night: "Do you think we can still win the war?" Schaefer-Kuhnert, contemplating the vast armoured force Germany had assembled, replied: "If we can't do it with what we've got here, then it's the beginning of the end." The panzers did not "do it" at Kursk. Yet the gunner was shocked by the conspiracy of German officers against Hitler in July 1944. He thought the bomb plot was "utterly wrong," and did not change his mind for many years.

By the autumn of 1944, "We recognized the inevitability of defeat, but we had to consider what we owed to our honour as soldiers. We had to stick together." He was appalled by the breakdown of discipline he saw during the retreat from France, "men fleeing loaded down with loot, taking girls, driving commandeered civilian vehicles ... already there was a breakdown." One battery in his own regiment was now equipped with captured Russian mortars, because it lacked sufficient 105mm guns. Yet he found confronting the U.S. Third Army in Lorraine a very much more acceptable experience than the Eastern Front. "You were fighting against human beings, who shared broadly the same philosophy. Once we agreed a truce with them, to remove dead and wounded from the battlefield. One of our men carried a wounded American from no-man's-land to their lines, and came back loaded with chocolate and cigarettes the 'Amis' had given him. That could never have happened in the east." Schaefer-Kuhnert "took it for granted that we must go on to the end, whatever that meant."

Lieutenant Helmut Schmidt expressed sentiments that were widely shared: "I knew that I was against the Nazis—but I did not know what I was *for*. Like most German soldiers, I thought that it was my duty to fight, and by day we did fight. But at night we prayed for the war to end. I felt no personal sense of shame. Once, when I saw a train loaded with Russian prisoners, I felt a stab of pity. But then I also felt: 'Such is war.' I didn't know the 'German Resistance' existed. I read Marcus Aurelius. From him, I learned that it makes no sense to fight what you cannot change." Sergeant Otto Cranz said: "I get so angry when people ask why we did not join the heroic resistance to Hitler. One could do nothing."

"I wonder what Hitler's thinking now," mused General Weiknecht, a Wehrmacht captive in Soviet hands. General Friedrich von Paulus, the vanquished commander of Stalingrad, said savagely: "He's trying to find some way of inspiring the nation to new sacrifices. Never in history have lies been such vital instruments of diplomacy and policy. We Germans have been tricked by this usurper." Colonel-General Strekker asked: "Why has the Lord been so angry with Germany as to send us Hitler? Is the German nation so base as to deserve such a punishment?"

POSTERITY IS bemused by the banality of Hitler and the coterie of gangsters who formed the leadership of the Third Reich. It is scarcely surprising that during the 1944–45 campaign they sought refuge in military and political fantasies, and committed themselves to a struggle to the end. Most tacitly acknowledged that their own lives were forfeit, and they were therefore indifferent to the fate of others. Through the last months of the war, many Nazi officials, Gestapo agents and SS men showed themselves eager to encompass the deaths of as many enemies of the Third Reich as possible before their own time came. Beria reported to Stalin on 19 September the discovery of a concentration camp near Tallin in Estonia. A squad of sixty SS had been rushed there, on the eve of its liberation by the Red Army, and 1,600 Jews—"mostly doctors, artists and scientists"—together with 260 Russian PoWs, had been murdered in a matter of hours, leaving only eighty survivors. Such actions were commonplace. In the spring of 1945 there was a rush to kill surviving critics of National Socialism within the Nazis' reach before they could be delivered by the Allies.

It is much harder to comprehend the behaviour of the generals such as Guderian and von Rundstedt, with their intelligence, high military competence and pretensions to honour, than that of the senior Nazis. Most of Germany's senior commanders had been dismissed for suffering defeats on the battlefield, only to be reinstated when their successors proved incapable of doing better. The generals complained constantly about the humiliations to which they were exposed, professed to despise Hitler, privately acknowledged that the war was lost. Yet, month after month, they attended the Führer's military conferences, endured his ravings about "wonder weapons," Wallenstein and Frederick the Great, then returned to their headquarters to continue the direction of his doomed war.

It is interesting to compare the German command structure with that of the Allies. The Russian system worked remarkably well from 1942 onwards, once Stalin showed himself willing to delegate to able commanders. Stalin shared Hitler's monomania and paranoia, but acquired vastly better strategic judgement. The U.S. Chiefs of Staff directed their forces with great managerial skill, though their effectiveness was weakened by inter-service rivalries. Roosevelt displayed no inclination to play the warlord as Churchill did, nor to impose his authority upon the military decision-makers except on the largest issues. Churchill's generals often complained about their master's military fantasies, eccentricities and egotism. In small matters, Britain's prime minister could behave high-handedly and pettishly. But on great decisions, however loud his protests, he accepted the advice of the military professionals. He possessed an extraordinary instinct for war. The partnership of Brooke and Churchill created the most efficient machine for the direction of the war possessed by any combatant nation, even if its judgements were sometimes flawed and its ability to enforce its wishes increasingly constrained.

By contrast, for all the tactical genius displayed by German soldiers fighting on the battlefield, they could never escape the consequences of serving under the direction of a man who rejected rationality. Hitler believed that his own military skills and judgement were superior to those of any of his professional advisers. He immersed the leadership in a morass of detail, wasting countless hours of his commanders' time, about armament design and the movements of trifling numbers of men and tanks. He allowed Göring, his old political crony, to remain leader of the Luftwaffe even when it was plain that it was collapsing as a fighting force through huge errors of policy and management. He gave Himmler a battlefield command which caused that master of mass murder to suffer a nervous collapse. His insistence upon sustaining to the end of the war heavily garrisoned German "fortresses" in the Channel Islands, Scandinavia and the

Aegean for reasons of prestige deprived Germany of prodigious numbers of men and quantities of precious arms and matériel, which might significantly have influenced the battles of 1945 if they had been withdrawn to Germany while there was still time.

One of Hitler's greatest follies in the last years of the war was the devotion of enormous scientific and industrial effort to the so-called *Vergeltungswaffen*— "retaliation weapons." The V1 was a small pilotless aircraft powered by a pulse-jet engine, catapulted from launch ramps located at hundreds of sites in Holland after the loss of those in France and Belgium. The first was fired at England on 13 June 1944, and in the weeks that followed 2,451 others followed. About two-thirds crashed prematurely, were toppled by British fighters (which perfected a clever manoeuvre of flying alongside the bomb, then flicking a wingtip under its fins) or were shot down by anti-aircraft fire. Many of the remainder fell on and around greater London, bringing renewed misery to a people exhausted by years of blitz and privation. The most destructive single V1 explosion took place at the Guards Chapel near Buckingham Palace during a service, in which 121 people died. By March 1945, over 10,000 V1 "flying bombs" had been fired, causing 24,000 casualties in England and many more in Belgium.

The V2 was the world's first ballistic missile, fuelled by alcohol and liquid oxygen, impossible to intercept and destroy because it travelled at supersonic speeds. The first V2 crashed on Chiswick in west London on 8 September 1944, killing three people and injuring seventeen. By 27 March 1945, some 1,050 rockets had fallen on England, killing 2,700 Londoners. A further "wonder weapon," the V3 long-range gun designed to fire on London, was used only briefly in the winter of 1944 against Antwerp and Luxembourg, to little effect. The V-weapons caused great apprehension and misery among the civilians of England and Belgium, but it should have been evident to the rulers of Germany that dumping small payloads of explosive with indifferent accuracy on the enemy could not conceivably justify the slave labour, materials and commitment of highly skilled personnel and technology necessary to create the delivery systems. The technology was extremely advanced, but it was futile, as even Hitler seemed to grasp in the last months. On the night of 17 December, a V2 crashed into the Rex cinema in Antwerp during a crowded show. When Hitler was informed that 1,100 people including 700 soldiers had been killed or wounded, by a characteristic irony he was reluctant to credit the report. "That would finally be the first successful launch," he observed sarcastically. "But it is so fairytale that my scepticism keeps me from believing it. Who is the informer? Is he paid by the launch crew?"

Had Hitler forsaken the propaganda rewards of raining V-weapons on England—to negligible military and industrial effect—and concentrated his firepower on the Channel ports, the consequences could have been serious for the Allied armies. Yet there was never the remotest possibility that any of the "wonder weapons" could change the outcome of the war. The Germans had made no significant progress with developing the only device that might have done so—an atomic bomb. The folly of persisting with the V-weapon programme, which drained Germany's shrinking resources merely to torment the enemy's population, highlighted the irrationality of Nazi behaviour as defeat beckoned.

Three forces determined Germany's ability to sustain the war. The first was the organizational genius of Speer. It was ironic that the most cultured member of the Nazi leadership, and the only one to display practical concern for the fate of the German people in the midst of defeat, alone provided the means to enable Hitler to fight on until May 1945. The second factor was the effectiveness of the machinery of internal repression, for which Himmler was responsible. One of the bleakest lessons of modern history is that while half-hearted dictatorships often collapse, those willing to sustain policies of implacable ruthlessness, slaughtering all enemies real or imagined, frequently survive until the natural death or military defeat of their principal. Himmler's task was made easier by the fact that hundreds of thousands of his agents knew that their crimes irretrievably committed them. Goebbels's contribution was also vital. His programme of national indoctrination, maintained over a decade, perverted the reasoning processes of one of the best-educated societies on earth. Here was a significant difference between the German and Soviet tyrannies. Whatever the Russian people's commitment to the war, many were privately cynical about Stalin's rule. By contrast, a formidable proportion of Hitler's subjects retained their belief in his policies. The self-delusion of the German people flagged only when the fabric of their society literally collapsed about their heads.

The third force in enabling Hitler to continue the war was the support of the Army. The only people who realized that Germany was doomed, and also possessed the power to do something about it, were its generals. Beyond the Army's feeble attempt in July 1944, they failed to act upon their knowledge to save the German people from Hitler. This is the basis for their claims upon the contempt of history. On 10 September, two months after the dismissal of Field-Marshal Gerd von Rundstedt as C-in-C West, he was once more summoned to Hitler's presence and invited to resume his role. He was sixty-eight, and showing signs of age, stress and some over-indulgence in alcohol. He was taking a cure at Bad Tolz when Hitler's message came. The lean, leathery old veteran tersely accepted recall to duty, observing later that he considered it his duty as a German officer. "Duty" and "honour" were words constantly on the lips of Wehrmacht generals, both then and afterwards. Yet von Rundstedt's pretensions were crippled by his participation in the so-called Court of Honour which presided over the dismissal of many officers from the German Army for their roles in the July bomb plot, in most cases as a preliminary to their execution. Von Manstein, who was regarded for some years after the war as an honourable man as well as a brilliant commander, has been exposed by modern research as deeply implicated in massacres of Jews and prisoners in the east. He happily accepted large cash hand-outs from Hitler, which in a moment of sublime optimism he used to buy an estate in East Prussia as late as October 1944. If von Manstein, von Kluge, von Rundstedt and others had faithfully followed Hitler's military instructions in the second half of the war, it would have been over much sooner. As it was, however, again and again they defied the Führer's demented orders, in the exercise of their best professional judgement.

The deaths of some five million Germans, as well as those of millions more of their enemies and captives, may be blamed as much upon such "men of honour" as von Rundstedt, who continued to support Hitler and to direct his armies, as upon the Nazi leadership. He appeared a caricature of the aloof, unemotional, aristocratic Prussian General Staff officer. In the 1944–45 campaign, von Rundstedt was granted little latitude by Hitler. The field-marshal remarked acidly that he was permitted only to post the guards outside his own headquarters. Yet he continued to show outstanding gifts as a commander, directing the defence of western Germany against overwhelming forces, his Führer's interventions foremost among them. There was nothing to love in von Rundstedt, but his professional skills commanded the respect of his subordinates and his enemies.

Militarily, Germany's generals in the winter of 1944 could not escape a fatal conundrum. Even if Hitler's decisions were demented and his refusal to sanction retreats condemned hundreds of thousands of men to die, what alternative strategy could be deemed rational, except surrender? Phased withdrawals to shorten the front and save troops from encirclement, which senior commanders constantly advocated, were militarily logical but offered no realistic prospect of changing the outcome of the war. The Allies profited at least as much as the Wehrmacht by every German withdrawal from a salient or abandonment of a beleaguered "fortress." Guderian, von Rundstedt, Model and their disgraced comrades such as von Manstein knew that any course of action could only delay the inevitable. It is hardly surprising that a substantial number of senior officers in the final months suffered nervous collapses or shot themselves. The strain of presiding over carnage which could not save Germany, but which merely deferred the day of reckoning for the Nazi leadership, proved unbearable for many officers, save the most brutally insensitive such as Schörner. Most of the military leaders who continued to serve Hitler to the end justified themselves by pleading that they were pursuing the salvation of the German people from Soviet vengeance. Yet such claims can hardly explain the ingenuity and determination with which they also defended the Western Front.

The German Army, with its perverted vision of honour, failed the German people, and the world, by maintaining its loyalty to Hitler. For the rest of their lives, senior soldiers cited their oath of loyalty to Hitler to justify their continued participation in the war. Even after 1945, many German veterans refused to see that a pledge of allegiance to a man who had created an illegal tyranny could possess no conceivable legitimacy. More pragmatically, the Army's leaders seized upon the Soviet threat to justify fighting on, when any rational analysis demonstrated that the war must be ended at any price. Continued resistance to the Russians made sense only if this was coupled with swift admittance of the Western allies to Germany. The American historian Omer Bartov, in his merciless analysis of the wartime Wehrmacht, argues that its behaviour was dictated by a far closer attachment to Nazi ideology than most of its officers acknowledged, then or later. "Even officers with little reason to be enamoured with Hitler and his regime often shared many of Hitler's prejudices," he writes. Bartov argues that many German commanders shared Hitler's fantasies of conquest and grandeur, racial genocide and Germanic world rule, along with his obsessive loathing of communists and Jews. He overstates his case, but there is something in it.

Hitler's generals, whether SS officers or old Prussian aristocrats, allowed themselves to lapse into fulfilling their duties in a moral vacuum. They abandoned coherent thought about the future and merely performed the immediate military functions that were so familiar to them. The old cliché about the robotic mentality of the German soldier is ill founded. On the battlefield, the Wehrmacht displayed much greater tactical imagination and energy than its opponents. But Germany's generals in the last months of the war indeed behaved as automatons, amid the whims and obsessions of their monstrous master. Most turned against Hitler not because they acknowledged that he was evil, but because they realized that he was losing the war.

Many of Germany's wartime soldiers became brutalized. It is untrue that mass killings were carried out only by members of the SS. On the Eastern Front, the Wehrmacht was often involved in the slaughter of civilians and prisoners. Its men had been subjected throughout their childhood and youth to conditioning of an extraordinary intensity, especially about the sub-human status of Jews and Slavs. The Potsdam Military History Institute's monumental history of the 1939–45 experience demonstrates conclusively the complicity of the Wehrmacht in the Barbarossa plan, which required the starvation of millions of Ukrainians not as an accident of war but as a specific military objective, to enable the diversion of Ukrainian wheat to feed Germany.

Germany's soldiers perceived themselves as a vastly more civilized people than their Soviet enemies. In everyday matters such as table manners, so they were. Some Western allied officers, especially after the war, allowed themselves to be deluded by German social courtesy, and sometimes by prisoners' impressive command of the English language, into respecting German combatants not only as skilful adversaries, but as men not unlike themselves. British fighter pilots, for instance, hastened to embrace Luftwaffe counterparts such as Galland and Knoke as fellow "knights of the air." Such sentimentality ignored the fact that these men were dedicated Nazis, who had eagerly supported Hitler's crimes. Likewise, many officers and men of the Wehrmacht were complicit in actions and policies, especially towards partisans, which placed them beyond the pale of civilization, and betrayed the very values they professed to be upholding against the Soviets.

Most of the courageous Germans who had dared to oppose Hitler were now dead or in cells awaiting execution, where their grace and dignity did more to redeem the German people in the eyes of posterity than anything achieved by the Wehrmacht on the battlefield. "A remarkable year is drawing to a close for me," Helmuth von Moltke wrote in December to his wife Freya from Tegel, where he lay imprisoned for his role in the Resistance to Hitler.

> I spent it predominantly among people who were being prepared for a violent death, and many of them have suffered it meanwhile...With all these people I lived in the same house, took part in their fate, listened when they were taken away for interrogations, or when they were removed altogether, talked with almost all of them about their affairs, and saw how they coped with it all...here at Tegel, already about ten of my group have been executed.... These violent killings eventually became such an everyday matter that I accepted the disappearance of individuals sadly but as a natural event. And now I tell myself, it is my turn.

A total of 5,764 people were executed in 1944 for their alleged roles in the German Resistance, and a further 5,684 in 1945. Of these, barely 100 were directly implicated in the July plot. Von Moltke concluded his last letter before the Nazis hanged him: "The grace of our Lord Jesus Christ and the love of God and the fellowship of the Holy Spirit be with you all. Amen."

CHAPTER SEVEN

Hell in the Hürtgen

FIGHTING IN THE FOREST

THOUSANDS OF Americans were now fighting inside the borders of Germany. Sir Alan Brooke wrote in his diary, on beholding the wreckage of Aachen: "It was a relief to see at last German houses demolished instead of French, Italian, Belgian and British!" The occupiers were somewhat bemused by their first encounters with Hitler's people in their own homes. German civilians of both sexes seemed without humility about their responsibility for the predicament in which they now found themselves. Civil Affairs, a large military bureaucracy whose personnel possessed varying degress of competence, enthusiasm and integrity, followed in the wake of the armies to assume supervision of the vanquished German people. Near Hürtgen, the U.S. 30th Division Civil Affairs officer was summoned to the mansion of a Luftwaffe colonel's wife, one Frau von Reventlow, who complained bitterly about intrusions upon her privacy by refugees. The American suggested that, since Germany had started the war, it seemed not unreasonable that she, like other Germans, should accept some responsibility towards the refugees caused by it.

Only the Russians possessed clear policies for the lands they occupied. Among the Americans and British, from the humblest footsoldier to the greatest statesmen, deep uncertainties persisted, about whether to treat Germany as a nation of criminals, a threat to world peace that must be permanently emasculated, as U.S. treasury secretary Henry Morgenthau urged; or whether to adopt Churchill's view, that one could not indict a whole people. The British prime minister preferred to leave great decisions about how to deal with the Germans until after they had been defeated, when the passions of war had abated: "It is a mistake to try to write out on little pieces of paper what the vast emotions of an outraged and quivering world will be either immediately after the struggle is over or when the inevitable cold fit follows the hot," he wrote to Eden, his foreign secretary.

176

Among the Allied forces entering Hitler's dominions, there was an instinctive indifference to German property, reflected in everything from bombing policy to looting. "One advantage of being in Germany is that one can liberate any article which he needs," Staff-Sergeant Harold Fennema of the 66th Signals Battalion wrote to his wife in Wisconsin. "Since you spoke of wanting a sewing machine, there are lots of them to be liberated here. Washing machines are a little harder to liberate, but we have hopes of getting one soon." American and British soldiers faced strict injunctions about "non-fraternization" with the enemy. GIs were subject to a fine of $65 for breaking the rules. Soldiers puzzled over how this whimsical figure was determined. In any event, the regulations were heeded more in the breach than in the observance. Many soldiers displayed pity, and even kindness, to individual German civilians. Had it been otherwise, the values for which the war was being fought would have been lost.

A significant number of U.S. soldiers appointed to Civil Affairs were themselves former refugees, picked for their language skills. Corporal Werner Kleeman had been born in Bavaria twenty-five years earlier. A Jew, he spent some months in Dachau concentration camp before achieving the extraordinary good fortune of a passport to England, and thence to America. He found life very tough as an infantry trainee: "Most NCOs were hill-billies who thought Jews wore horns. They had never seen a Jew. They liked to say: 'Latrine duty for the refugee!'" But then Kleeman was posted to Civil Affairs on the strength of his knowledge of German. He cherished the sensation that he was taking a small personal part in the destruction of Hitler's empire. The former refugee once found himself interrogating a shot-down Luftwaffe pilot who hailed from a Bavarian village three miles from his own. Yet sometimes Kleeman's American superiors expected more than he could deliver. Colonel Charles Lanham, the flamboyant officer commanding the 22nd Infantry, told the interpreter one day: "Now we're in Germany, the velvet gloves come off. These cows on the roads are getting in the way of my vehicles." Kleeman wondered if the colonel expected him to harangue the cows in German.

One of his colleagues was Sergeant J. D. Salinger. "In those days, he was very normal," Kleeman said of the novelist, "except that he would never let anybody read his letters home, and always forged the signature of a censoring officer." Sometimes Salinger would say: "Let's go look up Papa." They would head for the press camp where Ernest Hemingway was ensconced, asserting that he was hiding from his wife, Martha Gellhorn. Both Hemingways were serving as war correspondents. Jim Gavin of the 82nd Airborne somehow found leisure to conduct a brief affair with Ms. Gellhorn, which involved playing a lot of gin rummy in bed. Salinger and Kleeman admired Ernest Hemingway's unflinching enthusiasm for getting up front. The novelist had formed a close friendship with Colonel Lanham of the 22nd Infantry, a moody, self-consciously heroic figure who was by no means displeased to find himself the object of Hemingway's admiration in print. Lanham, who "led from the front, even to the point of fool-hardiness," was now to find himself and his regiment, along with a substantial part of the U.S. First Army, plunged into fighting more painful than any which they had known since Normandy.

"THE STAGNATION OF the war weighs heavily," the Dresden Jewish academic Victor Klemperer wrote in his diary on 2 November. "Another winter, that is a dreadful thought." So it seemed also to the Allied generals. At Eisenhower's strategic planning conference in Brussels on 18 October 1944, it was acknowl-edged that the British would be unable to launch a major thrust into Germany before winter. Montgomery's hopes of spearheading a breakthrough had died at Arnhem and on the Scheldt. If there was now to be a dramatic advance, it would have to be achieved by Bradley's men. It was agreed that Hodges's First Army should push towards Cologne, while Ninth Army attacked on the left, between Hodges and the British. Patton's Third Army was placed lowest in the queue for support and supply. Alan Brooke wrote gloomily in his diary on 8 November: "I do not like the layout of the coming offensive, and doubt whether we [will] even reach the Rhine, it is highly improbable that we should cross over before the end of the year." Brooke had become so desperate to see a land force com-mander appointed in place of Eisenhower, "[who] is detached and by himself with his lady chauffeur on the golf links at Rheims," that the sharp, brusque Ulsterman now favoured giving the job to Bradley, with Montgomery com-manding all Allied troops north of the Ardennes, and Patton doing the same job in the south. "[Eisenhower] *quite* incapable of understanding real strategy... Among other things discovered that Ike now does not hope to cross the Rhine before May!!!" Such was the gloom of some Allied commanders after their euphoric visions two months earlier.

A few miles inside Germany, south-east of Aachen, lay a cluster of large expanses of wooded hills collectively known to the Americans as the Hürtgen Forest. The ridge lines, occupied by the German 275th Division, had been cleared of timber, which increased their dominance of the forests below. The 275th were poor-grade troops, who—like the garrison of Aachen—posed no plausible threat to the flanks of an American advance to the Roer. Yet the strange decision was taken that the Hürtgen should be cleared of Germans before another major attack eastwards was made. The American historian Rus-sell Weigley has wisely observed: "The most likely way to make the Hürtgen a menace to the American army was to send American troops attacking into its depths. An army that depends for superiority on its mobility, firepower, and technology should never voluntarily give battle where these assets are at a dis-count; the Huertgen Forest was surely such a place."

The U.S. 9th Division had suffered much unpleasantness during its early attempts to push through the Hürtgen in October, while Aachen was still in German hands. By 16 October, the formation had suffered 4,500 casualties in advancing two miles. At the beginning of November, the 28th Division of V Corps took over the task. Some early successes alarmed the Germans, and caused them to reinforce the area heavily. When the fresh U.S. 18th Infantry was pushed into an assault on 8 November, its battalions suffered 500 casualties in five days. The executive officer of one regiment of 28th Division wrote: "We're still a first-class outfit, but not nearly as good as when we came across the beach. We have a great deal more prodding to do now." In the thickly wooded country where the tracks had become quagmires, it could take six or eight hours to move rations and ammunition forward a mile or two. The 121st Infantry charged eleven men with refusal to return to the line—the first such case V Corps had recorded. An American officer said bleakly: "We are taking three trees a day, yet they cost us about 100 men apiece."

Yet, instead of recognizing the folly of attacking on terrain that suited the Germans so well, Courtney Hodges reinforced failure. The Americans poured men into the long succession of battles which became known to all those who participated as "the hell of the Hürtgen Forest." This network of woodlands some eight miles deep by twenty wide, almost impassable by tanks, eventually cost its attackers some 25,000 casualties. The terrain made it impossible to deploy American firepower effectively. The defenders' weapons could cover every narrow access with devastating consequences for advancing infantry. "The trees were so dense that even when the sun shone, the day seemed gray," wrote Lieutenant William Devitt of the 330th Infantry. "My first impression of the Hürtgen was the unremitting noise of the artillery. It sounded like a thunderstorm that went on and on without stopping."

Devitt was a thoughtful twenty-year-old Minnesotan, posted to the 83rd Division in December as a replacement. "Until that time, the war hadn't seemed very real or very deadly to me ... I was anxious to learn what combat was like. I wanted to have the experience, probably to be able to talk about it after I got home." As he took his platoon into the line, he was horrified by the sight of the 4th Division men his unit was relieving, their faces and field jackets caked in yellow mud: "They looked like a collection of ghosts ... a grim lot, hollow-eyed from the constant pounding of shellfire, and fear of impending death."

Many of the trees around their positions had been hacked short by shellfire. There were craters and fallen branches everywhere, together with German corpses, which fear of booby traps made the Americans unwilling to remove. Because it was hard to bring hot food forward, they lived chiefly off K-rations: processed meat, cheese, cooked eggs, crackers, dried fruit. Devitt's company commander once asked him to breakfast, thinking he was doing the young officer a favour by offering him hot food, but the lieutenant hated the captain for making him risk the journey to his CP. Their SCR536 radios worked only intermittently among the trees. Incessant and dangerous effort was needed to splice broken field telephone lines. Devitt developed a personal obsession with toilet paper, because lack of it inflicted such humiliations when he, like most men, suffered an outbreak of "the GIs"—chronic diarrhoea. He carried one stash of paper in his helmet, another in his shirt pocket.

As an officer, he felt grateful that he had less time to be frightened than his men, because there was so much to do. The U.S. Army did not allow junior officers batmen—personal servants—as the British did, because it was thought demeaning to ask enlisted men to do such work. Omar Bradley was among those who deplored American scruples. He thought the British system militarily sensible, because overtaxed officers could do their jobs better if they did not also have to dig foxholes and prepare their own rations.

Devitt, like most young officers, learned a great deal from his veterans. His runner, a twenty-year-old from Indiana named Ernie Elliott, wounded in Normandy, put him wise to the shirkers: "Lieutenant, I wouldn't be too soft on so-and-so—he's always been a gold-bricker and will do whatever it takes to duck real work." Yet Devitt found it hard to learn how to rally men subjected to the strain of incoming barrages. He recorded a shouted conversation in the Hürtgen as German shells smashed into the trees around his platoon's foxholes:

"Lieutenant, will you come over here."

"Yeah, what d'ya want?"

"It's Smith. Can you talk to him?"

"Okay, just a second."

He found the man huddled in a foxhole, weeping uncontrollably.

"Smith, just take it easy. You'll be all right."

"Lieutenant, I just can't take it any more. I've just got to get out of here."

"Well, Smith, we all want to get out of here, but we can't. It'll let up soon."

After half an hour or so, the man recovered himself, and gave no more trouble. When a shell wounded two of his platoon, Devitt found himself struggling to put a field dressing on a large hole in one man's chest as it smoked in the icy air, giving off a stink of burning flesh. The other wounded man said: "Lieutenant, he won't make it. Come and help me." Sure enough, a few moments later as the stretcher-bearers lifted the chest case, he shuddered and was dead.

A new officer arrived to take over a neighbouring platoon, where his sergeant, Haney, urged him to dig his foxhole deeper. The lieutenant ignored this suggestion. Soon afterwards a near-miss gave him a slight shrapnel wound in the hand. The officer leaped up, yelling to his NCO: "Look, Haney, that's my ticket home! Talk about a million-dollar wound, this is it. Call the medic to put on a bandage, then it's the rear for me. I've had enough of this place." Devitt's com-

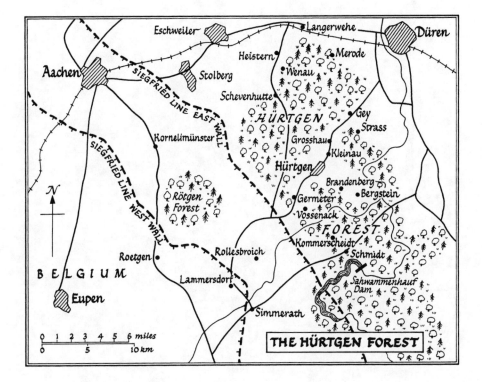

THE HÜRTGEN FOREST

pany suffered thirty-six casualties in a single week in the Hürtgen, without achieving anything of significance.

A MAJOR AMERICAN offensive began early in the afternoon of 16 November with an attempt to push eastwards from a start line north of the Hürtgen, along the so-called Hamich Corridor towards Cologne. Nothing did more to boost the precarious morale of the American attackers than the spectacle of their own fighter-bombers pounding the Germans. "It was a beautiful sight to us," wrote a U.S. infantryman watching a P-47 strike. "We could see the tracers bouncing off their targets, then they would dig down and let their bombs go. For a second or two, it would look as if they were duds; then a grey geyser of dirt and smoke would erupt." Inevitably, however, there were mistakes, and mistakes in wars cost lives. Again and again, especially amid the confusion of the woodlands, friendly aircraft strafed Allied positions, causing much bitterness and—more serious—corroding trust among units which had been hit, making them reluctant again to summon air support. Neither side had much idea exactly where the enemy was, except during an attack. The U.S. 28th Field Artillery fired 7,421 rounds of 105mm ammunition during the month of November in the Hürtgen. The regiment acknowledged, however, that most of these—6,520 shells—were blind and unobserved.

Even as the Hamich Corridor push was in progress, the unfortunate 26th Infantry were attacking inside the Hürtgen. Among the trees, the Americans suffered familiar, bloody difficulties in advancing a few hundred yards. In the corridor, where progress was made the lead elements found themselves under fire from German-held high ground on both sides. The first two days' fighting reduced the lead battalion of the 16th Infantry to an average of sixty riflemen per company, less than half its established strength.

The U.S. 109th Regiment fighting among the trees was deemed close to collapse. Its survivors were withdrawn. The 121st Infantry was so battered that one company broke and ran under artillery fire. On 24 November, both this company's commander and his battalion superior were relieved. In the next four days, two other company commanders and another battalion CO were sacked. Two days later, the regimental commander was also relieved, along with the 8th Division's commander, Major-General Donald Stroh. No one could accuse the U.S. Army of tolerating failure in its officers. The anger of the higher command was understandable, since the 121st had suffered only sixty known dead in an attack which petered out without gaining a yard. Private Robert McCall, a Connecticut farmworker, was sent as a replacement to the 121st. As he and some bewildered comrades waited to be allocated to companies, they saw Weasel tracked vehicles carrying out wounded. McCall reflected on the likelihood that he would soon be taking the same route. The first casualty he saw was a sergeant who leapt into a foxhole as shelling started, causing a grenade to fall out of his belt, which exploded and killed him.

McCall took part in his first attack on 28 November. Catching a glimpse of a German helmet, he fired, and was rewarded by the sight of an enemy soldier as frightened as himself emerging from a hole, his upheld hands shaking. The Americans broke out of the woods and began to advance across open ground towards their objective. They were stopped by heavy fire. "To stay where we were would have been suicide, so the whole outfit ran back across the field." McCall crawled into a foxhole recently vacated by the Germans, and was disconcerted to hear a cry of "*Kamerad!*" from the next trench. He saw a German helmet, and fired. Examining the corpse of the first man he had ever killed, McCall removed his watch and wallet. The following day, as his unit advanced into Hürtgen, he heard the shriek of an incoming shell. "Next instant, it felt like someone had hit me in the small of my back with a club." Two men dragged him to the roadside and left him for the medics. A few days later, he was on his way home to Connecticut. After a year of training, McCall's active service career had ended after just ten days in the line. Many men thought him lucky, and so indeed did he himself.

The 121st's total casualties were around 600 out of a strength of 3,000, but most of these were combat-fatigue cases. Its commanders concluded that the regiment had succumbed too readily to the misery of the Hürtgen. It was striking to contrast what the best American troops could achieve with the performance of their less effectual brethren. "Attacking forces were interfered with by mud, rain and sleet," wrote Sergeant Forrest Pogue with V Corps. "Enemy personnel were not of a high quality. The forces consisted principally of regiments of numerous units that had been disorganised in France. Numerous *Kampfgruppen* were formed of exceptionally young or old soldiers. Poor observation interfered with the use of artillery by the Americans." When repeated efforts failed to seize a peak named Castle Hill, on 7 December a battalion of the Rangers, who had achieved miracles on D-Day, was sent to do the job. They stormed the hill. Powerful artillery support enabled them to hold it against ferocious German counter-attacks. By the day's end, only twenty-five men remained in action among the two Ranger assault companies.

Lieutenant Tony Moody joined the 112th Infantry in the Hürtgen late in November. "It was very cold and very wet, and I had lost my bedding roll." He met his company commander for the first time in the middle of an incoming barrage, which frightened him considerably. He was then taken to meet his platoon: "Their morale was pretty bad. I'm sure we inflicted as many casualties on the Germans as they did on us, but somehow they didn't seem to get as upset about them as we did. We lost quite a few combat fatigue cases." Moody was a twenty-one-year-old graduate in architecture from Missouri, with ambitions to be an artist. His first hard test of leadership, he felt, came when a man returning from the latrines failed to hear a challenge and was shot dead by an American sentry. Writing to the man's wife, Moody struggled to find words to make her husband's death sound less ugly and futile.

Unglamorous jobs incurred inflated dangers. Prominent among these was that of signal wireman. It was critical to maintain communications between the forward positions and unit headquarters. Telephone lines were constantly severed by fire. Wiremen had to find the breaks and repair them, often while bombardment persisted. "Telephone wiremen were the first to die in every battle," observed Captain Karl Godau of 10th SS Panzer. Private Ralph Gordon of the U.S. 18th Infantry was called out at 0300 one night: "It was so dark that it was impossible to see your hand in front of your face, and the only reason I knew where I was, was that I followed my wire line till I reached the breaks. I must have fallen down a dozen times, and one time my pistol fell from my belt when I walked into a trench. I spent 15 minutes feeling around in the dark trying to find the pistol, and during those minutes I cursed everyone that had anything to do with starting the war."

Gordon and his unit emerged from the Hürtgen utterly traumatized by the experience: "We were thankful we were still alive, but for how long no one knew... The day after, a few fellows just couldn't take the strain any more, just went psycho, shouting and running all around like madmen. They got these fellows out as soon as possible, as it was bad on the morale of the other men." Wilmer Pruett, an eighteen-year-old from the woods of North Carolina serving with the 281st Combat Engineers observed again and again in the Hürtgen: "If there's another war, the only way they get me is to burn the forest and sift the ashes."

STRESSES OF BATTLE

BOTH THE AMERICAN and British armies pondered deeply the problem of combat fatigue, the cause of serious losses of fighting soldiers, above all infantrymen. In some units committed to the Hürtgen battle, combat fatigue reached epidemic proportions. A British medical report concluded that "the act of going sick, of giving in, is an all-or-nothing phenomenon, and is damaging to the personality." Most men, it concluded, were less effective soldiers after returning to duty, as did more than 50 per cent. The same report observed the paradox that a soldier who ran away from the battlefield was treated as a criminal and harshly punished, while the man who reported sick with combat fatigue was sympathetically received, although "the physical escape of the deserters and the psychological escape of the hysteric were expressions of the same mechanism." The report noted that the problem seemed much smaller in the

German Army, "though precipitating trauma was obviously greater." This was a polite way of suggesting that the German soldier, in defeat, was experiencing a tougher war than his Allied counterpart, on the road to victory. The report failed to remark the small but obvious point, however, that suspected Wehrmacht malingerers were shot. Although combat fatigue was recognized only with the utmost reluctance in the German Army, and not at all in Stalin's formations, there are no grounds for supposing that German or Russian soldiers were less afflicted by the shock of battle than men of other armies. They were simply denied the sympathy accorded to American and British sufferers.

A British analysis concluded: "Battle exhaustion cases occurred chiefly among men of poor type who, during training have constantly been guilty of petty crimes." The U.S. Army rejected this thesis, and took the view that many good men succumbed to combat fatigue and could be rehabilitated for return to duty. In the course of the north-west Europe campaign, British Second Army recorded twelve men per thousand as psychoneurotic admissions to hospitals. Comparable American ETO figures were fifty-two men per thousand, a total of 102,989 cases. Some 8.9 per cent of all men who passed through the U.S. Army in the Second World War were recorded as suffering at some time from combat fatigue. Martin Van Creveld, writing of the "enormous number of psychiatric casualties" the U.S. Army suffered in that war, suggests that the condition was regarded by the ordinary soldier and his superior as "a legitimate, almost normal complaint." The problem was especially prevalent among newly arrived replacements. Although combat fatigue was far less readily acknowledged in the German Army, the consulting psychiatrist at Second Panzer Army recorded in 1943 that it was especially common "among men who had not had time to form strong comradely ties with buddies." Together with trench foot, which was invariably highest in units where morale was low, combat fatigue represented a huge drain on Allied fighting manpower. Twenty-six per cent of all those who served in combat formations in the ETO between June and November 1944 at some time reported sick in these terms. "Combat fatigue was one of the most important causes of non-effectiveness among combat troops," concluded a U.S. Army post-war report. "News spread among the troops that they could avoid distasteful duty at least temporarily by getting into medical evacuation channels. It was very difficult under combat conditions to distinguish between malingering and mild combat exhaustion."

Officers who succumbed were often treated more generously than enlisted men. Lieutenant Colonel Ferdinand Chesarek, commanding the 28th Field Artillery, relieved a major of his duties and sent him to the rear, with a report simply recommending that he should not again be employed forward of a corps command post: "The strain of battle in a field artillery CP is greater than he can undergo and still function efficiently ... when the situation becomes involved, he works himself into such a state as to make impossible the continuation of his duties."

In the winter of 1944, Allied fighting strength was further eroded by the loss of thousands of men who simply quit. "There were increasing signs of plummeting morale," writes Carlo d'Este, "manifested by a rapidly rising desertion rate so serious that Eisenhower...became the first [U.S. commander] since Lincoln in the Civil War to order an American soldier executed for desertion." No reliable figures are available for overall losses caused by desertion and absences without leave, but Martin Van Creveld suggests "several hundred thousand," of whom a mere 2,854 were ever brought to trial. Available statistics show that the desertion rate in U.S. armies in Europe reached 45.2 per thousand in 1944 and 63 per thousand in 1945. On 1 January 1945, the U.S. provost-marshal acknowledged that more than 18,000 American deserters were roaming the ETO, while the British admitted to more than 10,000. A further 10,000 British soldiers were charged with the lesser offence of Absence Without Leave.

Unsurprisingly desertion, like combat fatigue, was overwhelmingly an issue in combat units. A sample of British offenders in north-west Europe revealed that more than 80 per cent of deserters had absconded from infantry rifle companies. This represented a serious haemorrhage of fighting manpower. The figures suggest that Eisenhower's armies were deprived of the equivalent of several divisions, men who disappeared from their units to become scavengers, supporting themselves by lives of active or passive criminality. They became familiar flotsam in every urban area of western Europe. This teeming horde sustained a huge traffic in stolen military rations, fuel, equipment and even vehicles, feeding the black markets of impoverished France, Belgium—and Britain. In Brussels in December 1944, an average of seventy jeeps *a day* were being reported lost. A significant proportion of supplies destined for the armies was diverted into civilian hands. More than a few men in General Lee's ComZ and its British counterpart did not desert but instead made their contribution to the war effort by selling stores which they were entrusted with moving to the front. Fortunes were made in those days, in those ways. In the British Army, concern about organized looting, black-marketeering and theft of military equipment became so widespread that a restriction was imposed on the value of postal money orders soldiers were permitted to send home. Disciplinary problems of all kinds were a serious issue. Eisenhower was driven to suggest the public execution of men convicted of rape.

The U.S. Army suffered severely in north-west Europe for the grave policy error it had made earlier in the war, of according a low priority to manning infantry formations and providing replacements for their casualties. "We are about to invade the continent," General Marshall wrote to Stimson, the U.S. secretary of war, in May 1944, "and have staked our success on our air superiority, on Soviet numerical preponderance, and on the high quality of our ground combat units." Marshall might have added: "and on the willingness of the Soviets to accept the overwhelming burden of ground casualties." It was also debatable whether the Chief of Staff had, indeed, given the emphasis he claimed to ensuring the quality of fighting manpower. The U.S. Army's belief that quality personnel were wasted in ground combat units is readily demonstrated by the manner in which it allocated recruits after educational testing. Only 27.4 per cent of American infantry soldiers attained grades I or II in initial army testing, while 29 per cent were grade IIIs, and 43 per cent grades IV or V, which reflected "low intelligence and suitability for training." The educational standard of men shipped to combat arms ranked far below that of those posted to administrative branches. For instance, 89.4 per cent of soldiers sent to the army's Finance Department had achieved grades I or II, as had 35.3 per cent even of those sent to the military police. Many riflemen in the U.S. Army felt themselves abandoned by God and by their own country. Charles Felix's unit was outraged to read in *Stars & Stripes* that men sentenced to imprisonment for rear-area disciplinary offences were being offered a transfer to infantry as an alternative: "So that's what they really think of us!"—shades here of Hollywood's *The Dirty Dozen.* To put the matter plainly, infantry—the core of every army's fighting power—reposed at the bottom of the U.S. War Department barrel. For those who had to fight America's battles in Europe, the cost of this monumental misjudgement was painful indeed.

"Replacements . . . are not satisfactory. They never have been," wrote Lieutenant Colonel C. Ware, G-1 of the U.S. 1st Division. "It seems the infantry has been the last thing to be taken care of." Orders to other commands to release men for infantry service were treated with shameless cynicism. One batch of 514 men released by the USAAF to the army was found to muster 231 court-martial convictions between them. In the words of the U.S. official historian, commanders "saw in the emergency retraining program an opportunity to rid their units of misfits and undesirables." Senior officers remarked on the absurdity of maintaining 198 anti-aircraft units in the U.S. armies in north-west Europe, when the Luftwaffe was almost moribund. It was a measure of the scale of manpower waste that even a modest reduction to 146 AA battalions freed 38,000 men for transfer to infantry. Far more decisive action could have been taken to reduce the grotesquely long support tail and to strengthen infantry units. The British Army gained some benefit from the fact that, unlike its ally, its best foot regiments possessed a prestige which allowed them to recruit quality manpower. However, overall British policy towards infantry was no more imaginative than that of the Pentagon. In a withering memorandum to the War Office, a British divisional commander deplored the fact that many high-ranking officers regarded the infantry "as a legitimate dumping ground for the lowest forms of military life."

Yet the root cause of Eisenhower's chronic manpower difficulties was an earlier Washington policy decision. The U.S. had created a ground army far smaller than its population would have allowed because the War Department woefully underestimated the size of the force that would be needed to defeat Hitler. Millions of potential recruits were rejected by medical boards, which were encouraged to set high standards. It was true that America needed a much bigger navy than Germany. The U.S. Navy's outstanding performance made it probably the most impressive of America's three wartime services. The U.S. decision to create a huge air force represented a rational exploitation of the nation's technological brilliance. But it remains astonishing that only eighty-nine U.S. Army divisions were deployed for active service. It may be argued that, given the difficulties of supplying America's armies in Europe, the commitment of more ground soldiers would merely have compounded these. Yet, even among the five million men drafted to the U.S. Army, only two million served in combat roles, in the loosest interpretation of that phrase. Barely 300,000 men were available in north-west Europe even in 1945 to confront direct German fire, as members of rifle companies or armoured units. It remains insufficiently understood that, while overall casualty rates on the Western Front in the Second World War were vastly lower than those of the First World War, a rifleman's prospects of surviving the entire campaign unwounded were not much better than those of his father in Flanders. The campaign could have been won more quickly, and Allied forces might have advanced much further east, if Eisenhower had been given more soldiers, and especially more infantrymen.

BOGGED DOWN

THE GERMAN SOLDIER found the experience of the Hürtgen Forest battle every inch as unpleasant as his American counterpart. "It's Sunday, my God, it's Sunday," wrote a German infantry medic of the 1058th Regiment. "With dawn, the whole of our front receives a barrage. The earth trembles. The concussions take our breath away ... We go forward to counter-attack. The captain is leading it himself. We cannot go far. Our people are dropping like tired flies. Suddenly, the artillery begins its monstrous song again ... If only we had the munitions and heavy weapons the American has, we would have sent him to hell a long time ago."

The same man noted on 26 February, near Grosshau: "Two wounded are brought to my hole, one with a torn-up arm, the other with both hands shot off. I am considering whether or not to cut off the rest of the arm. I'll leave it on. How brave those two are. I hope to God all this is not in vain. When the Ami really attacks again, then he has got to break through. I can't believe that this ground can be held any longer. Many of our boys just ran away, can't find them, and have to hold out with this small group." The U.S. 22nd Infantry noted that between 16 November and 3 December it captured 764 Germans, against some thirty-seven of its own men taken prisoner. The figures highlighted the reluctance of many of the defenders to fight to the last.

Willi Pusch, an eighteen-year-old soldier of the German 3rd Parachute Division, had seen his company reduced from eighty men to fifteen in Normandy, from which he emerged convinced that the war was lost. After two months refitting the unit in Holland, on 22 November they were committed to the last stages of the battle for the Hürtgen Forest. Pusch, a heavy, cheerful man with the huge hands of the East Prussian peasant, once again saw his company shattered. "The forest was a very brutal place," he said. They were withdrawn and attached to an improvised battle group, which was then given the support of a single tank for a counter-attack. As they advanced to the start line under heavy American artillery fire, the tank swerved off the road and promptly ditched in the mud and snow. The footsoldiers expressed profound relief. "That's it for us," they agreed, and trickled away to the rear.

They were in a village a few days later, on 11 December, when word came of Americans nearby. Pusch and his depleted unit were ordered to push the enemy back. The men, most of whom scarcely knew each other, trudged miserably forward. They occupied the first few houses, just as the Americans approached and opened fire. The Germans could see a score or more Shermans. A young lieutenant told Pusch: "Get a faust." When the paratrooper seemed reluctant to comply, the officer ran for one himself, fired, and set the leading tank on fire before he staggered back into the porch of their house, hit in the legs. The other men dragged him in, then ceased firing and retired to the cellar.

They heard Americans closing in. Two Germans cautiously climbed the steps to meet them, hands held high. A torch probed down from the ground floor upon Pusch and his remaining comrades. An American voice told them to come out. They dumped their weapons and ascended into captivity. Their wounded officer still clutched his Schmeisser, doggedly determined to fight on. The other Germans removed the gun, laid him on a door and carried him out. Pusch felt moved by the care with which an American medic treated his friend from Hamburg, Werner Mittelstrauss, who was badly wounded in the legs. German shells were now falling around them. The paratrooper was slightly wounded by splinters in his lip and eye. Yet he was overwhelmed with gratitude that his war was over: "It was like a reprieve from cancer." The following two years that he spent as a prisoner, initially working in a fertilizer factory at Norfolk, Virginia, were among the happiest of his life: "I was in heaven. I met no hostility in America." His story is important, because it highlights the experience of a German soldier no more eager for glory than most of his Allied counterparts. Pusch embraced escape from the war.

THE AMERICANS at last inched out of the Hürtgen Forest in the first days of December. They had won their battle, at fearsome cost. The 4th Division suffered terribly—some 4,053 battle casualties, together with a further 2,000 cases of trench foot and combat fatigue. Some of the division's companies were reduced to fifty men. Robert Sterling Rush writes of the 4th's 22nd Infantry: "The soldiers of the regiment did not quit, but at the end there was no attack left in them. The soul of the regiment had been ripped out when it lost its experienced junior leaders, NCOs, platoon officers...Although the unit remained above 75 per cent strength through a constant influx of replacements, once all its veterans were lost, its effectiveness declined dramatically." Meanwhile 1st Division, the "Big Red One," had lost 3,993 casualties, 1,479 of these in the 26th Infantry Regiment, to advance four miles. On 29 November, in an attempt to take the town of Merode, just north-east of the Hürtgen, the regiment lost two companies cut off and almost wiped out.

At last, the way seemed open to the Roer plain. Yet at the head of its river stood the Roer dams. These offered the Germans scope to flood the low ground at will. Control of the dams was critical, and this had been understood by Allied intelligence staffs since the beginning of October. The obvious solution was to destroy the dams by bombing before the armies reached them. This task was delegated to the RAF, which had made much of its 1943 success in bursting the Möhne and Eder dams by precision attack. Unfortunately, the Roer dams—like the vital Sorpe in 1943—proved resistant to air attack. Three attempts by Bomber Command failed. The RAF then abandoned the operation. The Roer dams remained potent threats in the hands of the Germans. No Allied ground force could advance into the plain until they were taken.

The dams might be reached through the so-called Monschau Corridor, a narrow strip of open ground just south of the Hürtgen, difficult country for an attacker because of its gorges, streams and pillboxes. Its seizure must inevitably be an infantry task. Back in October and November, the Americans had persuaded themselves that they could not advance up the Monschau Corridor while German forces remained on their flank in the forest. Yet the enemy in the trees were not elite mobile formations but infantry dependent upon their own feet and horse-drawn carts to go anywhere.

When the Americans finally addressed the Monschau Corridor in December, Gerow's V Corps at first made uncommonly good progress. His fresh divisions, especially the 78th, advanced without artillery preparation, exploiting friendly fog on 13 December. The 2nd Division made much slower work of the

Monschau Forest. It may have been "battle-hardened," to use one of the most abused clichés of war, but it was also very tired. Its 9th Infantry Regiment suffered 400 losses from trench foot and exposure, and a rather smaller number of battle casualties. "The German Army almost until its final extremity rotated units out of the line more frequently and regularly than the American Army," a U.S. historian notes. "The effect was to undermine an effective American division's asset of experience by sheer weariness." By the morning of 16 December, the Monschau Corridor attack was stuck. There was also a lurking sense of menace. While the 78th Division confronted the German 272nd Division, there was growing evidence of larger enemy forces beyond, with more ambitious purposes than those of merely checking the U.S. V Corps.

SOUTHWARDS IN LORRAINE, Third Army launched a new attack on 8 November, across a front of almost sixty miles. An assault on such a broad front represented a dispersal of hitting power which puzzled those who admired Patton's rare grasp of the importance of concentration. The conditions were dreadful. It was at this period that Patton enlisted the aid of Colonel James O'Neill, Third Army's senior chaplain: "Do you have a good prayer for weather? We must do something about this rain if we are to win the war... We must ask God to stop." If this request strengthened the widespread belief that Patton was not wholly sane, it inspired O'Neill to write a prayer which was afterwards circulated to every man in Third Army alongside its commander's Christmas greeting: "Almighty and most merciful Father, we humbly beseech Thee, of Thy great goodness, to restrain these immoderate rains with which we have to contend. Grant us fair weather for Battle." When it began to snow soon afterwards, opinion was divided about interpretations of the divine response.

Sergeant Bill Mauldin became a legend in the U.S. Army long before he achieved the same status in the United States as a cartoonist, by creating his two dogface GIs Willie and Joe for *Stars & Stripes*. Patton loathed these characters, whose shaggy mien and unheroic behaviour he deemed "subversive." He summoned their creator for a personal reprimand. Mauldin afterwards provided one of the most vivid portraits of Third Army's commander:

> There he sat, big as life... His hair was silver, his face was pink, his collar and shoulders glittered with more stars than I could count, his fingers sparkled with rings, and an incredible mass of ribbons started around desktop level and spread upward in a flood over his chest to the very top of his shoulder, as if preparing to march down his back too. His face was rugged, with an odd, strangely shapeless outline; his eyes were pale, almost colorless, with a choleric bulge. His small, compressed mouth was sharply downturned at the corner, with a lower lip which suggested a pouting child

as much as a no-nonsense martinet. It was a welcome, rather human touch. Beside him, lying in a big chair, was Willie, the bull terrier. If ever dog was suited to master this one was. Willie had his beloved boss's expression and lacked only the ribbons and stars. I stood in that door staring into the four meanest eyes I'd ever seen.

Mauldin observed: "I always admired Patton. Oh, sure, the stupid bastard was crazy. He was insane. He thought he was living in the Dark Ages. Soldiers were peasants to him. I didn't like that attitude, but I certainly respected his theories and the techniques he used to get his men out of their foxholes." For all Patton's bombast, however, in south-eastern France Third Army was still struggling to win ground. The Germans had thickly sown their positions with new plastic and wooden mines, impervious to American detectors. On 25 November, Patton belatedly but triumphantly entered the city of Metz. The local German corps commander sent a message to the remaining encircled forts in the hands of his men, warning them that if they gave up they "would surrender not to fighting troops...and in all probability to coloured troops." The last forts did not yield until 13 December. Enemy officers pricked their captors by expounding on the feebleness of the garrison. There had been no SS fanatics among them, said the Germans proudly, but rather a mix of old men and young replacements, in the usual muddle of units.

On 22 November at Nancy, an SS general galled Patton, who was interrogating him personally, by asserting: "The combat efficiency of the troops on the Eastern Front is far above the sector here." Patton asked why, if that was so, the SS officer had let the side down by remaining alive. Third Army's commander implied that the German's undamaged condition might not prove permanent. The general replied coolly that he was a prisoner of war of the Americans. Patton said: "When I am dealing with vipers, I do not have to be bothered by any foolish ideas..." Third Army's commander likewise questioned a Wehrmacht colonel about why his men were still bothering to fight. This officer replied: "They will continue to fight until such time as they receive orders to lay down their arms...It is the fear of Russia that is forcing us to use every man who can carry a weapon." He added that he hoped he would be taken to a PoW camp in the U.S. rather than Britain. Patton said this was likely.

In the last days of November, Third Army's offensive ran out of steam. It had reached the West Wall and made some penetrations after initial difficulties. On 1 December, American troops crossed the Sarre river. The Germans abandoned their efforts to hold a line on the west bank, and withdrew on the U.S. XX Corps's front. The men of every formation in the American advance had suffered heavily from exposure and trench foot. All Patton's infantry units were seriously short of men. They were weary, and morale was flagging. The mud made it impossible for either side to use tanks off-road, and thus drastically reduced the scope for bold initiatives. Further south in Alsace, Devers's 6th Army Group overcame weak German opposition to drive through the Vosges Mountains and take Strasbourg on 26 November. Patton urged that at least a part of Devers's forces should push on eastwards, to cross the upper Rhine and threaten the German First Army with outflanking. Eisenhower vetoed the proposal. He saw no purpose in crossing the Rhine so far south. Devers's divisions, like Patton's, were intended to swing northwards. By mid-December, their spearheads had begun to engage the positions of the old French Maginot Line, which the Germans were now defending backwards. Almost everywhere, from the Ardennes southwards, U.S. and French forces had closed up to the borders of Germany. Yet for Patton of all men, the great exponent of speed and dash, the battles of October and November had been deeply disappointing. All hope of a dramatic drive into Germany was gone with the coming of winter weather. After ten weeks of painful slogging, only more slogging seemed to lie ahead.

Some men cracked. Staff-Sergeant Bill Getman of the 254th Infantry spent thirty-one days in the Vosges before his unit began to push forward towards the Alsatian plain. One day during an attack, Getman suddenly turned and ran screaming towards the rear across a blazing field. A medic injected him with morphia and took him to the rear. He found himself unable to speak. After tests, he was taken to the 682nd Neuro-Psychiatric Hospital, where he had more tests. In the months that followed, he received narco-synthesis, narco-analysis and sodium-pentathol treatment. He began to speak again, stammering, and recovered some memory. He felt desperate to escape the army, and after a further examination he got his way. A doctor noted "my misery, my pains, my shaking body and poor speech. It was then that I heard the words: 'Sergeant, no more duty for you, limited or otherwise.'" Early in 1945, Getman went home.

"Many people here are resigned to a static winter," wrote Bradley's aide Colonel Chester Hansen on 22 November, "which is hard to understand ... Germany is now flat on her back and still resisting furiously. With good weather, we might smash on through with the help of our fighter-bombers, but the weather has been miserable and does not seem to want to cooperate." A visiting group of U.S. industrialists asked Bradley himself on 30 November whether he thought it possible that the armies might still be fighting over the same ground six months on. "I think it's entirely possible," answered 12th Army Group's commander, "unless we get a great deal more of ammunition and matériel."

"The average infantryman was nearly always certain that everyone else had quit the war except his own platoon," wrote Sergeant Forrest Pogue with the U.S. V Corps. "They knew whether fire came from left or right, and what casualties, but had little clue about time, or where they had been." Pogue noted the flat, dreary lull that descended upon the campaign towards the end of November:

Such periods always seemed marked by growing doubts on the part of the soldiers as to the wisdom of the war. In a typical discussion one evening, several of us talked of the listlessness of the American soldier, and the fact that he seldom seemed to know what he was fighting for. Some of them argued that there had never been any reason for our coming over, that all the U.S. needed was a strong navy. I doubted if we could ever make people see what they were fighting for, unless we were invaded. I said that most of them in 1942, soon after Pearl Harbor, seemed to think they knew why they were fighting, but as time went on it was harder to show them.

By the end of the Hürtgen battle, 24,000 Americans had become combat casualties, and another 5,000 had succumbed to trench foot, respiratory diseases and combat fatigue. Overall U.S. casualties in the autumn fighting were 57,000 combat and 70,000 non-combat, to achieve insignificant territorial gains, though the Americans could claim to have inflicted substantial losses upon the enemy. These totals masked harsher realities for individual units which had suffered most severely. A Company of the 4th Division's 22nd Infantry landed on D-Day with 229 soldiers of all ranks. By 16 November, only fifty-four of these men remained in the line; 275 replacements had been received. Among 500 soldiers all told, 70 had been killed, 41 were missing or captured, 235 were wounded and 91 had become non-battle casualties—trench foot or combat fatigue cases—though most of these returned to duty. Between 16 November and 4 December, 59.4 per cent of the 22nd's officers were either killed, wounded or missing, or became non-battle casualties, together with 53.9 per cent of their men.

Carlo d'Este has called the Hürtgen "the most ineptly fought series of battles of the war in the west." It is hard to disagree. A fatal combination of unimaginative command decisions by Bradley and Hodges and undistinguished combat performance by some of the units committed enabled the Germans to inflict greater pain than they suffered in the Hürtgen. While the British floundered in Holland, the U.S. 12th Army Group became almost literally lost in the woods. There is an argument that it was simply not feasible to make substantial advances in terrain such as that of the German border amid winter weather, but Hitler's panzers were soon to prove otherwise. "We never do anything bold," Eisenhower's Chief of Staff Bedell-Smith complained at a staff conference. "There are at least 17 people to be dealt with, so [we] must compromise, and compromise is never bold."

"If we were fighting a reasonable people," wrote Bradley's aide Chester Hansen on 6 December 1944, "they would have surrendered a long time ago. But these people are not reasonable. They have nothing to quit for." He added five days later: "I believe we have committed a smug and profound psychological error in announcing a program for unconditional surrender, since the German is obviously making capital of this in his effort to fan the fanaticism of the

German defence...Our demands do nothing to persuade him to realise the folly of his fight. They give him nothing to quit for."

Hansen's bewilderment about German persistence reflected in part the absence of any profound American hatred towards the enemy. Germany's defeat was inevitable. No conceivable throw of the dice by Hitler could prevent the Allies from completing the eventual destruction of his empire. The Nazi leaders' rejection of surrender was readily comprehensible, for only the gallows could await them. But why did the ordinary German soldier, or even his military commanders, fight stubbornly on, when the only consequence must be to add hundreds of thousands more names to the rollcall of the dead, and to ensure the ruin of such areas of the *Heimat* as had survived Allied bombing? Greater devastation was wreaked in Germany by air attack and ground fighting in 1945 than had occurred in the entire war before December 1944.

Colonel Hansen was surely right that German determination was strengthened by the Allies' insistence upon unconditional surrender. Some historians have echoed his conviction that the policy was thus mistaken. Yet it seems extraordinary to suppose that Roosevelt or Churchill could have offered negotiable terms to any faction within Germany, military or civilian. We know that Churchill was taken aback by Roosevelt's unscheduled assertion of the doctrine of unconditional surrender at the Casablanca conference in 1943. The British prime minister would almost certainly have avoided explicit use of those words. His consistent private advocacy of mercy for the German people, once they had been defeated, reflects his greatness of spirit. After May 1945, the Western allies treated the Germans with vastly greater generosity than they themselves had expected while the war was being fought. Had Germany's generals been granted a window into their nation's future, many might have perceived early surrender to Eisenhower as a tempting option.

Yet while the war was still being fought it was unthinkable for the Western allies to offer any olive branch. It would have been profoundly damaging to the motivation of ordinary American and British soldiers suddenly to have informed them that the Germans whom they were being asked to die fighting were merely lost souls who had been unfortunate enough to fall into the hands of evil leaders. Any such equivocation by Washington or London would also have provoked a crisis with Moscow. The time for offering mercy could come only when Germany had been militarily abased. It was a serious blunder by Washington to allow leakage of the Morgenthau Plan, calling for the reduction of Germany to a nation of peasant rustics. Stimson, as secretary of war, opposed this folly from the outset. At a meeting in Washington on 5 September to discuss the Plan, he observed wryly: "I'm the man in charge of the department which does the killing in this war, and yet I am the only one who seems to have any mercy for the other side." It was regrettable that Washington never formally abandoned the Morgenthau absurdity until the Potsdam conference in

July 1945. Yet, given the unspeakable suffering which the German nation had brought upon the world, nothing less than its unconditional surrender could be acceptable. It is surprising that some historians have supposed otherwise.

On 7 December, Eisenhower met Montgomery, Tedder and Bradley for a planning conference at Maastricht. In recent weeks, Montgomery had resumed his familiar written and verbal bombardment about the need to concentrate allied efforts upon a thrust to the Ruhr, "the only worthwhile objective on the western front." He argued that since Normandy the absence of a single ground commander had caused allied efforts to fail. He now proposed that 21st Army Group, with a U.S. army of at least ten divisions under command, should attack in pursuit of a Rhine crossing between Nijmegen and Wesel. Eisenhower, however, refused to accept the British view that the autumn campaign had been a failure. He suggested that it might be compared to Normandy. German forces had been steadily "written down," to create the circumstances for a decisive breakthrough. This was fanciful in the extreme. But so was Montgomery's proposal. The British commander's credibility as a strategist had been greatly diminished by the events of the autumn. Since June he had rendered himself so obnoxious in American eyes that most senior U.S. officers detested him.

As Supreme Commander, Eisenhower continued to display exemplary patience and discretion in avoiding a breach with the British field-marshal. Because relations between the two were somehow maintained, it is easy to forget that Montgomery provided Eisenhower with plentiful reasons to demand his dismissal. This would have been a disaster. The 21st Army Group's commander was a British hero. He was also, despite Antwerp and Arnhem, by far the ablest professional the British Army possessed. Later, in the spring of 1945, Montgomery's excesses caused Brooke seriously to fear that the Americans would insist upon supplanting him with Alexander, the only credible alternative. Alexander was much beloved by Churchill, and by the Americans, as a delightful military gentleman, an authentic hero of the First World War gifted with good looks, charm, courtesy and exquisite sartorial judgement. These merits, however, masked laziness and lack of intellect. Brooke dismissed Alexander as "a very, very, small man [who] cannot see big."

It was vital to the Allied cause that Montgomery should keep his job. Eisenhower was perhaps the only man with the diplomatic skills to make this possible, despite Montgomery's relentless provocation of the Americans in general and the Supreme Commander in particular. By December, all possibility of a quick end to the war was gone, under any commander and by any strategy. From Alsace to Holland, the tired soldiers of the Allied armies faced a strongly reinforced German defence. The winter weather made off-road movement almost impossible, and crippled the air forces. At the Maastricht conference,

Montgomery secured Eisenhower's agreement that he should push towards the Rhine early in January, supported by Simpson's Ninth Army on his right. But this would not be at the expense of other Allied operations further south—the "broad-front strategy." By this stage, no other policy was credible. An assault on a narrow front merely invited the Germans to move troops from a quiet sector to the threatened one. The relative passivity of the British since September had already enabled the enemy to shift forces southwards from Holland to face the Americans. There was every reason to suppose that they would do the same wherever they were granted a breathing space. In American eyes, since D-Day Montgomery had established a reputation for repeatedly promising more than he and his armies could deliver on the battlefield. Since September, whatever the disappointments and frustrations of U.S. ground operations, it was indisputable that the Americans had borne the brunt of the fighting.

By the standards of the Western allies, if not by those of the Russians or Germans, they had accepted painful casualties. Between 1 September and 16 December 1944, the U.S. First Army lost 7,024 men killed, 35,155 wounded, and 4,860 missing and captured; Ninth Army had suffered 10,056 casualties of all kinds during its brief existence; Third Army's losses were 53,182. The three armies had sustained an additional 113,742 non-battle casualties, mostly trench foot and combat fatigue. They had also lost almost a thousand tanks. Some of these were recoverable, and all were easily replaced. They had taken 190,000 German prisoners.

Yet, "to put it candidly," wrote Bradley later, "my plan to smash through to the Rhine and encircle the Ruhr had failed . . . Between our front and the Rhine, a determined enemy held every foot of ground and would not yield. Each day the weather grew colder, our troops more miserable. We were mired in a ghastly war of attrition." Eisenhower at Maastricht committed himself to more of the same, a continuation of the slow, dogged advance across the front. Hodges's First Army would maintain its advance across the Roer. Patch's Seventh Army would continue to support Patton, whose Third Army would launch a new offensive on 19 December, for which its commander cherished high hopes. Not one of the great men who gathered at Maastricht, not to mention the humble footsoldiers slogging through hills and forests in the snow and mud of mid-December, possessed any inkling that Hitler might have plans of his own.

CHAPTER EIGHT

The Bulge: An American Epic

THE SEASON OF "NIGHT, FOG AND SNOW"

A S WE HAVE seen, many German soldiers asserted in 1944, and have maintained ever since, that they fought until the end in fear of Soviet vengeance. It was ironic, therefore, that the next phase of the titanic struggle for Germany—Hitler's winter offensive in the Ardennes—inflicted a severe check upon the advance of the Allies on the Western Front and gravely weakened the Wehrmacht's ability to resist the Russians in the east. It is true that the Allied zones of occupation had been fixed, but no lines had been drawn for halting the armies. If the Anglo-Americans had been able to advance further faster, many Germans would have been spared the fury of the Red Army in the last days of war.

None of this, of course, was of the smallest interest to Hitler, who had no intention of remaining among those present if Germany was defeated. As far back as August, when his panzers' assault at Mortain was being destroyed by Allied fighter-bombers, he formed a design for a major counter-attack in the west. He told Keitel (Chief of Staff of OKW, the armed forces), Jodl (Chief of OKW's Operations Staff) and Speer that in November, the season of "night, fog and snow," he would strike at the Allies when they could not deploy their air-power. On 16 September, he informed his operations staff at the Wolf's Lair, his headquarters in East Prussia, that the attack would be made in the Ardennes, and codenamed *Wacht am Rhein*. His intention was to lunge sixty miles across Luxembourg and Belgium; seize Antwerp, the Allies' vital supply base; and separate the Americans from the British and Canadians. He did not delude himself that the German Army could expel the Allies from the continent altogether. But he believed that sufficient damage could be inflicted to fracture the Anglo-American alliance, buy time to strike anew against the Soviets, and allow his swelling arsenal of V-weapons to change the course of the war. He believed that a resounding defeat could persuade the Western allies, whom he held in little respect, to make terms. By contrast, he recognized that no military reverse would deflect the Russians.

Hitler's generals never for a moment shared their Führer's fantasies. It was true that the Americans in 1944 had followed the French in 1940 by deploying only a thin screen of troops in the Ardennes, which could easily be pierced by a determined assault. But in the Second World War the outcome of an offensive against a powerful enemy was seldom decided by the events of the first hours or even days. It hinged upon the ability of the attackers to sustain momentum, reinforcing constantly as fresh troops passed through tired ones, feeding forward the huge supplies of ammunition and fuel necessary to keep punching, while the defenders were rushing men, tanks, aircraft to the battlefield. In the winter of 1944, even after shifting large armoured forces from the east while the Russians were relatively quiescent, the Germans no longer possessed the resources to achieve this. Worse, they lacked fuel even to get their armour as far as Antwerp, unless they captured large stocks. Every German tank went into the Ardennes battle carrying just 150 gallons, enough for 150 miles, perhaps two or three days of combat. Once these were gone, the panzers would be in the hands of God or the devil. Germany's generals did not doubt that they could give the Americans a bloody nose, by hitting hard where the Allies were weak. But they anticipated that, when the offensive ran out of steam against strengthening Allied resistance, Germany would have expended its last strategic armoured reserve to gain only a few hundred square miles of snow-bound fields and woodlands.

Model and von Rundstedt—who was deliberately kept in ignorance of Hitler's plan until December—instead proposed a limited operation, designed to maul the American divisions holding the Ardennes front and dislocate Allied preparations to cross the Roer. Germany's warlord rejected this out of hand. He decreed that an assault should be made on the grandest scale: 200,000 men of Fifth Panzer, Sixth SS Panzer and Seventh Armies would strike a sector in which the Americans deployed only 83,000 troops. In the famous words of Sepp Dietrich, once the Führer's chauffeur and now commander of Sixth SS Panzer Army: "All Hitler wants me to do is to cross a river, capture Brussels, and then go on to take Antwerp. And all this at the worst time of the year through the Ardennes when the snow is waist-deep and there isn't room to deploy four tanks abreast let alone armoured divisions. When it doesn't get light until eight and it's dark again at four and with re-formed divisions made up chiefly of kids and sick old men—and at Christmas."

"He [Hitler] was incapable of realising that he no longer commanded the army which he had had in 1939 or 1940," said General Hasso von Manteuffel, the brilliant little forty-seven-year-old Prussian who had risen swiftly to command Fifth Panzer Army. Von Manteuffel was adored by his men, as a commander who always led from the front. Once, in a battle on the Eastern Front, a young tank officer heard a knock on his turret hatch, and thought it was Soviet shrap-nel. Instead, it was von Manteuffel's stick, as the general personally brought his tanks new orders. Now, von Manteuffel wrote of the chasm between Hitler's ambition and his army's capabilities: "It was not that his soldiers now lacked determination or drive; what they lacked were weapons and equipment of every sort." Von Manteuffel also considered the German infantry ill trained. Lieu-tenant Rolf-Helmut Schröder, adjutant of the 18th Volksgrenadiers, agreed. He felt confident of the quality of his unit's officers, but not of the men: "some were very inexperienced—and paid the price." Schröder held the Waffen SS in high respect, yet he was irked by the manner in which they were always given the best available equipment, at the expense of the Wehrmacht. His own unit was issued with new assault rifles before the Ardennes, only to have them withdrawn a few days later, with the explanation that such weapons were solely for SS use.

Von Manteuffel and his fellow generals were disconcerted by Hitler's appearance when they reported to him for a personal briefing at his headquar-ters near Ziegenburg in Hesse on 11 December: "a stooped figure with a pale and puffy face, hunched in his chair, his hands trembling, his left arm subject to a violent twitching which he did his best to conceal, a sick man apparently borne down by the burden of his responsibility. When he walked he dragged one leg behind him ... he talked in a low and hesitant voice."

Yet many rank-and-file German soldiers showed themselves more willing to believe in the Ardennes offensive than their commanders. Autumn Mist—the plan's new codename—revived briefly, but in surprising measure, flagging hopes: "Our soldiers still believed, in the mass, in Adolf Hitler," wrote von Manteuffel. "Somehow or other, they thought, he would once again turn the trick, either with the promised miracle weapons and the new U-boats or some other way. It was their job to gain him time." Colonel Gerhard Lemcke, com-manding the 89th Volksgrenadiers, said: "My comrades and I entered the battle with great confidence."

The Allies' failure to anticipate Hitler's assault was the most notorious intel-ligence disaster of the war. It derived chiefly from over-confidence. For years, thanks to the fabulous Ultra decoding operation, German deployments and intentions had become known to the Combined Chiefs of Staff before orders had even reached German forward positions. American and British command-ers had come to take for granted their extraordinary secret knowledge and even—in Montgomery's case—sometimes to profess that this stemmed from personal insight, rather than from his privileged view of the enemy's hand. Allied intelligence officers puzzled somewhat about the whereabouts of some German forces. An Allied summary of 13 December pondered "how long Sixth [SS] Panzer Army can remain isolated from the battle ... There is much the enemy can gain by holding his hand with these formidable formations, and much to lose by committing them prematurely."

But "orbat" intelligence about German unit deployments had diminished as the Germans withdrew across Europe, because they made more use of telephone landlines, impervious to interception. Moreover, Hitler imposed the strictest security on the build-up for Autumn Mist, including wireless silence. Allied air reconnaissance, anyway hampered by the winter weather, was unable to penetrate the great green canopy of the Ardennes forests, beneath which the panzers were gathering. German tank officers were ordered to adopt infantry uniform when reconnoitering the assault sector, though precious little prior inspection of the American lines was permitted at all. In a gesture reminiscent of Napoleon's wars, the hooves of horses bringing guns forward were muffled with straw. Men were issued with charcoal for cooking, to prevent woodsmoke from betraying their presence.

The Allies' most conspicuous error was to expect rational strategic behaviour from their enemy. There were clear pointers from intercepted communications, not least those of the Japanese ambassador in Berlin, that an offensive was brewing. There was much logistical evidence from Ultra of German accumulations of ammunition and fuel behind the quiet Ardennes sector, while these commodities were in desperately short supply in other, heavily engaged areas. Yet such pointers were ignored, because a German offensive seemed futile. Eisenhower, Bradley, Montgomery and their staffs made the same calculation as Germany's generals. Yet during five years of war the Allies had been granted plentiful opportunities to recognize Hitler's appetite for gigantic follies against the advice of his commanders. Five months earlier, the Anglo-Americans had profited from one of the greatest of these. The Führer had refused to allow a phased withdrawal in the west and insisted that Army Group B should fight in Normandy until it was largely destroyed. Yet in the winter of 1944 some Allied staff officers even suspected that his control of events was slipping. Hobart Gay, Patton's Chief of Staff at Third Army, wrote in his diary on 16 November that he believed Hitler was no longer in charge of Germany.

The outcome of all this wishful thinking at the highest level was that, when the Germans attacked on 16 December, the Allies were wholly unprepared. "Madness," wrote Winston Churchill, "is...an affliction which in war carries with it the advantage of SURPRISE." On the south of the front, the U.S. 6th Army Group had closed on the upper Rhine from Basle to the German border, save that the enemy still held out in the Colmar Pocket. Third Army had achieved some penetrations of the Siegfried Line, and was preparing a big new assault. First Army was close to the banks of the Roer, and preparing to attack its dams. Ninth Army and Montgomery's 21st Army Group were still struggling in eastern Holland. SHAEF Intelligence estimated that the Germans possessed seventy-four nominal divisions in the west, equivalent to less than forty full-strength formations. The Allies mustered fifty-seven divisions.

The three German armies fell on the Americans some thirty miles south of the Roer sector upon which Bradley's attention was focused. In the Ardennes three American infantry divisions—the 4th, 28th and 106th—were extended across a frontage of eighty miles, supported by the inexperienced 4th Armored. The 2nd and 99th Divisions faced the northern wing of the German assault. The 4th and 28th Infantry were weary and much depleted after their sorrows in the Hürtgen. The 106th was newly arrived and unpractised. The essential ingredients of a successful defence are obstacles covered by fire. Because the Americans were not expecting to be attacked, they had done little in the way of laying wire and minefields or digging deep bunkers. They occupied a few pillboxes inherited from the Germans, but had prepared no demolitions of bridges and culverts. The U.S. Army had traditionally paid little attention to defence, and in December 1944 saw little reason to do so. When American soldiers halted and entrenched, they did so only to pause between assaults. "Neither the 99th nor 106th divisions had dug in or made proper provision to meet an attack," wrote Sergeant Forrest Pogue at V Corps after the battle began. "There is not the sort of all-night minelaying done by 2nd Division." In some places, GIs even lacked good foxholes, because the frozen ground was impenetrable to entrenching tools, unless assisted by explosive charges.

Somewhat lackadaisical American patrolling, together with reports from local civilians, indicated heavy activity behind the German front, but this was not taken seriously. Noticing that most American units withdrew from outposts at night, the Germans exploited their absence. Even after the 106th Division heard tanks and vehicles moving on the night of 14 December, no one thought of investigating. The overriding enemy for every American soldier in Belgium and Luxembourg in the hours before the storm was not Germany, but the cold. It ate into men's spirits as much as their bodies, seeped into every corner of foxholes and tents, ruined houses and vehicles, where fires flickered and sentries stamped their boots in the icy darkness. There was a very unAmerican shortage of antifreeze, which caused difficulties for soft-skinned vehicle drivers. Some men still lacked proper winter clothing. Many formations were suffering alarming casualties from trench foot. GIs explored desperate expedients. A buddy of Private Eugene Gagliardi in the 7th Armored Infantry Regiment tried to keep his hands warm with his Zippo lighter. "We couldn't sleep, so we took our shoes off and took turns sticking our feet under the other guy's armpit," said Private First-Class Jack Pricket of the 393rd Infantry. Private "Red" Thompson desperately needed to wear his overcoat, but found that he could not run in it. He compromised by cutting off the bottom twelve inches of cloth, which cost him a reprimand from his disgusted platoon commander. A few hours later, officers had more urgent things to worry about.

On the evening of the 15th, the Germans who were to make the assault received a bottle of schnapps and a hot dinner apiece. There were peaches in rice for the engineers of 12th Volksgrenadier Division, "a feast for us," in the words of Private Helmut Stiegeler. Then they began to advance in "goose march" formation—single file—in silence through the darkness. Light reflected off the snow enabled each man to see those in front of him quite clearly. There were spasmodic halts, as officers checked the route. "The villages through which we marched lay peaceful in the December night," wrote Stiegeler. "Perhaps a dog barked here and there, or people were talking and looking at the passing soldiers. Out of an imperfectly blacked-out window a vague light shone out. With all these sights, most of our thoughts were of home in the warm houses with our families." Suddenly, a glow spread across the night sky. The Germans had switched on searchlights, deployed skywards to guide the advance of 3rd Parachute Division, traversing paths cleared by the engineers. A short, sharp, furious German bombardment began to play upon the American positions. At 0530, the armour and infantry attacked.

As the first column of German tanks emerged from the trees near Losheim, the local American outpost commander called for artillery fire. Nothing happened. The defenders' guns and mortars were, in many sectors, unready to fire effectively in front of their own positions. When the Germans closed in, they encountered pockets of brave and dogged resistance. But their spearheads were able to pierce the line in many places. There were far too few American soldiers to man a continuous line. On the 394th Infantry's front, anti-tank guns had been positioned for a week, but their gunners had not bothered to emplace them. As German shells started falling, the crews fled into the infantry lines. Two anti-tank men tore the cover off a K Company foxhole, and were promptly shot by its occupants. Soldiers of the 394th's B Company watched a German medical orderly work steadily at tending his unit's wounded in front of their positions. He glanced up only once, to shake his fist at the Americans. Soon afterwards, the company's survivors attached a white undershirt to a machine-gun cleaning rod and waved it aloft. Firing stopped, and they were herded to the rear as prisoners.

The 28th and 106th Divisions, in the centre of the front, held most of their positions on the first day largely because the Germans were content to bypass them and clear up later. The 28th Division, however, inflicted some sharp reverses on poor-quality German infantry formations. The attackers' difficulties were increased by the fact that, in the interests of security, some units had been forbidden to carry out reconnaissance. "I never took part in an attack which was worse prepared," said Colonel Wilhelm Osterhold of 12th Volksgrenadier Division. Some of his men cut the telephone wires to their own artillery, mistaking them for American booby-trap cables. This communications breakdown caused German shells to start falling among the Volksgrenadiers, inflicting serious casualties and stalling the regiment's advance.

From the outset, there was a remarkable gulf between the performance of German armoured and infantry formations. The panzers, and especially the SS, attacked with their familiar energy and aggression. The infantry displayed a

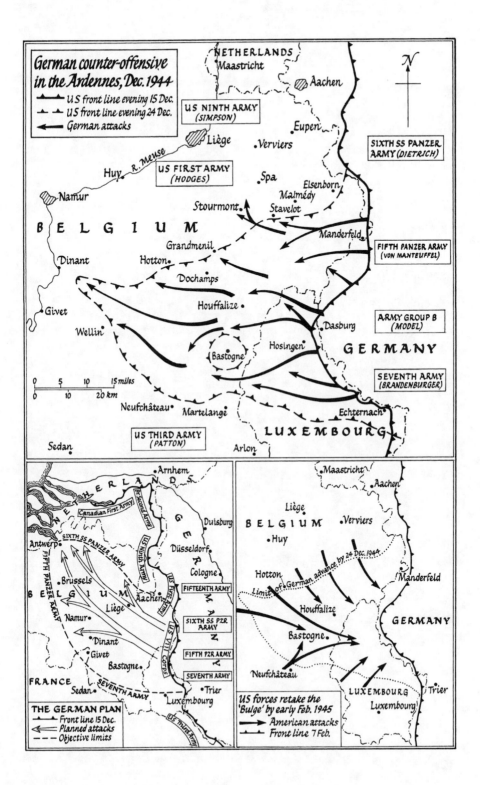

German counter-offensive in the Ardennes, Dec. 1944

- US front line evening 15 Dec.
- US front line evening 24 Dec.
- German attacks

NETHERLANDS
Maastricht
Aachen

US NINTH ARMY
(SIMPSON)

Eupen

SIXTH SS PANZER
ARMY (DIETRICH)

Liège
Verviers

US FIRST ARMY
(HODGES)

Huy
R. Meuse
Spa
Elsenborn
Malmédy
Stavelot

Namur
Stourmont

B E L G I U M
Grandmenil
Manderfeld

FIFTH PANZER ARMY
(VON MANTEUFFEL)

Dinant
Hotton
Dochamps

Houffalize
Dasburg

ARMY GROUP B
(MODEL)

Givet
Hosingen
GERMANY

Wellin
Bastogne

SEVENTH ARMY
(BRANDENBURGER)

0   5   10   15 miles
0   10   20 km

Neufchâteau
Martelange
Echternach

US THIRD ARMY
(PATTON)

Sedan
Arlon
LUXEMBOURG

Arnhem
NETHERLANDS
Maastricht
Aachen

Br. Second Army
Canadian First Army
Duisburg
Liège
Verviers

SIXTH SS PANZER ARMY
US Ninth Army
Düsseldorf
BELGIUM
Huy

Antwerp
FIFTH PANZER ARMY
Cologne
Hotton
Limit of German advance by 24 Dec. 1944
Manderfeld

Brussels
US First Army
FIFTEENTH ARMY
Aachen
Houffalize
GERMANY

BELGIUM
Namur
Liège
SIXTH SS PZR ARMY
Bastogne

Dinant
US VIII CORPS
FIFTH PZR ARMY
Neufchâteau

Givet
Bastogne
SEVENTH ARMY

FRANCE
Sedan
SEVENTH ARMY
Trier
Luxembourg
LUXEMBOURG
Luxembourg
Trier

US Third Army

THE GERMAN PLAN
- Front line 15 Dec.
- Planned attacks
- Objective limits

US forces retake the 'Bulge' by early Feb. 1945
- American attacks
- Front line 7 Feb.

lack of enthusiasm, skill and training which shocked their own officers and contributed importantly to the German failure. This was emphatically not the Wehrmacht of 1940. Officers' narratives resemble to a marked degree the tales of woe familiar in Allied accounts of offensive operations.

The forward American positions were bound to fall sooner or later, once the panzers had crashed through gaps in the line. A directive from Sixth SS Panzer Army emphasized the importance of such tactics, before the offensive began: "Watch for every opportunity to make flanking movements. Bypass enemy strongpoints and large towns." This indeed the Germans did, seeping through the front wherever they encountered weakness, leaving isolated defenders to be mopped up by the following waves.

Private Donald Doubek's platoon of the 106th Division had moved into the line on 15 December, with little idea where they were going or what they were supposed to do. They were ordered to dump their greatcoats and packs in a hamlet named Eigelscheid. Early next morning they found themselves being shelled and were ordered to fall back, which further confused and dismayed them. They took up defensive positions in the south-west corner of the village of Winterspelt, and lay awake all night listening to distant firing and watching flares go up. There were explosions nearby. Ray Ahrens, their scout, scuttled hastily through the door of a neighbouring house and found himself in a toilet. He stayed there for a while, feeling safer. The shelling became more intense next morning, 17 December. Their company commander was killed. His replacement told the men, "I'm going for help," and disappeared, not to be seen again. Men began to slip away towards the rear, "not wounded, but dazed and wandering aimlessly." At dawn Doubek's platoon was sixteen strong. By the time the Germans took the survivors prisoner, there were only four of them. Doubek, hit in the hip by grenade fragments, found himself loaded into a captured Dodge weapons carrier, and driven away towards a PoW camp. His mother was handed a telegram reporting him "missing" just as she walked down the main street of El Dorado, Kansas, to buy stock for her little hat and dress shop. She collapsed and had to be taken to hospital.

Many men learned of the German assault the hard way. Lieutenant Feinsilver, supply officer of the 2/12th Infantry, was riding his jeep to Berdorf in 4th Division's sector to collect laundry when he suddenly saw German soldiers advancing across a field beside the road. The jeep was fired upon as it performed a hasty U-turn, wounding the driver. Feinsilver seized the wheel and raced to the divisional CP in Consdorf with his companion slumped beside him. Soon afterwards, the officer commanding 12th Infantry's cannon company drove up, having bailed out of Berdorf after a fierce firefight. Battalion headquarters was near the church, where there was a big crowd of civilians. They were gathered for a local double wedding. The two brides and grooms walked from the ceremony in the burgomaster's office to the church for a service. An American officer said: "For God's sake, get this thing over with and tell these birds to get the hell home. I'll marry them myself if it'll help." A few minutes later, German shells started falling around them.

Word came to evacuate the entire 800-strong civilian population of the town. To the bafflement of the Americans, many preferred to remain in the cellars of their homes. Behind the front, "the tension in Luxembourg City was very great," said an American officer, "and could be seen written all over people's faces." Private Murray Mendelsohn, a combat engineer from New York, was initially exasperated by the German offensive because he had left a precious roll of unit snapshots to be developed by a chemist in the village of Ettelbruck, which was burned out in the first days. When he first heard that the Germans were closing on Bastogne, the name rang a bell. Just a week or two earlier, he had bought some perfume for his mother there.

On 28th Division's battlefield, a young officer of the 109th Infantry, Lieutenant James Christy, found himself struggling to persuade two tanks and a platoon composed of unwilling new replacements to advance into action. When Christy told Technical-Sergeant Stanislaus Wieszcyk that he was now platoon sergeant, the horrified NCO said: "Listen, lieutenant, I got these stripes for running a consolidated mess hall at Camp Fannin, Texas!" On the road to Fouhren at the southern end of the front, in deepening darkness, the tanks refused to go further without infantry leading them. Christy ordered his sergeant to take a squad to the point, and Wieszcyk said: "The guys have had more than enough today. They won't go." Lieutenant Christy doggedly set out down the road, leading the tanks alone. After a few minutes, Wieszcyk and a squad caught him up. "OK, lieutenant," said the sergeant resignedly, "you made your point." They marched on. The 28th Division inflicted significant damage upon the advancing Seventh Army, an overwhelmingly infantry force, though the 28th's positions were demolished one by one over the days that followed. The Division's 110th Infantry lost 2,750 men, virtually its entire strength, before the battle was over.

Further north, in the 99th Division's sector, Lieutenant Lyle Bouck's outpost of the 394th Regiment overlooking the Losheim Gap maintained one of the most dogged defences of the first day, until towards evening Bouck was wounded and his position overrun. He spent his first night as a prisoner lying among a crowd of Germans in a café in Lanzerath. Suddenly a King Tiger roared up the road and halted outside. A cluster of panzer officers swaggered in. They pulled out a map, pinned it to the wall with a couple of bayonets and began to berate the local infantry commanders for their sluggishness. The tankers' leader was Colonel Joachim Peiper, commanding a battle group of 1st SS Panzer designated to form the spearhead of Sixth SS Panzer Army. Peiper, a Knight's Cross holder, was the archetypal brave, gifted Waffen SS commander, just twenty-nine years old, with a record of brutality on the Russian Front which commanded respect even in SS circles. In one advance, Peiper's battalion claimed 2,500 Russians killed and just three captured. In his burning haste that first day in the Ardennes, the beak-nosed panzer officer wilfully ordered half-tracks into minefields, accepting the loss of six, to clear a path for his tanks. Like almost everything else in Peiper's savage but effective existence, half-tracks were expendable. Now, he demanded infantrymen to accompany the armour. Colonel Helmut von Hoffman, commanding 9th Parachute Regiment, acceded only after fierce argument. Peiper wrote: "I had the disgusted impression that the whole front had gone to bed instead of waging war."

At last, the SS officer and his men mounted their tanks once more and roared off into the early-morning darkness with paratroopers clinging to the Tiger hulls, leaving the café at Lanzerath to a few resentful German soldiers and their American prisoners. Lieutenant Bouck, of course, had understood nothing of the row he had witnessed, save that the SS were extremely cross. Shortly before dawn, the young American realized that his badly wounded platoon sergeant was dying. He laid the man's Bible and girlfriend's photograph on his chest and said a few words of prayer. He pledged his sergeant that, though they were now to be separated, they would meet again back in the States. The man's hand squeezed that of Bouck. Then he died.

Beyond chaos at the front as panzers crashed through the snowclad trees, disarray prevailed at most American headquarters. The Ardennes assault inflicted a psychological blow upon the Allied command at least as severe as the tactical damage to its front. The German bombardment had cut many phone lines, above all those from forward positions to artillery. Wireless communications were impeded by enemy jamming and poor terrain conditions.

Courtney Hodges, the taciturn fifty-seven-year-old Georgian who commanded First Army, was among the less esteemed American generals in Europe. He had started his military career as a private soldier, having failed his exams at West Point. His courage was not in doubt, and he was famously considerate for the welfare of his men. Bradley held him in great respect. But Hodges lacked force and presence. Many senior Americans asserted scornfully that First Army was run by its Chief of Staff, the unloved Major-General William Kean. In the early days of the German attack, First Army headquarters lapsed into an almost catatonic state, which appalled those obliged to do business with it. Three American pilots who flew their L-4 spotter planes out of Bullingen a few hundred yards ahead of Peiper's spearheads on 17 December reported to First Army HQ about their experience. They were soothed by a staff officer who assured them that 2nd Division had reported nothing amiss; since the pilots themselves were new to combat, they had "probably got spooked." Why didn't they just find their way to the mess hall and get themselves something to eat?

Throughout the first day, Hodges declined to cancel his planned attack on the Roer dams. Then he panicked. An officer who called on his HQ at Spa early on 19 December was bemused to find the table laid for breakfast, a decorated Christmas tree, phones and papers strewn around the offices, but only a lone woman civilian in occupation. Hodges had shifted his headquarters in acute alarm that it would be overrun. In the early hours of 20 December, a British liaison officer reported to Montgomery that "it was evident that the [First] Army commander was completely out of touch. His Chief of Staff was more completely informed but cagey or out of date. Neither of them seemed to be aware of the urgency of the situation."

Initial information was so scanty and confused that, on the evening of the 16th, Bradley believed the Germans were merely making a local counter-attack, and was no more willing than Hodges to dislocate deployments for his own impending attack. That first night, a bewildered Allied intelligence officer wrote: "Until more is known of this new enemy venture, it is probably unwise to speculate about its scope...There is no immediate objective of any special importance, and an advance limited to local gains of ground has nothing to recommend it. If he is bent on striking, the enemy is looking further afield." At this critical moment, Eisenhower's instinctive caution proved inspired. He ordered 7th Armored Division from Ninth Army in the north, together with 10th Armored from Patton's Third Army in the south, to move to cover the flanks of the threatened sector—just in case the German operation turned into something big. Patton, who believed himself on the brink of a breakthrough into Saarland, protested strongly, but acceded.

As every fresh signal, together with the capture of enemy documents, reinforced awareness that the Germans were making a huge effort, some Allied commanders remained bemused. "Pardon my French," said Omar Bradley, "but I think the situation justifies it. Where the hell has this sonofabitch gotten all his strength?" Eisenhower's Chief of Staff Bedell-Smith said: "Well, Brad, you've been wishing for a counter-attack—this is it." Bradley answered: "Yes, but I hadn't wanted it to be this strong." By the evening of 17 December, an Allied intelligence officer was writing: "Big issues are involved...If the venture is desperate, it is also well staged." German officers would have contested the second part of this assessment, but it is scarcely surprising that a shaken Allied headquarters should take such a view when the panzer vanguard was already twenty miles behind the Allied front. Model's forces had advanced further in two days than most of Eisenhower's men had moved in the preceding three months. They had demonstrated that neither the terrain nor the weather need be insuperable obstacles to a breakthrough, though both factors soon began to exert a baleful influence.

It is impossible not to detect perverse satisfaction in Montgomery's first comments to Brooke. The British field-marshal perceived a vindication of all his bitter criticisms of Eisenhower:

It looks as if we may now have to pay the price for the policy of drift and lack of proper control of operations which has been a marked feature of the last three months... The present American tendency is to throw in reserves piecemeal as they arrive, and I have suggested a warning against this. I have myself had no orders or requests of any kind. My own opinion is that the general situation is ugly, as the American forces have been cut clean in half, and the Germans can reach the Meuse at Namur without any opposition.

This was a wilful overstatement. Indecision at American higher headquarters was being redeemed by some cool and professional performances nearer the front. Gerow, commanding V Corps at the northern edge of the German thrust, decided by noon on the first day that the Germans were serious, and cancelled his formations' preparations for their own attack. He pulled back 2nd Division four miles under heavy German fire, to meet the threat to the Allied left flank alongside the 99th. At the headquarters of the U.S. 30th Infantry Division, the staff was engrossed in planning its crossing of the Roer. The G-3 interrupted to report to Hobbs, the commander: "General, there's some rumor that there's some sort of German attack going on down in front of VIII Corps. We don't know anything about it yet." The 30th Division knew all about it soon enough, as its units took post between Malmédy and Stavelot, and found themselves suffering heavy punishment. As the scale of the crisis became apparent, and amid the shattering of one of his regiments, the 119th, Hobbs turned to his assistant commander, Brigadier-General William Harrison, and asked: "What shall I do?" The brigadier urged the immediate relief of the local commander, and himself drove forward to take over the defence north of Stoumont.

Also in the north, Collins of VII Corps placed 1st Division on six-hour alert by 1100 on the first day, well before the Allied army commanders perceived the weight of the German assault. The "Big Red One" moved forward to join the battle that night, and was engaged next morning. Major James Woolnough, commanding its 16th Infantry Regiment, described the advance to the front as "the most frightening thing you can imagine: no intelligence, all those rumors of paratroopers dropping in, getting strafed. It was pitch black, and people were running every which way." Eisenhower's strategic reserve, the Airborne Corps, was rushed forward from its camps at Rheims. The 82nd Division went north, to move into line on the right of 30th Division. The 101st was sent south, to the vital road junction of Bastogne, which its leading elements reached around midnight on 18 December. The British 6th Airborne was hastened across the Channel from its camps in England to join 21st Army Group.

The Germans were making ground, and taking thousands of American prisoners in the forward areas. In the village of Honsfeld alone, a rest area of 99th

Division, Peiper's men seized intact some fifty American reconnaissance vehicles including half-tracks. The Germans also captured useful quantities of American petrol, and set prisoners to work emptying cans into their panzers. "The enemy was in total confusion," said Captain Werner Sternebecke, commander of Peiper's reconnaissance group, describing their arrival at Bullingen. "There was no organized resistance apparent." In one respect, Hitler's hopes were fulfilled: through the first week, interminable as it seemed to the Allies, poor weather prevented the air forces from joining the battle. In the rear areas, tens of thousands of American stragglers, service and support units, refugees from the initial German assaults, clogged roads and villages, fleeing in unashamed terror.

Some American armoured units performed poorly. Tank crews showed themselves reluctant to move at night, even in the face of desperate emergency. The German 276th Volksgrenadiers, supported by just seven self-propelled guns, deterred 102 Shermans of 10th Armored Division from engaging seriously in the first days of battle around Echternach. The American historian and Ardennes veteran Charles MacDonald passed withering comment upon the reluctance of either 9th or 10th Armored Divisions to provide effective support for the infantry of 4th Division, even though these U.S. formations suffered negligible casualties in the early stages of the battle. They seemed as protective about the welfare of their tanks, McDonald wrote, as an old-time cavalryman about his horse. Many American armoured crews endured the experience of Sergeant Jones of the 743rd Tank Battalion. An infantry captain warned him that a German tank was approaching. Jones fired as soon as he saw it—and watched the shell ricochet off its armour. "Did you see that?" said the infantry officer wonderingly over the radio.

MOST HUMAN BEINGS in peace or war are disorientated by finding themselves victims of the unexpected, whether a car crash or bank robbery or—in December 1944—the arrival of Germans in places where Americans had not the remotest expectation of encountering them. Men who have been briefed and trained for a military operation, who know what they are doing and where they are going, possess an immense advantage over those who are surprised. In the first two days of the Bulge offensive, tens of thousands of Americans found themselves in predicaments for which they were unprepared psychologically or militarily. A soldier of the 394th Infantry wrote, after being captured by Joachim Peiper's men in Honsfeld: "I hated to give up like that, but I guess it was the best thing to do. If we had started shooting we would have been slaughtered like a bunch of cattle."

All along the front, the impact of sudden appearances by enemy armour, together with the infectious fever of retreat, was compounded by rumours about the activities of Colonel Otto Skorzeny's commandos in American uniform. A few German paratroopers were also dropped in the American rear areas. They made no impact upon the battle, but provoked an outbreak of fifth-column paranoia. In the clear icy air, sound carried for miles. Men who heard shooting often supposed it to be far closer than it was. Colonel Pete Heffer of VI Corps recorded in disgust the panic-stricken behaviour of an officer in charge of a fuel dump who, upon hearing unfounded rumours of approaching Germans, personally smashed open 4,000 gas cans with an axe: "lots of equipment and matériel was prematurely destroyed."

The morning report of Company G of the 112th Infantry on 23 December recorded a long list of men "Missing In Action—Battle Casualty at Evacuation Hospital Unknown—Circumstances: Position Overrun by the Germans." The combat-fatigue toll included two technical-sergeants, six staff-sergeants, three sergeants, two technical personnel, and thirty-four other ranks. The executive officer of one battalion survived the battle, but died of a heart attack a few days later. Many other units suffered similar losses. On the night of 17 December, the officer commanding the 2/394th Infantry was described as "a quivering hulk."

Fierce anger spread through the American ranks at news on the second day of the offensive that SS panzer units were killing prisoners—nineteen at Honsfeld, fifty at Bullingen, eighty-six in the "Malmédy massacre" by men of 1st SS Panzer, the Leibstandarte Division. The Germans in the Ardennes offensive shot prisoners on a substantial scale, and even more contemptibly, murdered in cold blood more than a hundred Belgian civilians. Yet it was absurd to pretend—as did Allied propaganda at the time, and war crimes prosecutors later—that the killing of prisoners was a uniquely German practice. Some American formations were notorious for dealing summarily with captives. The 90th Division had a joke about the officer who asked what had happened to nineteen prisoners sent to the rear and was assured that five had reached the PoW cage. From top to bottom of the U.S. Army, the Malmédy massacre intensified a reluctance to take SS prisoners. Bradley expressed surprise on Christmas Eve, hearing that four PoWs from 12th SS Panzer had been brought alive to the cage. "We needed a few samples," said an officer apologetically, "that's all we've taken, sir."

A soldier of the 22nd Infantry remarked on the difficulty of taking prisoners to the rear amid intense artillery fire during the Hürtgen Forest fighting: "If you try to take them back you're taking your life in your hands twice. Once going through that terrain to get them back. If you get through it safely that time and don't get killed then you still have to go back up front after you get rid of them. So a lot of them never reached the rear that way." Private Bill True of the 101st Airborne was shocked when he saw a sergeant walk up to a wounded German lying in a ditch, exchange some words with him, then fire two rounds into the man's chest and walk on.

Sergeant Forrest Pogue at V Corps wrote:

The whole matter of killing prisoners has been on my mind since the Hürtgen Forest fight. I recalled ugly stories about a unit's record in regard to the killing of prisoners... [In the Ardennes battle] I visited a headquarters on the Malmédy road and was told that a sniper had just shot one of their men on an outpost. The men were looking for the German, and said that if they captured him they would shoot him. An armored infantry lieutenant, noting my surprise, said that his outfit had captured enemy soldiers on a recent occasion and, after saving two for questioning, disposed of the rest. His excuse was that, being tankers, they couldn't handle the rest. Others spoke of opening fire on enemy soldiers who seemed on the point of surrendering, so that there would be no need to shoot them later... A massacre like that at Malmédy is brutal only because it is larger, or calculated to provoke terror.

Few men in the line, however, possessed Pogue's academic objectivity about such matters. The Malmédy massacre provided a focus for all the fears, losses and humiliations of the first days of the American retreat. It generated a sense of grievance which possessed little rational justification amid brutalities which differed only in scale, not in kind, on the two sides of the line. But outrage about the atrocity was of great service to the American defence at a critical time. It aroused among GIs a hatred of their enemy that was conspicuously absent for much of the north-west Europe campaign. It helped to make many Americans fight harder in the vital days of December, and it made them disinclined to mercy. "This was the only time I saw American troops kill German soldiers that were trying to surrender," wrote Private Donald Schoo of the 80th Infantry Division. "If they wore the black uniforms of the SS, they were shot." Like many men, he did not know that every German tank crew wore black.

All over the battlefield, groups of Americans cut off from their own people and their own formations were struggling to regain cohesion and purpose amid chronic uncertainty about what was going on. Nothing did more harm to the morale of ordinary American soldiers in those first days than their ignorance. "We were in a state of confusion and without much of a leadership," said Corporal Max Lehmann of the 99th Division's 394th Infantry. "We had no idea what was going on in the next town to us, let alone the big picture," said Private Murray Mendelsohn, a combat engineer. Major Melvin Zais found himself sheltering in a cellar with two other officers, the more senior of whom set about slicing some potatoes he found and cooking them over a candle. Zais thought wryly: "If this is the way it is for a full colonel, I don't want any part of this army." On 20 December at V Corps, Sergeant Pogue scribbled in his diary:

remarkable how little we know of situation; how much the high-ranking officers deal in rumor-mongering. It seems remarkable that few expected counter-attack. It was only way Germany could relieve pressure, restore waning hope of her people, forestall unrest, disrupt our plans, postpone the war of attrition. When the attack is beaten back, if we have enough stuff to follow them through, we may gain the Rhine and beyond quicker than we would have done otherwise.

Stalin agreed. "Very stupid," he observed, when he heard of the German offensive. The German Army was already thinking likewise.

STEMMING THE TIDE

FOR THE WEHRMACHT, the first days of the offensive yielded a brief surge of exhilaration and hope. "Enemy morale was higher than at any time during the campaign," acknowledged a U.S. Army post-war report. A certain Lieutenant Rockhammer, whose tank unit is unidentified but who was evidently an ardent Nazi, wrote to his wife on 22 December:

> For once, we find ourselves a thousand times better off than you at home. You cannot imagine what glorious hours and days we are enjoying. It looks as if the Americans can't hold our big push. Today, we overtook a retreating column and flattened it...we got past them by taking a back road through the wood; then, as if we were on manoeuvres, we lined up along the road with 60 Panthers. This endless column approached us, their vehicles side by side, hub to hub, filled to the brim with men. We were able to concentrate the fire of 60 tank guns and 120 machine-guns on them. It was a glorious bloodbath, vengeance for our devastated homeland. Our men can still show the old zip...Victory never seemed as close as it does now. The decisive moment is at hand. We shall throw these arrogant bigmouthed apes from the New World into the sea. They will not get into our Germany...If we are to save everything that is sweet and lovely in our lives, we must be ruthless at this decisive hour of the struggle.

Far away on the Italian front, Allied troops occupying a house vacated by the Germans found a letter on the kitchen table addressed: "For English soldiers." It read: "Dear Kamerad, on the Western Front German troops are attacking the line of Americans. German tanks have destroyed a great deal of the enemy troops. The new German Luftwaffe is on the West Front and she is very, very good. The war is in a new station, she is over when the Germans are victorious.

Germans are fighting for their lives. The English are fighting for the Jews. AN GERMAN SOLDIER."

"The roads are littered with wrecked American vehicles, cars, tanks," Lieutenant Belmen of the Wehrmacht's 1818th Artillery gloated in his diary on 19 December. "Another column of prisoners passes. I count over a thousand men. Nearby there is another column of 1500, with about 50 officers, including a lieutenant-colonel who had asked to surrender."

The Germans had given the Americans an impressive tactical demonstration of how to launch an assault in difficult terrain, using infiltration and encirclement rather than allowing themselves to be pinned down in front of pockets of resistance, as the Allies so often did. In the first five days of the Ardennes battle, the Germans destroyed 300 American tanks and took 25,000 prisoners. Some American historians have sought to argue that only support troops or isolated individuals broke and fled. "A belief would long persist that when the Germans first struck, some American troops fled in disarray," wrote Charles MacDonald. "…That was patently false. No front-line American unit fled without a fight." It is impossible to accept this view. Eyewitness evidence of panic in some units, and of pathetic tactical failure in others, is overwhelming. When 1st SS Panzer attacked Stoumont, for instance, eight American tank destroyers were overrun without firing a shot after being abandoned by the infantry company alleged to be supporting them. On the first day, the 394th Regiment suffered 959 casualties, of which just 34 were dead and 701 "missing." There is no reason to regard any of this, however, as ground for unique national embarrassment. Men of every army run away when their front is broken or they find themselves enveloped by superior forces. The British often did so, and the Russians—and the Germans. If guilt and shame were appropriate, these belonged at American higher headquarters.

A critical point about the Ardennes battle is that instances of American chaos, of hysterical men fleeing for the rear, created a misleading picture. Any soldier might be forgiven for succumbing to fear as seventeen enemy divisions crashed without warning into his front. The wider reality, however, was that from its first day the ill-conceived German assault went as wrong as the British drive to Arnhem three months earlier. Much has been made of Allied blindness to the offensive possibilities of the Ardennes forests. Bradley had manned the region weakly, because it was considered difficult country through which to move large bodies of men and vehicles. So indeed it proved. From the first hours of 16 December, massive German traffic jams developed behind the front, as vehicles struggled to advance along the constricted approaches, while engineers made slow work of bridging rivers and streams.

German vehicles suffered immense difficulties on steep, narrow, twisting mountain roads. Guns sometimes had to be winched round hairpin bends. On 17 December, von Manteuffel and Model met on foot, both commanders having abandoned their transport in despair. Peiper, leading his battle group of 1st SS Panzer, had to walk six miles when the tanks became stuck. During its November retreat, the Wehrmacht had blocked the road between Dasburg and Clerf with fallen trees. Now, these proved frustrating obstacles to the German advance. Panzer Lehr was seriously late getting across the Our river. Von Manteuffel called the collapse of the German timetable in the first days "a very grave disappointment." In 1940, Hitler's armies had achieved a breakthrough in the Ardennes in summer weather, against a weak enemy. In December 1944, it proved a nightmare to move tanks and horse-drawn guns and equipment along forest roads and tracks that became slush-filled morasses. The terrain did much more than the defenders to check German deployment in the first vital days. And all this, of course, was before the weather allowed the allied air forces to intervene.

While German armour displayed its usual proficiency, the performance of supporting infantry, especially those of Seventh Army on the southern flank, was as feeble as von Manteuffel had feared that it would be. Ill-trained replacements, some of them newly transferred from the navy or air force, stumbled bewildered on to the battlefield. They proved completely lacking in the skills indispensable to German success. American defenders were taken aback to see some enemy soldiers advancing as uncertainly as sheep, clustering together and going to ground under fire, just as Allied infantrymen were often criticized for doing. Ferocious young Nazis such as Peiper and Skorzeny were exasperated by the poor showing of the footsoldiers. It was no more use for German tanks to advance deep into enemy territory without effective infantry support than for Allied ones to do so. The panzers had broken through on a forty-mile front and were driving west. But the infantry had shown themselves "incapable of carrying out the attack with the necessary violence," recorded a bitterly frustrated von Manteuffel. Officers were disgusted to find their men lingering to loot the prodigious quantities of American equipment and rations which fell into their hands. Wehrmacht discipline in December 1944 was nothing like that of the German Army which had died in Russia. The offensive lacked the sustained power to fulfil its objectives.

This became plain to the German commanders as early as the second or third day, when von Rundstedt appealed in vain to Hitler to break off the operation. On both flanks, American forces were holding their positions, with reinforcements arriving to shore up the shoulders of the front, preventing the Germans from widening their penetration. Kampfgruppe Peiper missed a notable opportunity after taking Bullingen. Had its tanks continued onwards to Wirtsfeld and Krinkelt–Rocherath, they could have turned the flanks of two American divisions, the 2nd and 99th. Major-General Lauer of the 99th said afterwards: "The enemy had the key to success within his hands, but did not know it." This was an overstatement, yet there is no doubt that Peiper could

have caused much trouble for the Americans. Whatever the achievements of
Germans at regimental level and below, in the Bulge battle their command and
control were lamentable. Army and corps commanders, hampered by poor
communications and misjudgements, again and again missed opportunities.
Bullingen provided a striking example. If Peiper had been allowed to exploit a
local situation where he discovered American weakness, instead of being
obliged to persist rigidly with the plan devised before the operation began, he
might have fared better. Instead, the Americans used their breathing space to
plug a dangerous gap. As darkness was falling on the evening of 17 December, on
a reverse slope between Bullingen and Dom, Lieutenant-Colonel Derrill M.
Daniel of the 2/26th Infantry told his company commanders that no one should
think his battalion proposed to emulate those who had broken or quit. "We fight
and die here," he said. The performance of Daniel's men during the days that
followed was among the most impressive of the battle.

Henceforward, weakened German units began to meet powerful, well-led
U.S. formations, thrown into battle knowing that they were expected to fight for
their lives. Lieutenant Rolf-Helmut Schröder of 18th Volksgrenadiers, fresh
from the Eastern Front, was reluctantly impressed by the physical quality of
American prisoners, "so many big, fit, well-fed men." In defence, winter darkness was invaluable to the Germans for resupply and redeployment beyond the
reach of Allied airpower. But, in attack, Model's forces were badly handicapped
by the short December days, for it was so hard to move tanks at night. Ever since
Normandy, Allied commanders had complained about high tank losses. General "Pip" Roberts of 11th Armoured Division observed: "Whenever you attack
the enemy with tanks, you get heavy casualties. When you inflict the casualties
is when he attacks you." Now, it was the Germans' turn to confront that reality,
and they possessed vastly fewer reserves than the Allies.

The once-mighty Panzer Lehr Division went into the Ardennes battle with
just fifty-seven tanks, barely the strength of an American armoured battalion,
and it was soon losing them. As the Germans pushed westwards, they suffered
mounting attrition from pockets of resistance at crossroads and villages. At
St. Vith and Stavelot and scores of other Belgian villages, their dash was
impeded sometimes for hours, sometimes for days, by groups of Americans supported by Shermans and tank destroyers. Even the inadequate 57mm anti-tank
gun took its toll. Artillery, the outstanding arm of U.S. forces, began to play
havoc with the German columns once it had restored communications and forward observation lost in the first stages of the battle. A single 105mm howitzer
battalion fired 10,000 rounds in one day.

Seventh Armored Division, in the north, inflicted one of the first important
checks on the German advance. On 17 December, 1st SS Panzer Division
approached the vital road junction at St. Vith, in the midst of the German
assault front, and some ten miles west of its start line. Beyond lay open country

towards the Meuse and the Belgian plain, together with the huge American fuel dumps, which the German tanks desperately needed, north-westwards at Stavelot. The tale of Peiper's panzers being cut off from the dumps by a wall of fire, from fuel set alight by the defenders, is mythical. The German never got near the 2.5-million-gallon treasure trove. Belgian guards indeed created a wall of flame, but this caused delay only for units of the U.S. 30th Division, hastening to get past it into action. The Americans ordered the fires put out. The first units of 7th Armored arrived just in time to block the Germans. Led by Brigadier Bruce Clarke, the 7th's Combat Command B conducted an eight-day stand which was as critical, and as courageous, as the defence of Bastogne. St. Vith was later abandoned for a time, but the defence achieved its vital objective—delay. An American historian suggests that here was some belated consolation for the miseries of the Hürtgen Forest fighting in November. If U.S. forces had not held the Hürtgen and its outlying villages, it would have been harder to present a "strong shoulder" to the right flank of the German assault.

The Bulge battle provided many examples of achievement by improvised American units, fighting in the sort of battle groups which the German Army routinely assembled but which were unfamiliar to the Allies. A battalion of combat engineers was assigned to the defence of Wiltz on 17 December, supported by six tanks, four assault guns, four three-inch tank destroyers, a battery of artillery and some bandsmen, clerks and cooks from 28th Division headquarters. Three days and nights of battle later, a third of the survivors were recommended for Silver or Bronze Stars. Two NCOs, Garland Hartsig and Eugene Baker, received battlefield commissions.

The "Twin Villages" of Krinkelt and Rocherath were scenes of some of the fiercest fighting. The officers of 12th SS Panzer were already fuming because traffic jams behind the front had stranded much of the division behind the West Wall, while its spearheads strove to achieve a breakthrough. The Germans suffered heavy losses of armour attempting to secure the villages with scanty infantry support. German recovery crews achieved their usual miracles in restoring some damaged tanks and tank destroyers to service within hours. Several immobilized German tanks were remanned and used as static pillboxes. But none of this diminished the Panzers' difficulties, when they found themselves bogged down in village fighting. "I spotted our battalion commander," wrote Lieutenant Willi Engel, a Panther platoon commander in Rocherath. "His face mirrored dejection and resignation. The failed attack and painful losses obviously depressed him severely. The knocked-out Panzers offered a distressing picture. At that moment, a single panzer approached the Command Post. Suddenly, only about 100m away, it turned into a flaming torch...It was later determined that an immobile but otherwise serviceable Sherman had scored the hit...Both sides fought with bitter determination."

Lieutenant Willi Fischer said: "When I reached the vicinity of the church [at Rocherath], a gruesome picture was waiting for me. Beuthauser was bailed out... His loader was killed by rifle fire as he bailed out... Brodel's tank stood next to me, burning brightly. He sat lifeless in the turret. In front of me, more panzers had been put out of action and were still burning." The U.S. V Corps had suffered serious casualties, but could afford them vastly better than the Germans. It had inflicted a notable defeat on one of the best formations in Hitler's armies. A 12th Army Group staff officer watching reinforcements moving forward experienced an unaccustomed surge of respect and understanding for the American infantryman: "Everywhere there is a feeling of humility—we know that his fight is the only real fight in this war."

Many of the actions that saved the American front reflected cool professionalism. On the extreme northern flank of the German push the 38th Cavalry Reconnaissance Squadron laid eighty truckloads of barbed wire, thickly laced with trip-flares and booby traps, in front of its positions. None of its men attempted to fight from houses, which often promised more protection than they provided. The defenders dug or blew foxholes in the steel-hard ground. The squadron lost only fifteen men. Its colonel, Robert O'Brien, said afterwards: "The whole action was an example not of any heroic action, but of what an efficient, active defense can do. There was no great lot of leadership: the men didn't need it." O'Brien's men did not endure the weight of attack that fell on units further south, but as American forces began to recover their balance the Germans found themselves facing ever-increasing attrition. The 37th Field Artillery was supporting the 1/23rd Infantry of 2nd Division. The Americans watched German infantry advancing towards their positions near Murringen. What followed was a textbook affair. The gunners dropped a round right, another left, one short, one beyond the approaching grey lines. Their forward observer in the church steeple, Captain Charles Stockwell, then called: "Fire for effect!" The 1/23rd's commander, Lieutenant-Colonel John Hightower, wrote: "Everything fired right on target. Charles yelled for them to fire the concentration again, and then once more. He then said: 'That is perfect. The infantry thanks you, and I thank you.'" The Germans fled back into the woods whence they had come. When they regrouped and renewed the attack, they suffered the same fate.

Many American officers on the battlefield maintained cooler heads than those at higher commands. "Headquarters continues to be a madhouse," recorded Hansen at Bradley's 12th Army Group on 20 December, "with too many people running in and out—too many telephone calls. Traffic is heavy, too, with the new divisions coming to reinforce our effort... they have helped at least to abate the alarmist sentiment that was so evident yesterday." When officers of reinforcement units asked local headquarters for information, again and again they heard only: "The front is fluid." The drivers of Allied tank columns rolling through the night hours to reach the front struggled to hold the road amid snow and ice, their only guide dim masked headlights, and the tiny reflector on the stern of the vehicle ahead. Amid the relentless engine roar of his Sherman of the 743rd Tank Battalion, Lieutenant Joseph Couri watched flares go up in the distance and glimpsed the tail glow of German V1 rockets heading for Liège: "My eyes were red, swollen and irritated from the grime and dust travelling behind another tank at close quarters with the turret open and standing all the time." Fighting a tank in the depths of winter was almost as tough as living in a foxhole. The Sherman's air intake sucked a constant icy blast into the turret, causing the commander and gunner to suffer special misery. Periscopes frosted. Condensation formed into icicles inside hulls. Starting up was often a major operation, and crews had to use "little joe" generators to keep batteries charged when their engines were still. Nervous infantrymen were grateful for armoured support, but complained about the noise generated by tanks in close proximity, fearful that it would draw German fire.

ON THE MORNING of 19 December, Panzer Lehr advanced to within two miles of the key road junction at Bastogne, on the south side of "the Bulge," as the shape of the German penetration was already causing the battle to be known among the Allies. Just a few hours earlier, the 101st Airborne had arrived in the town after a hundred-mile dash through the darkness from its rest camp at Rheims. Many of its soldiers lacked winter clothing, arms, ammunition. As they filed forward into action, they scrounged weapons from the broken fugitives and ravaged units falling back on Bastogne from the old front. The 101st possessed just enough arms, just enough men and more than enough old-fashioned guts to close the road to Panzer Lehr. The German formation was a shadow of its pre-Normandy greatness, but it remained a powerful threat to lightly armed paratroopers. Brigadier-General Anthony McAuliffe, commanding the 101st, was lucky to have the support of some forty tanks and the 705th Tank Destroyer Battalion.

Major William Desobry, commanding some fifteen Shermans of 10th Armored Division at Noville north-east of Bastogne, kept meeting stragglers "who told us horror stories about how their units had been overrun." He tried to persuade them to join his own outfit and stiffen the defence, "but their physical and mental condition was such that they would be more a burden than a help." He let them stumble on through his positions towards the rear. A unit of combat engineers which he embodied turned out to be a liability rather than a reinforcement: "They just weren't effective." But he acquired an armoured infantry platoon of 9th Armored, which proved somewhat more useful.

At 0400 on 19 December, Desobry heard a firefight up the road. He went out and stood listening by Noville church. His outpost men pulled back into the town, headed by an NCO shot in the mouth, who reported that German half-tracks were on the way. When the outpost team first heard vehicles, they had thought these might contain retreating Americans. Only when the Germans opened fire at close range were they disabused. There was an interval of silence in Noville, during which the Americans lay over their weapons, waiting apprehensively. Then through the thick dawn fog they heard the clatter of armour. Desobry thought: "Oh brother! There really is something out there!" As the first units of von Manteuffel's 2nd Panzer Division appeared, the Americans opened fire. They hit the two leading vehicles. As the Germans paused and began to deploy across their front, Desobry sent engineers forward to lay charges on the disabled enemy half-tracks, to ensure that they stayed where they were, blocking the road. A tank destroyer unit rolled up from Bastogne to stiffen the defence.

The Germans now occupied ridge lines overlooking Noville, from which they brought down heavy fire on the little town. Desobry felt that it was essential to regain this high ground. The 1/506th battalion of the 101st Airborne arrived and prepared to attack, some of its men begging weapons from Americans in the town even as they deployed. Yet just as the Airborne moved forward, so did the Germans. The rival attackers met, and a furious two-hour battle took place. Desobry could not rid himself of a sense of unreality, as he saw German prisoners being brought back: "These guys look funnier than heck." When one of them gave the Hitler salute, he thought: "This is getting like a Charlie Chaplin movie."

The Americans were simply not strong enough to make ground against the *schwerpunkt*—the principal concentration of force—of a panzer division. The Airborne abandoned the attack on the ridge line. "We said 'okay, good try—but let's pull back into the town.'" Just as the paratroopers were reorganizing, an American maintenance vehicle drove into Noville and stopped by Desobry's CP. The Germans spotted it and immediately called down painfully accurate artillery fire, which inflicted severe American casualties. Desobry himself was hit in the hands by shell fragments. As he was being driven to the rear in a casevac jeep, they were stopped by Germans. When the panzergrenadiers saw wounded men on litters, they waved the vehicle on. The driver got lost. Desobry was the only one of four casualties on his jeep to reach a field hospital alive, though he became a prisoner. A counter-attack by the 101st next day, 20 December, enabled the Americans encircled at Noville to withdraw into the Bastogne perimeter. The robust defence of the little town had imposed an important twenty-four-hour delay on 2nd Panzer's advance.

The 101st Airborne's stand at Bastogne became one of the American legends of the Second World War. Just praise has been heaped upon the achievement of the "Screaming Eagles." Less has been said about the medley of stragglers and survivors from all manner of units who found themselves participating in the town's eight-day siege whether they liked it or not. Staff-Sergeant Charles Skelnar, a baker from Omaha, Nebraska, now serving as a cook with the 482nd Anti-Aircraft Regiment, first heard of Bastogne as he manned a .50 calibre machine-gun on the kitchen truck of his unit on the Longvilly road, feeling very frightened in the midst of "absolute chaos." Until 16 December, he and his unit had scarcely heard a shot fired in anger. Now, they were suddenly ordered to abandon their half-tracks and pull back to Bastogne. About half his battery made it. The rest were lost on the road.

Dr. Henry Hills was a member of one of six field surgical teams which were landed by glider outside Bastogne on 26 December, to relieve the desperate shortage of medical aid. Three surgeons were killed by German fire before they landed, and every glider was hit in the air. As soon as they crashed, the medics dashed out of the wreckage and ran into the town perimeter. They were taken to a garage.

> As soon as you lifted up that [garage] door to go in, you could smell gas gangrene. There were some women trying to help, giving them water and so forth. [Men] were dying like flies. They'd been there for ten days. The only light was on the far side, where mechanics did repairs. There was a field stove there with coffee brewing, and four tables set up—stretchers on saw horses. After a case, we dumped all the instruments into a great big vat filled with alcohol. We had no gowns or masks, of course. The bottom floor of the garage had 400 serious casualties. The top floor had 400 walking wounded. We didn't bother with them.

The doctors had lost all but six pints of plasma in the glider crash. They had sulpha but no penicillin. As they worked, an infantry colonel came in and said he had received complaints that there were too many amputations: "Understand you're taking them off right and left here." Hills nodded: "Yep, those that need to come off." The colonel said: "Well, I'm not sure they do." Hills picked up a discarded limb and handed it to him. The colonel turned ashen, and left without another word.

Fifty hours after the medics arrived, they were relieved. Hills's last case was a minor compound fracture of the forearm. The anaesthetists were busy, so the doctor instructed a cook on how to inject the man progressively with a syringe of pentothal. When they finished the operation, the cook said: "Now I've done everything in this army."

The Germans bypassed Bastogne, leaving the town surrounded, and pushed on beyond St. Hubert, only twenty miles from the Meuse. But with the 101st in their rear it was immensely difficult for the panzers to exploit their advance. Von Manteuffel considered it one of the major German errors of the battle to leave Panzer Lehr to deal with Bastogne while pushing forward 2nd Panzer without support. Each division was independently too weak for its task.

Meanwhile on the northern flank, early on the morning of 21 December 12th SS Panzer launched the strongest attack thus far on the positions of the 2/26th Infantry north of Bullingen. German artillery and mortars began their bombardment long before dawn, and engineers had laid mines on the road approaching Colonel Daniel's positions. The colonel called for an artillery "ring of steel" to support his infantrymen. Twelve American 105mm howitzer battalions, drawn from three divisions, were made available to give fire support. The Americans were amazed by the suicidal courage of the advancing German infantry. It was in vain. The artillery swept them away in a storm of explosives, smoke and heaving earth. Corporal Henry F. Warner became one of the American heroes of the battle, fighting a 57mm anti-tank gun until he was mortally wounded by machine-gun fire from a Mark IV he had knocked out. German armour achieved a brief breakthrough on the 2/26th's right flank, and began crushing infantrymen in their foxholes. But an American tank destroyer entered the fray and hit seven German tanks in succession. Five others continued to advance, but two were wrecked by two Shermans before they, in turn, were knocked out.

The surviving Germans began to fire on the manor house which sheltered Daniel's command post. Just when his position began to seem desperate, a platoon of American self-propelled 90mm guns arrived. Under cover of a smokescreen, they hit two of the German tanks. The last survivor retired. Several hundred Germans had died, and the enemy had lost some forty-seven tanks and self-propelled guns. The Americans suffered 250 casualties. Colonel Daniel's force was now so weakened that he began to wonder if he should pull back. Yet the arrival of an additional company of reinforcements persuaded him that he could hold on. He was right. The Germans had exhausted themselves. The 2/26th had performed a memorable feat of arms, of the kind which decided the outcome of the battle. The regiment's performance caused the commander of 12th SS Panzer to describe 21 December as "the darkest day of my life." At Hitler's insistence, Sepp Dietrich's men continued to press forward against the Elsenborn Ridge for four more days. But the critical moment had passed. Model now recognized that, if a breakthrough was to to be achieved anywhere, it would have to be made by Fifth Panzer Army in the south, not Sixth SS Panzer Army in the north.

ON 20 DECEMBER, despite Bradley's bitter protests, Eisenhower gave Montgomery command of the entire northern flank of the Bulge, placing most of Hodges's First Army and Simpson's Ninth under his orders. This was a stroke of wisdom of the kind which justified all the Supreme Commander's claims to his authority. Montgomery, as has been observed, was the object of intense dislike among his American peers. It would have been understandable if Eisenhower had thus felt unable to give the British field-marshal authority over U.S. troops. Yet in this crisis he showed his statesmanship and was rewarded by a highly competent performance from Montgomery. Now that the Germans had broken wireless silence, Bletchley Park was decoding a flood of signals about their deployments and intentions. Montgomery therefore possessed advantages denied to his American counterparts in the first days. Yet other generals, possessing the same access to intelligence, remained unnerved by the German lunge. At a time when there was disarray, if not panic, at First Army headquarters, the foxy little field-marshal kept his balance. Coolly and calmly, he redeployed British and American forces to create a solid northern front against the German advance.

The British XXX Corps at Dinant was shifted to block the last miles to the Meuse. It was scarcely called upon to fight, for the Bulge was an American battle. But Montgomery displayed the quality most vital to a commander in a crisis—grip. Many even among those Americans who detested him applauded his contribution to the defence against Germany's winter offensive. When Brigadier William Harrison of the 30th Division met 21st Army Group's commander, he thought: "Here is a guy who really knows what he is doing." Von Manteuffel asserted afterwards that the Allied response to the Ardennes offensive was very much better co-ordinated than the original German attack.

Yet even in this crisis Montgomery could not bring himself to behave gracefully. At a meeting with Hodges of First Army and Simpson of Ninth, instead of inviting the Americans to brief him on the battle situation as they huddled over maps on the bonnet of his Humber staff car, the British commander turned to his young British liaison officer, Major Carol Mather. "What's the form?" demanded Monty, inviting Mather to explain the battle situation. The British officer wrote: "Our American friends...looked severely discomfited. It was a slight uncalled for." Montgomery's official biographer, Nigel Hamilton, said of his treatment of Hodges: "He humiliated the shyest...of American generals in his hour of shame." Bill Simpson, fortunately, seemed impervious to Montgomery's discourtesies. The gaunt, lanky, unassuming Ninth Army commander was a West Point classmate of Patton, and passed out of the Academy second from bottom. A rancher's son from Texas, much decorated in the First World War, Simpson proved himself one of the most sympathetic as well as most competent American officers in Europe. Not least among his virtues was a patience and good nature towards the British in general and Montgomery in particular, which deserved a more generous response than it received.

From the beginning of the battle, it became evident that Montgomery intended to exploit the crisis to pursue his familiar demand that an overall Allied ground commander should be appointed. On the very day Eisenhower gave the field-marshal command of the northern flank of the Bulge, Brooke felt obliged to send Montgomery a weary, strongly worded letter urging him to abandon his delusions about taking over the Anglo-American armies: "I think you should be careful about what you say to Eisenhower himself on the subject...especially as he is now probably very worried over the whole situation." The next day, Brooke reinforced his message: "I would like to give you a word of warning. Events and enemy action have forced on Eisenhower the setting-up of a more satisfactory system of command...It is important that you should not even in the slightest degree appear to rub this unfortunate fact into anyone at SHAEF. Any remarks you make are bound to come to Eisenhower's ears sooner or later."

The Bulge battle began at a time when American enthusiasm for the British was at a low ebb. James Byrnes, director of the Office of War Mobilization and sometimes known as Roosevelt's "assistant president," noted that even before the events of mid-December U.S. generals in France had been complaining about the "passivity" of Montgomery's 21st Army Group. There was ferocious U.S. criticism of British military intervention against the communists in Greece, which was considered to reflect not only Churchillian imperialism but a willingness to enforce this by diverting British troops from the west European battlefield, thus increasing the burden upon the Americans. Roosevelt told Stimson that he was frankly "fed up" with the British. "Something very like a crisis exists beneath the surface in the relations between the Allies who are fighting this war," the columnist Marquis Childs wrote in the *Washington Post* on 8 December 1944. "...I believe that most Americans who think about these things are deeply troubled about the turn of events in Occupied Europe." Representative Barry of New York said in Congress: "We Americans haven't suffered more than half a million casualties to divide Europe between Great Britain and Russia." The *Manchester Guardian* observed in a considerable understatement: "Anglo-American relations seem rather unhappy just now." With the trauma of the German assault in the Ardennes overlaid upon existing tensions, this was no time for a British commander to provoke the Americans.

Yet on 22 December the field-marshal wrote to Brooke in terms which reflected the conceit and self-delusion which he would soon afterwards expose in public: "I think I see daylight now on the northern front, and we have tidied up the mess and got two American armies properly organised. But I can see rocks ahead and no grounds for the optimism Ike seems to feel. Rundstedt is fighting a good battle." The following day, Montgomery reported: "I do not think Third U.S. Army will be strong enough to do what is needed. If my forecast proves true, then I shall have to deal unaided with both Fifth and Sixth Panzer Armies. I think I can manage them, but it will be a bit of a party."

Patton had been deputed to restore the southern front of the German penetration. He responded with a feat of command and staff work which won the admiration of history, by wheeling three divisions of Third Army through ninety degrees in seventy-two hours, to launch a drive north to Bastogne and beyond. Montgomery did not have to "deal unaided" with Fifth and Sixth SS Panzer Armies, nor was it ever likely that he would. By 22 December, the crisis of the Ardennes battle was over, though plenty of hard fighting still lay ahead. The field-marshal displayed admirable professionalism in reorganizing the northern front. But he did nothing then or later in the battle which suggested brilliance.

Moreover, his rhetoric deprived him of gratitude even from those who might otherwise have been willing to offer it. On 28 December, he reported smugly to Brooke about a meeting with Eisenhower:

> I said he would probably find it somewhat difficult to explain away the true reasons for the "bloody nose" we had just received from the Germans, but this would be as nothing compared to the difficulty we would have in explaining away another failure to reach the Rhine...[Eisenhower] was definitely in a somewhat humble frame of mind, and clearly realised that present trouble would not have occurred if he had accepted British advice and not that of American generals.

Even after the initial crisis of the battle had passed, some American units continued to suffer pain from the Germans' furious, frustrated thrashings. "Our outfit broke," Private John Capano of the 30th Division's 120th Infantry said frankly. His unit's first inkling that the Germans were moving came from Belgian civilian women, who trickled into their positions around the Lingueville–Malmédy road early on 21 December and volubly proclaimed that the enemy was close. "When the trouble started, we had no foxholes dug. Suddenly, there was the Luftwaffe bombing us. We'd been told the Luftwaffe was washed up. When we heard tanks, we all started to run for cover. We didn't know which way to go. We were firing into the trees. We figured that we just ought to make as much noise as we could. We thought: 'Somebody's fouled up.' The armored guys were our saviors. We rode out on top of their tanks." In reality, it should be said, although the 120th was badly mauled by the 150th Panzer Brigade—led by some of Otto Skorzeny's men in American vehicles and uniforms—the regiment later rallied.

Lieutenant William Devitt of the 330th Infantry was hit one night by mortar fragments which also brought down his platoon sergeant. "My first reaction was fear. I was afraid I was going to die. Concurrent with the fear came a prayer, something like 'God help me!' But simultaneously, I started to talk to myself: 'Don't panic. Seek help.'" He called quietly for a medic. The corpsman who responded explained apologetically that he had lost his torch. But within ten minutes stretcher-bearers took Devitt to the rear, with shrapnel wounds in his hand and abdomen. A few days later, he found himself sharing a room in a Welsh hospital with a young officer who had lost his leg. "I really don't give a

Goddam any more," said his roommate. "How'll I play tennis? I had a football scholarship from Texas Christian waiting for me. I just don't want to live this way." The boy got his wish, for he died of septicaemia. Devitt, who had been so eager a month earlier to experience combat, was profoundly grateful now to be through with it.

Major Hal McCown, commanding the 2/119th Infantry of 30th Division, was captured on 21 December while visiting forward positions, along with his wireless-operator and orderly. He was taken before Joachim Peiper, and conversed with the SS officer through a German interpreter who had spent sixteen years in Chicago. McCown said later: "The Germans' morale was high, despite the extremely trying conditions." He talked to Peiper for most of the night: "I have met few men who impressed me so much in so short a space of time as did this German officer. He was completely confident of Germany's ability to whip the Allies." Peiper waxed lyrical before the American about V2s, new submarines, fresh divisions. In the two days that followed, heavy American artillery fire fell around Peiper's headquarters, killing one American prisoner and a guard. On the afternoon of 23 December, McCown was summoned once more to Peiper. His panzers had run out of fuel. He was withdrawing on foot, leaving behind the wounded prisoners, but taking the American major with him. In the early hours of the next morning, 800 Germans slipped silently into the woods. Two hours later, the fugitives heard the first explosions as charges on their abandoned tanks began to detonate. All next day, the Germans probed for an escape route, once being challenged by an American sentry. Peiper and his staff disappeared. The other Germans pressed on, carrying their own wounded, until that night the column collided with American positions. In the ensuing firefight, Major McCown was able to escape into friendly hands, and tell his story to men of the 82nd Airborne.

The weather had cleared on 23 December. "There was an other-worldly beauty in the battlefield for those who had the comfort and leisure to observe," wrote the Australian war correspondent Alan Moorehead.

When you drove past the frozen canals and the tobogganing children up to the heights of the Ardennes, the sun broke through and it was like a spotlighted stage, mile upon mile of untrodden snowfields under the clear and frosty lamp of the winter sun. If you turned your back to the ruined villages and forgot the war for a moment, then very easily you could fancy yourself to be alone in this radiant world where everything was reduced to primary whites and blues; a strident, sparkling white among the frosted trees, the deep blue shadows in the valley, and then the flawless ice-blue of the sky.

For Allied defenders gazing up at the sunshine, lyrical beauty was to be found in the fact that their aircraft could fly. Supply drops rained down on Bastogne. At last, fighter-bombers descended in full force upon the battlefield. In St. Vith, Lieutenant Rolf-Helmut Schröder watched the impact of the first strikes on his depleted unit of the 18th Volksgrenadiers and thought bleakly: "This is not going to be easy." A veteran of the Eastern Front, Schröder had never before experienced heavy air attack. His commanding officer was wounded. They began to retreat under the command of a colonel newly arrived from Norway who, Schröder noticed with dismay, wore a tunic bare of battle decorations. His fears were confirmed during an American counter-attack. The colonel excused himself, saying: "Schröder, I'm afraid my foot is playing up." It should never be supposed that the Wehrmacht was led only by brave men.

American control of the battlefield reasserted itself slowly but surely. German tanks reached the furthest point of their advance, sixty miles from their start line and a few miles short of the Meuse, on 24 December. The panzers' clockwork had run down. Most enemy armoured units were starved of fuel. They were battered by aircraft and concentrated artillery fire. The American genius for mobility had enabled the defenders already to double their infantry numbers and treble their armoured strength in the embattled sector. The Bulge looked alarming on the map, yet no longer presented a strategic threat. "The fact that the Hun has stuck his neck out," wrote Tedder at SHAEF as early as 22 December, "is, from the point of view of shortening the whole business, the best thing that could happen. It may make months of difference." Time was always the friend of the Allies, the enemy of the Germans. Hitler's armies had lost their race.

Matthew Ridgway, commanding XVII Airborne Corps, was absent in England when the German offensive began. Gavin of the 82nd filled his place superbly through the first days, returning to his own division when the corps commander arrived. The force of Ridgway's personality is stamped upon every line of his correspondence, every record of his conversations. After days in which some senior officers who should have known better panicked, it is striking to contrast Ridgway's remarks to his formation commanders on Christmas Eve: "The situation is normal and completely satisfactory. The enemy has thrown in all his mobile reserves, and this is his last major offensive effort in this war. This Corps will halt that effort; then attack and smash him...I want you to reflect that confidence to the subordinate commanders and staffs in all that you say and do." Ridgway told Gavin: "Now, I know your men are tired, they've done a magnificent job out there, and they need you to go and pep them up a little bit. I don't know of anyone who can do that better than you. Will you get that across?"

Ridgway sent a biting letter to the officer commanding the 75th Division in his corps, asserting that its performance had been sorely inadequate: "I want every man imbued with the idea how lucky he is to be here, where the decision of this war will be reached, and where he can contribute his utmost to putting the 75th up alongside of the best divisions in our army. That upclimb starts today."

At least one man of the 75th Division which Ridgway was addressing, Harold Lindstrom, a twenty-two-year-old farmboy from Alexandria, Minnesota, felt nothing like "lucky to be here." A bespectacled rifleman in F Company of the 2/289th Infantry, Lindstrom arrived in France on 15 December and had been growing steadily more unhappy ever since. First, the tough, respected staff-sergeant who had been with his company through training succumbed to combat fatigue on their sixth day in the war zone, without hearing a shot fired. Lindstrom himself was nursing a feverish cold. The unit chaplain, a man he had never cared for, came by. To his own surprise, the soldier found himself grateful to see the priest: "things were different. I was ready to listen. I was afraid of the future and was looking for all the help I could get."

His company trudged forward, cold, weary, hungry and thirsty. They passed jeeps loaded with wounded, wrecked vehicles crushed into twisted steel and broken glass, trucks with their tyres still burning. Abandoned kit lay everywhere: "It was scary to see equipment just like that I was using. They had to have been guys just like me … After seeing that mess I was deathly afraid of German tanks, and I think most other guys were, too." Their neighbours in K Company were strafed by American P-38s. On Christmas morning, the 289th deployed for an attack, three battalions in line, towards the blazing Belgian village of Grandmenil. Tracer streaked towards them. As Lindstrom's platoon mortarman set up his tube, a German round ricocheted off the baseplate, striking sparks. For hours, they lay inert while German machine-gun fire hosed monotonously up and down the line, wounding a few men. Lindstrom felt the snow melting under him as he lay. Darkness came. At last their platoon leader, a thirty-five-year-old named Lavern Ivens, shouted: "Men, we can't lay here all night and wait to get hit. Start crawling up the hill towards that clump of trees." They were thrilled to receive orders and gingerly started moving. Then they heard an engine start, a German voice, and laughter. They lay still again. Rollie Combs called to Roy Mitchell: "Mitch, Mitch, which way should I lay? Facing or away from them?" Then somebody cried: "Let's get the hell out of here before they start shelling us." They trickled miserably back down the hill. A wounded man begged Lindstrom for his overcoat, but he felt so cold that he refused. Somebody else obliged and made Lindstrom feel guilty: "I am sure I would have given him mine. I just had to get used to the idea. I suppose I came across kind of poorly." They reached a field kitchen and sat gratefully eating their chow. That night, their battalion CO was relieved of his command.

Next morning, they were told to be ready to attack again. "That made me feel kind of desperate … I had never been so frightened as I was the night before, and now we were back at it again. I asked God to help me." F Company scouting officer asked for volunteers for a patrol. No one moved. At last, a few came forward. As they began to advance, American shells fell close. The line broke and ran towards the rear. Lindstrom looked in horror at a man with one eye hanging out; another with his legs blown off, smoking a cigarette under a tree; a stray boot with a foot in it; a sergeant being carried screaming to the rear by stretcher-bearers. He noticed that the NCO's body was a bloody mess below the waist, and wondered if he had lost his penis and testicles.

For four days after that, they lay in foxholes under shellfire. They had no idea where they were, nor that they were taking part in "the Battle of the Bulge." Lindstrom wrote: "Most of the time, I responded to simple dog-like commands such as 'move out,' 'hold up,' 'set up firing positions,' 'keep your head down.' I was always thinking about how cold I was." When he saw his first dead Germans, he envied them their peace: "The war was over for them. They weren't cold any more." Everybody was familiar with a U.S. government propaganda film about how the war was being fought for a typical all-American family and their dog Fido. Now, men would say to each other: "Remember, we're doing this for Fido."

Lindstrom's portrait of the experience of combat, in all its discomfort, bewilderment and fear, possessed a far greater resonance for most men who took part in the Second World War than the reminiscences of those who won medals. If anyone had told the Minnesotan and his comrades in their foxholes that merely by hanging on in there, by the fact of their survival, they had helped to win a great battle, they would have been bemused. Yet such was the reality. With such top-class American divisions as the 1st, 2nd Armored and two airborne formations reinforcing the line, the Germans were now simply beating themselves to death against the Allied positions, or struggling to win a breathing space for retreat. Bridges across the Ourthe had been blown in advance of 116th Panzer, and indeed at every turn American demolitions denied river crossings to the enemy. Joachim Peiper fumed about "the damned engineers." Only very late in the battle, as units began to capture large numbers of German panzers abandoned with empty tanks, did Allied commanders begin to grasp the scope of the Germans' fuel difficulties. When the U.S. 743rd Tank Battalion got into La Glieze, its men were excited to find thirty Tigers and Panthers standing intact, with empty tanks. The Americans enthused briefly about taking over the panzers, but the maintenance problems seemed insuperable.

At 1650 on 26 December, elements of Patton's 4th Armored Division broke through to the 101st Airborne. Brigadier Anthony McAuliffe hastened out to the perimeter to meet the tank men. Captain William A. Dwight saluted and asked: "How are you, General?" McAuliffe said: "Gee, I'm mighty glad to see you." The 101st Airborne had suffered 1,641 casualties, 10th Armored 503, while 4th Armored Division lost 1,400, and other units in proportion. The fighting around Bastogne was not over, and the link between the town and the main American front remained precarious. But it was no longer in doubt that the positions could be held.

The Bulge crisis provoked a hasty combing of rear areas for service corps personnel who might replace the heavy infantry casualties. Private Charles Felix, an artilleryman, was stricken by despair when told in late December that he was being transferred to infantry. An unwilling draftee, Felix had been relieved to see his papers stamped "Limited Service" because of poor eyesight. He was correspondingly crestfallen to be sent overseas at all. On arrival at his battalion, he seized the opportunity to claim non-existent radio experience and to his overwhelming relief was posted to battalion CP rather than to a rifle company. Omar Bradley liked to tell a story of a man who kept telephoning the *Stars & Stripes* Paris office for news of the battle. After repeated calls, he was asked which commander he was calling for. "I don't represent any general," the man responded gloomily. "I'm one of the Com-Z people slated for transfer to infantry." At one moment during the frantic search for reinforcements, Eisenhower asked Washington to make available 100,000 Marines, an extraordinary admission of desperation. His request was rejected.

IN THE NORTH in the last days of December, 2nd Armored Division from Hodges's First Army met its German counterpart 2nd Panzer Division just west of Dinant, and destroyed almost every one of von Manteuffel's tanks that had not already run out of fuel. 2nd Panzer started the battle with 116 tanks and assault guns and ended it with virtually none. Far southwards, in front of Patch's Seventh Army, the German Army Group G launched a second offensive in the Saarland, designed to increase pressure on the Allies, and make it harder for Eisenhower to reinforce the Ardennes. The initial assault gained a little ground and inspired a resurrection of Hitler's hopes. But this German assault, too, faltered and died in the first days of 1945.

On 27 December, SHAEF Intelligence recorded: "The tempo of the enemy's efforts has slowed almost to nothing." Corporal Iolo Lewis, a Welsh wireless-operator in one of Montgomery's Shermans, waiting for the Germans with XXX Corps above the Meuse, watched the enemy's tanks advancing in extended line, infantry among the panzers. The British felt relaxed and confident, their own tanks deployed hull down in overwhelming strength, as backstop for the American front. "As the sun came out, we knew the Germans were finished," said Lewis. "When the Typhoons came down on them, you could see crews jumping out of the panzers even before they were hit." On New Year's Day 1945, the Luftwaffe made its last big effort on the Western Front. Its fighters destroyed on the ground 140 Allied aircraft, including Montgomery's personal transport, in a series of surprise strafing attacks on airfields. But the German pilots suffered punishing casualties they could not afford, while Allied losses were quickly made good.

Since 24 December Guderian had recognized the failure of the Ardennes offensive, and begged Hitler in vain to allow the panzer divisions to be withdrawn east, in readiness to meet the Soviet onslaught which OKH, army high command, knew was approaching. Only Hitler's personal folly maintained the Ardennes battle, encouraged by Jodl, who persuaded him that maintaining pressure in the west was dislocating the Anglo-Americans' offensive plans. Indeed, it was Jodl who ordered the subsidiary attack in Alsace-Lorraine at this period, in defiance of Guderian's insistence that the vital priority was now the Vistula Front. Only on 3 January did Hitler belatedly sanction a withdrawal.

MOPPING UP

FROM THE FIRST days of the Ardennes offensive, the ebullient Patton urged that the panzers should be allowed to drive for Paris if they wanted. He was confident that the further the Germans pushed west, the fewer of them would ever go home. "Provided the two 'gateposts' hold," Alan Brooke wrote in his diary on 21 December, "there may be a chance of annihilating a great many of the sheep that have broken through. If only the Americans are up to it." Allied strategic superiority was overwhelming. The obvious challenge, once the Germans' momentum was spent, was to attack their salient at its base, cutting off their retreat. From 29 December onwards, von Manteuffel and his fellow commanders were urgently warning OKW of this peril to their exhausted and exposed formations. Yet Eisenhower, Bradley and Montgomery showed no enthusiasm for exploiting success. They were content patiently to shepherd the retreating enemy eastwards, hitting him from the air at every turn, destroying large numbers of his tanks and vehicles, but never seriously attempting to deny the Germans an escape route from the battlefield. Patton stood alone in urging a more imaginative stroke, to envelop the flagging enemy.

Third Army's dramatic drive north to Bastogne had filled the front pages of America's newspapers. Patton's Chief of Staff Hobart Gay reflected in his diary for 1 January 1945 on the irony that his chief was once again a national hero, a year to the day since he had been sacked as commander of Seventh Army, following the notorious "slapping incidents" in Sicily: "It's a fickle world... It is a crime that newspaper people, particularly men whose own standards are not very high, can take it upon themselves not only to try to ruin an individual, but also to react very adversely towards the success of the armed effort of a great nation."

Patton's pleas to strike at the base of the German salient were rejected. Gay was correct in asserting that his chief had once again become a national hero, for Third Army's energetic publicity apparatus ensured that Patton's soldiers were loaded with laurels for their drive north. Yet this stirring tale, which America was eager to hear after the humiliations of earlier days, masked some embarrassing truths about Third Army's role. Patton had indeed performed a notable feat of command and staffwork by dispatching two corps to support First Army within forty-eight hours of Eisenhower's initial request. Yet thereafter the piecemeal commitment of formations across a broad front cost his men substantial pain and casualties. On 3 January, Patton commented ruefully to his staff on the German Seventh Army: "They are colder, hungrier and weaker than we, to be sure. But they are still doing a great piece of fighting." It was argued that the Germans possessed the advantage of holding some formidable natural defensive features, but these had not proved decisive in American hands a fortnight earlier. Third Army's notoriously poor radio discipline also gave the German interception service generous notice of its movements and intentions.

Once again, Patton had shown himself skilled in driving his forces into action and gaining credit for their successes. But he proved less effective in managing a tough, tight battle on the southern flank. The Americans prevailed, but they did not destroy their enemy as comprehensively as von Rundstedt and Model feared was inevitable. Patton loudly advocated decisive action, but himself contributed to the failure to make it good. "Lightning Joe" Collins, that outstanding American corps commander, remarked with characteristic feistiness as the campaign approached its close: "I'm sure that, 50 years from now, people will think that Georgie Patton won the war...but he couldn't hold a candle to Bradley in the broader sense." Collins spoke as a loyal subordinate of Bradley's, and in truth there is little doubt that Patton was a vastly more imaginative warrior. But Collins's words reflected the view of many able American officers, that Patton talked a better game than he played when the going got tough.

The Allies opted for slow, steady pressure to squeeze out the Bulge, in an unglamorous series of operations which lasted until mid-January. It was a familiar story, resembling the failure to close the Falaise Gap in August 1944: the Allies were content with success. Until the last weeks of the war, they neither seriously sought nor successfully accomplished a triumph on a heroic scale. Even when Bradley belatedly achieved an envelopment in the Ruhr three months after the Bulge, it was of debatable significance. The allies knew how hard the German soldier could fight, especially to break out of an encirclement. The piecemeal destruction of the enemy sufficed. They declined the risks of pursuing the wounded tiger into the thicket.

The world was told only on 5 January that Montgomery had assumed temporary command of American forces north of the Bulge during the battle. On 7 January, the field-marshal held a press conference at his headquarters which proved one of the most lamentable episodes of his career. It was plain to every thoughtful British officer that the Americans felt chastened, even humiliated by the mauling the Germans had given them in the first days of the battle. Indeed, some U.S. officers overdid this sentiment and forgot that what matters on a battlefield is which combatant remains upstanding after the tenth round. In this case, it was certainly not the Germans. American soldiers and airmen had inflicted a major defeat on von Rundstedt's forces. It had been the function of the British merely to hold the ring. Yet for days British newspapers—which reached many Americans in Belgium—proclaimed with shameless relish that the British Army had been called upon to pick American chestnuts out of the fire. Bradley's aide Chester Hansen wrote on 1 January: "Their [the British] press is building up a well of resentment among our American troops that can never be emptied, a distrust that cannot be erased."

Yet on 7 January Montgomery emptied a petrol can on to Anglo-American tensions, then used the personal pronoun to ignite it: "As soon as I saw what was happening in the Ardennes, I took certain steps myself to ensure that if the Germans got to the Meuse, they certainly would not get over that river," he told assembled correspondents at his headquarters. "...You have thus a picture of British troops fighting on both sides of American forces who have suffered a hard blow...The battle has been most interesting; I think possibly one of the most interesting and tricky battles I have ever handled..."

Even after sixty years, it remains astonishing that a highly intelligent man who had reached the summit of command could be capable of such vainglorious folly. From Eisenhower downwards, every American who read Montgomery's words reacted with disgust. Beyond the absurdity of making such exaggerated claims for British participation in the battle, it was baffling that Montgomery felt able to regard the Bulge as a great feat of generalship. In reality, it was a battle fought by men in tanks, planes and foxholes with few imaginative interventions from their commanders. The defeated enemy was allowed to make a measured retreat—just as Rommel had been able to do after the Battle of Alamein in November 1942. A British intelligence officer recorded with rueful admiration on 10 January: "Without haste and without any trace of disorder, the enemy has today carried his withdrawal a stage further, and has left the snow and minefields to check Allied efforts to follow up." Zhukov would never have allowed to the Germans the licence which Eisenhower, Bradley and Montgomery accorded them when they were plainly whipped in the Ardennes.

"Monty did a good job, but I think it could have been done quicker," conceded Major Tom Bigland, one of his staff officers. "Monty privately admitted later that he underestimated American powers of recovery. The Americans, it must be remembered, had good equipment and fresh troops, whereas we had been at war for five long years, and were very tired." Montgomery represented the most extreme example of a conceit that ran through his nation's army: a belief that the Americans, having entered the war late and only under Japanese compulsion rather than as a matter of principle, were less competent fighting soldiers than the British. Alan Brooke regarded Eisenhower with contempt and Marshall with condescension. He believed that he himself could and should have been Supreme Commander in Europe. Churchill observed to Brooke in July 1944: "The Arnold–King–Marshall combination is one of the stupidest strategic teams ever seen. They are good fellows and there is no need to tell them this." Churchill once described Spaatz, the American air C-in-C in Europe, as "a man of limited intelligence." Air Chief Marshal Sir Arthur Harris said: "You pay him too high a compliment."

The British have always considered Americans boastful. Yet Churchill's people, impelled by regret at their own shrinking power, during the Second World War often spoke and behaved less graciously than their transatlantic allies. Churchill's private secretary wrote: "The more I contemplate the present trend of opinion and of events, the more sadly I reflect how much easier it will be to forgive our present enemies in their future misery, starvation and weakness than to reconcile ourselves to the past claims and future demands of our two great Allies. The Americans have become very unpopular in England." Dwight Eisenhower was a steelier and less genial figure than his public persona allowed. Yet the Abilene boy who grew up in classically humble rural American circumstances, the poker-player who retained a lifelong enthusiasm for dime Western novels, always behaved in public as one of nature's gentlemen. Montgomery, the bishop's son educated at St. Paul's and Sandhurst, never did. He was a cleverer man and a far more professional soldier than his Supreme Commander, but his crassness towards his peers was a fatal impediment to greatness.

No Allied general on the Western Front matched the verve displayed by Zhukov and his fellow marshals in the east. The Germans were persistently surprised by the sluggishness of the Western allies in attack, especially when the tide of battle was running as strongly their way as it was after the Ardennes offensive collapsed. Yet it can be argued that Allied generals achieved as much, or as little, as the performance of their soldiers would allow. It was a source of constant frustration to aggressive American commanders such as Ridgway and Gavin that on the battlefield U.S. troops failed to match their high ambitions. After the failure of an attack on 13 January, Ridgway sharply quizzed Leland Hobbs, commanding 30th Division, about "the poor showing of the 119th Infantry." Hobbs said apologetically that one of its battalion commanders had been summarily relieved. Ridgway declared that there had obviously been a failure of leadership all the way through the regiment. Demanding to be given its casualty figures, he exploded on hearing that just fifty-eight men had been lost to all causes. "He said that confirmed his view that enemy resistance had been insignificant."

Gavin raged at the limitations of other formations beside whom his paratroopers had to fight. "We are training our men to drive tanks and tank destroyers, since our armoured supporting people frequently abandon their vehicles when threatened in an attack," he wrote in his diary on 18 January.

If our infantry would fight, this war would be over by now. On our present front, there are two very weak German regiments holding the XVIII Corps of four divisions. We all know it and admit it, and yet nothing is done about it. American infantry just simply will not fight. No one wants to get killed...Our artillery is wonderful and our air corps not bad. But the regular infantry—terrible. Everybody wants to live to a ripe old age. The sight of a few Germans drives them to their holes. Instead of being imbued with an overwhelming desire to get close to the German and get him by the throat, they want to avoid him if the artillery has not already knocked him flat.

In the second week of January, even German propaganda broadcasts were obliged to recognize the reality of failure in the Ardennes. "The Winter Battle," as the Ardennes offensive had been described, now became "the defensive battle." German listeners were encouraged to translate their hopes to Alsace. Berlin's pundits emphasized "the miracle" of continued German resistance. After the surge in Wehrmacht morale in mid-December, now many men once more succumbed to despair. "If only this idiotic war would end!" Private Heinz Trammler wrote miserably in his diary in the Bulge. "Why should I fight? It is only for the survival of the Nazis. The superiority of the enemy is so great that it is pointless to struggle against it."

On 7 January near Bastogne, a battalion commander in 9th SS Panzer Division wrote to his friend Otto Skorzeny, complaining bitterly about the quality of the replacements that were reaching him—

> mostly Ukrainians who do not even speak German. There is a shortage of everything, but here it is the men that count. I have learnt what it means, for instance, to have to attack without heavy weapons, because there is no transport to bring forward mortars and anti-tank guns. We have to lie out on frozen ground, a target for enemy fighter-bombers. Still, it is not going any better for the Americans. If only we had just one division here, trained and equipped and with the élan we both knew in 1939, so long ago! Well, we shall and must win one day. My best regards to you and also to my old comrades of Vis and Orianberg. *Heil Hitler!*

Major William DuPuy, commanding the 1/357th Infantry, believed that the Germans at the end of the Bulge battle "didn't so much lose heart, as they lost organization. They just finally fell apart. They were strained beyond the elastic limit." Lieutenant Rolf-Helmut Schröder of 18th Volksgrenadiers felt bitterly disillusioned. "That's it—we've lost the war," he thought. He took over command of a battalion which was reduced to just eighty men. Yet as late as 13 January British Second Army Intelligence recorded respectfully: "The enemy can claim to have wrested the initiative from the Allies...He has provided his people with a tonic which they sorely needed, and for at least a week took their minds off the gloomy situation at the end of a disastrous year... he has gained time... Against this, however, the cost was tremendous for the results achieved."

As the Allies renewed their advance, they were plagued by the profusion of mines laid as usual by the Germans as they retreated. In mid-January, the 743rd Tank Battalion lost fifteen tanks to mines in two days. They were crossing ground that had been the scene of savage fighting. Private Ashley Camp leaped up in horror when he discovered that the snow-clad mound on which he sat down to eat his chow was composed of bodies. Sergeant Cockperry Kelly's tank track hit the feet of a frozen corpse, which sprang rigidly upright against the hull. From positions near Bellevaux, Lieutenant Joseph Couri wrote on 14 January: "This was the coldest night that I experienced in the war. After going through the forest with the turret open and the snow tumbling down from the trees, I was completely wet. The tank... was a Frigidaire, and we were going to try and sleep in it. We were better off than the infantry, for it was impossible to dig a foxhole... They asked if they could bed down under our tanks, and they did. There was not much sleep that night. The shelling from both sides was continuous."

The Germans were losing ground steadily, but showed no sign of outright collapse. Incautious actions were punished as brutally as ever by Model's soldiers. The British 13 Para was approaching the Belgian village of Bure down an open hillside one afternoon early in January when the Germans, who could see them coming, unleashed a mortar and artillery bombardment. Within the space of just fifteen minutes, the unit suffered 160 casualties, including sixty-five dead. During fighting in Diekirch on 25 January, men of the 3/2nd Infantry captured thirty-seven Germans. As they routinely disarmed and searched their captives, they were taken aback to find that one of them was female. Sergeant Clifford Laski reported laconically: "It wasn't until she took her helmet off and revealed those long locks of hair that we knew her to be a woman, because she wasn't particularly chesty." Staff-Sergeant Charles Skelnar's last memory of Bastogne after its relief was of a 101st Airborne sergeant herding prisoners towards the cage. Every time he saw a German wearing GI boots, the NCO smashed his rifle butt down on the man's feet. "They fought to the bitter end," recorded a sardonic Allied intelligence report on 29 December, on the interrogation of 1st SS Panzer prisoners, "and they are still insolent." Yet Private George Sheppard of the 319th Infantry enjoyed taking prisoners, and found their arrogance broken: "I felt proud. Here was the army of the Master Race, they've got their hands up, they're shouting '*Kamerad!*' they're down on their knees begging for you not to shoot them." Interestingly, a British expert on the Waffen SS believes that Joachim Peiper, symbol of German fanaticism and brutality in the Ardennes, suffered some kind of moral or physical collapse following the offensive's failure. Peiper's name disappears from all Waffen SS unit records until he emerges again in Hungary late in February 1945. If this is true, it reflects a tendency to hysteria not uncommon among fanatical young Nazi warriors. More than a few killed themselves, like Hein von Westernhagen of the 501st Heavy Panzer Battalion, under the stress of defeat. Not unreasonably, the Americans shot eighteen of Otto Skorzeny's men whom they captured in GI uniforms. The night before their execution, their captors allowed some German nurses who were also prisoners to sing carols to them in the cells.

"LIGHTNING JOE" COLLINS said he was convinced the Bulge battle had shortened the war by six months. While the drastic depletion of Sixth SS Panzer Army and Fifth Panzer Army was obviously significant, it is hard to accept Collins's judgement. At the summit of American command, the most notable consequence of victory was a despondency which persisted even after German failure was plain. Colonel Chester Hansen, Bradley's aide, recorded: "There was a serious discussion at the top about sitting down and waiting for spring." During the half-hearted German offensive in Alsace, there was talk at SHAEF about allowing 6th Army Group to retire into the Vosges. The battle inspired a resurgence of caution among Allied commanders and intelligence staffs. Alan Brooke believed that it "considerably retarded the defeat of Germany." The victors recognized that the battle had destroyed Hitler's principal armoured reserve. But they failed to perceive how desperate the overall predicament of the Third Reich had in consequence become, and thus to exploit the new situation with vigour. Fears were expressed at SHAEF that, unless the Allies could finish the war quickly, new German weapons, above all jet aircraft, would enable the enemy to continue the war through the summer of 1945. "Upon the conclusion of the Ardennes campaign," declared the official U.S. army post-war report on the campaign, "it was estimated that the Allies had no marked superiority over the Germans in ground force strength." This assertion would have aroused hysterical mirth at any German headquarters. SHAEF determined to establish the Allied armies in "strong defensive positions" along most of the front, "to free others for attack ... In late January, the enemy's combat strength was not considered markedly inferior to that of the Allies."

The Bulge offensive cost the Germans between 80,000 and 100,000 casualties. The Americans lost 4,138 men killed, 20,231 wounded and 16,946 captured or missing, between 16 December and 2 January. In the second phase of the battle between 3 and 28 January, American casualties totalled a further 6,138 killed, 27,262 wounded and 6,272 captured or missing. Defeating Hitler's winter offensive thus cost an overall total of 80,987 men, making the Bulge the most costly battle the Americans fought in north-west Europe, though one for which the "butcher's bill" was far smaller than that for any major eastern encounter. The

January figures illustrate how toughly the Germans continued to fight, even when they were being forced back after the failure of their own operation, starved of fuel and under constant air attack.

The Ardennes struggle rendered Eisenhower less willing than ever to take risks. His nerve had been badly shaken. The best U.S. corps and divisional commanders on the battlefield had shown more pepper and grip during the battle than their superiors at 12th Army Group and SHAEF. Hodges should have been relieved of First Army's command after his poor showing. But the mood among the Americans in mid-January inclined towards celebrating heroes rather than sacking scapegoats. The Western allies did not recommence major offensive operations on their own account until mid-February. It took seven weeks for Eisenhower's armies to recover their balance after the shock of the Ardennes.

Yet from the outset it was hard to envisage a scenario for German success. Von Rundstedt's armies lacked the power to sustain such a vastly ambitious operation to its conclusion in the face of overwhelmingly superior forces. American mobility was decisive. German movements were crippled by difficult terrain and inadequate fuel. Indeed, it is arguable that the fuel shortage contributed at least as much as allied resistance to stopping the panzers, even before Allied air power was committed. During 1944–45 Hitler's armies achieved remarkable feats when they were immobile and dug in, for they were hard to see and to hit. They were savagely mauled, however, whenever they moved and exposed themselves to air attack as they did in December and January. The Allies were able to move forces freely to the battlefield with their huge inventory of vehicles and almost unlimited fuel, amid negligible interference from the Luftwaffe. Tactically, the Ardennes was one of the worst-conducted German battles of the war, perhaps reflecting the fact that none of the generals giving the orders saw any prospect of success. The sorrows of those American soldiers who proved unable to resist the German panzers were erased by the triumphs of those who finally defeated them.

The principal beneficiaries of the Bulge battle were the Russians. The German Seventh Army was never impressive, but Fifth and Sixth SS Panzer Armies were among the most formidable forces Hitler had possessed in December. Their absence from the Eastern Front when Stalin launched his Vistula offensive was of significant value to the Soviet armies. Even when the panzer formations were belatedly transferred eastwards late in January, they had been devastated by their experience in Belgium and Luxembourg. It is unlikely that Dietrich's and von Manteuffel's tanks could have altered the outcome of the eastern battle, but their presence would have made the task of Zhukov and his colleagues much harder. The German fuel famine was strangling the ability of Hitler's empire to maintain its resistance, almost irrespective of events on the battlefield. But the Ardennes attack imposed in weeks a level of attrition upon

German armoured forces which might have taken months had they been deployed in defence. Stalin was always contemptuous of the battlefield contributions of his American allies. But he owed them a debt for the defeat they inflicted upon the Germans in December 1944. He might better have appreciated their achievement if his nature had allowed him to care more about the tens of thousands of Russian lives saved by the failure of Autumn Mist.

CHAPTER NINE

Stalin's Offensive

THE STORM BREAKS

T HERE WAS A Red Army saying: "Where Zhukov is, there is victory."
Georgi Zhukov was forty-eight, a shoemaker's son from a village some
ninety miles south of Moscow, who had fought in the First World War
as a tsarist cavalryman. He rose to prominence in the Mongolian conflict of 1939
between Japan and Russia, which remains almost unknown in the West. He
played a leading role in the councils of the Soviet high command from the first
days of the war in June 1941. Critics argued that luck and German blunders did
as much as Zhukov's own generalship to win his laurels in the battles of
Leningrad and Moscow, but this seems ungenerous. In January 1943 he received
his marshal's star. His wholesale executions of men suspected of cowardice or
desertion demonstrated a ruthlessness which did Zhukov no disservice in the
eyes of Stalin. During the defence of Leningrad, he directed that any man who
abandoned his post without written orders should be shot. He deployed tanks
behind the forward positions not to kill Germans but to shoot down mercilessly
any Russian who fled. Zhukov's high intelligence and grasp of all military matters, matched by a sobriety unusual among Soviet senior officers, were generally acknowledged. He had been leading large armies for longer than any other
Allied commander. While Zhukov was directing the defence of Leningrad back
in 1941, Eisenhower was still Chief of Staff of Third Army in Louisiana, newly
promoted to brigadier. The Russians did not always get it right—indeed, their
mistakes were on a scale as extravagant as everything else about the Eastern
Front. But Soviet generals in the last two years of the war handled large forces
with much greater assurance than their American and British counterparts.

Zhukov's perfectionism, his meticulous staffwork and summary dismissal of
any officer who failed to meet his standards made him a harsh taskmaster. Yet he
was the servant of an even harsher one. In 1941, he burst into tears after a
tongue-lashing from Stalin. Reading the memoirs of Russia's wartime com-

manders, it is easy to be deluded into supposing that they inhabited a rational world, recognizable to Americans and west Europeans. They did not. From the first day of the war to the last, they existed and fought in a universe more fearsome than that of Hitler's commanders. Under Stalin, failure signalled death. Not even the greatest marshal was secure from degradation, torture and execution. One day in 1941, Russia's senior airman became drunk and complained to his supreme warlord: "You're making us fly in coffins." Stalin responded quietly: "You shouldn't have said that." The general—Pavel Rychagov—was shot, along with much of the Red Air Force high command. Stalin's military subordinates existed in a state of permanent fear. It is not easy to compare relative evils, rival monsters, yet it is a matter of fact that the senior subordinates of Adolf Hitler enjoyed a much better prospect of survival than those of Joseph Stalin, until military defeat overtook Germany.

Such a man as Zhukov could scarcely be less than utterly ruthless. Yet he inspired enthusiasm among his soldiers, for the reason common to other great commanders throughout history: he was a winner. "Zhukov was very popular, much more popular than Stalin," said Corporal Anatoly Osminov. The marshal's stern, unbending presence utterly dominated his headquarters. "He was a hard case," said one of his artillery staff officers. "He was slow, stubborn, and never said much. It was difficult, if not impossible, to change his mind." The marshal's office was studiedly austere—a metal table, maps, a thermos water container with the painted words "drinking water" misspelt on it, and a tin mug chained to the urn. In his operations room in the midst of a battle, Zhukov savagely reprimanded an officer whom he noticed working in a black fur coat, for being improperly dressed. Lieutenant Vasily Filimonenko trembled when Zhukov appeared in his artillery forward observation post, and spent ninety minutes studying the German line through his periscope. "I must see for myself," said the marshal, and quizzed the young officer closely about his living conditions and the gunfire support plan. There was no warmth there, but a steely, uncompromising professionalism of the highest order. "Everyone was terrified of him," said Lieutenant Evsei Igolnik. "We knew that he was not above using a cane on his own staff officers." On one occasion, he dispatched a divisional commander to a penal battalion for displaying inadequate energy on the battlefield. Zhukov was the most effective military commander of the Second World War.

Yet, in the Soviet Union's great advance west from the Vistula and into East Prussia, the glory was not intended for any marshal. For more than two years, to a remarkable degree Stalin had deferred to his subordinate commanders in the conduct of the war. They rewarded him with victories. Stalin's resentment of Zhukov's celebrity and popularity had grown, however, eating into what passed for his soul. All his life, the ruler of Russia displayed towards able comrades a blend of admiration and envy which impelled him to murder most of them sooner or later. Although his marshals would fight the great battles now impending, and Zhukov would play the decisive role on the Vistula front, Stalin was determined that in the eyes of the Russian people and of history the January offensive of the Red Army should be identified as his own achievement.

Among the men of the Red Army, attitudes towards the nation's leader were complex and various. Many soldiers avowed less respect for him than for Zhukov. "Stalin won the war, but he was responsible for so many deaths," said Corporal Nikolai Ponomarev of the 374th Rifle Division. Major Fyodor Romanovsky of the NKVD was, unsurprisingly, a passionate admirer of his nation's leader: "He saved the Soviet state. He possessed a very good mind and picked good people. The leaders of England and America did not have to fight the war with a fifth column in their midst. We did. Stalin destroyed our traitors. We were real communists in those days." Yet for every party zealot like Romanovsky there were scores of men whose families had suffered badly at the hands of Stalin. Nikolai Senkevich, a Red Army doctor, often asked himself: "Is there no one to rid us of this cannibal?" His father, an illiterate Belorussian peasant, had died in the Gulag after being convicted of hoarding flax seed. His brother had served ten years in a labour camp for "political crimes." Yet Senkevich would never have voiced aloud a harsh thought about Stalin. Corporal Anna Nikyunas said: "We were fighting for our country, not for Stalin." Major Yury Ryakhovsky's father told him: "You should obey Stalin not for what he is, but because he is the leader of our nation." Ryakhovsky himself said: "Stalin seemed like a god to us."

To the frustration of the Party, however, Christian religion still touched the hearts of many Soviet soldiers. Men and women in imminent danger of death reached out to a deity who promised a hereafter, rather than to a national leader likely to consign them there. "I often prayed to God for deliverance," said Nikolai Ponomarev, who wore a crucifix through his entire front-line service. Corporal Anatoly Osminov always carried an icon given to him by his mother. He knew that he would have lost his Party membership if a political officer had heard about it, "but many men crossed themselves privately, and prayed for their lives. There was a little bit of religion somewhere in most of us." Lieutenant Alexandr Sergeev's men liked to recall the Russian proverb: "We all stand together beneath the hand of God." Seventeen-year-old Yulia Pozdnyakova had never been taught the words of any prayer, but when she found herself being bombed, she invented some.

HITLER HAD ALWAYS opposed the building of fixed fortifications, on the ground that they discouraged the offensive spirit which he demanded from his armies. Yet in the weeks before the Soviets struck on the Vistula some 1.5 million German civilians were belatedly struggling in the snows to drive spades and

mattocks into the frozen soil of the Reich from the Rhine to Königsberg, to create anti-tank ditches and trench lines against the Allied flood. In East Prussia
alone, 65,000 people of both sexes and all ages and conditions were engaged
upon defensive works, almost all of them futile. Hitler fiercely rejected Guderian's proposal to withdraw the main German forces in Poland from the forward defence zone—the *Hauptkampflinie*—to positions further back—the
Grosskampflinie—beyond the range of the initial Soviet bombardment. Germany's warlord lost his temper when this was mooted, "saying that he refused to
accept the sacrifice of 12 miles without a fight." The *Grosskampflinie* was thus
established only two miles behind the front, in accordance with the Führer's
wishes, beneath the immediate path of Soviet artillery. This was in absolute
contradiction of German military doctrine, and destroyed the prospects of a
successful counter-attack even before the battle began.

Worse, Hitler transferred to Hungary two of the fourteen and a half panzer
and panzergrenadier divisions available to face the Russians on a 750-mile front
from the Baltic through Poland, because of his obsessive anxiety about the Lake
Balaton oilfields. "If something happens down there, it's over," he told Guderian. "That's the most dangerous point. We can improvise everywhere else, but
not there. I can't improvise with the fuel. Unfortunately, I can't hang a generator
on a panzer [to power it electrically]." The Russians were delighted by this folly.
"A very stupid disposition," Stalin observed on learning of the German diversion of forces to Hungary. On 1 January 1945, the only major German armoured
reserve on the Eastern Front was thrown into Operation Konrad, to relieve
Hitler's forces beleaguered in Budapest. The counter-attack came within sight
of the Hungarian capital before it was halted on 13 January. Hitler's obsession
with Hungary caused seven of the eighteen panzer divisions available in the
east to be deployed there, while four were in East Prussia, two in Courland and
just five faced Zhukov and Konev. In January on the Eastern Front the Germans
could deploy only 4,800 tanks against the Red Army's 14,000, and 1,500 combat
aircraft against 15,000.

Soviet propaganda loudspeakers blared music towards the German lines
night after night of early January, to drown the engine noise of thousands of
tanks and guns moving towards their start lines on the east bank, or preparing
their breakout from the western beachhead already established at Sandomierz.
Some of the men who occupied listening posts beyond the Russian lines, watching the Germans, lay prone all day in the snow. Only when darkness fell could
they rise to relieve themselves, to force some movement back into paralysed
limbs. Sergeant Nikolai Timoshenko, one of the Red Army's superbly skilled
patrol leaders, spent Russian New Year's Eve, 7 January, crawling for hours
across the ice of a frozen river to reach German positions on the far bank. As
always ahead of an attack, the Red Army needed prisoners. His patrol stormed a
house where they had identified a German machine-gun post, killed three and

captured three of the enemy, and returned across the ice before dawn. In the early days of January, such operations were repeated a thousand times along the entire front from East Prussia to Yugoslavia.

Until the very eve of Stalin's assault, Hitler's fawning military courtiers Keitel and Jodl continued to feed their Führer's belief that the Soviet threat was a bluff. There were scant grounds for such a delusion. A steady stream of reports from prisoners and deserters—how strange it seems that Red Army soldiers were still deserting to the Wehrmacht in these last months—confirmed the scale of Russian preparations. "A deserter from 118th Guards Army at Baranov says the Soviet attack will start in three days, aims to reach the German border in a single bound, and will mask Cracow," observed a Wehrmacht situation report sent to Berlin on 9 January. A prisoner from 13th Guards Division likewise declared that the attack would start in three days, and that the River Nida was his unit's first objective. Another PoW from 370th Guards Division said his formation had been given the cheering reassurance that its assault would be preceded by a penal battalion's "fighting reconnaissance." Soviet mine-clearing, bridge-building and reinforcement on a huge scale were reported to OKH.

The deluge of foreign equipment which had descended upon the Red Army caused some difficulties for those obliged to use it, especially American radios. Yulia Pozdnyakova, a signaller, puzzled desperately over the English-language instruction manuals for the sets she was expected to operate, together with the English labelling on their controls and dials. To confuse matters further, she was attached to a Polish formation of the Red Army, most of whose men spoke little Russian. She was horrified at being ordered to wear a Polish uniform. Her own family were descended from old Russian nobility, and indeed her grandparents had fled from the Bolsheviks, never to be seen again. Her father died in 1930. She lived with her mother and stepfather until they were arrested for "political crimes" in 1940. She and her two sisters found themselves alone in Moscow.

When the war came, though she was only fifteen she enlisted in the Red Army, claiming to be two years older. She discovered a companionship in its ranks which had been entirely missing from her lonely childhood at home. "I always felt an orphan, but you cannot be entirely lonely when you are eating every day from the same soup pot as a lot of other people." The soldiers called her "the kindergarten kid." She had a good musical ear, a sense of tone and timing which proved invaluable in learning Morse transmission. Yet the campaign was always an experience of discomfort, fear and bewilderment for a girl of seventeen. "We weren't living proper lives. We were simply surviving, and doing a job that had to be done." Corporal Ponomarev said: "In January 1945 we could see the end in sight, which seemed wonderful." He himself had been a soldier since 1940, fighting from Moscow westwards with all three Baltic Fronts at different times, twice wounded. Now, he yearned to finish the business and go home to Omsk to fulfil his ambition to become a doctor.

Though the Red Army was incomparably better supplied in 1944 than it had been earlier in the war, shortages remained endemic. Lieutenant Valentin Krulik's unit found itself without lubricants for its weapons, and tried to substitute sunflower oil. This was not a success. All its tommy-guns jammed. The favoured Guards divisions were generally well provided, but lesser Soviet formations still relied heavily upon scavenging for equipment, vehicles and above all food. Early in 1945, units were given advance warning that they would be required to carry out the harvest on German territory when summer came, to reduce the requirement for bringing flour from Russia. As far as possible, the Red Army lived off the land, in the manner of European armies centuries earlier.

Its enemies, however, were in a far worse case. On 11 January, an OKW report on the condition of Germany's forces acknowledged that morale was low in many units. On all fronts, there were serious shortages of clothing, machine-guns, motor tyres, trucks. Army Group E revealed that it had been forced to destroy much of its own artillery because it lacked means to move the guns; "the men's ability to march is handicapped by the number of worn-out boots." Fifteenth Army reported shortages even of mess-kits and horses. All units lacked men, and especially trained NCOs. Army Group Centre said that many replacements were inadequately trained in the use of weapons, and physically unfit. Klaus Salzer, an eighteen-year-old paratrooper, wrote home describing how a local farmer had invited him and some comrades for a great Christmas dinner—the last of his young life, as it happened—with chicken and pork and roast potatoes: "When you haven't had a lot of food for ages and that sort of feast is put in front of you, it's hard not to stuff yourself," he told his parents. "A lot of us were horribly ill next day as a result."

After an acrimonious argument about the deployment of reserves, Hitler surprised Guderian by becoming suddenly calm and declaring emolliently that he respected his Chief of Staff's anxiety to strengthen the line in Poland. Guderian said bluntly: "The Eastern Front is a house of cards. If it is broken at one point, all the rest will collapse." On 12 January, British Naval Intelligence sent a dispatch to London from Stockholm, detailing the latest information from agents about the mood inside Germany. Civilian morale had improved a little, said the report. There was optimism about the coming of the new jet fighters. There was no expectation of a new Allied push in the west before early summer, but a Russian offensive in south and central Poland was anticipated at any moment: "Germans who had hitherto held some hope of making terms with the Russians no longer count upon this possibility." This was a prudent concession to reality. The Soviet Union indeed possessed no interest in negotiation with any faction inside Germany. Vengeance, the destruction of Hitler and the spoils of victory were the objectives of the vast armies which Stalin now unleashed. He professed to the Western allies that he had advanced the timing of his onslaught in order to ease their difficulties in the Bulge battle. In reality, the essential schedule of the offensive had been determined back in November. Churchill expressed Allied gratitude anyway. "May all good fortune rest upon your noble venture," he cabled to Stalin. "...German reinforcements will have to be split between our flaming fronts."

The Soviet offensive began with an assault by Konev's 1st Ukrainian Front, from the western bridgehead across the Vistula some 120 miles south of Warsaw. The cold was even more brutal than on the Western Front in the Ardennes. Fog and intermittent blizzards cut visibility. At key points, 300 artillery pieces were allocated to a single kilometre of front. The bombardment began at 0435 on 12 January, directed against the positions of Fourth Panzer Army. The frozen ground was torn open in a thousand places. Houses crumbled to rubble. Bunkers collapsed on their occupants. The survivors lay stunned and traumatized by the cacophony unleashed by the Soviets. The assault began at 0500, with Soviet "forward battalions"—penal units—probing the German front, bypassing strongpoints and advancing up to half a mile beyond the outpost line. This was a mere reconnaissance, however, before a new barrage began at 1000, pouring fire upon the defences to a depth of six miles. This phase lasted almost two hours. The Germans estimated that the bombardment cost them 60 per cent of their own artillery and 25 per cent of their men, together with the destruction of Fourth Panzer Army's headquarters.

The main Russian infantry attack began late in the morning, and by 1700 hours had advanced some twelve miles across the snowclad landscape. The Germans paid an immediate and heavy price for Hitler's insistence that much of the German armoured reserve was deployed in the forward zone, within easy reach of the Russian guns. One Tiger unit was destroyed while refuelling. The commander of 17th Panzer Division was wounded and captured. On the second day, Soviet spearheads penetrated fifteen to twenty-five miles on a forty-mile frontage. LXVIII Panzer Corps ceased to exist, and German infantry fell back as best they could, covered by the surviving tanks of 16th and 17th Panzer Divisions. LXII Corps found itself being outflanked, and retreated on foot with the loss of all its heavy equipment.

"We now had to pay for our tardiness in retiring from the great salient which in any case was bound to be lost in the end," wrote von Manteuffel, lamenting the belated transfer of his formations from the Ardennes to the Vistula Front; "...our troops were more tired even than we had expected, and were no longer capable, either physically or mentally, of coping with a tough, well-equipped and well-fed enemy. Replacements received in January were inadequate both in quality and quantity, being mostly older men or of a low medical category, and ill-trained as well."

On 14 January, forty-eight hours behind Konev, Zhukov's 1st Belorussian Front launched the principal thrust of the offensive, breaking out of its two small bridgeheads west of the Vistula. On the first day, his men advanced twelve miles into the positions of the German Ninth Army. By the night of the 15th the Russians had reached the Pilica river, which they were eager to secure before the enemy could stabilize a line behind it. Infantry crossed the ice, but it proved too thin for vehicles. Engineers fortunately discovered a ford, and blew holes in the ice to open a path. Six tanks and two assault guns were abandoned in the river after their engines flooded, but two dozen Soviet tanks reached the western bank. By nightfall on 15 January, Soviet bridgeheads west of the Vistula were linking up across a front of 300 miles. Zhukov's leading tanks and infantry had advanced sixty miles from their start lines. Hitler's Army Group A was reduced to ruin.

The Germans mounted repeated counter-attacks with tanks, assault guns and infantry. All failed. It is impossible not to contrast the manner in which the Russians brushed aside German spoiling operations with the checks to which the Americans and British submitted in similar circumstances. The Germans considered the Western allies absurdly nervous about their flanks. Again and again on the Western Front, local counter-attacks caused assaults to be broken off. Russian aggressiveness was indeed sometimes punished by the encirclement of their spearheads, but Russian forces became accustomed to this predicament and were relatively untroubled by it. Men spoke with pride of having survived two, three, four encirclements. Sooner or later, either the isolated troops broke back to re-establish contact with the Soviet main positions or a relieving force fought its way through to join the spearhead. In the early days of the Vistula offensive, poor weather restricted Russian air support. But the entire operation demonstrated the Soviets' mastery of the setpiece attack; their dash in exploiting success and their resolve in dismissing counter-attacks.

Alexandr Sergeev, one of Zhukov's gunner officers, found the mood of the Red Army at this time quite different from that which he had known in the years of struggle for the motherland and the long winter lull in Poland. "In the trenches, we all knew each other intimately. We were together for a long time. Now, people seemed to come and go so quickly. We once got a new battery commander whom I never even met, because he was killed so quickly. His replacement was shot by a sniper a few hours after he arrived. I lost ten replacement gunners in a single morning. At this stage of the war, some of them were very poorly trained." Yet Lieutenant Gennady Klimenko, fighting further north with 2nd Ukrainian Front, said: "Morale was very high."

As early as 15 January, OKH's war diary acknowledged: "The Russians have achieved their breakthrough. It is to be feared that within two days they will have reached the Upper Silesian border. The forces of Army Group A are hopelessly inadequate . . . the divisions moved from the west by the Führer on the 13th will not arrive before the 19th, which will be too late." Army Group A reported: "The battle in the Vistula salient continues at undiminished intensity, and threatens a major crisis . . . 16th and 17th Panzer Divisions are no longer coherent forces, having lost all their tanks...Our available forces have been gravely weakened. We are conducting piecemeal withdrawals to more secure positions. These movements are still in progress, and details are not available." Details were unnecessary. The overarching reality was that the remains of Hitler's armies on the Vistula were retreating in disarray. On the 15th, Hitler belatedly ordered two divisions of the crack Grossdeutschland Panzer Corps south from East Prussia to prop up the sagging front in Poland. Guderian was aghast, since it was plain that a big Russian offensive was looming in that sector too. These reinforcements never reached their intended destination in front of 1st Ukrainian Front, but became entangled in the Polish shambles created by Zhukov. The Grossdeutschland detrained near Lodz on 18 January, amid a mass of fleeing ethnic German civilians. Its tanks covered the withdrawal of Ninth Army, and then themselves joined the retreat across the vast white, flat plain where the only landmarks were blackened vehicles and buildings. Guderian fumed at the absence of Sixth SS Panzer Army in Hungary. He had wanted the Ardennes formations for a strategic counter-stroke in Poland. Hitler refused to commit further forces against Zhukov. He merely replaced the Wehrmacht's commander on the Polish Front, Josef Harpe, with the brutish Nazi Field-Marshal Ferdinand Schörner.

Schörner's first report to OKH was a catalogue of woes: "Thousands of soldiers are fleeing in the region of Litzmanstadt [Lodz], especially support, police and administrative units. Numerous vehicles—even armoured ones—are being abandoned. Measures to halt this tide have so far proved fruitless...I must demand urgent assistance to restore order in the rear areas. The enemy's breakthrough can be checked only by rounding up every man in uniform who is running away."

The famous General Walther Nehring of XXIV Panzer Corps performed one of the most notable feats of the Polish campaign. He withdrew his forces in a series of night marches punctuated by fierce local battles with Russian troops. Nehring's men encountered terrible scenes, where Russian columns had smashed through columns of trekking refugees, leaving roads strewn for miles with shattered humanity and vehicles. When they reached the Pilica river, they found a single small bridge which they reinforced with tree trunks, to carry trucks and light armour. Finally, they drove two tanks into the water under the bridge, to reinforce it for the passage of Panzer IVs. Many vehicles were lost when they ran out of fuel, but on 22 January the vanguard of Nehring's force reached the comparative safety of the Warthe river, after covering 150 miles in eleven days. Other units trickled in during the days that followed. Coolness, luck and exceptionally shrewd map-reading by their commander had enabled them to sidestep the main Russian forces. Nehring's units were finally able to cross the Oder westwards at Glogau.

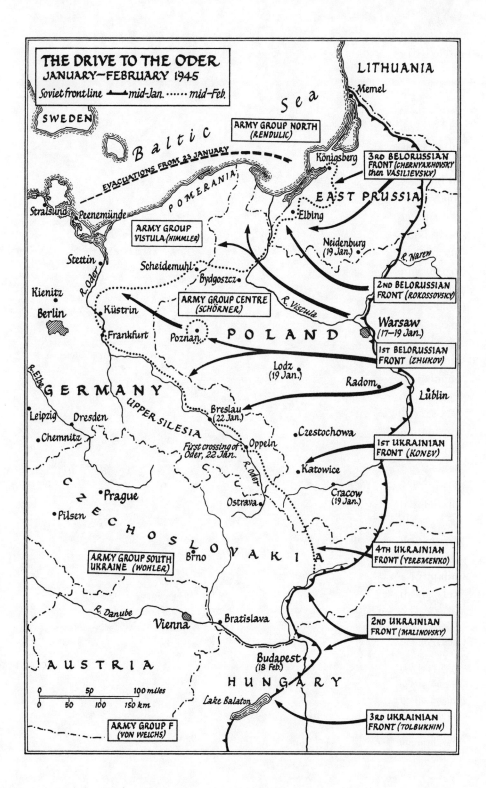

THE DRIVE TO THE ODER
JANUARY–FEBRUARY 1945
Soviet front line ▲▲▲ mid-Jan. ······ mid-Feb.

LITHUANIA

Baltic Sea

SWEDEN

ARMY GROUP NORTH
(RENDULIC)

Memel

EVACUATIONS FROM 23 JANUARY

Königsberg

3RD BELORUSSIAN
FRONT (CHERNYAKHOVSKY
then VASILIEVSKY)

POMERANIA

EAST PRUSSIA

Stralsund
Peenemünde
Elbing

Neidenburg
(19 Jan.)

R. Narew

ARMY GROUP
VISTULA (HIMMLER)

Stettin

Scheidemuhl
Bydgoszcz

R. Vistula

2ND BELORUSSIAN
FRONT (ROKOSSOVSKY)

Kienitz

R. Oder

ARMY GROUP CENTRE
(SCHÖRNER)

Berlin

Küstrin

Frankfurt

Poznan

Warsaw
(17–19 Jan.)

P O L A N D

1ST BELORUSSIAN
FRONT (ZHUKOV)

R. Elbe

G E R M A N Y

Lodz
(19 Jan.)

Radom

Lublin

Leipzig
Dresden

UPPER SILESIA

Breslau
(22 Jan.)

Chemnitz

Oppeln

Czestochowa

1ST UKRAINIAN
FRONT (KONEV)

First crossing of
Oder, 22 Jan.

R. Oder

Katowice

C
Z
E
C
H
O
S
L
O
V
A
K
I
A

Prague

Ostrava

Cracow
(19 Jan.)

Pilsen

ARMY GROUP SOUTH
UKRAINE (WOHLER)

Brno

4TH UKRAINIAN
FRONT (YEREMENKO)

R. Danube

Vienna

Bratislava

2ND UKRAINIAN
FRONT (MALINOVSKY)

A U S T R I A

Budapest
(18 Feb.)

H U N G A R Y

0   50   100 miles
0   50   100   150 km

Lake Balaton

ARMY GROUP F
(VON WELCHS)

3RD UKRAINIAN
FRONT (TOLBUKHIN)

The Russians were now advancing up to forty miles a day, exceeding the most optimistic estimates of the Stavka. Yet in the exhilaration of such a dash, with the enemy fleeing in disarray, death came upon many men unexpectedly. Lieutenant Vasily Kudryashov was driving at full speed down a long, empty Polish road in a tank column behind his company commander, Victor Prasolov. For hours they had not heard or seen gunfire, nor any sign of the enemy. Kudryashov was leaning on his turret hatch, smoking. Prasolov was sitting on top of his T-34, singing exuberantly, though no one including himself could hear his words above the roar of the engines. The column emerged from a forest into open fields on both sides of the road. A German tank concealed behind a haystack a thousand yards away fired a single shot which struck Prasolov's tank. A shrapnel splinter neatly severed the commander's head. Kudryashov, behind him, stared in horror as it bounced among the shell fragments on the road.

Captain Abram Skuratovsky, a signals officer, finished supervising the laying of telephone lines fifteen miles behind the front one morning and prepared to drive back to corps headquarters. A group of pretty girl soldiers begged a lift. The unit's deputy political officer said peremptorily: "I'll take the girls—you take the men and lead the way." Their little column of vehicles had just set off when the Luftwaffe made one of its rare appearances. Four German aircraft strafed the column. Skuratovsky and most of his men sprang out of their trucks and ran hard for the fields. A bomb scored a direct hit on the commissar's staff car. The planes disappeared. Badly shaken, Skuratovsky stood smoking a cigarette and contemplating the dreadful wreckage on the road. Suddenly the divisional commander drove up, and sprang out. "Fuck you!" he shouted. "Is this your idea of being an officer? Don't just stand there looking at wreckage—get the road cleared!" The signallers dragged out the bodies of the political officer, his driver and the six girls, dug a common grave for them, and pushed the remains of the vehicles into the ditch. Then the survivors drove soberly towards corps headquarters.

A bizarre little episode of this period concerned a Soviet general named Mikahylov. A man in his forties, he possessed a much younger wife. Returning unexpectedly to Moscow, he found her with a young captain and a newborn baby. He was overcome with despair. "*O blad! Generals na kapitana zamyenila!*" he said drunkenly one night, back with his division, "What a whore! She prefers a captain to a general!" A few days later, Mikahylov personally led a suicidal assault on the German lines. He was badly wounded, but survived to become a Hero of the Soviet Union. "If we could have made good use of all the futile heroic deeds we witnessed, we could have won five wars," Major Yury Ryakhovsky mused sardonically.

Konev took Cracow on 19 January, before the Germans had time to demolish it. Next day, the first Russian troops crossed the German border east of Breslau, pushing for the city. On the southern flank in Upper Silesia, the German Seventeenth Army possessed only seven feeble divisions, 100,000 men, to hold a front of seventy miles in an industrial region which contained the most important mines and factories left in Hitler's empire. Konev had been ordered by Stalin to do his utmost to secure the area intact. The marshal launched his forces upon a grand envelopment, while simultaneously pressing the Germans frontally. Schörner recognized that Upper Silesia was untenable. He ordered a wholesale retreat. The field-marshal telephoned Hitler and told him: "If we don't pull out, we'll lose the whole army ... We're going back to the Oder." Hitler stunned his staff by acceding without protest. He knew that if Schörner, most blindly loyal of his commanders, said that the line could not be held, he must be believed. By 29 January, the Russians had overrun all of Upper Silesia. They had also taken Auschwitz.

Red Army signaller Yulia Pozdnyakova was one of those sent to help the doctors coping with the 7,600 survivors of the largest death camp in Hitler's empire. The ovens had been cold for ten days, but the stench of death lingered, though at first the girl did not recognize this for what it was. She gazed upon the great heaps of children's shoes, the hoards of human hair, the mass of files and paperwork in the camp offices, and was perplexed that the Germans had left behind such a gigantic collection of documentation and evidence about their unspeakable actions there, not least 348,820 men's suits and 836,255 women's coats and dresses. As she sorted through clothing and papers, "I felt somehow guilty that I was touching all these things. The ghosts of the dead were all around us. It was very hard to sleep at night. For weeks afterwards, I could not stand the smell of fried meat." Each night when they returned to their billets, they heated water and scrubbed themselves desperately, seeking to wash from their bodies the taint of genocide.

It is curious that, though Konev was told what his men had found at Auschwitz, he did not trouble to visit the camp for himself. The marshal said after the war that his duties on the battlefield did not permit him to "abandon myself to my own emotion." It seems more plausible to suppose that any Russian who had lived through the mass murders of Stalin was incapable of excessive sentiment in the face of those perpetrated by Hitler. Moscow made no public announcement about Auschwitz, or about what had been found there, until after the war ended.

On 14 January, Guderian ordered the mobilization of the Volkssturm along the entire length of the Eastern Front. The military value of this measure was negligible. It was quickly found necessary to mingle the VS with regular army units in forward positions. "Used in isolation [the Volkssturm] possesses only limited military value and can be quickly destroyed," Hitler himself acknowledged in a general order of 27 January. The consequences of the VS mobilization were disastrous for German industrial production, emptying whole factories of their workforces, provoking a flood of complaints on this score from regional gauleiters, and driving another nail into the coffin of Speer's armament production. Keitel reminded all commands that the Volkssturm should be deployed only when there was an immediate local threat. But he continued to urge the virtues of Germany's citizen defenders: "The VS consists of men of all ages engaged in the defence of the Reich, many of whom have suffered severely from the terror-bombing, and most of whom have long experience of important war work. They have been mobilized to assist the defence of the Reich in its most dangerous hour." In justice to the Nazis, they committed the Volkssturm in exactly the circumstances for which the British trained and prepared their own Home Guard, "Dad's Army," in the event of a German invasion in 1940. The Volkssturm's military value proved small, not least because few weapons were available for its units. In the battle for Germany, some teenagers fought with frightening courage. But most of the Volkssturm's old men wanted no part of the struggle, and drifted home as soon as they dared.

Even as the front collapsed before the Russian onslaught, however, some Germans impressed the Red Army by the tenacity of their resistance. A Pole quoted a Wehrmacht prisoner saying: "A terrible end is better than terror without end." A report to Beria from 1st Belorussian Front declared: "There are still a lot of Germans fanatically confident of Germany's victory." The same document complained that resistance was being encouraged by the promiscuity with which some Soviet units were slaughtering German prisoners:

> Soldiers of 1st Polish Army are known to be particularly ruthless towards Germans. There are many places where they do not take captured German officers and soldiers to the assembly points, but simply shoot them on the road. For instance, [in one place] 80 German officers and men were captured, but only two were brought to the PoW assembly point. The rest were shot. The regimental commander interrogated the two, then released them to the Deputy Chief of Reconnaissance, who shot these men also. The deputy political officer of 4th Infantry Division, Lieutenant Colonel Urbanovich, shot nine prisoners who had voluntarily deserted to our side, in the presence of a divisional intelligence officer.

The NKVD's objections to such practises were practical rather than moral, but the killing of prisoners had plainly attained epidemic proportions if it provoked a protest to Moscow.

Yelena Kogan was an interpreter who spoke fluent German and was often charged with interrogations:

For everyone else, a German was simply an enemy with whom it was impossible to have any human contact. But I could talk to them. I saw in their eyes their awful uncertainty about their own fate, as they wondered if they would be shot. The younger Germans were professional warriors. But the older ones had families, civilian jobs, some experience of the world. I tried to find a common denominator among the fascists, and I usually failed. It seemed to me that they were simply victims of their country's madness. I only met one real fascist in the whole war—in the spring of 1942, a German navigator who bailed out when his Heinkel was hit while he was bombing us. I asked him: "Didn't it bother you to bomb defenceless women?" He shrugged: "It was fun."

By January 1945 the Soviet Air Force, which had begun the war with pitifully primitive aircraft, had become a formidable ground-support arm, equipped with machines as good as anything its enemies possessed. As the Luftwaffe's squadrons declined steeply in both quantity and quality, those of Russia had improved dramatically. Pilot training was never of the same standard as that available to British and American aircrew, who flew for a year or longer before being committed to combat. Alexandr Markov, a boyish-looking twenty-one-year-old from the Caucusus, spent three and a half years in pilot training among 800 other air cadets at Grozny, because there were no aircraft available for them to fly. After an eternity of boredom and frustration—"we wanted to go out and conquer Germany, but all we were able to do was study the theory of flight"—he won a place in flying school by getting into the school band. His commanding officer was captivated by the fashion in which Markov played the balalaika. But, even in 1944, they were expected to train on old aircraft, which constantly failed them. "Sometimes, there were three funerals in a week." Forty-seven per cent of all wartime Soviet aircraft losses were the consequence of technical failure rather than pilot error or enemy action. They learned next to nothing about fighter tactics, because they were forbidden even to loop: "We were just taught to make figures in the sky." Markov qualified in May 1944, with 100 hours' dual and solo experience. When he was finally sent to a squadron, he was expected to learn to fight in the air over the German lines.

The Soviet Union devoted little effort to strategic bombing. Its air force was a branch of the army, overwhelmingly committed to tactical operations. Russian units never received the sort of "cab-rank" close support from fighter-bombers that was available to the Western allies, because they lacked sophisticated ground–air radio links. But in 1944–45, the Soviets possessed overwhelming air superiority over the battlefield, protecting their advancing armies from the sort of devastation they had suffered from the Luftwaffe between 1941 and 1943. Most Russian bomber operations were carried out by daylight formations of Ilyushin-2s and American-built Bostons, attacking with heavy fighter escort. "I was testing my own skills to the limit," said Alexandr Markov of his days as an escort pilot. "Right to the end, the Germans had some pretty good fliers. We were sometimes flying four missions a day, each one from half an hour to two hours. Nobody asked whether we could take it. The tired pilots were simply the ones most likely to die." Unlike British and American pilots who were rested after a "tour," Russian aircrew flew until they died, or won the war. On the ground, their planes were serviced almost entirely by women. The girls did everything for them—bombing up and arming the aircraft, manning communications, washing their clothes. One Soviet night-bomber wing was entirely crewed by women, twenty-three of whom became Heroes of the Soviet Union.

Markov fell in love with his unit's meteorological officer, twenty-six-year-old Lydia Fyodorovna. She was married, but her husband serving on the Leningrad Front wrote suggesting that the couple should part: "He had found someone else, of course." Markov married Lydia after the war. At their airfield behind the Polish front, the pilots partied every night. Yet in most respects their war was more austere than that of their British and American counterparts. No one painted names or cartoons on their planes, any more than they did on Russian tanks. They had enough to eat, and almost unlimited supplies of alcohol. But there were few creature comforts, and no leave. There was only the war, and the comradeship of the unit.

BREACHING THE ODER

At the end of January, the Russians seized bridgeheads across the upper Oder, upstream and downstream from Breslau. The Germans first learned of their coming when Russian tank gunfire sank a steamer proceeding blithely downriver from the city. Breslau was designated by Hitler as a fortress, and doggedly held by the Germans for many weeks to come. But Konev's southern offensive had now achieved its principal purposes. It had opened a path into the heart of Germany across the last great river barrier. The loss of Upper Silesia caused Albert Speer to dispatch a memorandum to Hitler, copied to Guderian, in which the armaments minister asserted that without Silesia's factories Germany's war was lost.

Meanwhile, further north, General Vasily Chuikov had seized Lodz against negligible resistance on 19 January. Soviet and Polish flags burgeoned across the city. The Russians had enveloped Warsaw. Its garrison, such as it was, fled without resistance. The occupiers found that the Germans had systematically razed every landmark: St. John's Cathedral, the Royal Palace, the National Library, the Opera House. There was no military purpose behind the devastation. It reflected only Hitler's nihilism. Captain Abram Skuratovsky, a Soviet signals officer and also a Jew, wandered among the ruins of the Warsaw ghetto. Like many Russians who had already seen so much horror and destruction, he felt regret, but no sense of shock. For Skuratovsky, this was "just another bloody page in the history of the war." Beria's men were already arresting Polish Jews. As early as December 1944, the NKVD chief had reported to Stalin the arrest of a group who had established an organization in Lublin, with the intention of sending a delegation to the planned Polish Jewish Congress in the United States. Beria declared that he had evidence the Lublin Jewish leader was a British agent.

The Soviets estimated that between two-thirds and three-quarters of Warsaw's buildings had been destroyed. Most of the population, expelled by the Germans, scavenged like animals in the surrounding countryside across a radius of ten or fifteen miles. "In order to re-establish order in Warsaw," Beria's local commander reported to him on 22 January, "we have formed an executive group composed of members of the Department of Public Security and NKVD, with orders to locate and arrest members of Army Krajowa and other underground political parties. 2nd NKVD Frontier Guards Regiment has been moved to Warsaw to implement these measures." In Poznan, the NKVD reported that a third of the housing and half the city's industry had been destroyed, and that more than half the pre-war population of 250,000 had fled. The Germans blew all the bridges before they retired. The speed of the Soviet seizure of Lodz took the Nazi leadership and local population by surprise, though "all members of the city's administration have fled to Germany." No demolitions had been conducted, and 450,000 residents remained from the pre-war population of 700,000. Of these, almost half were Poles, about 100,000 Ukrainians, Russians and Belorussians, together with some 50,000 Germans. The Russians immediately embarked upon the massive task of shipping each racial group in its tens of thousands to the homelands which Moscow deemed most suitable for them.

Even as the Red Army was storming towards the Oder, its relentless rear-area campaign continued, to clear Soviet-occupied territory of "hostile elements." These operations required the deployment of thousands of NKVD troops. A report to Stalin from Beria in January described one action in which the 256th Escort Regiment was sent to liquidate a 200-strong partisan band; 104 were killed and 25 captured, including their leader. In another action, eighty-seven were killed and twenty-three captured. Among the dead were five Germans. A further Wehrmacht straggler was taken prisoner. An armoured train was dispatched to deal with another such group, which included draft-evaders as well as "bandits." In a further action, seven "bandits" and 252 draft-evaders were captured. Some of these, said Beria, were wearing SS uniform. A captured Wehrmacht officer proved to be a White Russian who had left his country in 1918 and who admitted that he had been serving as an intelligence officer for

Vlassov's Cossacks.* The validity of Beria's claims is, of course, highly doubtful. But his reports provide a vivid picture of the bloody chaos which persisted for many months within the territories reconquered by the Red Army.

On 24 January, Beria reported that 110,000 people had now been returned from the occupied territories to Russia, including 16,000 children. Of these, 53,610 had been sent home; 7,068 drafted for military service; 43,000 dispatched to NKVD camps for "further screening"; 194 "collaborators and betrayers of the motherland" had already been identified. Stalin ordered that all liberated Red Army officers about whose behaviour there was the smallest doubt should be sent to penal battalions. "One had to be very vigilant at Front HQ," said Major Fyodor Romanovsky of the NKVD. "There were so many kind of nationalists, and Whites who were urging men to desert, and assuring them of good treatment from the Germans." He added gravely: "We would never convict innocent people. We looked into every case." It was acute awareness of the significance of the Soviet tide for the people of eastern Europe, above all the Poles, that caused Churchill to send to a friend a greeting for this "New, disgusting year." How perverse it seemed that, amid Stalin's smashing victories, Jock Colville, one of Churchill's private secretaries, should observe: "The prospect of the end of the war and the problems it will bring with it are depressing the PM." Churchill said to Colville: "Make no mistake, all the Balkans, except Greece, are going to be bolshevised; and there is nothing I can do to prevent it. There is nothing I can do for poor Poland either."

Roosevelt raised the Polish issue half-heartedly at the Yalta conference of the leaders of the Grand Alliance in February 1945, reminding Stalin that the United States possessed seven million inhabitants of Polish stock. As an elected national leader, the president had to consider their concerns. Stalin dismissed this assertion with a shrug: of those seven million Poles, only 7,000 voted, he said. A British junior minister, H. G. Strauss, resigned from Churchill's government over Yalta, observing that he found it "impossible to approve of the treatment of the Polish people by the Crimean conference." When New Zealand's prime minister remonstrated about the abandonment of the Poles to Stalin, Churchill answered: "Great Britain and the British Commonwealth are very

---

*General Andrei Vlassov was a very able and experienced Soviet officer prominent in the defence of Moscow, before being captured by the Germans in July 1942. Vlassov, embittered by what he saw as Moscow's betrayal of his army in the field, and seduced by the Germans' judiciously humane treatment, agreed to raise an anti-Stalinist force from Russian PoWs. He was successful in recruiting several infantry divisions, whose members preferred German service to certain misery and likely death in German camps. They were notorious for indiscipline and indeed brutality in Italy and Yugoslavia, though some fought with fierce determination in the last phase of the war, knowing what their fate would be in Soviet hands. Vlassov himself was hanged in 1946, aged forty-six. Most of his men who had served in Wehrmacht uniform were either summarily executed or died in the Gulag.

much weaker militarily than Soviet Russia, and have no means, short of another general war, of enforcing their point of view. Nor can we ignore the position of the United States. We cannot go further in helping Poland than the United States is willing or can be persuaded to go. We have therefore to do the best we can." Poland's doom was sealed—to be passed with the acquiescence of the democracies from the bloody hands of one tyrant into those of another.

When Hitler heard that Warsaw had fallen, he ordered the arrest and interrogation by the SS of three senior staff officers at OKH who were deemed to have connived in this act of weakness. As a gesture of solidarity, Guderian insisted on sharing his subordinates' ordeal. In the midst of one of the climactic battles of the Third Reich, its senior commanders were obliged to devote hours to this black farce. Guderian was then grudgingly permitted to return to his duties. OKH's chief of operations was dispatched to a concentration camp. Another of the three staff officers was shot.

"Germany's leadership faces its greatest challenge of the war," acknowledged a Berlin radio broadcast on 22 January. "Retreats and disengagements are no longer possible, because our armies are now disputing territory of vital importance to German war industry...The utmost effort is required from every man and woman. The German people will respond willingly to the call, because they know that our leader has never failed to restore the situation, however grave the difficulties." On the same day, Bradley's aide Colonel Hansen wrote in his diary: "It is incredible to view the advance of the Russian front and realise how the East has suddenly become the cynosure of American and allied attention." After many months when commanders in the west had scarcely considered events in the east, now as they pored over their maps and perceived the Soviet line of battle drawing so close to Berlin, the movements of the Red Army began to cast a long shadow over the operations of the Anglo-Americans.

For the Western allies, the frustrations of communicating with the Russians about practical military problems, such as bomb lines, remained as great as ever. To the end, Stalin rejected all demands for liaison officers to be attached to Soviet field headquarters, just as Russian officers were attached to SHAEF. He insisted that contacts should be conducted exclusively through Moscow. In addition to refusing to refuel Allied aircraft seeking to aid the Poles, the Russians denied requests that RAF and USAAF planes crippled on bomber operations should be allowed to land at Soviet forward airfields. A British SOE mission parachuted to the Army Krajowa, led by a full colonel, was detained, disarmed, interrogated, humiliated, imprisoned and finally shipped to Moscow. The Russians were seriously tempted to shoot its members, as they had already shot some SOE personnel in Hungary. It was two months before the British embassy in Moscow could gain exit visas for the SOE group. Allied commanders, conscious of the huge volume of vehicles, equipment and supplies delivered to the Soviet Union, were increasingly exasperated by Russian recalcitrance. Yet from Stalin's viewpoint his policy was perfectly rational. The consequences would be gratuitously embarrassing if Allied liaison officers witnessed at first hand the conduct of the Red Army in eastern Europe, and reported it to Washington and London.

An American officer who did glimpse the Red Army in motion was amazed by the spectacle of this teeming host, mingling the modern and the medieval, drawn from a hundred races and tribes, burdened with equipment and loot, accompanied by horse-drawn carts, civilian vehicles, bicycles, trucks of every shape and size interspersed with tanks and guns: "I'll never forget those Russian columns and the crap they had. Holy smoke, you wondered how the hell they marched all that distance with that kind of stuff." A New Zealand doctor liberated from captivity by the Soviet advance watched Zhukov's men stream across Poland in late January:

> What a disorderly rabble they looked. Terrible congestion and utter chaos...During my whole eight weeks as a guest of the USSR, I saw absolutely nothing in the way of medical organisation...Before leaving a Polish hospital, I was attracted by a commotion outside. I went to the window and saw a stretcher containing a wounded German officer being carried down the steps. As I looked, a young Cossack officer hurried after the stretcher, drew his revolver, and shot the German through the head. It was a ghastly exhibition, but even more nauseating was the sight, some few minutes later, of Polish children stripping the body of clothing as it lay in the street.

Even after the doctor's recent experiences in the hands of the Nazis, he experienced a surge of pity when he found himself on a train at Odessa halted alongside wagonloads of Germans on their way to Siberia: "it was difficult not to feel sorry for the blighters."

"There seemed to be little difference between [Russian] treatment of the peoples they were supposed to be liberating and those they were conquering," wrote Peter Kemp, one of the SOE party mentioned above, who observed the Red Army's behaviour to the Polish residents of a building commandeered as a corps headquarters.

> The soldiers...behaved with calculated brutality and contempt. They broke up furniture for firewood, they pilfered every article of value and marked or spoilt what they did not care to take away; they urinated and defecated in every room...the hall, the stairs and passages were heaped and spattered with piles of excrement, the walls and floors were splashed with liquor, spittle and vomit—the whole building stank like an untended latrine. It is a pity those communists who declared that they

would welcome the Red Army as liberators never saw that particular army at its work of liberation.

Discipline within the Red Army was indeed erratic. Pyotr Mitrofanov, the forty-five-year-old driver of Vasily Kudryashov's T-34, was supposed to be on watch one night when the lieutenant found him asleep in their tank. Kudryashov lashed out at him: "You traitor! You know you could be shot for this!" Mitrofanov fell trembling on his knees before the officer, pleading for mercy. He was brusquely forgiven. Next day, the driver said: "Comrade commander, will you write a letter to my family for me?" Mitrofanov, like many Red soldiers, was illiterate. Kudryashov shot back, intending humour: "Yes—we can tell them how you were guilty of dereliction of duty!" Mitrofanov turned ashen once more: "No, no, no!" he cried. "Send me to Siberia—tell them anything but that." The Soviet Army was a maze of contradictions. Sentiment and terror, comradeship and cruelty, devotion to duty and reckless indiscipline marched together in a fashion that could confuse its own men, never mind the rest of the world. Mitrofanov was killed in action three days afterwards.

When millions of very young men were entrusted with weapons, fatal accidents became endemic. For fun, a soldier in Valentin Krulik's unit of Sixth Guards Tank Army dressed himself one day in a German smock and helmet, then dashed into his section's bunker waving a Schmeisser and crying "*Hände hoch!*" This was agreed to be extremely funny. But one of his comrades shot the cross-dresser before he was recognized.

ZHUKOV DETACHED several divisions northward, to secure his flank against the German forces in Pomerania. But, with the collapse of organized resistance in the path of his 1st Belorussian Front, the exultant marshal began to think that he might be able to advance to Berlin "on the run." This was certainly the fear of German Intelligence, which reported to OKH on 20 January: "From the enemy's behaviour and reports received, he is aiming to complete operations rapidly and not to permit any pause. We must therefore reckon that, against his usual behaviour pattern, he will continue to press forward without worrying about short-term threats to his flanks."

Everything seemed to hinge upon whether Zhukov could seize a bridgehead across the Oder in the Berlin region before the Germans regrouped. Through the last days of January, the Russian advance towards the river slowed, as it met new German lines of resistance. None amounted to much, but each imposed delay and some casualties. On 30 January, on the northern flank men of Fifth Shock Army reached the Oder. Next morning an officer and a few men walked across the frozen river and took possession without opposition of the small town of Kienitz. The local stationmaster nervously approached the Russian officer and demanded: "Are you going to allow the Berlin train to leave?" The Russian expressed ironic regret: "The passenger service to Berlin will undergo a brief interruption—let us say until the end of the war." Although the Germans rushed forces to Kienitz, Zhukov's men were able to reinforce their foothold west of the river. On the night of 2 February, the Soviet 301st Rifle Division crossed the Oder ice under heavy German fire, to strengthen the bridgehead. The Germans still held ground eastwards at Frankfurt and Küstrin. But elsewhere the Russians had secured vital ground on the western bank. Here was the final prize in an operation which had overrun a large part of Hitler's remaining territory in three weeks. On 2 February, the Stavka formally declared 1st Belorussian Front's Vistula–Oder operation concluded.

Zhukov's dash to the Oder inspired the Germans to a last Herculean effort. The Wehrmacht's difficulties now far exceeded those of September 1944, when new defences were forged in the west after the Anglo-American rush across France. Men, weapons, aircraft, fuel were drastically diminished. Yet German reaction was effective enough to crush Zhukov's hopes, briefly shared by Stalin's Stavka, of a dash for Berlin. On 19 February, the artillery commander of 1st Belorussian Front was told to prepare for an immediate attack on Hitler's capital. But these orders were almost immediately countermanded in the face of intelligence reports of large-scale German movements on the northern flank: "The Front commander took the decision to liquidate enemy forces in Pomerania before starting the Berlin attack." In reality, of course, the decision was Stalin's. The Russians felt obliged to delay their final assault by almost two months, vastly increasing the price they paid for Hitler's capital. In February, with the Russians within sixty miles, the city lay almost undefended. By April, when the climactic encounter took place, hundreds of thousands of men had been summoned from every corner of the shrunken Reich to fight its last battle.

We shall never know how the Russians would have fared in February had their spearheads pressed on. Chuikov, the hero of Stalingrad, now commanded Eighth Guards Army, which had advanced 200 miles in fourteen days. He vociferously asserted until the day of his death that Hitler's capital could have been seized in February. His Soviet peers strongly disagreed. First and Second Guards Tank Armies could almost certainly have got to Berlin. But even the Soviets, often so bold about exposing their flanks, feared that after driving a deep salient into the enemy's line it was too dangerous to go further, leaving large German armies behind their front both north and south, in Pomerania and Hungary. To Stalin's Stavka it seemed reckless to risk disaster, having achieved overwhelming success. Zhukov's and Konev's men were tired. They faced problems of supply immensely more challenging than those of the Anglo-Americans in France in September. Distances were greater, roads worse and transport limited. The Anglo-Americans were still far away, and seemed to pose no threat of pre-empting Stalin's triumph in Berlin. It was decided to defer the final assault until the Soviet armies north and southwards had caught up; the enemy had been further battered; and reserves of men, guns and ammunition could be brought forward.

As always, the Germans seized the respite. They threw themselves into rendering the Oder line defensible. In the last days of January aircraft bombs, power saws, demolition charges were employed in attempts to breach the frozen river. Then God took a hand. On the night of 1 February, it began to rain. In the days that followed, a premature blush of spring brought a thaw. The snows melted—and so did the Oder ice. Hitler had been given a moat. More than that, and as always when seasonal thaws came, the roads of eastern Europe deteriorated dramatically. The task of providing daily supply for Zhukov's and Konev's armies became dauntingly harder, when every ton had to be trucked 300 miles or more through chronic mud from the nearest railheads.

The Germans rushed 88mm flak guns from all over the Reich to reinforce the anti-tank defences beyond Berlin. Almost the entire remaining strength of the Luftwaffe was thrown into the eastern battle. The Germans were able to mount some damaging air attacks on Soviet positions. By St. Valentine's Day, fourteen German divisions were deployed against Zhukov's front. In February, while just sixty-seven new and repaired tanks were sent to the west, 1,675 were shipped east. German counter-attacks on Soviet positions west of the Oder failed. The Russians slowly but steadily enlarged their bridgeheads. The outcome of the impending struggle for Berlin was hardly in doubt. But each day of respite granted to the Germans would increase the price the Soviets must pay for final victory.

BEHIND ZHUKOV's front in Poland, the bitter struggle between the "London Poles" and the communists continued unabated. On the night of 19 February, men of Army Krajowa stormed the communist-run prison in Lublin, killed two guards and released eleven AK prisoners, along with twelve guards who also defected. Seven of the prisoners had been awaiting execution for "political crimes." On 2 March, the commanding officer of 28th Regiment of the 9th Polish Division of the Red Army persuaded 380 of his men to desert on their way to the front. Most set off for their homes, to which they were pursued by NKVD detachments. On 7 March, a junior officer at the Polish army tank school at Holm, a secret member of Army Krajowa named Kunin, persuaded seventy cadets to quit with their weapons, and to join the anti-Soviet struggle. In the days that followed, the deserters were ruthlessly hunted down by the NKVD. Most were killed or captured. So alarmed was the NKVD by the political threat that a draconian order was issued to remove all personal radio sets from members of Polish units of the Red Army, to prevent them from listening to broadcasts from London. This ban was soon afterwards extended to make possession of radios illegal even among Polish civilians. The Russians had now "liberated" almost all Poland. Yet the plight of most of its citizens was, if possible, worse than their lot under the Nazis. Beria received permission from Stalin drastically to reinforce the NKVD's forces in Poland.

While Zhukov paused at the Oder, further south Konev renewed his own massive operation to clear south-east Germany. First, his men closed upon the ancient city of Breslau, Silesia's capital. At 0600 on 8 February, at first moving sluggishly through the quagmire created by the thaw, the Russians advanced from their bridgeheads on the upper Oder. Against slight resistance from the remains of Fourth Panzer Army, the attackers gained almost forty miles on the first day. By 15 February, 35,000 troops and 80,000 civilians in Breslau were encircled by Konev's armies. The Germans of Seventeenth Army attempted a counter-attack which met some of the Breslau fortress troops on 14 February, but were then driven back by overwhelming Russian forces. The only consequence of the German effort was to impose a delay on Konev, during which he was able to rest and resupply his men. Like Zhukov his great rival, the marshal had cherished his own hopes of reaching Berlin in a single bound. He, too, was now obliged to acknowledge that this was unrealistic.

Nehring's XXIV Panzer Corps launched an ambitious counter-attack in the south on the night of 1 March, which surprised the Russians and inflicted substantial casualties before it ran its course—Konev lost 162 tanks to the Germans' ten. Goebbels joined Schörner for a parade in the recaptured town of Lauban on 8 March, at which the field-marshal, a devout Nazi, flattered the propaganda minister outrageously. Next day, amid snow showers, a new German counter-attack began at Streigau, forty miles eastwards. This recaptured the town. Revelations of atrocities committed by the Russians during their brief occupation may have done something to stiffen the determination of Schörner's soldiers. The Russians did not make an impressive military showing during these operations. They had grown over-confident, allowed themselves to be taken by surprise, and retired in disarray.

German Intelligence was still making extraordinary efforts to gather information from behind the Russian front. Four Ukrainians were parachuted from a Ju-88 on the night of 27 February, led by a former Red Army sergeant, carrying a radio and 206,000 roubles. They were immediately captured. On the night of 4 March, troops of the 1st Ukrainian Front met a twenty-two-man German patrol nine miles beyond the Oder. After a protracted firefight in which thirteen Germans and five Russians were killed, the survivors were found to be members of Abwehr Group 306, guided by three Red Army defectors. It seems remarkable that even the legendary Reinhard Gehlen, chief of German Intelligence for the Eastern Front, still considered operations of this kind practicable or worthwhile, though as late as New Year's Day 1945 a U-boat landed two German spies on the Maine coast, to conduct ill-defined intelligence operations against the United States.

German counter-attacks seemed irrelevant. It was meaningless to expend lives and irreplaceable equipment to recapture small fragments of lost Reich territory, which were doomed to be lost again within a matter of days. Army Group Balck reported miserably from Hungary on 5 February: "Amid all the stresses and strains, no improvement in morale or performance is visible. The numerical superiority of the enemy, combined with the knowledge that fighting is now taking place on German soil, has proved very demoralizing to the men. Their only nourishment is a slice of bread and some horsemeat. Movement of any kind is hampered by men's physical weakness." The staff officer cataloguing these dismal realities concluded in wonder: "In spite of all this, and six weeks' unfulfilled promises of relief, the men still fight tenaciously and obey orders." Yet for how long?

The counter-attacks inside Germany took place in sectors lightly held by the Russians, and lacked the weight to achieve anything beyond local successes. They exerted no influence upon Konev's latest big push, against the Germans further east in Upper Silesia. This was the last important industrial area in the east which remained in German hands. Konev attacked on 15 March. His men gained a Neisse crossing the following night. Reinforcements began to pour over a pontoon bridge. By 31 March, the Russians had gained Ratibor and Katscher, claiming to have killed some 40,000 German troops and captured a further 14,000. The bulk of Hitler's forces in the region were able to pull back intact, above all First Panzer Army. But Konev's left flank was now secure.

Between 12 January and 3 February, the drive to the Oder cost 1st Belorussian Front 77,342 casualties, and 1st Ukrainian Front 115,783—more than twice U.S. losses in the month-long Bulge battle. OKH posted eastern casualties for the months of January and February of 77,000 dead, 334,000 wounded and 192,000 missing—a total of 603,000, at least five times German losses in the Ardennes. Soviet forces in Hungary stood eighty miles from Vienna. Konev was 120 miles from Prague. Zhukov's spearheads were forty-five miles from Berlin.

Yet, even as the eyes of the world were fixed upon Allied forces approaching Hitler's capital, further north a vast human tragedy was unfolding. The Soviet drive into East Prussia, northern axis of Stalin's assault upon Germany, was to cost the lives of up to a million people, and inflicted a wound upon the consciousness of the German people which has never healed.

CHAPTER TEN

Blood and Ice: East Prussia

AN IDYLL SHATTERED

THIS BOOK TRACES a descent into an inferno. Its early pages have described chiefly the lot of soldiers, some of whom endured traumatizing experiences. Hereafter, however, as the pace of the Third Reich's collapse quickened, the civilian population of Germany began to suffer in a fashion dreadful even to those already familiar with aerial bombardment. Leave aside for a moment questions of guilt, military necessity, just retribution. It is here only relevant to observe that in 1945 more than a hundred million people, who found themselves within Hitler's frontiers as a consequence of either birth or compulsion, entered a darkening tunnel in which they faced horrors far beyond the experience of Western societies in the Second World War.

The great flatlands of East Prussia extended southwards from the Baltic, between the ports of Danzig and Memel. They had been ruled variously over the centuries by Prussians, Poles, even Swedes, yet the population in 1945 was almost exclusively composed of ethnic Germans, 2.4 million of them, to which should be added some 200,000 Allied prisoners and forced labourers, and many thousands of German refugees from the Baltic states. The 1919 Treaty of Versailles severed East Prussia from the rest of the Reich, by granting Poland a corridor to the sea at Danzig, soon followed by the transfer of the province of Posen to Warsaw's governance. In September 1939, East Prussians rejoiced when their land link to Germany was restored by Hitler's Polish invasion.

The region's character was strongly influenced by its great aristocratic families. "East Prussia was a province very untypical of Germany," observed Helmut Schmidt, "owned chiefly by the gentry and nobility, in which the ordinary people were dependent peasants. It was a peculiar society, with this very thin upper crust of counts and barons and princes, and beneath them hundreds of thousands of people who possessed barely enough food to live." Henner Pflug, who worked there as a teacher, said: "The Nazis seemed to take second place in

East Prussia. The aristocracy was still on top." The middle class, such as it was, lived chiefly around the provincial capital of Königsberg. The grandees occupied some wonderfully beautiful country houses, in a semi-feudal relationship with the peasantry who tilled their fields. For centuries before the Nazis came, the Germans of East Prussia perceived themselves almost as missionaries, fulfilling a civilizing mission, maintaining the values of Christendom amid the barbarians of eastern Europe. *Heimat*—homeland—is an important word in German. It possessed special significance for the people of East Prussia.

Graf Hans von Lehndorff, the doctor who composed one of the most moving narratives of his *Heimat*'s experience in 1945, wrote of its "mysterious splendour. Whoever lived through those last months with receptive senses must have felt that never before had the light been so intense, the sky so lofty, the distances so vast." Since 1939, East Prussia had been a backwater, largely sheltered from the impact of world conflict. "It was incredibly quiet," said Ursula Salzer, daughter of a Königsberg railway manager. "We had no sense of the war going on, and plenty to eat."

Matters began to change in the late summer of 1944. Königsberg, which had been desultorily bombed by the Russians, was attacked by the RAF's Bomber Command. Its aircraft came first on the night of 26 August, when most failed to find the city. Three nights later however, on 29 August, 189 Lancasters of 5 Group struck with devastating effect. Bomber Command estimated that 41 per cent of all housing and 20 per cent of local industry were destroyed. Unexpectedly heavy fighter activity over the target accounted for fifteen Lancasters shot down, 7.9 per cent of the attacking force. Yet the people of Königsberg cared only about the destruction which the RAF's aircraft left behind. When a bailed-out Lancaster crewman was being led through the ruined streets by his escort, a young woman shouted bitterly at him in English: "I hope you're satisfied!"

Her name was Elfride Kowitz. Her family's dairy business and their corner house in Neuer-Graben had been utterly destroyed in the attack. When she emerged from a shelter after the raid was over, she stood gazing in horror at the ruins of her family home. She saw a man in a helmet. It was her father. They fell into each other's arms, and sobbed in despair. "Both my parents were completely destroyed," she said. "They had lost everything they had worked all their lives for." Her father saved only the family's radio set. Everything else was gone. Her bitterness never faded: "That raid was so futile—it did nothing to shorten the war." Never again before May 1945 did Elfi fully undress at night. She began to shake as soon as she heard sirens.

A few special people beneath the Allied air attacks shared the common fear, but also found the bombers symbols of hope. Michael Wieck, a sixteen-year-old Königsberger, could not enter the city's air-raid shelters, because he was a Jew. Instead, when attacks came, he resorted to a coal bunker. He listened to the distant buzz of aircraft as it grew to a roar, then heard the angry bark of the flak. He was still above ground when the RAF's "Christmas tree" pyrotechnic markers drifted down through the night sky. "I was not so critical of bombing then as I became after the war," said Wieck. "We knew that the only thing that could save our lives was the victory of the Allies, and this seemed a necessary part of it." Yet even for Wieck and his parents the RAF's second raid on Königsberg seemed a catastrophe. "Schoolbooks, curtains, debris of all kinds rained half-burned from the sky. The heat was so enormous that many people could not leave their cellars. Everything was burning. Some people took refuge from the flames by jumping into the river. When it was over, the scene was like the after-math of an atomic explosion." Local Hitler Youth leader Hans Siwik, a former member of the Führer's bodyguard, was as appalled as Wieck, from a somewhat different perspective. Siwik was disgusted by the "immorality" of the British assault: "It seemed crazy that people should destroy such a place. People in Königsberg were unaccustomed to raids. We didn't have a lot of flak. I was hor-rified by the idea of such vandalism." Yet worse, much worse, was to come.

In the chilly autumn days of 1944, Hans von Lehndorff watched the storks begin their annual migration southwards. He fancied that many other local peo-ple shared his own impulsive thought: "Yes, *you're* flying away! But what of *us?* What is to become of us, and of our country?" East Prussians recognized that they were doomed to suffer Germany's first experience of ground assault, because they were nearest to the relentless advance of the Red Army.

The province's gauleiter was one of the most detested bureaucrats in the Third Reich, Eric Koch. Earlier in the war, as Reich commissioner in Ukraine, Koch had delivered a speech notorious even by the standards of Nazi rhetoric: "We are a master race. We must remember that the lowliest German worker is racially and biologically a thousand times more valuable than the population here...I did not come to spread bliss...The population must work, work and work again...We did not come here to give out manna. We have come here to create the basis for victory."

Throughout 1944, as the Red shadow lengthened beyond the borders of East Prussia, Koch delivered an increasingly strident barrage of bombast about the government's commitment to preserving the province from the Soviets. He set his face against any evacuation by the civilian population. To countenance such a flight would be to acknowledge the possibility of German defeat. It was the duty of each citizen of the fatherland, Koch declared, to hold fast to every inch of its soil in the face of the monstrous hordes from the east. Nor was it only Nazis who saw a special significance in the defence of East Prussia. Every German now knew that, by agreement between the Soviet Union and the Western allies, if their nation was defeated the province would be ceded to Poland, in compen-sation for eastern Polish lands which were to become part of the Soviet Union.

It had been settled between the "Big Three" that some sixteen million eth-nic Germans throughout eastern Europe—whether recent immigrants who had formed part of Hitler's colonial plantations or historic residents—would be deported to the new post-war frontiers of Germany. This was to be a colossal, historic transfer of populations, which was accepted by the Western allies with remarkably little debate or hesitation on either side of the Atlantic. "The President said he thought we should make some arrangements to move the Prussians out of East Prussia the same way the Greeks were moved out of Turkey after the last war," recorded Harry Hopkins in 1943; "while this is a harsh procedure, it is the only way to maintain peace and . . . in any circumstances, the Prussians cannot be trusted." Churchill asserted the justice of this pioneer exercise in "ethnic cleansing" to the House of Commons on 5 December 1944: "A clean sweep will be made," he said. "I am not alarmed by the prospect of the disentanglement of populations, nor even by these large transferences, which are more possible in modern conditions than they ever were before. The disentanglement of populations which took place between Greece and Turkey after the last war . . . was in many ways a success."

The purpose of this vast compulsory migration was to ensure that never again would Germans be motivated to act aggressively by the interests of their ethnic brethren in eastern Europe. Germans would be ring-fenced in their own country. Prussia, historic heart of German militarism, was to be dismembered. There would be no more German minorities elsewhere. Such Allied action would also redress, and more than redress, Hitler's treatment of the regions of Poland annexed to the Reich, from which he had expelled almost a million Poles since 1939.

German generals in Soviet hands, whose conversations were monitored by the NKVD, railed at the immense injustice which they saw looming over their nation. "They want to take East Prussia from us," said von Paulus, the vanquished commander at Stalingrad. "We can't just say to them: 'Here it is. Take it.' In this respect the Nazis are better than us. They are fighting to preserve our homeland. If German land is given to Poland, there will be another war." General Strekker agreed: "If they take East Prussia from us, it will mean another war, and of course the German people will be blamed again—this time undeservedly."

The first Russian incursions into East Prussia took place on 22 October 1944, when 11th Guards Army captured Nemmersdorf and several other border hamlets. Five days later, General Friedrich Hossbach's Fourth Army retook the villages. Hardly one civilian inhabitant survived. Women had been nailed to barn doors and farm carts, or been crushed by tanks after being raped. Their children had been killed. Forty French PoWs working on local farms had been shot, likewise avowed German communists. The Red Army's behaviour reflected not casual brutality, but systematic sadism rivalling that of the Nazis. "In the farmyard stood a cart, to which more naked women were nailed through their hands in a cruciform position," reported a Volkssturm militiaman, Karl Potrek, who entered Nemmersdorf with the Wehrmacht. "Near a large inn, the 'Roter Krug,' stood a barn and to each of its two doors a naked woman was nailed through the hands, in a crucified posture. In the dwellings we found a total of 72 women, including children, and one man, 74, all dead…all murdered in a bestial fashion, except only for a few who had bullet holes in their heads. Some babies had their heads bashed in." Even the Russians displayed subsequent embarrassment about what had taken place. Moscow's official history of the Great Patriotic War of the Soviet Union, usually reticent about such matters, conceded: "Not all Soviet troops correctly understood how they had to behave in Germany…In the first days of fighting in East Prussia, there were some isolated violations of the correct norms of behaviour." In reality, of course, what happened in October in East Prussia was a foretaste of the Red Army's conduct across Poland and Germany in the awful months to come.

Koch and Goebbels turned the tragedy of Nemmersdorf into a propaganda banquet. Photographers and correspondents were dispatched to record every detail of the Russian atrocities. The story was broadcast far and wide as a sample of Soviet barbarism, and as a spur to East Prussia's defenders. Posters showing the victims were distributed throughout the province, newsreels shown in every cinema. Many women who saw them took steps to acquire poison as a precaution against capture. More than a few subsequently used it.

Like most senior Nazis, Koch himself lived lavishly, if not stylishly. He occupied an estate outside Königsberg named Gross-Friedrich, dominated by a big modern house, for which he had somehow secured bricks when they were available to no one else. Small, squat, moustachioed and prone to outbursts of uninhibited rage, Koch shared the paucity of physical graces common to most of the Nazi leadership. But his acolytes basked in his patronage, the parties and private film shows, access to the gauleiter's personal box at Königsberg's theatre. Koch possessed his leader's monumental capacity for self-delusion. When the RAF bombed Königsberg, he was furious that an errant stick of bombs landed at Gross-Friedrich. As he supervised the clearing up, he observed between clenched teeth: "*That* won't be allowed to happen again." When some of his female staff expressed fears after the Soviet incursion at Nemmersdorf, Koch said authoritatively: "That's as far as they'll be allowed to get. We can stop them here." The women found the gauleiter so plausible that they almost believed this. Lise-Lotte Kussner, a twenty-three-year-old East Prussian girl who acted as one of Koch's secretaries, drafted a joint note from Koch and Robert Ley, the labour minister, reporting on East Prussia's contribution to the "wonder weapon" programme. Even as late as the winter of 1944, she found it intoxicating to draft correspondence to her Führer on the special typewriter with ultralarge letters to indulge his poor eyesight: "I was so young. I believed in the wonder weapons; that our army would protect us; that the Russians could be stopped. I had faith."

Koch still forbade any civilian evacuation except in the frontier area, where some villages were fortified against the assault. Posters appeared in every community, decreeing that anyone who sought to abandon his home would be executed as a traitor. The gauleiter sent a Christmas message to East Prussian soldiers at the front: "We all know that this battle—which is a matter of 'To be, or not to be'—must and will give us only one outcome, victory, if we are to preserve our nation, our freedom, our daily bread, our living space and a secure future for our children." Koch paid ritual tribute to the performance of the Volkssturm, and highlighted the "bestial murders" in Nemmersdorf, Tutteln, Teichof. He concluded brightly: "The *Heimat* wishes you a healthy Christmas."

"For us Prussians," wrote General Heinz Guderian, "it was our immediate homeland that was at stake, that homeland which had been won at such cost, and which had remained attached to the ideas of Christian, Western culture through so many centuries of effort, land where lay the bones of our ancestors, land that we loved...After the examples of Goldap and Nemmersdorf, we feared the worst for the inhabitants." Many Germans, and especially the Prussian and Silesian aristocracy, envisioned their nation's eastern lands much as the plantation owners of the Confederacy perceived the old South in the American Civil War. Their vision was imbued with the sense of a romantic rural idyll that gripped their whole imagination and loyalty, most readily understood by readers of *Gone with the Wind*.

Cattle were among the first fugitives to be seen in East Prussia. Vast herds accompanied the winter flood of refugees from the Baltic states. The beasts roamed bewildered across the snowclad countryside, harbingers of the terror that was approaching. The province's defenders were in no doubt about the magnitude of their task. A Wehrmacht report from Königsberg on 5 January observed that the city would have to be garrisoned by formations retreating from the main battlefield, on which they were bound to suffer severe losses, especially of armour. It was all very well for Gauleiter Koch to mobilize ninety local Volkssturm battalions, but 22,800 rifles and 2,000 machine-guns were required to arm them. Most of these did not exist, though the province had been given preferential treatment for the allocation of weapons.

The Russian thrust into East Prussia and northern Poland was, of course, subordinate to the assaults of Zhukov and Konev further south. Yet it was vital to generate pressure on the Germans here, to prevent them from either shifting forces to Zhukov's front or launching counter-attacks against 1st Belorussian Front's exposed flank. Even if the Soviets spurned the "broad front" strategy adopted by Eisenhower, they could not allow any one of their army groups drastically to outpace the others, lest they provide the Germans with an opening for one of their legendary envelopments. The Russian armies attacking East Prussia under Chernyakhovsky and Rokossovsky possessed overwhelming superiority. They outnumbered the Germans by ten to one in regular troops, seven to one in tanks, twenty to one in artillery. By early January, 3,800 Russian tanks and assault guns were massed on the border. The two Soviet commanders were to drive forward into German territory, seizing Königsberg and severing East Prussia from the rest of Germany, then securing the great ports of Danzig and Stettin. Rokossovsky's armies were also charged with protecting Zhukov's right flank. Amid the huge tracts of territory to be addressed, how was Rokossovsky to stay in touch with Zhukov, while supporting Chernyakhovsky? This important issue was still unresolved when the offensive began.

Stalin never doubted the strength of resistance his armies could expect on the soil of the Reich. "The Germans will fight for East Prussia to the very end," he told Zhukov. "We could get bogged down there." Chernyakhovsky's 3rd Belorussian Front began its bombardment of the northern sector in thick fog on the morning of 13 January, when Konev's men had just opened their drive in southern Poland. In the still, icy air the thunder of Soviet artillery, delivering 120,000 rounds in a few hours, was audible sixty miles away in Königsberg. Hans von Lehndorff's windowpanes rattled. "It sounded as if a lot of heavy lorries were standing round the building with their engines running uninterrupted." In East Prussia, however, the Germans had been able to do what Hitler forbade in Poland—withdraw the bulk of their forces from the outpost line, beyond the reach of the Soviet barrage. When the first Russian troops swept forward, they met fierce resistance.

The Germans had located strongpoints in the cellars of houses commanding crossroads and key strategic points. Some bunkers boasted guns mounted in cupolas. German propaganda slogans had been painted in huge letters on many buildings: "WAR HAS ARRIVED ON OUR DOORSTEP, BUT TILSIT SURVIVES DESPITE THE TERROR"; "SOLDIERS! ALL OUR HOPES NOW REST UPON YOU"; "THE DESTINY OF THE FATHERLAND LIES WITH YOU"; "OUR CITIES CAN BE STILLED, BUT NOT OUR HEARTS."

A matching message had gone forth to every Soviet soldier of 3rd Belorussian Front:

> Comrades! You have now reached the borders of East Prussia, and you will now tread that ground which gave birth to the fascist monsters who devastated our cities and homes, slaughtered our sons and daughters, our brothers and sisters, our wives and mothers. The most inveterate of those brigands and Nazis sprang from East Prussia. For many years they have held power in Germany, inspiring its foreign invasions and directing its genocides of alien peoples.

In the days before the Red Army crossed the border, political officers held meetings explicitly designed to promote hatred of the enemy, discussing such themes as "How shall I avenge myself on our German occupiers?" and "An eye for an eye." Later, when orders came from Moscow to adopt a less savage attitude towards Germans, to encourage surrenders, it was far too late to change an ethos cultivated over years of struggle. "Hatred for the enemy had become the most important motivation for our men," writes a Russian historian. "Almost every Soviet soldier possessed some personal reason to seek vengeance."

Early signals to Moscow from advancing Soviet forces reported that the civilian populations of Tilsit, Hurnbigger, Tallin, Rognit and other towns had vanished. Water and electricity were cut off, but the occupiers were gratified to discover houses still well endowed with personal property. Prisoners told Soviet interrogators that the civilians had been evacuated from the forward area several weeks earlier. Russian soldiers, who had never set foot beyond their own homeland, looked in wonderment at the prosperous towns and villages of East Prussia. Many Russian soldiers asked each other: "Why did the Germans want to come to Russia when they had so much here?" Lieutenant Gennady Klimenko said: "German villages looked like heaven compared with ours. Everything was cultivated. There were so many beautiful buildings. They had so much more than we did." Vladimir Gormin shared his enthusiasm: "Great country! So clean and tidy compared to ours!" Political Departments expressed alarm during the months that followed about the ideological impact upon the Red Army of perceiving the wealth of Germany. This contradicted years of propaganda about the triumph of socialist economics over that of fascism. The spectacle of a rich Germany implied the failure of an impoverished Soviet Union. In the view of some Russians, rage about the wealth of the enemy, in contrast to their own destitution after decades of sacrifice, helps to explain Soviet soldiers' manic destruction of artefacts of beauty and symbols of riches during the battle for Germany.

Throughout the campaign in the east, an ugly contest persisted between the propaganda arms of the rival tyrannies, to expose each other's atrocities. Even as the soldiers of Chernyakhovsky and Rokossovsky were killing and raping their way across East Prussia, the NKVD found time to send a report to Moscow about the discovery of a mass grave in a forest a mile north-east of Kummenen, containing the remains of a hundred Jewish women, who appeared to have been tortured and shot. The majority were aged between eighteen and thirty-five, said the report, and each woman wore a yellow star and five-digit number. "Mugs and wooden spoons were tied to their belts. Some had potatoes in their pockets. They had all been starved."

A Soviet officer describing the emptiness of the countryside said that, when his unit crossed the border into East Prussia, the only civilians they saw were two very old men, "whom," he added casually, "my soldiers promptly spitted on their bayonets." It took Marshal Chernyakhovsky a week, together with heavy casualties, to break through the German defences. When he did so, many

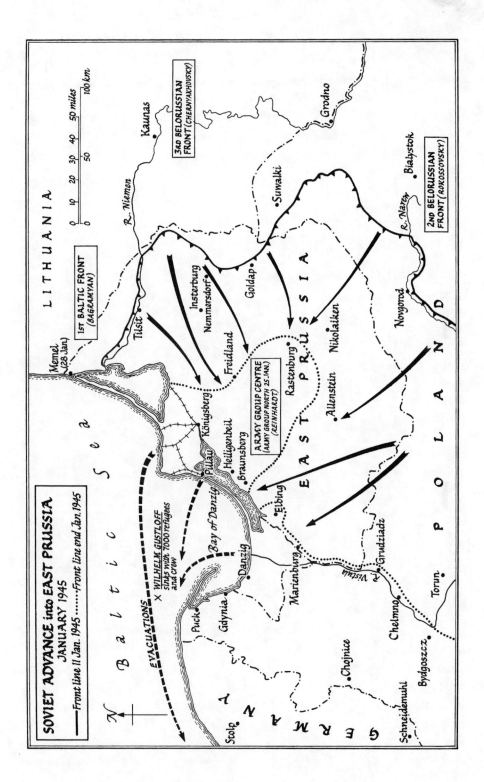

SOVIET ADVANCE into EAST PRUSSIA
JANUARY 1945

——— Front line 11 Jan. 1945 ······· Front line end Jan. 1945

LITHUANIA

1st BALTIC FRONT
(BAGRAMYAN)

3rd BELORUSSIAN
FRONT (CHERNYAKHOVSKY)

2nd BELORUSSIAN
FRONT (ROKOSSOVSKY)

ARMY GROUP CENTRE
(ARMY GROUP NORTH 25 JAN.)
(REINHARDT)

Baltic Sea

Bay of Danzig

EAST PRUSSIA

POLAND

GERMANY

EVACUATIONS

X WILHELM GUSTLOFF
sinks with 7000 refugees
and crew

N

Memel
(28 Jan.)

Tilsit

Insterburg
Nemmersdorf

Freidland

Königsberg

Heiligenbeil

Pillau
Braunsberg

Elbing

Marienburg

Danzig

Gdynia

Puck

Stolp

Schneidemuhl

Bydgoszcz

Chojnice

Chelmno

Torun

Grudziadz

Vistula

Goldap

Rastenburg

Nikolaiken

Allenstein

Novgorod

R. Narew

Suwalki

Grodno

Bialystok

Kaunas

R. Niemen

0   10   20   30   40   50 miles
0   50   100 km.

defenders from the Volkssturm and Volksgrenadier divisions streamed away in rout. Rokossovsky's men, whose attack had begun on 14 January from the Narew bridgeheads, were already racing forward on Chernyakhovsky's left. By 23 January, Soviet forces had crossed the rivers Deime, Pregel and Alle, the last natural defensive lines before Königsberg. Four days later, the Russians had almost completed the encirclement of the city. The Germans retained only a narrow corridor to the sea.

It is hard to overstate the naivety of most Russian soldiers. They had never seen indoor sanitation. Nikolai Dubrovsky was an intelligent and educated man, yet when his friend caught venereal disease he was perfectly ready to accept that this represented the work of a special German women's unit which, Stalin's people were told, sought sexual relations with their enemies in order to disable them. Major Yury Ryakhovsky never doubted the truth of a rumour at his front headquarters that for capitalistic reasons of their own the Americans were selling vehicles to the German army. The paranoia fundamental to Stalin's Russia infected millions of Soviet soldiers. Vladimir Gormin's corporal dragged a ten-year-old East Prussian boy in front of the regimental commander, asserting that he had just seen him poisoning a well. The colonel, with uncharacteristic restraint, told the corporal to give the child a cuff and let him go.

From the first day the Soviets drove into East Prussia, they began to loot on an epic scale. This was a practise institutionalized by the Red Army, which allowed every man to send home a monthly parcel of his spoils. On German soil, the invaders found booty beyond their dreams—food, drink, furniture, livestock, clothing, jewellery. Corporal Anatoly Osminov spotted in a billet one day a soldier playing a piano with his toes, while staring fascinated at his own image in a huge gilt mirror placed on the opposite wall. Soldiers in their white camouflage smocks fought, died and pillaged in a rhythm slowed only by the desperate cold, the chronic difficulties of movement in a world in which men ploughed through the snow with the clumsiness of spacemen.

When Captain Vasily Krylov gazed out on the flat, white plain of East Prussia, he thought that it looked like a beautifully pristine bedsheet. "YOU ARE NOW IN ACCURSED GERMANY," said a Red Army sign at the border. "ON TO BERLIN!" Krylov was his regiment's reconnaissance chief. Earlier in the war, he was badly wounded when a German shell landed by his truck, showering his face and eyes with glass from the windscreen. It took a surgeon six months to extract the splinters. He was then recommended for rear-area duty, but preferred to return to the front. As the advance moved deeper into the country, the long truck column of his Katyusha regiment was often slowed by fleeing refugees. As the Russian vehicles forced a passage through the throng, his own men succumbed as readily as those of every other unit to the opportunities for rape and looting. "We did our best to keep control, but it was very hard." Belated efforts by commanders to restrain soldiers' excesses were dismissed with contempt. David Samoilov, a poet who served in the Red Army, said: "Soldiers didn't understand this sudden change of course. In the emotional state prevailing in the army at the time, men could not accept the notion of amnesty for the nation which had brought such misery upon Russia."

Where civilians were foolish enough to remonstrate about looting, the troops simply torched their homes. Once some Russian women, forced labourers, appeared at Vasily Krylov's headquarters and began to explain the difference between good and bad local Germans. An officer said roughly: "We don't have time to start classifying fascists." The scale of plunder in East Prussia overwhelmed the officers' 32-pound monthly parcel allowance: "You could hardly send an accordion." But Krylov's orderly managed to dispatch a magnificent tea set to his family, and when he himself got home to his collective farm near Novgorod after the war he found his mother and sister wearing clothes he had sent them from East Prussia in January 1945.

The invaders swiftly overran the Wolf's Lair at Rastenburg, the vast headquarters complex from which Hitler had directed the operations of his eastern armies. Russian soldiers wandered curiously among the buildings, awed by the sophistication of its defences and bunkers. The German staff and guards were long gone, but in the commandant's office the occupiers found an order dated 8 January, instructing all personnel that they were bound by a lifelong oath of silence about everything they knew concerning the Führer's affairs. A Russian flicked curiously through the headquarters telephone directory. Hitler's extension number, he reported, was inevitably "1."

Lieutenant Alexandr Sergeev's infantrymen were fascinated by the ghostly emptiness of most East Prussian villages. They kicked open the doors of houses, and found ovens still warm, food on tables. The only people they met were foreign forced labourers on the farms, abandoned among the livestock. Special units following the advance were deputed to herd captured beasts into Russia, to replace the enormous numbers which had perished since 1941. They also herded "liberated" slave labourers into the Red Army, the factories, or—in the case of hundreds of thousands of "suspicious elements"—NKVD camps. Soldiers became warier about looting after early experiences with booby traps, which the retreating Germans had left behind in large quantities, wired to tempting prizes. "Our boys would open a door, we'd hear a loud explosion, and that would be that," said Lieutenant Alexandr Markov. His artillery unit learned to attach a telephone cable to a door before opening it from a safe distance. But such precautions offered no defence against the Red Army's terrifying vulnerability to alcohol. Markov's brigade captured a railway station in which they found a tanker wagon full of neat spirit. Many men were reduced to helpless stupor before the Germans counter-attacked. The unit only narrowly avoided disaster.

The Red Army did not behave with universal brutality. Indeed, many Germans were bewildered by the whimsicality with which they were treated. In one village, local people were praying in church, awaiting their end, as the first occupiers arrived. The villagers were astounded when instead a Soviet officer brought them bread. One German woman marvelled: "The Russians have been here half a day, and we are still alive!" Forward units often behaved in a punctilious, even kindly fashion, but warned local inhabitants: "We can vouch for our people, but not for what is coming behind"—the great undisciplined, wantonly barbaric host which followed the spearheads. It was in East Prussia that the Red Army began to rape women on a scale which surpassed casual sexual desire and reflected atavistic commitment to the violation of an entire society.

At first, it seemed that Königsberg would fall immediately, that the entire defence of East Prussia would collapse. Yet, once again, the Wehrmacht took desperate action. The 372nd Infantry Division, supported by assault guns, was rushed into the line north of the city, and by a margin of minutes was able to stem the Soviet assault, destroying some thirty tanks. Königsberg, together with a narrow coastal perimeter, was now besieged. It would maintain its defence for two terrible months. Naval action was decisive in enabling the Germans to maintain supplies and gunfire support for ground formations fighting with their backs to the Baltic.

Boys and old men in their thousands were summoned to active duty with the Volkssturm. When seventeen-year-old Joseph Volmar reported for morning *Appel* at his Luftwaffe glider school outside Königsberg on 20 January, he and his class were hastily marched to the nearest station, almost two miles through driving snow. They fought their way on to a train for the city, through a mob of terrified civilians. On arrival, they were paraded before a harassed infantry captain. "Men or boys or whatever you are," he said, "you have been assigned to my command for the heroic defence of Königsberg. I hope you will do justice to yourselves when the time for combat comes." They were issued with French long rifles of 1914 vintage, and twenty-five rounds of ammunition. One boy was given a Czech machine-gun. To their sergeant's fury, only Polish ammunition proved to be available for it. They were loaded on to a city bus, under command of a Hitler Youth leader, and drove slowly through the street. An NCO coaxed them into song. They joined hesitantly in a chorus of "Edelweiss." As they gazed from the windows at the throng of refugees stumbling through the snow, the early morning's sense of adventure gave way to mounting unease, then to fear: "Hundreds of frostbitten faces stared up at us as we sped in the opposite direction. One face was like another, each showing hunger, fatigue and fear as a pair of weary eyes peered out from under a scarf. Small children were bundled up in a sled or riding uncomfortably in baby carriages stuffed with clothing and household goods. Often, the carriages were abandoned at the roadside."

They travelled some thirty miles into deepening darkness. They began to pass soldiers, plodding in the opposite direction. Then, without warning, they heard shellfire. The bus stopped in a village which had been abandoned by its inhabitants. They were told to bed down in two houses beside the church. "What about food, Scharführer?" someone asked their NCO. He shrugged: "You're out of luck today." They wandered among the buildings until they chanced on a supply dump that had been set on fire, and salvaged a few wheels of cheese and bottles of wine. Then, wrapped in their greatcoats, they drifted into anxious sleep.

They were roused four hours later by their sergeant: "Everybody up and outside! The Russkis are coming!" Some ninety-strong, they were marched to an embankment in front of a railway line at the edge of the village. They had just begun to dig holes in the snow when Russian mortaring began. One boy groaned and slid down the embankment, rolling in agony as he came. Lying at Volmar's feet, he muttered, "Say farewell to my mother," and died. They could hear screams from other wounded. When Volmar tried to load his rifle, he found the bolt was frozen. He attempted to put a tourniquet round the bloody leg of their machine-gunner. There were cries of "*Sanitäter! Sanitäter!*"—"Medic! Medic!" As Russian fire intensified, the boy crawled among dead comrades, searching for ammunition. For four hours, they lay and fired as best they could at the Russians, who advanced steadily closer. Finally their NCO shouted: "Let's get out of here! We can't hold on any more! Everybody get across the tracks and make for the river! Bring the wounded if you can."

They could not. They simply ran, more boys falling to a Russian machine-gun. One, hit in the leg, cried as he lay: "Help me across the tracks! I don't want to be taken prisoner." Volmar began to drag him, but suddenly saw a Russian soldier fifty yards away, holding a machine-pistol. The young German abandoned his screaming comrade and started running again, throwing away helmet, gas mask and finally a beloved camera. Just as he crossed the railway tracks, he heard a burst of fire and felt a hammer blow in his arm. He stumbled on across a frozen river, until at last he saw a medical orderly who roughly bandaged his throbbing wound. He was given a swig of wine and fell into instant sleep. Somebody put him on a truck. At a Königsberg hospital, he was helped into a bed as its previous occupant was wheeled away to the morgue. A 7.65mm bullet was removed from his arm without anaesthetic. He later found that the futile stand of his company had cost the lives of twenty teenage student pilots.

One of the men who commanded Hitler Youth units such as Volmar's was Gefolgschäftersführer Hans Siwik. He was a twenty-five-year-old Berliner, though his father came from Austria. Before the war, to his immense pride he had served in the Leibstandarte, Hitler's personal bodyguard. He warmed to the memory of the Führer's small personal attentions to him, such as discussing a presentation samurai sword one afternoon when Siwik was on duty in his private quarters: "Hitler could be a real softy." His SS career foundered, however, after he failed the officer course at Bad Tolz. He was sent to East Prussia as a Youth leader.

In the first days of 1945, Eric Koch ordered Siwik to form "Hitler Youth bat-tle groups"—"do it any way you like that will stop tanks." Siwik banded his sixteen-year-olds in companies of 200. They were issued with First World War Mauser '98 rifles. "The oldest boys were about 16, but there were others who could not have been more than 13," wrote a German soldier who saw such a body march out.

They had been hastily dressed in worn uniforms cut for men and were car-rying guns which were as big as they were. They looked both comic and horrifying, and their eyes were filled with unease, like the eyes of children at the reopening of school... Some of them were laughing and roughhous-ing, forgetting the military discipline which was inassimilable at their age... We noticed some heart-wringing details about these children, who were beginning the first act of their tragedy. Several of them were carrying school satchels their mothers had packed with extra food and clothing, instead of schoolbooks. A few of the boys were trading the saccharine can-dies which the ration allotted to children under 13... What could be done with these troops? Where were they expected to perform? Was Germany heroic or insane? Who would ever be able to judge this absolute sacrifice?

Siwik's group was at first employed digging anti-tank ditches. Then, on the morning of 20 January, he was ordered to take a company in trucks with a single anti-tank gun to occupy positions some thirty miles south-east of Königsberg. They drove through deep snow, the boys at first excited rather than fearful. They dug trenches beside a sunken road, and sited their gun. After a long, shiv-ering wait, they saw Russian infantry advancing towards them, three T-34s fol-lowing. "Open fire," Siwik told his company. They began enthusiastically enough, but soon the aged Mausers began to jam. The soldier ran from foxhole to foxhole, helping to clear them. The nearest Russians came within eighty yards before, to the Germans' surprise, pulling back in failing light. The chil-dren fell asleep in the snow where they lay.

Early next morning, the Soviet advance recommenced, this time supported by accurate mortar fire. Siwik, who had once told the Führer that he yearned for a posting where he might win a medal, found that his interest in decorations had now faded: "the issue wasn't winning. It was delaying the Russians long enough for the refugees to escape." He hardly knew the names of any of his boys, he simply addressed them as "you." In the middle of the morning, a truckful of fausts arrived. No one knew how to use them. They fired some twenty without effect before a lucky shot hit a T-34, which brewed up. Russian mortaring was causing casualties. They could only use strips of torn shirt to bandage wounds.

After hours of indecisive firing, there was a muffled roar of armoured vehi-cles behind them. A panzer officer dismounted, and gazed in amazement at the children. "What the hell's all this?" he cried in some disgust. He told Siwik and his company to make themselves scarce. Gratefully, they scrambled out of their holes and plodded towards the rear. They had lost six killed and fifteen wounded. "The boys were traumatized. Their patriotism had shrivelled away," said Siwik. His own enthusiasm for combat had also waned. As they marched towards the coast among the throng of refugees, he told his company to throw away their weapons and try to find civilian clothes. "They were all from towns the Russians now held. I could not send them home." Siwik kept his own uniform, and with a handful of boys eventually secured space on a naval supply ship leaving Pillau. It may be assumed that he was able to exercise his authority as a Party functionary. After two days at sea, he reached the temporary safety of Stettin.

THE WORST JOURNEY IN THE WORLD

FROM LATE JANUARY onwards, with most of East Prussia in Soviet hands, the German Army struggled, first, to hold its surviving enclaves—notably Königsberg and the nearby port of Pillau—and, second, to keep open a line of retreat along the coast south-westwards to Germany for hundreds of thousands of teeming refugees. The fortunes of the battlefield, and of the precarious escape routes, seesawed violently, tragically, through ten weeks that followed. On 30 January, a Russian assault towards Königsberg's rail line to Pillau brought ghastly consequences for a trainload of fugitives. The engine was halted by a T-34 on the tracks. The passengers jumped out when Red soldiers started firing on the carriages. Russian infantry embarked on a familiar onslaught of looting and rape. Königsberg's principal defenders were 5th Panzer Division and the East Prussian 1st Infantry Division. In mid-February, the garrison and the German forces on the Samland peninsula staged a ferocious counter-attack, to reopen the link to Pillau. This was achieved on the 20th, a notable feat of arms. Once again, refugees began to flee from the city towards the port, somewhat reducing the burden of hungry mouths among the besieged. Some 100,000 people fled during this lull. On 26 February, the Russians decided that for the present it was foolish to commit further resources to the seizure of Königsberg. The German forces in the city and on the Samland peninsula north-east of it represented no possible threat to the grand Soviet design. Chernyakhovsky's Thirty-ninth and Forty-third Armies were ordered to hold their existing positions, masking the German garrison until time and forces could be spared to finish it off.

Meanwhile further south and west, 2nd Belorussian Front under Rokossovsky, whose advance had begun on 14 January, cleared most of East Prussia while Chernyakhovsky was still hammering at its capital. As the defences were rolled up, German commanders pleaded with Berlin to allow

Fourth Army to make a major withdrawal, to avoid envelopment. Inevitably, Hitler refused. On the 19th, Fourth Army reported that a desperate shortage of munitions of all kinds was crippling its ability to hold ground: "Any further losses would precipitate a serious crisis." Yet, early on the 21st, Guderian told the commander of Army Group North, Hans Reinhardt, that Fourth Army would have to maintain its existing positions. "But that's quite impossible," protested its commander. "It means everything is going to collapse." "Yes, my dear Reinhardt," said Guderian wearily. When at last a modest withdrawal was authorized, it was too late.

Stalin was irked by Chernyakhovsky's failure quickly to secure Königsberg. As he watched from Moscow the sluggish progress of 3rd Belorussian Front, on 20 January he ordered Rokossovsky's armies of 2nd Belorussian Front to wheel north, towards the Baltic coast, and sever East Prussia from the rest of the Reich. The weight of two Soviet fronts smashing into Prussia and thence Pomerania wrought havoc among millions of German soldiers and refugees. Yet this was achieved at the cost of opening a wide gap between Rokossovsky and Zhukov, who was appalled to find his right flank exposed—here was the blunder which destroyed any possibility that Zhukov could have reached Berlin "on the run" in February. It was the Stavka's worst strategic decision of the last phase of the war—and the Stavka was, of course, Stalin. Rokossovsky's forces became embroiled in a long succession of battles along the Baltic coast. In all of these the Soviets triumphed, yet they seemed strategically irrelevant. Once Berlin fell, surviving pockets of German resistance could be addressed at leisure. By sending Rokossovsky north, Stalin importantly weakened the drive for Hitler's capital. The Stavka's decision did not, of course, threaten final victory, but it may have delayed this by two months.

Rokossovsky's tanks crashed into the long, exposed flank of Fourth Army around the Frisches Haff—the vast frozen coastal lagoon south-west of Königsberg—and into hundreds of thousands of trekking refugees. On 21 January, Soviet spearheads began shelling throngs of fugitives struggling to escape through Elbing towards the Reich. The Russians reached Allenstein on 22 January, overrunning German reinforcements detraining there from the east. On 23 January, Fifth Guards Tank Army entered Elbing, temporarily halting the refugee trek. Having suffered substantial casualties from local defenders and Panzerfausts, the Russians were obliged to withdraw. They did not enter the town again for a fortnight, but now held much of the near shore of the Frisches Haff. Only a thin, sandy tongue of land between the lagoon and the sea—the Frisches Nehrung—still offered a passage for a host of fugitives, if Rokossovsky's armies could be pushed back a few miles.

With considerable courage, the German commanders on the Baltic decided to defy Berlin, to save their 400,000 troops and the great mass of civilians milling helplessly across thousands of square miles of snowbound countryside, searching for a path westwards. On the moonlit night of 26 January, Fourth Army launched a counter-offensive which drove back the Russian Forty-eighth Army and broke through to Elbing. Once again, a land passage for the refugees was open. Reinhardt of Army Group North was sacked for his disobedience, as was Fourth Army's commander, Hossbach. Hitler was wholly uninterested in the plight of his suffering people. Hundreds of thousands of fugitives, however, had cause to be grateful to the dismissed generals.

Across the entire battlefield between the Baltic and Yugoslavia, the rival forces' tanks, artillery, infantry, machine-guns were now conducting their deadly contest amid throngs of civilians fleeing westwards, and the merciless winter weather. The plight of East Prussia's fugitives was worst of all. Women and infants huddled upon columns of carts laden with possessions, figures shuffling through the snows with children crying out in their wake, became doomed extras in the drama of the armies. The civilians' sufferings, the march of so much despairing humanity towards extinction, became to the combatants a spectacle as familiar as the frozen rivers, snowbound forests and burning villages among which they met their fate.

Russian attitudes towards the refugees ranged from indifference to deliberate brutality. When advancing T-34s met trekkers, the tanks smashed through their midst, mere battlefield flotsam. Again and again, Russian artillery and machine-guns raked columns of trekkers or blocked their flight. Cold and hunger also killed huge numbers. To this day, surviving East Prussians place the heaviest burden of blame for their fate upon Gauleiter Koch, who denied them licence to flee before the Russians came. But Soviet gunfire was directly responsible for the slaughter of tens of thousands. The Russians' policy owed little to military necessity and everything to the culture of vengeance fostered within the Red Army over almost four years by such manic Moscow propagandists as Ilya Ehrenburg.

Once the Soviet commitment to fire and the sword became evident, the German army in East Prussia performed extraordinary feats of courage and sacrifice, to hold open paths to safety for the civilians. The saga of East Prussia's winter of blood and ice is one of the most awful of the Second World War. Russians said: "Remember what Germany did in our country." It was indeed true that for each German killed by the Red Army could be counted the corpses of three, four, five Russians killed by the Wehrmacht, the Luftwaffe and the SS in their glory days. Yet few modern readers can escape revulsion in contemplating the fate of the East Prussian people in the first months of 1945. Since the expulsion of the German population from East Prussia had already been agreed between the Allies, it is scarcely surprising that the Russians were untroubled by the mass flight of refugees. It seems strange, however, that when the depopulation of the province was a matter of Moscow policy, the Red Army acted so savagely to impede the westward passage of people who were anyway doomed to expulsion.

WALTRAUT PTACK was only thirteen, but in her schoolroom early in the new year all the children's chatter was about possible suicide when the Russians came. There was a rumour that the Ivans would use poison gas. Waltraut was the daughter of a cobbler in Lötzen who made boots for the Wehrmacht. The family had spent a sad Christmas, lacking even the decorated tree the children had wanted so much. Her eldest brother Günther had died in the battle for Aachen. On 23 January, they left home a few hours ahead of the Russians, towing a family sled. This carried only the barest essentials—food and blankets. The child pleaded to take her doll, but her father sternly insisted that it must stay behind. Every few hundred yards of the trek to the nearest station, some family treasure was abandoned to lighten the sled. When they reached the tracks amid the familiar mob of hysterical people, they waited hours. Passing trains carried only troops forward, wounded back. At last, a soldier took pity on the misery of the Ptack children. He allowed them to climb on a freight train, which crawled through the countryside for many hours, stopping repeatedly. Then they heard that the Russians were in Elbing. The trucks and their despairing human cargo were shunted eastward again. After a few miles, all the passengers were ordered off. They stumbled through darkness the few miles to the edge of the Frisches Haff. Through the days that followed, they scavenged for food and a path to safety, as Russian artillery fire grew steadily closer. They slept in barns, cowsheds, abandoned houses.

On 5 February, their father was successful in begging places for the children and his eighty-year-old mother on a truck crossing the lagoon. At the military police checkpoint, there was a bitter argument when the soldiers wanted to insist that sixteen-year-old Horst Ptack stayed to join the Volkssturm. "My father knew that it must mean death for him." Herr Ptack won the battle for his son, but lost it for himself. At the age of fifty-seven, he was now required to fight for his fatherland. He left the family at the edge of the ice. It was raining hard, and the snow was turning to slush. They began to fear that the ice underfoot would melt. Waltraut stared curiously at the frozen corpse of an old man lying beside her. They crossed the lagoon safely and, on the far side, crowded into a earthen shelter among scores of others to rest: "Human warmth kept us alive." Next morning, the skies cleared, the sun shone and the Soviet Air Force came. They watched the bombs leave the aircraft above, so small in the air, and then saw huge explosions all around them, blasting holes in the ice and killing many people who stood upon it. The aircraft maintained a shuttle all through the daylight hours: "Many, many people died that day." Waltraut's eleven-year-old brother Karl-Heinz caught a stampeding horse and stood trying to calm it through the attacks, while everyone else lay prostrate, hugging their fear.

At Pillau, they lingered for three days, praying that their father would be able to rejoin them: "People were roaming the streets demented with grief, searching for loved ones." Their father did not come. The Russian guns were getting closer again. They fought their way on board a freighter and lay terrified on a bed of straw in its hold through the sea passage to Danzig, where they arrived on 20 February. The family spent the balance of the war as refugees in an abandoned seaside villa in Pomerania. They never heard of their father again.

Twenty-year-old Eleonore Burgsdorff had returned to her mother's home in East Prussia in December 1944, after serving her statutory two years with the Reich Labour Service. The family lived in a beautiful baroque house named Wildenhoff, which belonged to her stepfather, Graf von Schwerin. A typical German aristocrat, he had declined to join the July plot against Hitler. "First, the Russians—then the Nazis," he said. The family shared Christmas together with their staff of twenty and the miscellany of Russian, Polish and French PoWs who worked on the estate. They gave each other small gifts of wool, to knit clothes. "We all recognized that we were living on a volcano. Our Russians knew that, for them, the coming of the Red Army meant death." For the last time in their lives, the prisoners sang carols in the courtyard. There was plenty to drink at Wildenhoff, because over the years of Germany's triumphs visiting officers had brought Scotch whisky, Grand Marnier and champagne to fill the cellars.

As soon as the festivities were over, "Kaps" von Schwerin departed for the front. Almost certainly because the Nazis suspected his loyalty, he was given a thankless role, commanding a Volkssturm unit. He always wore a cherished gold pin. When he left home for the front, he did not take this with him. "I know I shan't be coming back," he said. On 16 January, Eleonore picked up the telephone at Wildenhoff and took a call from her stepfather's unit. Her mother had gone into Königsberg the previous day. Eleonore took the train to the city, and went to her mother's room at the Park Hotel. She walked in and said simply: "Kaps is dead." Her mother slumped back, dragging the bedclothes over her head. The two women sobbed together for a time. Thereafter, the forty-one-year-old widow behaved as if she had been turned to stone. To her daughter's despair, she would not focus at all upon practical issues—above all, flight. When they returned to Wildenhoff, the girl felt that she could not leave her mother, lest she kill herself. Day after day, though they knew they should flee, they postponed the decision. Many of the treasures of Königsberg Museum had been evacuated to Wildenhoff. Gauleiter Koch had told Gräfin von Schwerin that, if it ever proved necessary to evacuate the area, he would arrange special railroad space for the works of art. None of this came to pass.

As the Red Army drew near, the von Schwerins walled up family papers and valuables in the cellars, and tried to choose a few special favourites to take with them. Eleonore looked wonderingly upon the shelves of priceless volumes in the library, and finally selected those which looked oldest and most splendid, with seals hanging from their leather bindings. A Ukrainian woman art historian was billeted with them as curator of the art treasures, which included a priceless hoard of icons looted by the Wehrmacht from Kiev. She refused to abandon her cherished charges. "When the Russians come," said the Ukrainian, "I shall set fire to the whole place and everything in it."

The estate tenants and staff also declined to leave. "We had the Russians here in 1914," they said, "and in the end they went away again. It'll be the same this time." Eleonore asked a French prisoner to look after Senta, the family's beloved Great Dane. At last, they set off for the station in horse-drawn carts. After an emotional farewell, their coachman took the horses back to the house. The two women boarded a train for the hour-long journey to Braunsberg, where a cousin lived. The trip took eighteen hours. They arrived to find their cousin preparing his own trek. The women clambered on to a cart. The roads were crammed, and the pace was painfully slow amid the chaos of the living and dead. Worst of all were the corpses of babies lying in the frozen snow. Their party was fortunate enough to be among the first to cross the ice of the Frisches Haff, on 24 January. Soldiers helped them with the wagons. At one point they came close to disaster as a wheel tilted over open water, and their horses almost slipped into the abyss. Yet, travelling by night and resting by day, they escaped westwards into Germany. The horrors of their war were not yet ended, but they had left behind the nightmare of East Prussia. They never saw Wildenhoff again. The Ukrainian art historian fulfilled her dreadful promise. She immolated the house, its contents and herself in a great blaze as the Russians approached, a vision reminiscent of the burning of Manderley in Daphne du Maurier's novel *Rebecca*.

On 21 January, Gauleiter Koch, the man personally responsible for refusing to allow any prior evacuation of East Prussia, burst into his secretary's office on his estate at Gross-Friedrich. "You must go—quickly—tonight," he told Lise-Lotte Kussner. "Take the rest of the village people." She responded instinctively: "But I can't—there are posters everywhere saying that it would be treason." So indeed there were—drafted by Koch himself. Now, he said: "No, no—that means nothing. Just go." The gauleiter was distraught. In two hours, a little convoy of tractors and trailers was assembled. There were three Belgian PoWs, five women, a grandfather, eight small children and a fourteen-year-old boy. Lise-Lotte went into the house to tell Koch they were ready. She met his wife, Lilo. "Where are you going?" Frau Koch demanded.

"We're off," said the girl.

"No, you're not."

"It's the gauleiter's order."

"You're staying here."

Frau Koch was visibly confused, no less so when her husband appeared and confirmed his orders, adding that his wife must remain. A Russian prisoner and his Polish girlfriend begged to join the trek. Lise-Lotte said: "But you're going to be liberated!" The couple said: "No, we want to get out." Koch, however, refused to let them leave. They took some snow-chains off a Wehrmacht vehicle to equip one of their own. Their privileged little convoy had progressed just six miles when one of its tractors broke down. Lise-Lotte telephoned Koch to ask what to do. He responded furiously: "Just keep going. You must go faster. The Russians are at Elbing already!" Their road, unlike most of those throughout East Prussia, proved curiously deserted. They were flagged down by a Wehrmacht patrol, who told them that the way ahead was closed by the Red Army. They lingered fearfully for hours before the orders changed. German troops had regained some ground. They could drive on. They heard Russian guns every yard that they travelled, but they reached the Vistula ferry without serious incident. Here there was a long, long queue. Irma, one of the women in the convoy, said: "Get the little ones screaming." They awakened the sleeping children, and set them to howl. The apparent plight of their small charges persuaded the soldiers to allow them to bypass the queue. The tractors drove forward to the ferry, past long lines of silent, resentful refugees.

Even as Lise-Lotte's group was crossing the Vistula, her mother telephoned Koch from their home, some thirty miles from Königsberg. "Where is my daughter?" she asked. Koch said untruthfully that he had put her aboard a ship: "I got her a place—on the *Wilhelm Gustloff*." Frau Kussner demanded to know how she herself was to flee, when her grandmother was immobilized with a broken rib. Koch sent a car manned by two uniformed Party officials to take the Kussner women to an airfield, where he arranged places for them on a plane to Breslau. Even the Kussners' dulled consciences were pricked by the experience of speeding for miles across East Prussia through columns of refugees who could seek safety only on their feet in the snow.

At Stralsund, Lise-Lotte's tractors ran out of diesel, but a cousin of hers was stationed in the port, a sailor. He found them fuel in exchange for food. Late in April, after many halts and delays, they crossed the Elbe. Most of those who fled from East Prussia in less privileged circumstances would have begrudged them every moment of their good fortune. Lise-Lotte Kussner said: "I know Koch was responsible for terrible things, but that was not how I knew him." Just so. Later, however, she was careful to tell no one in whose service she had spent the war years.

In the heart of Germany, the news from East Prussia and Silesia seemed a harbinger of the doom that was approaching. "The first shattering reports of the terrible happenings were brought to Berlin by refugees…" wrote Paul von Ste-mann. "They told about people being trampled to death on the platforms in the fight to get seats on the last trains, and dead bodies being thrown out of the moving, unheated goods trains, and young mothers who were driven to insanity and would not believe that the babies they carried in their arms were long dead… Many women gave birth in the open, and soon followed their newborn in death." Shocked refugees told stories of German soldiers killing their cattle and horses, even looting their houses. A grand Silesian landowner described in disgust how one of Germany's supposed defenders had fired a Panzerfaust at a baroque chest in the hall of his mansion. On Berlin station platforms, soup kitchens were established to feed refugees, and clothes provided to replace those they had lost. It is interesting to speculate whether these grieving people would have recoiled had they known that many of the warm woollens which they were given had been collected by the SS from the wardrobes of Jews trans-lated into ashes in the death camps.

"Berliners are receiving the first visible warning that the Red Army stands before the frontiers of the Reich," wrote the German correspondent of *Stockholms-Tidningen* on 24 January. "Columns of trucks crowded with refugees and baggage and bags and sacks roll through the streets on their way between one railway station and another. Most of the refugees are typical German peas-ants from the East, and only women and children—no men. They peep wide-eyed from under their headscarves at the ruined streets of the capital they are now seeing for the first time in their lives."

Yet Berliners did not receive the easterners with unmingled sympathy. For four years, the people of East Prussia, Saxony and Silesia had lived in tranquil-lity, while the cities of the west were bombed to destruction. More than a few Berliners were by no means displeased now to see their smug fellow country-men from the east dragged down into the common misery. The Wehrmacht estimated that 3.5 million ethnic Germans were already in flight, and this num-ber increased dramatically over the weeks ahead. In mid-January in Berlin, said Paul von Stemann, "we expected the Russians to arrive any day. The East was like a flood which had broken all dykes… Berlin sat back and prepared itself for the flood to roll over it, only hoping that it would be short and sharp." Berliners even professed to laugh at the tales of mass rape brought by the eastern fugi-tives. There was a ghastly joke: "I would rather have a Russian on my belly than a bomb."

IN THE LAST days of January, seventeen-year-old glider-pilot cadet Joseph Vol-mar lay in a Königsberg hospital recovering from an arm wound. He talked defi-antly about rejoining his comrades and getting even with Ivan. His roommate, an old soldier, dismissed his pretensions: "Look, boy, why not give up on this hero stuff? You're lucky to have made it this far—don't push it." As Russian shells began to fall around them, on 30 January the walking wounded were told to make for Pillau. "What a motley group we were! Soldiers with head wounds, arm wounds and even some leg wounds walking with sticks were making a bid for escape. Anything seemed better than letting the Russians get you." At the beginning, whenever a shell fell close, he dashed for cover. Another man said: "You can't do that—you'll miss the boat. You've got to keep moving." A merciful truck, one of the handful still moving, carried them the last few miles to Pillau town square. Volmar's arm was still intensely painful, but a fat sergeant insisted that he must strip the bandage and show his wound before he was allowed to join the queue for a boat. There were many deceivers cringing among the casualties.

The waterfront was a shambles of abandoned carts and wagons. Refugees and wounded men clustered in thousands around a small ship with a great jagged bomb hole in its foredeck. The column of casualties was forced through the mob, clambering over discarded trunks, crates, suitcases and at last up the gangway. A stench of blood, urine and excrement drifted up the companionway. They lay shivering until darkness fell and they put to sea. Thus they retched and vomited their way to Swinemünde, and onward by train to Lübeck, where an X-ray revealed that a bone in Volmar's arm was shattered. He cared only that he had escaped from East Prussia and gained a month's reprieve from the war.

Twenty-year-old Elfride Kowitz was likewise struggling on the dockside at Pillau. She watched people fighting to gain space aboard ships, sometimes crashing into the water as they lost their hold on the quayside or were thrown overboard by rivals. Russian warships intermittently shelled the harbour. Elfi nearly secured a place in a ship loaded with coffins, only to be frustrated at the last moment. Finally, she abandoned the struggle and returned to the Luftwaffe unit outside Königsberg, in whose offices she had been working. She departed in its truck convoy westwards and crossed the ice of the Frisches Haff amid the familiar scenes of terror and horror. "Again and again I thought: 'We're doomed.' All that mattered was to escape the Russians. There were so many people struggling ruthlessly to survive—including myself." The temperature was 25 degrees centigrade. Women were abandoning babies in the snow. The lorry beside them was obliterated by a direct hit from a Russian shell. Their little contingent was one of the few military convoys driving west. One of the trucks broke down and had to be towed by another.

Among the refugees, the very young and the very old suffered most of all. Once, military police sought to have Elfi evicted from the Luftwaffe truck, to make room for old people. She felt no urge for self-sacrifice. She was only grateful when their lieutenant insisted: "She's one of us." Some trekkers, seeing the dead and dying around them in the snow, turned round and went home, saying: "Maybe the Russians aren't as bad as people say," a judgement they later regretted. Elfi Kowitz reached the Vistula ferry to find cows abandoned by their owners mooing hopelessly in their unmilked agony: "We knew what was happening. The poor animals did not." At last, the Luftwaffe convoy was able to cross. The unit was posted to a new airfield in Mecklenburg. Elfi Kowitz never returned to East Prussia, "but the memory still hurts. Sometimes, it seems as we had dreamed it all." For the rest of her life, she could not bear to hear the grinding of tank tracks, because of the frightening memories the sound evoked.

"The highway along the Frisches Haff is now the only route open between the German garrison in Königsberg and Brandenburg," the Soviet 1st Baltic Front reported to Moscow early in February 1945.

It is under systematic fire from our artillery, machine-guns and mortars. But the enemy is still getting food and ammunition through on foggy days and at night. According to our intelligence reports, in addition to the garrison there are still a million civilians in the city [Königsberg], both residents and refugees. They include many senior fascist figures, landowners, businessmen, and government officials and their families. People are living in huts and cellars. Food is short... Typhoid is rife. There are many wounded and sick in the city. Some refugees have tried to get to Pillau across the ice, but they drowned. The ice is now very thin, after so much shelling by our guns. Every day, the Gestapo arrest and execute hundreds of people for looting and robbing food depots, and also for urging surrender. Prisoners say the city is prepared for a long siege.

The military defenders of Königsberg nursed few illusions about their prospects, shelled and bombed relentlessly, but the Nazis could offer the garrison only the aid of a barrage of fantasy. A National Socialist propaganda officer addressed the wounded at a hospital in the city late in February, announcing with shameless falsehood that several hundred new tanks had just been unloaded at Pillau, and that a German armoured thrust was pushing north from Breslau towards Warsaw. Those who fled East Prussia now, said the Nazi, "would be home in time for the spring sowing... This was the Führer's long-cherished plan, to let the Russians in, the more surely to destroy them." When a doctor expressed scepticism about this nonsense, he was rebuked by colleagues for defeatism—and for risking his life. Soldiers and civilians alike were urged to attend screenings of Goebbels's new propaganda epic, *Kolberg,* which was being shown in the city's theatre. "A capering café violinist in uniform, along with ten other unmilitary musicians, played the latest sentimental popular tunes to the wounded." Looters scrambled for booty among the ruins—how odd that, when the end of everything was at hand, such men still craved property, possession of which had become meaningless. Military police combed cellars and wrecked buildings for deserters. Every man and boy who could bear arms was herded ruthlessly to join the garrison manning the snowbound defences.

Dr. Hans von Lehndorff, a devout Christian, found himself perversely light-headed as he contemplated his predicament in the beleaguered city: "I tramped through the powdery snow in a curiously exalted mood, as if the whole town and its fate belonged to me alone. As I went, I sang a hymn in praise of God, and my voice moved me to tears of joy. The greatest moments of a man's life arise when the Last Judgement is near at hand; the world rolls round like a ball beneath his feet."

Among the very few people in Königsberg who prayed for the coming of the Red Army were sixteen-year-old Michael Wieck and his family. They were musicians from a distinguished artistic background. His mother was a Jew, and he himself was reared in the faith. His elderly gentile father had always proudly rejected official demands that he should disown his wife. In childhood, Wieck experienced the familiar escalation of humiliations which Nazi Germany heaped upon all his kind. Back in the mid-1930s, his parents had instructed him not to greet his teachers with the Nazi salute each morning. The headmaster had insisted. When Hitler honoured the school with a personal visit, Wieck was pushed into the back row of the welcoming ranks. He felt bitterly the exclusion of being forbidden to join the Hitler Youth. Then he was expelled from school altogether, and the family were evicted from their home. His father was dismissed from the directorship of his musical seminary. Michael Wieck's sister Maria had mercifully escaped to Scotland with a *Kindertransport* in 1939, but Michael was thought too young to accompany her. Once, he asked his mother despairingly: "Why am I treated as different from all the others?" She answered: "It is more honourable to belong to the persecuted than to be a persecutor." His childhood ended, said Wieck, at the age of fourteen. Even at the height of the siege of Königsberg, if he was careless enough to walk on a pavement with his yellow star, some German—probably young—would order him into the gutter. He was sent to work ten hours a day in a small soap factory among Russians, Gypsies, homosexuals and other outcasts. Only four out of twenty survived the siege. His parents waited, waited, waited for deportation or death. They had heard nothing of gas chambers, but they knew that Jews were marked for extinction. Unbeknown to the Wiecks, late in 1944 an order was sent from Berlin to Königsberg to kill all Jews, but this was implemented only in respect of those already held in camps. The handful who still dwelt in local communities were carelessly omitted.

Michael's father feared that the Germans would kill the last Jews just before the Russians arrived. A man of sixty-four, he cherished at home a little hatchet, his pathetic weapon. "If the Russians are coming and the block warden sends for us," he would say, "that is the moment to resist." They clung to life amid the deluge of Soviet bombs and shells, almost despairing of deliverance.

"IT WAS OUR HOLOCAUST, BUT NOBODY CARES"

BETWEEN 23 JANUARY and 8 May 1945, German merchant and naval shipping evacuated more than two million refugees from the Baltic coast, under the orders of Admiral Oskar Kummetz, naval high commander in the east. Freighters and launches, naval escorts and colliers were all pressed into service. Several large passenger vessels had been lying idle for years thanks to the Allied blockade. The *Wilhelm Gustloff* was a 27,000-ton pre-war "Strength through Joy" Nazi cruise ship, which since 1940 had served as a U-boat depot vessel. In the last days of January, its ageing captain was warned to take on fuel and prepare to transport refugees westwards from the port of Gdynia, near Danzig. As soon as it was known that the *Gustloff* was to go, a desperate struggle began to gain boarding passes. Most berths were quickly filled by those with money or influence. Stabsführerin Wilhelmina Reitsch, sister-in-law of Hitler's favourite test pilot, Hanna, clamoured for space for some of the 8,000 naval auxiliaries in the port, whom she commanded. They were all girls between seventeen and twenty-five, acutely conscious of their likely fate at the hands of the Russians. Only 373 were embarked. So were 918 naval personnel and 4,224 refugees.

For three days, they waited in anguish in the crowded passenger decks for permission to sail. A special maternity unit was established on the sun deck, for some refugees were heavily pregnant. One hundred and sixty-two military casualties, many of them amputees, were brought aboard on stretchers and placed in an emergency hospital. On the night of 27 January, the entire complement was ordered ashore during an air raid. They spent hours of icy misery in the port's shelters, before straggling aboard again at dawn. At the last minute, the Führer Suite on B Deck was taken over by thirteen members of the family of Gdynia's burgomaster, along with the city's kreisleiter, his wife and five children, their maid and parlour maid. Some of the Nazi functionaries complained sourly about overcrowding.

On 30 January, the morning of the ship's departure, there were renewed dramas. Military police boarded, to search every living space for deserters. As the *Gustloff* finally cast off at 1100 hours, a flotilla of small boats scrambled alongside, filled with refugees shrieking to be taken aboard, women holding high their babies. Pitying crewmen let down scrambling nets. The ship's peacetime complement was 1,900 passengers and crew. The manifest on 30 January showed more than 6,000 souls. Some 2,000 more are believed to have struggled aboard during the final rush. There was a further delay offshore, where the *Gustloff* anchored to await a second ship, the *Hansa*. Finally, the port authorities determined that it was too dangerous for the ship to wait. Escorted only by an aged torpedo boat, the liner set course westwards. The *Hansa*'s captain signalled: "Bon voyage."

A surge of relief swept through the decks of the *Gustloff*. At last, the passengers saw the prospect of safety after the terrors of the shore. A doctor persuaded a small orchestra to play for the military wounded. The ship's barber began to do a brisk trade among refugees seeking to improve their dishevelled appearances. Those with money and clout were able to eat a better dinner afloat than they had seen for many weeks, with wine and meat. Unfortunately, however, the *Gustloff* was a poor sea boat. It began to wallow heavily in the Baltic chop. Ice formed on deck. Many, perhaps most, passengers were soon prostrate with seasickness. Some of those who had eaten dinner wished that they had not.

Shortly before 1900, between broken snow showers, thirty-three-year-old Captain Third Class Alexandr Marinesko of the Soviet submarine *S-13* sighted a large ship, which to his amazement—as a result of German negligence—was not zig-zagging and was showing lights. Even in a service notorious for heavy drinking and indiscipline, Marinesko had achieved a reputation for reckless behaviour ashore which had incurred the displeasure of the NKVD. He was suspected of counter-revolutionary tendencies. He had been at sea for three weeks on his current patrol, without sighting a worthwhile target. Now, he exerted himself. *S-13* began to stalk the *Gustloff* on the surface, taking up a position down-moon, between ship and shore. It took him two hours to overhaul the liner and turn into a firing position. At 2104, at point-blank range of less than a thousand yards, he fired a salvo of torpedoes, daubed with the usual slogans "For the Motherland," "Stalingrad," "For the Soviet People." There were three devastating explosions. The *Wilhelm Gustloff* listed heavily, and began to sink.

Most of the girl naval auxiliaries were fortunate enough to die instantly, when a torpedo detonated below their living space. The old, the sick and wounded could not move, but perished more slowly. There were screams from those trapped behind watertight doors, which rolled down immediately after the attack. Some naval personnel fired rifles to control panic-stricken mobs of passengers surging up from the lower promenade deck. A waiter running through a cabin flat heard a gun go off and opened a door, to see a naval officer standing with a pistol over a dead woman and child, while another terrified child clung to his leg. "Get out!" shouted the officer, and the waiter did so, leaving the father to finish his business. Suicide seemed perfectly rational when just twelve of the ship's twenty-four lifeboats were on board, those in the davits were not swung out and the mortal cold of the Baltic awaited.

Most of the crew behaved contemptibly. A lifeboat with capacity for fifty pulled away carrying only the captain and twelve sailors. Another was lowered so recklessly that its load of passengers was upended into the sea. Several boats were never launched at all. The ship was soon lying broadside to the sea. It finally disappeared seventy minutes after the attack. Some people tore off their clothes before leaping into the water, an absurdly rational gesture at a moment of catastrophe. Many never escaped from the passenger spaces. There was no dignity aboard the foundering ship, only the nightmarish sights and sounds that accompanied several thousand helpless people fighting in panic to save themselves, or choosing a swift death by gunshot. The *Gustloff*'s distress signal was heard by the heavy cruiser *Admiral Hipper,* which was also sailing west that night with 1,377 refugees. As her course drove the cruiser past the grave of the liner, survivors struggling in the water waved frantically, clutching a moment of hope. The *Hipper*'s churning screws ended their suffering. The big warship could not risk heaving to, with a submarine close by. Alexandr Marinesko missed a far more useful target than the *Gustloff* that night. After his attack, he took *S-13* as deep as the shallow Baltic would allow, to escape depth-charge attack. He never saw the *Hipper.*

The torpedo boat *T-36* was the only vessel to render immediate assistance. It closed the scene in time to pick up 252 survivors. Many even among those who had found places in lifeboats froze to death before other rescuers arrived at daybreak. A naval petty officer who boarded one boat full of corpses next morning found an unidentified baby, blue with cold but still breathing. He adopted it. The child became one of just 949 known survivors of the greatest maritime disaster in history, its 7,000 dead far outstripping those of the *Titanic, Lusitania, Laconia.* Yet, amid global tragedy on the scale of 1945, the horrors of the *Wilhelm Gustloff* remain known only to some Germans and a few historians.

Alexandr Marinesko's role in the Baltic tragedy was not yet complete. On 9 February, he spotted and fired upon a new target. The 17,500-ton liner *General Steuben,* carrying 2,000 wounded and 1,000 refugees, sank swiftly. A mere 300 survivors reached Kolberg. Marinesko returned to his home port in triumph. This sensation did not last long. The captain was already the object of NKVD scrutiny. Now, he was told that his claims to have sunk two liners were rejected. They had probably fallen victim to air attack. A bitter man, a few months later he was cashiered from the Soviet Navy. After further instances of drunken indiscretion, he was sentenced to three years in a labour camp. Only in 1960 were his claims to have sunk the *Gustloff* and the *General Steuben* finally accepted, and his service pension reinstated.

The anguish of the Baltic fugitives continued until the very end of the war. On 16 April the 5,000-ton motorship *Goya,* carrying 7,000 refugees and service personnel, was torpedoed sixty miles off the coast of Pomerania by the ancient Soviet minelaying submarine *L-3.* One hundred and eighty-three survivors were rescued. On 3 May, rocket-firing Typhoons of the RAF sank the 27,561-ton liner *Cap Arkona* at Lübeck. When British troops reached the port a few days later, they found its waters still strewn with corpses. Contrary to the view of many Germans from 1945 to the present day, all the ships sunk were legitimate targets, since they were being employed at least partially for the transport of military personnel. But, by a dreadful irony, 5,000 of the dead from the *Cap Arkona* were concentration-camp inmates, shipped from Poland.

History has paid little heed to the doings of the wartime German Navy, beyond the U-boat campaign and its few big-ship actions. Yet in the last months of war, in the face of huge difficulties and heavy losses, the Kriegsmarine displayed energy and courage in the Baltic, supplying beleaguered German garrisons and evacuating refugees. Despite the horrors of the big-ship sinkings recounted above, many people owed their lives to Germany's sailors, most of whom behaved much better than the crew of the *Wilhelm Gustloff.*

THE MISJUDGEMENT by Stalin's Stavka, in ordering Rokossovsky's armies to pivot northwards towards the Baltic coast, where their principal achievement was the slaughter of refugees, enabled most of the German Second Army further south to withdraw across the lower Vistula, where its units consolidated. If Rokossovsky had instead remained close upon Zhukov's right flank, far fewer German troops would have escaped to fight again. On 13 March, the Soviets turned their attention to destroying the German Fourth Army in the "Heiligenbeil Cauldron," the pocket on the Frisches Haff south-west of Königsberg. The 280mm guns of the *Lützow* and *Admiral Scheer* supported the efforts of fifteen ruined German divisions which sought to maintain the Baltic struggle. Marshal Alexandr Vasilevsky, who had taken over 3rd Belorussian Front when Chernyakhovsky was killed by shell fragments on 18 February, mustered seven armies against them. Hitler refused a request to allow troops and heavy equipment to be evacuated from the port of Rosenburg. A few thousand Germans escaped from Rosenburg in the last days, but most perished in the battle which ended on 28 March. The Russians claimed to have killed 93,000 German troops and captured 46,448.

The Red Army now resumed its assault on Königsberg. The city was encircled by a chain of fourteen ancient forts half a mile apart, each 900 yards wide, surrounded by a water-filled moat. They possessed stone walls, were roofed with concrete fifteen feet thick, and were manned by some 800 men apiece. Behind the moats and anti-tank ditches, trenches had been dug all the way into the city itself. The cellars of houses had been fortified with concrete blocks, protecting their apertures on to the street. On the rail tracks, an armoured train was mounted with mobile batteries of artillery and flak guns. These defences enabled the garrison to mount a formidable resistance, despite the knowledge that the final outcome was inescapable. By early February, PoWs and deserters were telling the Russians that the mood in Königsberg was grim. "Now that the evacuation of civilians has stopped, there is panic," said an NKVD report. "The bread ration has fallen to 300 grams for soldiers, 180 for civilians. Some of the inhabitants want a surrender, but many have been frightened by Goebbels's propaganda, and fear the coming of the Red Army. On 6 February, the corpses of some 80 German soldiers executed for desertion were displayed at the north railway station bearing signs: 'They were cowards, but they still died'."

General Otto Lasch, the able officer commanding the city's 35,000-strong garrison, suffered acute political as well as military difficulties. Gauleiter Koch commuted into Königsberg by Storch light aircraft, to meddle in the direction of its defence. The Russians deployed 1,124 bombers, 470 close-support aircraft and 830 fighters in the air bombardment to soften up the defences. As fires raged out of control in the streets, refugees braved artillery fire to continue streaming towards the port of Pillau. Russian assault troops had to fight yard by yard through the outer defences of Königsberg, and many defenders fought with the courage of despair.

"The Königsberg battle was very hard indeed," said Corporal Anatoly Osminov of Thirty-second Tank Army. "The fortress was a desperately tough nut to crack. Many of those Germans hung on in their trenches until we crushed them under our tracks. Our own losses were terrible." Lieutenant Alexandr Sergeev of the 297th Infantry Regiment was startled to see civilians among the soldiers firing fiercely at them from the German lines. He was a handsome, reflective young man whose father, chairman of a collective farm, had ridden with Budyenny's Cossacks in the Civil War. He completed training and joined 3rd Belorussian Front only in the summer of 1944, but already he found himself commanding a company at the age of nineteen, after two of his regiment's company leaders were killed. More than half his own machine-gun platoon were casualties. The arrival of thirty-five bewildered replacements brought the company strength up to sixty. "I have never seen such violent resistance as we met at Königsberg," he said. His own divisional commander was wounded in the head, leading one attack personally. On 28 March, it was Sergeev's own turn, as Fifth Army launched a new assault. The spring thaw made the ground almost impassable for tanks and threw the full burden of battle upon the infantry. No rations got through on the morning of the attack. Like his men, Sergeev approached the start line having eaten only a couple of American biscuits. A Kazakh platoon commander waved to his men: "Okay, time to go!" The Russians advanced in extended line, dragging their machine-guns and mortars with them: "The men were moving forward, then they began to fall down." When Sergeev saw the crew of a heavy machine-gun lying dead beside it, he took over the weapon himself. Seconds later, a German bullet hit the gun's cooling-jacket, and water gushed out.

German Nebelwerfer fire was falling all around them, accounting for many of Sergeev's men. He himself was hit in the side by a fragment which pierced his stomach. He collapsed over the machine-gun, and lay stunned and bleeding, gazing blankly up at aircraft criss-crossing the clear blue sky. "What a pity to die on a beautiful day like this," he thought, exactly like Prince Andrei wounded on the field of Austerlitz in Tolstoy's *War and Peace*. Then pain attacked him, and he began to scream, cursing compulsively: "The whole front must have heard." One side of his body was laid open and pouring blood. His men dragged him to the rear, where he was put on a horse-drawn cart and taken to a field hospital, still screaming. The rags of his tunic were cut off. He lay naked on a stretcher, staring in revulsion at a pile of severed limbs on the floor of the tent, while a nurse anaesthetized him with an ether pad, restraining the waiting surgeon: "No, no—he isn't asleep yet." One in a hundred stomach cases such as his own survived. He was the one. While recovering from his wound, he contracted pneumonia and spent the rest of the war in hospitals.

Russian after-action reports on the battle for Königsberg paint a picture of confusion, improvisation and often bloody mistakes among the attackers. In the west and north-west of the city, the Russians were compelled to use flamethrowers and Molotov cocktails to set ablaze buildings in which the defenders had emplaced themselves for a fight to the death. There were frightful "friendly fire" incidents, in which artillery observers lost contact with the infantry, and called down shelling on their own men. Rubble and ditches dug by the Germans made it necessary to manhandle Russian field guns forward under fire, by human exertion alone. A severe shortage of radios hampered communication. There was no room for tactical sophistication here, merely murderous hammering at the German positions line by line, until each in turn collapsed.

When the Russians reached the streets of Königsberg, the first white sheets appeared at shattered windows. Shelling and bombing intensified. In the operating theatre of a German hospital, Dr. Hans von Lehndorff found the lights crashing down on to him from the ceiling after a direct hit. German troops ran back among the buildings, emptying their rifles in futility at the strafing aircraft. Von Lehndorff, whose hospital now lay in no-man's-land, watched his countrymen re-forming a defence line among ruins behind the once-beautiful lake that stood in front of Königsberg castle. "The further side of the pond looks like a cabbage patch destroyed by hail," he wrote on 7 April.

One is involuntarily reminded of pictures of Douaumont and other shattered fortifications of the First World War, except that those had been erected specially for war, whereas the Königsberg pond seems to have taken a perpetual lease of civilian quietude. Now it is being completely ravaged. Nerves are beginning to give way among us ... Lest the idea of suicide become infectious, I gave a little address in the operating theatre on the text "Fear not those which kill only the body, but cannot kill the soul. But fear that which can destroy both body and soul."

General Lasch, commanding the garrison, at last concluded that no more could be done. He surrendered Königsberg on 10 April. Berlin demanded explanations from Fourth Army's commander. General Friedrich-Wilhelm Müller had achieved notoriety when he was unwillingly propelled into command six weeks earlier by telling Army Group HQ: "I am a good NCO and I know how to carry out orders, but strategy and tactics are quite beyond me. Just tell me what I ought to do!" Now, Müller signalled: "The reasons for the fall of Königsberg, beyond Russian superiority of men and tanks and aircraft, concerns the morale of our own troops. The impression of the city lit up by flames and strewn with unburied dead dampened the spirits of the defenders. Whether the commander also failed in his duty cannot with certainty be established." Hitler was uninterested in either rationality or obfuscation. He declared Lasch a traitor, arrested his family and sentenced him *in absentia* to death by hanging. One hundred and twenty police and SS fought to the end in the old castle, even after the capitulation. In long, wretched columns, 60,526 prisoners and refugees marched out, according to NKVD figures, watched by Russian soldiers who plundered them as they passed. Beria reported that there were 32,573 Germans, 13,054 Soviet citizens—slave labourers—and 13,054 people of other foreign nationalities. Some Volkssturm in civilian clothes were shot out of hand as partisans, just as the Wehrmacht in Russia had executed their counterparts in thousands. The Russians claimed to have killed 42,000 Germans and captured 92,000 prisoners, including 1,800 officers, in the Königsberg operation, but this was probably an exaggeration. Beria announced to Stalin that eight NKVD groups, each of 120, were searching Königsberg for "spies, traitors and collaborators." These had already detained 14,901 people, though their progress through the streets was rendered difficult by mountains of rubble. Eight NKVD regiments had formed a cordon around the city, to deny escape to fugitives.

Germans on the Samland peninsula, north-east of the city, held out for two weeks longer. The final position to fall, Major Karl Henke's Battery Lemburg, was defended to the last man until 1530 on 27 April. Dr. Karl Ludwig Mahlo, a Luftwaffe medical officer, was among the final party to escape from Pillau. For months, he had been struggling to treat thousands of wounded people, soldiers and civilians alike, to whom he could offer pitifully little: "What we could do was a drop in the ocean." He found that he had become frighteningly inured to suffering, consumed by fatalism: "Germany was destroyed. There was a feeling that, after us, there would be nothing." Mahlo owed his escape to friends in the navy. His bitterness about what happened in East Prussia, his own birthplace, never abated.

WHEN CAPTAIN Abram Skuratovsky and his 168th Signals Unit of the Red Army reached the Baltic at Pillau, he dipped a bottle into the sea and filled it as a souvenir of their campaign. "We were in tearing spirits." Skuratovsky had somewhere acquired a splendid horse, which he rode until some Lithuanians stole it one night. He marvelled at the empty landscape they had inherited, with its fruit trees just coming into blossom, abandoned houses and lowing cattle. "The cowsheds in East Prussia seemed grander than the houses we lived in at home," he said. Skuratovsky came from Kiev, where his father sold fish. It was a revelation for his men to find themselves in billets with running water, to see livestock confined by miles of barbed-wire fencing, a commodity which in his own experience was employed only on battlefields.

Corporal Anatoly Osminov's unit was exhausted by the long, brutal campaign. Outside Königsberg, they leaguered their tanks. Osminov's driver, Boris, a veteran who had served eight years in the same unit and had experienced eight tanks burning under him, took his tommy-gun and went off into a nearby forest in search of something edible. Suddenly, he came upon a group of men digging trenches. Thinking they were Germans, he raised his tommy-gun and called "*Hände hoch!*" They were Russians. Their officer killed him, for which he could scarcely be blamed. They brought Boris's body in to the tank leaguer just as the signal came through announcing the capitulation of Königsberg. The soldier was much beloved in the unit. The men clubbed together and sent thirty-six gold watches, spoils of the battle, to his widow.

Even by the standards of the Red Army, the cost of triumph on the Baltic was very high. Between 13 January and 25 April, 2nd Belorussian Front lost 159,490 men dead and wounded, and 3rd Belorussian Front 421,763. During three months in East Prussia, therefore, the Red Army suffered almost as many casualties as the Anglo-American armies in the entire north-west Europe campaign.

THERE WERE HUNDREDS, if not thousands of suicides when the Russians took Königsberg. The family who lived above Margaret Mehl's apartment, a bank director and his wife and daughter, made a cool decision to kill themselves. Others died in less spectacular fashion. Margaret Mehl's aunts Helena and Else decided to stay behind and await the return of their husbands from the war. They simply starved to death. Dr. Hans von Lehndorff saw terrible scenes of murder and pillage: "We stood close together, awaiting the end in some form or other. The fear of death...had been entirely dispelled now by something infinitely worse. On every side we heard the despairing screams of the women: 'Shoot me! Shoot me!' But the tormentors preferred a wrestling match to any actual use of firearms." Some women were raped in hospital maternity wards, within days of giving birth.

Through the siege of Königsberg, the Jewish Wieck family had clung to life in their cellar. The Wiecks' first glimpse of the forces of freedom was a solitary soldier on a bicycle. The men of the Red Army always seemed fascinated by the opportunity to ride bikes. Soon afterwards, a single T-34 drove by. Finally, a self-propelled gun halted in front of their apartment building. Soviet troops streamed through the streets. Dreadful disillusionment now befell the Jewish survivors. "It was hell," said Michael simply. "We wanted to receive the Russians as liberators, but how could we? They killed every man they saw, and raped every woman between seven and seventy. We heard the screams and cries for help far into the night. They locked some people in the cellars and then set fire to the houses above. They herded civilians from the city to the battlefield outside to be shot or burned." The boy, his mother and his father, whose beloved violin was snatched from him, were herded under guard with a crowd of others into a field, at first without food or water.

"My father had led a very sheltered life. He could not cope with these circumstances at all. My mother, who was ten years younger, managed a little better." She escaped rape only, said Wieck, "because the Russians found enough younger ones." Their Mongol captors had no idea of the significance of the yellow stars on their sleeves. The Wiecks experienced a spasm of hope when they met a Jewish Russian officer, who spoke both German and Yiddish. Their optimism was swiftly crushed. "If you were really Jewish," said the soldier contemptuously, "you would be dead. Since you are alive, you must have thrown in your lot with the Germans." And so the family tore off their yellow stars and shared the plight of their fellow prisoners.

There had been 120,000 civilians in Königsberg before the siege. The Wiecks were among 15,000 people who now remained. They were herded back into the city under guard to bury the dead. "I saw the murdered women," said Michael Wieck, "the corpses that had lain in cellars for weeks. We found people who had hanged themselves in their houses. We put them all in bomb craters in the streets, horses and humans together, before a snow plough filled them in." The burial parties lived on the verge of starvation, suffering in turn malaria, dysentery, lice and inflamed lungs. Wieck's father caught typhoid.

By a supreme irony, in the midst of their misery the Wiecks "rediscovered a certain community with the Germans." In April, Michael was taken to a notorious special camp run by the NKVD at Rothenstein, where Dr. Hans von Lehndorff was also incarcerated. Persons under investigation were held in a large cellar, jammed so thickly together that they could not lie down or even sit. They stood or kneeled, hour after hour and day after day. "We were glad when people started to die, because the living got more room." Once a day, they were let out for exercise. At night, the Russians descended by torchlight to fetch suspects for interrogation. The victims returned bleeding, sometimes lacking teeth. One man with tuberculosis coughed incessantly. Food was given only to those who possessed a receptacle to put it in. Michael Wieck unscrewed the globe of a lamp above their heads to hold his portion of mouldy bread. He offered to let the TB case share it with him. "No, no," said the man, "keep away from me—

you will only catch my disease." He died three days later. Wieck said: "Those sixteen days in the cellars at Rothenstein were no less terrible than Auschwitz. First Hitler and the Nazis had tried to destroy us, now it was the Russians. I had given up, I wanted to die. I began to refuse food and water. Then someone persuaded me to accept a spoonful of sugar. I felt the desire to live seeping back."

Wieck, an impish, electric personality possessed of both brilliance and charm, was finally released by the Russians after an officer befriended him. Unlike one fellow prisoner who, despairing of the future, hurled himself off a bridge and drowned when freed from Rothenstein, Wieck proved a survivor. For three years after the fall of Königsberg, he eked out a living playing a violin to entertain the Russian occupiers, before escaping to West Germany in 1948 and forging a distinguished career as writer and musician. His parents also survived. Was he robbed of his childhood? He shrugged. "It does as much harm to have a normal childhood as to have a difficult one." His story and his moral generosity represent a triumph of the human spirit.

THE NUMBERS OF those who died in the flight from East Prussia will never be precisely established. By the end of the war, some eight million people were thought to have abandoned or been driven from their homes in the eastern provinces of the Greater Reich, and a further eight million followed during the first years of Soviet hegemony. It is known that 610,000 ethnic Germans were killed in Rumania, Poland, Czechoslovakia and Yugoslavia. Well over a million disappeared, and are presumed to have died, escaping from East Prussia, Silesia and other areas of Hitler's eastern empire. They perished from exposure, cold, hunger and Russian gunfire. To this day a profound rage persists in Germany, that a world still obsessed with the events of the Second World War knows so little, and appears to care less, about the horrors in the east in 1945. "The bulk of those who fled, and of those who died, were not the kind who can write books, or even tell their stories," remarks Helmut Schmidt. "They were very ordinary people." One East Prussian woman's choice of words would find scant modern favour outside Germany, but reflects a common passion among her fellow countrymen: "It was our holocaust, but nobody cares." Both before and after the coming of peace, the Western media was economical in its reporting of the horrors that took place in East Prussia and Silesia, despite a multitude of witnesses occupying the displaced-persons camps of Germany. Revelations were still fresh about the concentration camps, the mass slaughter of Jews, Russians, Gypsies and other victims of Hitler's homicidal mania. The victors were in no mood to perceive Germans as victims. The Nazi gauleiters in East Prussia, Pomerania and Silesia bore a heavy responsibility for their refusal to permit, far less to facilitate, the flight of the population before the Red Army came, but inevitably they pleaded orders from Berlin. To seek compassion from the Nazis even for their own people was, of course, an absolute contradiction.

For the victorious Americans and British, it was far more difficult to pass judgement upon the conduct of the Russians, and it remains so today. "You have, of course, read Dostoevsky?" demanded Stalin of Milovan Djilas, when the partisan leader complained of the rape of Yugoslav women by liberating Russian soldiers.

> Do you see what a complicated thing is man's soul, man's psyche? Well then, imagine a man who has fought from Stalingrad to Belgrade—over thousands of kilometres of his own devastated land, across the dead bodies of his comrades and dearest ones? How can such a man react normally? And what is so awful in his having fun with a woman, after such horrors? You have imagined the Red Army to be ideal, and it is not ideal, nor can it be... The important thing is that it fights Germans... The rest doesn't matter.

Russians have often displayed a spirit of indulgence towards barbarities within their own society which does not extend to those committed against their people by foreigners. Why should it do so? Hitler and his armies had aspired to enslave the Russian people, no more and no less. Millions of Russian captives in Germany had already died, and millions more had become serfs of German farmers, factory-owners, householders—some of them in East Prussia. Stalin's people knew this. The Red Army had performed feats which would have been unthinkable for Western soldiers, and paid a price that no American or British army would have accepted. As Russians fought their way painfully west through 1943 and 1944, every man in the ranks saw the legacy of German occupation: blackened ruins, slaughtered civilians and ravaged countryside.

In 1945, in Soviet eyes it was time to pay. For most Russian soldiers, any instinct for pity or mercy had died somewhere on a hundred battlefields between Moscow and Warsaw. Half a century earlier, the great Gorky had observed the paradox that a group of Russians who might individually be humane, decent people were capable, when gathered in a mob, of extraordinary bestiality. An ethos of hatred and ruthlessness had been deliberately cultivated in the Red Army. It would be wrong simply to dismiss Soviet soldiers as savages. Though there were many primitive people in the Red Army's ranks, there were also cultured and thoughtful ones, some of whom this narrative seeks to bring to life. It is indisputable, however, that in 1945 the Red Army considered itself to deserve licence to behave as savages on the soil of Germany, and its men exploited this in full measure. They dispensed retribution for the horrors that had been inflicted upon the Soviet Union of a kind familiar to Roman conquerors, who also thought of themselves as a civilized people.

Dwight Eisenhower painfully exposed himself to the charge of naivety by the description of the Russian soldier in his post-war memoirs: "In his generous instincts, in his devotion to a comrade, and in his healthy, direct outlook on the affairs of workaday life, the ordinary Russian seems to me to bear a marked similarity to what we call an 'average American.'" If the detail of what took place in eastern Europe was still unfamiliar to SHAEF's Supreme Commander, by 1948 (when his memoirs were published) he must have possessed a general understanding of the Red terror which disfigured the Allied victory over Germany. His remark must be considered an exceptionally unhappy example of political tact.

To this day many Russians—and indeed the Moscow government—deny the scale of the cruelties the Red Army is alleged to have inflicted in East Prussia and Silesia, and later beyond the Oder. Private Vitold Kubashevsky, for instance, who speaks frankly about every other aspect of his experiences with 3rd Belorussian Front, still refuses to discuss what he saw in East Prussia. Yet eyewitness testimony is overwhelming. "All of us knew very well that if the girls were German they could be raped and then shot," wrote Alexandr Solzhenitsyn, who served as a Soviet artillery officer in East Prussia. "This was almost a combat distinction." It is striking that such a man as Michael Wieck, the young Königsberg Jew who welcomed the Russians as his saviours, bears witness to the horrors they committed. Even Professor John Erickson, whose monumental history of the Red Army is the most admiring by any Western author, acknowledges its conduct in East Prussia: "Speed, frenzy and savagery characterised the advance... Villages and small towns burned, while Soviet soldiers raped at will and wreaked an atavistic vengeance... families huddled in ditches or by the roadside, fathers intent on shooting their own children or waiting whimpering for what seemed the wrath of God to pass... men with pity for no one."

The Russians themselves, of course, paid most heavily of all for their policy of fire and the sword. A belief that there could be no purpose in surviving Soviet victory overtook much of the German Army in the east. The huge casualties Stalin's nation suffered during its drive into Germany reflected, in considerable part, the fact that the victors offered the vanquished only death or unimaginable suffering. Even after sixty years, it is difficult to extend to the German people the pity due to innocent victims of Nazi tyranny. However bitterly many Germans may have regretted this by 1945, Hitler and Nazism were the creations of their society. The horrors the Nazis inflicted upon Europe required the complicity of millions of ordinary Germans, merely to satisfy the logistical requirements of tyranny and mass murder. Yet now they saw the first fruits of retribution.

"We were forced to leave a land where generations of our families had been born, where they had lived and died, which they had loved and tilled the land and yes, defended it against many enemies," wrote Graf Franz Rosenburg, one of East Prussia's landowners, venting the bitterness of his entire people. "Everything we cherished was lost in a single night!" The Red Army was responsible for massive destruction of art treasures, almost certainly including Peter the Great's Amber Room, though, like so much else, this was subsequently blamed on the Nazis. At his post on the shore at Pillau, Private Vitold Kubashevsky of the Red Army watched curiously as the tides came in. Each one bore with it a harvest of German corpses, a flotsam of failed fugitives, to swing to and fro upon the waves beside the *Heimat* they loved so much, and which was now as irredeemably forfeit as their own lives.

At Yalta on the evening of 6 February 1945, in a spasm of compassion Churchill said to his daughter Sarah: "I do not suppose that at any moment of history has the agony of the world been so great or widespread. Tonight the sun goes down on more suffering than ever before in the world." Churchill knew little, when he spoke, about what was taking place in East Prussia. Yet its people's fate formed a not insignificant part of his vision.

CHAPTER ELEVEN

Firestorms: War in the Sky

THE BOMBER BARONS

BY THE WINTER of 1944, bomber operations against Germany had attained awesome destructive power. On 14 October, U.S. and British air forces launched a joint operation, Hurricane, to demonstrate to the Germans—and also to the Allied Chiefs of Staff—the scale of force they could unleash in a single twenty-four-hour period. First, in daylight, 1,251 aircraft of the U.S. Eighth Air Force attacked rail centres at Saarbrücken, Kaiserslautern, and Cologne, escorted by 749 fighters. Six bombers and one fighter were lost. Meanwhile, 519 Lancasters, 474 Halifaxes and 20 Mosquitoes of RAF Bomber Command mounted a daylight raid on Duisburg, escorted by British fighters. They dropped 4,918 tons of bombs, for the loss of thirteen Lancasters and one Halifax. With the coming of darkness, a further 498 Lancasters, 468 Halifaxes and 39 Mosquitoes again attacked Duisburg in two waves, two hours apart. A total of 4,540 tons of explosives and incendiaries were dropped, for the loss of five Lancasters and two Halifaxes. German casualties in the city were unmeasured, but heavy. On the same night, 233 Lancasters and seven Mosquitoes struck Brunswick. Only one Lancaster was lost. The old city centre of Brunswick was totally destroyed—an area of 370 hectares—and 561 people died. It was never thought necessary for Bomber Command to visit Brunswick again.

Meanwhile—still during the night of 14 October—the RAF sent twenty Mosquitoes to Hamburg, sixteen to Berlin, eight to Mannheim and two to Düsseldorf on nuisance raids, designed to drive the inhabitants of those cities into their shelters and force the defenders to expend weary hours manning guns and searchlights. One Mosquito was lost over Berlin. Another 141 bombers manned by crews completing operational training launched a diversionary sweep across the North Sea. One hundred and thirty-two RAF aircraft mounted electronic counter-measures operations, to frustrate German radar and communications. By the time the last aircraft turned homewards, a total of 10,050 tons of bombs had been dropped on Germany, the highest total attained in any single twenty-four-hour period of the war.

Yet what did all this mean? What were the fruits of this huge effort, which absorbed a substantial part of the war-making powers of the United States, and consumed a proportion of Britain's industrial capacity equal to that devoted to the entire British Army? The bombing of Germany destroyed almost two million homes and killed up to 600,000 Germans, many of these in the war's closing months. From beginning to end, the Western allies encompassed the deaths of two or three German civilians by bombing for every German soldier they killed on the battlefield. Yet did this shorten the conflict, or achieve an impact commensurate with its human and industrial cost both to the victors and to the vanquished?

Between 1918 and 1939, the apostles of air power had preached the gospel of strategic bombing, which they argued could render redundant the bloody struggles between armies on the ground by destroying the industries essential to a nation's war effort. Airmen in Britain and America also saw in bombing the key to their own struggle for independence from the older fighting services, proof that an air force was much more than a mere appendage of armies and fleets. Before the war, many European politicians, not to mention the public, were much alarmed by visions of cataclysm inflicted from the skies, and by such early manifestations of the totalitarian states' contribution to history as the destruction of Guernica and Nanking, Warsaw and Rotterdam.

From 1940 onwards, however, the combatants surprised themselves by learning to live with the consequences of aerial assault. They found that bombing inflicted great misery, hacked brutally at the culture of centuries, and imposed pain on industry. It would be ludicrous to imply that the German people found the experience of being bombed acceptable, or to deny that Hitler's war production suffered not only from damage to plant, but also from absenteeism and chronic dislocation to the lives of the labour force. After the Luftwaffe had tried and failed to break the British in the blitz of 1940–41, however, a more rational and less absolutist view of bombing supplanted pre-war expectations of doom, among all save the Allied air chiefs.

The airmen remained messianically committed to strategic bombing. In America, the USAAF argued that the Luftwaffe had failed against Britain because it had not systematically addressed precision targets vital to the nation's infrastructure—oil, transport links, the power grid. The RAF believed that the German attack upon Britain had merely lacked the sustained weight to strike a mortal blow. In 1941, the Chief of Air Staff Sir Charles Portal demanded from Churchill a commitment to create a force of 4,000 heavy bombers, a fantasy which remained unfulfilled even in 1945 by the combined might of the RAF and USAAF's squadrons in Europe. Churchill was always sceptical about the airmen's visions. "All things are always on the move simultaneously," he wrote to Portal in October 1941, "the Air Staff would make a mistake to put their claims too high."

Throughout 1940 and 1941, however, the RAF's bomber offensive was the only means by which Britain could carry the war to Germany. The prime minister threw his weight behind the creation of a great bomber force. Unless the British could convince themselves that air attack might eventually defeat Hitler, what course was open to them save a negotiated peace? Even Churchill at his most optimistic never supposed that Britain's armies could alone beat the Axis. It was ironic that the RAF thus set about attempting to do to the Germans exactly what the Luftwaffe had signally failed to achieve against Britain. The bomber offensive was to be lavishly endowed with ironies.

In 1942, even as the skies over Britain brightened immeasurably with the accession of the United States and Russia as allies, the Combined Chiefs of Staff agreed that bombing remained vital, because it would be years before the Anglo-American armies could undertake a decisive land campaign. In the secrecy of Whitehall, the British were obliged to acknowledge the failure of their precision air attacks upon German industrial targets, for which the RAF's night bombing force was too weak and ill-equipped. They embarked instead upon the policy of "area bombing"—a systematic assault upon the cities of Germany with a mixture of high-explosive and incendiary bombs, designed to break the morale of the enemy's industrial workforce, as well as to destroy his means of production. For the rest of the war, this offensive gathered momentum, as the RAF's Bomber Command grew in strength, despite heavy losses of British aircrew—56,000 highly trained personnel were killed by the war's end, almost double the fatal casualties suffered by the American bomber men in Europe.

The USAAF's Eighth Air Force was slow to build up forces in Britain with which to launch its own precision campaign. In 1942, it confined itself largely to attacking short-range targets in France. In 1943, when formations of B-17 Flying Fortresses and B-24 Liberators began to attack Germany, their losses against German fighters were alarming, sometimes horrendous. In the worst single month, October 1943, the Americans lost 186 heavy bombers—a 6.6 per cent casualty rate. In January 1944, during the RAF's so-called Battle of Berlin, Bomber Command lost 314 aircraft, or an average 5 per cent of its strength on every raid. Since a British bomber crew was obliged to carry out thirty operations to complete a tour of operations, and an American crew twenty-five, it needed no wizard of odds to compute that an airman was more likely to die than to survive his personal experience of bombing Germany.

Yet in 1944 the offensive was transformed. The Americans achieved a decisive breakthrough. Their pre-war doctrine of the self-defending bomber formation had proved unsustainable. Their bombers became, instead, dependent upon fighter escort for protection. It had always been assumed that it was tech-

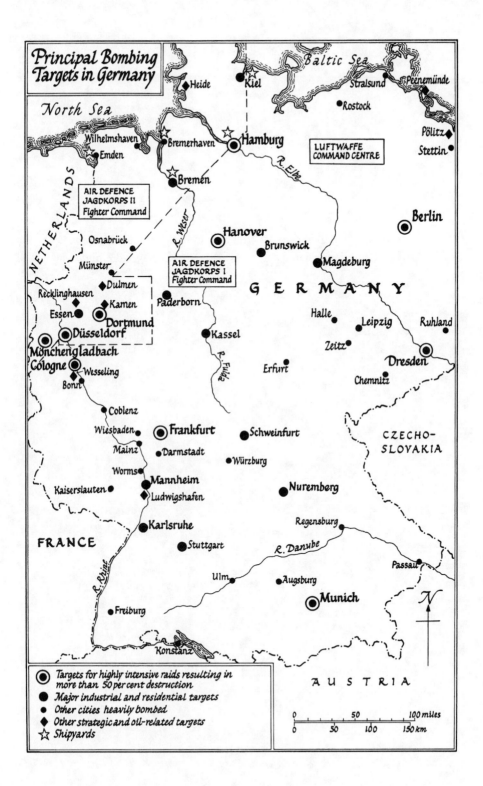

Principal Bombing
Targets in Germany

Baltic Sea

North Sea

Heide
Kiel
Stralsund
Peenemünde
Rostock

Wilhelmshaven
Bremerhaven
Hamburg
Pölitz
Emden
Stettin

LUFTWAFFE
COMMAND CENTRE

Bremen

NETHERLANDS

AIR DEFENCE
JAGDKORPS II
Fighter Command

R. Elbe

Berlin

Osnabrück
Münster

Hanover
Brunswick
Magdeburg

R. Weser

AIR DEFENCE
JAGDKORPS I
Fighter Command

G E R M A N Y

Recklinghausen
Dulmen
Kamen
Paderborn
Halle
Leipzig
Ruhland

Essen
Dortmund
Kassel
Zeitz

Düsseldorf
R. Fulda
Erfurt
Dresden

Mönchengladbach
Chemnitz

Cologne
Wesseling
Bonn

Coblenz

CZECHO-
SLOVAKIA

Wiesbaden
Frankfurt
Schweinfurt
Mainz
Darmstadt
Würzburg
Worms

Kaiserslauten
Mannheim
Nuremberg
Ludwigshafen

FRANCE
Karlsruhe
Regensburg
Stuttgart
R. Danube
Passau

R. Rhine
Ulm
Augsburg

Freiburg
Munich

N

Konstanz

A U S T R I A

◉ Targets for highly intensive raids resulting in
more than 50 per cent destruction
● Major industrial and residential targets
• Other cities heavily bombed
◆ Other strategic and oil-related targets
☆ Shipyards

0   50   100 miles

0   50   100   150 km

nically impossible to build a fighter with the range to fly deep into Germany, together with the performance to match that of the enemy's single-seat interceptors, Messerschmitt 109s and Focke-Wulf 190s, once it got there. By fitting the British Rolls-Royce engine to the American P-51 Mustang aircraft, however, a miracle was accomplished. Equipped with fuel drop tanks, the Mustang could fly with the bombers to Berlin, then outfight the Luftwaffe. After months of failure in its efforts to destroy Germany's aircraft production by bombing factories, by the summer of 1944 Eighth Air Force's fighters were wrecking the Luftwaffe in the sky, killing irreplaceable German pilots as well as shooting down their planes. Between January 1941 and June 1944, the Luftwaffe had lost 31,000 aircrew. Between June and October 1944, it lost 13,000. In 1944, the USAAF destroyed 3,706 enemy aircraft merely in daylight operations over Germany. This was an extraordinary achievement, which conferred dominance of Europe's skies upon the Allies.

The RAF's night attacks, which were already exploiting improved technology, now also profited from the decline of the German fighter force. During the spring and early summer of 1944, the Allied air forces were largely diverted from attacking Germany to strike targets in France and the Low Countries, in support of D-Day. When the bombers returned to Germany once the Allies were established ashore, the enemy had lost most of his coastal air defences. From July onwards, American and British bomber losses fell steeply. There were still some painful days and nights. But average Allied casualties seldom exceeded 1.5 per cent, and were often less.

Yet by the late summer of 1944 enthusiasm for bombing had waned within the Allied leadership. The politicians, generals, admirals, were weary of the airmen's extravagant forecasts. Sir Arthur Harris, C-in-C of Bomber Command, would forever be haunted by his promise to Churchill in the winter of 1943 that, if his Lancasters achieved another 15,000 sorties against Berlin, the Germans would inevitably be forced to surrender by 1 April 1944. Harris achieved his quota of Lancaster sorties, amid dreadful casualties, but by April Fool's Day there was not the smallest sign of Germany's collapse. Only two months before D-Day, General Carl "Tooey" Spaatz, America's air commander in Europe, suggested that the impending triumph of bombing made a descent on Normandy redundant, and urged a less hazardous assault on Norway. The British Army and Royal Navy, in particular, were embittered by the losses they had suffered in their ground campaigns and in the Battle of the Atlantic because the RAF's obsession with strategic bombing crippled its ability to provide support for land and sea operations.

All the available evidence showed that Germany continued to achieve miracles of industrial production despite the Allies' huge commitment to bombing. Politically, Churchill had exploited the strategic air offensive in his long struggle to reconcile Stalin to delays in launching the Second Front. But that was now over. The minds of the mightiest war leaders on both sides of the Atlantic were fixed upon the land campaign in north-west Europe. The importance of tactical air support for the armies was undisputed. But no one much cared any longer what Bomber Command and Eighth Air Force, supported by Fifteenth Air Force from Italy, were or were not doing to Hitler's empire. The extravagant advocates of air power, both American and British, were discredited in the eyes of their peers. The "new warfare" had plainly failed to destroy Hitler's empire. The footsoldiers were being obliged to fight their way through Germany in the "old warfare" way.

Now, however, there was a new irony. After almost discrediting themselves by the extravagance of their claims, in the spring of 1944 the American airmen had indeed identified Germany's vital weakness: oil. To continue the war, Hitler was overwhelmingly dependent upon the production of synthetic fuel. The Germans found it incomprehensible that, until May 1944, no systematic attempt had been made by the Allied air force to strike their oil plants. When Eighth Air Force began to do so, alongside Fifteenth Air Force flying from Italy, the results were remarkable. Petroleum available to Germany fell from 927,000 tons in March 1944 to 715,000 tons in May, and 472,000 tons in June. Luftwaffe supplies of aviation spirit declined from 180,000 tons in April to 50,000 tons in June, 10,000 tons in August. Germany needed 300,000 tons of fuel a month to fight the war, yet by September reserves had fallen to half that amount. Speer's spectacular achievements in sustaining aircraft production became meaningless without fuel. These statistics were, of course, unknown to the Allied leaders, but Ultra provided important clues. Even though the first USAAF raids in May had limited effect, intercepted signals traffic showed how much the attacks had alarmed the enemy. So low had the credibility of the Allied "bomber barons" sunk, however, that no one important in either Washington or London was persuaded that here, at last, the airmen had found Hitler's vital weakness, a short cut to ending the war. During the armies' advance into Germany, the RAF and USAAF begged SHAEF to emphasize to media correspondents that the devastation they met was the proud fruit of the air forces' efforts, rather than of mere artillery. Yet Bradley's aide Chester Hansen wrote on 7 December: "The gross claims of our airmen on the winning of the war by airmen are discounted by our ground force people." In October 1944, so disenchanted had Marshall and the U.S. Chiefs of Staff become with the airmen's unfulfilled promises that they seriously contemplated ordering the USAAF to abandon all strategic operations which did not promise directly to diminish German fighting power.

Air attacks on oil plants achieved dramatic successes in late May and June. They were somewhat interrupted during the summer invasion support campaign, but the American airmen were now convinced of their decisive importance, and threw immense effort into the oil campaign through late summer. As autumn gave way to winter, the weather provided the enemy with just sufficient breathing spaces from American precision bombing to enable the Germans to keep their armies moving. Almost every synthetic plant proved capable of repair within two or three weeks of a given attack. Repeat visits to targets were therefore essential. When these did not take place, because of thick overcast or unavailability of forces, a thin stream of oil flowed once more to Germany's forces.

The Americans also focused sharply on transportation targets, as urged by SHAEF's deputy Supreme Commander, Air Chief Marshal Sir Arthur Tedder, and his scientific advisers. In the final months of the war, at last the American airmen could claim that they were playing a vital role in strangling the Wehrmacht. It was extraordinary that German production continued at all. It should never be forgotten that, despite all the efforts of the air forces, until May 1945 ammunition continued to reach Hitler's forces in sufficient quantities to sustain the struggle. But, from the end of 1944 onwards, the loss of vital factories and raw materials to the Russians, damage to rail links, together with the acute shortage of oil, combined to create immense difficulties for the Germans in producing armaments and in using them effectively on the battlefield. The Luftwaffe, already crippled by disastrous failures of aircraft design and management, was now rendered almost impotent by lack of fuel either to train new pilots or to fly operational aircraft.

Amid the ruins of Germany and impending Allied victory, the USAAF and its leaders received less credit than they deserved for this success. All military achievements can be judged only in the wider context of grand strategy. For instance, if the RAF's Bomber Command had succeeded in its efforts to sink the pocket battleship *Tirpitz* in 1941, 1942 or even 1943, this would have made a notable contribution to the war. Yet, by the time the airmen destroyed the great vessel in November 1944, its sinking had become strategically irrelevant, a mere clever circus trick. Likewise, and far more important, had the Allied air forces been able to strike effectively against Germany's oil supply earlier in the war, they might have received the laurels for dramatically foreshortening the outcome. As it was, by the time the Americans identified the vital arteries of Hitler's war machine, the armies saw themselves on the brink of victory, without much need to acknowledge the contribution of the bombers.

The success of the USAAF could have been both swifter and more complete if the British had also committed themselves with real resolve to the oil campaign. In the autumn of 1944 some important British airmen, including the Chief of Air Staff and the Director of Bomber Operations, became convinced that the RAF should shift its forces from destroying cities to hitting oil plants. Sir Charles Portal was also persuaded of the merits of Tedder's "Transportation Plan"—battering the rail, road and water links of Germany. Yet both these policies foundered upon the same rock: the obsessive determination of Bomber Command's C-in-C, Sir Arthur Harris, to complete the programme of destroying Germany's cities which he had begun in March 1942. By the autumn of 1944, the British aircraft-construction programme undertaken back in 1941 at last reached fruition. Heavy bombers were pouring off the production lines, giving Harris a striking force of unprecedented power. His squadrons could call upon ever-more sophisticated radar navigation, marking and aiming devices. German defences were crumbling. Harris's power to inflict fire and death upon the cities of the enemy reached its zenith at the very moment when sensible strategists had become persuaded that there were much more useful ways of deploying Allied air power. That shrewd scientific civil servant Sir Henry Tizard acknowledged as far back as 1942 that Bomber Command might eventually inflict *catastrophic* injury upon Germany. He expressed doubt, however, about whether such injury would prove *decisive*. By late 1944, scepticism about the decisive value of destroying German real estate had become widespread in the Allied corridors of power.

Between its assaults upon cities, Bomber Command did attack transportation and oil targets. In the heated conflict of opinion which developed between the Air Ministry and Harris in the winter of 1944, Bomber Command's C-in-C kept his critics at bay by paying some lip-service to their demands. But he never disguised his determination to employ the chief weight of his forces where he wanted them. Between July and September 1944, some 11 per cent of British sorties were directed at oil targets and 20 per cent against cities. Between October and December, 14 per cent of RAF bomber attacks fell upon oil, 58 per cent upon cities. Repeated Air Ministry missives to Bomber Command, urging greater concentration on oil, vanished swiftly into Harris's waste-paper basket. In a letter to Portal on 1 November 1944, he deplored the range of demands on his resources and urged the importance of persisting with the assault on cities:

> In the past 18 months, Bomber Command has virtually destroyed 45 out of the leading 60 German cities. In spite of invasion diversions, we have so far managed to keep up and even to exceed our average of 2 cities devastated a month... There are not many industrial centres of population now left intact. Are we going to abandon this vast task, which the Germans themselves have long admitted to be their worst headache, just as it nears completion?

All that was required to complete his grand design, said Harris, was the destruction of Magdeburg, Halle, Leipzig, Dresden, Chemnitz, Nuremberg, Munich, Coblenz, Karlsruhe and some undamaged areas of Berlin and Hanover. Harris never wavered in his opposition to attacking oil and transportation—indeed, everything save Germany's cities. He derided those who advocated such wishy-washy policies. He wrote contemptuously to Portal on 25 October 1944: "During the past few weeks, every panacea-monger and 'me too expert,' to many of whom we had already (we hoped) given the quietus in the past, has raised his head again."

Portal responded on 5 November: "At the risk of your dubbing me 'another panacea merchant,' I believe the air offensive against oil gives us by far the best hope of complete victory in the next few months..." On 12 November, the Chief of Air Staff returned to the charge, rejecting Harris's argument for completing the destruction of Germany's cities: "I know that you have long felt such a plan to be the most effective way of bringing about the collapse of Germany...If I knew you to be as wholehearted in the attack on oil as in the past you have been in the matter of attacking cities, I would have little to worry about."

In November, 24.6 per cent of Bomber Command's sorties were devoted to attacking oil plants, delivering a larger tonnage of bombs than the USAAF's Eighth Air Force. Portal wrote again to Harris on 8 January 1945, urging even greater efforts. He pointed out bluntly that, but for the success of the Americans in creating a "favourable air situation," Bomber Command's attack on cities might well have ceased to be sustainable. This was indeed a remarkable admission from the head of the RAF: only the success of American air policy had saved that of Britain from humiliating failure. None of these arguments moved Harris, however. He was a man of elemental passions. Churchill observed after the war that Bomber Command's C-in-C was "a considerable commander," but he added: "there was a certain coarseness about him." Harris told Portal defiantly that he would resign if the Air Staff had lost confidence in his direction of the bomber offensive.

In the face of such obduracy, Britain's Chief of Air Staff retreated. On 20 January 1945, he wrote to Harris: "I willingly accept your assurance that you will continue to do your utmost to ensure the successful execution of the policy laid down. I am very sorry that you do not believe in it, but it is no use my craving for what is evidently unattainable. We must wait until after the end of the war before we can know for certain who was right..." This was an extraordinarily feeble letter for the head of the Royal Air Force to write to a subordinate commander. But propaganda had made "Bomber" Harris one of the most celebrated war leaders Britain possessed. At a time when it was plain that the war would end within months, Portal lacked the stomach for the huge row that must accompany Harris's dismissal. While Churchill no longer revealed much interest in the bomber offensive, he had always displayed respect for Harris's leadership. It was most unlikely that the prime minister would welcome, even if he was willing to acquiesce in, the dismissal of Bomber Command's C-in-C when victory was at hand. Harris should have been sacked in the winter of 1944 for his defiance of the policy approved by the Combined Chiefs of Staff, and for his insubordination towards Portal. Contrary to widespread belief, Harris did not invent area bombing. This was established before he assumed command of his forces. But he executed the policy with a Cromwellian zeal which ensured that his name is forever identified with the destruction of Germany's cities in the Second World War.

The USAAF focused its attacks through the closing period of the war upon oil and transportation targets. "We should never allow the history of this war to convict us of throwing the strategic bomber at the man in the street," declared General Ira Eaker, Eighth Air Force's commander, in January 1945. Yet such fervently moral observations would not have impressed the Germans beneath Eighth Air Force's assaults. It was true that American targeting specified rail junctions, bridges and suchlike, rather than city centres. But, given the mean error of aiming accuracy, a great many American bombs landed on civilian residential areas rather than on infrastructure targets. When conditions were overcast and it was necessary to bomb by radar, as was often the case, the destruction wrought by the USAAF was broadcast almost as widely as that generated by the RAF's area attacks. The British found it convenient publicly to deny the existence of any moral issue about striking at German centres of population. The Americans did acknowledge a moral issue, but killed many civilians anyway. There is no evidence that the German people, then or later, recognized much practical distinction between the brands of misery imposed upon them by the respective Allied air forces. To an extraordinary degree, and especially in the last months of the war, the air chiefs were left to make policy as they saw fit. On the American side, writes the historian Michael Sherry, "after September 1944, no one outside the air force carefully examined its methods of bombing. Whether it chose to blast factories, mine sea-lanes or level cities was largely for [General "Hap"] Arnold and his subordinates to decide... The leaders and technicians of the American air force were driven by technological fanaticism."

It is important to establish the background against which the last phase of the bomber offensive took place, because this proved overwhelmingly the most destructive. Between September 1944 and April 1945, the Western allies dropped more than 800,000 tons of bombs on Germany, 60 per cent of the total tonnage delivered between 1939 and 1945. German industrial production peaked in September 1944, and thereafter declined relentlessly as plant and raw materials in occupied territories were lost. In January 1945, with considerable courage Speer informed Hitler that the German economy was within weeks of collapse. From an Allied viewpoint, there was an overwhelming case for maintaining air attacks on oil installations and transport links. It would have been unthinkable to stand down Bomber Command and the U.S. Eighth and Fifteenth Air Forces while the Germans continued fiercely to resist Allied assaults on the battlefield. It is hard to imagine, however, that any strategic purpose was served, or might rationally have been expected to be served, by continuing the destruction of cities. Yet this is what happened, on a vastly greater scale than ever before. In August 1943, its most active month of that year, Bomber Command dropped 20,149 tons of bombs on Germany, and Eighth Air Force 3,999. In

October 1944, Bomber Command dropped 61,204 tons, Eighth Air Force 38,961 tons. In February 1945, British and American tonnages were 45,889 and 46,088 respectively; in March, 67,637 and 65,962. In all, in the first four months of 1945 the British dropped 181,740 tons of bombs on Germany, and Eighth Air Force 188,573. In the whole of 1943, the British had dropped only 157,367 tons. Such statistics emphasize how much destruction was done to Germany's cities at a phase of the war when "de-housing" civilians had become meaningless to everyone except the wretched Germans beneath.

Bishop Bell of Chichester, one of the most prominent British civilian critics of area bombing, had delivered a stinging rebuke in February 1944:

> I desire to challenge the Government on the policy which directs the bombing of enemy towns on the present scale, especially with reference to civilians who are non-combatants... It is of supreme importance that we, who are the liberators of Europe, should so use power that it is always under the control of Law. It is because our bombing of enemy towns—this "area bombing"—raises this issue of bombing unlimited that such immense importance is bound to attach to the policy and action of His Majesty's Government.

It is a tribute to the maintenance of democracy in Britain that such a statement could be made, and publicly debated, in the midst of a world war, even if after years of suffering at the hands of the Luftwaffe few among the bishop's British audience were in a mood to heed him.

Most people believed that the German people deserved their fate. Yet it seems debatable whether Allied aircraft were appropriately employed in belatedly administering punishment to the German people, as distinct from inflicting strategic damage upon their capacity to continue the war. The bomber offensive may be perceived in four phases. From 1940 through 1942, it inflicted negligible damage upon the Germans, but represented a heroic earnest of British defiance. In 1943, the impact of intensified bombing was assuaged by increased industrial output, but air attack obliged the Nazis seriously to address the defence of the Reich. From the spring of 1944 onwards, the bomber offensive achieved a terrible maturity. It made mounting inroads on Germany's industrial capacity, and brought the Luftwaffe to its knees. Richard Overy, among others, has justly highlighted the importance of bombing in forcing Hitler to devote huge resources—above all some 10,000 of his excellent 88mm guns—to the home defence of the Reich when these deadly weapons would otherwise have been deployed on the fighting fronts, to the detriment of the Allied armies. This drain on battlefield armaments would have been even greater had not Hitler professed an unconcern, even satisfaction, about the destruction inflicted by bombing: "[it] actually works in our favour, because it is creating a body of people with nothing to lose—people who will therefore fight on with utter fanaticism."

Up to 1945, there seems little difficulty in justifying the bomber offensive militarily and morally, as a matter of both desirability and necessity. In all wars, combatants must pay a moral price for military actions, and painful choices must be accepted. Churchill agonized before D-Day about the inevitable deaths of thousands of French civilians if France's rail links were bombed. He reluctantly concluded that the greater good—the success of the invasion—must be held paramount, and he was surely right. Few British or American people worried much about the fate of the people of Germany during the war years. Why indeed should they have done so? The Germans had brought unspeakable misery upon the world.

Yet in the early months of 1945 Bishop Bell's remarks a year earlier attained a new relevance. By this last phase, the moral cost of killing German civilians in unprecedented numbers outweighed any possible strategic advantage. The wholesale destruction of some great cities, Dresden foremost among them, could have been averted, even if attacks on urban rail centres had continued. Ironically, and although the leaders of the USAAF never admitted this, Spaatz's aircraft joined in many area attacks in the last weeks, because they ran out of identifiable precision targets. The performance of the strategic air forces at this period was a murderous, largely futile muddle. "I felt that again our efforts were rather disconnnected," wrote Tedder, as Eisenhower's deputy. "We were attacking more or less simultanously oil, cities, depots, marshalling yards, canals and factories. In this I could discern no comprehensive or economical use of our overwhelming air forces." Churchill or Portal should have stopped Harris's manic assault on Germany's surviving cities. Neither did so, Churchill because he was preoccupied elsewhere, Portal because he lacked the steel indispensable to great military commanders.

The USAAF's strategic offensive achieved formidable success, in winning air supremacy over Europe and in crippling German oil production and transport links. By contrast, the final stage of the area offensive against Germany's cities contributed little to the defeat of the Nazis, and cast a moral shadow over Allied victory which has never been lifted. It is impossible to fight any war wholly humanely. In most respects, the Western allies displayed commendable charity in their conduct of total war against an enemy bereft of civilized sentiment. Aerial assault, however, provided the exception. It was a policy quite at odds with the spirit in which the Americans and British otherwise conducted their war effort. The remoteness of bombing rendered tolerable in the eyes of Western political leaders and military commanders, not to mention their aircrew, actions which would have seemed repugnant and probably unbearable had the Allies confronted the consequences at close quarters. Eisenhower's soldiers frequently found themselves killing local inhabitants in the course of battles for Germany's towns and village. They would have surely revolted at the notion of systematically slaughtering civilians by artillery bombardment or machine-gun fire. This is what the Allied air forces did, nonetheless, protected by the curious moral absolution granted by a separation of some thousands of feet of airspace, together with the pragmatic excuse that it was impossible to hit targets of military relevance with air-dropped missiles without inflicting what is now called "collateral damage."

We should recognize, however, that it is far easier to pass such judgements amid the relative tranquillity of the twenty-first century than it seemed in 1945, when Hitler's nation was still doing its utmost to kill American and British people, together with millions of Nazi captives, by every means within its power. Some Germans today brand the bombing of their cities a war crime. This seems an incautious choice of words. It is possible to deplore Harris's excesses without accepting that they should be judged in such emotive language. For all its follies and bloody misjudgements, the strategic air offensive was a military operation designed to hasten the collapse of Germany's ability to make war. It stopped as soon as Hitler's people ceased to fight. Most of Germany's massacres, by contrast, were carried out against defenceless people who possessed not the slightest power to injure Hitler's empire. They were murdered for ideological reasons, devoid of military purpose.

LIBS, LANCS AND FORTS

THOSE WHO CARRIED out the Allied bomber offensive never saw themselves as persecutors of innocent women and children. They were young, and far too preoccupied with their own vulnerability to death to have much sentiment to spare for the sorrows of the enemy. The bomber crews of the United States and Britain suffered wartime casualty rates almost as dreadful as those of Hitler's U-boat crews. For an Allied flier, the skies over Europe represented a terrifying environment. Flak guns, fighters, the hazards of weather, collision and mechanical failure rendered the experience of bombing Germany among the most alarming assignments of the war. Those who flew bombers never witnessed the human consequences of their actions. They knew only that they were striving, at great personal risk, to cripple the industrial and military might of Hitler's empire.

Among airmen, opinion was divided about whether formation flying with the USAAF Eighth and Fifteenth Air Forces was preferable to the loneliness experienced by the crews who carried out the RAF Bomber Command's night attacks. Some men found fighting in daylight, watching comrades die in stark proximity, frighteningly cold-blooded. The Americans stationed in England felt very far from home. In the huts on their bleak airstrips in Norfolk and Suffolk, they were wakened for briefing around 0400, about the time their RAF counterparts were going to bed. Out on the desolate stands where the bombers were dispersed, pilots watched for the green flare arching into the sky, the signal to start engines. In a long procession *Four of a Kind, Little Audrey, Piccadilly Commando, Miss Carriage, Liberty Belle* and the rest of their exotically named silver sisterhood swung around the perimeter track on to the runway. One by one, the "Forts" and "Libs" lumbered into the air to take up their places in the rigid formations demanded by U.S. tactical doctrine. The least popular slot was that of "tail-end charlie," "Purple Heart corner," first target of German fighters. The crews switched on oxygen at 8,000 feet, and usually approached the enemy coast around 1000 hours. The waist gunners pulled away their hatches, exposing the fuselage to a blast of icy air which chilled every flier, even in a heated suit. Staff-Sergeant John Romine wrote of the special loneliness of the tail gunner: "The few feet that separated us from even the waist gunners seemed like a thousand miles." Crews tested their thirteen guns before entering German airspace, then settled down for the long run to the target.

For six to ten hours, any flier doing his job properly was required to make a fierce effort of concentration. "In bright sunlight, even with dark glasses our eyes grew tired from squinting," wrote Carl Fyler, a Kansan who flew B-17s from Molesworth in Cambridgeshire. On overcast days when they were sometimes obliged to rely upon instruments, every crew was haunted by the fear of collision. In these last stages of the war, interference from the Luftwaffe diminished dramatically, even when Göring's handful of Me-262 jet aircraft joined the battle. The German fighters often found themselves outnumbered forty to one. "Each time I close the canopy before take-off," wrote a young Luftwaffe pilot gloomily, "I feel that I am closing the lid of my own coffin." But on bad days the Fortresses and Liberators fought running battles against Focke-Wulfs and Messerschmitts across hundreds of miles of German sky. Flak remained a mortal danger until the last days. There was no counter to anti-aircraft fire save luck. American aircraft were more strongly built than their British counterparts, which relied upon darkness for protection. The heavy armour fitted to USAAF planes required them to carry smaller bombloads than the RAF's Lancasters and Halifaxes, but they could also survive more punishment. Again and again, American aircraft were desperately damaged, but some of their crewmen survived. A gunner in Carl Fyler's squadron was hit by shrapnel which tore off his left arm and inflicted mortal internal wounds. The doomed man crawled forward to the wounded waist gunners, whose arms were broken. He buckled on their parachutes and helped them to bail out before he himself went down with the stricken plane. He was recommended for a posthumous Medal of Honor, for a display of courage and sacrifice of the kind which was often asked of bomber aircrew.

Formation-flying was an intensely demanding discipline, requiring relentless commitment by every pilot, and above all from the lead aircraft. Returning from bombing oil refineries in Rumania on 13 September 1944, Arthur Miller's squadron were appalled to find themselves flying headlong towards a mountainside. They pulled up steeply, prompting a storm of abuse over the radio, directed against their leader. "You fucking bastard," shouted a pilot, "trying to kill us all for shoe shines." After a shocked pause, the colonel commanding the formation said: "This is Red Leader—plane making comment, identify yourself *now*." There was another silence, then laughter, snickers, and an outpouring of fearful anger from other aircraft: "Red Leader, why don't you go and sit in a corner and play with yourself and shine your balls, if you have any"; "You turd-eating son-of-a-bitch, you almost had your day of reckoning"; "If you had marched today and your uniform was on straight, you wouldn't be flying into mountains, you cocksucking motherfucker." At last, they landed in Italy to refuel. Miller was surprised to see only five planes fire flares to indicate casualties aboard—fewer than he had expected, after meeting heavy and accurate flak over the target. As they taxied in, they were amazed to hear the voice of their deputy leader: "I apologize to you all. I almost killed the whole squadron. I should never let up until we touch down. I am sorry."

Staff-Sergeant Delbert Lambson, a gunner, was a nineteen-year-old small farmer from New Mexico. A deeply religious young man, Lambson was married to a seventeen-year-old girl, and had a baby son. He once hit a man who said in the mess that there wasn't a woman in the world who could be trusted. He pitied those who found the job unbearably hard, including their own ball-turret gunner: "Soldiering and especially combat never did agree with him. Before each mission, even on cold winter mornings, the sweat would be running down his face. I liked him because he was uncomplicated, honest, and made few demands. He seemed grateful to be with me, and that made me feel at ease." On one trip, Lambson found himself assuming the job of a gunner who was found mentally unfit to fly.

Over Regensburg with the 390th Bomb Group, his plane was badly hit, and a 20mm cannon shell struck Lambson in his turret: "Streaks of fire shot through my brain. My hands shot up to my face. Blood trickled through my fingers and down my chest. My left leg was numb and my left shoulder felt as if a hot branding iron had been thrust into it. The left leg and arm of my padded flying suit was ripped to shreds, and was soaking up the blood that poured from my wounds." On escaping from his turret, he made the alarming discovery that the rest of the crew had already jumped without him. He bailed out, and pulled the ripcord of his parachute at 5,000 feet, terrified of bleeding to death before he reached the ground. He lost consciousness, and awoke to find a group of unsmiling German soldiers peering down at him. He had lost an eye, and remained comatose for a week. In the air, Lambson had never thought much about the nature of the task he and his comrades were performing. Yet in hospital he was tended with wonderful solicitousness by Marie, a German nurse. She went on leave to visit her mother in Berlin. Lambson was shocked to hear that she had been killed on the train by strafing Allied fighters.

While the heavy bombers attacked Germany from fields in England, their medium counterparts flew missions from strips in France, where they enjoyed nothing like the comforts of fighter and bomber crews stationed at English bases. The French grass fields, overlaid with pierced plank runways, offered accommodation not much less cold and dirty than those of rear-area ground troops. Yet Lieutenant Robert Burger, a B-26 navigator based near Cambrai, found his job in the last months of the war almost routine: "I can go out on a mission now wondering what we are going to have for dinner." Major Jack Ilfrey said: "Whenever I heard any griping about food and living conditions, I always reminded the men they were better off than most of the other boys scattered around the world. They had places to go and things to do. It wasn't like home, of course, but it wasn't Africa or sleeping in tents in Italy, or fighting in the South Pacific. We all had a hell of a lot to be grateful for." Yet life in tents alongside the French strips was always dreary and cold. Robert Burger experienced a stab of envy when he landed at a fighter base near Brussels one day and found the pilots sitting down to eat "on cushioned chairs, covered tables and pitchers of lemonade, Belgian girls waiting on table. The pilots ordered a cocktail from the nearby bar as a string quartet played soft music. It was unbelievable—shangri-la to us!"

Most of the medium bombers' short-range operations were carried out at the request of army commanders. Each day, the crews stood by, waiting upon the pleasure of the generals. "Nice day, but nothing for us. Played horseshoes all afternoon. Big bull session round the fire at night," Captain Marvin Schulze of the 397th Bombardment Group wrote in his diary one typical autumn day of 1944. As the weather worsened, there were many days when flying was impossible: "Stood down early. Big drunken brawl that lasted till early morning. Major Hamilton got two broken ribs out of the deal ... Pretty foggy all day long. Sawed wood for about three hours. Peeled potatoes and made French fries. No mail in over a week now ... A beautiful raid this morning. Target a railway road bridge at Prayen, Germany. No flak, no fighters. Flew number four." But then there were the days when the enemy intervened, sometimes ferociously. On 23 November, "two ships blew up before we got to the target ... two more were lost to fighters. The whole of Capt. Stephenson's flight went down, with the exception of Lt. Neu, who landed the most shot-up plane I ever saw ... It's a pretty sad outfit tonight." Schulze's B-26 Group lost fifty-one men in two days. The big picture, of overwhelming Allied dominance, masked the intimate reality, of some bad days which maintained the tempo of fear.

The people who fight wars are customarily referred to as "men." Yet in truth, irrespective of their ages, most of those engaged in combat behaved, thought and talked as boys—exuberant and emotional, careless and naive. "Dear Mom," a pilot of the 95th Bomb Group, Harry Conley, wrote home.

No air battle manufactured in Hollywood can approach the thrills and sights of the real thing. They rarely last over half an hour, but the thrills of a lifetime are contained in that short space of time. It's a funny reaction. I sit there flying my airplane and I can hear and feel all my boys' guns going off. The only enemy planes I can see are those coming from the front or side, and I can see whatever flak appears in those regions. You sit there quite calmly and watch the flak explode around you in little puffs of black smoke... as if it were a movie. Then a couple of hours after you are back on the ground, it begins to dawn on you, and it is then that you get properly scared. The German boys are marvellous pilots and really have guts.

On 4 November 1944, the crews of 408 Squadron Royal Canadian Air Force prepared to fly from Linton-on-Ouse in Yorkshire, on one of Bomber Command's great night raids against Germany's cities. A force of 384 Halifaxes, 336 Lancasters and 29 Mosquitoes was to attack Bochum. The 408 Squadron was scheduled to take off at 1600, but to the bitter frustration of the crews bad weather caused repeated postponements. David Sokoloff's crew were specially tense, because it was the thirteenth trip of their tour. "We had to hang around the Halifax, *F-Freddie,* checking and re-checking for something to do, smoking cig after cig in the clammy half-dark of the English winter evening," wrote the nineteen-year-old bomb-aimer, Alan Stables from British Columbia. Dave Hardy, the rear gunner from Saskatoon, felt nervous and gloomy. Jon Sargent, the navigator, an accountant from British Columbia, said: "Why the hell don't the bastards scrub it in this weather?" Their spirits were further depleted by a friendly visit from the base's Catholic chaplain.

The planes finally took off at 1930, carrying fourteen tons of fuel and bombs, slipping into the familiar routine: "Lock throttles—adjust pitch on the starboard outer—wheels up and locked—synchronise engines—adjust trim tabs—throttle back to climbing boost." "Sok," the pilot, always worried about putting his chocolate too close to the heating outlet, where it would melt. He was a twenty-four-year-old Londoner who had been studying architecture at Yale in 1939. He went north to Montreal to join up, which is how he now found himself captaining a Canadian crew. He was dismayed to find the aircraft struggling to reach operational height, a familiar problem with Halifaxes, whose ceiling was 2,000 feet below that of the Lancs. Sok told Stables to ditch part of their bombload, a practice which infuriated Bomber Command's senior officers, but was commonplace in some squadrons.

F-Freddie gained 1,000 feet, but the plane was still 5,000 feet below the bomber stream's designated altitude and ninety minutes short of target when Hardy in the rear turret yelled, "Fighter port—go!," and they pitched into violent corkscrew evasive action. When they resumed their course, the gunner said he had seen a Ju-88, but it was gone. A nervous, jocular voice on the intercom said: "How many engines did it have?" Sok said briefly: "Cut the chatter." They saw other aircraft around them catching fire and falling through the sky. Then oncoming tracer streaked up to meet *F-Freddie* and lashed into the wing. Stables, in the nose, closed his eyes and prayed. The engineer yelled: "Port engine on fire, skip, let's get the hell out." Sok said coolly: "Feathering port inner, hit the graviner switches, Dick, prepare to abandon aircraft everyone. Bomb doors open. Drop your bombs, bomb aimer." The graviner switches released CO_2 on to the engines, but this failed to extinguish the fire. The crew left their stations and went to the hatches. Sok threw the aircraft into a steep dive, to put out the fire. This was a terrifyingly risky manoeuvre. Sometimes it succeeded. Often, however, it created a blowtorch effect which melted the wing off the aircraft. The seven men in *F-Freddie* were lucky. Levelling off at 4,000 feet, they found that the fire was out.

The crew returned to their positions—except Hardy, the rear gunner. His turret was traversed sideways, and empty. He had bailed out—a wise move, for it was notoriously difficult for rear gunners to escape from a stricken aircraft. They set a course for home, hampered by the loss of all their maps and logs, which had been sucked out into the slipstream by the great blast of air that swept through the fuselage when the hatches were ditched. The main fuse panel had been destroyed by German fire. The fuel gauges and radar were gone. They suffered another moment of terror when the mid-upper gunner reported seeing two fighters, provoking Sokoloff to corkscrew again.

By late 1944, bomber crews possessed one huge asset for survival: if they were badly hit, they no longer had to struggle home across the North Sea, where so many met their ends earlier in the war. *F-Freddie* crash-landed on the flarepath at Brussels without flaps or brakes, bouncing so violently that the undercarriage collapsed. The aircraft skidded rasping on its belly past the end of the runway and over a ditch, earth exploding upwards into the fuselage through the shattered nose. It lurched to a stop seventy yards short of a cluster of houses. There was a mad scramble to get out before the aircraft caught fire, though mercifully there was no blaze. They counted a hundred holes in the aircraft. Later, Sok's mother asked anxiously if the pilot would have to pay for the damage.

The exhausted and traumatized crew were taken by truck to the Imperial Hotel in Brussels. In addition to their own aircraft, twenty-nine others were lost by Bomber Command that night. A thousand people died in Bochum, where the steelworks was badly hit. After three weeks' survivors' leave, David Sokoloff's crew returned to operations from Linton and flew a further twenty-three trips. Among every hundred RAF Bomber Command aircrew in the course of the war, fifty-one died on operations, nine were lost in crashes in England, three seriously injured, twelve were taken prisoner, one was shot down and escaped capture, and just twenty-four completed a tour of operations. One night just before Sok's crew were due to take off again, they found their new rear gunner drinking beer. If he ever did such a thing again, they said, they would kill him. Survival depended on luck, but also upon relentless vigilance through each minute of every hour that men braved the airspace over Germany.

From the autumn of 1944 onwards, Bomber Command conducted a growing number of daylight operations, alongside its night attacks. As the Luftwaffe's powers declined, and with France and Belgium now in Allied hands, daylight "ops" offered a chance of more accurate bombing and reduced casualties. Daylight raids were initially conducted against easy targets. Most groups committed their less experienced crews to them. Yet this bred resentment among those who were still flying long, dangerous night sorties to eastern Germany. Eddie Lovejoy, a navigator with the RAF's 75 Squadron, was one of a crew serving their second tour. They were exasperated to see others racking up several trips towards their quota of thirty operations on short daylight "milk-runs," while Lovejoy's men were flying through the darkness for nine or ten hours to targets such as Stettin. In September, their pilot formally protested to the commanding officer, who duly rostered them for some daylight ops against German V-weapon sites in Holland. "It was thus that I saw the enemy coast approaching in full daylight for the first time in the war," wrote Lovejoy wonderingly. After flying so often over Europe in darkness, he found it strange now to do so in sunlight, and was even more amazed when he saw a German Me-262 jet fighter streak past them. At the end of October, his crew took part in a tactical raid on German gun positions near Flushing. The neighbouring Lancaster was a wingspan away when Lovejoy, in the astrodome, saw a 105mm shell strike its bomb bay. The ensuing explosion caused the entire formation to lift in the air. Lovejoy was hurled against the side of the astrodome by the force of the blast, "and to my utter horror was gazing at a few dark pieces of debris drifting down to earth... By flying at night, we had missed the spectacle of horrors like these, but seeing it happen close to was an experience to shake one clear down to the soles of one's shoes... It was a rather silent and melancholy journey home."

All heavy bomber crews found it a strange experience, creating a special kind of strain, to drink one night in a pub in rural Lincolnshire or Norfolk, then to be thrown next day into a battle that might end in a PoW camp or in death. Most men's loyalties became fiercely focused upon their own crews. "Other people in the squadron were just acquaintances," said Sergeant Bill Winter, a Lancaster wireless-operator. "The crew was everything—you slept together, drank together, ate together, went on leave together—and fought together. My biggest fear was of being sent on a trip as a 'spare bod' with a strange crew." On the ground, little was asked of bomber aircrew save that they should rest, attend briefings, check and test equipment. At Winter's 106 Squadron, there was intense resentment when, during a period of poor weather which permitted little flying, aircrew were ordered to muster for a morning jog around the airfield perimeter track. There was even greater fury when they were issued with shovels and told to help clear snow off the runways. They believed, not unreasonably, that enough was asked of them over Germany to merit forbearance on the ground.

If there was a common strand among young men of the wartime generation, whether American, British, German, Russian, it was their passion for flying. They were seized by the romance of escaping from the earth. The air corps was first choice of assignment for millions of disappointed conscripts who finished up in armour, infantry, artillery. Richard Burt, a Liberator gunner from Utah, found that flying above cloud "made you feel as if they had cleaned up the earth . . . it has a peaceful, mind-washing effect on me." Until he met the enemy, he simply gloried in the aesthetic beauty of the sky.

"I thought a lot about our guys down there on the ground with the army," said another B-24 gunner, Ira Wells. "We had all the glory. I realised how fortunate we were to be in the air." Wells was a dentist's son from Staten Island who volunteered for the air corps in 1943, but realized during training on Piper Cubs that he would never make the grade as a pilot. His crew formed in Lincoln, Nebraska, a wonderful amalgam of Americans at war. There were two Jews, two Catholics and five Protestants. The pilot was from Michigan, the bombardier from Iowa, the top turret gunner from Illinois, waist gunners from Oklahoma and Massachusetts, tail from Ohio; the other three were New Yorkers. "We were the Lindbergh generation," said Harold Dorfman, their navigator. "I wanted to fly like I could taste it." The only one among them who seemed less than enamoured with their Liberator was the pilot. Before being drafted, he had been an inspector on a B-24 production line. "I know all the things that are wrong with these aircraft," he announced gloomily. "I'm more frightened of them than any of you."

They joined the 448th Bomb Group at Seething, a remote Norfolk airfield, in September 1944. They slept two crews to a Nissen hut, and found themselves moving into the beds of men who had gone down the previous day. Their surviving roommates had done fifteen trips. The newcomers quizzed them about what it was like, and were told: "pretty scary." Wartime bomber crews were mere passing visitors on their bases for the few months of their tour, amid a huge permanent population of ground staff and maintenance personnel. The only exception at Seething was George, a cook who had been there since the base was built, and suddenly volunteered to reclassify as an air gunner. George had made himself so cosy that he spent most of his off-duty time in the cottage of villagers who lived at the end of the runway, whose daughter Daphne was "just a little bit pregnant" by him.

Wells's and Dorfman's crew made their first trip on 13 September, a milk-run to a marshalling yard. Their second trip was more hazardous. They flew at 200 feet over Arnhem, pushing out supplies to the beleaguered British paratroops, glimpsing the Dutch waving and the German tracer slashing up at them. "We dropped our supplies in the right place," said Harold Dorfman, "right on the Germans, of course." Dorfman was a passionate amateur photographer and snatched some remarkable images from the cockpit during their tour, not least those of Liberators disintegrating in mid-air. "I stood at the window and cried as I photographed our wingman breaking up," said Dorfman. His own crew was lucky. They trusted each other—"Sometimes I think we were too young to be as scared as we should have been," said Corporal Wells. He himself felt no great animosity towards the Germans they were bombing. "We knew Germany was the ally of Japan. That was enough. In those days, people were just patriotic. It never occurred to us to ask ourselves whether what we were doing was right." But Harold Dorfman said: "I'm a Jew. I knew what was going on. I had no sympathy whatsoever for the Germans." Likewise the RAF's Bill Winter, who said: "We never thought about what was underneath—if you saw a lot of fires you just thought: 'We've really given them a pasting tonight.' "

Sergeant Jack Brennan, a B-17 radio-operator/gunner in 200th Group, belonged to an unhappy crew. They neither liked nor trusted their pilot, "a phoney ... There was a real personality problem. We got hit just about every trip. Mostly, we survived thanks to the skill of our navigator. None of us was in the mould of heroes." Brennan was a twenty-two-year-old baker's son from Staten Island, and his family were furious when he volunteered in 1942. They had been confident of getting him a deferral. As his pilot blundered through the skies over Germany, hardly a day passed when Brennan did not regret his eagerness to join the Air Corps. His only consolation was that he felt very conscious of how much better they lived on their base at Royston in Hertfordshire than did GIs on the ground in Germany.

On their twenty-fourth mission, they were hit amidships by flak over Berlin. To the disgust of some of the crew, the pilot set course for neutral Sweden, a destination favoured by Allied airmen who had seen enough of the war. "We'd always known that if something happened, the pilot wouldn't be there—and he wasn't." Seven members of the crew jumped over Sweden. Only Brennan, the navigator and bombardier survived. A U.S. legation representative, who came from Stockholm to visit Brennan in the Swedish hospital where he was recovering from arm and leg injuries, said anxiously: "Don't say anything detrimental about your pilot." The gunner observed wearily: "They had to think everybody was a hero."

In the air, attacking in their vast formations, American bombardiers scarcely used their Norden bombsights; they simply flicked the switches to release their loads in unison with the mission leader. A combat historian asked each of

Wells's crew after their first trip what they had thought about as they approached their target. The pilot answered: his wife; the co-pilot: his baby; Dorfman, the navigator, said he was too busy to think at all, trying to see they didn't get lost. By the end of 1944, the huge accompanying forces of escort fighters overwhelmed the dwindling Luftwaffe on most sorties. Wells never fired his guns in anger. He occasionally glimpsed German jets in the distance, but they were too far away and too fast to offer a shot. Wells retained a profound fear of having to bail out because, like his navigator, he was Jewish. But he claimed to have experienced more fear visiting his girlfriend in London during the German V2 rocket attacks than he did over Germany.

By 1945, every heavy bomber carried an extraordinary weight of high technology and skilled manpower to operate it. A B-24 Liberator contained 1,550,000 separate parts. British Lancasters required crews of seven, American Fortresses and Liberators nine or ten. The functions of pilots, flight-engineers and navigators were self-evident. It sometimes seemed debatable, however, whether a dedicated wireless-operator was necessary. The bombardier—bomb-aimer, in British parlance—was a passenger until the five or ten minutes of a bomb-run, though he sometimes operated a radar set. In American formations, where following aircraft merely released their bombs when their leader did, many men wondered whether a bombardier was required in every crew. British "heavies" carried three gun-turrets and two dedicated gunners. They learned early in the war that with their small-calibre .303 machine-guns they were most unlikely to shoot down a well-armoured German night-fighter. Some critics urged dispensing with the heavy hydraulically powered front and mid-upper turrets to improve aircraft ceilings. However, the presence of the guns was thought essential to crew confidence. The chief function of gunners was as look-outs, watching for fighters and triggering evasive action from the pilot. "Our gunners never fired in anger," said Bill Winter. "The only time we were really plastered, we never even saw the fighter."

Flying as a gunner imposed stresses almost equal to those facing the pilots or specialists, because a man had much less to do and more time to think. When an American daylight formation was under attack, the gunners' purpose was to contribute to the geometrically calculated barrage, interlocking between the aircraft of a formation, through which a Luftwaffe attacker must pass. It was essential to fire repeated short bursts rather than to press the trigger continuously. The barrel of a .50-calibre machine-gun overheated and bent if it remained in action for more than eight seconds. For all their extravagant claims, only a tiny number of gunners ever hit a German aircraft. In the last months of the war, escort fighters provided the defensive capability that mattered. The two waist gunners, at least, might have been dispensed with. But the barrage generated by the Fortress and Liberator .50 calibres was thought to be morale-building. The bombers' large crews were maintained to the end. It did not go unnoticed, however, that the most successful British aircraft of the war was the twin-engined Mosquito, which carried no guns in its bomber role, and relied solely upon speed and agility for survival. "Mossie" losses to enemy action, especially towards the end, were negligible. The Mosquito, with a crew of only two, could carry a formidable bomb-load.

Now that overwhelming forces of escort fighters dominated the skies over Germany, crews feared flak much more than the Luftwaffe. Each exploding shell left an image of smoke in the sky like an inverted Y ten feet high, tilting in different directions. Formations weaved to confuse the gunners until they reached their "IP"—the "initial point" ahead of the target. From there on, they were required to fly straight and level for the ten minutes of their bomb run, ignoring the hailstorm rattle of shrapnel on the fuselage, praying for the bomb release to be over. "There would be seconds when you felt your lungs would burst because you forgot to exhale," wrote a crewman. "Instants would occur when you believed your eyes were seeing more than they could behold. There was an unreal sensation of having your body feel moist all over, and then . . . your mouth felt like it was stuffed with dry cotton . . . for no reason at all your lower jaw would quiver and you couldn't speak."

There were very bad days when even the Luftwaffe in its decline committed substantial forces of fighters. On 11 September 1944, a mission to the Ruhland synthetic oil-plant on the Czech border met some fifty Focke-Wulfs and Messerschmitt Bf-109s. On the 1,300-mile round trip, Eighth Air Force lost forty-five bombers and twenty-one escorting Mustangs. Of thirty-six aircraft of the 100th Bomb Group, fourteen failed to return. It was often the case that once a formation had been broken open and some aircraft lost, the enemy was able progressively to cut down its survivors. Over the Ore Mountains on the Ruhland raid, ten American aircraft crashed within a six-mile radius.

On 31 December 1944, thirty-seven aircraft of the 100th Bomb Group attacked Hamburg, a coastal target which was usually considered far less hazardous than objectives inland. After making a landfall south of the Danish border, the formation turned south-west down the Elbe at 25,000 feet. "The flak was brutal. We flew through flak clouds and aircraft parts for what seemed like an hour," said Lieutenant William Leek, from Washington State, making the twenty-second trip of his tour. Luftwaffe fighters attacked the formation as it left the target, battling into a strong headwind. Ten U.S. aircraft went down in the space of a few minutes. Leek's first pilot, Lieutenant Glenn Rohjohn from Greenock, Pennsylvania, was manoeuvring to fill a gap in their formation left by a neighbour's demise when there was a tremendous impact. They had suffered a disaster of a unique kind. Another B-17, piloted by Lieutenant James Macnab, was flying immediately below that of Rohjohn. Suddenly, it lurched upwards, and locked on to the Fortress above. The top turret pierced the lower fuselage of Rohjohn's B-17. "We were like creeping dragonflies," said Leek. The ball-turret gunner in Macnab's aircraft cranked his turret manually until he could escape into the fuselage. The plane began to burn. Rohjohn attempted in vain to break his own aircraft free by gunning the engines. Three of the lower aircraft's four motors were still turning. Rohjohn now feathered his own propellers and rang the "bail out" bell. His ball-turret gunner was saying Hail Marys over the intercom. The man knew he could not escape, that he was doomed. "I couldn't help him," said Leek, "and I somehow felt that I was invading his right to be alone."

Ammunition began to explode as fire spread through the lower aircraft. Rohjohn told Leek to go, but the co-pilot refused, knowing that alone the pilot could not control the B-17. Shortly before 1300, they crashed into a field at Tettens, near Wilhelmshaven. On impact, Rohjohn's plane at last slid free of Macnab's. It ended a mad career across the grass when the left wing sliced into a wooden military headquarters building. By a miracle, both Rohjohn and Leek survived the crash. They crawled out on to the wing, into the hands of a German soldier. "All that was left of the Flying Fortress was the nose, the cockpit and the seats we were sitting on," said Leek. Four men survived from Macnab's plane. In all, 100th Group lost twelve aircraft that day.

Bombing Germany was never a safe activity. To the very end of the war, some crews and some missions suffered horrible experiences. But the overall rate of attrition had declined steeply since the bloody days of 1943, when a bomber crew was more likely to die than to survive. Throughout the war, both the RAF and USAAF periodically varied the number of operations a crew had to complete before being relieved. In the worst days, American fliers had to fly twenty-five missions. By the winter of 1944, with the progressive collapse of the German defences, this had risen to thirty-five. Yet throughout the war fliers based in England were cosseted by their commanders, as befitted men called upon to perform extraordinary tasks and live with exceptional strains. After seven trips, Wells's crew was sent for a week's "R & R" in delicious comfort at "the flak house," a country mansion near Salisbury maintained specially for U.S. bomber aircrew. They felt they needed it.

Earlier in the war, many squadrons had suffered serious problems with airmen who "Section-A'ed"—succumbed to combat fatigue. But nobody at Seething did so in the final months, though a pilot once panicked and bailed out over Germany, leaving the rest of his crew to bring the plane home. Wells and Dorfman flew their last mission to Berlin in March 1945, awed by the vast armada of which they formed a part. Their designated targets were usually bridges or marshalling yards, but that day they were told explicitly that they were hitting the centre of Hitler's capital. On their return, they exultantly buzzed the control tower at Seething to celebrate their own survival. The pilot, alone among them, volunteered for a further tour of operations. Everybody else went gratefully home.

There sometimes seemed a peculiar bloodlessness about the routine of massed bomber operations in the final months of the war. The fliers tripped their switches 21,000 feet above Germany, and those who had not suffered misfortune or disaster went home to see that night's movie or to head for the huge dance hall in London's Covent Garden that was their favourite rendezvous. Meanwhile, far beneath, flame and death engulfed a chosen tract of Hitler's shrinking empire. "We just wanted to get it over with," shrugged Ira Wells. "If we could bring the end closer by dropping bombs on Germany, that was fine by us. We were kids." It was ironic that the surviving bomber crews went home to their loved ones without ever having seen at close quarters the land upon which they had wreaked such havoc.

FIGHTERS

THERE WERE SIGNIFICANT gradations of pleasure and pain about flying combat operations in different types of aircraft. Both USAAF and RAF fighter pilots pitied their counterparts in the heavy bombers, as a man in a sports car might condescend to a trucker beside him. More than a few fighter pilots actively enjoyed the experience of war, in a fashion denied to most bomber aircrew. Yet, in fighters as in bombers, much hinged upon the luck of a man's assignment. Ground attack was infinitely more hazardous than flying escort missions. In both roles, men continued to die until the very end. In Squadron-Leader Tony Mann's RAF Typhoon wing, two squadron commanders were shot down and killed over Holland in the last week of the war. Not every pilot found fighter operations tolerable. A man who joined the same group as Marvin Bledisloe quit after three missions, because he preferred the humiliation of being stripped of his wings to going on. A few pilots seized upon any mechanical excuse to abort a mission.

Bledisloe had spent almost two years as an instructor in California before being drafted to a P-47 Thunderbolt squadron in England late in 1944. This made him an exceptionally experienced flier, and thus more likely to survive. But as a married thirty-year-old, he came to combat flying with no heroic ideal, merely a determination to fly the 300 operational hours necessary to complete a fighter tour, and get home to his family. He was taught at the outset that the job of an escort fighter was not to pursue Luftwaffe fighters to destruction, but to stick close to the bombers. On Bledisloe's first mission, he was shocked to see one of his group's most experienced pilots blown out of the sky by flak. Luck, as well as skill, played a critical role in survival. The Thunderbolt was a much heavier and stronger aircraft than the Mustang, but also a poorer performer.

The gravest crime for a "fighter jock" over Germany was to hog the radio, sacred for the passage of split-second word about the enemy. One day, a new pilot suddenly burst into a monologue across the airwaves: "Hey, this is Jerry!

My coolant is haywire. The indicator is in the red. What'll I do? This thing is liable to quit on me any minute. Where are we? What'll I do if my engine quits?" "Jerry" faced the rage of the entire group when he got home. In air combat, at collision speeds with enemy aircraft of 700 or 800 m.p.h., seconds were vital. The strain of flying long single-seat missions over Germany told on most men. By autumn, as Bledisloe neared the end of his tour, "my nerves were on edge, I was fidgety, eating little and not getting enough sleep. My butt was killing me from sitting on the hard raft. I was hollow-eyed and weak from the diarrhoea that hit me after every briefing. My weight was down from my normal 160 pounds to 130." Halfway to Germany on his last trip, he was ordered to abort and escort home an aircraft with mechanical failure. He embraced the break. He was simply happy to finish alive. He returned to California after flying seventy missions in 103 days.

Yet Major Jack Ilfrey of the 79th Squadron believed that morale was always higher among the fighter pilots than among their bomber counterparts. Losses were lower, "and we did not have death brought so close. When a fighter was lost, he just failed to come home. But many times crippled bombers returned to base with one or more dead on board, and the men got a first-hand view of death." Ilfrey, a twenty-four-year-old Texan, had an extraordinary and by any standards heroic war. He started out flying P-38 Lightnings in North Africa, then moved to England, committed to four- or five-hour bomber escort missions. In the summer of 1944, he took over command of a squadron deployed on ground support. On 11 June, he bailed out over the German lines after being hit, but successfully evaded capture and rejoined his squadron in nine days. He was temporarily demoted a rank for the riotous celebration which followed.

On 20 November, Ilfrey's wingman Duane Kelso was hit while they were attacking German positions near Maastricht. Kelso set down on a German runway, amid heavy flak. Ilfrey made a split-second decision: "I thought of several instances that my comrades had saved my life." He landed his own Mustang alongside Kelso's crippled aircraft, stopped, jumped down on the wing, threw out his dinghy and parachute, then pushed Kelso into the seat. He climbed in on top of his wingman and gunned the engine for take-off before the astounded Germans could react. With four legs in the cockpit, Ilfrey could not operate the rudder, so crossed his own and let Kelso work the pedals. The other pilot was understandably shaken. "For Christ's sake, Kelso, don't get a hard-on and send me through the canopy!" exclaimed Ilfrey from his lap. They landed safely back in England. A month later, Ilfrey was posted back to the U.S., after flying 142 combat missions.

Most pilots who gazed down from their cockpits upon the battlefields of Germany reckoned that their lot was enviable alongside that of the fighting soldiers far beneath them. "The landscape looked just like Passchendaele," wrote an RAF Typhoon pilot of 197 Squadron, Richard Hough, staring down on the Reichswald early in 1945, "amid the splintered trees and countless shell-holes, the zig-zag of never-ending trenches, the long columns of lorries snaking up towards the front line, the sparkle of guns from the east."

The RAF's Typhoon pilots expected to fly two missions a day of an hour apiece, though in emergency this might extend to four. Most pilots flew a hundred such operations before being relieved, though a flier who was showing the strain could be grounded sooner. Their aircraft normally carried two 500-pound or even 1,000-pound bombs, in addition to their cannon, on a variety of ground-attack missions exotically codenamed Ramrods, Lagoons, Jim Crows, Roadsteads, Rhubarbs. In the last months of the war, "anything that moved on the road was fair game, as only the military had petrol. But sometimes military traffic mixed in with the refugees in their horse-drawn vehicles. I saw open trucks crammed with infantry, with innocent ox-drawn carts in front and behind. Of course we killed civilians—we couldn't help it." Hough, like most pilots, acknowledged that it was much easier to overcome scruples if the consequences of one's own actions were invisible. "You sometimes saw too much with ground strafing. At the same time, with the hunter's instinct, the heart lifted with excitement at the sight of a target below, and the hunter's blood ran faster as you pushed down the stick, opened the throttle wide, made a quick intercept calculation, switched on the sight and slipped the shield from the gun button." Every ground strafer hated flak gunners as personal enemies, and would take extraordinary risks to get in a shot at them after bombing a target.

An age ago, in the innocent days of 1940, a British fighter pilot in France was appalled to see the Luftwaffe's "knights of the air" machine-gun refugees on the roads. "They *are* shits after all," Paul Richey observed in shocked dismay in his officers' mess. Yet by 1945 few of the leaders of the American and British air forces found anything to trouble them in their orders for Operation Clarion, an assault on German communications links which was unleashed on 22 February. Clarion was allegedly designed to inflict a massive blow on the remaining German transport net, by striking with 9,000 American and British bombers and fighters across the widest possible area. The bombers, as usual, were deployed against railroads and bridges, but their attacks also covered many small towns. All those concerned with Clarion's planning recognized that, whatever the targeting pretext, its real purpose was explicitly terroristic—to demonstrate the power of the Allies to strike at will into every corner of the Reich. General Ira Eaker of Eighth Air Force expressed concern that Clarion would demonstrate to the Germans "that we are the barbarians they say we are, for it would be perfectly obvious to them that this is primarily a large-scale attack on civilians, as, in fact, it of course will be." General Charles Cabell, an adviser to General Arnold, scribbled bitterly on a copy of the Clarion proposal: "This is the same old baby-killing plan of the get-rich-quick psychological boys, dressed up in a new kimono." Clarion went ahead anyway. Allied fighters were committed to attacking road movements of every kind. "CLARION hit people who had never been bombed before," notes a German historian. "The psychological effect was very great." The civilian casualties inflicted by the operation were never documented, but certainly ran into thousands. For the rest of the war, Allied pilots attacked German civilians with growing promiscuity. Who could blame them, after the lead Clarion had given them from the top?

The Allied fighter-bomber pilots, like those of the Luftwaffe in 1940, were very young men. Few denied the adrenaline rush that often transcended the terrors of operational flying: "I could see the cannon strikes dancing along the road like a hysterically fast fuse racing to its point of detonation," wrote Richard Hough. "The car was packed with passengers—there must have been five or six inside, and not one with the sense to keep a look-out through the window. My glimpse of them, alive, intact, perhaps talking together and smoking, was one frame from a film, flickering like the Odessa Steps sequence from Eisenstein's *Potemkin*. The next frame, as the full weight of my shells tore in, was all blood and fire." In the spring of 1945, even in rural Saxony German civilians became reluctant to go shopping because of the danger of being strafed by passing fighter-bombers. They learned to throw themselves flat on the ground whenever aircraft approached. It was so easy for a bored young man to touch his gun-button, to relieve the monotony of a patrol. "We sometimes thought the Allied pilots were playing a game with us," said fifteen-year-old Helmut Lott, who grew weary of ditching his bike and running for the nearest cover as soon as a Jabo peeled off into a dive.

During a firing pass at 600 m.p.h. in the dive, wrote Lieutenant Jack Pitts of the 371st Fighter Group, "you feel as if you are flying the guns, not the plane. You see where the bullets are hitting, and make minor adjustments with the controls to 'walk the stream of bullets' onto the target." Pitts's Thunderbolt squadron sometimes flew three missions a day from their French bases, spending perhaps thirty minutes each time over enemy lines. On 19 December, he and his squadron were looking for "targets of opportunity" across the Rhine. He fired some 2,400 rounds of ammunition and wrote in his diary: "I really did enjoy this mission. I probably killed a lot of German civilians. Tough luck. *C'est la guerre*." Afterwards he recalled:

I was barely 22, probably still quite immature, and didn't take much of anything seriously except when I was flying... It *was* fun. Most small boys like to tear things up; the most fun with toys was not in building a windmill, but in knocking it down. Well, we had graduated from being small boys into being big boys, but we still liked destroying things, especially since that was what we were expected to do. It was great fun watching a locomotive blow up, or seeing a truckload of ammunition explode, with parts of the truck flying through the air.

Pitts's squadron suffered few casualties. He experienced little fear, even when engaged by the Germans' shrinking force of Focke-Wulfs. He felt: "This is what I was trained for; I'm better than they are, my plane is better than theirs; let's get it on!" Sometimes, he sang to himself in the cockpit:

> *It may be in the valley, where countless dangers hide,*
> *It may be in the sunshine, that I in peace abide*
> *...If Jesus is with me, I'll go anywhere!*

The RAF's Squadron-Leader Tony Mann, a Typhoon reconnaissance pilot, even found it in his heart to pity the plight of the Luftwaffe in those last months: "I felt sorry for the German air force because they were let down by their commanders and their industry. When the dreaded Hun just stopped turning up, you began to wonder if they were frightened or something. It was only afterwards that we realized they simply couldn't do it."

The recklessness of some aircrew persisted on the ground. Jack Pitts and his fellow pilots used aviation fuel for almost every purpose, including cleaning clothes. Once, the gasoline stove in the house in which they were billeted exploded, killing one pilot and severely burning several others. The house burned down. Towards the end, however, even frankly callous young fliers began to feel spasms of pity for the beaten enemy, just as Tony Mann did. "There were four men unloading some stuff from the back of a caisson," Jack Pitts wrote in his diary on 18 March 1945. "They evidently heard me just before I fired, because they all turned round, and I could practically see a look of surprise. I squeezed the trigger and these four just seemed to melt away. The caisson burned and the horses dropped... All in all, I got one truck, 14 horses and six Germans. It's almost sickening because these poor devils don't have a chance. Oh well, they started it."

Bradley's aide Chester Hansen recorded a conversation among America's top soldiers in which his chief suggested:

> that it would be good to fight the Germans all the way to Berlin, to teach them the lesson of death or destruction they have carried to the world. Everyone is in hearty assent. I suggested to Bull [G-3 at SHAEF] that we bomb each town in our path, but "Pinky" protested that this was not our way of waging war. Patton promptly declared that if it was necessary to have military objectives to bomb, he would declare every switchboard in

every town a military objective. The need for harsh treatment of Germany is now more apparent than ever.

TARGETS

MOST OF THE citizens of the Third Reich, great and small, cherished a sense of outrage about the Allied air assault. Guderian used the opportunity of a radio broadcast to deliver what he called "an appeal to the chivalry of our adversaries. I referred to the Anglo-American air terror. I regret to say that this desperate plea of mine was without success. Humanity and chivalry had both disappeared during those months." Even those Germans who possessed no love for Hitler, and yearned for an end of the war, felt deep bitterness towards the Allied air forces. Lieutenant Helmut Schmidt, a post-war chancellor of Germany, witnessed the destruction of Hamburg. "The sky became black, the sun disappeared. The worst thing was the stench—like being in the kitchen of McDonalds... a smell of beef... but the beef was people." Schmidt lost his parents, grandparents, parents-in-law and home to Allied bombing. "It was wholly unjustified, indeed it was inexcusable," he said passionately, long afterwards.

Few Germans ever acknowledged the legitimacy of the role in which the Allies cast them, shareholders in a monstrous evil which placed them beyond the pale of civilization and the right to mercy. Instead, most of those on the ground perceived themselves as victims of a great injustice. They were oblivious of concentration camps and murdered millions. They saw only their own law-abiding, hard-working, civilized communities reduced to rubble by Germany's boundlessly vengeful foes. In 1944–45 air attack and its consequences became the dominant realities of most Germans' lives. "It was a war of despair and mounting torments," wrote Paul von Stemann, the Danish correspondent in Berlin. "There were no signs that the bombings would lead to a collapse. It was incomprehensible how people struggled on... but there did not seem to be a breaking point. It was the great fallacy of the war, that civilians could be brought to succumb by conventional bombing."

"I'll describe to you today how our home town looks," a Heuchelheim woman wrote in misery to her husband at the front.

The middle of Ludwigshaven is flat, and Ludwigstrasse a heap of ruins, only the *Bürgerhaus* is standing. Bismarck street is almost burnt out. Schiller, See Krak and Neidermann completely gone. Ludwig arrived on leave in the morning, and had the most terrifying experience that night: incendiaries on the house. He put them out, but all around is a ruin... he got terrible burns on his left hand. One horror follows another. Last week, Frankenthal and Opal Oppau got it. Mannheim and Ludwigshaven are dying cities. Helene Kruck can't take it any more, she simply can't...she hasn't got even a bed, so I'm taking her in here so she can at least rest at night. Each successive attack is more terrible than the last. Horror and fear run through every street.

Frau Rothmeier of Idstein wrote to her husband: "We spend most of our lives in the shelters. Our little girl sleeps for 15 minutes, and then I have to get her up again...At noon today it was especially bad. Squadron after squadron of bombers were followed by fighters which fired on people and houses. They fly so low you can almost touch them."

On 1 December 1944, Private Heinz Trammler went home on leave. "At 4 o'clock, I arrived in Hamburg," he wrote in his diary.

> At 5:30, I was standing in the ruins of my house. My heart stood still. It was here that I lived with my wife and children in peace and comfort. Who is to blame for all this? The English? The Americans? Or the Nazis? Had a Hitler not come, there would have been no war. If the Nazis had not talked so big, or put on such a show, or done so much sabre-rattling, we would have peace with those who are our enemies today. Had we retained democracy in Germany, we would still be in accord with England and the United States. It was with those thoughts that I stood before my ruined home.

Few Germans thought as clearly as Private Trammler, but his uncommonly penitent reflections availed him nothing. The diary was found on his corpse by American troops advancing near Hennamont on 13 January 1945.

Dr. Marcus Scaff-Howie was shocked to find villagers near his Bavarian home raking through the debris of a crashed Liberator, searching the pockets of the dead crew for cigarettes and chocolate. "It seemed monstrous that even these decent country folk had lost their reverence for death," he wrote in his diary. The British Joint Intelligence Committee agreed. Its members suggested in a report composed in the autumn of 1944 that the emotional reactions of the German people had been dulled by the innumerable horrors they were experiencing:

> Everyone is convinced that no opposition could prevent the tragedy of the German people taking its fatal course...even bombing does not seem to have any influence on people's morale. It is accepted as an inevitable fate. Nevertheless, there is much more interest in bombing than in events on the fields of battle, not because bombing is expected to hasten the end of the war, but because it directly affects the personal life of the individual. The main question for every German today is: "Shall I be bombed?"

"We discussed why the Germans carried on," wrote Paul von Stemann.

Our answers were all inadequate. We said it was because they were apa-
thetic, because they were tired, because they had no civic courage or initiative. They were mentally exhausted, and did not have the strength to
end the war. When I came home to Denmark I was asked how the feeling
was in Berlin. The answer was that there was no public feeling one way or
the other. There was no reaction to be observed to the great events of the
war. When the army tried to get rid of Hitler and did not succeed, there
was no more reaction than if they had been told that the moon was not
made of green cheese. It was all now beyond them.

The Berlin diarist "Missie" Vassiltchikov remarked upon the paradox that
daylight bomber attacks mesmerized people by their terrible beauty as well as
by the horrors they inflicted. When civilians were not in the shelters, they
watched the perfect formations of glittering aircraft parade across the sky,
inscribing signatures in condensation trails, their bombs often clearly visible as
they fell.

The black-out was a dominant reality. "We lived in a dark world," said Klaus
Fischer, who lived in Jena in central Germany. "Even in the daylight hours you
couldn't see where you were going in the street cars with their windows painted
black. At night you sometimes saw people in the street trying to read newspapers by moonlight." The first alarm sounded when enemy aircraft were 120
miles away—perhaps forty minutes' flying time. As soon as the sirens were
heard, people knew that it was time to turn on the radio, fill the bath with water,
turn off the gas. Families checked that luggage, thermoses, torches and gas
masks were ready in the hall, and dressed children. In cinemas, a big V appeared
on the screen. A second alarm sounded when raiders were much closer. The
words *Flieger Alarme* appeared on cinema screens. The big feature stopped until
the all-clear sounded. It was time to descend to the shelters, there to sit reading
uneasily, listening in silence to the dull thunder above, or chatting in tense,
muted tones to relations and neighbours. In Hamburg, Mathilde Wolff-
Monckeberg recorded in February 1945 that she and her fellow citizens had
suffered five early warnings and three proper alarms in a single day and night
"during this period of vast, general distress, of certain extinction."

Although Germany's armament production figures continued to rise
through much of 1944, these would undoubtedly have been very much higher
but for the effects of bombing on both plant and the workforce. In 1944, the Ford
plant in Cologne reported 25 per cent absenteeism, and BMW in Munich 20 per
cent. Such figures represented severe disruption of shift patterns and orderly
working. Anyone who said that he was not frightened of being bombed was a liar
or a fool. There was a glass-blower in Jena who always refused to go down to

shelters when there a raid: "Either it gets you or it doesn't," the man shrugged fatalistically. "It" finally got him, like so many other people, in March 1945. Fires often burned for days, because there were too few engines to address the hundreds of conflagrations started by a big attack.

It would be mistaken to suppose that air-raid shelters represented havens of security. Many thousands of people asphyxiated in their subterranean gloom. Amid the fires created by a heavy attack, intense heat killed. Sometimes burst boilers or water mains drowned or cooked underground fugitives. During every attack, scenes of terror were played out among those seeking sanctuary. Twelve-year-old Vilda Geertz, in Hamburg, like many children treated the first raids as a game. But, as the attacks intensified, she saw the naked panic in the streets when alerts sounded, the tearful adults, people fighting each other to get through the doors into the shelters. Once inside, when the bombs began to fall, the whole world seemed to shake. Almost everyone suffered in some degree from claustrophobia. "I came to live in a fantasy world, in my books, because reality was so terrible."

Frau Husle of Cologne wrote to her husband, a corporal in Model's army, "The streetcars don't run, the Neumarkt looks as if it had been ploughed. We have no water or electricity and very little gas. Candlelight may be romantic at Christmas, or if two people are together, but when I am so lonely it makes me very unhappy. My nerves are completely finished. One day you will see me again, but it is better not to think about it. If my hair has turned white it won't matter—or will it???" Early in the air war, the authorities urged city-dwellers to send a trunk of clothes and possessions to some friend or relation in a less vulnerable area. That way, if their house was destroyed, they could retain some of the bare necessities of life. When Joyce Kuhns fled westward from Breslau with her three small children in January 1945, after many adventures she arrived at last on the doorstep of a friend in Halle. With the help of the caretaker, she gratefully dragged from the cellar a trunk of clothes she had sent there months before. Next night there was an air raid. When she and her children returned from the shelter, the house and the trunk had disappeared. Only the body of the caretaker remained.

When Allied aircrews saw black puffs of flak pockmarking the sky around them, they felt fear and often animosity towards the gunners beneath. Yet most of the crews of those hated flak guns were teenagers, too young to have been allowed to fly. Hans Moser was the sixteen-year-old son of a government official from Nuremberg, manning a 105mm gun named Bertha at a synthetic-oil plant in Upper Silesia. Between attacks, he and his comrades were expected to continue with homework, and even to attend some school classes in the battery huts. The teenage gunners were supposed to receive an allowance of a pint of milk a day to build their strength, though this never reached them. Moser, who was nicknamed "Moses," walked to church every Sunday with a friend named

Georg, who intended himself for the priesthood after the war. They sat in the pews among a congregation of sturdy local peasants. "We were so young that we didn't think very deeply about things," said Moser. "We simply accepted that this was how life was."

In their chilly barracks after hours, girls played no part in their thoughts. They talked about schoolwork, played chess and read Karl May Western novels. They slept a lot and nursed their hunger, because they were at an age when boys are always hungry. Most of the time, their greatest enemy was boredom. Perhaps every three weeks, there was a raid. As they stood to their guns, there was a long, tense period of expectation. The smoke generators masking the oil plant began to pour forth steep columns of oily fumes, designed to confuse the enemy's bomb-aimers. The unit doctor told the boys sternly that they should try to empty their bowels before an attack, because it would thus be easier to treat them if their intestines were pierced by shrapnel. When a raid began, as the gunners sweated to load and fire Bertha, they gazed up at the huge silver formations, resenting what they saw as the arrogant security of the crews, so confident of dumping their loads of terror and returning home for supper.

The gun crews cheered uproariously when they saw a plane suddenly bleed black smoke and plunge downwards. Once, an American flier fell beside their battery on his parachute. He had lost a leg, but remained conscious. The boys crowded curiously around him, and were amazed to hear him address them in fluent German. His name was Richard Radlinger. "Why do you come here attacking us?" the gunners demanded. The airman replied easily: "We'll all have a beer together after the war." Then he was taken away to a military hospital. After every raid, the oil plant looked a mess of wreckage and tangled steel. The gunners were amazed that within two or three days it always seemed able to resume production.

Throughout the air war, there were many cases of Germans wreaking summary vengeance upon shot-down airmen. When Richard Burt, a Liberator gunner from Utah, was being escorted through Vienna after being shot down, an elderly civilian began to curse him and belabour him with his umbrella. Burt's guard restrained him. As Carl Fyler was taken to Bremen rail station after parachuting from his B-17, civilians shouted at him: "*Terrorflieger! Schweinhund!* Chicago gangster!" Sometimes, German bitterness had much deadlier consequences. Lieutenant Henry Docherty, co-pilot of a B-17, was badly beaten up in front of the mayor of Spandau. Docherty reported seeing four RAF fliers hung from telegraph poles. A Nazi SA man drove up to a house where a British airman was being held and asked: "Where is the pig?" The flier was lying on the floor, his face bleeding. The SA man shot him in the stomach, and told one of the guards to finish him off, which the man did.

On 28 February 1945, two Spitfires hit by flak crash-landed almost beside each other north of the village of Bohmte. The pilots, Flight-Lieutenant Taylor and Sergeant Cuthbertson, were uninjured. They were taken under guard to the local inn. Soon afterwards Norbert Mueller and Fritz Buchning, two Nazi SA officials, arrived. They demanded to see the prisoners. Buchning delivered a raving harangue about "murderers of innocent women and children." The fliers were then marched into a nearby wood and shot. The SA said they were acting in obedience to an order issued on 26 February by the local kreisleiter, that all pilots of strafing aircraft were to be executed. Interrogated later, one of the firing squad said: "I was of the opinion that the Orstgruppenleiter was acting correctly, because I knew of the order." Many other such incidents are recorded in war-crimes investigations files. Aircrew who found themselves confined in prison camps may have suffered privations, but in the hysterical atmosphere of Germany under bombardment in early 1945 they could think themselves fortunate to survive.

It was ironic, of course, that in the last stage of the war many PoWs themselves died in air attacks. Large numbers of Polish prisoners were killed during an RAF raid on Lübeck. Next morning, those who survived found themselves the objects of intense local bitterness: "An angry crowd of civilians gathered outside the camp shouting abuse at us," wrote Piotr Tareczynski, a Polish gunner officer in captivity since 5 September 1939. "Rightly or wrongly, they blamed us for their misfortunes. Some of the crowd carried staves. That was the only time we were glad to have barbed wire around us." Cloud obscured Coblenz during a raid against the city on the night of 22 December 1944. The RAF's markers drifted towards Stalag XIIA, twenty-five miles eastwards. Several PoW medical personnel were killed by stray bombs, along with civilians in the neighbouring village of Diez. Bud Lindsey, a nineteen-year-old Texan, was disgusted to find himself strafed by a U.S. Thunderbolt as he was led to the rear after being captured in the Vosges Mountains in November 1944. He had stumbled into the German lines while collecting platoon reports days after he joined the 100th Infantry Division, without ever having fired a shot in anger. The American fighter caught his group of prisoners a few hundred yards behind the front, bullet strikes throwing sparks from a nearby house: "I don't know why the pilot suddenly decided to fire on a small group of men of which five were American PoWs," wrote Lindsey bitterly. "...Perhaps it had been a dull day for him."

In the aftermath of a big raid, prisoners of war and slave labourers could often be seen in the cities manning rescue equipment, pumping air into ruins where survivors were believed to be trapped in rubble. Every city-dwelling German became accustomed to walking to work through streets on which glass from uncountable shattered windows scrunched underfoot at every step. Ruined buildings bore chalked inscriptions, guiding friends and relations to the new abodes of survivors. Half of Europe, in those days, seemed to be searching for lost loved ones. Some were only temporarily mislaid. Others were gone for ever. And there was worse, far worse, to come.

After a USAAF raid on Berlin on 3 February 1945 local rumour alleged that 15,000 people had died, though the real total was much smaller. Paul von Stemann wrote: "That everything was dissolving in confusion became clear to me as I walked unchallenged through the battered buildings of the Foreign Office. They had been hit by a big stick of bombs, and all the doors were open, so that I could stroll freely through the offices. Documents, papers, books lay about the floor covered with chalk, rubble, broken glass and ink running from shattered bottles. Among the crowd was von Ribbentrop himself, spruce as a cadet in his fine uniform, but with bewilderment in his face." For some weeks, the winter snows had rendered Berlin's miles of ruins wonderfully picturesque. Now, instead, amid the February thaw they looked grey and wretched. People tramped through streets thick with mud created by rain falling upon ubiquitous dust and rubble.

Von Stemann sometimes drove the 120 miles from Berlin to Dresden, to experience the blissful tranquillity of that city after the relentless air raids in the capital. Installed at Dresden's Bellevue Hotel, "all around us was the manmade beauty we were starving for," he wrote, "August the Strong's castle, the Zwinger, the baroque Hofkirch, the museums with their huge collections of china, ivory, sculpture and paintings, and further behind the Alt Stadt with its winding streets and many antique shops well stocked and eager to make a sale."

Gotz Bergander, a young Dresdener, had been twelve when the war began. In the early years, his father returned laden with luxuries from duty with a Luftwaffe flak unit in France. The boy quizzed him eagerly about how many British planes he had shot down. In 1941, Gotz was surprised to see his mother burst into tears when the invasion of Russia was announced on the radio, yet his favourite pastime remained the depiction of lurid battle scenes in his sketchbook. At school, he and his classmates regarded air-raid drill as a game. They lit balls of paper to simulate falling incendiaries, and practised extinguishing them. They gazed at pictures of bombed cities. Until 1945, however, Dresden was a distant and low-priority target for Allied aircraft. "I had a lot of imagination, but not enough to conceive what air attack might mean for us." When Bergander himself was drafted to join a local flak-gun crew, his romantic illusions about war were swiftly shattered. The work was hard, the routine relentlessly boring. A few mis-aimed bombs occasionally fell on Dresden, but the guns seldom fired. One cold, clear night, they saw the distant glow of Leipzig burning. But local opinion held that Dresden's great cultural heritage rendered it immune from Allied devastation. As the front came closer, and defeat loomed, another rumour held that their city was designated for preservation, to serve as the Allied occupation capital.

Bergander's father Emil had been released from his flak unit to run the well-known Bramsch company, manufacturing yeast and schnapps at a distillery close to their home. When the teenager was sketching in his room and heard a radio warning of an air raid, he would hang a towel out of the window, as a signal to his father to halt production in the works. They preferred to do this at the last possible moment, because the yeast spoilt if the plant was shut down. In the late afternoon of 13 February 1945, the boy spent some time with his mother at Dresden station, watching the great throng of soldiers, travellers and refugees. They took the streetcar home at 9 p.m. Soon after they reached their house, which stood in the inner suburbs, there was an alarm. The building was owned by his father's company, which had its offices on the ground floor. The managing director had ordered the cellar specially strengthened as a shelter with steel shutters, rubber seals and a telephone line. The family descended into its safety, and sat there through the storm of concussions which followed. Only twenty-five minutes after the raid began, the planes departed. The Berganders emerged into the darkness to find that no bombs had fallen near by, but a great pink glow suffused the sky above the city. Gotz climbed on to the factory roof, and used sand to extinguish a few incendiaries which had fallen there. The largest local landmark was a big cigarette factory, domed like a mosque, and surmounted by minarets. Everything upon the horizon as far as its gates was burning. Gotz marvelled at the beauty of the flames, reflected in the yellow glass of the dome. He was awed, and afraid. This first attack had been carried out by 244 Lancasters of the RAF's 5 Group, which had dropped more than 800 tons of bombs.

Even at a safe distance from the vast conflagration engulfing the city, the teenager felt its heat. He descended again to the street, and saw the first trickle of terrified fugitives approaching. "Everything is burning!" they cried. Their coats were covered with ash, and many were coughing violently from smoke inhalation. Some carried bags laden with a few possessions. A small, stunned crowd gathered in front of the Bergander house, discussing the nightmare. Suddenly somebody shouted: "Alarm again!" They looked at each other in disbelief. "Impossible!" said a man. The teenager shouted fiercely at the sky: "Criminals!" It seemed so utterly unjust. They retired to their cellar again, listening in terror to explosions which seemed much heavier and closer than during the earlier wave of bombing. So they were. Five hundred and twenty-nine RAF Lancasters delivered more than 1,800 tons of bombs with deadly accuracy. Just six were lost. The impact upon Dresden was catastrophic.

After forty minutes, the attack stopped. The Berganders emerged from the shelter to find that their own house and factory were almost the only buildings in the area which survived undamaged. When the boy went back on to the roof, he descended to tell his parents that he could see only a white wall of flame. Sporadic explosions persisted, from delayed-action bombs. The lower part of their own street was burning. The crowd of fugitives was swelling constantly. At last, Gotz Bergander tired of the awful spectacle, and sank exhausted into sleep.

Next morning, the residents of Dresden stumbled out into the streets, to behold the utter devastation of their city. Victor Klemperer, a sixty-three-year-old Jewish academic, yearned as much as any man in Europe for the defeat of the Nazis, yet he was appalled by what he now saw before him:

We walked slowly, for I was now carrying both bags, and my limbs hurt...Above us, building after building was a burnt-out ruin. Down here by the river, where many people were moving along or resting on the ground, masses of the empty, rectangular cases of the stick incendiary bombs stuck out of the churned-up earth. Fires were still burning in many of the buildings...At times, small and no more than a bundle of clothes, the dead were scattered across our path. The skull of one had been torn away, the top of the head was a dark red bowl. Once an arm lay there with a pale, quite fine hand, like a model made of wax such as one sees in barber's shop windows. Some people...pushed handcarts with bedding and the like, or sat on boxes and bundles. Crowds streamed unceasingly between these islands, past the corpses and smashed vehicles, up and down the Elbe, a silent, agitated procession.

Another Jewish family in Dresden made a special pilgrimage that terrible day: to satisfy themselves that the Gestapo headquarters had gone. "It was terrible, the bodies, the city burning," said Henni Brenner; "...but from a distance we saw that it [too] was burning. Well, then, we felt some satisfaction." Klemperer's own home was destroyed. He and his wife cut the yellow stars from their clothes, because they knew that only as Aryans did they have any chance of securing food, shelter, mercy. When they heard the distant sound of aircraft once more, and threw themselves to the ground amid renewed explosions and rubble dust trickling over their heads, Klemperer thought fervently: "Just don't get killed now!"

As Gotz Bergander ventured down to the street, he met a throng of people from the city begging for water—the factory had its own supply. Bizarrely, a worker arrived on his bicycle. "Why have you come?" asked the boy. "I wanted to see if the old place was still standing," said the man, one of their most conscientious workers, in his strong Saxon accent. They were all emotionally exhausted: "We could not grasp what had happened to us. I felt no hatred for the airmen, but a great anger. I felt they were cowards. Why didn't they face us man to man?"

When the sirens sounded again, they looked blankly at each other. Somebody said: "But there's nothing left to bomb." Almost a hundred people, most of them hysterical, crowded into their shelter at the same time as Victor Klemperer lay hugging his fear in the street. Three hundred and eleven USAAF Fortresses had come to complete what the RAF's Lancasters had begun, delivering a further 771 tons of bombs on Dresden. The Berganders heard the first sticks falling, very close. It felt as if they were standing under a railway bridge as a train thundered overhead. All the lights went out. Torches revealed a thick cloud of white dust choking the air of the cellar. A sudden shock of blast drove the breath from their lungs for a moment. They were too stunned even to cry out. The Bergander family threw themselves on the floor. They were exceptionally fortunate in the strength of their shelter. A stick of 500-pound bombs had landed within yards of the house. Somehow, both the building itself and the neighbouring factory survived almost unscathed, save for the loss of every pane of glass and most of the roof tiles.

They came out to find the strong west wind fanning flames through almost every surrounding building. The Berganders ran among the buildings, dousing with wet blankets burning fragments of debris that had drifted through the air before falling to the ground. They thanked their good fortune, in having saved not only their lives and possessions but also a store of potatoes which alone fed them through the days that followed. They began carrying water to the neighbouring hospital, which had none. They laboured to restore power to the factory, while giving such help as they could to the tide of refugees. Gotz Bergander possessed a camera. He photographed everything that he could see, for posterity. His father was furious: "Why waste your time? Besides, it's forbidden!" In the weeks that followed, they had little time to talk to each other or even think about what had happened. They were simply engaged in a struggle for survival. His mother suffered a heart attack. She was just forty-four.

In a single night and day, Dresden had suffered devastation more comprehensive than any other great urban centre of Germany save Hamburg and Berlin. At least 35,000 of its people had died. By a characteristic irony, the city's railway links, pretext for the Allied bombardment, were relatively unscathed. Trains were again running through the city within a few days. "The bombing of Dresden was an extravagance," observed Bergander almost sixty years later, with the detachment of an historian, most unusual among Germans of his generation.

> Even in war, the ends must relate to the means. Here, the means seemed wildly out of proportion to the ends. I will not say that Dresden should not have been bombed—it was a rail centre, and thus an important target. I will not say Dresden was an exceptional case as compared to other German cities. But I do not understand why it had to be done on such a huge scale. The only answer, I suppose, is that the Allied policy of bombing had developed a dynamic of its own.

Enormous scholarly effort has been expended since 1945 upon exploring the Allies' motives for destroying Dresden. Many researchers, especially Germans, find it hard to comprehend that, in the minds of the Allied planners, the city possessed no special significance. It was merely one among a dozen undamaged urban areas which had been listed for months on Sir Arthur Harris's target board at High Wycombe—his notorious schedule of unfinished business in Germany. The demolition of itemized cities was essential to the fulfilment of his vision for the triumph of air power. Harris was specifically encouraged to address targets in eastern Germany by Churchill, on the eve of the Yalta conference. The prime minister was eager to demonstrate to the Russians the power of the Allied air forces. Freak meteorological conditions created in Dresden a firestorm—a wall of flame driven by fierce wind—of a kind which Bomber Command aspired to create every night of its offensive, but only three times accomplished: at Hamburg in 1943, Darmstadt in 1944 and Dresden in 1945.

When researching the bomber offensive a quarter of a century ago, the author chanced upon, and revealed for the first time, the RAF's briefing notes to its squadrons which attacked Dresden. "In the midst of winter," these read in part,

> with refugees pouring westwards and troops to be rested, roofs are at a premium...Dresden has developed into an industrial city of first-class importance...its multiplicity of telephones and rail facilities is of major value for controlling the defence of that part of the front now threatened by Marshal Konev's offensive...The intentions of the attack are to hit the enemy where he will feel it most, behind an already partially collapsed front...and incidentally to show the Russians when they arrive what Bomber Command can do.

The banality of this document accurately reflects the almost casual spirit in which the assault on Dresden was mounted. Great horrors in war are not always, or even often, the product of commensurate reflection by those who unleash them. Churchill himself regretted the destruction of Dresden after it had taken place, when the cultural implications were drawn to his attention. But amid the relentless pressures of prosecuting a war, to the prime minister as much as to Harris, Dresden seemed merely a placename on a map until the attack took place. Afterwards, of course, it was scarcely even that.

"This misery has got to stop," Luftwaffe Unteroffizier Erich Schudak wrote in anguish in his diary after an air raid on 5 March. "What has become of our beautiful Germany?" Yet Schudak could not bring himself to accept that there was only one fashion in which "this misery" would end. On 18 March, he wrote: "Most of the squadron is convinced we have lost the war. To that, I can only say: 'What weaklings!' I know things don't look bright and are getting desperate, but I'm sure we could turn the situation around." Sir Arthur Harris might have said that, as long as such a spirit persisted among Germany's defenders, his assault upon Germany's people had to continue. And so indeed it did.

Henry Kissinger, perhaps surprisingly given his own Jewish background and subsequent political history, is among those who believes today that the area bombing of Germany was wrong: "Yet when a nation had tolerated the murder of so many people, they did not seem to deserve much sympathy." This point will continue to be argued, with special passion among the people of Germany, through generations yet unborn.

The bombing of the cities and industrial centres of the Reich continued to the very end, destroying some targets useful to the Nazi war effort, and many that were not. On Monday 12 March 1945, a massive USAAF raid on Vienna destroyed its great Opera House. Some 160,000 costumes, together with sets for 120 productions, were consumed in the pyre. Two hundred and seventy people died merely in the cellar of the Jockey Club, which received a direct hit. It took rescuers a fortnight to burrow through the rubble and recover the bodies. "The smell is nauseating and clings to one's nostrils for days," wrote "Missie" Vassiltchikov, who had left Berlin to work in a Viennese hospital. The last performance to be staged at the Opera House was that of Wagner's *Götterdämmerung*.

CHAPTER TWELVE

Marching on the Rhine

ROADS TO THE RIVER

IT WAS LATE January 1945 before the Americans and British were done with the Bulge battle, and ready to address operations of their own creation. Hitler's offensive and its aftermath had already imposed six weeks' delay upon the advance into Germany. Long before the Ardennes actions were over, however, Montgomery was once more urging upon Eisenhower the case for a concentrated punch at the Ruhr from the north, by his own 21st Army Group with Simpson's Ninth U.S. Army under command. Bradley was disgusted. At a conference at SHAEF on 31 January, he told Eisenhower that since the Ardennes offensive and the publicity Montgomery had generated, "friendly and intimate co-operation between him and the Field-Marshal was out of the question. He stressed strongly the political importance in the United States of giving the big thrust to an American commander. At present his troops, and to some extent their families, were either indignantly loyal to him, or had had their confidence in the leadership severely shaken. Neither reaction, he said, was healthy."

Russell Weigley has observed that, while Eisenhower never wholeheartedly committed himself to Montgomery's cherished northern axis, he showed himself far more sympathetic towards it than the British commander allowed or than American generals thought reasonable. "If the field-marshal had not been too deficient in understanding and tolerance towards Ike to recognize this fact, he might have been able to exploit it to his advantage." In the aftermath of the Bulge, Eisenhower accepted that Montgomery should be given the chance to make a big push. To Bradley's fury, he agreed to place Ninth Army under British command until the Rhine was crossed. But he insisted that Montgomery's offensive should be delayed until the second week of February, to give Bradley's 12th Army Group the opportunity to recover ground in the Ardennes before the British moved.

Montgomery chafed at this. On the old Bulge battlefield, where First Army stood, the Germans were no longer in any position to go anywhere except backwards. "So far as I can see," Montgomery wrote contemptuously to Brooke on 22 January, "the Ardennes battle is being continued for the sole reason of keeping Bradley employed offensively...I am not consulted in any way about plans for centre or south, or about plans for the front as a whole, and I have no idea what is the long-term plan... The real trouble is that there is no control and the three Army Groups are each intent on their own affairs." The British Chiefs of Staff supported Montgomery's view that Eisenhower's armies possessed supplies sufficient only for one immediate big push, which should take place in 21st Army Group's sector, on the Dutch–German border. In the spring of 1945, shortfalls in supply were still causing immense difficulties. Each month from December 1944 onwards, discharges from all the ports in Allied hands fell short of estimated capacity by 15 to 20 per cent. The British argued once more for giving priority to the northern axis.

At the Malta meeting of the Combined Chiefs of Staff which preceded the Yalta conference at the end of January, this issue caused some of the most bitter arguments of the war. It provoked Marshall to threaten resignation if the British did not fall into line with Eisenhower. America's chief soldier "lit out so vigorously that he carried everything before him," wrote Stimson admiringly. Men great and small were growing weary and fractious after years of war. The Americans' patience with their allies was wearing thin. Strategy and national pride apart, Montgomery's personal behaviour in the wake of the Bulge had been so outrageous that there was no possibility his aspirations would be heeded. There were now three Americans in north-west Europe for every British soldier. U.S. predominance was increasing daily. It is no exaggeration to say that, after the Ardennes battle, the Americans scorned Montgomery and anything he proposed. Malta gave Marshall the opportunity "to express his full dislike and antipathy to Montgomery." The public courtesies of the alliance were maintained, but privately Eisenhower and his colleagues had had enough of 21st Army Group's commander, and of British pretensions.

The British delegation at Malta understood this, even if it was gall and wormwood to them. "An unsatisfactory meeting with the Americans which led us nowhere and resulted in the most washy conclusions," Brooke wrote after the war. "I did not approve of Ike's appreciation and plans, yet through force of circumstance I had to accept them...we were dealing with a force that was predominantly American, and it was therefore natural that they should wish to have the major share in its handling. In addition there was the fact that Marshall clearly understood nothing of strategy." Churchill advanced an impulsive proposal that his favourite general, Alexander, vastly better than Montgomery at rubbing along with the Americans, might replace Tedder as deputy Supreme Commander. The prime minister cherished a delusion that Alexander would put more spine into the direction of the ground campaign. This seemed unlikely, given Alexander's notorious indolence. Posterity owes a debt to the American Chiefs of Staff for squashing such a folly. Unsatisfactory as might be the existing command structure, with its poisoned relationship between Montgomery and the Americans, it would now persist unchanged until the end.

The great captains of history have always been conscious of what the enemy might do, but they have focused chiefly upon their own intentions. It is one of the strangest aspects of the north-west Europe campaign that, even as Hitler's armies sank to their knees, they retained psychological dominance on the battlefield. The most baleful consequence of the Bulge was that it reinforced Eisenhower's fears about German counter-threats. "We must make certain," he told Montgomery on 17 January, "that he [the German] is not free, behind a strong defensive line, to organize sudden powerful thrusts into our lines of communication. As I see it, we simply cannot afford the large defensive forces that would be necessary if we allow the German to hold great bastions sticking into our lines at the same time that we try to invade his country." In other words, Eisenhower intended his armies to continue a cautious broad-front advance to the Rhine.

In the early years of the war, the German army conducted offensives of stunning daring: against the British and French in 1940; against the British and later the Americans in the North African desert; against the Russians in 1941 and 1942. German generals felt able to expose their flanks with impunity, because they faced adversaries who lacked the skill and imagination to exploit opportunities. On the Eastern Front, the Wehrmacht was forced to change its attitude after Stalingrad and other dramatic envelopments showed how well the Russians had learned their lesson. In the west, however, the Germans were able to withdraw at their own speed from the Bulge, because the Allies made no attempt to cut them off. Allied commanders remained fearful about exposing their own flanks in attack, even when the Germans no longer possessed the resources or mobility to intervene with conviction. Eisenhower's armies had suffered severe embarrassment in the Bulge battle. The Supreme Commander had no intention of exposing them to further setbacks. After the massive intelligence failure in the Ardennes, he felt no temptation to act aggressively upon the basis of the latest SHAEF assessment—that the German army in the west had shot its bolt. He refused to acknowledge that von Rundstedt's armies were indeed, at last, on the ropes. He wrote, spoke and behaved as if the Wehrmacht was still the same enemy as that of Normandy.

Montgomery's demands for boldness would deserve more respect from history if either the British or American armies had displayed the determination and fighting skills to make good his visions. Yet since September 1944 many Allied commanders had expressed dismay about the lack of aggression shown by their troops, save exceptional units such as the airborne and Rangers. After counter-attacking in the Bulge, the Allies had signally failed to seize the opportunity to translate the repulse of the German forces into their destruction. "The Germans appear to be beaten and beaten badly," Gavin wrote in his diary on 3 February. "With better troops, I see no reason why we could not run all over them. The public will never know nor appreciate this. Our American army individually means well and tries hard, but it is not the army one reads about in the press. It is untrained and completely inefficient... certainly our infantry lacks courage and élan."

Gavin was equally scornful about the manner in which trench foot had been allowed to assume epidemic proportions. He argued that while this was a genuine medical condition, it was preventable by good unit discipline—foot examination and changing socks. In truth, defective American winter footwear was the principal cause. In some formations, however, trench foot had undoubtedly become a convenient alternative to combat fatigue as a means of escaping from line duty. "Poor discipline was reflected by a high trench foot rate," observed a U.S. Army post-war report, "as it was reflected by a high VD rate, a high court-martial rate and a high AWOL rate." Several officers were relieved of their commands for failure to address trench foot effectively in the winter of 1944–45. A total of 46,107 cases were reported in Bradley's armies between October 1944 and April 1945, around 9.25 per cent of all casualties, the equivalent of three combat divisions lost to Eisenhower. By contrast, and as the Pentagon noted with some chagrin, under far worse battlefield conditions the French army in the First World War suffered a 3 per cent trench-foot rate.

At the beginning of 1945, Eisenhower commanded seventy-three divisions in north-west Europe. Of these, forty-nine were infantry, twenty armoured and four airborne; forty-nine were American, twelve British, three Canadian, one Polish and eight French. A further seven American divisions reached the front by February, most of them fresh from the United States. On the other side, seventy-six German divisions were deployed in north-west Europe; a further twenty-four in Italy; seventeen in Scandinavia; ten in Yugoslavia; and 133 on the Eastern Front. This paper order of battle was, of course, misleading. The average German armoured division was now reduced to some forty tanks and self-propelled guns, compared with almost 300 in its British or American equivalents. On 6 February, the Wehrmacht reported a total manpower deficiency of 460,000 men. Many German soldiers would have been medically disqualified from service in the Allied armies. Even with their teenagers and cripples, most Wehrmacht formations mustered less than half the men of their Anglo-American counterparts. While the Allies were extravagantly equipped, the German army was starved of the most essential fighting material. Speer's efforts yielded a final substantial delivery of new aircraft to the Luftwaffe, but since there were neither trained pilots nor fuel to get them airborne, this achievement was meaningless. Wehrmacht tanks and vehicles suffered flooded filters and clogged carburettors from "Moselle petrol," a violet-coloured blend of gasoline and alcohol on which they were now dependent, and which made it necessary for tank crews to pre-heat their exhaust manifolds with blowtorches, at severe risk of fire. German tanks were designed to provide five hours' reliable continuous running, a vital requirement on the battlefield, yet by now it was rare indeed for any armoured unit to be able to achieve this. "Our battery was still fully equipped, and receiving ammunition," said Karl Godau, a gunner officer of 10th SS Panzer. "Gas, always gas was the problem."

Godau's unit profited from the fact that the Waffen SS was always first in line for whatever weapons and ammunition were available. In the Wehrmacht shells were in chronic short supply. Germany's only dubious advantage was that of diminishing lines of communications. Despite the best efforts of the Allied air forces, rail links across the Reich were somehow kept open until the very end. But traffic flow was vastly reduced, and troop movements which should have taken hours required days amid diversions and persistent disruption. Panzer Lehr Division found itself stranded at Mönchengladbach for lack of fuel. The only way the formation could move to the front was to load every one of its vehicles on to railway flatcars, a desperately time-consuming process. A sergeant-major of 12th SS Panzer was appalled when his unit took delivery of brand-new tanks at Memmingen, to discover that there was no fuel with which to drive them into battle: "We had to blow them up without firing a shot." The Germans were so starved of means of mobility that sometimes one tank towed another. Units found themselves forced to move into battle with a hotch-potch of commandeered transport, charcoal-fuelled vehicles, horse-drawn carts and—more often than not—men's own two feet.

"It was 'subsistence warfare,'" said Sergeant George Schwemmer of 10th SS Panzer. "Scrounging for ammunition and weapons. We were very, very envious of the Americans' plenty." Increasingly desperate measures were adopted to urge on Germany's despondent defenders. Model promised extra rations for any unit which shot down a ground-attack aircraft, and ten days' special leave for any man who accomplished such a feat with small arms. The reverse of the coin was reflected in a warning by the commander of 7th Parachute Division on 14 February: "The sternest measures will be taken against any further unauthorized rearward movements by individual soldiers or small units, of the kind that have been seen during the past two days."

Sergeant Schwemmer took part in one of innumerable hopeless counter-attacks at the end of January on the U.S. Third Army's front. His men left their carefully camouflaged foxholes with the deepest regret and began to advance across open ground. Devastating American automatic-weapons fire swept their ranks. "This is suicidal," said the company commander, an amiable man who was the son of an Austrian hotel owner. He was killed minutes later. Schwemmer took over. He rallied the survivors and took shelter for a time in a shell hole. Then there was a lull in the firing, and they began to pull back. Heavy

American shelling descended again. They sank into what cover they could find. The cold was terrible. When darkness fell, they stumbled towards the rear, only to be checked by a major who fiercely ordered them forward again. All night, they struggled to gain ground, until they lapsed shivering into a ditch, where they remained until dawn. Schwemmer spent the next month hospitalized with acute frostbite.

To launch the Ardennes offensive, Hitler had temporarily transferred forces from east to west while the Russians were comparatively passive. This process had been reversed when Stalin struck on the Vistula. German formations were hastening eastwards. "It is essential that the change in our priorities should be concealed from the enemy for as long as possible," Keitel signalled to von Rundstedt on 22 January. "Every day is vital. OKW has available a range of options for feints and diversions to give the enemy the impression that the forces removed [notably Sixth SS Panzer Army] will be redeployed in Holland." In reality of course, Ultra intelligence swiftly conveyed news of the German redeployment to American and British commanders.

A deserter from 12th SS Panzer told his captors on 16 January: "You could walk through to Cologne if you wanted. There is nobody to stop you." Lieutenant Helmut Schmidt wrote of returning from leave in January: "When I reported back to my commander in the Eifel, it was plain to everybody that the end of the war was approaching. I said: '*Hauptmann*, it would make more sense for us to shift everything east against the Russians, and let the Americans keep coming here in the West.' He answered: 'I'll pretend I didn't hear that.' We scarcely knew each other, but not every officer was a Nazi, and he didn't report me." U.S. Ninth Army captured a report on two enemy sentries condemned to death *in absentia*, having disappeared from their posts and presumably deserted. The men were also sentenced to dismissal from the Wehrmacht and loss of their civil rights. "Sentence will be carried out," declared German Fifteenth Army optimistically, "as soon as the two deserters return from captivity." Patton interviewed a captured German commander, General Graf von Rothkirch, commanding the LIII Corps. The American asked the familiar question: why did the Wehrmacht continue to fight? He received the familiar answer: "We are under the orders of the High Command, and must carry on as soldiers in spite of personal opinions and beliefs." A German staff officer from 331st Volksgrenadier Division told his American captors with some disdain that his comrades expected the Allies merely to continue to grind down German resistance through overwhelming firepower, "rather than attempt any bold and brilliant tactical stroke."

To many men of the Allied armies, it seemed increasingly painful to risk their lives in the final stages. Lieutenant Howard Randall joined the U.S. 76th Division as a replacement platoon commander late in January. His first experience of bloodshed was prompted by a man who shot himself in the leg one night, to avoid attacking at dawn. "My flashlight revealed his greatly swollen calf with a gaping hole in it filled with bloody hamburger and bits of shiny bone. I could see steam rising from the wound as the brightened blood rushed through the hole...I stood up and found that my knees were weak. I thought to myself—Lord, if a little wound like that has such an effect on me, how will I stand up when blood is the order of the day?" Yet Lieutenant Tony Moody of the 28th Division marvelled at the courage with which some men endured horrifying wounds. On a night patrol in Colmar, a recently arrived replacement, a nineteen-year-old from Michigan named Dennis Wills, trod on a mine. He never screamed, nor indeed made a sound, while they laid him in a shelter half and struggled through the snow back to the American lines. He simply said resignedly: "I guess I'll never jitterbug again."

In a monastery on the edge of Eindhoven, a British maxillo-facial unit, known to its staff as the "Max Factors," addressed the wounds inflicted by shrapnel, burns, blast. "The casualties themselves were uncomplaining beyond belief," wrote Sister Brenda McBryde.

> Those who were unable to speak, like the Guardsman who was being kept alive on eggnogs poured down his nasal tube, would hand me little notes: "Steak and chips tonight, Sis? Or shall we try the duck à l'orange?'...One day a sergeant of the 51st Highland Division was carried in, propped upright on a stretcher by rolled blankets. "Let him fall back and he's a goner," the M.O. had warned the bearers. A flying chunk of mortar had carried his lower jaw clean away, and an emergency tracheotomy had been carried out. After resuscitation, he was on the operating table for two and a half hours while the surgeons removed the earth and grit of the ditch and shreds of khaki cloth from the pulpy mess which was all that remained below the sergeant's upper lip.

As Sister McBryde dressed the man's wounds later, she noticed by his bedside "a photograph of a good-looking young soldier in Scottish dress with his arm about the waist of a smiling girl...if this was our sergeant, his girlfriend was in for a shock."

IN THE FEBRUARY drive to the Rhine, Allied forces were to advance across a front of some 250 miles. From Strasbourg south to the Swiss border, French divisions would hold firm in their positions on the upper Rhine. Further north the forces of Bradley and Montgomery, together with Patch's Seventh Army, would close up to the Rhine through a series of river assaults and exploitations. Patton's Third Army had furthest to go—some eighty miles. Simpson and Hodges, together with the British and Canadians, faced an advance of just over thirty miles. They knew it was overwhelmingly likely that the Germans would destroy all the Rhine bridges, but cherished hopes of a lucky break, a chance to seize at least one intact crossing which would enable them to push on across Germany without a pause.

Following the Bulge operations, twenty-one of the forty-seven U.S. divisions deployed on the Western Front were concentrated between the Hürtgen Forest and the Moselle. First Army began its attack on a front some ten miles wide, south of the Hürtgen and the Roer dams. Its units faced hard going through the thick woodlands of the Eifel before reaching open ground. On the eve of the new offensive, Bradley had to repulse a rash last-minute proposal from Eisenhower, to transfer several divisions southwards to finish off the Colmar Pocket. The German toehold there looked messy on the map, but was strategically irrelevant. Bradley lost his temper with SHAEF when this plan was telephoned to him during a meeting with Hodges and Patton. Patton said: "Tell them to go to hell and all three of us will resign. I will lead the procession." Eisenhower backed off. The French, with American armoured support, finally closed the Colmar Pocket on 9 February.

Bradley's attack began well, despite freezing weather. It was led by Ridgway's airborne divisions, who showed all the dash in attack for which they were famous. By 4 February, the Americans were well inside the first defences of the West Wall. On the right, the U.S. VIII Corps at first made less headway against 9th Panzer Division before eventually gaining momentum. German counterattacks delayed the advance, but lacked the punch to stop it. By 12 February the Americans had taken the town of Prüm, and closed up to the Prüm river.

The assault crossing of the Sauer river, which began on the night of 6 February, proved a painful experience. The same early thaw which so cheered the Germans on the Oder swelled the modest Sauer into a fast, treacherous fifty-yard-wide torrent. Under fierce German fire, assault boats drifted out of control or sank, troops were lost, engineers struggled to create pontoons. A dozen American-built bridges were broken. Private Charles Felix was at a battalion headquarters with his colonel, whom he much admired, on the night of 6 February, when VII Corps began its crossing. A signaller, Felix recorded the CO's radio conversation with one of his platoon commanders as they confronted the difficulties of launching boats under German mortaring:

"Lieutenant, are you across yet?"

"We had to turn back. We were under heavy fire."

"Where are you now?"

"We're in the woods."

"Lieutenant, you've got to get those men moving. You're holding up the advance."

"These men have had it, sir! They won't budge for me or anybody else! I've tried everything! They won't move!"

"Lieutenant, I know it's tough up there, but you're going to have to go over right now. The longer you wait, the worse it'll be ... quit screwing around."

After a further altercation, the reluctant platoon set off. But it was a night of disasters across the whole front of the advance. Felix's Colonel Rudd was enraged to discover that men were seizing litter handles to provide themselves with an excuse to get to the rear by carrying casualties. Rudd barred all riflemen from litter-bearing. He demanded court-martials for three men suspected of incurring self-inflicted wounds, and fumed when their company commander reported that since there had been no witnesses there was no evidence on which to charge them. The same company commander complained about the behaviour of his replacement riflemen: "They keep their heads down and won't look up. They think if they just lie there, the krauts can't see them. They're getting killed without firing a shot." In Private George Sheppard's company of the 319th Infantry, one man killed himself to escape from the attack. "He overdid it," said Sheppard laconically. "Some guys actually thought it was easier to die than to go on." Patton delivered a personal reprimand to the commanding general of the 94th Division after its initial failure to cross the Sauer, remarking scathingly on the fact that his units had reported more non-combat than combat casualties.

Major William DuPuy personally briefed every platoon and squad commander of his battalion of the 357th Infantry for the Sauer crossing. DuPuy had inherited command a few weeks earlier, when his predecessor walked into the CP and announced that he couldn't take it any longer. As H-Hour approached, DuPuy checked every sub-unit: "A few of the men we had to put into the boats at pistol-point. I suppose that is not an approved leadership technique." When the boats reached the other side after taking the first wave across the river, "a lot of the engineers simply abandoned them and wouldn't go across again. So my guys had to scarf up the boats and drag them right up the bank right across from the pillboxes, in the middle of the night. Those engineers were not brilliant. They probably thought they were in with a bunch of madmen."

Yet it is important to match tales of men who gave way to fear with those of others who pressed on. Lieutenant William Devitt of the 330th Infantry saw his own sergeant spin and fall after a German machine-gun burst caught him. To the officer's amazement, the sergeant then got up, held up his helmet in surprise to reveal two holes in it and ran on forward. Devitt reflected that not a man in the platoon would have held it against the NCO if he had said: "That's enough. I quit. I'm leaving. I'll see ya after this war's over."

Sergeant Tony Carullo's company of 2nd Infantry got across the Sauer intact, but then ran into trouble among the German positions on the far side. They were pinned down when Carullo's platoon commander, a Californian named Marvin Shipp, crawled over and said: "Come on, get up, we're going to make it to the rail tracks." The men reluctantly followed, but Lieutenant Shipp was shot a few minutes later. "He never even knew he'd just made it to captain," said Carullo sadly. His platoon was enraged. They shouted at the German position: "*Kommen sie hierher! Hände hoch!*" When a German cautiously showed himself, a Pennsylvanian named Johnny Komer shot him at once: "We were all so mad because they'd killed our lieutenant."

It was three days before the Sauer crossing was secure. Yet though the Americans suffered difficulties, they were able to keep moving. Hitler signalled his displeasure in the usual fashion, by sacking the commander of Seventh Army on 20 February. It is hard to see what any German general could have done better or differently, however, faced with attacks in such overwhelming strength. When the U.S. 5th Division crossed the Prüm on the night of 24 February, it met little resistance. For the first time, many Germans seemed ready to surrender without a fight. Patton's formations broke through the West Wall on a front of some twenty-five miles, and were also making good progress further south. Walker, commanding XX Corps, staged an imaginative operation on the night of 23 February, when in advance of an attack by the 94th Division he sent 5th Ranger battalion to create a roadblock around Zerf, to prevent German reinforcements from intervening. The Rangers did the job with their usual drive and effectiveness. When the 94th Division's advance stalled in the face of an ambush manned by the usual German mix of a tank, an 88mm gun and some infantry with fausts, the Rangers about-faced and attacked the Germans from the rear, driving them off. Patton's men took Trier on 1 March, capturing a useful Moselle bridge intact. His XII Corps began to drive a deep salient into German Seventh Army. At last, the great pursuit commander's offensive was achieving the sort of pace and drive he yearned for.

On the night of 9 February, after days of bitter fighting and some severe setbacks and losses, Hodges's First Army finally gained possession of the Roer dams, focus of so much anxiety for five months. The Germans had not, as had been feared, demolished the structures. They merely opened the discharge valves to release a torrent which flooded the river valley for a fortnight. This delayed the start of Simpson's attack, Operation Grenade, until the waters in front of his army's positions subsided.

All along the Allied front, it was apparent that German resistance was weaker than the attackers had ever seen it. American units met Germans surrendering in substantial numbers without a fight. When the U.S. 90th Division captured six 120mm mortars, some paratrooper PoWs proved perfectly willing to instruct GIs on how best to use the tubes against their own people. Aggressive American formations were rewarded with dramatic rewards, above all on Third Army's front. Patton himself stood on the road, urging his men forward with his usual theatricality and frequent losses of temper. When two armoured divisions became snarled at an intersection and an MP died in the consequent traffic jam, Patton insisted that the responsible corps commander should spend the next nine hours personally directing vehicles, to learn not to make the same mistake again. Such stories contributed to the Patton legend, and also to suspicions of his derangement. "There was something a bit scary about Patton," observed Eisenhower's son John. "To pretend to love war like he did, there had to have been a screw loose somewhere."

When 4th Armored Division found itself facing little resistance, it raced north-eastwards. In one bound, it covered twenty-five miles, taking 5,000 prisoners and killing several hundred Germans for the loss of 111 of its own men, before reaching the hills above the Rhine. If only others had done likewise. "For a victorious army," said Lieutenant Glavin, G-3 of 6th Armored Division on 22 February, echoing German opinion, "our divisions are too sensitive to their flanks... the result of this timidity is that we do not exploit local weaknesses, and unless the whole army moves forward along a broad front, nobody moves." If every American formation had shown the same drive and enthusiasm as the best of Patton's troops, the Allies might have secured their line on the Rhine weeks earlier. A major opportunity was missed on Hodges's front because of Eisenhower's commitment to Montgomery. Collins's VII Corps was making dramatic progress towards Cologne when the order came to halt the drive, because it was time to pass the baton—and the necessary logistic support—to Montgomery, in accordance with Eisenhower's undertakings to the British. A more flexible and imaginative commander—or one unconstrained by the demands of inter-allied relations—would have allowed Hodges's forces to keep going to the river and delayed Montgomery for the necessary few days.

As it was, 21st Army Group's big push south-east from Nijmegen, spearheaded by the Canadians, was launched as scheduled on 8 February. The attack, Operation Veritable, was a characteristic Montgomery setpiece. It began with a five-hour barrage by 1,034 guns, the heaviest of the war in the west. Five infantry divisions supported by three armoured brigades advanced on an eight-mile front with the Rhine on their left flank and the Maas on their right. The Germans had flooded much of the countryside and strongly fortified the area. They now drained their reserves to meet the attack, throwing in five divisions and the remains of Panzer Lehr. "Everybody hated Veritable," said Brigadier Michael Carver. The British found the fighting tough and miserable from beginning to end.

In theory, only 30,000 Germans supported by seventy tanks were left to face the U.S. Ninth Army when it launched Grenade on 19 February. This began with a crossing of the Roer on a fifteen-mile front. There was a supporting artillery piece for every thirty-two yards. A vast smokescreen was laid over the crossings, rising 2,000 feet into the air. Yet as the Americans began to move, they found themselves floundering in the waterlogged morass left behind by the floods. When they reached the river proper, boats were swept relentlessly downstream by a five-knot current. Private David Williams of the 104th Combat Engineers was struggling with an assault boat when there was a blast close by and his leg went numb. Shrapnel had gashed open his upper thigh. His buddy Ray, beside him, cried out, "Dave, Dave, Dave—oh dear, oh dear," slung him over his shoulder and carried him to the rear.

The advancing Allies were becoming bolder about using darkness. The U.S. 30th Division staged a highly successful night attack on Altdorf, which they took almost without loss. However, when they tried another such operation on 26 February, two tanks at once tipped into unseen craters, in what turned out to be a minefield. German fire then brewed up two Shermans, and the flames brilliantly illuminated the attackers. American gunners spotted armoured movement on their left flank and knocked out four tanks. These were British mine-clearing flails, attached for the assault, which had strayed off-course in the darkness. A single day's fighting on 27 February, attacking the town of Königshafen, cost one U.S. regiment nine tanks.

Many officers and men felt desperately tired. "It has been quite bloody awful for days," Lieutenant-Colonel George Turner-Cain wrote in his diary on 2 March, "we have fought day and night...I am extremely tired and very nervy." He added a few days later: "It is quite time I left command, as I am no longer fit to conduct stiff operations." Even in retreat, the Germans remained unimpressed by Allied tactics: "Infantry do not press forward energetically," observed an Army Group B report. "They merely follow the armoured forces and occupy ground. There are long pauses after the objective of a given attack has been taken. They are very sensitive about exposing their flanks."

When the 92nd Reconnaissance Squadron of 12th Armored Division entered the little town of Linderburgerhof near Trier, in seconds the German defenders brewed up three light tanks leading the column. Private Frank Rumph dashed into the house nearest his wrecked vehicle. A Sherman roared forward, only to be knocked out at once. Its commander, the only survivor, crouched behind its immobilized hull. Rumph yelled at the man to join him. The two Americans retired into the cellar and munched some dried carrots they found there, until at evening more American light tanks arrived to rescue the survivors of the armoured party. Next day infantry cleared the place street by street, as so often proved necessary.

The British found the experience of fighting their way through the Reichswald forest especially painful. "The Reichswald was the nastiest battle we had fought since Normandy," said Lieutenant Edwin Bramall. The Germans had constructed five successive lines of defence, manned chiefly by paratroopers. Flooded ground on both flanks forced the British and Canadians to advance on a narrow front. The thick woodland was almost impenetrable to tanks. Foliage jammed turret traverses. The Shermans were anyway unable to use their armament effectively—it was too dangerous to fire high-explosive shells lest they hit trees above their own infantry. The tanks were also highly vulnerable to faust ambushes in the dense cover. Lieutenant Kingsley Field, commanding a

Churchill troop of the King's Own Scottish Borderers, was enraged when a British infantryman mistook his tank for a German and fired a PIAT bomb at it. Field sprang down from his turret and kicked the man. Shellbursts among the tree canopy caused many infantry casualties from splinters. The movement of supplies was a nightmare in the cold and mud. The rain scarcely abated for a single day.

The British 7th Somersets set off from Nijmegen aboard Shermans on the evening of 9 February, in a heavy downpour. The sky was lit up by flames from a brief and unusual German air raid on the Dutch town. The infantrymen clung to the tank hulls in sodden misery, fearful of falling off into the path of the vehicle behind. The rain was interrupted only by sleet. Early on the morning of the 10th, the column paused for the men to drink a few cans of self-heating soup. Private Len Stokes found that his hands and feet were utterly numbed, "at the last stage before frostbite." They rode onwards all that day, and in the middle of the night reached the Reichswald. They crossed their start line at 1600 hours on 11 February, under orders to take the village of Hau. The attack stopped for a time, when the leading company reached a crossroads which was under heavy artillery fire. "Everyone was exhausted," Stokes wrote in his diary, "the conditions were appalling—cold, wet and sleet, very dark between farms." Eventually they all fell asleep on the floor of a farmhouse. The battalion reached its objective, but spent the following day and night under incessant mortar and shellfire. Late on 14 February, they were attacked by three German tanks with infantry support. The British had seen the Germans forming up, but were unable to make wireless contact with their supporting artillery. Stokes was sent as a runner to the rear, to pass map references orally. He had gone only sixty yards under German fire when he met the battalion commander, moving forward in a Bren-carrier to see for himself. The colonel dismounted, sprinted forward, checked the positions, ran back to his radio and called down devastating artillery fire which crushed the German advance in its tracks. Such was a typical single-unit action in Germany in February 1945.

The 21st Army Group's month-long battle in the Reichswald became as miserable an experience as that of the Americans in the Hürtgen. Dai Evans, a private in 53rd (Welsh) Division, saw his neighbour looking ashen after a German mortar "stonk" and called to him: "What's up, Frank? Are you hit?" The man replied simply: "No. I've shit myself." His mates helped to get his trousers off, and wiped him with grass as best they could. Here was an uncommonly vivid demonstration of comradeship. Nor was it only private soldiers whose fears overcame their bodily processes. Soon after, as the platoon advanced Evans was dismayed to see their officer fall, apparently wounded. "It's my ankle," he said. Evans looked at the lieutenant's leg and could see no blood. The officer said again: "I think I've sprained my ankle. I can't go on." Evans "suddenly realised that he was a bundle of nerves, scared almost out of his mind." The private said, "You'd better stay there, sir. I'll tell the stretcher-bearers where you are," and marched onwards with the leaderless platoon. Evans was honest enough also to record, as few unit war diaries ever recorded, an occasion when his platoon simply ran away. They were in the midst of a Reichswald attack when he suddenly found himself alone. He called out by name to some of his squad. Nothing happened. "In the end, I had to give up the search and admit that they had done a bunk..."

On 14 February, Montgomery reported to Brooke that the British were opposed by all or part of four parachute, three infantry and two panzer or panzergrenadier divisions: "This is a pretty good party." Three weeks later, he acknowledged grimly: "It is tough going, and many of the enemy paratroops refuse to surrender even when they have run out of ammunition, and have to be shot." Allied soldiers often felt unembarrassed respect for German courage. One night, an enemy patrol crossed a river in front of the 6th Cameronians. The Germans were obliged to withdraw after being fired on, leaving a wounded man under the British bank. When daylight came, the British were amazed to see a German soldier run down to the far bank, launch a rubber boat, paddle furiously across under machine-gun fire, seize the wounded man and return unscathed. "It was the bravest thing I've ever seen," said Lieutenant Cliff Pettit admiringly. "Every night, we kept wondering when the Germans were going to pack it in," said Captain John Langdon of 3rd Royal Tanks. "I can't say one felt sorry for them. Our object was to kill them. Theirs was to kill us. But they fought fairly against terrific odds."

Allied armour found itself increasingly impeded by rubble in towns devastated by heavy bombing. The city of Cleve, for instance, became a much more difficult obstacle after the Allied air forces had visited it. Mistakenly, 1,384 tons of high explosive had been dropped instead of the incendiaries requested by the army. "Bomb craters and fallen trees were everywhere," recorded a British officer, "bomb craters packed so tightly together that the debris from one was piled against the rim of the next in a pathetic heap of rubble, roofs and radiators. There was not an undamaged house anywhere, piles of smashed furniture, clothing, children's books and toys, old photographs and bottled fruit were spilled in hopeless confusion into gardens from sagging, crazy skeletons of homes." Ruins provided better defensive positions for surviving Germans than undamaged buildings. One platoon of the 7th Somersets found a Panther tank crunching relentlessly towards its positions. A PIAT operator, Private Hipple, crawled to the edge of a bomb crater and was preparing to fire at the great brute from a range of twenty-five yards when the Panther's gun went off. The blast, at point-blank range, blew the hapless soldier into the bottom of the crater. Astonishingly, he recovered and crept upwards again with his PIAT. He fired several bombs which seemed to strike the Panther, without disabling it. The German occupants, however, were sufficiently discomfited to beat a retreat.

Overall statistics showed that the Allies were suffering only modest casualties. But, for those unlucky enough to serve at the tip of the spear, there were some terrible days. On 26 February, the Canadian Cameron Highlanders were attacking in the Rhineland between Calcar and Udem. The attack began in mud and darkness, and the Camerons in their vehicles found themselves under heavy fire. One of their company commanders, Major David Rodgers, jumped down from his Kangaroo (a turretless Sherman used as an infantry carrier) and ran into the nearest house defended by German paratroopers, which he cleared alone before his men reached him. He did the same with a second house, killing four of the enemy and capturing a dozen. He returned to his battalion headquarters to report, and found the CO dead, his intelligence officer severely wounded and the position being sprayed by enemy automatic weapons. Rodgers, accompanied only by his batman, ran headlong across open ground to a house from which the Germans were firing, kicked open the door and pressed the trigger of his Sten gun. It clicked dead. The magazine was empty. He grabbed his pistol and started firing, wounding two Germans and causing the other occupants to surrender. He went on to clear the rest of the house room by room, killing or wounding nine Germans and capturing twelve. He then returned to assume temporary command of his battalion, and toured each of its company positions on foot to ensure its security before he handed over to the unit second-in-command. For his morning's work Rodgers was recommended for a Victoria Cross, though he received only an immediate DSO. Once again, it was shown how the behaviour of a single determined man could influence the outcome of a battle, if he was fortunate enough to survive to complete the business. "Bomber" Harris once memorably remarked that "any action deserving of the VC is, by its nature, unfit to be repeated as an operation of war."

The 156th Brigade of the British 52nd (Lowland) Division suffered a less happy outcome of an action a few days later. The Scots were committed on 7 March to attack the village of Alpon, just short of Wesel on the Rhine, the last German pocket west of the river. The British assault battalions spent the night before the attack under German shellfire. Next morning, the unit attacking the village, 4/5th Royal Scots Fusiliers, soon became stuck among the houses, against energetic resistance from troops of First Parachute Army, supported by two self-propelled guns. The 6th Cameronians started the battle in some disarray. Their commanding officer had been blown out of his jeep for the second time in a week and was unfit for battle. His replacement was crippled by malaria, but insisted on conducting the operation. The battalion's officers were thoroughly unhappy about attacking over ground they had been unable to reconnoitre and where the enemy's strength was unknown. The Cameronians were ordered to carry out a flanking movement around Alpon, but in the first hours two of their platoons became entangled in fighting in the village itself, and lost several men before being pulled back.

A mile or so away, men of the 4th KOSB were advancing to join the Cameronians' attack. "As usual, the rough plan on paper looked delightfully simple and free of snags," wrote one of its platoon commanders, Peter White, "a feeling that was helped by one's normal wishful thinking...that Jerry would have pulled back over the river by the time we arrived to do battle. To add to the dejected look of the sections trudging up the road, it was a chilly, raw day, and rain began to fall and soak into our clothing. I wondered if a newspaper reporter would have described us as 'straining at the leash to be at the enemy, with morale at a new high.'" The Scots were deeply respectful of the tenacity of the Germans. When the KOSBs reached their objective, they found "one young German still firing his MG with his jaw shot off and standing in a trench on the body of a dead comrade."

That night, the attack on Alpon was resumed under cover of darkness. The three fighting companies of 6th Cameronians were given widely separated objectives. D Company reached its destination without opposition and dug in. A Company ran into serious trouble on a railway embankment, which was raked by German machine-gun fire on fixed lines. At one point, its commander had his map shot out of his hands. The company finally withdrew when it lost radio contact with battalion HQ, and the time drew near for a scheduled British bombardment of its position.

C Company got across the railway tracks in a single dash, but halted short of a road that its commander had been told was the British boundary with the U.S. Ninth Army, which was alleged to be conducting a parallel attack. No Americans appeared, due to a breakdown of communications. C Company found itself exposed, some 400 yards behind the German front, with only forty-five minutes to dig in before dawn broke on 9 March. There was no time to create effective foxholes. Germans began to appear, including a Volkswagen field car which the Scots shot up. A tank clattered forward. The Cameronians loosed two PIAT bombs, which bounced off the hull. Supported by tank fire, German paratroops then assaulted and overran the British positions piecemeal. By 1000 it was all over for C Company. It had lost twenty-seven men killed and wounded. The other sixty surrendered.

At 156th Brigade headquarters, there was chaos. The divisional commander turned up in person, raging. Uncertainty about the whereabouts of the U.S. Ninth Army resulted in a decision not to allow any artillery support on the southern flank, lest shells fall upon the expected Americans. Radio contact had been lost with all the Cameronians' companies. Poor weather made it impossible to call for air support. A request for tanks was refused, because the situation was so confused. Tensions became apparent between all the senior officers involved—indeed, they had lost control of the attack. The brigade commander paced the floor wretchedly, telling his staff that the divisional commander had taken the battle out of his hands. To compound the gloom, the BBC nine o'clock news announced that the U.S. Army had captured Alpon, when in reality the British were still struggling unaided to secure the village.

Meanwhile the Cameronians' B Company had launched its own attack. One platoon successfully crossed 200 yards of open ground to reach its objective, a factory. But as soon as Jocks entered the yard the Germans fired on them, severely wounding the platoon commander. His men spent the rest of the day pinned down in the factory's outdoor earth latrines. By the time another platoon followed across the open ground, the Germans were thoroughly awake. The rear two sections and platoon HQ were almost wiped out by machine-gun fire. The platoon commander, nineteen-year-old Cliff Pettit, found himself pinned down in a gully with some twelve survivors, alongside a dozen German prisoners. "We were completely surrounded," he said. When they attempted to reach cover, several prisoners as well as six Cameronians were shot down. Pettit was left with just six men of the thirty with whom he had started the day.

At 1900 that evening, the Germans withdrew under orders. Hitler had acknowledged that the west bank of the Rhine was no longer defensible. Alpon was the last significant British action on the near shore. That night the Allies heard heavy explosions as the river bridge ahead of them was blown. Sixth Cameronians had lost four officers and 157 men. Next day, 10 March, the battalion searched the battlefield for its dead. They found one officer of C Company, Lieutenant Ken Clancey, still alive but mortally wounded. He was the third son of his parents to die in the Second World War. Bill Kilpatrick, Cliff Pettit's platoon sergeant, was awarded a DCM for fighting on through the battle after being three times wounded.

Cliff Pettit felt afterwards that his first serious action exposed the inadequacy of his training. He had been taught how to handle setpiece operations, but was at a loss about how to behave when command broke down. "I'd no idea how to operate with tanks. I had no wireless training. I felt very conscious of the lack of flexibility in British Army tactics. We had not learned nearly enough about how to cope with unexpected situations." Nor, it seemed, had his senior officers. The brigade commander was sacked after the battle. The 6th Cameronians were relieved that their CO returned to take over command from his incompetent temporary replacement. The men of 4th KOSB, who had seen hard fighting on the Cameronians' flank, were infuriated to hear the BBC describe the German stand at Alpon as "of nuisance value only." In reality, this little battle for an obscure German hamlet displayed the defenders' usual energy and determination, together with familiar shortcomings among the attackers. Here, once again, was a situation in which the Allies had been unable effectively to employ the huge paper advantage of their firepower. There was never an easy way to win the struggle for Germany, but bungling on the scale which took place at Alpon on 8 and 9 March 1945 contributed mightily to the Allies' difficulties.

GERMANS

As THE ARMIES drove deeper into Germany, many American and British soldiers recoiled from the human misery they beheld. "I do loathe all this destruction and suffering," Captain David Fraser wrote home on 15 March.

> I haven't got at all the right temperament for war. I loathe the sufferings of the old and the children, of whatever nationality. It is only possible to hate from a distance. You know people chuckle and say "1000 more bombers over somewhere last night" with glee, but when one sees the results one feels nothing but pain. Please don't misunderstand me—I know very well that the Germans started it... They deserve it back and it's probably no bad thing that they've had it—but it's still impossible to relish the sufferings of civilians.

It was a nice question whether the young British officer would have considered twenty-five-year-old Maria Brauwers deserving of his sympathy. She found it harder than most to accept impending defeat, because she had been an ardent Nazi. Brought up in a village near the Dutch border, her family found modest prosperity under Hitler, after much hardship in the 1920s. From 1941 to 1943, she served as a National Socialist propaganda worker in Poland, before coming home to marry a factory book-keeper fifteen years older than herself, and giving birth to a son. In December 1944, they were living near Jünkerath on the Moselle, thirty miles west of Frankfurt. "I was very disheartened," she said. "I had so much idealism, I had believed so much in Hitler. Now, one could only pray." They had watched the war come closer by the day. In December, the German armoured columns had streamed past, full of hope, on their way north to participate in the Ardennes offensive. Then occasional bombs began to fall on the town, one of which destroyed the house next door. As her husband August bicycled home from work one day, an American fighter machine-gunned the road. August fled into the forest, and came home full of anger about the cruelty and unfairness of such behaviour. Knowing that worse must come, like many of their neighbours the couple dug a shelter in the woods. By late December, they were spending most nights in it. When American shells began to land near by, the shelter became their home. Maria's husband left the woods only to search for food.

One night, in the darkness they heard repeated cries of "August! August!" Maria said: "Don't answer. They want to conscript you again." They huddled together with the baby, very frightened. Then a torch shone in their faces and a shocked voice exclaimed "Maria!" It was her brother Berndt. His Wehrmacht unit was retreating through the area. The local pastor had told him where his sister was hiding. Now, he began to cry. He had not even known that Maria had a child. He was overcome by the spectacle of his own loved ones cowering in a hole in deep snow. His unit was immobilized for lack of fuel. "You've got to get out," he said, "across the Rhine. This is a battlefield!" Berndt stayed two days with them. He purloined two cans of Wehrmacht petrol to enable them to bribe a passage across the river. One night, somebody stole the stolen fuel. Berndt spent most of their hours together asleep. When at last they parted, he said blankly: "The war's lost. We're never going to see each other again," and disappeared back to his unit, with which he fought until the last days of Berlin.

The family camped in the frozen woods until February, tearing up sheets to make diapers for Hermann the baby, washing in the snow. The artillery fire grew in intensity. A farmer finally took pity and allowed them to sleep in his cellar, giving Maria milk from his cows. Parties of filthy, exhausted soldiers occupied positions close by, bringing lice. Maria was horrified to find the crawling misery upon her baby. They cursed the Americans: "What are they doing here, when they've got all the space they need back home?" Some men denounced Hitler. Maria still blamed the Treaty of Versailles. She learned that her home had received a direct hit and was now a ruin.

At last, on 6 March, as she climbed the steps out of the farmhouse cellar to visit the lavatory, she heard the squealing clatter of tank tracks. She felt so overwhelmed by relief that fighting was finished that she fell back down the stairs. "It's over, it's over," she cried. August said more cautiously: "Maybe it's true that the Americans are here, but the war isn't finished." A brusque American voice called down to the cellar for them to come out. They filed out into the daylight, clutching their fears. A U.S. officer lifted aside the baby's shawl and said something kindly. Maria felt reassured. Later, however, she was shocked by the carelessness with which GIs behaved in the houses. When she saw that men were using washbasins to relieve themselves, she demanded of their sergeant: "Is this how gentlemen behave?" The man laughed and shrugged: "It's how soldiers behave." Her son Hermann contracted tuberculosis after his experiences, and suffered for years from the consequences of malnutrition.

Many Germans were shocked by the ruthlessness with which their own soldiers behaved towards civilian homes and possessions. The CO of the 17th SS Artillery Regiment felt obliged to draft an order reminding his men that they were no longer fighting in occupied territories, where licence was permitted: "The reputation of the Waffen SS cannot tolerate the confiscation of bicycles and horse teams at pistol point. It seems to me that some NCOs and other ranks have still not recognized that they are in their own country again." Civilians were shocked to discover that their own forces ruthlessly bombarded German towns and villages occupied by the Americans and British.

Twenty-two-year-old Katharina Minniger spent seven days in the cellar of her family home in the village of Hausbach as battle raged around it. A Wehrmacht Nebelwerfer battery was deployed close by, provoking fierce counter-fire and air attack from the Americans. In a lull, Katharina ventured out to ask an officer what was happening, and realized that the end was close. The mortar teams were packing to go. A soldier who had been billeted in the Minniger house bade her a wistful farewell. The soldiers could not hitch up one tube, and abandoned it in their garden. Infantrymen began to trickle through the village towards the rear, some wounded, some sobbing, some riding horses. Many were terrified boys. Bizarrely, the civilians found themselves trying to calm the soldiers' fears. Katharina's elder sister Maria played draughts with one teenager in their cellar. Shell-severed telephone lines lay strewn across the road. The American bombardment began again. Dragging a wounded man with her, Katharina returned to the cellar.

They lay there through the night, listening to intermittent shelling and screaming. Then she heard a noise above, and went cautiously to investigate, thinking that it was the Americans. Two ashen-faced young soldiers, who had been billeted in the house, were begging sanctuary. "It's been terrible up here," said one, "as bad as I've ever seen. There's not much left." They all went underground again, and huddled shaking with terror. A few hours later, on 21 March, the Americans came. The soldiers filed upstairs clutching a white flag and were marched off to captivity. Every window in the Minniger house was shattered by blast, but the structure survived. Katharina received permission to feed the stock. The Minnigers' cow survived, but the fields were littered with dead animals and dead men. Other civilians emerged from their refuges to shuffle about in shocked silence. The stench of death was terrible, and most people held pads over their noses and mouths. The nearby woods which they loved so well were blackened and stripped of leaf, many trees torn to stumps. Katharina was horrified to see fragments of a man hanging from a branch. A headless soldier hung over the fence outside their home. Yet her chief emotion was an overwhelming surge of relief.

In the middle of February, retreating German troops seeped through the little village of Dorweiler, a few miles east of the Moselle near the Luxembourg border. Twenty-two-year-old Hildegarde Platten watched them fearfully— "They were in a terrible state, a gun painfully towed by a single ox." Since 1940, life in the village had been miserably dreary, with all the young men away and social life suspended. Her father had always predicted that the war would "end in tears." Fugitives came to the village from bombed cities, desperate to barter their remaining possessions for food, or to find sanctuary. It was a poor district, and Hildegarde was the only child of a smallholder with a few cows, pigs, chickens and an ox plough for his three small fields. One morning, a retreating soldier said: "We're pulling out. You'd better go and hide in the woods." At first, they were reluctant to leave their stock, and sat in the cellar as desultory shells began to fall from American guns six miles away, on the far side of the Moselle. Devout Catholics, they prayed constantly. At last, they followed most of their neighbours to a nearby slate quarry, where they took refuge through the nights, returning at daybreak to milk the cows. One morning Hildegarde got home to find every window broken. Dough which she had left to settle on the kitchen sill was strewn with splintered glass. Another day, she discovered a terrified sixteenyear-old German deserter cowering in the cellar. As she returned to the quarry, she suffered the unnerving experience of being shelled by a battery directed by a Piper Cub overhead. She hid in a crater, because someone had told her that the same place was never hit twice.

Then came a morning when a villager came to the quarry and announced "The Amis are here." They made their way cautiously into the village, led by a man bearing a white flag. There was no firing, but they found a hive of American activity. Tents were being pitched, soldiers were washing and cooking. In her own house, she was shocked to find a GI frying eggs with the family's cherished silver cake-knife. Another was wearing her favourite shawl. "That's mine," she said. "No," the man replied easily, "it's mine." Her father said wearily: "These are only the first. There will be many more. Say nothing." Then he sat down outside and burst into tears. "So this is what my whole life has been for," he exclaimed brokenly, "losing everything."

When the Americans left, they had wilfully damaged nothing, though they removed all the family's portable valuables, especially cameras and watches. The villagers of Dorweiler learned to count their blessings, however. At least there had been no battle among their homes. At nearby Bucholz, a group of Waffen SS fought to the bitter end, defending roadblocks on both sides. At Beltheim, one officer and a handful of men held out until American gunfire obliterated every building around them. "Ridiculous ... ridiculous," said Hildegarde Platten. Yet when she and her parents heard afterwards about what had happened in the east, the family recognized its good fortune.

SOME ALLIED SOLDIERS were merely bemused by their first encounters with German civilians. Others recoiled. Soon after Dai Evans and men of 53rd (Welsh) Division occupied billets in a house, "the farmer went into a spiel we were to hear so often in the months to come: how he had hated the Hitler regime; how he had never agreed with the Nazis. He even hinted that he and his wife had been in danger due to their outspoken animosity towards the local

Nazi officials. We soon learned to treat such statements in the way we treated those of the French who bragged of their activities with the Resistance."

The Allies strove to find means by which their soldiers might distinguish Nazis from the rest of the civilian population. A notable example of the perils of enlisting psychologists in the service of armies may be found in an intelligence circular sent to all British commands, summarizing identifiable Nazi traits: "undue acceptance of parental authority, with a resultant docility to those above and an expected right to dominate those below; exaggerated awkwardness or shame on the subject of tender relations between parents and children ... the over-valuation of male friendship and masculinity associated with a social depreciation of the female sex ... a marked unconscious tendency to read one's own traits or impulses into the actions of others, to seek scapegoats."

At the age of twenty-one, Staff-Sergeant Henry Kissinger of the U.S. Counter-Intelligence Corps found himself running the city of Krefeld, rounding up Gestapo agents and Nazi officials. Although he himself had grown up in Germany, "this was the one period of my life when I felt completely American. I even thought I had lost my accent." Yet he cherished a fierce determination not to allow himself to be angry with the Germans: "I felt that I had seen what it was like to be discriminated against. It seemed wrong to go back and do to the Germans what they had just done to us."

Almost all German attempts to deploy "werewolf" groups, to wage guerrilla war behind the lines against the Western allies, failed miserably. Ten-year-old Jutta Dietze and her schoolmates in Saxony were instructed not to approach a certain local wood, because werewolves were digging in there, but when the time came and the Americans arrived, there was no resistance. It was the same across much of Germany. Helmut Lott, a fifteen-year-old junior Hitler Youth leader in Griessen, near Frankfurt, was mobilized for the Volkssturm in January. He was initially excited by the promise of a chance to fire live ammunition, and became even more so when he found that he was an instructor for his eighty-strong group, which included his own grandfather. Reality proved disappointing. They possessed only dummy fausts, a single MG42, and two machine-pistols. "For the first time, I sensed the absurdity of what we were doing." His father, an infantry captain who was also a Nazi Party member, was taken to hospital suffering from wounds he had received in Courland. When the boy went to visit him, proud in his uniform, and described the preparations to resist the Allied armies, his father exploded: "Now I really believe the war is lost!" he said. "This is ridiculous. Stay as far away from it as you can." The boy was deeply shocked: "I still thought we could win." His Volkssturm unit was never mobilized, for there were no weapons to arm the men, "and I doubt whether they would have obeyed a call-up anyway." The boy was only grateful that he and his family survived unscathed when the Americans came.

Almost the only visible success for werewolves was the assassination of the American-appointed mayor of Aachen on Palm Sunday 1945. Other isolated attempts were made: on 16 March Dr. Alfred Meyer, gauleiter of Westphalia, appealed to the local SA commander for "a few selected personnel of 17 and over…fanatical Nazis who will not hesitate to make the supreme sacrifice, to offer their lives. Absolute secrecy [is necessary] even to their immediate families. I expect every district leader to designate three men who fulfil the above specification. The selected men should be equipped with clothing which can stand abuse, strong shoes, one change of underwear, eating and cooking utensils, food coupons and identity cards. *Heil Hitler!*" There is no evidence of any response to this appeal. The guerrilla concept was alien to the German military tradition. Only a few teenagers fulfilled Berlin's hopes. Peter Carrington of Guards Armoured once took over a farmhouse for his squadron headquarters and relegated its German occupants to the cellar. On waking next morning, "I was dismayed to look out of the window and see the German son of the house attempting to fix a charge to my jeep. I decided to commit an atrocity. I gave the family five minutes to clear out, told my sergeant-major to pour ten gallons of petrol on the house, and put a match to it." Carrington, epitome of English aristocratic good nature, recalled bathetically, but without evident regret: "The fire went out."

As the German armies fell back mile by mile and day by day, one of Captain Karl Godau's gunners in 10th SS Panzer, a gloomy Westphalian, observed: "I'm going to end up defending the rabbit hutch at the end of my garden." A relative of Heinrich Himmler serving at a corps headquarters in the west continued to proclaim noisily: "Those who weaken must be broken!" But his commander eventually found these protestations intolerable, and had the officer transferred. During the last months, even in a crack regiment such as the Grossdeutschland, morale became perilously fragile. Lieutenant Tony Saurma's loader jumped down from their tank during an action, supposedly to clear their gun. Once on the ground, he mysteriously disappeared. The crew heard a Russian propaganda loudspeaker urging seductively: "Come this way, comrade—this way to freedom." Saurma assumed that the loader had seized the opportunity to desert. His troop sergeant, a Mecklenburger, often teased him: "Aren't you afraid of dying?" Saurma said afterwards: "When a soldier had time to think, he began to brood about home, even to think of killing himself. I always tried to keep my men busy, so that they did not have the opportunity to brood. I kept talking to them. Sometimes one felt that their nerve had gone. Some would talk about shooting themselves."

In the frenzied movements of those last months, tanks of the Grossdeutschland once found themselves engaging the Russians from the railway flatcars on which they had been brought to the battlefield. At night, when the tanks leaguered to rearm and perform maintenance, the crews now had to provide their own local defence, for they lacked panzergrenadiers to do the job for them. Rations shrank. They found themselves obliged to eat the army-issue cheese which everyone detested, because there was little else. Some days, there was only bread.

Once, after Saurma's troop had spent a night on a serious drinking binge, he sensed them to be on the edge of mutiny. "For God's sake, let's end this," they said. The young officer gathered his tank crews together and harangued them: "You were born—some time you're going to die," he said. "In between, there is a parabola of life, which has its good moments and its bad ones. You must not think of yourselves, but of others who depend on you. You can't just give up." Heaven knows what Saurma's men thought of these lofty sentiments, but they fought on. Between 15 January and 22 April 1945, his division suffered an astounding 16,988 casualties, 170 per cent of its strength. In the three years of its existence, the Grossdeutschland lost 50,000 men and 1,500 officers.

"Most German soldiers realize the hopelessness of their country's predicament," observed a Soviet intelligence report on 2 March, "but a few still express faith in victory. There is no sign of a collapse in enemy morale. Germans still fight with dogged persistence and unbroken discipline, and some prisoners express their pride about this. A captured company commander said: 'We must hold to the last man.' A soldier named Viktor Schubert said: 'The war will end this year, and we shall win it.'" It is hard to deny bemused respect to Germans capable of addressing Soviet intelligence officers in such terms in the spring of 1945.

The Ardennes was the last large-scale armoured battle Hitler's armies fought on the Western Front. Thereafter, the Wehrmacht was obliged to fight a campaign against the Americans and British which was overwhelmingly dependent upon footsoldiers with hand-held anti-tank weapons. There was no further scope for grand strategy, because Germany possessed no more choices about how or where to fight. A few officers were already discreetly telling their men to go home, and more did so with every week that passed. Commanders instructed to fight to the last round frequently interpreted this as meaning the last artillery shell. Even where tubes and ammunition still existed, lack of trained personnel and prime movers critically hampered the deployment of heavy guns. Units overwhelmingly composed of untrained replacements lacked the tactical skills to mount counter-attacks. So incompetent were some novice armoured crews that, when they collected new tanks direct from the factories, they frequently ditched or crashed them on the road to the front.

"I have four divisions, facing 22 Soviet divisions with two in reserve," the officer commanding the Hermann Göring Parachute Corps reported to OKH on 12 March. "Each of our divisions is holding six miles of front. I have 41 tanks and self-propelled guns against four tank brigades. I have 58 artillery pieces against 700. In the first two months of 1945 the Corps has lost 37,000 men; of 106 grenadier companies, 45 are commanded by NCOs, the remainder by young and untrained officers. The average company changes its entire personnel in 9 to 12 days."

On 13 March, the Luftwaffe's Luftflotte 6 reported that it possessed fuel for its aircraft to make just one sortie apiece, and pleaded for further supplies before the Russians launched their next offensive. It was impossible, said Luftflotte 6's commander, to take any action at all against the enemy's Oder bridgeheads without more fuel: "In this sixth year of the war, the Luftwaffe requires from the army understanding and co-operation on supply issues."

Many soldiers had become desperate to escape from the war, if they could only identify an opportunity to surrender. On 17 March, twenty-two-year-old Corporal Henry Metelmann lay over his elderly rifle and watched with considerable bewilderment as the American Seventh Army advanced on Speyer. "The whole cavalcade looked like a Sunday school outing. What a strange army! Infantry spread out in line with tanks." Metelmann came from a working-class Hamburg family and was an ardent Nazi when he marched into Russia as a volunteer with the Wehrmacht in 1941. Three years later, his idealism had evaporated. He yearned only to survive. He had been transferred to an improvised unit in the west after being wounded in the east. As they paused in Speyer, housewives pleaded with them not to fight in the town. When he laid down his faust by a wall, it disappeared. Women in the vicinity merely giggled when he begged for its return. The soldiers discussed among themselves what to do next, and agreed to surrender as swiftly as possible.

When they heard American tanks a few cobblestoned streets away, they retired to the cellar of the nearest house, took out cards and played the first of many games of *Skat*. The young son of the house eventually came in, contentedly munching a chocolate bar which a GI had given him. Their moment had come, the soldiers decided. They stepped apprehensively into the street. Some chattering women laughed and said something about "Hitler's last hope." The men hung a white towel on a broomstick, and walked cautiously forward until they met two Americans strolling towards them with hands in their pockets. Metelmann said, "Surrender! Surrender!," and was disconcerted when the enemy soldiers hastily turned and fled. Five minutes later, some infantry and armoured cars appeared, told the German to drop his broomstick and herded the prisoners into willing captivity. When they ate their first American rations, these half-starved men decided "that with food and beverages of that quality and quantity, we could have conquered the world."

"SINCE THE ISSUE of the Yalta communiqué," suggested a Second Army Intelligence Report on 22 February, "the very hopelessness of Germany's fate after the war may be one of the reasons for the continuance of a struggle which daily becomes more desperate. Death is better than slavery. Smashed cities are better than seeing them handed over to the Poles or occupied by the Allies." A German company commander fighting near Oppeln, Lieutenant Patteer, addressed his men: "Friends, this isn't about our lives any more, it's about the fate of Germany. We soldiers must prove that we are real Germans. Imagine what the fate of our own families will be if the Russians get to them. It will mean death." Likewise Lieutenant Hummel: "Men, we must fight to the end, or we're all dead anyway. Think of East Prussia and what the Bolsheviks are doing there!" Within the British Army, a marked class division influenced attitudes towards the tide of Soviet vengeance now sweeping into Germany. "Other ranks" had been incited by their own country's propaganda and by a fashionable sense of socialist solidarity to regard the Russians and "Uncle Joe" with enthusiasm. Many of their officers did not share this view. David Fraser, a twenty-five-year-old captain of the Grenadiers, wrote in disillusionment to his family on 25 February, after hearing news of the Yalta conference: "It fills me with utter gloom...Poland has been sold, which one knew would happen but is nonetheless disgusting and humiliating when it occurs...All this has been ratified, and yet are the very things against which...we went to war."

Fraser felt little animosity towards the Germans, but profound hatred for the Soviets: "I cannot see that this war has or will have accomplished anything except a military decision as unimportant as a victory in one of the dynastic wars. The root evil still flourishes, and everybody knows and daren't say. Wretched Europe!" Fraser could never remove from his mind the belief— entirely correct, but in 1945 still keenly disputed—that the Russians, rather than the Nazis, had murdered thousands of Polish officers at Katyn in 1940. "To most [of our officers]," he wrote, "this possibility, let alone likelihood, was often regarded as near-disloyal to the Allied cause if mentioned. I had bitter arguments with friends, who were not stupid but were determined to believe only good of those who were fighting the same enemy."

AT THE SUMMIT of the Nazi leadership, fantasy still held sway. At one of Hitler's conferences in February, Speer drew Dönitz aside and sought to persuade him that the military situation was now hopeless, that steps must be taken to mitigate the catastrophe facing Germany. "I am here to represent the Navy," responded the Grand-Admiral curtly. "All the rest is not my business. The Führer knows what he is doing." Even at a much humbler level in the nation's hierarchy, fantastic delusions persisted. After Cologne fell, Sergeant Otto Cranz of the 190th Infantry was surprised to hear one of his comrades insist mechnically, yet with utter conviction: "My Führer must have a plan. Defeat is impossible!" Even as Königsberg stood besieged in February, Dr. Hans von Lehndorff wrote in his diary: "Most people are still convinced that the Führer's present conduct of the war is in accordance with a pre-determined plan. And the fact that the Russians have already reached the Oder, and we are now living on a little remote island, is hardly realised."

General von Thadden, commanding the ruins of the 1st Division in East Prussia, met a local artist who expressed his delight in the extraordinary scenes he was able to paint amid catastrophe. Von Thadden asked where the artist's family was. They were still at home and quite well, said the man easily.

"But isn't there too much shelling going on? The Russians are no more than a thousand yards away from you."

"That's true. The top storeys have had one or two hits. But we live on the ground floor."

The general suggested that the artist should evacuate his family.

"Do you think that's necessary, Herr General?"

"Necessary? That depends on ... your feelings towards your family."

To such a perversion of rationality had Nazism brought an entire generation of Germans.

REMAGEN AND WESEL

VANITY AS MUCH as military necessity caused Montgomery to lavish extraordinary care and resources upon his crossing of the Rhine. It was plain that this would be the last great setpiece operation of the campaign. Twenty-first Army Group's commander intended it to be a fitting memorial to his own achievement. No fewer than 37,000 British and 22,000 American engineers were deployed to conduct the river crossing. For the assault, the British Second Army collected 118,000 tons of supplies, and the U.S. Ninth 138,000 tons. Landing craft, amphibious DUKWs and Buffaloes in profusion were trucked or driven to the crossing points at Wesel. One American and one British parachute division were to assist in securing the far bank, but here they would descend only two thousand yards beyond the front, rather than sixty miles as at Arnhem.

An operation on this scale, and of this complexity, required laborious preparation. A party of Intelligence Corps NCOs, drinking tea in their cosy farmhouse billet, were irked to receive a visit from a gunner officer, who told them that next day a battery of medium artillery would be digging in outside their door. " 'Mind you,' said the gunner amiably, 'you're very welcome to stay, provided you don't mind squeezing up a bit. The windows will fly out with the blast, of course, and we'll probably lose a good deal of the roof.' "

Having reached the west bank of the river on 10 March, Twenty-first Army Group proposed to cross, together with the U.S. Ninth Army under command, on the 24th. For two weeks, Montgomery's forces planned, briefed and amassed matériel. Perhaps this was unavoidable. But, with the Wehrmacht in ruins, it seemed to many Americans then, and to history since, regrettable that so many men dallied for so long. As early as 7 March, when Collins of VII Corps met Hodges beside the Rhine in the newly captured ruins of Cologne, he told First Army's commander that he hoped the Allies would not sit tight in front of the river, giving the Germans a chance to recover. Bill Simpson urged Montgomery to allow Ninth Army to make a fast crossing at Urdingen, where there were few German troops. The field-marshal turned him down flat.

Yet on 7 March events took a hand. As 9th Armored Division headed towards Remagen, south of Bonn, they learned that the Ludendorff rail bridge, which ran across the river between a low ridge on the west bank and a sheer cliff on the east side, was still intact. Just before 1300, the lead American platoon commander reached high ground overlooking the river and saw German troops still retreating across the bridge, a formidable structure of three arches supported by four stone piers, landmarked at each end by sooty, mock-medieval towers. Wooden planking had been laid across the twin rail tracks, to ease the passage of marching soldiers. Two hours later, 9th Armored's commander decided to risk the bridge being blown while his men were crossing, and ordered his infantry to storm it. A German civilian told them they had better hurry: he had heard that it was to be demolished at exactly 1600. The Americans believed that they had an hour in hand.

Yet it was already 1600 when men of the 27th Armored Infantry, led by Lieutenant Karl Timmerman, reached the bridge approaches under small-arms fire from the towers. There was a heavy explosion. When the debris settled, the smoke and dust cleared, the Americans saw that the bridge was holed somewhat, but still standing. Timmerman ordered his men to push on across it. Pershing tanks provided fire support, while three engineers followed the lead riflemen, cutting every wire they could see. With amazingly little difficulty, Timmerman's company was soon across the 350-yard span. Two of his platoons deployed to cover the bridge's eastern approaches, while one began to climb the steep cliff overlooking the river. 9th Division's commander ignored orders to divert most of his formation to another bridge across the Ahr river, and threw the rest of his armoured infantry across the Rhine at Remagen. When III Corps heard the news at 1630 that men were holding a crossing, 9th Armored was formally ordered to exploit the opportunity.

Not everyone rejoiced, however. Eisenhower's G-3 from SHAEF, that unconvincing officer General Harold "Pinky" Bull, happened to be visiting Bradley when word of Remagen reached 12th Army Group. Bull recalled a staff study which showed that a Rhine crossing between Coblenz and Cologne offered scant opportunities for exploitation on the eastern side. He said as much, declaring brusquely that Remagen was the wrong place for First Army to cross the river. Bradley exploded: "What in hell do you want us to do—pull back and blow it up?" A telephone call to the Supreme Commander yielded more sensible orders for 12th Army Group: "Hold onto it, Brad. Get across with whatever you need—but make certain you hold that bridgehead." Eisenhower suggested committing four or five divisions. Yet even as Americans streamed triumphantly across the precarious bridge at Remagen, Bull persisted with his stubborn objections. He displayed the mindset which made the Allied advance across Europe such a cautious affair. Even as the Americans reinforced at Remagen, Eisenhower made plain his intention to close up his armies at the river, before allowing any grand exploitation on the east bank. He remained fearful that, as long as some German forces survived on the western side of the Rhine, the potential existed for another unpleasant surprise, a counter-attack across an exposed American flank. Any senior German officer would have heaped scorn on this notion. But SHAEF regarded the threat most seriously.

AT HITLER's headquarters in Berlin, the atmosphere grew ever more frenzied. Like exhausted jugglers, Germany's commanders struggled to sustain their efforts to rush formations across the Western Front. On 2 March, Hitler inveighed perversely against von Rundstedt's proposal to move men south from the 21st Army Group sector: "It just means moving the catastrophe from one place to another."

Hitler responded to news of the Remagen crossing in his usual fashion—by sacking von Rundstedt as commander in the west. The haughty old man was replaced by Kesselring, "Smiling Albert," an implausible former airman turned general, who had nonetheless conducted a stubborn fighting defence of Italy for eighteen months. Kesselring now found himself concluding his military career by presiding impotent over a catastrophe. His initial task was to deploy every available man against the Remagen bridgehead. In the first twenty-four hours, the Americans had pushed across 8,000 men, supported by tanks and anti-aircraft guns. Thereafter, huge traffic jams built up on the west bank, as units surged towards the bridge under German artillery fire. On 13 March, the engineers insisted on closing the Ludendorff entirely, to repair the serious structural damage inflicted by the initial German demolitions. Troops continued to cross the river near by, using landing craft and rafts. Surviving Luftwaffe aircraft and even German frogmen attacked again and again in the hours of darkness. They were frustrated by American guns and searchlights.

On 15 March, the battered Ludendorff bridge suddenly collapsed into the river with a thunderous roar, killing twenty-eight of the engineers working on it and injuring many more. By now, however, its loss scarcely mattered. By 21 March, five engineer pontoons were open across the Rhine at Remagen. Elements of nine German divisions were concentrated north of the American positions on the east bank. Yet these formations were desperately weak, and deployed piecemeal. Men like Captain Walter Schaefer-Kuhnert of 9th Panzer recognized that "what we were doing was no longer fighting a war in any proper military sense." His unit was able to move only by night. Air attack had destroyed most of its vehicles and killed all his battery's radio-operators and telephonists. They retreated across the Rhine at Düsseldorf just as the U.S. First Army crossed at Remagen. Schaefer-Kuhnert's regiment was ordered to proceed to Frankfurt, but within a few miles was urgently redirected, to support a counter-attack through the hills against the American bridgehead. Desperately short of fuel, they were reduced to begging a few litres here, a few there, at the gates of factories they passed on the road. Somehow, they reached the Remagen battlefield, sited their guns in quarries a few thousand yards from the river, and opened fire on 10 March. Model himself arrived. The stocky little field-marshal strode about behind the front, overseeing the battle with increasingly visible desperation. The Germans were doing their utmost, but their commander knew that this was not enough. The American bridgehead was invulnerable to Model's enfeebled formations.

Meanwhile further south, on 13 March Patton launched his own attack south-eastward across the Moselle. Four days later, Third Army had trampled over the remains of the German First and Seventh Armies. American armour passed through the infantry and began a dramatic drive across the Saarland. As Patch's U.S. Seventh Army attacked north-eastwards through the last remaining sector of the West Wall still in enemy hands, Patton's men were already pushing far behind the German front. The attackers faced local spoiling actions, which could change nothing but only inflict delay. Moving east out of Neustadt towards Speyer on 23 March, for instance, the spearhead of 10th Armored Division met a Panther and promptly blew off its turret.

A young American armoured engineer officer ran alone on foot ahead of the tanks, looking for a way round the barricades blocking the road. The lead tank drove through an underpass before being hit. The Americans spotted two panzerjäger, covered by infantry, tucked in beside a nearby building. A Sherman fired at them and missed. Its next shell did better, hitting one of the German armoured vehicles at the junction of its gun and shield, jamming the recoil mechanism. The German tried to retire, but lost a track to another shell. The panzerjäger collided with its mate, wedging it against a wall. Both German armoured crews bailed out and fled, except one driver who remained in his seat, concussed by the first hit. As the Shermans engaged the infantry with their machine-guns, the commander of the leading American tank collapsed in his turret, shot by a rifleman. His tank pulled aside, allowing its successor to overtake and drive on. This little firefight had lasted only four minutes. The Americans now drove on into Speyer in thick fog which reduced visibility to a hundred yards. They suffered a steady trickle of casualties for some hours before the town was secured.

Such small encounters, repeated again and again every day along the front,

made hard pounding for the men of the Allied vanguard. Yet it was plain that
organised resistance was collapsing. Patton's spearheads were moving fifteen to
twenty-five miles a day. Third Army collected 68,000 prisoners and Seventh
Army 22,000 in the Saarland–Palatinate operation. Patton's men suffered 5,000
casualties, Patch's some 12,000. This was a small price to pay for rolling up a
major part of the surviving defences of central Germany.

THERE WERE FEW jokes in the north-west Europe campaign, and indeed it was
never easy to be funny about events which were matters of life and death. But
the U.S. Army relished to the utmost the spectacle of Montgomery's forces
preparing to stage a huge, formal military pageant on the Rhine, more than two
weeks after its own soldiers had crossed seventy miles further south. It was true
that the bridgehead at Remagen did not diminish the need for Allied forces to
secure big crossings north of the Ruhr. Montgomery's Operation Plunder had
not become redundant. But the Americans' spectacular achievement robbed
Plunder of glamour and glory.

For ten days before Montgomery's forces crossed, a smokescreen shrouded
the Allied bank of the river at Wesel, to conceal troop and vehicle movements
from German artillery observers. A massive bombardment preceded H-Hour.
Patton twisted Montgomery's tail by staging another assault crossing of his
own, on the middle Rhine at Nierstein and Oppenheim, just south-west of
Frankfurt, on the night of 22 March, twenty-four hours before Montgomery's
big moment. Third Army's 5th Division met negligible resistance. On the morning of 23 March, Patton triumphantly telephoned 12th Army Group and
announced: "Brad—don't tell anyone, but I'm across . . . I sneaked a division over
last night. But there are so few Krauts around that they don't know it yet. So
don't make any announcement." Patton's bulletin to 12th Army Group further
taunted the British, by describing how his forces had crossed "without benefit of
aerial bombing, ground smoke, artillery preparation and airborne assistance,"
all of which 21st Army Group was employing on a prodigious scale.

For ten days before Montgomery's forces crossed, a smokescreen shrouded
the Allied bank of the river at Wesel, to conceal troop and vehicle movements
from German artillery observers. A massive bombardment preceded H-Hour.
At 2100 on the evening of 23 March, 51st (Highland) Division staged a diversionary crossing near Rees. The Scots traversed the great river in seven minutes and
were soon secure on the eastern bank, having met slight resistance. At 0200 on
the 24th, the main crossing began north-west of Xanten, led by 15th (Scottish)
Division, even as the first wave of 120,000 men of Simpson's Ninth Army
launched their own American landing craft. Tracer flew overhead, to guide the
course of the assault vessels amid the fierce current. The U.S. 30th and 79th
Divisions suffered just thirty casualties in crossing the great river which had
been the focus of so many Allied hopes and fears for so long. The Germans had
abandoned the attempt to defend the Rhine shore against overwhelming firepower, and dispatched many of the Wesel defenders to the Remagen perimeter.

Yet an easy success for Montgomery was now succeeded by an equally spectacular shambles. The 21st Army Group's commander had determined that, alongside the amphibious assault on the Rhine, Allied parachute forces should be committed. Eisenhower gave him not only the British 6th Airborne, which had done so well in Normandy, but also a division of Ridgway's U.S. XVIII Airborne Corps. Their task was to secure the higher ground behind the river, together with six bridges over the River Issel. To ensure that the airborne landing did not disrupt the artillery preparation, the paratroopers and gliderborne forces were committed only after the river crossings had been made, at 0900 on 24 March. This was the last great airborne operation of the Second World War.

Whatever surprises the Allies had been able to inflict on the Germans elsewhere on the Rhine, at Wesel for weeks the defenders had anticipated Montgomery's crossing. The amphibious assault units profited greatly from the Germans' transfer of forces to Remagen. But behind the river bank, beyond reach of significant damage from the British bombardment, the Germans had deployed formidable anti-aircraft power. Some 357 German flak positions—about a thousand gun barrels—had been identified. Four wings of RAF Typhoons mounted a standing anti-flak patrol through the attack. Yet, as the great airborne armada approached for Operation Varsity, ferocious ground fire rose to meet it. The British gliders, in particular, suffered severely. It was a painful irony that, despite the negligible losses of the waterborne divisions, on 24 March the American 17th Airborne took some 1,500 casualties, including 159 men killed. The British lost 1,400 men, including a quarter of their glider pilots, out of 7,220 landed. Forty-four transport aircraft were destroyed and 332 damaged. Twenty-two of the seventy-two C-46 aircraft dispatched were lost. "The casualties to glider pilots and their passengers, though by no means light, were not sufficient to affect the course of the battle, though the loss of equipment was serious," concluded a British after-action report soothingly. Yet about half the gliders in the American sector and 60 per cent in the British zone suffered flak damage. Their passengers found the experience of the assault horrendous, and remain bitter that it has received so little attention from posterity.

The American 17th Airborne, making its first drop into battle, was to seize the Diersfordter Forest, from which it was feared that the Germans could fire upon the river crossings. The original plan called for the commitment of the U.S. 13th Airborne as well, but shortage of aircraft caused them to be excluded. The men of the 17th took off from twelve airfields around Paris after a hefty pre-dawn breakfast of steak, eggs and apple pie. Their formations rendezvoused with those of the British 6th Airborne over Brussels, then swung north-east for the last 103 miles of the approach to the river, where Eisenhower, Churchill, Brooke and a host of other Allied luminaries waited to witness this last great spectacular of the Anglo-American campaign.

Private Patrick Devlin of 6th Airborne's Royal Ulster Rifles attended mass the day before he boarded his platoon's glider for the Rhine. He had just returned from home leave in County Galway, after surviving the Normandy campaign. His mother begged him to stay snug in Ireland, "but to me it was all a big adventure which I would not have missed." A sniper by trade, for this operation he preferred to carry a Bren gun. On the runway at Rivenhall near Colchester, he and his mates kicked a football before take-off. Then he dozed, not discontentedly, through the three-and-a-half-hour flight into Germany.

Dr. David Tibbs of 13 Para was moved by the "wonderful spirit of the men." Yet not all were eager for action. The night before the assault, the doctor was woken twice to deal with self-inflicted wounds. He also found himself ministering to an Irishman who displayed a urethral discharge and suggested himself as a VD case. Tibbs was confident that the man had used toothpaste to simulate the symptoms. "Here's your tablets," he told his patient brutally. "Tomorrow you jump, clap and all!" The paratroopers were assured that the opposition would have been flattened by air and artillery strikes. The medical teams, however, were briefed to expect heavy casualties.

At the airfield, Tibbs and his comrades were a trifle disheartened to hear that their American pilots had never before carried paratroopers. The fliers inquired innocently about the long cylinders attached to parachute packs and clipped beneath the fuselage—"Are those things explosives?" Yes indeed, said the British, bangalore torpedoes. At that moment, the whole plane lifted and there was a resounding thud as the bangalores were dumped on the tarmac. A head leaned out of the cockpit: "Just testing the clips!" the pilot cried cheerfully. The frightened doctor shook his fist at the American, and helped the signals officer to reattach their dangerous cargo. When most of Lieutenant Peter Downward's platoon were already aboard their Dakota, a young soldier suddenly broke down and announced that he could not go on. Downward took the boy aside and remarked that, since he would be one among 8,000 men of 6th Airborne dropping, the odds were that he would make it. "Also, that as a young man he would hate himself if he looked back on this act of cowardice. He had to think of his family. How would they feel, to have a son labelled a coward by a court martial?" The boy boarded the aircraft, jumped, survived, and afterwards thanked his officer, little older than himself.

One of Downward's men, Porrill, relieved the monotony of the long flight by serenading the aircraft with his mouth organ. As David Tibbs's C-47 approached the dropping zone, the doctor was horrified to see through the door a long stream of men descending into a thick forest. Their dispatcher gestured at their own stick to jump. Tibbs's sergeant, No. 1 in the C-47's doorway, shook his head violently, pointing down at the trees and a row of pylons. Then the landscape cleared, and they threw themselves into the air. The doctor watched curiously as a German 88mm gun crew beneath him loaded and fired their piece. He hit the ground 200 yards from the battery. Seeing two paras close by, he pointed to the enemy guns. Weighed down with equipment, the soldiers waddled towards them with agonizing sluggishness. But every German eye was on the sky. The British threw grenades and successfully rushed the guns.

Colonel Edson Raff and 700 men of his U.S. 507th were dropped two miles off target, because their transport pilots were confused by haze. Marching through the woods towards their rendezvous, he chanced upon a German artillery battery, which his "Ruffians" immediately stormed, killing most of the gun crews. By 1400, Raff's men had secured all their objectives. Brigadier-General William Miley, commanding the 17th, was also landed miles from his intended dropping zone and separated from his staff. Indeed, all he could initially see on the ground were three soldiers and a container labelled as a .30 calibre machine-gun. The general took the weapon and the soldiers in charge, and started his battle commanding a single machine-gun crew, which opened a brisk fire on the enemy.

At least part of the 507th had landed where it was intended. By contrast, Colonel James Coutts's entire 513th Parachute Infantry suffered an awkward trip. First, while still in the air their C-46 transports passed over a German flak belt. Twenty-two American aircraft were shot down in flames, the nightmare mitigated only by the fact that all their paratroopers were able to jump before the C-46s crashed. The undamaged aircraft dropped their men not on the designated DZ-X, but on 6th Airborne's glider landing zone at Hammelkiln, which was under heavy German fire. The American paratroopers found themselves engaging enemy gun positions even as gliders crashed in around them. Ridgway was so dismayed by the readiness with which the C-46s had caught fire that he gave orders that the type was never again to be used for carrying paratroopers into action.

This was the most ambitious glider operation of the war. The British Hamilcars carried loads of eight tons. 6th Airborne's glider lift alone landed beyond the Rhine 4,844 men (dead and alive), 342 jeeps, 348 trailers, three gun trailers, seven Locust tanks, fourteen lorries, two bulldozers, eleven Bren-carriers, nineteen five-hundredweight cars, fifty-nine portable motorcycles, 127 heavy motorcycles, sixty-eight bicycles, twenty field cycles, ten 4.2-inch mortars, two 75mm guns, fifty six-pounder anti-tank guns, twelve seventeen-pounders, and two twenty-five-pounders.

Lieutenant Jack Curtis Goldman flew an American glider carrying the combat surgical team of 17th Airborne. As they approached the landing zone, he could catch only glimpses of the ground through holes in the vast riverside smokescreen. They cast off and approached the LZ undamaged, "but then as we were about six or eight feet off the ground, it sounded as if a giant popcorn machine had exploded in the back of the glider—machine gun bullets ripping our fuselage to shreds." He was sickened to feel the glider's wheels bumping over the bodies of dead paratroopers. At last they shuddered to a halt. The occupants leaped out and ran to the shelter of a belt of trees. When Goldman got there, he found that he was so shaken that instead of bringing his Thompson gun, he was clutching a big can of fruit cocktail. Lacking anything else useful to do, he sat down and ate it. It was two hours before gunfire subsided sufficiently for him to return to the glider and retrieve his weapon and equipment. He saw lying in the wreckage the bodies of several men whom he knew well. He unclipped the reserve parachute from a dead man and later sent the silk to a girl in Brownfield, Texas. She took it as a proposal of marriage.

One British platoon leaped from a glider as it shuddered to a halt, deployed around the wreckage and opened a brisk fire. A British loudspeaker broadcast a hasty message: "You are in friendly territory...cease firing...you have been dropped short of your target." Harry Pegg's glider of the Royal Ulster Rifles crashed disastrously. He was one of only three men out of thirty-two who were unwounded. American medics who came to their aid reported grimly that they had recovered sixteen unattached legs from the wreckage. "It was chaos," said Pegg. As most of his platoon was dead, he found himself acting as bodyguard for the battalion CO. He remained concussed for the rest of the day. Private Harry Clarke of 2nd Ox & Bucks was appalled by the dead and wounded strewn around the wrecked gliders: "At the front of one burning aircraft was its pilot, still wearing his headphones, arms outstretched and forming the shape of a crucifix in the flames."

Pat Devlin's glider was one of only five in his battalion which got down undamaged. His stick jumped out to find themselves on the right landing zone, but a thousand yards from their objective, a T-junction just west of Hammelkiln. He saw some Germans by a farmhouse and threw himself down with his Bren, too late to get a shot at them. Someone shouted: "Tanks!" Spotting two big half-tracks packed with Germans, Devlin fired a long burst, and heard screams as their heads disappeared beneath the hulls. The vehicles sped on past the British, leaving the Irishman pleasantly elated. He had emptied seventeen twenty-round magazines since landing. He felt that, whatever happened next, he had made a small dent in the German Army. He called to his sergeant, a Belfast Protestant: "Geordie, we'd better start moving to the objective." Picking up a fistful of empty magazines and his gun, which had jammed from overheating, he trotted forward. There was a burst of fire. Suddenly, he suffered a jolt and gave an exclamation, dropped the Bren and fell flat. Devlin had been hit in the right side and forearm. "It felt as if somebody had struck me a severe blow across the small of my back with a big stick. The pain wasn't too bad, like a nagging toothache, but I couldn't move." He was disturbed, however, to find his thigh soaking wet. Would he bleed to death? Then he realized that a bullet had pierced two condensed-milk tins in his side-pack. A glider pilot crawled past. Devlin begged the man to drag him into a ditch. The flier ignored him and moved on. Then McCrea, one of his platoon mates, appeared and pulled him into cover, observing: "This'll serve you bloody right for playing silly soldiers." Devlin was a volunteer. No Irishman faced conscription.

There was another shout of "Tanks!" McCrea promptly disappeared. Two German armoured cars dashed past, their hulls draped with wounded. One crashed into a wrecked glider near by and was shot to pieces by the British. A German officer slid into the ditch beside Devlin and sat clutching his head in his hands in shock, muttering repeatedly: "*Deutschland kaputt*." Two other Germans walked forward with their hands in the air. McCrea returned, excusing himself for abandoning him by saying: "You don't hang around when there's tanks about!" Devlin was taken to an aid post.

David Tibbs, 13 Para's doctor, found himself some 400 yards from his intended landing point. He walked across the field towards the rendezvous, gazing in horror at crashed gliders and dead men in scores. He later found twenty-four of his own battalion hanging dead in their harnesses in the forest where they had been misdropped. The CO of the 1st Canadian Parachute Battalion was shot by the Germans, like Tibbs's comrades, as he hung helpless from the trees in his harness. The enraged Canadians stormed the neighbouring town of Schnappenburg, giving short shrift to those Germans they encountered on their passage, though in truth it was no more rational to expect mercy for a paratrooper in transit than for a bailed-out tank crew. The business of war is not to give the enemy a fair chance, but to do everything possible to deny him one.

Tibbs came upon the corpse of a staff-sergeant to whom he was much attached, turned over the man's body and was repelled by the sight of an earwig crawling out of the man's nose. He thought: this is the reality of war. Tibbs had just begun to treat British wounded when a tall, distinguished-looking German Army doctor presented himself and gave a smart salute. "Good morning," said the man in English. "Why have you been so long? We have been up all night waiting for you." For some hours, the British and German medical teams worked beside each other: "We got on well. The Germans were always pretty good on these occasions." "The landing zone was a pretty horrific sight. People were deeply upset—about a third of our gliderborne element were casualties."

Peter Downward was overwhelmed by the spectacle of parachutes in the thousands filling the air, each one differently coloured to denote whether it bore man, ammunition or medical supplies. Every company commander of 13 Para possessed a hunting horn, and sounded this as he hit the ground in differing Morse letters to summon his men. One of Downward's NCOs inquired after his health, and only then did he realize that the lieutenant was bleeding from a tiny fragment of shrapnel which had struck his nose during the drop. He was lying among his men, peering cautiously over the rim of a ridge to pinpoint his position, when his attention was distracted by the spectacle of his colonel, Peter

Luard, cantering up to him astride a large captured German farm horse. "For God's sake, Downward—there's your objective!" Luard pointed. "Take it!" Thus inspired, the young officer got up and sprang forward with his platoon towards a barn which he found already occupied by men of the battalion. "Things were starting to fall into place amid this absolute mayhem." As he stood among the casualties at the regimental aid post, he saw a popular Canadian officer lying motionless on a stretcher. Downward said how sorry he was to see that the boy had been killed. This provoked an angry cry from the stretcher: "I'm not fucking dead—I've been hit and I can't bloody well move." The young man was paralysed for the rest of his life.

The third American unit of 17th Airborne, 194th Glider Infantry, landed in the right place, at the cost of twelve C-47 towing aircraft shot down and almost every glider damaged. The men, led by the relatively elderly forty-five-year-old Colonel James Pierce, spewed out of the wreckage to find themselves instantly engaged with German flak-gunners, who depressed their weapons to fire at the airborne soldiers on the ground. By the time the shooting stopped, the 194th had captured forty-two guns, ten tanks, two mobile flak-wagons and five self-propelled guns.

One of the stranger cargoes in 6th Airborne Division's gliders was a team from the British intelligence organisation SOE. Two British officers were landed with a group of agents, mostly Polish, whom they were instructed to infiltrate into the German lines, with orders to gather information as far forward as they could get. Major Arthur Winslow reported that he had taken one man to the forward British positions and left him in the hands of the local company commander, to penetrate the German line as best he could: "I cannot say I was altogether hopeful about his chances." He left three more Poles on a road near Osnabrück. "They had shown a certain amount of doubt about getting away," he said, but finally each agent in turn kissed the British officer on both cheeks and started walking towards the last fragment of Hitler's empire. Winslow watched "three rather forlorn-looking figures disappear into the blue." Nothing is known of their fate.

General Matthew Ridgway, who had characteristically decided to jump with 17th Airborne, almost became its last casualty of the Rhine operation. Late on the night of the 24th, the two jeeps carrying him and his aides left a meeting with the British and were driving back to the American zone. Suddenly, they saw Germans in front of them. The paratroopers hastily stopped and jumped out of the vehicles. There was a brisk firefight, in which a German grenade landed among the Americans. Ridgway's jeep took most of the blast, but a fragment wounded the general in the arm and shoulder. The Germans retired, no doubt as surprised and shaken as the Americans. The Americans crowded into their surviving jeep, and reached the 17th CP unscathed. Ridgway needed major surgery on his arm, but pronounced himself too busy to have the grenade fragment removed until the war was over. He suffered severe discomfort from it through the weeks that followed. Airborne command was no sinecure.

IF MONTGOMERY's Rhine operation was plodding and over-insured, those who crossed the water could be grateful that their objectives were gained at small price. But the casualties incurred by the airborne assault were out of all proportion to its contribution. Gliders were never again employed in war. Operation Varsity was a folly for which more than a thousand men paid with their lives— almost as many as 1st Airborne lost killed at Arnhem. Once again, a baleful reality had been permitted to steer events: the airborne divisions existed, and consumed rations. So they had to be used. Thereafter, however, for the remaining weeks of the campaign American and British paratroopers fought as infantry.

Alan Brooke expressed relief when he got Churchill safely home after witnessing the crossings at Wesel. He had been alarmed by the old statesman's eagerness to expose himself to German fire, his exultation when the odd shell landed near him. "I honestly believe that he would have liked to be killed on the front at this moment of success," Brooke wrote in his diary. "He had often told me that the way to die is to pass out fighting when your blood is up and you feel nothing." Yet if Churchill had reached a stage of his life at which personal survival seemed unimportant, younger men did not share his indifference. Exploitation beyond the Rhine by the American and British armies proved embarrassingly sluggish. Once again, the Allies found themselves engaged in sharp fighting against remnants of such formations as 116th Panzer. Town by town and village by village, the Allies pressed on into the surviving strongholds of the Reich, halting where they met opposition, bombarding the defenders into submission whenever this was possible. The effectiveness of German resistance in the west was diminishing daily, but there always seemed just enough men and just enough guns to sustain some kind of defence. "With hindsight," observed Kurt von Tippelskirch sagely, "following the breaching of the Rhine, the last symbolic and military obstacle in the west, it becomes difficult to perceive any purpose in the continuance of the war. But the struggle continued, because there was no one who would or could end it, as long as the man who had begun it all remained at his post."

A few, a very few Allied soldiers enjoyed the battles in Germany. "My only experience of war was being on the winning side," said Captain John Langdon, a twenty-three-year-old officer with 3rd Royal Tanks. "It may sound a terrible thing to say, but I found it all terrifically exciting. I loved it." Most of his comrades did not. "There was an impatience, even desperation to get this thing over," said Major John Denison of 214th Brigade. "The liberation of Germany is a sight to see," wrote George Turner-Cain, "hardly one stone left upon another, furniture taken out and burnt, china and bottles all broken. I do not like to see this kind of action, and do not encourage my men to do it. It is the Canadians and Yanks who are determined to create such havoc." Every soldier supposed that excesses were the prerogative of some army other than his own.

They all hated street fighting. Supporting artillery, so effective in open country, became almost irrelevant. Among houses tactical radios, unreliable at the best of times, ceased to function at all. Tanks were vulnerable to grenades or petrol bombs dropped from above on to the turrets, always their most vulnerable points. The whole weight of endeavour fell on the infantry. "Clearing a town is an arduous process which cannot be hurried," observed a British briefing note. Men were told to leave behind packs which caught on windows, and warned that German paratroopers customarily occupied ground floors and cellars of houses. Clearing a street, infantry squads covered each other as they ran from house to house, sometimes grenading and sub-machining every room before entering. It was a laborious business which became ever more painful as the same routine had to be repeated through towns and villages across Germany, wherever resistance was met.

WILHELM PRITZ had endured a terrible war: two years on the Eastern Front and three wounds as an infantryman, before he gained the merciful deliverance, as it seemed to him, of a posting as a heavy mortar NCO with the 766th Regiment in Saarland. They blew up their remaining tubes and escaped across the Rhine north of Heidelberg in March 1945, suffering the bitter reproaches of civilians west of the river: "So—you're quitting and leaving us to face the enemy." When a *Kettenhunde*—military policeman—tried to herd him into the ranks of a battle group on the east bank, Pritz said simply: "Try to stop me and I'll kill you." He and some fifteen other stragglers banded together for protection against further MPs and began walking towards Heidelberg. At first, they also led a horse pulling a 37mm gun, but they wearied of this burden, and abandoned horse and gun in a shed. At the small town of Schlecheim, they took refuge among the local inhabitants in the cellar of a house. They had made up their minds to surrender. But surrender could be intensely dangerous.

Early next morning, 1 April, they sent a small boy into the town to look around. He returned to report that American troops were already searching houses. The civilians with them insisted that the soldiers should pile their weapons in another room, which they did. They were frightened, "but nothing to what we would have been if we had been facing the Russians." At last, an American shouted from up the stairs: "*Kamerad! Kommen!*" They filed out of the cellar, hands high. A GI briskly removed their watches and medals. An American officer demanded in perfect German: "So what are we going to do with your

Hitler and your Himmler?" "You can do what you like as far as I am concerned," said Pritz wearily. He felt a surge of relief that his own war was over.

In the last weeks of the war, there was a dramatic increase in attrition from fausts. In Normandy, these had accounted for just 6 per cent of British tank losses, rising to 9 per cent in Belgium and Holland, 7 per cent in western Germany—and a startling 34 per cent east of the Rhine. Statistics were similar for American armoured units. Crews adopted increasingly desperate methods to protect their tanks, shielding them with sandbags and bundles of logs laced with chicken wire. When the U.S. 3rd Division captured a cement factory at Stolberg, crews ignored warnings that overloading hulls could wreck suspensions, and mixed concrete to lay on the front of their Shermans. "They would grab at any straws," wrote an armoured officer, "they were desperate to survive."

By February 1945, new tanks were being sent into service which belatedly matched those of the Germans. The British Comet and American Pershing were formidable weapons, with heavier protective armour and bigger guns. Infantry had to be warned to stand well clear of the Pershing's high-velocity 90mm cannon when it fired, because of the terrific blast deflected by the muzzle brake. The Pershings fought their first battle in Cologne, and amazed the Germans by their ability to fire on the move, with gyro-stabilized gunsights.

Yet, to the very end of the war, it was remarkable how much damage well-handled enemy tanks inflicted upon the Allied juggernaut. On 30 March, a troop of King Tigers from a German armoured school encountered a column of Shermans advancing along a road with half-tracks loaded with infantry, and three tank destroyers. As the Americans approached a road junction, the Tigers cruised down the line in the opposite direction. "Observers said it looked more like a naval engagement than a land battle." One Sherman hit a Tiger on the thin armour above its engine compartment, and another German crew bailed out when hit by a white phosphorus smoke shell, convinced that its Tiger was on fire. But the Americans suffered appallingly: seventeen Shermans, seventeen half-tracks, three trucks, two jeeps and a tank destroyer were knocked out in a matter of minutes.

Complaints about the quality of infantry replacements became a strident chorus in the last weeks, as both Americans and British scraped the manpower barrel. A U.S. rifle company commander, Lieutenant Jack M. Brown, lamented the quality of soldiers joining his unit: "The men as a whole are not well trained... They will not return enemy fire. They are not fit physically or mentally." Brown described how an NCO came back from a patrol, complaining that his men went to ground and refused to move when friendly artillery fire was heard passing overhead. "A private came to the First Sergeant recently and complained of having nervous indigestion. He wanted to go on sick call, and as a result was evacuated. Upon questioning this man, I found that the ripple of friendly artillery fire was making him nervous...several men suddenly develop aches, pains etc on outpost duty, and request to be relieved. Someone has scared these men to death."

Likewise in British units, the quality of replacements caused exasperation. David Tibbs ruefully contrasted the paratroop volunteers he had known in Normandy with newcomers in 1945. "Under stress, not infrequently they fell apart morally." Lieutenant Roy Dixon said: "There was a certain reluctance towards the end to do anything exciting." Major Bill Deedes: "The willpower to keep going forward under fire weakened as time went on. You don't become 'battle-hardened.' One of the tank commanders we worked with had been brewed up three times. Inevitably, the nerve weakens. We weren't nearly as good in 1945 as we had been in 1944." The desperate shortage of British replacements made it necessary to break up more units and send their men to new regiments, creating unhappy misalliances. The 6th Cameronians were fiercely proud of their Scottish Calvinist lineage. When thirty Catholics arrived one day as replacements, they were not made welcome. The Protestant riflemen marched out behind an Orange banner, singing that anthem of intolerance "The Sash My Father Wore." A bitter sectarian brawl broke out behind the lines. A young officer who tried to intervene was brushed aside by a man saying simply: "You bugger off—this is nothing to do with you."

Given the desperate need for infantry, the U.S. Army hastily extended the use of African-Americans in combat roles. Their behaviour inspired some encouraging reports from field commanders. Major Roderick R. Allen reported: "they are performing very well. There has been no running away, and there have been some individual acts of heroism which were awarded the Bronze Star." But others remained sceptical. Brigadier-General Fred Ennis, a senior officer of 12th Armored Division, reported: "We are having disciplinary trouble with some of them along sexual lines, and it would be distinctly helpful if we had latitude in plucking out the trouble-makers." Lieutenant-Colonel Wells, commanding 66th Armored Infantry, said: "The colored troops as yet are definitely not first-line combat troops, but their performance has been good at sentry and outpost work. They have been very alert and will shoot at anything, but I would say that they are more jumpy than white troops." It was scarcely surprising that African-Americans incurred problems in combat roles after generations of cavalier, even brutal treatment at the hands of the U.S. Army.

As the British fought their way into Osnabrück in the last days of March against some dogged resistance, a sergeant medical orderly went forward to treat a wounded German and was promptly shot. Shortly afterwards, the defenders sent a message to the British lines apologizing for the mistake, and said that the man had been taken to the city hospital. David Tibbs climbed into a jeep with the battalion padre, a driver and an immense red-cross flag. They drove unimpeded through the German line and into the city, through a vast throng of refugees, a hand pressed down hard on the jeep's horn. "The devastation was enormous." At the hospital, they found a dozen British wounded in one ward—most, as a German officer told them with bleak satisfaction, PoWs who had fallen victim to British shelling. Bill Webster, the man they had come to see, had been hit in the neck, and lay paralysed. The German surgeon who was treating him said he thought the sergeant had a chance of making a recovery, and indeed he later did so. The British visitors drank schnapps with the mother superior and the colonel in command. They toasted an early end to the war. Then they drove unscathed back to the British lines, amid spasmodic explosions as the retreating Germans blew up their ammunition dumps.

An officer of the Highland Light Infantry advancing into Osnabrück told a man to escort a young German prisoner to the rear. Hearing a shot, he asked who had fired. The same soldier answered: "It was me, sir. He kept saying 'I die for my Führer, I die for my Führer' ... well, the bugger's dead. Aye, he is." The officer resignedly ordered the man back to his post.

On every side, the Germans were cracking, the Allied sense of victory was growing. Attacking an enemy-held village at the head of a troop of Crocodile flame-throwing tanks, Lieutenant Andrew Wilson felt himself gripped by an "unfeeling madness":

> He looked for places where the enemy might still be hiding. There was a wooden shed. As the flame hit it, the wood blew away in a burning mass, and there in the wreckage was the body of a Spandau ... The gunner gripped his trigger. Swinging the turret down the front of the burning village, he began firing off the seventy-five at point-blank range. Where, oh where, was the infantry? As always in action, he lost count of time. Wherever he swung the cupola, he saw fire and smoke and the track of destruction ... Then all at once it was over. By the barn a little group of grey-clad Germans appeared, without helmets or weapons, waving a sheet on a pole. He gave the order to stop firing and opened the hatches. The air was full of smuts and the sickly-sweet smell of fuel. He made a sign for the Germans to come out into the open. They moved slowly. At first there were ten; then there were 30 or 40. In the hush of the moment, he felt a great elation; if ordered, he could have driven through the smoking village and right on to the enemy's divisional headquarters. Nothing could have stopped him; he couldn't be harmed. Then the infantry came swarming into the village, dodging the mortar shells which the enemy had started dropping now. In the confusion, the Germans began to bring out their wounded, blinded and burned, roughly bandaged beneath their charred uniforms. Some of them looked at the Crocodile. What were they thinking? He went back to

refuel, and remembered his letters. One was from his mother. It said: "We are proud of you."

Total casualties in the British 21st Army Group for February and March were 5,180 men killed, 21,170 wounded and 2,850 missing. Such numbers did not indicate fighting of great intensity, by the standards of the European war. Yet they represented the equivalent of thirty-five or forty infantry battalions lost to the British order of battle. The overwhelming preponderance of Americans was still increasing. On 15 December 1944, there were 3.24 million men in Eisenhower's armies, including 1,965,601 U.S. troops in Europe, 810,584 British, 293,411 French and 116,411 Canadians. On 4 February 1945, overall Allied strength had risen to 3.38 million. By the end of March, there were four million uniformed men under Eisenhower's command, of whom 2,550,037 were American and 866,575 British. In these final weeks of the war, at last the divide between the manpower commitment of the Western allies and that of the Soviets was narrowing. Churchill feared that the world would soon forget the scale of Britain's sacrifice. He told the Cabinet Office: "Get me the best figures available of the losses sustained by the English in this war... Another calculation which might be made would refer to the loss of cockneys. Would it perhaps be true to say the citizens of London, military and civil, have lost more than the whole of the British Empire?"

The prime minister received in response statistics of relative mortality among the Western allied nations in the Second World War: by April 1945, one in 165 Englishmen had died, one in 130 Londoners, one in 385 Australians, one in 385 Canadians, one in 175 New Zealanders and one in 775 Americans. The Western allies possessed no idea of how many Russians had been killed, and no one in Moscow was likely to tell them. The dying was not over yet, but at last the men of the Allied armies were beginning to dare to hope that they might live. By April 1945, Captain David Fraser spoke for millions of his comrades when he observed: "The sense that, with luck, one might be able to see the end became a dominant emotion."

CHAPTER THIRTEEN

Prisoners of the Reich

THOSE INVOLVED in the cataclysmic struggle for Germany fell into three categories. First, there were perhaps twenty-five million active participants, who fought in the uniforms of one army or another. These men were subject to orders and vulnerable to the brutal fortunes of the battle-field, yet they were protagonists in determining the fate of Europe. Then there were the onlookers—the civilian inhabitants of Germany. Wilfully or no, they had brought a terrible evil upon the world. Yet now they found themselves supine, impotent, mesmerized, as catastrophe descended. The third group were victims—prisoners of many nations held in thrall by Hitler and his minions, powerless to influence their own fates save by the act of survival. This, for most, was challenge enough. It is hard to bridge the cultural abyss between the man-nered, comfortable, fatly fed, impeccably uniformed ethos of Eisenhower's headquarters, from which the liberation of Europe was being directed, and the conditions of animal subjection in which Hitler's prisoners in their millions waited for Eisenhower's soldiers to come. Until the very end, the Nazis contin-ued to inflict suffering and death upon the innocent as if the Thousand-Year Reich remained a realistic prospect.

By 1945, the custody, exploitation and murder of prisoners had become the largest activities in Germany beyond the military struggle. In computing scale, it is impossible to distinguish accurately between voluntary and forced labour-ers. Only approximate estimates are feasible. Even after the killing of nine mil-lion German captives since 1939, between eight and ten million foreign men, women and children remained in Hitler's dominions, held in varying degrees of proximity to death. These figures take no account of entire nations still held captive, such as the Dutch. From every country which fell under Hitler's sway after 1939, the Nazis herded men and women in vast numbers into the Greater Reich. The circumstances of their bondage varied greatly. First, there were American and British military PoWs. Although these suffered hunger and intermittent brutality, most were treated in accordance with the Geneva Convention. Their captivity was relatively humane until the last months of the war. Many were then marched hundreds of miles under dreadful conditions, as the Germans sought to prevent their liberation. Some thousands died in consequence.

Next down the hierarchy came French, Polish and Italian PoWs, who were treated less well. Many were sent to work for German factories and farms in conditions that ranged between tolerable and barbaric. Some 1.8 million PoWs were directly employed in the German war economy. Beyond these, some 7.8 million paid and forced labourers from all over Europe sustained German industry in the absence at the front or in the grave of much of its workforce. Some 500,000 Ukrainian women, for instance, were shipped to Germany between 1942 and 1944 to boost civilian morale by reinforcing the ranks of domestic servants. Nothing gave greater impetus to Resistance movements throughout occupied Europe than the anxiety of young men to escape deportation for forced labour. Many of those shipped to Germany were treated as slaves. Hundreds of thousands died. Six hundred thousand Italian "military internees" were treated with special cruelty by Germans embittered about the perceived betrayal of the Reich by Italy's 1943 surrender.

Beyond these again were the last categories: Jews, together with political prisoners and Russians. The Jews were singled out for extermination, and in that sense their fate was unique. In the last year of the war, the pace of killing quickened. Those who survived did so merely by accident, because the Nazi death machine faltered amid the disruptions and administrative inconveniences imposed by defeat. But in considering Nazi servitude as a phenomenon it should be remembered that Germany also presided over the killing of a host of people who were not Jewish. At least three million Russians and hundreds of thousands of other enemies of Hitler died in captivity. Two million Soviet prisoners, Poles, Gypsies and other "anti-social elements" were killed at Auschwitz alone, in addition to two million Jews. Many victims were merely allowed to perish in the concentration-camp system, rather than being deliberately gassed. Every Western allied prisoner who glimpsed a compound inhabited by Russians recognized how fortunate were his own circumstances in comparison. Germany's excuse was that the Soviet Union was not a signatory to the Geneva Convention, and thus that Stalin's soldiers could not expect its protection. Every day in every camp in which Russians were held, men died of disease, hunger or cruelty.

It is an odd reflection of the Nazi psyche that Hitler chose to keep millions of Russians on the brink of death rather than to shoot or gas them. The Third Reich's immense network of camps required tens of thousands of staff to service and guard its inmates, men who might otherwise have rendered service at the front. The SS directly employed some 300,000 prisoners manufacturing consumer goods for commercial sale and small quantities of ammunition, but these activities were so inefficiently and corruptly organized—to the despair of Speer—that they brought no advantage to the German war economy. Hundreds of thousands of prisoners were provided with unproductive tasks merely to occupy their days. As Germany's labour shortage became a critical issue, it was rational enough to exploit captives to sustain the Reich's industry. It remains baffling, however, that a Nazi leadership willing to murder millions of people without scruple should have allowed other millions to cling narrowly to life. A highly structured, finely tuned hierarchy of suffering, offering pitiful rewards and appalling punishments, persisted in Germany until the end.

By 1945, the millions who languished within the camps of the Third Reich awaited deliverance in the knowledge that they were doomed unless relief soon came. When staff officers in the armies of Montgomery or Bradley, Zhukov or Rokossovsky asked themselves what need there was for haste in completing the defeat of Hitler's empire, any man and woman confined behind the wire encircling a thousand Nazi barracks could have given an answer. "They could have been quicker," said Nikolai Maslennikov, for three years an inmate of concentration camps. "The Western allies only started to fight when the Germans were almost beaten. They were bloody slow. They were too late for too many."

THE PRIVILEGED

The most fortunate, or least unfortunate, of Germany's prisoners were American and British soldiers, sailors and airmen, though they could scarcely be expected to see their own predicament thus. Under the terms of the Geneva Convention, officers were not liable to work, while other ranks could be conscripted for labour. Ironically, many officers suffered greater psychological stress from the privilege of idleness than some of their men who were put to work. As a PoW, Private Ron Graydon worked without resentment as a coal miner. "You just accepted it." One of his comrades, a big Guardsman named "Chalky" White, managed to conduct an affair with the landlady of a local bar. Graydon's circumstances deteriorated when he was transferred to work in a benzine plant outside Chemnitz among slave labourers.

Among those drafted for agricultural service, some were brutally treated by German farmers. Others, however, forged surprisingly close relationships with the families to which they were dispatched. Tom Barker, from Eastbourne in Sussex, was a twenty-two-year-old private in the Royal Engineers, captured in France in 1940. From his prison camp in Poland, he found himself sent to work every day for a local German farmer, Hugo Otto. At first, Barker was merely a clumsy city boy. Within months, however, he found himself managing a horse plough, scything corn, slaughtering pigs, as if to the manner born. He grew to love Laura the mare and her foal Lorchen. The farm grew potatoes and rye, some barley and oats, roots for the animals and a few peas. Barker learned to speak German, and ate with the family: "It always mystified me how, with so few basic things to use, they always managed to produce the most delicious food." Hugo Otto occasionally offered him a glass of schnapps. Gerda, the family's teenage daughter, became a close friend, though her somewhat starchy mother tried to insist that, as a PoW, Barker should always walk behind Gerda rather than beside her. In the evenings before he returned to camp to sleep, the girl sometimes sang to Tom's accordion, while another prisoner played a violin. He was taught to shoe horses, and even to do some iron-working in the forge.

This was the young soldier's life for more than three years, of a kind shared by hundreds of thousands of others. It would be foolish to assert that many prisoners achieved as rewarding a relationship with their captors as that of Tom Barker. His prison life was not an idyll. Like every other PoW, he suffered a long interruption of his youth. But the experience was redeemed, rendered tolerable, by his engagement with simple peasants. "You may perhaps think that the life of a prisoner as I have described it does not compare with what you have learnt from books and films," Barker wrote. "We were better treated than the French, which seemed rather odd, as they had made peace with Germany; better than the Poles...the brutality to the Russians was indescribable." The camp guards were mostly Ukrainians. The only interruption of a lax regime came one night when a prisoner sought to indulge a familiar practise of slipping through the wire to visit his Polish girlfriend. The guards shot him. He hung screaming on the fence until he died. Thereafter, none of the prisoners sought to test their captors' goodwill.

By 1944, there was scarcely a farm in Germany which was not dependent upon PoWs or foreign forced labourers to replace absent soldiers. Stanislas Domoradzki, a Pole, was among those treated far less humanely than Tom Barker. He was regarded as a slave by the first family for whom he worked near Kitzingen on the river Main. "Stan" was just fourteen when he was detained in a summary round-up near his home, herded on to a train and shipped to Germany. He was issued with a yellow "P" armband, and sent to a farm where he was relentlessly beaten and bullied by Herr Schmitt, his elderly employer, and Schmitt's daughter-in-law. "You'll fill in for my sons who are away fighting," said the farmer sourly. Stan was eventually returned to the local mayor's office, as not worth his keep. He was not strong enough to manage heavy labour. He fared a little better with his next employer. The father of the house was a harsh taskmaster, but his eighteen-year-old daughter Guedraut befriended Stan, and eventually provided his first sexual experience.

As an officer, Captain John Killick was not liable for work. He spent his time as a prisoner in a room with three other men captured at Arnhem. The adjutant of I Para occupied himself almost exclusively, it seemed to Killick, in polishing his boots. He himself played a guitar in the camp band. The paratroopers were

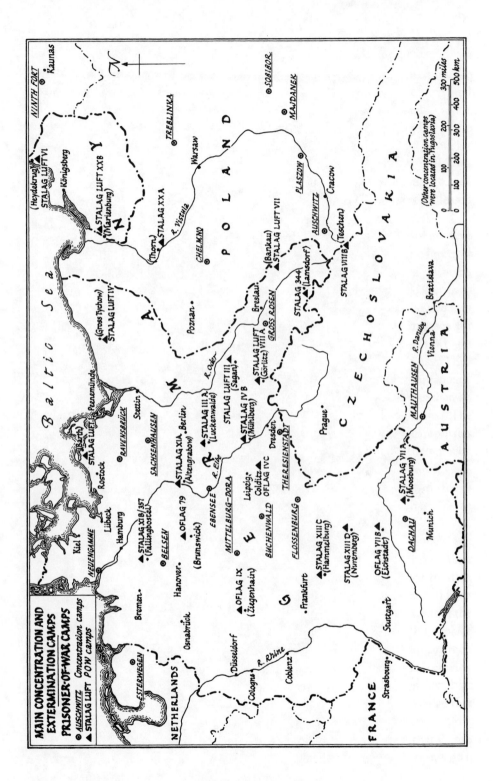

MAIN CONCENTRATION AND
EXTERMINATION CAMPS
PRISONER-OF-WAR CAMPS

● AUSCHWITZ Concentration camps
▲ STALAG LUFT POW camps

exceptionally fit when they arrived, so that it was several months before hunger began seriously to corrode them. They were appalled by the mental state of some of those who had been captives for four or five years. "Many had become deeply withdrawn. Several were frankly psychotic." When Richard Burt, a Liberator gunner, arrived at Stalag IVB after being shot down in November 1944, "we were told by the guards not to stare at our fellow-prisoners, because many of them had been here a long time, and acted a little peculiar. If we were to see them sailing their little boats on the fire pond, we were not to make fun of them. I guess before it was over, we were all a little peculiar."

Yet it often fell to long-serving prisoners to lend support to bewildered, traumatized new arrivals. At Stalag IVB, the British were horrified by the state of some of the Americans who joined them after the Bulge battle: "their morale was at rock bottom. They were shocked, frightened, suffering from frostbite," and in need of help and leadership. In all the camps, unlikely people held the prisoners together and strove to keep spirits alive. In Stalag IVB, the guiding light was a forty-year-old dental officer, who had been "in the bag" since 1940. Another veteran, Regimental-Sergeant-Major Andy Samuels, earned the lifelong admiration of other inmates for his leadership in the last months of the war.

The tedium of camp life was dreadful. It was shattered at intervals, however, by incidents which emphasized the prisoners' circumstances. At Stalag IVB, three PoWs were shot dead during 1944: one was caught stealing coal; another crossed the perimeter tripwire; a third broke the curfew. A twenty-year-old Liberator gunner from Pittsburgh, Charles Becker, believed that the guards at his camp, Stalag IV in Pomerania, behaved well enough as long as men obeyed the rules: don't cross the warning wire, ensure that windows are barred and no lights shown at night: "I thought they did the best they could under the circumstances and conditions." Yet Becker suffered the usual chronic malnutrition. His teeth loosened. The diet of starch, bread and potatoes inflicted constant constipation, sometimes for eight or ten days at a stretch. Most of the daylight hours, prisoners walked round and round the perimeter wire talking to friends, or eked out the simple tasks that assumed much importance in a world in which there was so little to do.

Self-respect was deeply corroded by confinement, and that of some prisoners collapsed altogether. "I have seen men degrade themselves to beg for an inch or so of a cigarette being smoked by a guard," wrote Sergeant Robert Harding. "I have seen men sell the very clothes from their backs for a single fag." Corporal Denis Thomas observed: "People say: 'Oh, you were only inside for six months.' But they were the worst six months of my life." Many men felt outcasts, cut off from their own kind, their lives deprived of purpose and dignity. Grievances and frustrations became obsessional. Denied privacy, they took refuge in hiding small items, especially food. "Even reasonable men would waste hours in childish kicking against the pricks," wrote Squadron-Leader Peter Campbell, an RAF officer in Sagan. Tiny events assumed extravagant proportions. One day in the autumn of 1944, some prisoners were allowed out of the perimeter under escort, for a walk. Campbell found this "an overpowering sensation." New arrivals were intently questioned about the outside world: "How're we doing? Is London still standing?" In some camps, the dissemination of news received by secret radios was highly organized. New Zealand doctor Richard Feltham was amazed on his first morning in Stalag XXA to receive a smart salute from a Guards sergeant-major who handed him two duplicated sheets, saying: "*The Times*, sir!"

Morale improved in 1944. When news of D-Day reached Tom Barker's camp, a big Londoner named Bob, who had been attempting with indifferent success to grow tomatoes, dashed to his vegetable plot and joyfully tore up every plant: "I shan't need the bloody things!" Bob was premature, but at nights thereafter prisoners could see the glow of war on the eastern horizon and hear the rumble of explosions. "We were never satisfied unless we heard the Allies were advancing very rapidly," wrote Peter Campbell, "and we had no patience when they were stopped for any period."

Some men became involved in escape plans not because they possessed a serious hope of gaining freedom, but because fantasies of escape provided a focus for lives that were otherwise purposeless. Only a tiny number of Allied prisoners made successful "home runs," or indeed tried to do so. The difficulties were enormous, even if one spoke good German and was granted extraordinary luck. Peter Campbell felt grateful that a leg injury sustained when he parachuted into the Channel from his Spitfire in April 1942 disqualified him from taking part in Sagan's 1943 "Great Escape," which provoked the Nazis to shoot fifty of the officers recaptured. A giant sign was thereafter displayed in the camp by the Germans: "ESCAPE IS NO LONGER A SPORT." Campbell wrote: "Escape starts as a madness, then the PoW adjusts and becomes institutionalised." He himself worked in the props department of the camp theatre, and attended Spanish classes. Every man was hungry, and matters worsened dramatically in the last months of the war. Campbell lost over forty pounds. Private Jerome Alexis of the U.S. 110th Infantry, who had been captured in the Hürtgen Forest in November 1944, was among a group of enlisted men working in the officer camp Oflag LXIV at Altburgund. There were educational classes of all kinds. Alexis studied French and German, but still found the boredom crippling.

John Killick suffered a special difficulty, that his marriage was unhappy. He had to think through his personal problems under exceptionally unpromising circumstances. "But I discovered inner resources. I read a lot of Dickens, wrote up my Arnhem diary." It is dismaying to notice the number of women who felt no scruple about informing husbands behind the wire in Germany of their defection, or even of pregnancy by another man. This added emotional anguish to conditions that were already wretched enough. British officer George Millar became obsessively determined to get home to his adored wife. He made three bids for freedom before finally achieving the miracle of a successful escape from Stalag VIIA in 1944. "The only thing that would end everything," Millar told his wife when they were at last reunited in their London flat, "would be if you had fallen in love with somebody else…" She replied coldly: "Perhaps I have." Millar wrote of himself: "He began then to wish that he had not come home." Utterly distraught, the young officer volunteered to parachute back into Europe as a secret agent, and indeed did so.

Cold was the worst hardship in the winter of 1944, and prisoners spent many hours in bed to escape it. Killick became a smoker for the first time in his life— "People said it helped"—and rolled cigarettes from an unlikely blend of dried vegetable leaves. He began imprisonment weighing 189 pounds and emerged weighing 140. Some of the tensions between Allied forces persisted into PoW camps. Most British and American prisoners pitied the Russians, despised the French and thought the Poles unhinged. In Stalag VIIA at Moosburg, near Munich, by the time of its liberation 80,000 prisoners were confined in an area of eighty-five acres, including 38,000 French, 8,000 British, 6,000 American and 14,000 Russian. Nineteen-year-old American Bud Lindsey intensely disliked the three British NCOs who ran Hut 53: "Their demeanour was aloof, conceited. They gave the impression they considered American GIs to be inferior, which did not sit well with our group… especially with me, the best soda jerk in central Texas."

Lindsey and his companions readily measured the fluctuations of the war by the behaviour of their captors. The Germans enjoyed a burst of elation in December, during the Ardennes offensive. This was supplanted two months later by a newfound eagerness to make Allied friends. A guard took Lindsey's little work gang into a Munich café and bought his charges a beer. The man plainly realized how soon he would be changing places with them. There was a last spasm of German jubilation when news came of President Roosevelt's death, which some guards, like their Führer, deluded themselves would precipitate the break-up of the Grand Alliance. To the end, their captors strove to maintain their authority. On 3 April, Lindsey was sentenced to thirty days' punishment for stealing a Red Cross parcel. A German officer told the American that he would be court-martialled as soon as the war was over.

Early in 1945, as the Russians began to sweep across the territory of the Greater Reich, Hitler entertained the notion of murdering all PoWs before they could be liberated. He was enraged by reports of German soldiers surrendering in large numbers to the Western allies. This, he said, was "the fault of that stupid Geneva Convention. We must scrap the idiotic thing." He argued that, if the Nazis killed their own prisoners, such action would put a stop to the

Allies' humane treatment of Germans who surrendered, and thus destroy any incentive for his soldiers to betray their duty. Jodl and Guderian with difficulty dissuaded Hitler from this course. Yet the Nazi leadership remained determined not to allow Allied captives to be liberated. Göring pointed out to Hitler at a conference on 27 January that 10,000 Allied aircrew were held captive at Sagan, in the path of the Red Army. It had been suggested that these men should merely be left to the Russians. The Luftwaffe's chief strongly objected to making the Allies a present of 10,000 trained airmen. "They must leave," agreed Hitler, "even if they march on foot. Anyone who runs away will be shot. That must be done by all means." Göring said jovially: "Take off their trousers and shoes, so they can't walk in the snow."

Hundreds of thousands of prisoners found it hard enough to walk in the snow even when they retained their trousers and shoes. Not only from Sagan, but from scores of camps throughout the eastern Reich, during the first weeks of 1945 the inmates were herded forth on marches westward that continued for weeks and even months, inflicting terrible suffering. Dragging their pitiful possessions, escorted by guards in little better case than themselves, they trudged through the thick snows amid unending columns of refugees already clogging the roads. Almost every route westward from Poland was crowded with suffering humanity, together with their abandoned possessions. At least 750,000 concentration-camp prisoners were driven west. More than a third died. Many were simply shot out of hand by guards impatient with the difficulties of moving exhausted and starving skeletons barefoot in deep snow. Others perished from hunger or exposure, others again from air attack—Allied pilots were often unable to distinguish between columns of enemy soldiers, refugees and prisoners on the roads of Germany flashing beneath their wings.

Military prisoners suffered less than concentration-camp inmates during these marches. Yet the last months of the war provided the worst experience of their captivity. One morning early in January 1945, Private Tom Barker's camp was alerted to move. The young British soldier walked for the last time to the farm of the Otto family, where he had worked for three years. They, too, were preparing to flee from the Russians. Frau Otto was holding Laura the mare while Hugo shod her, in readiness to pull their cart. Their daughter Gerda was baking bread: "To the other children, it was all an exciting joke, but Gerda was old enough to realise that this was a tragedy, and it showed in her face." Barker gave her his accordion. She offered him two loaves of bread and a piece of bacon. He borrowed the family sledge, in the hope that the prisoners would be able to use it to take with them some of the remarkable accumulation of possessions they had assembled since 1941.

We now had to say goodbye. You may think it strange that goodbyes between what were supposed to be enemies should be difficult, but difficult it was. I had long since become…one of the family. I wanted to hug them all, but because of everything I hesitated to do so, something I always regretted. I could still remember the agonies of the refugees in Belgium and France in 1940. I knew that, for these people, conditions would be almost unbearable, in the depths of a bitter winter.

And so the young British soldier and the German fugitives parted, to play their separate roles in the vast trek west, through months in which Barker suffered experiences far more dreadful than anything he had known during his three years in Poland.

American airman Richard Burt was among those who began to march in February from Stalag IVB. The prisoners were soon desperately hungry. They received their best break when RAF fighters strafed the column. Cannon fire killed the horses of their ration-wagon. The starving prisoners butchered the animals and enjoyed their first solid meal for weeks. Otherwise, they picked and boiled dandelion leaves, crushed grain and made soup. They journeyed across eastern Europe for three terrible months, scavenging every mile of the way. Burt was grateful for his own boy-scout training—"Some of the city boys found it very tough." They never washed, and were all riddled with lice and ticks: "I felt ashamed of myself for falling into such a sick state. We were weak, wet, hungry, and not much seemed to matter most of the time." The very act of walking became intolerable. They hated especially the hard cobbled streets of towns. No one knew what happened to many men who fell by the wayside in snowstorms or collapsed later from exhaustion or starvation. None had any thought of escape so close to the end of the war. Indeed, they feared being left behind by their columns, finding themselves at the mercy of a hostile population. The prisoners were taunted and cursed by many German communities through which they passed, and even stoned by children urged on by their parents. "We seemed most likely to be killed when they found out that we were *Americanisch Luftwaffe*," wrote Burt. When the prisoners finally met Allied troops in May, like most of his comrades Burt was obliged to spend a week in hospital before being fit even for a transit camp.

Bill Bampton, a private of the East Surreys captured in 1940, started marching with his column from Stalag XXB near Danzig on 24 January. They had some discussion about hiding in the woods to await the Russians, "but I preferred to stay with the crowd, a decision I later regretted." There were 500 of them, British and French, with intense animosity between the nationalities. The Polish civilians among whom their course first lay were kind, but the cold was deadly: "With our sled, I could not help thinking of Scott's expedition to the Pole." They slept mostly in farm buildings.

A crisis came when it was found that some men had pilfered tinned meat from the column's stocks. The commandant paraded all 500 men, and announced that unless the culprits confessed there would be no further issues of Red Cross parcels. There was a long silence. Then some prisoners urged the guilty to own up: "Be British! Show you've got British guts!" A few reluctantly stepped forward, some of whom denounced their fellow culprits. The mood of desperation intensified every day. Bampton was shocked to find his comrades stealing bread from each other's packs: "A shameful happening...I couldn't help noting another lesson in human nature. The British people are pleasant in pleasant circumstances, but otherwise..." He wrote in his diary: "I hate the way our boys behave, rushing and pushing and completely forgetting that they are British soldiers." He was disgusted by the spectacle of men fighting for possession of Red Cross parcels: "a shocking affair! Talk about wild animals."

Dr. Helmut Hugel, a German petroleum engineer and enthusiastic Nazi, was walking down a road behind the front when he overtook a column of American prisoners being hastily herded beyond reach of liberation. He was horrified to hear a guard shout: "Anyone who cannot go on will be shot!" Hugel wrote in his diary: "We thought this an empty threat, but soon we saw in the road ditch some prisoners who had indeed been killed. What sort of propaganda could the Americans make out of this, if they find them?"

In the last week of January, the inmates of Oflag LXIV began their own march westward, away from the distant sound of Soviet artillery fire. The prisoners were led by Colonel Paul Goode, a regimental commander captured in Normandy, who had run his camp with iron discipline. Goode was accompanied by his runner, Private Jerome Alexis. On their first day, the Americans covered twelve miles. The elderly guards were in such poor shape that the prisoners sometimes carried their rifles. They soon found themselves suffering dysentery from the local water. One morning, almost all the Germans disappeared. The German commandant, Colonel Schneider, formally surrendered himself to Colonel Goode, who sent a patrol in search of the Russians. Before this could return, however, some of the guards reappeared, accompanied by a detachment of Latvian SS. Colonel Schneider was reinstated. The prisoners' march continued. They moved westward, pitifully slowly among the mob of refugees. Alexis thought, however, that the American PoWs were treated better than those in British columns they met, among whom guards were using rifle butts ruthlessly. When some Russian prisoners attempted to beg cigarettes from the GIs, they were shot.

Four straggling British prisoners joined the Americans. One of them was a Scot who played the bagpipes. Colonel Goode appointed the soldier and his music to lead their column. To the prisoners' delight, a shipment of Red Cross parcels appeared. They crossed the Oder among the refugees on a ferry near Swinemünde on 28 February, and were then taken by train—how extraordinary that the Germans could still find rolling stock for such a purpose, at such a time—to Oflag XIIIB at Hammelburg. Thirteen hundred of them had set out from Poland. Just 400 prisoners arrived at Hammelburg. Most of the rest survived, but languished as stragglers up and down Germany.

Colonel Goode was appalled by the dejection and collapse of discipline he found in the new camp: "There was filth everywhere, the men were dirty and unkempt. An atmosphere of utter demoralization was easily discerned." Goode seethed, and sought to take a grip. "Slowly, things began to shape up as the colonel tried to instil a measure of self-esteem in the men once more," wrote his orderly. "He pointed out that becoming a prisoner-of-war was not a dishonourable thing, unless there had been cowardice, or a deliberate attempt to seek capture." But Goode could not produce food, because the Germans professed to have none.

On 26 March, the prisoners heard a rumour that American forces were approaching. What followed was one of the most extraordinary tragic farces of the north-west Europe campaign. At noon next day, the Hammelburg prisoners heard gunfire. A Sherman tank opened fire on the guard towers. The Germans responded. The guards fired warning shots towards the prisoners, who fled into their huts. Shermans killed some Yugoslav prisoners, whom they mistook for Germans. Suddenly three American PoWs including Colonel John Knight Waters, Goode's executive officer, walked forward carrying a white flag. They had been sent to negotiate with the American force by the camp commandant. A nervous guard raised a rifle and fired, wounding Waters. There was then an outburst of shooting from both American liberators and Germans. The wounded colonel was carried to the sickbay. Soon afterwards, the camp gates opened. Soldiers of Third Army poured in, mounted on jeeps and half-tracks. Colonel Goode conferred with the senior officers of the liberating force, Captain Abraham Baum and Major Alex Stiller, who identified himself as an aide of General Patton. Stiller said that he was accompanying the column "as an observer."

Baum said that he lacked the vehicles to take away all 1,291 U.S. prisoners, but would carry as many as he could. The story behind the arrival of his column defies belief. Hammelburg lay some thirty-six miles beyond the Allied front, in country still defended by elements of three German divisions. Baum had been dispatched on the personal orders of Patton, against the strong objections of the responsible corps and divisional commanders. Patton told them: "I'll replace every man and vehicle you lose." "Task Force Baum" started out with 294 men in sixteen tanks, twenty-seven half-tracks and assorted support vehicles. Colonel John Waters, Goode's executive officer, was Patton's son-in-law. The Third Army commander afterwards claimed he had no reliable knowledge that Waters was at Hammelburg, that he merely wished to liberate American prisoners known to be confined there. There is overwhelming evidence that Patton lied. The sole objective of the Hammelburg raid was the liberation of his own daughter's husband.

Baum's column set out in darkness to return to the Allied lines, every vehicle jammed with PoWs. Jerome Alexis rode on the hull of the third Sherman in the column. They passed some German soldiers without being challenged, and began to congratulate themselves. Thirty minutes down the road, however, they met their first opposition—German infantrymen with a faust who inflicted minor damage on a Sherman. This was enough to convince Baum that he faced a battle. He halted the column and conferred again with Goode. He explained that he could not fight with the PoWs aboard. There were no weapons for them and no space. To the prisoners' bitter chagrin, most were now marched back to the camp. They were soon followed by a thickening stream of wounded and stragglers from Baum's column, which found itself locked in combat with German forces. The Hammelburg infirmary filled to overflowing, its medical supplies exhausted. At 1500 next afternoon, the Germans marched all the unwounded prisoners down to the rail station and evacuated them to Stalag Luft III, which had been transferred from Sagan to Nuremberg. They were finally liberated at Moosburg on 29 April, after the U.S. 14th Armored Division fought a brief firefight with their guards. Colonel Waters and eighty other wounded prisoners remained at Hammelburg until they were freed on 6 April. Patton then dispatched his personal doctor and two Piper Cub aircraft to fly his son-in-law to hospital in Frankfurt. Both Baum and Major Stiller, who survived their battle with the Germans but themselves became prisoners, were deeply embittered. They did not become less so when Patton paid a personal visit to Baum's bedside after his liberation, to present the hapless officer with a Distinguished Service Cross.

Only fifteen men of Baum's liberating column returned safely to the Allied lines, along with twenty-five Hammelburg prisoners who made their own way across country. The remainder were killed or captured. Lieutenant Robert Harrison of the 101st Airborne, one of the Hammelburg PoWs who had been captured in the Bulge, set out to walk to the American lines. Back before D-Day, Harrison had endeared himself to his men when their pay did not come through. He advanced them $35 apiece out of his own pocket to tide them over. Many were killed before they could repay him. Now, Harrison covered fifty-eight miles before reaching a river, where Germans guarded the bridge. He tried to swim across and was shot in the water. It was just a month before the end of the war.

It is extraordinary that Patton was never subjected to disciplinary action for this act of egomania unmitigated by any possible military advantage. "I feel terrible," the general wrote to his wife on 6 April, "I tried hard to save him [John Waters] and I may be the cause of his death." When he heard that his son-in-law had been badly wounded as a result of his initiative, he burst into tears. He attempted to impose blanket censorship on the raid, but inevitably the story leaked to the press. Marshall, in Washington, was outraged. Eisenhower excused

Patton: "[He] is a problem child, but he is a great fighting leader in pursuit and exploitation." True enough, yet Patton's Hammelburg action seems far less excusable than the "slapping incidents" in Sicily, for which he had been dismissed from his command. The episode must be cited in any assessment of Patton's claims to greatness. It is impossible to imagine any other senior participant in the Allied campaign committing such a selfish, murderous folly or being pardoned for the loss of life which it incurred. At a moment when all Europe was on its knees, when Germany was a maelstrom of suffering humanity, an Allied army commander committed an act which argued that he cared only for his own.

THE DAMNED

WESTERN PRISONERS often caught sight of Russian PoWs in neighbouring compounds. German guards distributed Red Cross parcels and sometimes a thin gruel of humanity among the British and Americans, while presiding over unspeakable excesses to Russians a few hundred yards away. The Germans acknowledged the Western allies as fellow inhabitants of the same planet. They denied this privilege to Stalin's people. An American PoW at Thjorn was appalled to watch through the wire as Russian amputees shuffled through thick snow with the stumps of their legs bound with sacking. Thousands died there, as in every Russian camp conducted by the Nazis. They were buried in a common grave beyond the gates. "Every day a sort of tumbril rattled past outside the entrance with its load of naked bodies which were tipped unceremoniously into a hole." A Russian described how, when a man died during the night, they tried to prop him up in his bed until after *Appel*, so that the living might draw his rations. In Stalag XIB, Corporal Denis Thomas watched a German guard stroll over to a Russian boiling potatoes in the neighbouring compound and casually kick his mess-tin into the dirt.

Every American and British prisoner knew that he could consider himself fortunate compared with the Russians. In the course of the war over 5.7 million Red Army soldiers were captured by the Germans, of whom 3.3 million—58 per cent—died. Around 600,000 were summarily killed on or near the battlefield. The balance died in the camps of Germany and Poland. The saga of one of these men, Mikhail Petrovich Devyataev, is among the most extraordinary of the Second World War. Devyataev was the thirteenth child of a Moldovian blacksmith. His family suffered harrowing privations in the Civil War and its aftermath. In his childhood, an aeroplane made a forced landing near his home. From that moment, he was determined to become a fighter pilot, and in 1941 he did so: "I fell in love with flying and everything about it." He was twenty-seven and had flown some 200 sorties when one day in July 1944 his Yak-7 was jumped by German FW-190s. He lost consciousness as he parachuted from his stricken aircraft and woke to find a German soldier standing over him. His leg was broken, and he had been badly burned. He spent some months in the primitive hospital of his PoW camp, and retained a lasting gratitude to British prisoners in the next compound, who were generous with food and even found a few drugs for him. En route to a new camp near Königsberg at the end of 1944, he exchanged identities with a dead Red Army soldier, because Soviet pilots were subject to exceptionally brutal German treatment. At the beginning of 1945, he was shipped to Peenemünde, the island on the Baltic coast where Hitler's "wonder weapons" were developed and tested.

His destination was a slave-labour camp. Here, with an icy wind blowing off the sea, some 4,000 Russians were employed repairing runways and clearing unexploded British bombs in conditions of pitiless brutality. All the prisoners were starving by inches. None had ever escaped. They were beaten constantly, often fatally. One man who tried to swim to freedom was brought back and torn to pieces by guard dogs in front of the prisoners. Devyataev saw a bailed-out British bomber crewman killed by the dogs in a lake where his parachute fell. Most of the work gangs were sooner or later blown up by bombs they were moving. The crematorium fires never cooled.

By the beginning of February 1945, the Germans were in a visibly dangerous mood. Devyataev concluded that the prisoners had no hope of surviving the war if they stayed where they were. They would either starve or be shot. He told the nine other men in his gang that they must escape. "How?" they demanded. "I'll fly you out," he said. It took some days to convince them that he could do it, for they knew nothing of his credentials as a pilot. At last, in the early-morning darkness of 8 February, as their gang worked on the runway, Ivan Krivonogov struck their guard a savage, fatal blow with his crowbar. Petyor Kutergun hastily stripped off the man's uniform and himself put it on. The camp dogs, which they feared desperately, had recently been taken away for training to attack tanks with explosive charges. Their absence made escape seem marginally easier. The work gang, apparently escorted by a guard, stumbled a mile down the airstrip to the commandant's personal Heinkel. They opened the rear door and scrambled into the fuselage. Devyataev found and opened the battery box. It was empty. He slumped in despair.

It took them an agonizing quarter of an hour to find a battery trolley and connect it. More precious minutes slipped away before the pilot was able to start the engines. Daylight had come. The Russian now had to taxi past a line of other aircraft, on which German mechanics were already working. He tore off his striped jacket, thinking that the sight of a pilot half-naked in mid-winter would alert the Germans less readily than a man in the grimly familiar garb of a prisoner. The Luftwaffe men indeed gazed curiously at the Heinkel's cockpit, but did not intervene. Devyataev was struggling with the unfamiliar controls.

He got Krivonogov to sit beside him, pushing buttons and pulling levers at his direction. The other eight men huddled in the fuselage. The plane swung on to the runway. The pilot gunned the engines and released the brakes. As they lifted into the sky, they began to croak the words of the "Internationale." They lurched rather than flew through the sky. Devyataev, who had never flown a twin-engined aircraft, could not discover how to raise the undercarriage. They were scarcely in the air before he put the plane into a steep, almost fatal dive. He weighed only ninety pounds and lacked the strength to handle the flap lever. The entire cluster of desperate men threw their weight on to it, just in time to make the plane pull out of the dive. After an hour airborne north-eastwards over the Baltic, they turned over the coast and saw great columns of fugitives fleeing before the Red Army. Flak streaked up at them, slightly damaging a wing.

Devyataev was desperately cold, and got Krivonogov to pull his striped coat back over his shoulders: "My whole being was concentrated upon flying the plane." They followed the coast northwards. He risked losing height, and suddenly saw a bridge. There were Russian soldiers on it. He brought the plane in to land amid renewed firing from the ground. As the Heinkel touched the frozen snow, the undercarriage collapsed. They thrashed through the mush to a halt. A jumbled mass of bodies was thrown forward into the cockpit by the impact. But all were alive and uninjured. They scrambled clumsily out of the aircraft, walked a few yards in their wooden clogs, then found themselves so weak that they were obliged to clamber back into the fuselage. They had no idea where they were. After thirty minutes, a wary Russian cavalry patrol arrived from Sixty-first Army. The escapers explained themselves to the incredulous soldiers: "You got away from a rocket centre?" For some hours, they were treated as miracle men. Their rescuers hastened to feed, clothe and congratulate them.

Then the NKVD arrived. The prisoners were questioned relentlessly, hour upon hour and then day after day. At last, the interrogators gave their verdict: "What you claim to have done is completely impossible. This is obviously a German plot." The nine other men of Devyataev's work gang were fed for a few weeks, than drafted to penal battalions. Five died in the last weeks of the war, advancing into German minefields at the crossing of the Oder. The pilot himself spent the next year in solitary confinement. Once, he was escorted to Peenemünde, to retell his story on the captured rocket site. Then he was sent back to his cell. He was told nothing of VE-Day when it came, and on 20 May was shipped to the former Nazi concentration camp at Sachsenhausen near Berlin. A year later, following the testimony of captured Germans and Soviet survivors of the slave-labour camp, the NKVD grudgingly conceded that there might be something in Devyataev's story. He was released and demobilized. With his papers stamped as a former PoW, however, it was months before he could find work of any kind. He endured a life of grinding poverty: "Even friends with whom I had been at school turned their backs on me...the sun began to shine for me again only when Stalin died." In 1957, the truth of his astounding exploit was at last officially recognized. Mikhail Devyataev was made a Hero of the Soviet Union.

MANY JEWS, before they were shipped to concentration camps, passed months or years imprisoned and half starved within the ghettos of their own native cities. "Boredom is usually associated with the idle rich," wrote Jerzy Herszburg laconically, about his time in the Lodz ghetto, "it also existed in the ghetto and even in the camps." In July 1944, he and his fellow inmates were assembled for shipment to Auschwitz. "It may be difficult to comprehend...but the gathering of the Jews took place in an almost friendly atmosphere." They had all been enormously heartened by the Allied landing in Normandy. They believed that the war must end soon. Jewish police marshalled their charges at the station with carefully labelled suitcases. Only a few inmates mistrusted the atmosphere of goodwill, hid themselves—and survived. Herszburg, a sixteen-year-old, argued afterwards that at least the ghastly delusions of the passengers lent a spurious optimism to their last days. His own uncle, who had shown great kindness to him in the ghetto, rode the train to Auschwitz "in peace and hope."

Arrival at the camp shattered the fantasy. Their luggage was abandoned by the tracks, never to be seen again. The Kapos—"trusties" recruited from among prisoners—herded them into the camp, where more than half were gassed immediately. Once heads had been shaved, the survivors, who retained only their own belts and shoes, laughed nervously at each other about the dramatic change in their appearances. Their first hours were spent "in a strange mixture of very long waits and sudden bursts of activity." Herszburg was among those sent to the nearby camp at Birkenau, thrown into a barracks among a thousand prisoners in transit to either work camps or gas chambers Throughout his time in the camp, he suffered desperately from loneliness. Eventually he made a few friends. But, one by one, they died.

In his progress through the Nazi concentration-camp system during the ten months that followed, it is striking that Herszburg thought Auschwitz–Birkenau nowhere near as bad as some of its rivals, such as Belsen. "We remained reasonably clean. It was not a working camp. We grew suntanned, and did not suffer from lack of sleep. I was seldom hit, and seldom spoken to. I once saw the body of a man who had electrocuted himself hanging on the wire, but there were few suicides—we were far too preoccupied with trying to survive. I saw no hangings or shootings. I never saw anyone die." This was part of the demented genius of the Birkenau system: the inmates were maintained in a state of docility, because death took place beyond their vision. Yet every inmate knew the meaning of the "selections" which took place early in the morning or late at night. Sometimes, men were chosen on the basis of visible health, once by passing them under a horizontal bar: those who touched it lived, those too short or too stooped died. Sometimes the men selected chose to delude themselves that they were leaving Birkenau to work in Germany, though in reality they died. On other occasions, men were indeed sent to labour camps. After a selection, "we seemed able to erase it from our minds... and to carry on in the usual camp routine." Herszburg saw no examples of mental breakdown, "perhaps because we were not called upon to make any decisions."

After ten weeks in Birkenau, he was sent with a work detail to Brunswick. The journey, which provoked a brief spasm of hope, lasted two days. On arrival, however, this proved the worst camp in which he lived. The prisoners worked twelve-hour shifts, seven days a week, in an auto factory. Many died of starvation. "Some experts on concentration camps assure me that I must have had a very strong will to live. Simply because I did not die, I have some difficulty in proving them wrong. In spite of their knowledge, I feel that their theory... is wrong—I was at my lowest then." He noted that most of those who survived were short and stocky like himself. The only skills which he identified in himself was those of "absolute obedience to our masters and the ability to go without food for fairly long periods of time." The only relief, the only glimmer of hope, in these cruel days came with the air raids: "The sound of sirens always filled me with joy, as it did all other prisoners... The brave pilots... probably never realised how much hope and joy they gave us in the winter of 1944."

Early in 1945, after five months in Brunswick, Herszburg was transferred to the neighbouring camp of Watendstedt. He was dispatched from the compound each day to the V2 rocket component assembly line at the Hermann Göring works. The plant had been so badly damaged by bombing that there was little to do save clear wreckage: "I felt much better there." As the Allied armies approached, the prisoners were once more loaded on to trains. They travelled for three days across the shrinking Reich to Ravensbrück. For the first time since Herszburg had entered the Lodz ghetto, a guard chatted to them as human beings. At the camp, Jews were ordered to step forward. They were astounded to be handed Red Cross parcels. Fear of approaching retribution now moved even some SS guards to a perverted hint of generosity. Next day, the Jewish prisoners were handed another Red Cross parcel and once more herded on to a train. On 25 April, they were offloaded at Wöbbelin in Mecklenburg. They were pushed into a barracks in which bodies lay uncollected, "and our block had many... the living and the dead shared the damp floor in close proximity." To the very end, there was a rollcall every morning for the diminishing band of survivors.

It is interesting to contrast the policies of the rival tyrannies of Stalin and Hitler towards their captives. Both were indifferent to humanitarian issues, yet the former proved much more pragmatic. The Soviets realized that they could not allow prisoners to starve in excessive numbers if they were to extract useful service from them. Even Beria recognized that, unless German prisoners ate, they could not work. In September 1944, around 2,895 German PoWs died of starvation in NKVD camps. For the first ten days of October the figure was 1,366. The death rate caused the Russians to conclude that a marginal adjustment of rationing policy was necessary. Beria reported to Stalin: "We have taken steps to improve feeding of PoWs, to increase the productivity of their labour, with the coal industry being given first priority."

Hitler's servants, however, seemed content to allow their slaves to starve to death. Captain Vasily Legun weighed 189 pounds when his Yak-4 was shot down over the German lines in the Ukraine in September 1943, and 92 pounds a year later. He was imprisoned at a camp near Mühlberg with some 2,000 other Soviet aircrew. He expected to die there, like so many others. The twenty-seven-year-old son of a Siberian peasant family, Legun was suffering from a badly infected leg. The Russian doctor in the camp wanted to amputate it. But one day, beside his bed, the pilot found two American PoWs from the neighbouring compound, one of them a B-17 navigator. They opened a blanket they had brought, to reveal a jumble of wonderful things: chocolate, canned milk, marmalade. Legun wanted to eat everything at once, but the doctor warned him: "Food can be your enemy, too." He was given a modest ration each day through the weeks that followed. He gained a little weight, and his leg healed.

The only common ground between the Russians and Americans in the camp was that neither were free to leave. Legun and his comrades wore rags, and indeed depended on seizing the clothing of the dead to cover themselves at all. The Americans possessed uniforms, received Red Cross parcels and letters from home, did no work. The Russians were employed on stone-breaking and enjoyed no contact with their homeland. In their despair, they began to dig an escape tunnel, and had advanced thirty yards towards the perimeter fence when a spring thaw came, causing the excavation to collapse. In February 1945, a large group of Russians escaped. Most were brought back and executed in front of the other prisoners. After that, the survivors waited passively for death or deliverance.

"In the camps, many people died of despair, not hunger," said Nikolai Maslennikov. He was captured near the Peterhof outside Leningrad in 1942 at the age of seventeen, after a childhood dogged by the fact that his family's papers were stamped with the fatal words which indicated that they were "persons of the second sort," the brand laid upon the politically suspect. Maslennikov's father had once visited England and bought two English suits. In consequence, young Nikolai was forbidden to join the Communist Youth Movement, the Komsomol, and was unable to follow his ambition to study aerodynamics.

His participation in the defence of Leningrad was impeded by the fact that, like many of his fellow recruits to the Red Army, he lacked arms. Most of his unit was killed without the means of firing a shot. He fled homewards to join his parents. The Germans overran their village and rounded up all young men of military age. Maslennikov began his career as a Nazi prisoner working in factories making aircraft parts. Having incurred the displeasure of his captors, he was sent to a concentration camp at Gross Rosen in Poland, home to 60,000 inmates—Poles, Frenchmen, political criminals, Russians. He quickly learned some of the rules determining survival. He moved everywhere in a group, never alone. He avoided all eye contact with the guards. Friendship was a dangerous luxury. Almost any man would denounce another in exchange for a crust of bread. He consciously sought to suppress all emotion: "I knew that it would be the end of me if I began to give vent to feelings." Only once did he attract the personal attention of the guards, when he was deemed slow in removing his cap. An SS woman hit him with a gloved fist, breaking three ribs. All his conscious thoughts focused upon food: "We did not think about girls or our families, only about getting that tiny morsel of cheese out of the mousetrap." Men died every day of starvation or beatings. They knew very little about the progress of the war, save that Stalingrad sent every German into mourning. "After that, Russians were treated just a little better—no worse than other nationalities." Maslennikov was sustained by a lingering, unbreakable conviction that somehow it would all end soon.

Gross Rosen was not a designated mass-murder establishment. Like most Nazi concentration camps, it was simply a place where people died, usually within six months. It was not a site for sophisticated medical experiments, but prisoners were sometimes used for cruder research, such as testing army boots by marching interminably around the compounds while carrying heavy loads. Wholesale killings took place only occasionally. One day when prisoners returned from the stone quarries, from the window of his barracks Maslennikov saw a chain of wagons rattling past on the narrow-gauge railway to the crematorium, laden with women and children and old people. "The eyes of each bore a different expression," he said. "I have seen them in my dreams forever after." In the winter of 1944, there was an escape attempt in Compound 20, which housed political prisoners. A group killed a guard, threw blankets over the wire, scaled it and ran away. Most were swiftly recaptured and killed, in some cases by drenching them in cold water, which froze on their bodies. The next two batches of political prisoners who arrived at the camp were killed immediately, presumably lest they, too, should nurse ambitions of freedom.

At the beginning of 1945, when the camp was evacuated, Maslennikov was transferred to Nordhausen. Here, the rules were simple. Those who could not work were not fed at all. He was employed removing corpses from the compounds and burning them on great pyres: "You arranged a layer of wood, a layer of corpses, a layer of wood, and then poured sump oil on top." One day, an order came that radio specialists were needed. Maslennikov immediately volunteered, certain that any hazard must be preferable to Nordhausen. His only chance, as for most Nazi captives, was to prove himself useful. He was transferred to Sachsenhausen, where it was intended that he should be employed on the assembly of radio-detonated mines. By the time his group arrived, however, American bombs had destroyed the factory. Instead, gangs of prisoners were sent into the capital, to clear unexploded bombs. This assignment offered priceless opportunities to scavenge for food in wrecked houses, yet it was also highly dangerous. There were days when whole teams disappeared, having been unlucky in their experiences with bombs. Executions were commonplace in the camp, and increased in the last weeks of the war. Compared with Gross Rosen and Nordenhausen, however, Maslennikov felt that Sachsenhausen was "not at all bad."

Zinaida Mikhailova spent three years in Ravensbrück, because she refused to work in the Mauser armaments factory after being deported from the village near Leningrad where she lived. She was one of eight children of a peasant father, shot by the NKVD for reasons unknown in 1934. Her mother worked at the local railway station. She left school at fifteen in 1938 and found a job in the ticket office at Moscow station. She was unfortunate enough to be caught at home on the weekend that the Germans overran her village. Her papers showed her to be a Party member. This caused her to be consigned to slave labour, like all her kind. Yet while some deportees survived the war, none of those who remained behind in Zinaida's village did so. All were killed by the Germans sooner or later.

Several women in Zinaida's group declined to work in the munitions industry, and thus shared her journey to Ravensbrück, where 92,000 prisoners died in the course of the war. Her experience contradicted the view of many male concentration-camp prisoners, that to survive it was essential to live as an island, to trust no one. She believed that companionship, passionate group loyalty, preserved her. Each night when the guards left the compound, a little cluster of the women whose dresses bore the "R" in a red triangle that marked them as Russians gathered together, to talk or sing songs. "This was very important to us. I learned how important it is to make friends, to get on with people." They spoke about home, and cried. They exchanged information with the neighbouring men's compound by throwing notes over the wire.

The calendar of life in a concentration camp was like none other, because its landmarks were specially memorable encounters with death. One day became different from another because a woman was beaten until she died, or because they saw five men being hanged. Any prisoner faced the lash for possession of a book. Zinaida was once flogged and sent to solitary confinement after being denounced by a Polish inmate for writing poetry. "Yet the Jews," said Zinaida unsurprisingly, "suffered more than any of us." The prisoners' day began with "dirty tea," a muddy brew made of ersatz leaves. At *Appel*, they were counted in rows of ten, then she went to her work as a cleaner. There was soup at midday, with a slice of bread, and more soup in the evening. On Sunday, they made a kind of porridge.

"I always hoped," she said, "because without hope you could not survive. Though I was a Party member, I also believed in God. My family all went to church. I dreamed of home, and of food, and of my boyfriend Mikhail." Mikhail, inevitably, had been killed in action, but Zinaida did not know that, just as she and her group knew nothing about the progress of the war. By the autumn of 1944, however, they were aware at least that the Allies were advancing on Germany. This made them even more fearful, because it seemed inevitable that the Germans would kill them before their liberators could arrive.

Edith Gabor shared with Zinaida Mikhailova the experience of Ravensbrück, though the two women did not know each other. Like many Jews, Edith underwent a progression of horror which attained its nadir in the last months of the war. Her father was a wealthy Budapest diamond wholesaler. She herself trained as a furrier, because her mother believed that every girl should possess a skill. She completed her apprenticeship just as the Germans occupied Hungary in March 1944, when she was eighteen. Like most of the Budapest Jewish community, the family had always enjoyed close links with Germany, and indeed spoke German at home. Her boyfriend Ervin had been accepted for training as a singer at the Frankfurt Music Academy in 1939, a place which he did not live to take up. When the Nazis came, the Gabors concluded that their best chance of safety lay in making themselves useful. Her father started to repair watches for SS officers, while she was sent to work in a factory entirely staffed by Jews, manufacturing clothing for the Wehrmacht. They cut and stitched fourteen hours a day, and were soon at the edge of starvation. "We lived like animals," said Edith. "Each day we thought: 'What could get worse today?'" Her father cherished a pathetic flame of hope. He would say: "It will pass. The war will end." He was periodically summoned to perform forced labour, but allowed to return home at night. Edith slept in the factory, sharing a mattress with a heavy woman who almost crushed her whenever she turned over in her sleep. At weekends, she was allowed home for a few hours, sneaking through the streets like a hunted criminal. The family was now restricted to a single room of their big apartment. One day, she heard that Ervin had been conscripted to "Forced Labour Unit 101." He disappeared without trace.

Then her father was summoned. He left a large packet of diamonds in the custody of a Christian friend. "They are for you, my children," he said to Edith and her brother. "They will make you rich." But the diamonds were never seen again and nor was her father, last identified in a labour camp on the Austrian border. When next she went to see her mother, she found all the family furniture and china gone. There was one marvellous, terrible snapshot of hope. In

October 1944 Admiral Miklos Horthy, Hungary's ruler, announced that his country was abandoning the war. Edith's mother embraced her in tears of joy, and said: "Tonight, I make a chicken." But within a few hours Horthy was deposed by the Nazis. Germany's grip upon Hungary became absolute. Mrs. Gabor sobbed once more, and sent Edith running back to the factory "overwhelmed with fear and heaviness. I felt what was coming."

Her mother and six-year-old brother Georg were soon sent to join her in the factory, sleeping together in a bunk. Edith's meagre ration had to suffice among all three, for her mother was too frail to work. When the SS one day separated women between sixteen and forty from the rest, her mother seemed perfectly resigned. She said to Edith: "You just go, and take care. If I don't survive—" Edith interrupted tearfully: "No, no, you must! You must!" "If I don't survive, do three things: bring up Georg and give him a good education and see he learns some languages; take care of my daughter's grave"—this was a sister who had died as a child—"and visit my friend Ilona." Then they parted for ever. "Be strong!" her mother shouted after her. Everywhere in the factory were people sobbing and saying farewells. Edith's brother found himself pushed into a group with her mother.

The girls' party was led to the station by Hungarian SS and loaded into box-cars. Red Cross workers, surprisingly, were allowed to give them some water and a big can of tomatoes. Then they embarked on a journey which lasted for days, without air or light or exercise, or any hint of where they were going. At last they saw a station sign bearing the name RAVENSBRÜCK. Polish "trusties" and dog-handlers marched them into the camp. "Where are we?" asked Edith in bewilderment. "My dear," said another woman simply, "you are in a death camp." She was confused by the sight of a bakery, until it was explained to her that this was the crematorium. In a tent, they were ordered to strip. Edith shed her Rumanian hand-made shoes, angora-trimmed coat, blouse and tailored skirt. She laid down her favourite compact and crocodile handbag. "You won't need those again," said an SS woman contemptuously. It was December 1944. They were marched naked to another building where they were given clogs and camp uniforms, to which they were required to affix their numbers. They were led to showers, where they found themselves expected to wash with bleach rather than soap. "More! More!" shouted an SS woman. "Dirty Jews!" The soldiers laughed. Most of the group were genteel, bourgeois, highly educated young women, who had never in their lives been seen naked by any-one save their families. Their heads were shaved. A woman screamed: "What would my husband say?"

They worked in the fields, struggling pathetically to drive spades into the iron-hard winter ground. One morning at *Appel*, an SS woman threw a bucket of water over Edith, for the fun of seeing her eyelashes freeze and turn to lead within seconds. Whenever an SS guard spoke to her, she was convinced that her last hour had come. For a time, she stopped eating. Friends forced bread down her throat. Nine children had come with their group. All were were taken away. The mother of one nine-year-old boy succumbed to grief and died within days. After a month, their group was summoned for a new medical examination, once more naked while their hands and mouths were examined. An SS woman said: "Now I want to see if Jewish women are smart enough to stand this without complaining!" She advanced down the line inserting a rod in their private parts, one by one. Edith's friend Kathy screamed, "I am a virgin!," which provoked more laughter from the guards.

One day after an inspection, an SS man said: "Anyone who can speak fluent German, step forward." Several women did so. A civilian who was standing beside the officer pointed to two, of whom Edith was one. Two days later, she found herself among a group of 200, once more loaded upon a train. "It was impossible to feel relief, because one had no idea where we were going." After two days on the train, they were unloaded at the small town of Penig, near Magdeburg, and marched to a barracks. This was Ebensee concentration camp. An SS guard said: "Tomorrow, you work." They found themselves among Poles, Russians, Italians in a factory manufacturing aircraft parts, working twelve-hour shifts, often at night, every day walking two miles each way from the barracks to the assembly line. Their guards were not allowed into the factory. Their rations remained at starvation level. They suffered all manner of sores and diseases. Yet they were alive.

Edith was so weakened that she found it very hard to work, and lived in terror of being marked for extermination. She was saved by a German—their civilian supervisor, Herr Kaiser. In these most awful of circumstances, in a world from which almost all humanity had been banished, she received from this man an infinitesimal allowance of kindness, just sufficient to preserve her life. Kaiser would sometimes say to her: "If you feel too tired to work, you can go to sleep." He brought the girls a little food. He allowed them to hunt among the garbage for potatoes. "He was a fine man." In measuring the abominable deeds of the Nazi era, the charity of a few such men as Kaiser should be placed on the balance against the enormities of his countrymen. It required courage to retain even such small shreds of decency in Hitler's Germany.

Towards the end, Edith's health failed completely: "I had no more strength. I gave up. I knew I could not take it any more." Kaiser arranged for her to be hidden in the hospital, where the doctor granted her three days off work. Even a few months earlier, her flagging health would have provoked a death sentence. Yet now, in early April 1945, "we could see fear in the faces of the SS. They were not strict any more. They stopped shouting at us." Edith knew that she had been living on the very lip of the grave, from which so many millions of other Nazi captives toppled in. But she was held back. She survived. It is, perhaps, worth reflecting upon the predicament of Edith Gabor while reading the minutes of

British Foreign Office official Arminius Dew. He wrote on 1 September 1944, during the impassioned controversy about Allied policy in the face of increasing intelligence about the Holocaust: "In my opinion, a disproportionate amount of the time of the Office is wasted on dealing with these wailing Jews."

It is hard to fathom the logic which caused the Nazis to transport children along with parents to slave-labour camps in Hitler's empire, and then to keep some alive, while dispatching hundreds of thousands of others to the gas chambers. The administrative inconvenience, not to mention the cost of providing food, however little, for children, must have significantly outweighed the value of a mother's services. Gennady Trofimov was eight when he, together with his newborn sister Anna, was shipped to Latvia with their mother and grandmother from Novgorod, in the autumn of 1943. Their father had gone to the war in June 1941. Their mother, who worked in a local china factory, said later that watching her husband and hundreds like him board the train to join the Red Army seemed like watching wheat being scythed. She repeated again and again: "I don't care what state he comes home in, even if he is a cripple—I just want him back." Grigory Trofimov was killed in one of the first battles, fighting without training, without even knowing how to hold a rifle.

The surviving family members subsisted almost entirely on potatoes through two years of German occupation. Their journey to Latvia among a mass of other local peasants was a week-long nightmare, interrupted by interminable halts, because partisans had cut the rail track. Near Riga, families were separated. "The old people, we discovered later, went immediately to become soap," said Gennady Trofimov. "Children became blood donors. Mothers worked in the fields." They became the slaves of local farmers, fed only at their whim. Gennady earned his first pay, a loaf of bread, for a day's labour driving a horse which powered a loom to make fibre out of flax. "We did not even understand the meaning of the word misery," he said. "All we knew was that we were hungry all the time. If we found something to eat, that meant a tiny moment of happiness."

In the autumn of 1944, as the Red Army swept across Latvia, they were moved into a barracks in Riga. "We lived like animals, sleeping on the floor, scavenging for rubbish," said Gennady. His grandmother looked after little Anna, while his mother was sent out to dig trenches for the Germans. The Russians were already bombing the port. At the age of three, Anna could tell the difference between an aircraft bomb and an artillery shell, from personal experience. The whole family fell on their knees and prayed through the air raids. They celebrated every religious holiday. Their grandmother proved a woman of iron, one also possessed of great gifts. Though she was illiterate, she had spent much of her life working as a nanny for rich families. She had an extraordinary fund of proverbs, jokes and fairy stories, which for almost four years were the only entertainments they experienced. "It was a miracle that we survived," said Gennady. He spent the days wandering the town, searching for food. At the age of ten, he possessed no toys, had never attended a school, could not write or read more than a few words glimpsed on shop signs. Almost the only game known to him and scores of other hapless urchins around the barracks was to take turns to crouch in an old motor tyre and roll each other down the street in it. In the winter of 1944, the family was sent to another farm in southern Latvia, where they spent the rest of the war. "My only memory of life was as a struggle," said Gennady. "My mother seemed very ordinary. Yet she proved to be a heroine, because she kept us alive."

Viktor Mamontov was sixteen when he was captured by the Germans in 1942. He had survived the siege of Leningrad, in which his father died of starvation, while he himself worked twelve hours a day in a shell factory. His elder brother was killed in one of the first battles, fighting armed with a spade because there were not enough rifles. Mamontov was evacuated to a town near the Black Sea, and was in hospital recovering from pneumonia when the Germans overran the area. He fled for his life among thousands of terrified young soldiers who were throwing away their weapons and uniforms. After being wounded by a bomb fragment, he was taken into captivity by the Germans. He escaped, and roamed the Crimea for a time until he was caught riding on a German train without papers. He was shipped among a consignment of Jews, partisans and other "antisocial elements" to a concentration camp near Bremen.

At first, he worked among 800 others in a canning factory, sleeping on the concrete floor, starving. Then he was transferred to load ballast on to trains and clear air-raid salvage and unexploded bombs. Late in 1943, a group of prisoners were denounced for plotting an escape, and he found himself among them. The indicted men were transferred to a prison at Wissemünde, and then to the 21st Punishment Camp near Brunswick. This was his worst experience yet. All 400 prisoners were required to run rather than walk everywhere. Polish "trusties" ran the camp, which was entirely occupied by Poles and Russians. Polish guards rather than SS carried out most of the beatings. The prisoners were employed upon removing waste from a metalworks and crushing it into roadmaking material.

Mamontov was too weak to walk when he left 21st Punishment Camp after serving his eight-week sentence. He was sent briefly to a transit camp near Leipzig, and thence to Buchenwald. They did little work in Buchenwald. They merely lingered on the cusp between life and death. After a few months, he was transferred to Dora, an outstation of Buchenwald, from which the inmates marched every morning into a mountain factory where V2 rockets were assembled. "We believed that no one would be allowed to leave the place alive, because it was top secret."

They were an extraordinary miscellany. There were some French and a few British prisoners. Two of Mamontov's Russian friends, Pavel Ostrovsky and

Sergei Fomichev, had been sent there for attempted escapes. Both died. Yosef
Ardginski, an Uzbek, was suspected of helping partisans. He survived. They all
exchanged addresses soon after they arrived, so that if any man lived he might
inform families of the fate of others. There were a few German political prisoners, who had a radio. This kept them informed about the war. After the Warsaw
Rising, there was an influx of Poles. Alleged indiscipline was rewarded with
twenty-five lashes. German behaviour became much uglier when evidence
emerged that some prisoners were sabotaging rocket parts. Rations were cut.
Anyone suspected of sabotage was summarily executed, sometimes by hanging
in the workshops in front of the other slaves.

In 1945, "conditions became appalling," said Mamontov. Some days, there
was no bread, merely a few boiled potatoes. The camp possessed a small crematorium, but now there were too many corpses to burn overnight. Each morning
as the prisoners marched to work, they saw the dead heaped outside. Mamontov
attributed his own survival to some inner strength: "I never panicked. Those
who panicked and thought they would die did die." But in those first months of
1945 despair seemed very close. One night in March, the alarm sounded, and
they were suddenly marched to a train waiting near by. "We had no idea where
we were being taken. At stations, we would push a jug between the slats of the
boxcar, and sometimes a railworker would fill it with water." It took them a week
of hell to travel fifty-five miles. When the train stopped, they were marched
three miles to their destined camp. Stragglers who collapsed were shot beside
the road. Their new home was Belsen. When they arrived on 4 April the administration of the camp was collapsing. Prisoners received no food at all. Bodies
littered the compounds. They slept among corpses in the barracks. "The stench
was indescribable ... I cannot imagine how I survived."

Georgi Semenyak was a young gunner from Leningrad, captured in July 1941
after walking for three weeks eastwards, trying to stay ahead of the German
invaders. His subsequent experience was an odyssey through the hierarchy of
misery within the Nazi prison industry. He spent his first two years of captivity
in PoW camps in Poland. In November 1943, an informer denounced a large
group of prisoners for organizing an anniversary celebration of the Revolution.
Eighty-four men were sent to a slave-labour camp at Stutthof near Danzig,
where 12,000 Russian, Polish, Lithuanian, Latvian and French prisoners were
being literally worked into their graves. "The Germans obviously did not care
whether we lived or died. We believed that we were doomed." They were summoned to *Appel* each morning by a bugle call from one of the watchtowers. They
lived chiefly off beet soup. The work itself was futile—relentless earth-moving
designed solely to occupy the prisoners. He noted one grotesque irony—in
PoW camp, they had been forbidden to sing. At Stutthof, it was a privilege of the
damned to sing. "Every nationality was treated terribly, but Russians were
treated worse than anyone except Jews and Gypsies."

Every nationality save the Russians was allowed to send one postcard a month home, which had to be written in German. Semenyak spoke the language, and wrote endless cards for foreign fellow prisoners: "Dear mama and papa, I live well here. We get enough to eat and drink. Nevertheless, could you send us some bread…" As the Russians swept across East Prussia, the prisoners were evacuated from Stutthof and marched westwards away from the Red Army. By April 1945, their captors had run out of places to drive them to. Semenyak was among several thousand Stutthof prisoners whom the Germans determined to remove by sea. They were loaded on to barges, then towed by a tug from river estuary to estuary, searching in vain for a path into the Reich which had not yet fallen to the Soviets.

On Semenyak's barge were 600 men, crammed into the hold and on the decks. They were terrified of capsizing. Those on deck crowded into the hold as the swell rose. They began to die. The corpses were merely thrown overboard. They had no food, and some started drinking sea-water. It seemed unlikely that they would be allowed to live. The Germans had taken immense pains to evacuate Stutthof and keep its inmates out of Soviet hands, "because they feared that we would tell the story of what had been done to us." Day after day the barges wallowed uncertainly across the sea, with the trail of corpses on the swell lengthening relentlessly. "Despair? We were always in despair. Somehow, each of us persuaded himself that he would be the one to survive. But the barges were the worst thing that ever happened to me." On their tenth evening at sea, they ran aground on a sandbank. The tug abandoned its search for a landfall, cast off all its charges and steamed away into the darkness. At 6 a.m. next morning, they were sighted by a German naval ship, which put off lifeboats.

Pitying German sailors took the survivors on board and landed them on an island close by. Of several thousand prisoners who had been embarked, just 400 remained. The war was at its last gasp. So also were millions of captives like the stricken survivors of Stutthof.

STARVATION OF A NATION

UNTIL THE VERY end of the Second World War, several nations in their entirety, together with some large communities, remained captives of the Germans: Norway, Denmark, northern Italy, northern Yugoslavia, much of Czechoslovakia, the Channel Islands and most of the population of Holland. The Dutch experience was perhaps the worst. Between November 1944 and May 1945, some 4.5 million people lived not merely on the brink of starvation, but in the midst of its fatal consequences. In Holland during those months, the mortality rate of small children doubled, that of babies trebled. Twelve thousand people died outright of hunger, a further 23,000 as a consequence of Allied air raids on German rocket sites, 5,000 in German captivity and 30,000 as forced labourers. Of the 2,800 Dutch people executed in cold blood by the Germans, 1,560 met their ends in the winter of 1944–45.

The Dutch suffered an abrupt descent into misery. In 1939, as in 1914, Holland sought to escape conflict with its mighty neighbour through a declaration of neutrality. Hitler's invasion of the Low Countries in May 1940 snuffed out that aspiration. Yet, after the swift military collapse and the decision of the Netherlands royal family and government to choose exile, many Dutch people resumed a remarkably humdrum existence. There had been little anti-German sentiment in Holland before 1939. Now, most of the country's bureaucracies and institutions accepted Nazi authority, much as they detested the proconsul whom Hitler appointed to rule the Netherlands, the Austrian Arthur Seyss-Inquart. There was a small Resistance movement, whose courageous members ran an escape line for Allied airmen. But the flat, open terrain of a small country did not lend itself to guerrilla war. German intelligence penetrated the Dutch networks of Britain's Special Operations Executive with deadly consequences. "People soon realized that resistance was very, very dangerous," said twenty-two-year-old Ted Van Meurs, who suffered severely in German hands before escaping to freedom. "Adventurous young men preferred to try and flee the country."

For all the fame of Anne Frank's long concealment from the Nazis, the wider reality was that almost all Holland's Jews were identified, deported and killed. Of 117,000 shipped east, 5,500 returned. Just 20,000 Dutch Jews survived the war. "At first when they took Jews, people said: 'It's impossible, they can't do that,' " observed a young Dutchman. "But after a time such things become normal." Hans Cramer, the twenty-two-year-old son of a German Jewish father living in the Hague, said: "For most of the population life went on in an incredibly normal way. Okay, there was no coffee or tea, and a few people were in great danger, but lots of others still seemed to be playing tennis. Some of us were surprised by the willingness of the Dutch authorities to work with the Germans." More Dutchmen carried arms for Hitler—some 25,000, of whom 10,000 were killed—than wore the khaki of the Free Netherlands forces.

Both rival armies found Holland a bewildering place, full of contradictions. On the one hand, some Dutch people behaved with extraordinary courage in assisting Allied forces and fugitives. On the other, some inhabitants—especially those living near the German border—seemed more sympathetic to the Wehrmacht than to their Allied liberators. Fritz Hauff, an officer with 712th Fusilier Battalion, recorded in his diary on 21 October a conversation with a Dutch civilian: "His attitude is typical. He does not care who wins the war, as long as it is over soon." This view was echoed by George Turner-Cain, writing of his own experiences as colonel of a British battalion billeted among Dutch civilians in the winter of 1944: "There is considerable indifference to our presence, and some are downright unfriendly." War Office reports from the liberated area of Holland stated that "security doubts on the reliability of elements of the Dutch population" caused some houses and villages to be compulsorily evacuated; and "The discovery that liberation was going to increase the hardships and difficulties of living was a big disappointment to labour, and has tended to produce discontent."

Until the winter of 1944, when liberation seemed so close, most Dutch people unwillingly accepted their lot. The Netherlands was perhaps the most instinctively ordered middle-class society in Europe. "There were some nice German officers and soldiers," said Cas Tromp, twelve-year-old son of an Amsterdam court official. Once when his brother was hit on the head by a stone, a German hospital patched him up and a German soldier drove the boy home. Tromp's father was careful to avoid trouble with the occupiers: "He was a law-abiding man. He had three children to feed." Bert Egbertus's father, an Amsterdam house decorator, was able to slip back home from forced labour in Germany. "It was not so bad for Dutch people—nothing like as bad as for Poles and Russians. Though there was a war, for a long time it was not so terrible for us." The 8 p.m. curfew was an inconvenience, nothing worse. While those who resisted the occupiers suffered badly, for much of the war Germans treated those who obeyed them with civility. Bertha Schonfeld, a twenty-seven-year-old living in the Hague, was deeply irked when she tripped in the street and two German soldiers helped her up. She had an argument on a train with a uniformed Dutch Nazi who offered her his seat, which she refused.

Yet it would be wrong to confuse Dutch acquiescence with enthusiasm for the occupiers. Fritz van den Broek, a Dordrecht doctor, would not allow his children to go to the cinema, because he did not wish them to be exposed to German propaganda. The only film his twelve-year-old son had thus ever seen was *Snow White*, a few weeks before the 1940 occupation began. In the course of the war, some 7,000 young Dutchmen sought to join the Allied forces by the long perilous routes across the North Sea or the Pyrenees. Just 1,700 succeeded. Ted Van Meurs, a medical student, escaped repeatedly from German camps on his way to labour service. He was badly injured jumping from a train. After being patched up, he was sent to a labour camp near Lake Constance. Van Meurs swam the lake to Switzerland, amid the icy cold and the German searchlights, and eventually became a medical officer with the Free Dutch forces. When the German authorities in Holland demanded that every university student sign a pledge of loyalty to the Nazi regime, only a small minority acceded. The remainder were forced to abandon their studies.

Most of the Dutch people exulted as readily as the rest of Europe when deliverance from their oppressors seemed at hand. Rashly, even irresponsibly, Eisenhower declared in a broadcast to the Dutch people on 3 September 1944: "The hour of your liberation is now very near." To encourage open rejoicing, let alone active resistance, in a country as ill suited to guerrilla warfare as Holland was reckless. During the first six days of September, the Germans executed 133 prisoners. On 17 September, the day of the Arnhem drop, 28,000 of Holland's 30,000 railwaymen downed tools in a national strike. As millions of people all over the country heard the allied guns thundering closer each day, Orange flags and badges blossomed. The nation prepared to celebrate. Yet with the failure of Arnhem and the stagnation of the allied line, the Germans acted ruthlessly to tighten their grip. Leaders of the rail strike were imprisoned, and some died. Six thousand Germans began conducting demolitions in Rotterdam. Resistance activity was met with summary executions. After Dutch insurgents in Putten wounded ten Germans, eighty-seven of the town's 600 houses were burned. "Not a person was to be seen in the houses," wrote a young Dutchman who went to Putten to look for his parents on 4 October. "Everywhere there were white flags and sheets, as if the village was surrendering after a hopeless struggle, smoking ruins and a deadly silence." Three Dutchmen were shot in Rotterdam on 6 October, four more on the 24th. After a senior German intelligence officer was killed on 23 October in Amsterdam, twenty-nine hostages were killed. On 4 November the Germans blew up the Gothic town hall of Heusden, killing 134 refugees inside.

It was characteristic of the contradictions in the Germans' behaviour, a belief in their own honour and rectitude even as they enslaved an entire population, that the Nazi leadership clung to figleaves of respectability. On 30 September in Haarlem, a German staff car swerved around a corner, forcing a Dutch cyclist to leap on to the pavement. The Dutchman shouted angrily at the German driver. The officer in the car responded by tossing a grenade, which missed the cyclist but badly injured a bystander and a thirteen-year-old girl. The German C-in-C of the Netherlands, von Blaskowitz, issued a stern rebuke, cautioning all ranks to observe traffic regulations: "It is unacceptable that bad behaviour by German forces should unnecessarily provoke the civilian population."

The privations of the Dutch people, cut off from imports of food, worsened swiftly as winter approached. In Amsterdam there was gas for only ninety minutes a day, no trams nor phones nor electricity. Children played football in the streets, empty of all vehicles save those of the German army. Sixty-six thousand of Holland's 100,000 cars and 3,800 of the country's 4,500 buses, together with half of its four million bicycles, had been removed to Germany. There was no fuel for those motor vehicles which remained. People queued ceaselessly for the smallest trifles. In the Hague, communal kitchens were feeding 350,000 people a day with such provisions as were available. People in the capital were ordered to surrender blankets and clothing to the Germans. All Netherlanders became reluctant to walk far, because walking wore down shoes, and these were almost unobtainable. Eight-year-old Roelof Olderman rejoiced when he was given some beautiful new black shoes. Then it rained. He found that the soles were made of cardboard, which fell to pieces beneath his small feet. There was no legitimate source of fuel to heat Holland's offices, schools and homes. During the icy winter, trees were felled, fencing torn down. Even the wooden wedges between the idle tram rails were stolen. In the manic quest for fuel, graveyards were ransacked not to rob the dead but to seize their coffins for firewood. Cas Tromp was sent almost daily to search for wood around Schiphol airfield, near his home. Once, instead, he found an unexploded bomb. He danced along the casing, even jumped on it, because like most children he had no sense of peril.

The Germans needed more slaves, both in Holland and in the Reich. When they demanded labour to dig defences at Venlo, no one reported. In consequence twenty local hostages were shot, likewise ten in Apeldoorn. These examples produced a reluctant trickle of workers. Vastly more men were required, however, for industrial labour. Fifty thousand Rotterdammers were rounded up and shipped to Germany. Women offered butter, chocolate, brandy, even their own bodies, to their rulers, if their men could be spared. Families slept in terror of the tramp of German boots on cobbles in the night, and the cry of "*Aufmachen! Aufmachen!*"—"Open up! Open up!"—which signalled the seizure of husbands and sons. In all, some 300,000 Dutch people were deported.

One day, Bert Egbertus's mother was detained in a German round-up and held for ten hours. She came home at last at 2 a.m. The boy had lain alone in his bed, sick with fear, since 8 p.m. In the absence of light and heat, there was nowhere else. His father already lived in terror of discovery, after returning illegally from German labour service. Like some 300,000 other Dutch people, Egbertus was a "diver." Officially—and for ration purposes—he did not exist. So too were Jan and Tom Wempe, sons of a government official living in Apeldoorn. The Germans hounded their father when they failed to report for labour duty. Instead, the boys began months in hiding behind a false wall in the loft. "Don't worry. We'll pray, and it will be all right," said their father. So it was. The Wempes were fortunate enough to remain undiscovered. Many others were found, and suffered. Even for divers, the excruciating boredom of confinement seemed pain enough. The Wempe sons, twenty and twenty-four, read the same handful of books again and again and again. Their brother Theodore thought himself fortunate to have work for the Resistance. "The strain of such a life was very bad for family relationships," he said. "To have two people sleeping in the same bed, to conceal their presence in the house, is not nice."

By November, the weekly ration for Dutch people had fallen to 300 grams of potatoes, 200 grams of bread—five slices—28 grams of pulses, 5 grams each of meat and cheese. In total, this was about a quarter of normal human food intake. "Too much to die on, but too little to live by," the Dutch observed bleakly. The ration allocation provided just 900 calories, against the 2,500 of the British people, who were suffering hardship enough. People ate nettle soup, chaff and rye bread. Willem van den Broek's mother, who was pregnant, ate the starch she used for ironing in a desperate attempt to strengthen her body. Dogs and cats disappeared, as they were eaten by their owners or anyone capable of capturing them. "My mother was crying all the time," said Hans Cramer. "She couldn't bring herself to eat even when there was food. All our energies were devoted to survival." "The drapes have been torn aside," proclaimed Radio Oranje, broadcast station of the Free Netherlands, on 7 October, "bleeding and tortured Holland is exposed to the gaze of the world."

The Dutch prime minister in exile pleaded with Eisenhower's Chief of Staff, Bedell-Smith, for the liberation of his country by 1 December, before the worst of winter came. Prince Bernhardt of the Netherlands, son of the Dutch queen and leader of the Free Dutch forces, appealed in passionate terms to the Allies to hasten liberation. Eisenhower responded coolly that "military factors, and not political considerations," must determine Allied strategy. The echoes of Warsaw were unmistakable. In Holland, Allied policy caused special pain and resentment, because the voices of denial came from the armies of the democracies, not the implacable Soviets.

Among young Dutchmen, from September onwards there was a modest upsurge in recruitment to the Resistance, matching experience in France after D-Day. That winter, Holland harboured an estimated 5,000 fighters and 4,000 intelligence-gatherers, together with some 25,000 people engaged in secret publishing or working for escape networks. Between September 1944 and April 1945, American and British aircraft parachuted 20,000 weapons into Holland. It remains hard to balance the benefits to the self-respect of the Dutch people against the military futility and tragic sacrifice of the arming of civilians. To the very end, the Germans mercilessly executed anyone suspected of assisting the Resistance, together with countless hostages. All that winter, in squares and on street corners, the public murder of Dutch people continued, to discourage their compatriots from armed opposition. In Rotterdam 100 hostages were shot, in Amsterdam 200. When a prominent Nazi official was shot by the Resistance in March, Himmler demanded reprisal killings of 500 people. He eventually accepted the corpses of 250, of whom twenty-six were young men shot on a rubbish dump in the centre of Amsterdam. The Germans were in a chronically tense, dangerous mood. For years, the Dutch had grown accustomed to Wehrmacht units singing marching songs as they swaggered through the streets. There was no more singing in the winter of 1944.

The courage of the Resisters was extraordinary. One day in January, a Jewish mother and her two sons, desperate for food, went foraging from the house in Zeist where they had lived in precarious obscurity. They were detained by Germans who thought they appeared Jewish, and locked up in the local police station along with seven other Jews, until the SS could remove them. The father of the family sought the aid of the Resistance. Local fighters decided that a rescue attempt could be made, but that it must be carried out by men unknown by sight to the local police. A former policeman named Henny Idenburg enlisted the aid, willing or otherwise, of a Luftwaffe deserter whom the Resistance was hiding. A local garage owner agreed to turn a blind eye while a German truck he was repairing was "borrowed" for an hour. On 23 January, the Luftwaffe corporal in his uniform accompanied Idenburg, in his old Dutch police uniform, to Zeist police station. They produced a forged demand for the prisoners, who were duly handed over and herded out to the truck amid appropriate shouts and abuse. When the truck halted in a forest near Driebergen, the traumatized Jewish prisoners were convinced that they were to be executed. Instead, they found themselves taken into hiding in a church until they could be removed to safe houses. They survived.

"We call out to the free world," the Resistance signalled to London on 13 February. "An old, civilized nation is threatened with destruction by the German barbarians. Let the free world raise its voice . . . We shall hold out." Yet with so many peoples across Europe crying out for salvation, just as the Allies were reluctant to acknowledge the unique plight of the Jews, so also they paid scant heed to that of the Dutch. Everything, argued Churchill, Roosevelt, Eisenhower, must hinge upon the defeat of Germany, the fount of all these evils. Allied leaders were convinced that to be deflected from their central purpose to succour any special group of Nazi victims would assist only the cause of Hitler. The Allies were probably right. But it was very hard for people dying by inches to acknowledge it.

The liberators seemed so tantalizingly close. Their guns could be heard month after month, firing from positions only a few miles distant from the towns and villages in which many Dutch people lived under savage oppression. Almost daily, British fighter-bombers strafed Dutch trains and roads. Whatever the shortcomings of Allied bombing policy—and its cost in Dutch lives—it is hard to exaggerate the surge of hope and excitement which every passage of the Fortresses, Liberators and Lancasters gave to the occupied nations beneath their wings. Theodore Wempe thrilled each time he saw aircraft and told himself rapturously: "They come! They come!" People stood on their roofs waving, and often thinking enviously of the Allied pilots flying home to lunch in freedom. In those days, Holland was an intensely monarchist country. Fierce argument persisted about whether their queen should have chosen exile in 1940 or should have remained to share the sufferings of her people. But Netherlanders were much moved when Allied planes dropped leaflets showing pictures of their little princesses, living in exile with the rest of the royal family. On Queen Wilhelmina's birthday, some people set out their washing in Dutch national colours, provoking German soldiers to clatter angrily through the streets, tearing it down.

Transcending everything, there was hunger, the hunger of a nation. In every community in Holland, everyone knew the collaborators and black-marketeers,

for these were the only people who were not starving. The German commandant of the concentration camp at Amersfoort celebrated Christmas Day 1944
by cancelling all food for the inmates, and holding an *Appel* lasting from 7 a.m. to
1:30 p.m. amid the snow of the frozen parade ground. The guards' Christmas
geese were hung upon the wire to mock the captives, until they disappeared
into the German kitchens. Some food supplies were dispatched to Holland by
the International Red Cross, but the Nazi authorities proved obstructive about
distribution. Dutch people recalled that in 1918, when German and Austria were
starving after their defeat, German and Austrian children were sent to Holland
to be fed and cared for. Perhaps some of those young fugitives, they thought,
had grown up into their persecutors and tormentors of 1945.

Petty deceit became a way of life—stealing cabbages and carrots from gardens, seeking to deceive a shopkeeper into supposing that he had already been
given your ration coupon. City families waited weeks for their turn to hire a
small handcart. Then they walked miles into the countryside on *Hongertrochten*—
hunger treks—to find farmers with whom to barter furniture, sheets, clothing
for food. Some country people found the opportunities for exploitation irresistible—accepting a gold ring for a handful of potatoes. The city-dwellers of
Holland harboured lasting resentment against farmers who enriched themselves
amid their nation's agonizing privations.

By January, the daily ration had fallen to 460 calories. "Those who are hungry shout," observed a Dutch newspaper bitterly on 30 January, "but those who
are starving keep deadly still." A profound silence had fallen over Holland, as
people huddled in their houses, avoiding the smallest unnecessary activity to
conserve energy. Schools were closed by lack of heating. Industrial and commercial activity was at a standstill. Only Germans, and their Dutch creatures,
continued to use vehicles. Garbage piled in the streets, swarming with rats,
because there were no means of collecting it. When civilians had exhausted
supplies of pulped sugar beet, they began to eat tulip bulbs—140 million were
consumed that winter. "Take a litre of water," suggested a local recipe, "one
onion, 4–6 bulbs, seasoning and salt, a teaspoon of oil and some curry substitute.
Brown the onion with oil and curry, add water, bring to the boil, and grate the
cleaned bulbs into the boiling liquid." The outcome was repulsive, but possessed some vestiges of nutritional value. Jan de Boer, one of nine children of an
academic living in the Hague, saw an ill-nourished horse defecate in the snow
outside his home one morning. He was astonished to behold a passer-by
descend from his bicycle and poke through the steaming dung, searching for
undigested morsels of corn, which he ate as he crouched. A Dutchman said he
learned that winter that human beings "only consisted of a stomach and certain
instincts." Twelve-year-old Willem van den Broek dreamed not of exotic
adventures nor even of luxuries, but about bread, meat, cheese, sweets.

Medical research suggested that children aged between ten and fourteen suffered most from hunger. The average Dutch fourteen-year-old boy weighed forty-one kilos in 1940, but only thirty-seven kilos in 1945, and had become two centimetres shorter. Girls of the same age were a frightening seven kilos lighter and six centimetres shorter. Typhoid and diphtheria epidemics had broken out. Women stopped menstruating. Men became temporarily impotent. Corpses lay in churches awaiting burial. An Amsterdam old people's home reported that its death rate had doubled. A visitor to a cemetery wrote: "the shrunken bodies were lying next to each other. No flesh on thighs or calves. Most had bent arms and legs, the hands clenched as if the poor devil was still asking for food." On 17 March, a Dutch leader sent a new appeal to London for aid: "The expression 'starved to death' has been used so often in a figurative sense that it is difficult to realise that people are dying in the street...And when the question arises: 'But how can people stand it?,' my answer is: 'Those people cannot stand it; they are really going completely to pieces.'"

All these miseries were compounded by Allied bombing. Bertha Schonfeld felt irrationally safe at home, and simply buried her head in her hands as bombs fell close at hand. Rather than go down to a shelter, she and her mother protected themselves by putting saucepans on their heads. Once, a neighbour found a spent cannon shell in her bed. The Germans were launching V2 rockets against Britain from Holland. They had deliberately located launch and storage sites near to built-up areas. All the windows in the Schonfelds' apartment were broken by the premature explosion of some of the forty-five-foot monsters. V2s killed 2,724 British people in the last months of the war. The Allied air forces strove to frustrate them, and killed far more people doing so than did the V2s. On Saturday 3 March, fifty-seven Boston and Mitchell bombers of the RAF's Second Tactical Air Force, aiming at launch sites on the Haagsche Bosch near the Hague, instead plastered a residential area. The Germans refused to allow the fire brigade to enter the stricken streets, asserting that "the stupid Dutch have to learn what it is like." The raid killed 511 people and destroyed 3,250 houses, one of them the home of the local Resistance leader Henri Koot, who lost everything he owned. Twelve thousand desperately cold and hungry people now also found themselves without shelter. Churchill was infuriated by "this slaughter of the Dutch." The British Foreign Office told the Dutch ambassador that the responsible officer had been court-martialled, for confusing the vertical and horizontal co-ordinates of the target. In fact, there is no evidence that anyone was disciplined for the tragedy, but rumour within the RAF suggested that there had been a disastrous bomb-aiming error. Other raids involved less dramatic blunders, but inflicted a steady stream of civilian casualties. Misdirected Allied bombs caused the deaths of substantially more people in the nations of occupied Europe than the Luftwaffe killed in its blitz on Britain.

Dutch bitterness towards the Allies, as well as against the Germans, had become very great. Antoinette Hamminga, a teenager living near the Hague,

suffered no subsequent trauma about the months of starvation, but retained terrifying memories of her experience as a passenger on a train strafed by British
fighter-bombers, when a girl sitting behind her was killed and another was
drenched in the blood of a wounded woman. "People got very angry," said
Theodore Wempe. "We constantly asked each other: 'Why don't they come?
Will it be a couple of days? Or a week?' " Churchill spoke to the House of Commons on 14 March about the plight of Holland, but as late as the 27th Eisenhower asserted in response to questions from Washington that the best way to
assist the Dutch people remained "the rapid completion of our main operations." Yet those "main operations" seemed interminable, amid the inexorable
decline of Holland into ruin and of its people into shadows of humanity.

Through the very last days before freedom belatedly came to Holland, the
Germans continued to kill. Hitler's servants seemed eager to drag with them
into the grave of the Third Reich every innocent who fell into their clutches.
On 8 March, 263 Resistance members were executed in reprisal for an attack on
General Rauter, a senior SS officer in Holland. On 1 April, Canadians freed the
big east Netherlands town of Enschede. The night before they arrived, the
Gestapo executed ten people, together with two more just an hour before
Canadian tanks appeared. When the liberators entered Zutphen on 6 April,
they found the bodies of ten freshly executed civilians, some of whom had been
tortured. As late as 7 April von Blaskowitz, commanding the 120,000 German
troops remaining in Holland, was still frenziedly preparing demolitions and
giving orders for a last stand in the area of Noord-Holland, Zuid-Holland and
Utrecht which had been designated Fortress Holland. On 15 April, thirty-four
people were executed in Amsterdam. Two days later, the Germans blew up the
huge dyke guarding the Wieringer flatlands, flooding 50,000 acres, the granary
of western Holland, to add to the 230,000 hectares of the country already under
water. A. C. de Graaf, deputy leader of the local Resistance, emerged from hiding to save his wife and children from the inundations. He was caught and shot.

One of the most extraordinary episodes of the war, still scarcely known in
the West, began on 4 April 1945 on the Dutch offshore island of Texel. Its garrison, the 882nd Battalion of the Wehrmacht, comprised some 550 Georgians captured on the Eastern Front. They mutinied and ran amok, killing every German
they encountered. A local Resistance leader consulted with the Georgians, and
set off with three of them in the local lifeboat to seek aid from the British across
the North Sea. They landed at Cromer in Norfolk on 6 April. The British, however, received them without enthusiasm. They were subjected to six days of
interrogation, at the end of which the Georgians were dispatched to a PoW
camp. No action was taken to assist the Texel mutineers, or the local Dutch
people.

The Germans, even in these last weeks of the war, addressed the uprising
with unstinting ferocity. Hitler signalled personally to demand that "an exam-

ple should be made of the rebels." Some 3,600 men of the Wehrmacht were committed, in a battle that lasted more than a fortnight. The C-in-C Netherlands reported to Berlin on 17 April: "Extremely fierce fighting from strongpoint to strongpoint... success only possible if all available artillery and other heavy weapons are employed." Yard by yard, the Germans forced back the mutineers. A German officer who led the way into the local hospital shot five badly wounded Georgians in front of a Dutch nurse. The last fifty-seven mutineers capitulated on 20 April. "We had risen against the Hitler tyranny, we had made great sacrifices," one of the few survivors wrote bitterly, "but instead of receiving help we were betrayed and abandoned." The captives were stripped naked, forced to dig their own graves, then shot. The last four were kept alive long enough to fill in the holes. A total of 117 local Dutch people, 550 Georgians and 800 Germans perished in the Texel battle, which went entirely unremarked outside Holland, both then and later. This bloodbath ended barely a week before Hitler's death.

The agony of Holland was assuaged by the surrender of von Blaskowitz's forces on 5 May, yet it became the work of months to claw back the nation from the abyss of starvation, aided by enormous Allied air drops of food—Operation Manna. If the Dutch were not confined behind barbed wire, their sufferings were at least as great as those of most Allied prisoners of war. Incredibly, the occupiers continued to murder Dutchmen not only after Hitler's death, but in their rage and bitterness after VE-Day. Germans indulged an orgy of looting and killing before the Canadian liberation forces arrived. On 8 May, twenty-year-old Elsa Caspers remonstrated with an SS man standing over three bodies, which he said were those of "terrorists." Elsa, a Resistance courier, said: "Surely you must know the war is over?" The German sneered: "We did it just for fun." Annie van Beek, who was twenty-three in 1945, retained for the rest of her life her bitterness towards the Germans: "They took away what should have been the best years of my life. They gave us that awful last winter. My fiancé spent three years as a prisoner of war. My younger brother died in one of their terrible camps." If the law had been enforced against all Germans who committed crimes against humanity in the countries occupied by Hitler, post-war executions on a Soviet scale would have been necessary. The Dutch experience of war in the winter of 1944–45 was as terrible as that of any nation in western Europe. To the very end, the Germans showed no hint of mercy to millions held in the Nazi maw.

CHAPTER FOURTEEN

Collapse in the West

EISENHOWER'S DECISION

THE SEIZURE of the bridge at Remagen, one of the most melodramatic episodes of the Allied campaign, was followed by a march to victory on the Western Front that ended in anticlimax, for reasons that were inescapable. Bradley's forces staged their breakout from the Remagen bridgehead on 25 March, almost three weeks after the crossing was taken. Here again, caution had prevailed. After a slow start, making four or five miles a day, the pace of the advance quickened. German resistance was slight. Bradley, who had never achieved a successful envelopment, now became passionately committed to encircling the Ruhr and at last making the massive capture of Germans which had eluded his armies since Normandy. His plan was that the U.S. First Army, pushing up from the south, should link with Simpson's Ninth, swinging south-east from Wesel. It seemed to some observers strange that, after Eisenhower had repeatedly asserted the primacy of Berlin as the focus of all Allied hopes and aspirations since June 1944, the Americans should now throw overwhelming force behind a limited operation 250 miles west of the capital. The Ruhr's strategic and industrial importance stemmed from its production of raw steel rather than finished munitions. At this stage of the war, it was implausible that any steel leaving the presses could be converted into weapons in time to be employed by the Wehrmacht. Russell Weigley is among the fiercest American critics of Bradley's decision to concentrate on the Ruhr, "whose strategic significance was...essentially nil." Yet Bradley judged the capture of the remains of Army Group B, his adversary since Normandy, as the most substantial objective for his armies. In the light of subsequent events, he may have been right.

Some Allied units encountered stubborn local resistance. There was an unhappy episode on 30 March: as the U.S. 3rd Armored Division barrelled confidently eastwards, tanks from the SS Panzer Training School at Paderborn struck hard at the American column. A Tiger smashed into the jeep of the division's commander, the much admired Maurice Rose. The general was trapped on the road. He reached down to his waist, apparently to unbuckle his pistol belt to surrender. A German shot him. It was fancifully suggested that Rose had been deliberately killed because he was Jewish, indeed a rabbi's son. In truth, the general was merely a victim of the chance of battle.

In the days that followed, the Americans fought some fierce little battles with Germans seeking to escape capture, but nothing seriously impeded their advance. Whatever delays some spearheads suffered, overall American casualties were small, and armoured columns ate up the miles eastwards. In the first days of April, Bradley committed eighteen American divisions to tighten the Ruhr noose on 317,000 men, the ruins of Army Group B. As the Americans closed in, dogged German resistance persisted. Ridgway dispatched one of his officers to Model's headquarters under a flag of truce, proposing surrender. Model declined, declaring that his oath to the Führer required him to fight to the end. Ridgway told the German colonel who brought this message to his CP that he was free to return to his own lines. The colonel responded prudently that he would prefer to become a prisoner of war. Lieutenant Rolf-Helmut Schröder, a staff officer at Model's HQ, found himself carrying orders to corps commanders for renewed attacks. One general said furiously: "This is all nonsense—it's crazy!" Schröder shrugged apologetically: "I don't make the plans—I just bring them from Army headquarters." The other corps commander seized the operation orders which the young officer brought and tossed them into the wastepaper basket.

When the Germans in the Ruhr pocket finally abandoned the struggle on 18 April, the principal challenge for the Americans was to marshal their captives and put them into PoW cages. Flying in a B-26 high above the battlefield on 25 April, Lieutenant Robert Burger saw below him "what looked like a dark plowed field... To my disbelief, it proved to be acres of massed humanity. There must have been hundreds of thousands of German PoWs packed together closer than a herd of cows. How they were fed or kept clean, I will never know. This was probably the largest audience I will ever have—as we flew over, all those captives' eyes looked up. I don't doubt some of them were ones that formerly shot at us."

Since advancing out of the Remagen bridgehead, it had taken a month to complete the Ruhr envelopment. Ninth Army suffered around 2,500 casualties of all kinds, and First Army some three times that number. Model, Army Group B's commander, walked away into a forest and shot himself on 21 April.

Because Dwight Eisenhower presented a benign face to the world, even his commanders sometimes underestimated the pressures upon him, the relentless tensions under which he laboured. In mid-March, some of his staff feared that he was close to a nervous breakdown, a condition only slightly ameliorated by a forty-eight-hour break in the South of France. When Ike's son John arrived in Europe, assigned as an infantry platoon leader, Bradley insisted that the boy should instead be given a staff job. The previous autumn, the son of General "Sandy" Patch had been killed in action while serving with his father's own U.S. Seventh Army. The blow devastated Patch, and for some time rendered him all but unfit for his duties. Eisenhower's subordinates were desperate to ensure that no such emotional burden was laid upon the Supreme Commander. To John Eisenhower's deep embarrassment, he was kept out of combat. His father now faced decisions as important as any since Normandy.

Montgomery abruptly informed SHAEF on 27 March that he intended to drive for the Elbe, with the British Second Army's left wing touching Hamburg and the American Ninth Army's right brushing Magdeburg: "My headquarters will move to Wesel–Münster–Wiedenbrück–Herford–Hanover—thence by autobahn to Berlin, I hope." This signal infuriated Eisenhower. Next day in his headquarters at Rheims, he received a message from Marshall in Washington warning of the importance of clarifying demarcation lines with the Russians, to avoid any danger of an embarrassing, perhaps dangerous collision when the Eastern and Western allies met. The two communications forced upon Eisenhower some immediate decisions. He dealt first with the British field-marshal. Beyond arrogating to himself the Supreme Commander's authority to make strategic choices, Montgomery's assumption that the U.S. Ninth Army would remain under his command seemed intolerable. Eisenhower signalled 21st Army Group that, with the Rhine crossing operation complete, Ninth Army would revert to 12th Army Group's command on 2 April. Omar Bradley thus became master of 1.3 million men in four armies. Eisenhower decreed that Bradley's forces should address the main axis of advance eastwards. The 21st Army Group would fulfil a subsidiary role, covering the Americans' left flank, while Devers's 6th Army Group performed the same function on the right. It is unlikely that it cost the Supreme Commander much pain to give orders that would distress Montgomery.

Eisenhower's next action roused the fury of Churchill and has provoked controversy for sixty years. Without further reference to his political and military superiors, on his own initiative he sent a personal message to Stalin stating that his armies had no intention of advancing to Berlin. SHAEF hoped, he said, that the Anglo-Americans would meet the Russians on an axis Erfurt–Leipzig–Dresden—which meant around the Elbe, at least forty miles west of Berlin. He copied his cable to the Combined Chiefs of Staff.

Churchill personally telephoned Eisenhower on 29 March to express his dismay that a field commander should have communicated so vital a decision direct to Stalin, without prior reference to the Anglo-American leadership. The British prime minister asserted his strong belief in the importance of Berlin as

THE WESTERN ADVANCE
BEYOND THE RHINE
········· Allied front line 28 March
▲▲▲▲ Allied front line 7 May

0   50   100 miles
0   50   100   150 km

DENMARK

Baltic Sea

Kiel

Rostock

Bremerhaven

Lübeck

Hamburg

Emden

Stettin

Groningen

Amsterdam

NETHERLANDS

Belsen

Brandenburg   Berlin
Potsdam

ARMY GROUP H
(BLASKOWITZ)

Hanover

Arnhem

Osnabrück

Münster

R. Ems

Brunswick

Magdeburg

R. Oder

R. Elbe

21st ARMY GROUP
(MONTGOMERY)

Dortmund

Kassel
(4 Apr.)

Harz Mts

Nordhausen

Halle

Dresden

Düsseldorf

ARMY GROUP B
(MODEL)

R. Weser

Leipzig

Cologne

Marburg

Erfurt

Weimar

Bonn

Chemnitz

BELGIUM

Koblenz

Fulda

R. Rhine

CZECHOSLOVAKIA

Prague

12th ARMY GROUP
(BRADLEY)

Frankfurt

Luxembourg

Mainz

Würzburg
(5 Apr.)

Pilsen

Mannheim

Nuremberg
(23 Apr.)

Saarbrücken

ARMY GROUP G
(HAUSSER)

Regensburg
(26 Apr.)

6th ARMY GROUP
(DEVERS)

Karlsruhe

Nancy

Strasbourg

Stuttgart

R. Danube

Passau

Ulm
(23 Apr.)

Munich

FRANCE

R. Inn

Salzburg

Basle

Zurich

Innsbruck

AUSTRIA

SWITZERLAND

Brenner Pass
(4 May)

Klagenfurt

Bolzano

N

ITALY

U.S. FIFTH ARMY

Trieste
(2 May)

Turin
(30 Apr.)

Milan
(26 Apr.)

R. Po

Padua

Venice
(29 Apr.)

the final destination of the Anglo-American armies. Yet the American Supreme Commander no longer felt obliged to display the deference to the British prime minister which had seemed appropriate a year or two earlier. Churchill was visibly weary and audibly testy. Eisenhower was well aware that the wishes of the British government no longer exercised decisive influence where it mattered—in Washington. "The PM is increasingly vexatious," Eisenhower told Bradley. "He imagines himself to be a military tactician." Churchill said to Brooke: "There is only one thing worse than fighting with allies, and that is fighting without them."

One line in Eisenhower's signal to the combined Chiefs of Staff has remained the focus of fierce debate since 1945. He asserted blandly that "Berlin has lost much of its former military importance." He made plain that he had no intention of assaulting Germany's capital, unless he was instructed to do so. "I am the first to admit that a war is waged in pursuance of political aims," he wrote on 7 April, "and if the chiefs of staff should decide that the Allied effort to take Berlin outweighs purely military considerations, I would cheerfully readjust my plans and my thinking so as to carry out such an operation." No such decision was forthcoming. Marshall endorsed Eisenhower's decision, overriding the remonstrations of the British. The dying Roosevelt did not intervene.

Back in November 1943, the president had asserted that "there would definitely be a race for Berlin. We may have to put United States divisions into Berlin as soon as possible." The president sketched a plan for the post-war occupation of Germany, in which the capital stood in the American zone. By April 1945, Roosevelt's 1943 Berlin vision had evaporated. This was a reflection of the president's unwillingness to intervene in issues of military strategy, save on the largest questions; his failing health; circumstances on the German battlefield which had been quite unforeseeable sixteen months earlier, with the Russians further forward than anyone had envisioned; the reluctance of the U.S. Chiefs of Staff to make military decisions for political purposes; and the desire of the U.S. State Department to conciliate Moscow.

At the time of Eisenhower's exchanges with London and Washington, however, Bradley had no more knowledge than Montgomery of Eisenhower's decision—and it was overwhelmingly a personal one—to forswear any attempt to reach Hitler's capital. On 3 April, 12th Army Group's commander was still telling his own generals that for the last big advance of the war Ninth Army would head for Berlin, while First Army struck south-east for Leipzig. On 4 April, Simpson was ordered to "exploit any opportunity for seizing a bridge-head over the Elbe and be prepared to continue to advance on Berlin or to the north-east." As late as 8 April, Eisenhower visited Major-General Alexander Bolling, commanding the 84th Division in Hanover, and asked him where he was headed next. "General . . . We have a clear go to Berlin and nothing can stop us," responded Bolling. "Keep going," said Eisenhower encouragingly, putting a hand on Bolling's shoulder. "I wish you all the luck in the world and don't let anybody stop you." It seems extravagant to interpret this with hindsight, as Bolling did at the time, as a tactical mandate to drive for Hitler's capital; rather, these were simply a commander's loose words of encouragement to a junior subordinate. The conversation reflects the somewhat insouciant manner in which Eisenhower seemed to his generals to address the Berlin issue, together with his familiar imprecision of military purpose.

More than one major historian of the campaign has voiced the suspicion that, if American rather than British troops had occupied the Allied left flank, natural focus of a push for Berlin, Eisenhower would have unleashed them towards Hitler's capital. As it was, so deep had become his loathing of Montgomery, so determined was he to frustrate the field-marshal's "efforts to make sure that the Americans—and me in particular—got no credit" for the campaign, that he set his face against any course that would enable Montgomery to lead a triumphal march on Berlin. Stephen Ambrose, the Supreme Commander's biographer, has suggested that if Bradley had commanded in the north "Eisenhower might well have sent him to Berlin." Yet it seems implausible to suppose that Eisenhower's last big decision of the war was founded upon personal animosity, real though this was. He was still much troubled about the possibility that the enemy would make a last stand in south Germany, at the mythical "Alpine Redoubt" which preoccupied SHAEF intelligence.

There was a much more substantial issue. If the Germans defended Berlin with the desperation they had displayed in other last-ditch actions, Allied casualties would be enormous. When Eisenhower asked Bradley for his estimate of American losses in a drive for Berlin, 12th Army Group's commander suggested a figure of 100,000. This estimate does not seem unrealistic—it amounts to barely one-third of the casualties actually sustained by the Russians. It is true that in early April the Americans overestimated Germany's residual capacity to sustain the campaign. Yet it is striking that U.S. casualties in April 1945 declined only slightly against those of February, as the Germans maintained disorganized but often fanatical resistance. It is plausible that Germany's soldiers would have resisted an Anglo-American assault on Berlin much less vigorously than the Soviet one. But it would have been rash for Eisenhower to make any such assumption while Hitler lived, or indeed for history to do so.

When Russian forces were already within thirty miles of the city, while the nearest Americans were still four times that distance away, wherein lay the virtue of a commitment to conclude the Western allied campaign with a bloodbath? Berlin stood more than a hundred miles inside the designated, unalterable Soviet occupation zone of Germany. What would Eisenhower have said to the mother or husband of an American or British soldier killed in a battle for

Hitler's capital, which at best would have yielded only a symbolic triumph for the Western allies? Was any symbol worth tens of thousands of American and British lives? "I decided," he wrote in his post-war memoirs, "that [Berlin] was not the most logical nor the most desirable objective for the forces of Western Allies."

Eisenhower's decision provoked the wrath of his subordinate commanders at the time, and the censure of posterity informed by the Cold War. Robert E. Murphy, the influential American diplomat acting as political adviser to Eisenhower and the German Control Commission, expressed his dismay in a letter to Washington on 14 April. "Apparently," Murphy wrote, "there is on the part of some of our officers no particular eagerness to occupy Berlin first... One thing seems to be that what is left of Berlin may be tenaciously defended house by house, brick by brick. I have suggested the modest opinion that there should be a certain political advantage in the capture of Berlin, even though the military advantage may be insignificant." To put the matter bluntly—which, surprisingly, none of the Anglo-Americans engaged in this debate did at the time—somebody had to assume responsibility for capturing or killing Adolf Hitler, as well as securing his capital. Militarily, the fate of the Führer was merely incidental to the defeat of Germany, but he could hardly be permitted to depart into retirement in Buenos Aires. Once again, it was Stalin alone who knew exactly what he wanted—Hitler's capture alive, for the greatest of all show trials.

There is no doubt that the Anglo-Americans could have reached the Berlin area swiftly, whatever uncertainties persist about what might have happened once they had done so. Eisenhower's decision seemed to his critics to mark the nadir of an advance dominated by cautious and unimaginative strategic leadership since he had assumed command of the Allied ground forces on 1 September 1944. For the Americans and British, the new policy ensured an anticlimactic end to the greatest military campaign in the history of the world. The occupation of Bremen and Hamburg, Munich and Stuttgart scarcely offered the peerless drama of a march through the streets of Hitler's conquered capital.

Churchill's anger that Berlin was to be forsaken as a prize reflected the deeper grief which haunted the last months of his war, that Hitler's dominance of eastern Europe was now to be supplanted by that of Stalin. Yet the Washington administration refused to share the British prime minister's fear of the Russians. Staff-Sergeant Henry Kissinger said, half a century later:

If you look at the world geopolitically, the mistakes were avoidable. But if you look at them as Americans did in 1945, when they were trying to escape history, they were understandable. America was determined not to do what other nations had always done after winning wars—grab as much as they could. There was no excuse for the way Roosevelt treated Churchill. FDR was naive. But one must make allowances for the spirit of the time. If Roosevelt had resisted Soviet demands, a big slice of the U.S. intellectual community would have accused him of provoking Stalin.

If the Allies had identified seizure of Berlin and Anglo-American liberation of large tracts of eastern Europe as vital war aims early in 1944, it would have been necessary for the U.S. and British governments to order Eisenhower to pursue his advance across north-west Europe in a wholly different spirit, with vastly greater urgency. Washington and London would have needed to assert a political agenda for the last months of the conflict. Instead, from beginning to end, the SHAEF Supreme Commander's orders were explicitly military in character, directed towards the destruction of the Nazi regime. Stalin's suspicion, indeed paranoia, about American intentions was prompted by disbelief that any great nation could conduct a war without political ambitions, when those of the Soviet Union now dominated its military strategy.

Yet even before Roosevelt's health failed, America's conduct of the war was overwhelmingly determined by her Chiefs of Staff, military men. It was impossible, in the last weeks of war, abruptly to invite the army commanders in the field to adopt different priorities. And who in Washington was going to do this, in the last weeks of a dying president, or the first days of a novice one? No military action undertaken by the Anglo-Americans in the spring of 1945 could have undone the decisions of the Teheran and Yalta conferences about the Soviet occupation zone in Germany, to which Churchill had acceded. No belated Anglo-American military success could snatch the east European nations from communist tyranny, because the Russians already occupied them. It is true that geographical limits had not been agreed at Yalta for Allied military operations, because no one could guess in February where the armies' respective advances might end. This was why Eisenhower felt obliged to signal Stalin at the end of March about his intentions. But wherein lay the purpose of losing American and British lives to gain territory destined to become the responsibility of the Red Army? Millions of Germans were fleeing in terror from the Russians, and praying to be occupied by the Western allies. This was, however, a problem for the vanquished, rather than for the victors.

The Allies had tacitly, and in considerable degree explicitly, conceded Stalin's claims to a blood price, in recognition of Russia's sacrifice. Even in the last year of war, the Red Army had accepted casualties many times those of the Americans and British, to complete the destruction of the Third Reich. If the Western allies had dashed for Berlin, the Russians would unquestionably have pre-empted them. Stalin would never have stood by while the Anglo-Americans occupied Hitler's capital. Zhukov and Konev had held their line on the Oder since the end of January, when the Americans were still struggling above the Roer. If the Americans and British had made a rush for Berlin, exactly the kind of messy, perhaps politically disastrous collision Marshall feared could have taken place between the Russians and Anglo-Americans. Eisenhower's last major decision of the campaign lacked any Pattonesque "lust for glory." But it was surely the correct one. No Western military action in April 1945 would have changed the post-war settlement. The manner in which Eisenhower allowed the momentous decision to trickle down among his commanders, almost as an afterthought, scarcely suggested the behaviour of a man who was making an important considered judgement, conscious of history's eyes upon him. Yet Eisenhower's forbearance about Berlin highlighted his political common sense, together with his rare gift for bearing responsibility, which is too readily taken for granted in a man who had risen from the rank of colonel to five-star general in less than three years.

Staff-Sergeant Henry Kissinger observed: "America doesn't produce great generals. Eisenhower was the manager of an alliance. If Rommel had commanded the Allied armies, he might have got to Berlin in one go. But what did we have to gain by haste?" It is impossible to share the view of Cornelius Ryan and others that Eisenhower made an historic blunder in April 1945 by declining to drive for Berlin. The die was cast. Churchill's anguish about the plight of eastern Europe caused him to clutch at unrealistic hopes in April 1945. Even if the British prime minister possessed an historic vision lacking at the summits of U.S. power in those days, it was Churchill and not Eisenhower who displayed naivety about the options open to the Western allied forces to frustrate Soviet imperialism in arms, unless they were prepared to go to war with Stalin.

Among Eisenhower's last big operational decisions of the campaign, one was indeed political. Montgomery was ordered to abandon his earlier task of covering the American left flank and to strike fast for the Baltic coast at Lübeck, to "seal off the Danish peninsula." There were real fears that the Soviets might aspire to seize Denmark. Simpson's U.S. Ninth Army would march east towards the Elbe river. The remainder of the American armies would swing south, to take southern Germany and address Hitler's Alpine Redoubt, where large enemy forces including many SS fanatics were reported to be gathering. The Alpine Redoubt was, of course, a myth, and it was bizarre in the extreme that SHAEF intelligence embraced it. But it is impossible to argue that the Allied turn southwards made any significant adverse impact upon the last days of the campaign, as the remains of the German Army crumbled in their path. The U.S. Seventh Army drove south on a route that finally took it to Munich and the Brenner Pass. Patton's Third Army advanced in a great sweep which embraced Chemnitz, western Czechoslovakia and northern Austria. Hodges's First Army attacked south of the Harz Mountains, towards Halle and Leipzig, while Simpson's Ninth took an easterly line through Brunswick and Magdeburg which led, at last, to the historic junction with the Russians.

DRIVING TO THE ELBE

LATE ON THE afternoon of 11 April, the 67th Armored Regiment became the first American unit to reach the Elbe, after travelling almost sixty miles in a single day. They found themselves shooting their way through the streets of Schönebeck, south-east of Magdeburg, while other elements of 2nd Armored Division disposed of desultory resistance in the western suburbs of that city. Within a few hours, the Americans had thrown a bridge across the river and established forces on the eastern bank. The colonel of one American regiment, oblivious of Eisenhower's intentions, told his men exultantly: "You are on your way to Berlin." Many senior officers still shared this delusion, and the Supreme Commander seemed in no hurry to disabuse them. Only on 12 April did he inform Patton of his decision that most of the Allied armies would stop at the Elbe, unless there were local tactical reasons to advance a little further. Third Army would halt on a north–south line parallel with the river in western Czechoslovakia and northern Austria.

Yet although the Americans quickly secured several Elbe crossing points, incredibly the Germans continued to counter-attack. As late as 14 April, Ninth Army felt obliged to pull back from one of its bridgeheads under fierce enemy pressure, after taking more than 300 casualties. Eisenhower repeatedly checked the great joy-ride of Patton's Third Army to ensure that, to the very end, his forces maintained a more or less straight frontage. In the south, the Germans' Army Group G simply disintegrated in the face of Devers's 6th Army Group.

"There was little that was cheerful or exhilarating about the last stages of the war," wrote Air Chief Marshal Sir Arthur Tedder at SHAEF. The final Anglo-American drive across Germany offered few moments of glory, and many foolish little battles which wasted men's lives even more pitiably than all war wastes lives. For instance, as tanks of the U.S. 12th Armored Division entered the little town of Boxberg on 12 April, at first they encountered only a few snipers. When the column was halfway down the main street, however, enemy troops armed with fausts and small arms began to fire upon them from upper storeys. This was a battalion of officer cadets who were "young, tough and smart," Colonel Richard Gordon reported. The Americans hastily withdrew. "Then we converged the fire of our tanks, artillery and infantry on the town, and blasted it down," said Gordon.

A routine was established across the breadth of the American and British fronts. A tank column clattered across the countryside until it approached a town or village. Then vehicles halted, and officers peered forward through their binoculars. Any sign of movement provoked a radio call: "Put one through the window." A brisk succession of tank or howitzer shells smashed into the buildings, throwing up dust and smoke. Then the liberators pushed on, unless the town was unfortunate enough to be defended by SS or Hitler Jugend, in which case absolute devastation followed. Many communities pleaded with combatants of both armies to be spared from destruction. Allied officers often enlisted the services of local burgomasters to telephone ahead to the next village on the road, warning its people to put out white flags or face the consequences. Only Nazi fanatics remained heedless and allowed their own people to pay the price.

"The leading vehicle got knocked out sooner or later, and nobody enjoyed the 'honour' of leading the regiment," Lieutenant-Colonel Tony Leakey of the British 5th Royal Tanks wrote wearily. Once, all four tanks of his point troop were knocked out approaching a German strongpoint. Their lieutenant rallied the men who bailed out of the stricken Shermans, and they stormed the enemy position with personal weapons. There was much resentment in the unit that no one received a "gong" for this notable display of determination. As Leakey's tanks approached Bremen, "it was the same drill—keep going on the one road until the leading vehicle brewed up. Once, it was a scout car of recce troop, the crew killed, a young officer who'd joined three months before." The road was mined, and the enemy had taken up positions on both sides: "The infantry got a bloody nose, lost a number of men and had to withdraw. The leading tank hit a mine and promptly brewed up. The crew was killed. At this stage of the war, nobody was very keen to earn medals."

For men who had survived years of battle, it seemed especially cruel to meet death now. Lieutenant Kingsley Field's entire troop of the King's Own was destroyed by a single German tank in the space of a few minutes near Gock. "It seemed a stupid time to die," wrote Flight-Lieutenant Richard Hough, an RAF Typhoon pilot. OKH in Berlin signalled to all army groups on 18 April: "On the Elbe front a weakish assault troop of ours without effort brought in 40 American prisoners. The Americans surrendered for the reason that they had no idea of letting themselves be shot dead so near the end of the war. This fact is to be notified to the troops...German actions must prove to [the Americans] that their campaign is no pleasure trip through Germany."

In that final phase on the Western Front, the confrontation between reasonable men who aspired to behave in a reasonable way and unreasonable, often hysterical men and children willing to embrace death became more painful than ever. In the history of the Second World War, much has been written about the "fanatical" performance of the Japanese soldier. Yet Japan surrendered without fighting a battle for its homeland. It was Germans who fought to the last in the rubble of their own towns and villages, some of Hitler's soldiers who displayed a fanaticism matching and perhaps surpassing that of the armies of Nippon. Kesselring sent a withering signal to LXXXII Corps on 18 April, alleging that its resistance around Nuremberg had been crippled by "a deficiency of leadership, initiative and resource, for which responsibility must be brought home to individuals." This was a familiar Nazi figure of speech for selecting scapegoats for military failure to be shot.

Among the Allied armies, even in these days of victory, no man could assure himself of safety. Private Ralph Gordon of First Army's 18th Infantry was vastly relieved that after the Hürtgen Forest nightmare he and his friend Pete were posted from a rifle company to the regimental supply column. On 31 March, Pete took forward a jeep-load of ammunition without troubling to put on his helmet. He was hit in the head by shrapnel and died of wounds a fortnight later. Gordon "felt like I could kill every Jerry left in the country." Andy, a close friend of both men, appeased his rage by evicting the German occupants from the houses around their positions, telling them to sleep in the fields. A fortnight later, Gordon saw his old rifle company advancing in column up the road into the town of Hochstedt, among them an old buddy named Ben. "Take it easy, kid," his friend called after him. C Company met Germans, and Ben was fatally hit in the chest. It was just three weeks before the end. In Lieutenant Howard Randall's battalion of the 417th Infantry, a newly arrived lieutenant refused to risk his neck by going on patrol in the last days. This officer was transferred to Civil Affairs. Another lieutenant sought to diminish the risks of reconnaissance by placing German civilians in front of his own riflemen as they approached built-up areas.

As the advancing Allies entered German towns and villages thus far untouched by war, some sensitive men felt uncomfortable about their intrusion upon communities which looked close kin to their own, occupied by people who seemed not unlike those among whom they lived and worked back home. A squeamish Civil Affairs officer with the U.S. 30th Division complained in a report:

> Consideration was not given to sick and elderly people, and mothers with very young children. The attitude of higher command seemed to be that these people...should be made to feel the full significance of war and what their troops had done to other people. There were many complaints as to looting by troops, and a number of rape cases...The taking of personal belongings was rampant. The turning-in of arms, cameras etc was conducted, in my opinion, in a thoroughly disorganized and disgraceful manner.

A German woman handed Corporal Werner Kleeman the dogtags of a GI she sought to report for raping her. Kleeman threw them away: "I didn't want to get the boy into trouble."

As men of the British 7th Somersets ran into a farmyard in the face of desultory German fire, weapons cocked and grenades in hand, a company

A boy steals wooden wedges from the tramlines for firewood.

HOLLAND'S "HONGERWINTER"

A nation starved and thousands died because the Germans were determined to maintain their occupation, and the Allies declined to divert forces to liberate the Dutch.

The face of hunger

GLIMPSES OF THE GERMAN ARMY DURING ITS BRILLIANT, FUTILE FIGHTING DEFENCE OF THE HEIMAT IN 1944–45

Paratroopers with men of the 2nd SS Panzer Division

Fighting by Lake Balaton

Manning an anti-tank gun

A Mark IV tank, often mistaken by Allied soldiers for the dreaded Tiger.

The indignity of death: A German soldier on one of the last battlefields.

THE VICTORS ADVANCE—SOMETIMES VERY SLOWLY

An infantryman's classic view of the battlefield.

A British observer in Holland, where movement in the flat polder so often ended in death.

A horrendous image captured by Harold Dorfman, a Liberator navigator, as B-Baker plunged to earth after being blown apart by a German Me-262 jet fighter.

THE AIR WAR

February 1945. An American B-17 "Flying Fortress" over Berlin.

Harold Dorfman

*The Ludendorff bridge at Remagen, seized by the U.S. Army
in a dramatic coup on 9 March 1945.*

*A German civilian who appears to perceive the virtues of fraternization
with Private Ralph Gordon.*

Churchill lunches with Brooke and Montgomery beside the Rhine.
Brooke believed the Prime Minister would have been happy to die in action there.

ADVANCING

Pushing on towards Cologne

Germans submissive: Civilians in the thousands seek to make their peace with their new rulers—here, in Schweinfurt.

INSIDE GERMANY

Germans unyielding: Soldiers hanged for dereliction of duty. Each man wears a sign claiming: "I am a coward."

Germans captive: Reichsmarschall Hermann Göring

FACES OF
DEFEAT

A German officer nurses his misery after capture by the U.S. Seventh Army.

Fleeing Soviet terror: At mortal risk, Germans struggle westwards across the Elbe at Tangemunde.

The architect of global misery confronts his nemesis.

RUSSIANS IN VICTORY

Men of the Red Army fight their way into Königsberg.

Savouring triumph in Berlin

A liberated Soviet prisoner avenges himself on a former German persecutor.

A Russian girl soldier—perhaps his "field wife"—with her general.

Lee Miller, legendary American photographer, with a Russian officer, celebrating the Allied junction at the Elbe.

THE CAMPS: Germany's captives, liberated by the Allies at the brink of death.

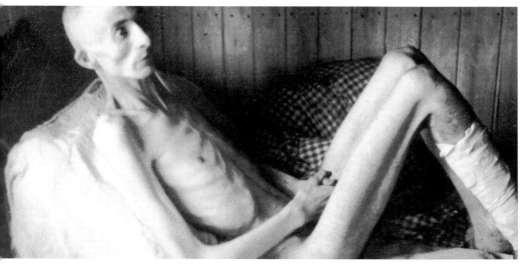

(ABOVE) *Not a concentration-camp victim but an American PoW*

(RIGHT) *Stalag 326 Prisoner of War Camp in Germany, where 30,000 Russian PoWs died. Nine thousand were still alive when it was liberated.*

(BELOW) *Two inmates of the Lager-Nordhausen concentration camp*

(BELOW RIGHT) *At Bergen-Belsen*

Stalin triumphant.

Churchill eclipsed.

LEADERS

Roosevelt approaching death.

(LEFT) *Field-Marshal Keitel ratifies the final German surrender in Berlin on 8 May 1945.*

THE END

(BELOW) *American soldiers at the great picture window of Hitler's ruined mountain retreat, Berchtesgaden.*

(BOTTOM) *Fireworks in Moscow*

sergeant-major kicked open a door and found himself confronted by some forty small German children, together with two teachers. They were all standing at attention, hands held high, staring fixedly ahead without even a tear on their frozen faces. After the first shock, the British soldiers and the German children gazed silently at each other for a few seconds, then the conquerors moved on. Lieutenant-Colonel Ferdinand Chesarek of the 28th Field Artillery drove up to an airfield where Germans were running briskly from plane to plane, throwing thermite bombs into the cockpits. "Christ almighty, what confusion—all those wagons, guns, troops, trucks and everything else. All these armed Germans mixed up with us. Everything was so crazy." One night a British sentry woke Captain Andrew Wilson of the Buffs to report the capture of a prisoner who had stumbled into their tank leaguer. A torch beam revealed a German sergeant-major, who protested vehemently that he possessed a leave pass to proceed home and could not legitimately be detained.

A contemporary British report identified three causes for sluggish forward movement: enemy resistance; difficulty of supply and repair; and "the desire of soldiers to enjoy 'the fruits of victory.' " Bing, one of 13 Para's Alsatian dogs which had jumped at the Rhine in special harnesses, disappeared one morning and was found hopelessly drunk in a German wine cellar. Loot had become the chief preoccupation of some men. "Did he have a Luger? Did he have a Luger?" a captain in Private Charles Felix's battalion demanded, almost jumping up and down with excitement, when he heard that his men had captured a German officer.

Lieutenant Howard Randall's company commander invited him to ride into the neighbouring town, which they found deathly quiet, the house windows draped in white flags. Outside the timbered town hall, they left one man to guard the jeep while the other four Americans wandered inside, pistols drawn, and made their way to the mayor's office. They met two white-haired men and an elderly woman, who pointed nervously to an immense heap of cameras, binoculars and weapons, obviously collected from the local population. The Americans kept pistols pointed at the Germans, who maintained an icy composure, while with their spare hands they delved into the hoard. "The captain suddenly spotted a handsome Leica camera and made a dive for it . . . Then I saw a nice blue-black pistol . . . I swooped down and grabbed it, and then some beautiful ceremonial knives. I grabbed them all and stuffed them hurriedly into my jacket pockets. The situation had become ludicrous. The three unruffled Germans never said a word, while the four of us were scrambling all over the floor." After the Americans left, it was a week before the town was formally occupied. When they returned, they found that SS men had hanged the mayor for displaying white flags.

A frightened German woman approached the British lines with a pretty girl and said to an officer: "Please do not let your men rape my daughter." Dr. David

Tibbs drew himself up in the approved stance of an affronted English gentleman and said stiffly: "Madam, these are British soldiers." Yet while nothing
remotely resembling the Russian orgy took place on the Western Front, many
Allied soldiers seized the opportunities granted to them for easy sexual inter-
course, whether through rape or some marginally less brutal arrangement. During street fighting in Bremen, a young officer of the KOSB lost two men of his
platoon. He found them reclining comfortably on bunks in a shelter by the railway station teeming with German civilians: "As though this was not enough,
each had lying beside him his rifle . . . and a German *fräulein*. It was not clear
whether fear or bribery with ration chocolate or cigarettes had induced these
girls to submit to the Jocks."

"The Germans were very hungry. The girls would get at my riflemen for a
tin of sardines," observed Major Bill Deedes. An officer of 52nd (Lowland) Division was shocked to come upon two German women "being shagged in relays
by American soldiers." A post-war U.S. Army report on military discipline concluded that in north-west Europe: "Rape became a large problem . . . A considerable percentage of offences is directly attributable to faulty unit leadership . . .
[Men's orientation for war] included propaganda of hatred towards the Germans. This made it easy for the soldier to justify looting, assault, burglary, robbery and even rape. The theory was that the fighting soldier must hate the
enemy . . . Its application complicated the problem of military justice." It seems
an awkward reflection on the administration of justice in 1944–45 that more
than 40 per cent of all death sentences passed in the ETO were imposed upon
African-American soldiers, though these constituted a tiny proportion of U.S.
Army strength.

Sergeant Colin McInnes gazed in awe at the shambles to which occupying
troops had reduced a German house. "We were struck at once by the tremendous physical energy of the looters," he wrote.

> Furniture was upended and flung about in heaps in a way that made move-
> ment from room to room as difficult as rock-climbing. Anything of glass
> was smashed, walls had their paper torn from them or were splashed with
> ink, wood was gouged out of cupboards and tables, upholstery had been
> sliced open on the seats and arms of chairs and sofas, and curtains were
> ripped to tatters. It seemed that all this expressed a hatred of organized
> life, and a yearning for primitive chaos on as large a scale as possible.

A British war correspondent was bemused one morning to hear a ferocious din
emerging from a house. He entered, and beheld a cluster of men manically
smashing a grand piano with axes.

In "Red" Thompson's platoon of the U.S. 346th Infantry, the last fatality of
the war was caused by a mortar bomb which fell on the head of their most ded-

icated looter, a man who emptied the drawers of every house he entered. Some men refused to loot at all, not on moral grounds, but constrained by fear of German booby traps. A few men plundered systematically, in planned pursuit of objects of value. Fortunes were made in Germany in 1945, by men sufficiently cool and acquisitive to choose their plunder judiciously, and with the rank or transport facilities to carry it away. Some British Special Air Service groups, profiting from the latitude they were granted about their own movements, devoted the last days of the war to systematic safe-blowing. Most soldiers, however, merely grabbed any artefact to hand, in the manner of warriors since time immemorial. They groped for tangible compensation for having risked their lives, and cherished the licence granted by dispensation from the customary laws of property. The Anglo-Americans were a great deal less brutal than the Russians, but they seized enemy property with almost equal abandon.

Lieutenant Tom Flanagan of the British 4th KOSB was appalled to see one of his men snatch a blanket from an old woman, observing: "You'll not be wanting that, missus." The man then grabbed an eiderdown and a watch. The young platoon commander sought to intervene, but his sergeant said firmly: "You'll be wanted at company headquarters, sir. I'll deal with this." Flanagan wrote: "I left... trying hard not to believe what I had just witnessed. Those men were behaving as I had always imagined German soldiers to behave, not like the image I held of 'Tommy Atkins' who was kind, tolerant, easily put upon, considerate to old folk and especially good with children. This conflict of fact and imagery confused me. My innocence had taken another blow."

The French Army, and especially its colonial troops, behaved with savage indiscipline in Germany, in some places perpetrating excesses on an almost Soviet scale. The French were indulged in some degree, because their thirst for vengeance against the Germans seemed understandable. General de Gaulle had fiercely insisted upon the French right to enter Germany in arms, and Churchill persuaded Stalin to accede to de Gaulle's demands for a designated occupation zone. French troops on the ground played out the role of victors with a ruthlessness which dismayed some of their allies.

The Americans and British behaved better than many victorious armies in history, but less well than the official record suggests. If rape was far less widespread than in the east, it was certainly not unknown. Looting was almost universal, mitigated only by spasms of bourgeois conscience on the part of the thieves. "Pitiable middle-aged lady in the house," wrote Corporal Stan Proctor of 43rd (Wessex) Division in his diary for 26 April, describing his billet, "and we found a young man hiding in what was left of the loft. It was her son, a deserter from a Hitler Youth unit. We had to hand him over to our police. He was a good-looking and quiet young chap. There was a photo of him in his Hitler Youth uniform which I took with me as a reminder of what somebody like Hitler can do to people. We also took two nice wireless sets from the house. I suppose we looked on them as spoils of war, but the lady was upset. I was ashamed of what we did." In 21st Army Group throughout the campaign, just seventy-two men faced disciplinary charges for looting, against 2,792 charged with being improperly dressed.

Even before they reached the concentration camps, men of the liberating armies were disgusted by their encounters with foreign prisoners of the Nazis, human skeletons scavenging across the countryside of Germany. "The countryfolk and their houses and farms are well cared for," wrote a British officer. "Only their slaves look miserably underfed and clothed." An escaped Canadian pilot approached 2nd Fife & Forfar Yeomanry one day, carrying a slave labourer he had met, who was dressed in two sacks and so weak that he could only mutter: "*Polski.*" British medics could not get food into him. The man lay moaning on a stretcher until he was placed in an ambulance. This was already occupied by a captured German officer who had lost a foot. The German spat upon the Pole. The British dumped the German in a ditch.

Outside the town of Büdingen near Frankfurt, a handful of SS mounted a last-ditch resistance, quickly suppressed by the Americans. The local Nazi officials fled. The grandfather of Helmut Lott, a teenage evacuee living in the town, returned home bearing a Party official's brown tunic and breeches as mementoes. His grandmother took one look and threw the uniform on the fire, demanding of her husband: "Are you crazy?" There was shelling during the night, which caused the fearful inhabitants to spend the night in their cellars. Next morning, however, a large crowd turned out on the streets to greet their occupiers respectfully. "Everybody was wearing their Sunday best, to demonstrate the whiteness of their consciences," observed Lott drily. The first vehicle that appeared in the main street, however, was not a tank but a red sports car full of laughing GIs. The people of Büdingen found this ridiculous, and faintly humiliating. "We thought: what is this?" said Lott. "These people are supposed to be occupying us, but they look as if they are on an excursion to the seaside."

In their turn, the Allies were bewildered by German behaviour. The whole nation seemed in denial of any responsibility for the war, and for the crimes of the Nazis. "The attitude of civilians was really rather typical of the master race," observed a report by the 2nd Battalion, Warwickshire Regiment. "They seemed to expect us to treat them in the politest possible manner. You would think from their behaviour that they had won this war. They only started to show any respect at all when we made it clear that we meant business." Some Americans were likewise bewildered to find that the Germans in towns they seized, while not hostile, were resentful of Allied interference in their normal lives. Even while firing continued, some enemy civilians voiced protests. "It sure makes you feel silly," observed Lieutenant Darrigo of Novotan Heights, Connecticut, "crouching or dashing around trying to get a shot at a sniper, while a civilian peddles by on his bike and a woman and child just tag along watching."

Private Denis Christian of 6 Commando was bemused to be reprimanded by the owner of the house in which he was billeted for failing to clean the bath. His unit's German interpreter subjected the British to a lecture about "how Germany had only lost the war because it lacked oil." A teenage girl whom 13 Para met in Graven not only spoke good English, but assured them severely that the Wehrmacht would soon retake the area. The Führer would then punish the Allies for daring to invade the fatherland. The English soldiers respected the girl's courage, but were horrified by the depth of Nazi indoctrination which the encounter revealed. The battalion's colonel, Peter Luard, announced flatly that the battalion would take no SS prisoners. When two Waffen SS indeed fell into their hands, an officer simply took them behind a tank and shot them. "With hindsight, it seemed very shocking," said Lieutenant Peter Downward. "Yet the SS were so truculent."

"A woman of a house in which I was billeted entered the room, looked at the wreckage and burst into tears with the words '*Es ist alles kaputt und es war so schön*,'" Captain David Chudleigh reported to his division headquarters early in April, in disgust rather than sympathy.

> Even after I had carefully explained to her what the war was all about, and that what she was suffering was little in comparison with what she and her kind had inflicted on the world for more than five years, the only reaction was a flood of tears. I do not believe her horizons were any broader for my efforts. A few minutes later this woman pointed out the body of a German soldier lying in the garden, and asked me to take it away and bury it, but not in her garden. Considering that she was a woman (of a sort), her indifference to the fate of one of her countrymen was astonishing. A long-term educational programme is obviously needed here.

Sergeant Robert Brookshire of the 609th Tank Destroyer Battalion was riding in a jeep flagged down by a tearful German woman waving a handkerchief. She was a teacher and told the soldiers desperately: "Some of my pupils, young boys, are up this hill in a cabin, armed with rifles, and have vowed that they will fire at Americans until they are killed. Will you please not shoot them, but come with me and try to convince them to surrender?" Between them, the German teacher and the American NCO induced the sheepish fourteen-year-olds to file out of the building without their weapons. Brookshire was always a reluctant killer. About the same time, he suddenly found himself confronted by six Germans. He froze, thinking his end had come. Then the Germans laid down their weapons. "Why didn't you kill them?" asked a buddy. Brookshire said: "Because I somehow knew that if I did, I'd never see my young daughter again."

As the U.S. 743rd Tank Battalion was mopping up near Lemgo, it came upon a German general outside a large house, at the head of 500 men, "lined up at attention, guns piled in one part of the courtyard, equipment piled neatly in another." The American unit suffered its last fatal casualty of the war in the battle for Magdeburg on 17 April. A faust hit a Sherman turret, killing the gunner and wounding the commander and loader. It was fired by a German woman. Aschaffenburg earned a reputation as one of very few towns—Hameln was another—where local civilians fought energetically against Third Army. "There was some of the hardest fighting of the war in that town," recorded an American officer. "Hitler had said that every man, woman and child should fight...this town was the only place where that was really carried out. Everybody fought the Americans." In the ruins of Aschaffenburg, men of XV Corps found the bodies of boys of twelve and thirteen, who had chosen to die fighting for their Führer.

In Friesoythe on 12 April, it was reported that the commanding officer of the Argyll & Sutherland Highlanders of Canada had been shot in the back by a civilian. The Canadian divisional commander, Christopher Vokes, was already angered by other incidents in which civilians had fired upon his men. He ordered the entire town bulldozed in retribution. Only when this process had been completed was it learned that in reality the Argylls' colonel had been killed by a German soldier with a Schmeisser.

The 21st Army Group faced spasms of hard fighting. Second Fife & Forfar Yeomanry fought one of hundreds of similar tiny actions on 5 April, at Glissen. Lieutenant Frank Fuller was leading the battalion, and as they approached the town could see little sign of enemy defences. "No washing," his operator reported laconically over the radio. Then they spotted enemy infantry in ditches. The tanks pulled off the road, making way for the infantry to move forward. A faust hit Fuller's tank. The young officer bailed out. He was promptly hit by machine-gun fire, as was his gunner. His shaken wireless-operator came on the air and announced that he was remaining in the turret. The rest of the crew were dead. After an hour of fighting, the surviving Germans raised their hands. They proved to be very young members of 12th SS Panzer, who were taken to the rear. The British always hated the Hitler Jugend Division. "Fanaticism is nasty," said Captain "Dim" Robbins. "They were absolute sods—incredibly arrogant, even as prisoners," in the words of Corporal Patrick Hennessy. On this occasion, however, a British officer observed bitterly that the young prisoners were "blubbering." Their action had changed nothing, save to delay the advance an hour or so and to kill a young officer and three men. A comrade noticed Fuller's body, "just recognizable," lying in a ditch as he drove past. He remembered that the lieutenant was newly married.

Two days later, Major William Steel-Brownlie drove his tank round the corner of a German village at 30 m.p.h., to ram full-tilt a large chest-of-drawers which a German family was struggling to remove from a burning house. "Clothing and underwear were caught up and whirled round in the tracks." His machine-gunner hosed a handful of German defenders fleeing the scene: "Was it cruel to batter retreating troops? There was always the thought that they might be reorganized and waiting for us next day or the day after, as well as thoughts about Frank Fuller and many like him. Not far away was another family rescuing furniture from their burning home, but in the circumstances one's reaction was simply: so what?"

"Once we got into Germany, we could do anything, knock down anything," said Captain David Fraser. "There were very few inhibitions. We were told: 'If you need to burn a village—burn it.' " On 12 April, the British director of military intelligence reported on the mood of civilians in the path of the armies: "Germans are becoming increasingly bitter at bombing of targets of negligible military value, and caution us against appointment of Jewish burgomeisters which [they say] is a pyschological mistake and which militates against co-operation of German civilian population."

As the advance gathered pace, at last for some men exhilaration overcame fear. Charles Farrell, a Scots Guards squadron commander, thought as he drove his Sherman across Germany of Christopher Marlowe's line: "Is it not passing brave to be a king and ride in triumph through Persepolis?" At Rathau on the Aller, the CO of 5th Royal Tanks advanced on foot to take a cautious look into the town before his tanks moved in. He encountered one of his own officers, a huge Welshman named John Gwilliam who later captained his country's rugby team, "carrying a small German soldier by the scruff of his neck, not unlike a cat with a mouse." The colonel said: "Why not shoot him?" Gwilliam replied in his mighty Welsh voice: "Oh no, sir. *Much* too small."

A British tank officer glimpsed some tiny figures beside a wood half a mile away, from which a German half-track had just emerged. He fired a few rounds of high explosive from his gun, then followed up with a long burst of Besa machine-gun fire. Trees caught fire. He saw survivors start to move towards the tanks, hands held high. "To my horror, they were civilians," wrote William Steel-Brownlie, "followed by a horse and cart on which were piled all kinds of household goods. They were children, a boy and a girl, holding hands and running as hard as they could over the rough ploughed earth. They came right up to the tank, looked up at me, and the small boy said in English: 'You have killed my father.' There was nothing I could say."

On 14 April, the Canadians at last secured the Dutch town of Arnhem, which had caused such bitter grief to the Allies six months earlier. But First Canadian Army was still making slow headway against the German opposition among the bleakly familiar rivers and canals of Holland. Montgomery, pushing northeastwards to cut off Denmark from the Russians, was suddenly urged by SHAEF to hasten. On 8 April, the British XII Corps got into a fight around Lüneburg which persisted for four days. Ritchie's men finally reached the Elbe on 19 April, and Hamburg only on the 23rd. They gazed in awe at the vast port city, reduced to rubble by Allied bombing. After a series of bitter actions, XXX Corps finally secured Bremen on the 26th. Eisenhower offered no congratulations to 21st Army Group. He believed, surely rightly, that the British did not try very hard in this last phase of the campaign. "In Germany it was a swan—a slow swan," said Lieutenant Roy Dixon. "Nobody wanted to get killed at the last minute, so nobody wanted to take any unnecessary risks." Bill Deedes said: "War is a very fatiguing experience. It works relentlessly upon the nervous system. By the end, we were all incredibly tired. In Hanover, I found that I no longer had the energy to discipline my soldiers for getting drunk."

On the evening of 14 April, the British approached the concentration camp at Bergen-Belsen. Guards hung out white sheets from their towers in surrender. Belsen's prisoners saw, and rejoiced as they watched the night sky lit by artillery fire. Viktor Mamontov, the eighteen-year-old from Leningrad who had survived two years in some of the most terrible camps in Germany, believed himself to be dying. He was now among those who stumbled out of the barracks in ecstasy. The guards on the watchtowers opened fire on the prisoners. Mamontov fell, hit in the leg. When he saw the Germans fire again and again upon wounded men who moved, he lay motionless. He remained where he had been hit hour after hour: "Until the very last moment, I thought I would die." At last next morning the British tanks came. For hours, the prisoners had to tend each other, until medical teams arrived. Those who could still walk smashed open the food store. Mamontov contracted typhus, and spent the next six months in hospital. He lost all his hair, and weighed just eighty-seven pounds. He was disgusted that the British executed only seven of Belsen's German staff.

America's legendary broadcaster Ed Murrow contrasted the healthy, well-fed Germans he saw ploughing the nearby fields with the human skeletons of Buchenwald liberated by the U.S. Third Army. He described the heaped corpses, the paralysis of the near-dead. "I have reported what I saw and heard, but only part of it," said the great reporter. "For most of it I have no words." R. W. Thompson of the *Sunday Times* wrote from Belsen: "When you gaze upon the human body distorted beyond recognition, and come to the point where there is literally no difference between the living and the dead, you are beyond shocking because you are beyond normal standards." At Dachau, in an outburst of spontaneous rage the American liberators summarily executed twenty-one guards, including seventeen SS.

The British buried 23,000 bodies on the site of Belsen, and evacuated a further 28,900 people, of whom 2,006 were already dead. One of the doctors who went to the camp in British uniform was by birth a German Jew. This man, Dr. A. R. Horwell, wrote to his wife: "The phrase 'that's what we are fighting for' never had so deep meaning for me..." Horwell watched each mass grave being filled in, and a sign placed on it "Grave No. 8 1000 bodies. 30 April 1945." A few days later, in a British officers' mess, he was deeply moved to find himself among a group "where there is no sign of discrimination, and where the Jewish padres were the most honoured guests. It made me realise it again: it *was* worthwhile to be in this war, it *is* an honour and distinction to wear this uniform." His wife had expressed her fears for his safety among the German people. He responded: "darling love, I must restrain myself, for fear to become too emotional. I can't help it, darling; it is a great thing to be back here after all these years—and after all these immense sufferings inflicted upon us and our people, to be here with the victorious army...I am very happy tonight, and sad at the same time. Happy, because I have survived, one of the few to see this day; and sad, because I am of the few—so few." "At Belsen, I felt a curious elation," said Dr. David Tibbs. "Looking at all these terrible things, I thought: 'Here is the justification for this war, for all the lives we have lost, for everything we've been through.' "

At 1640 on the afternoon of 25 April, a reconnaissance group of the U.S. 69th Division met men of the Soviet 58th Guards Division at Torgau on the Elbe. The scenes of warm greetings between allies, filmed by a host of cameramen and screened in cinemas across the Western world, masked a much harsher reality. "Take no initiative in organizing friendly meetings," a stern order from the Soviet front commanders warned all units. "Where meetings do take place, behave in a friendly way, but inform commanders immediately, and give no information about operational plans or unit objectives." An American corps commander found his Soviet counterpart eager to toast the armies of Roosevelt, and sought in vain to convince the Russian that Roosevelt was dead. Beria's representatives were soon reporting instances of "suspicious remarks" by Americans, including that of a U.S. officer who allegedly spoke disrespectfully about the competence of Soviet artillerymen. A British officer complained to the Russians about the treatment of some liberated British prisoners who were savagely interrogated by the Red Army before being thrown into a pigsty with German PoWs. The Russians replied icily that this letter was "grossly impolite, and that if any further such communications were received, they would not be answered."

Yet statesmanship demanded a loftier vision of the junction at Torgau between the crusaders for freedom and the agents of tyranny. "After long journeys, toils and victories across the land and oceans; across many deadly battlefields, the Armies of the great Allies have traversed Germany and have joined hands together," said Churchill in a broadcast that night. "Now, their task will be the destruction of all remnants of German military resistance, the rooting out of the Nazi power and the subjugation of Hitler's Reich." Field-Marshal von Paulus, surveying the ruin of his country from a Soviet prison cell, observed contemptuously: "If the British and Americans had not dilly-dallied so much, we could have got this whole thing over a great deal sooner."

ELEVENTH HOUR

BETWEEN THE ELBE and the Oder, the civilians of Hitler's shrunken dominions awaited their fate in a curious state of submission, even paralysis. "Berlin never seemed so peaceful to me as in the April days before the commencement of the battle," wrote Paul von Stemann, the Danish journalist, "girls dressed up for spring, little real work left to do, streets empty of traffic." Robert Ley, Hitler's labour minister, penned an article for *Der Angriff*, extolling the virtues of a society which had shed possessions and worries, was no longer encumbered with all the petty responsibilities of peacetime life and property. "Thus we are marching towards victory," wrote Ley, "stripped of all gratuitous ballast, and without the burden of materialistic baggage." Soviet pilots flying over Berlin described an uncanny stillness on the eastern side, with trains and trams standing idle, factory chimneys dead, while from the far suburbs of the city an endless stream of cars and carts and people on foot moved westward.

Hans Siwik, the Hitler Jugend leader who had escaped from East Prussia, called at the Reich Chancellery to see some old comrades from the days when he served with Hitler's personal SS bodyguard. Otto Günsche, the Führer's SS adjutant, ventured a notable banality to his old comrade: "Things are not going too well." When Siwik saw Hitler, whom he had revered so deeply for so long, he was appalled by the senile, broken figure before him. He received a perfunctory handshake and was disturbed to notice that the hand was ice-cold. The atmosphere around the Chancellery and the bunker was fevered, and on every side Siwik heard words of mistrust, bitterness, recrimination. It was plain that the end was close. "It all seemed so unjust," he said. Siwik was one among many of his fellow countrymen still incapable of comprehending what the Third Reich, in which he had been a minute but eager cog, had brought upon the world.

Even some sophisticated Germans remained remarkably naive about the prospect before them. Many who could have fled did not do so. "We pretended that, having been through these years of anguish and humiliation, we now wanted to witness the final and total destruction of the evil," recorded von Stemann. "Perhaps we were motivated by a vain and boyish pride to show that we could make it. Perhaps we had more unrealistic fantasies. None of us expected the end to come as it did. I believe we had a vision of a Cecil B. de Mille picturesque and well-planned parade of the Allied leaders, moving in a great cortège past the Siegssaule and through the Brandenburg gate."

Kertzendorf, the lovely mansion south of Berlin owned by Freddy Horstmann, a portly, moustachioed former diplomat, had been destroyed by bombing. Horstmann remained in the gardener's cottage, crowded with art treasures salvaged from the big house. He awaited the arrival of the British and Americans with equanimity, confident of patronage from prominent Allied acquaintances. "They are all my friends," he declared expansively. A former ambassador in Lisbon and Brussels, Horstmann had abandoned government service when told that his promotion would require a divorce from his half-Jewish wife Lally. An indolent sophisticate who lived in great style on the family newspaper fortune, he had endured the war by simply denying its reality. Horstmann and his friends agreed sagely that there could be no battle for Berlin, for the means no longer existed to defend the city. A friend arriving to stay in the spring of 1945 apologized for having been obliged to abandon a camembert cheese on his train when it was strafed. "*Ach*, a camembert!" said Horstmann regretfully. "What a pity. When shall I ever eat a camembert again?" He never did so, for he died in a Russian labour camp.

Until days before the Russians arrived, at great country houses around Berlin there were still liveried servants, fine wines and candle-lit dinners at the tables of the doomed Prussian nobility. The gravel of their drives was raked, the gardens tended by large staffs of prisoners, doing duty for family retainers absent at the front. "The participants appeared to take it all for granted, and behaved as if this life would go on for ever," wrote Paul von Stemann. "Most families had lived on their estates for hundreds of years, but were soon to join the stream of refugees, leaving the splendours behind to be looted and vandalised." At a big party one night in the house of his married daughter, General Geyr von Schweppenburg, former *Panzergruppe* commander in Normandy, lost his temper and denounced the reckless frivolity of dancing while Germany stood on the brink of catastrophe. The young guests ignored his outburst. They partied on far into the night. In Berlin itself, von Stemann observed that "dancing became uninhibited, drink for intoxication not enjoyment. Love became sex." Many people of both sexes became fiercely determined not to face the last act as virgins.

There was a Cuban dance band, which had appeared from no one knew where, performing nightly in the basement of a ruin in the Tiergarten. The Cubans became fashionable. Money seemed suddenly irrelevant, supplanted by barter. Unexpected stocks of coffee, cigarettes and cognac were unearthed. Half a kilo of coffee could be exchanged for twenty litres of petrol. There was heavy traffic in false identity papers and car number plates. Fatalism, lassitude gained sway everywhere outside the ranks of those soldiers preparing to fight their last battle. Prisoners of war alleged to be clearing city bomb rubble sat idle by fires lit in the debris, apparently unsupervised. Unarmed soldiers and deserters wandered the streets, with little effective interference from the military police. The Third Reich's deadly grip was loosening, its lifeblood seeping away into the horror-soaked soil of Germany. Labour gangs began to build defensive barricades in the suburbs. Berliners observed that they would hold up the Russians for exactly sixty-five minutes: an hour laughing, followed by five minutes sweeping the pathetic obstacles aside.

"The Berliners carried on forced by fear," wrote von Stemann. "They were frightened all the time: of their own secret police; of the bombers; of the Russians; and of the revenge of millions of forced labourers. They were frightened of their own past, and knew it would catch up with them." Yet despite all the preparations, there were welcome rumours among the inhabitants that the capital would not be defended at all. For a few brief weeks, Berliners thought themselves fortunate people, as elsewhere across Germany people fled for their lives in their millions.

Ilse Bayer, twenty-five-year-old daughter of a Berlin haulage contractor, was the wife of a naval petty officer based at Swinemünde on the Baltic. Through January and February, she had found refugees from East Prussia knocking on the door of her billet. Now, it was her own turn to become a fugitive. On the afternoon of 12 March, a secretary from naval headquarters ran down their street, warning families of an impending air attack. Frau Bayer scooped up her two younger children in her arms, while the eldest ran in front of her to a shelter. The bombing seemed to last an eternity. At one point, an admiral appeared and wanted to evict all the civilians from the shelter, since it stood on Kriegsmarine property. No one heeded him.

The Bayers emerged at last to find flames everywhere, their own home in ruins, the ships alongside the quays burning fiercely. Ilse believed that her husband Walter was at sea, but suddenly she saw him standing there in front of her. "I almost clawed him to see if he was real." The commanding officer of his destroyer, an uncommonly humane man, had sent Bayer ashore in a launch to retrieve his family. His wife found herself struggling desperately to get her small children, utterly distraught, up the side of the destroyer from the pitching boat. Next afternoon, the navy landed the refugees amid the ruins of Kiel. The Bayers were fortunate to find a lodging with an elderly couple in a village a few miles outside the city, where the children cried themselves to sleep. In the days that followed, there were renewed flashes of terror, when the roads were strafed by passing fighter-bombers, "which killed a lot of people at that time." But the Bayer family rejoiced in their unexpected good fortune. They lived.

Eleonore von Joest, who had trekked from East Prussia to Berlin in January, found herself once more on the road in April with her mother, seven children, a housemaid and a Polish farmworker called Miron. They could hear gunfire from both east and west as their carts plodded slowly onwards towards Holstein. They hoped desperately that the western ones were closer. This second trek proved even more frightening for the women than the first from East Prussia, because of constant strafing by American and British aircraft. All along the roadside lay dead horses, wrecked carts, dead people. The brilliant sunlit spring weather mocked their terror. They reached Holstein on 5 May, after a journey of almost 200 miles.

One day in April, Klaus Fischer and his mother were walking past the old

Lamsdorfer bridge in Jena when they saw soldiers working on it, laying cables in a trench, then carefully replacing the cobblestones on top of them. They were preparing the bridge for demolition, and indeed destroyed it hours before the Russians arrived. With meticulous efficiency even amid disaster, the city fathers arranged for Jena's streetcars to be divided, half placed on each side of the river before the bridge was blown. Everyone prepared for the end in different ways. Henner Pflug fell into conversation on a train with a young Waffen SS man. "Surely it's all over," said Pflug. The soldier said defiantly: "Oh we'll lick the Russians yet!" But then he added impulsively that he had two spare shirts. Would Pflug like them? "I shan't be needing them any more." The civilian took the shirts, and the two men parted.

Lieutenant Rolf-Helmut Schröder served briefly on the staff of General Walter Botsch, commanding LIII Corps near Bonn. Day after day, Schröder's principal duty was to move pins on the map, to mark Allied advances which German forces were impotent to arrest. He watched Russian prisoners digging emplacements to house guns which had long ago been destroyed west of the Rhine. One day Schröder ran into the command bunker pursued by a barrage of exploding grenades, and indeed carrying in the back of his head a fragment from one of them. "The Americans are here," he announced tersely. In a room adjoining the military operations centre, he glimpsed a cluster of Nazi Party officials, policemen and women, all very drunk—"a bad memory." His general hastily put on his overcoat inside out, so that the red lapels of high command were invisible. The staff wrecked the radio equipment, then decamped. In a few moments, the bunker was almost empty. The young officer was bemused when a civilian entered. It was the local museum director, who also happened to be the uncle of his girlfriend. "Herr Schröder!" exclaimed the visitor. "What are you doing here?" The lieutenant shrugged: "Waiting to die." "Don't you know your general's done a bunk?"

Schröder escaped on foot to his family home in Westphalia. Under a railway embankment on the edge of Hagen, his own town, he met two German tanks, waiting for the Americans. "We've got thirty rounds between us," said one of the commanders. "When they're gone, we're finished." To his mother's consternation, Schröder arrived home with a fellow officer, his driver and batman. They all put on civilian clothes, and Schröder buried his pistol. But he soon realized that escape was impracticable. He dressed once more in his uniform, and surrendered to two American NCOs. One said: "This is all crap—let him go home." But the other American insisted that Schröder must be held, removed his Iron Cross and started him on the journey to a PoW camp.

Late in March after his unit was overrun, Helmut Schmidt decided to try to get back to his wife in Hamburg, rather than allow himself to be taken prisoner. He and two other men set off eastwards from the American front, walking by night and hiding by day. At first, they received considerable help and kindness from German peasants. As they reached the north German plain, fear of Allied reprisals made local people become progressively more reluctant to shelter fugitive soldiers. They spent several nights huddled beneath bushes under the stars. At last, Schmidt reached his family.

When Sergeant George Schwemmer of 10th SS Panzer was discharged from the hospital where he had spent February being treated for frostbite, he was sent to command a platoon in a battle group north-east of Stettin. Discipline was visibly collapsing. There were increasingly bitter wrangles between the fanatics, determined to fight to the end, and those who recognized the futility of doing so. They were suddenly ordered aboard open rail trucks, and shipped south into Saxony, under Schörner's ruthless command. They called the field-marshal "the soldiers' claw," because he was not above personally arresting stragglers and herding them back into battle. Deserters were being shot daily—Schörner had executed three battalion commanders in a week for alleged dereliction of duty—but in mid-April Schwemmer decided that he would take the risk. He knew the Americans had already overrun Blankenburg, where his wife was living. The sergeant and a few others slipped away across the Oder bridge. They marched in formed ranks, to give an impression of moving under orders, and begged overnight shelter in houses they passed. The fugitives made one attempt to surrender, advancing with hands in the air towards Americans whom they encountered near Linz. They were met by machine-gun fire, which killed a twelve-year-old boy. After that, Schwemmer simply took to the countryside like tens of thousands of others. He walked and walked, until at last he became the first soldier from Blankenburg to reach home, a distinction for which he was deeply grateful.

In the path of Konev's armies, sixteen-year-old Corporal Helmut Fromm from Heidelberg was playing "Indians." He manned a periscope in his unit's positions beside a sniper, occasionally raising a helmet on a stick above the parapet to draw Russian fire. A sniper needed a counter-signature on his score-card, to qualify for the special leave granted to a man who achieved at least twenty confirmed kills. Once, to relieve the monotony, they put a round just in front of a horse, which bolted. Another time, they took a long shot at a cycling Russian who fell off, scrambled to his feet and ran away carrying the bicycle. If it sounds fantastic to imagine German soldiers behaving so childishly in the days before the last stand of Hitler's Reich, consider their age: many of these "men" were indeed children, who laughed at the things children laughed at. They were adult only in their candidacy for death.

On 5 April, Victor Klemperer sat in the darkness of a train to Munich, listening to the conversation of his fellow travellers. One young man said that his own father, who had believed passionately in victory, now no longer did so. "Only Bolshevism and international Jewry are the victors," grumbled the passenger. A young woman whose husband was fighting in Breslau announced that she still trusted the Führer, and believed that victory would come.

A delegation of diplomats from the Japanese embassy in Berlin visited von Ribbentrop, Hitler's foreign minister, demanding to know what steps he proposed to take for their safety. They received scant satisfaction. The British intercepted a signal to Tokyo from the Japanese minister in Lisbon, setting out a somewhat ambitious diplomatic plan for his country: "It is my belief that the only means by which Japan, confronted as she is by the present unparalleled national crisis, can bring about a turn for the better in her fortunes is by a radical re-orientation of her policy towards the USSR. The collapse of the German army is now unmistakably only a matter of time." The minister suggested that Japan should seek a bilateral treaty with Stalin.

Captain Walter Schaefer-Kuhnert of 9th Panzer Division spent the last days of his war supporting a Volksgrenadier unit—"hopeless people," he observed, with professional contempt. One morning in his captured jeep he found himself driving in the middle of a massive column of American armour. "My God," he thought, "we haven't got that many tanks in our entire army." His driver accelerated away, and they saw astonished GI faces staring after their field-grey uniforms. Finally, the Germans abandoned the vehicle and found a path on foot back to their battery. "It was rubbish to say that we fought to the end because of fear of the SS," he said. "We did so because fighting men understand that they must stick together." Even in the extremities of March and April, the gunner officer felt proud of the fact that some men who had been allowed home on leave as far afield as Silesia returned to the unit for its final battles.

The Russians had encircled the synthetic-oil plant in Silesia where sixteen-year-old Hans Moser had served with a flak battery back at the end of January. Moser and his young comrades watched while NCOs blew up their guns. A huge baulk of timber flew high into the air, landing almost on the top of the teenager, who thought his last hour had come. They were then given three minutes in which to pack a ration-bag and waterbottle apiece and marched away through driving snow towards the distant train station. Men and boys soon started falling out in the freezing cold. Moser suffered frostbite. In Niesse, a baker's wife allowed him to put his feet in her stove to thaw out. "Are the Russians coming?" she asked fearfully. "No, no," said the boy stoutly, because he could not face telling her the truth. He trudged onwards. By the wayside, he saw a neat fence beside a churchyard, with a notice proclaiming: "Joseph Eichendorff is buried here." The great nineteenth-century lyrical poet was one of Moser's idols. The teenager yearned to make a pilgrimage to the grave. But he did not dare to linger.

One icy night, he and his dwindling body of young companions encountered a terrible vision. A column of shrunken men in striped clothes came past, escorted by SS men with lanterns and dogs. "Who are these people?" he asked a guard. "Jews and gangsters," said the man tersely. Later, they heard shots, and came upon some of the prisoners lying dead by the road, falling snow already thick upon their bodies. For hours afterwards, they found themselves passing the corpses of prisoners and refugees, many of them old people. One dead face haunted his sleep for months afterwards, a tall man who had been shot in the back of the neck. The bullet had forced open his jaws. The man stared vacantly upwards, eyes and mouth wide open. Once, the gunners saw two elderly German civilians towing on their sled a concentration-camp prisoner who had collapsed. One of the young Luftwaffe men asked the couple roughly: "Why are you bothering to help this gangster?" Moser said nothing, and indeed felt nothing: "We were immersed in our own worries. We just wanted to get home."

As they crossed into Czechoslovakia, the tension, even hatred, among local people was palpable: "The Czechs were stirring." Military police patrols questioned every male traveller constantly, searching out deserters. Their party possessed only a single written movement order to cover them all, so they clung together. At Prague, they found a train westwards. At last, after weeks on the road, he reached home in Nuremberg. When the Russians overran his position, Moser had been officially reported "missing." Now, when he banged the knocker of the family house clad in his white snow smock, his mother opened the door and screamed. She thought he was a ghost.

Even elite units such as the Grossdeutschland were no longer willing to fight. Captain Mackert, one of its battalion commanders, described his shock when men began to flee under Soviet attack even when he drew his pistol upon them: "All my attempts to keep the company together failed ... The men would rather be shot than stay in their positions." Mackert was left only with one NCO, two wireless-operators and a runner. He never saw his soldiers again.

It is an extraordinary reflection of the fashion in which weapons and ammunition continued to the end to reach some units—and especially the favoured SS—that as late as 13 April at Wiener Neustadt 1st SS Panzer received a delivery of ten new Mark IV tanks. The division's paper strength before its final battles was 10,552 men. Yet its morale was no better than that of the Grossdeutschland. "The atmosphere was truly hopeless," said Werner Sternebeck, "the issue of orders sluggish, inconsistent and lacking conviction ... We were facing our last battle, and with our 17 Panzer IVs and Panzer Vs, we could only delay the impending collapse."

At the makeshift hospital in the school of a small town in Schleswig-Holstein where sixteen-year-old Melany Borck worked as a nurse, the last days were awful. There were few doctors. The men were riddled with lice. Those with families in eastern Germany were desperate for news of them, of which there was none. Drugs had run out. They were reduced to boiling birch-bark to make a primitive antiseptic. Melany administered anaesthetic by holding an ether pad over a man's mouth. Once, in her pathetic ignorance, she overdid the process so that a patient remained unconscious for eight hours. Beyond the casualties laid in rows on straw palliasses in the classrooms and corridors, others remained in bunks on the hospital train which had brought them, because there was nowhere else. At the beginning, the girl had found working at the hospital rewarding. For the first time in her life, she was treated as an adult rather than as a child. But when she found herself reliving the last battle for Pillau through the fevered nightmares of a dying man whose hand she held, the memory haunted her. Even after many months on the wards, she still found it hard to look upon shattered limbs, the ruins of so much youth.

"We're retreating again," Corporal Helmut Fromm of Ninth Army wrote in his diary on 19 April, on the road thirty-five miles south-east of Berlin in front of Konev's tanks, "nobody knows where to. The columns of men stumble along these dusty roads, horses dragging our grenade-launchers. The infantry pulled back past us while we were still in action. Our tanks are on the same road...Just now at least there is no air attack, but shells are falling right and left. I am filthier than any pig, we've nothing hot to eat, I'm smoking my last cigarette. How long can this go on?"

Piotr Tareczynski, a thirty-two-year-old Polish gunner officer, crossed the Oder with his PoW column in darkness, over a bridge being prepared for demolition. Stettin, some fifteen miles northwards, was being bombed. "The flares being dropped by aircraft made it look as if a pink blanket was suspended above the city." Next day, as they passed among prosperous farms, he pondered the likely fate of their inhabitants: "The time for settling accounts was approaching fast. Nemesis was at their door. Those farmers still viewed us as enemies, though we were hardly able to walk. They were afraid of us. To them, we were living proof of Germany's crimes against humanity." There were many belated deaths from Allied strafing. The neighbouring column of PoWs to that of British airman Trevor Peacock was attacked by RAF Typhoons, whose rockets and cannon inflicted some eighty casualties. Lieutenant Philip Dark, a British naval officer captured at St. Nazaire, watched in impotent horror as RAF Tempests swept down on his group. "One's nerves, after those three years, were in a poor state. It had been a cotton-wool existence. I noticed a body lying flat in the ditch as I upped and ran...I thought 'You silly bloody fools!' Being shot up by one's own boys, what irony!"

In the last weeks, there was a belated rush of killings in the concentration camps. Some enemies of the Third Reich seemed in danger of surviving its demise, and the Nazis hastened to eliminate them. At Dachau on 9 April, Johann Georg Elser, the communist who had tried to assassinate Hitler in November 1939, was executed. At Flossenburg the same day, Dietrich Bonhoeffer, Admiral Canaris and his Chief-of-Staff General Hans Oster were hanged, likewise Hans von Dohnanyi in Sachsenhausen. Thus too died many less famous names.

Never had the contrast been more brutally drawn between the experience of the Eastern and Western Fronts. As the last act of the battle for Germany approached, the American and British armies were advancing against only spasmodic resistance, suffering few casualties, knowing that their task was all but completed. Even after the shocking confrontation with the reality of the concentration camps, most of Eisenhower's soldiers had no thought for vengeance. They were preoccupied with their own survival, and with going home. The Western allies were ending the war as they had begun it, with anger in the hearts only of individuals with special reason to harbour it. Most men felt some pity for the vanquished. They succumbed to passion only when confronted with the most conspicuously impenitent or murderous Nazis.

Yet in the east, six million Russian soldiers were preparing for the day of triumph and retribution which they had been promised for so long. Their victory was not in doubt, but they now faced some of the Second World War's most savage encounters upon the battlefield. In the east, the last act was among the most terrible, as the Russians faced Germans ready to fight with the fanaticism of despair, amid a society collapsing into hysteria. Adolf Hitler had led one of the most educated and cultured societies on earth to a moral, political and military abyss. He now sought to ensure that as many as possible of his own people accompanied him over the brink.

CHAPTER FIFTEEN

"The Earth Will Shake as We Leave the Scene"

THE ABYSS

EVEN AS THE Americans and British were advancing eastwards in April, and while Zhukov and Konev marshalled their forces on the Oder, elsewhere Soviet armies were fighting gigantic battles along almost a thousand miles of front. In the west, Germans were surrendering. In the east they were dying in their tens of thousands. The testimony of Wehrmacht soldiers who survived the war is unrepresentative of the experience of Hitler's forces fighting the Russians in the last weeks, because so many such men perished. The fate of some units, especially those of the Waffen SS, is lost in fire and smoke, because no witnesses remained to record their destruction. Significant numbers of young soldiers, children of the Third Reich, betrayed no interest in surviving its collapse. Any temptation to applaud their courage is undone by an understanding of its futility, and of the depravity of the mindset which it reflected.

Hitler himself was indifferent, of course, and consumed by self-pity. "If the war should be lost," he said in one of the most notorious of all his utterances, "then the nation, too, will be lost... There is no need to consider the basic requirements that a people needs in order to live a primitive life. On the contrary, it is better to destroy such things, for this nation will have proved itself the weaker and the future will belong exclusively to the stronger Eastern nation. Those who remain alive after the battles are over are in any case only inferior persons, since the best have fallen." The Third Reich had always been in love with death. Now, its passion would achieve a final consummation.

Major Karl-Günther von Hase's father, Paul, commandant of Berlin, had been hanged for his part in the July bomb plot. His son was recalled from Italy for interrogation. Although he established his innocence, he was discharged from the General Staff, and sent in mid-January 1945 to serve as operations officer of one of Hitler's designated fortresses, Schneidemühl in East Pomerania.

Von Hase saw no dilemma in continuing to fight, despite his family's purgatory at Hitler's hands: "I was a professional—I had to do my duty. Obviously the war was lost, but there was an obligation to defend Germany, and a clear distinction between fighting the Russians and the Western allies. German behaviour in 1945 reflected a determination not to repeat the experience of 1918, when the German army was not defeated, but gave up."

As von Hase drove through the snow to his new posting, a black cat crossed the road. He found nothing in the "fortress" to discourage superstition. Its commander was an able regular officer a few years older than himself, Colonel Remlinger. Yet the garrison was pitifully weak. Beyond a few regular Wehrmacht troops, Schneidemühl was manned by 6,000 Volkssturm, the teenagers of an NCO cadet school and a few self-propelled guns from a local artillery school. There were no tanks. The entire civilian population of the town was recruited to dig defences. They were swiftly encircled by the Russians, and lost their airstrip at the beginning of February. Thereafter, they received only a few air-drops. Repeated requests to be permitted to break out were rejected. The garrison of Schneidemühl soon found itself some thirty miles behind the front.

Remlinger's men defended themselves with energy, mobilizing an armoured train which sallied from the perimeter to rescue a load of ammunition and supplies from beneath the Russian guns. Rationing was strictly enforced in anticipation of a long siege, with the result that much of the available food eventually fell into Soviet hands. It was ammunition that was lacking, and by mid-February almost exhausted. The Russians maintained a constant heavy mortar barrage, and bombed the defenders by night. Von Hase was dismayed by the fate of the fourteen- and fifteen-year-old NCO cadets: "It was terrible. They tried so hard to be brave. Whenever we needed volunteers for a patrol or a dangerous counter-attack, those teenagers put themselves forward. We had to get back lost ground—so we used them." Von Hase was presented with the Knight's Cross, pinned on him by Remlinger, for his own part in leading counter-attacks. "Discipline remained amazing to the very end."

As the situation grew desperate, von Hase thought of his fiancée, Renate, who was nursing in Thuringia. The Wehrmacht had long since established a system of proxy marriage for soldiers absent at the front. The landlines to Schneidemühl were cut, but the major sent a wireless message proposing their marriage, which Renate received. On 13 February, in accordance with the regulations, she went to her local registrar and took the vows with her hand upon a steel helmet, intended to symbolize her absent fiancé. It was impossible, however, to signal to Karl-Günther that the ceremony had been performed. When later asked by Russian interrogators whether he was married, he answered: "I don't know." On 22 February, when it was plain that the "fortress" was no longer defensible, Remlinger decided to defy his orders. The survivors of the garrison broke out and scattered into small groups to attempt escape. After walking for three days, Remlinger, von Hase and a dozen others fell into Russian hands. Remlinger died in captivity.

After the fall of Budapest on 14 February, the Russians expected a relatively untroubled advance through the rest of Hungary and on to Vienna. Instead, on 6 March, Hitler committed Sixth SS Panzer Army, veterans of the Bulge, to a dramatic counter-attack north and south of Lake Balaton, to save his Hungarian oilfields. Second Panzer Army was also directed to strike east towards the Danube. In a sea of mud, the Germans launched their offensive—and at first gained ground against the startled Russians. In Hungary, the Soviets were weak in armour. Russian infantry and anti-tank guns found themselves meeting the brunt of the German thrust. Lieutenant Valentin Krulik's motorized infantry unit of Sixth Guards Tank Army was ordered to take up defensive positions in a village near the Czech border. They were digging hard, and extremely scared at the prospect of facing tanks with only a few anti-tank grenades. Suddenly, Krulik saw an 85mm anti-tank gun being towed past. He waved down the driver and begged the NCO in charge of the gun to stay and support them, which the sergeant obligingly did. Krulik was pleased to see that the man was wearing a string of medals, indicating that he was a veteran. They dragged the gun into concealment behind the paling fence surrounding a vegetable garden. There were only two gunners, so the infantrymen helped sort armour-piercing ammunition from high explosive. Then they waited. At last, three German Mark IVs crawled slowly across the fields towards them, followed by infantry. The sergeant gunner said nonchalantly: "Oh, it's only those old things!" The Russians lingered minute by minute, allowing the range to close. Then the sergeant said: "Drop the fence!" As soon as they pushed over the paling, the gun fired. A tank caught fire. Its two consorts began to drop ineffectual shells around the Russians. Krulik's men swept the German infantry with automatic fire. After a few minutes, the surviving tanks and footsoldiers retired. This was not the German army of 1941 or 1942. These were the last writhings of desperate men. Krulik, deeply relieved, said to the gunners: "That's the first time we've had our own private artillery support. Nice evening, sergeant."

Once the Soviets recovered their balance after the shock of the Germans' Lake Balaton assault, they disposed ruthlessly of the attackers. German tanks and vehicles were anyway coughing to a halt all over the battlefield, for lack of fuel. The Germans ended the battle with fewer than 400 operational tanks and assault guns, against the 900 they had started with. The men of 1st SS Panzer Corps were exhausted. "We were at the end of our physical strength," said Corporal Martin Glade, of the retreat that began once more in mid-March, as the Soviets renewed their offensive.

At each orientation stop, comrades dropped to the ground where they stood ... [Our officer] distributed the company along a ridge in the darkness. "Dig in! Dig in!" I heard him shout, time and again. We ... dug shallow holes for ourselves. Mine was the depth of a spade. Then, fatigue overcame me. When I woke up again, I was hardly able to get to my feet. I was frozen right through. The sky was turning red in the east ... With my frozen fingers I dug in my haversack for a dry bread crust and a piece of sausage.

The Russians opened fire on the featureless hill, bereft of cover: "The effect was devastating ... to the right and left of me, men were lying motionless, silent, strangely curled up—more than half the company, I thought. Last night when we moved onto that damned hill, we had been 48."

The Germans abandoned their attack and began to pull back on 16 March. The Russians resumed their advance on Vienna, reaching the city outskirts on 4 April. Two days later, Valentin Krulik was sent with a reconnaissance patrol into the heart of the Austrian capital. He cared little for its illustrious history: "We didn't pay much attention. For us, it was just another battlefield." Alexandr Vostrukhin reached the suburbs with a T-34 battalion of the same brigade as Krulik. "The city looked amazingly untouched by the war, so quiet and serene, with no fires in sight."

Krulik led his men into the streets from the west in a couple of trucks, without meeting resistance. They caught sight of German troops, but found no organized defences. For a few minutes, they were bemused to find themselves following a column of Wehrmacht vehicles. "The silence was really creepy." But as night came on, despite Krulik's report that the path was open, his regimental commander felt uneasy about penetrating deep into the city without support. They pulled back to the suburbs. It was several days before the Russians were ready to address Vienna in force. In the interim, the Germans regrouped. SS panzergrenadiers fought ferociously through the streets for a week. Among them was Otto Skorzeny, Hitler's favourite commando. By 10 April, even Skorzeny despaired. He reported to Berlin: "The situation is hopeless. There are no defensive preparations, utter despondency. Organization has broken down ... Troops are bewildered and deprived of initiative. I ordered that three officers accused of treachery were not to be shot, but hung from the Floritzdorfer bridge. Withdrawal of the Luftwaffe is using fuel needed by tanks and fighting troops—and they are taking with them only women and furniture."

It cost the Red Army a week of bloody fighting to cover the ground Valentin Krulik's men had travelled so easily at the outset. "Our problem in 1945," said Krulik, "was that we were always in a hurry—being replenished on the march, very short of experienced officers, with a lot of very young and pretty old replacements filling the ranks. We were often confused about our own location. We would pore over the map and say: 'Well, we've been through here and here. We're going where? And after that, where?'" The Austrian capital was not finally secured until 14 April. On that date, Sixth SS Panzer Army sent a final signal to

Berlin: "The garrison of Vienna has ceased to exist. Despite their exhaustion, the troops are fighting with exemplary courage." Bombardment had reduced much of Vienna's beauty to rubble. The Soviet occupiers trudged through a city in which whole avenues blazed, littered with corpses and the wrecks of tanks and self-propelled guns destroyed by the score in the street fighting.

Rokossovsky's armies swung westwards during March, after gaining all of East Prussia save a few German strongholds. They smashed through West Prussia and Pomerania. Refugees and Wehrmacht soldiers alike were pressed relentlessly back upon the Baltic coast. Hundreds of thousands of them crowded into Danzig. It was defended by the remains of the German Second Army, while behind its positions huddled some 1.5 million refugees, most from East Prussia, together with 100,000 wounded jamming the hospitals. On 12 March, command was entrusted to the tough, effective General Dietrich von Saucken. "He was a son of East Prussia," in the words of German admirers, "and what mattered to him . . . was the seething mass of refugees, whom he was determined to save from the grasp of the Russians." The gauleiter of Danzig, Albert Forster, wrote: "I still believe in some kind of miracle. I still believe in Almighty God, who has given us our Führer . . . All that is left is for the West to recognize where its real enemy lies."

Instead, however, hysteria was overwhelming many of Forster's people. On 12 March, Russians found sixteen members of three families, including mothers and children aged between two and fifteen, in a shed a few miles outside Danzig. All had had their throats or wrists slashed by one Irwin Schwartz, a prominent local Nazi who said that this had been done at their own request. Some of those involved, who were still alive, persisted with their efforts to die even as a Red Army doctor attempted to save them. Schwartz, who survived cutting his own wrists, said that he had killed his own wife and three children, then offered the same service to his neighbours. "It is better to die than live with the Russians," he told his interrogators. Fifty-eight women and teenagers killed themselves by slitting their wrists in the town of Mednitz in 1st Ukrainian Front's sector. The same day, Konev's headquarters reported to Moscow: "Many Germans in areas we have occupied are dying of starvation."

On 15 March, six Russian armies began a simultaneous assault on Danzig. At last, the surviving heavy units of the German surface fleet, which had contributed so little to Hitler's war effort, found a role. The old battleship *Schlesien* and the cruisers *Prince Eugen* and *Leipzig* fired on the Russians from stations offshore, shaking the earth with the impact of their huge shells. The Germans remained faithful as ever to their doctrine of active defence. For four days, the line held. On 19 March, under fierce Russian pressure von Saucken's positions began to crack. On the 22nd, the first Soviet tanks reached the Baltic north of Danzig. The city centre came within Russian artillery range. A ferocious bombardment began. Civilians descended to the cellars, from which most did not emerge for many days. Russian fire was also raking ships in the harbour which were still attempting to evacuate civilians. A Russian soldier observed with satisfaction that once gunners accustomed to firing at ground targets adjusted to the demands of hitting ships, the results were devastating: "A gun would fire, then came the explosion of the shell, and another craft capsized and went to the bottom with its load of fascists."

Lieutenant Gennady Ivanov, commanding a Stalin tank troop, found the Danzig fighting as tough as anything he had known in three years of war: "The Germans fought very hard and very well, right up to the end." Ivanov's unit was dispersed by companies, to support the advance of Sixty-fifth Army's infantry. "I have never seen such a terrible battlefield—so much mud that we could hardly manoeuvre." Ivanov, a genial, exuberant twenty-one-year-old from Kazan in Tartary, had enjoyed an unusually untroubled upbringing, as the son of a successful Soviet bureaucrat. His elder brother had been killed early in the war—the family never knew when or where. An enthusiastic photographer, Ivanov took his looted Leica everywhere he went with the victorious Red Army.

On 19 March, his company stood just north of Danzig, peering at their next objective, a brickworks a thousand yards distant, flanked by a pine wood. When the supporting artillery barrage stopped, to Ivanov's surprise and dismay their company commander Chernyavsky, in whose judgement he had little faith, ordered the tanks to advance without infantry. The heavy Stalins thrashed clumsily forward on their bellies in the soft going, the lead troop eighty yards ahead of Ivanov's. They were firing half-heartedly at the brickworks, in lieu of any identifiable target. Suddenly, a German Panther crept out from the nearby wood, fired once at a range of 700 yards and disappeared behind cover again. It repeated this process three times in as many minutes. Three Stalins stood blazing, their crews running for the rear. The rest of the company retreated in confusion.

The Russian officers dismounted and were discussing what to do next when the divisional commander limped forward, leaning on the stick he had carried since he was wounded, and nursing a towering rage. "How long have you commanded armour?" he demanded of their company commander. "Is this your idea of how to fight a tank battle? What's the range of your guns? Eleven hundred metres? Then why don't you use it!" He started beating Chernyavsky furiously with his stick. "Now get on with it!" They remounted the tanks and resumed the advance. Within minutes, a Panther shell struck Chernyavsky's tank, setting it on fire and killing the crew—"which," said Ivanov laconically, "saved our captain from a court martial."

It took the Russians two days to get across that open field to their objective. Supporting infantry crept forward yard by yard towards the wood where German infantry and anti-tank guns were dug in, enfilading the attackers. When the tanks at last followed, "we found our tommy-gunners lying dead in heaps." Two brothers, Nikolai and Pyotr Oleinik, were gunner and driver in the same tank when it was hit. They bailed out alive, but Nikolai disappeared as they ran for their lives under fire. Pyotr, concussed, wandered hopelessly for hours searching for his brother, but never even found his body.

On 27 March, the regiment was ordered to advance to cut the railway north of Danzig. They set out in darkness, and halted when they believed they had secured their objective. Dawn revealed, however, that instead of the train tracks they had merely reached a tramline. On the radio net, the regimental commander told the point troop gloomily: "I've already informed Division we are on the railway." Reluctantly, he now reported their mistake. General Panov, commanding I Guards Tank Corps, radioed back personally, in one of the rages characteristic of Russian commanders: "You're all heading for court martial," he told the hapless colonel, "but I'll shoot you myself before the tribunal gets to sit." The tanks resumed their advance, until they found before them a blown rail bridge, with two trains deliberately driven into the gap, creating a tangled mass of wreckage, covered by German machine-gun fire. Russian engineers dashed forward. They lost a lot of men, but at last laid charges in the debris. The explosions blew a gap just large enough for the passage of self-propelled guns, though not tanks. Supported by infantry, the guns raced forward and forced open the road. "Everybody got medals," said Ivanov. But the Germans had delayed them almost until nightfall, in the sort of action that was fought a hundred times in a hundred places in those days.

Ivanov's tank column, still two miles from Danzig city centre, resumed its advance at first light. As they left open country behind and began to move among buildings, they met group after group of Hitler Youth armed with fausts and Molotov cocktails, who wreaked havoc. The regiment lost at least fifteen tanks to hand-held weapons in the street fighting that followed. Ivanov's own Stalin was hit in Hochenstrasse, in the first daylight hours of 30 March. He found himself soaked in blazing fuel, against which his fire-resistant suit provided scant protection. He was fully conscious and watched his cherished German boots burning before his eyes. He collapsed into the turret, screaming in pain. His crew dragged him out through the lower hatch, still under fire, and threw him into a big pool of melted snow by the roadside. Ivanov wrote gaily to his parents, in the tones of reassurance used by many soldier sons: "I am completely safe and well, and enjoying wonderful weather in Germany!" In reality, he spent twenty-two days in a field hospital. His regiment lost forty out of its fifty-five tanks in Danzig. All its company commanders were killed.

There was a black-comic song Russian tank crews sang, of which one line ran: "Our legs are torn off and our faces are on fire!" Ivanov's friend and fellow troop commander Vladimir Dobroradov, who led their column into Danzig, had a leg amputated after the battle. He was a dazzlingly handsome young man, an ardent dancer. When Dobroradov awoke from anaesthesia, he gave way to despair and shot himself with a small pistol. Ivanov believed that Dobroradov met his fate because over the preceding weeks he had diverted himself in off-duty hours by flirting with the "field wife" of his brigade commander. That officer, who was unamused, ordered his impertinent young rival to take point position in the Danzig attack. Ivanov always afterwards thought of the biblical tale of Uriah the Hittite. Their regimental commander, who had incurred Panov's wrath, also died in those days. A German woman walked up and shot the colonel at point-blank range, in an act of vengeance for her own rape by Soviet soldiers. "Such things were happening," shrugged Ivanov. "In Rokossovsky's mob, Rokossovsky permitted it." The woman survived only long enough to explain her motive, before being bayoneted.

IN THE STREETS of Danzig during the last days of its defence, the SS and field police hanged scores of men who had abandoned their units. Russian aircraft harried to destruction retreating columns of German troops and vehicles. On 25 March, a certain Colonel Christern passed through Danzig to assume command of 4th Panzer Division. Given the urgency of his appointment, his signals officer was astonished when the panzer leader halted beside one of the city's few surviving churches.

> The colonel looked about inquisitively, and then a delicate smile lit his battle-scarred face. He shot a silent glance at me to indicate that I was to seat myself on a bench, thereupon he and the driver climbed a steep flight of steps to the loft...I was somewhat uncomfortable sitting there while the rumble of combat carried from outside. Then I nearly jumped out of my skin...the organ roared into life...I knew that the colonel was devoted to music...but this was the first time I had heard him on the organ—and he played it like a master.

Von Saucken ordered the final evacuation of the ruined city, which had become indefensible, on the night of 27 March. The surviving German troops in the area were now isolated on the Hela peninsula, where some remained until the end of the war, and on the coastal plateau of the Oxhofter Kampe, from which von Saucken was able to evacuate several units by sea in the week following the fall of Danzig. Until the very end of the war, soldiers and refugees continued to be rescued by sea from the marshy meadows of the Vistula delta.

Fourteen-year-old Erich Pusch, a fugitive who had lost his parents on the ice of the Frisches Haff, lay in a cellar in Danzig with his young brother and a dozen or so other terrified people, mostly women and children. The first Russian entered their refuge early on the morning of 31 March. The man demanded to know if there were any German soldiers present. Assured that there were not, he collected all watches and rings, then left. Young Erich put his head cautiously into the street to investigate, and saw some very young Russian soldiers standing around their tanks. Occasional shells were still exploding, fired by German naval guns. Erich returned to the cellar. They all sat in dread, awaiting the worst. The next Russians to arrive were very drunk. They took all the women into the adjoining room and raped them, amid hysterical pleas for mercy. Returning, the Russians noticed lying on the floor a young Russian PoW, who had lost a leg before his capture. One Red soldier bayoneted him and then, when the doomed man screamed, shot him. Every soldier in the Soviet armies had been thoroughly briefed that fellow countrymen who had surrendered to the fascists were traitors. The soldiers then demanded the shoes of everyone present, collected these in a bag, and departed. The women were left sobbing. Late that night, Mongolians came, and raped a fifteen-year-old girl. After that, successive waves of Russians reappeared all night, bent on the same business. They ignored the old men and children, but raped the women repeatedly.

Next morning, the Pusch boys and their companions emerged traumatized from the cellar, to find the city in flames. People were streaming from their houses clutching such possessions as they could carry. Erich saw German soldiers hanging from the tram pylons, executed as deserters. The great column of refugees shuffled through the streets, watched by throngs of Red soldiers. Russians began to pull men from the line and examine them. Some, presumably suspected of being soldiers in civilian clothes, were shot. Then the Russians began to pick out girls. One or two clutching babies handed these to older women to take away, then went sobbing after the Russians to meet their fate. Twenty-five-year-old Frieda Engler, a cousin of Elfi Kowitz, was raped eighteen times by Russian soldiers outside Danzig.

On and on the Pusch boys walked westwards, beyond the city and its suburbs. They were exhausted and desperately hungry. They slept that night in a ditch. Next day, a woman saw them walking in their stockinged feet and took pity. She led them to her house, where her two teenage daughters were hidden behind the bedroom wardrobe. There they lived as scavengers through the two desperate, ravening months that followed.

The same fate befell eleven-year-old Anita Bartsch. The Russians swept into the air-raid shelter where she was hiding with her family, demanding watches and women, "*Uri! Uri! Frau! Frau!*," in their usual fashion. After being relieved of their watches, the fugitives unwillingly ascended to the street, to perceive a pile of corpses. Anita's eldest sister Maria was raped, then sent to a Russian detention camp with their mother and teenage brother. Anita found herself living alone with her four-year-old brother and three-year-old nephew in a derelict flat. Through the weeks that followed, she scavenged and stole just sufficient fragments of food to keep them alive: "We lived like little animals." The ruined city was a ghastly place for survivors of any age. Once, she came upon a shallow river bed, filled with the bloated and decayed corpses of German soldiers. After six weeks, the Russians released the rest of the family. By a miracle, Anita's sister Maria found them: "She was in a bad way, and all of us were suffering from severe malnutrition. My mother scarcely had any flesh left on her bones." Soon afterwards, the Russians began evicting all Germans from Danzig to make way for the new Polish occupants. The traumatized survivors of the Bartsch family rode a railway flatcar to Berlin, and thereafter to a displaced-persons camp where they spent the next three years. "My mother never got over it and died five years later—she was just fifty," said Anita Bartsch. "My father was very sick when at last we were reunited. He never worked again." Photographs of the family at that time show faces imprinted with imperishable pain.

In the streets of Danzig, Captain Vasily Krylov watched the manic looting of abandoned shops. "The whole place stank of corpses." He saw soldiers cheering the discovery of a tanker wagon of alcohol. They emptied their weapons into it until spirits spouted from a hundred holes, then stood open-mouthed beneath the fountains of liquor. Many men, said Krylov, were angered by the splendour in which they perceived the Germans to have been living, the riches of their houses. "They were bitter about what the Germans had done to us, when they saw how Hitler's people lived at home." "It was very difficult to maintain order as we advanced into Germany," admitted Major Fyodor Romanovsky of the NKVD. There was considerable confusion in the upper ranks of the Red Army about the limits of tolerable behaviour. Yelena Kogan's commanding officer took a call one day in Poznan from a Polish unit complaining that two Russians had raped a local woman. "Shoot them!" ordered the Soviet officer. Kogan observed drily: "His attitude proved to be behind the times. Our colonel did not know what the rest of the army was doing in Germany."

The old Pomeranian coastal fortress of Kolberg was cut off by the Russians on 4 March. Its garrison consisted of only 3,300 men, mostly stragglers and Volkssturm, commanded by an elderly veteran of German South-West Africa, Colonel Fritz Fullriede. They could call on the support of four broken-down tanks, which had to be towed into action by trucks, and naval gunfire from two destroyers offshore. Fullriede was also obliged to assume responsibility for 68,000 civilians. Russian attacks began on 13 March. Fullriede dismissed calls for Kolberg's surrender. Warships continued the evacuation throughout the siege, taking off refugees to Swinemünde. It was painfully slow work. Some families killed themselves, despairing of escape. Yet Fullriede's garrison, at the cost of almost half its strength, held the line until the evacuation of civilians was complete on 16 March. The colonel then achieved a last small miracle, supervising the evacuation of his soldiers from their coastal perimeter only a mile wide and 400 yards deep, early on the morning of 18 March. Fullriede was awarded the Knight's Cross for what was, indeed, the fulfilment of a heroic humanitarian purpose.

For most of March, 105,000 men of Third Panzer Army retained one major German foothold east of the Oder, a sixty-mile strip of front known as the Altdamm bridgehead, commanded by Hasso von Manteuffel. The Russians attacked here on 14 March. Next day Hitler began systematically stripping Third Panzer Army of troops to reinforce Berlin. Von Manteuffel decided that his position was untenable. He withdrew all his surviving forces across the Oder next night, demolishing the river bridges. On 21 March, the Russians mopped up the survivors in Altdamm town, capturing large quantities of abandoned equipment and armour.

Germany's generals were stunned by Hitler's appointment of Heinrich Himmler, whose skills lay solely in the field of mass murder, to military command of the Vistula front late in January. Guderian described Himmler's role as "preposterous ... I used such argumentative powers as I possessed in an attempt to stop such an idiocy being perpetrated on the unfortunate Eastern front ... all in vain." Once arrived at his headquarters, the Reichsführer SS proved wholly unable to exercise command functions, even with the assistance as his chief of staff of another accomplished killer, SS General Heinz Lammerding, whose men had carried out the Oradour massacre in France. Himmler's tenure as Vistula commander proved as disastrous as the Wehrmacht had anticipated. On 18 March, Guderian discovered that the SS chief had abandoned his headquarters and was said to be nursing a bad cold in a sanatorium at Hohenlychen. In truth, he had suffered a nervous collapse. Guderian had little trouble persuading Himmler that he should ask to be relieved of responsibility for command of the front, and there was no resistance from Hitler.

On 22 March, General Gotthard Heinrici, commander of First Panzer Army in the Carpathians, a dogged little old soldier, went to see Guderian at his headquarters in the complex of low, camouflage-painted concrete buildings at Zossen, nerve centre of the German Army's war effort. Guderian told him that a big counter-attack was being planned from the Frankfurt-on-Oder bridgehead, against the Russians threatening Küstrin. This fortress, once the prison of Frederick the Great, stood on an island in the Oder some fifty miles east of Berlin. The Russians had briefly penetrated its defences early in February, before being evicted.

Now, Hitler insisted that an attempt to relieve Küstrin should start in two days. The hapless Heinrici must assume responsibility. Yet before the attack could be launched, the Russians themselves attacked, on that same morning of 22 March. When the German counter-attack was launched on the 23rd, it was halted in its tracks by Soviet artillery fire. Heinrici urged Hitler to abandon Küstrin, which was isolated. As usual, the Führer demurred. He insisted on further counter-attacks. On 27 March, three divisions of Ninth Army launched an assault which so surprised the Russians that the leading German tanks reached the outskirts of Küstrin. But there they were stopped, and ruthlessly destroyed.

"It was a massacre," said Heinrici grimly. Eight thousand men had died for nothing. Next day, Hitler dismissed Guderian, asserting that his health required an immediate six weeks' convalescent leave. The last of Germany's great field commanders was replaced as Chief of Staff by General Hans Krebs on 29 March. The same day, the Russians launched an intense bombardment of Küstrin. The garrison broke out and escaped on its own initiative that night, though a few survivors lingered to die fighting as the Russians occupied the fortress. On reaching the German lines, Küstrin's commander was immediately imprisoned by Hitler.

Breslau, capital of lower Silesia, held out through an epic siege of seventy-seven days, which only ended a week after Hitler's death. The city was encircled on 16 February. It took the Russians a fortnight to fight their way through a bare mile of southern suburbs, against determined resistance. The garrison, some 50,000 strong, still looked for relief from Schörner's Army Group Centre. After the flight west of many Silesian refugees, plunging into snows and perils that brought death to thousands, some 80,000 civilians remained in Breslau. Behind the front lines, scores of houses had been destroyed by the defenders to open a fire zone. Firemen, industrial workers, service personnel threw themselves into the defence with a courage worthy of a better cause. Factories continued to produce ammunition, cigarettes—600,000 of them a day—heavy mortar bombs. The garrison even constructed an armoured train. Luftwaffe night sorties maintained deliveries of mail and some stores.

The gauleiter, Karl Hanke, was among the most repellent officials of the Third Reich. He hanged Breslau's burgomaster for suggesting that the city was indefensible. He sent exuberant daily reports to Berlin, prompting Goebbels to remark in delight: "If all our gauleiters in the east were like this... we should be in better shape than we are." Hitler described Hanke admiringly as "a devil of a fellow." Yet Hanke's interventions in the military conduct of the defence were disastrous. He pressed constantly for a breakout to reach Schörner's army, a notion which the army's commandant dismissed. Such an initiative would have required several divisions. Thousands of Breslau men and women were forced to work almost to death, building a new airstrip at Hanke's bidding.

The gauleiter established his own headquarters in the cellars beneath the city's university library. He proposed to demolish the building above, to render his own quarters impregnable beneath its rubble, and was dissuaded from incinerating half a million books only by fears that the pyre would spread flames across the city. By 1 April, the Russians were bombarding Breslau with huge guns of up to 280mm calibre. The cathedral tower fell, the botanical garden burned, and large areas of the south and west became uninhabitable. Yard by yard, the Russians pushed back the defenders into the city centre.

Everywhere along the Eastern Front, Germany's forces were cut off, or disintegrating as they fell back to the last bastions of the Reich. When survivors of

10th SS Panzer were refused permission to break out of encirclement on 19 April, "we saw it as our death sentence," said Captain Karl Godau, a gunner. He still had his battery, but no fuel to move it. Command and control had broken down. On the 20th, they fired off the last of their ammunition, then blew up the guns and trucks within sight of the Russians: "It was horrible—like being stripped naked." A few men escaped. Godau's battalion commander, a much admired officer named Harry Jops, swam the Elbe to escape imprisonment. The remainder surrendered. To their surprise, at first the Russians treated them quite well. It was later, during the long march to imprisonment in Silesia and afterwards in Russia, that their descent to misery took place, with stragglers shot down and many men perishing of starvation or despair.

Germany's armies were crumbling one by one. In the west, resistance had almost ceased. In the east, men manned their positions conscious that to hope even for personal survival was extravagant. Fanatical Nazis aspired only to make an end in keeping with their demented, heroic vision of the Third Reich. Yet every other foothold of German resistance paled into insignificance alongside Hitler's capital. It was there, the world knew, that the last terrible melodrama must be played out. All eyes now turned upon the grimy, battered, desperate streets of Berlin.

"HITLER KAPUTT! HITLER KAPUTT!"

IT IS IN the nature of war that many people find it impossible to acknowledge that the horrors they witness represent reality, or that a familiar environment is doomed. How can the heart accept the signals of the brain, however powerful and rational, that a known universe, in which the blotter stands where it has always stood on the office desk, the sofa in the lounge of the house, the shop on the corner of the street, is about to disappear for ever? If this phenomenon is true for ordinary mortals, then it becomes unsurprising that the Nazi leadership, with the notable exception of Speer, retreated into fantasy even as the Allied armies closed in for the kill. A regime that had suborned a nation and sought to conquer the world sustained its giant edifice of self-delusion to the last. Grand-Admiral Karl Dönitz had directed Germany's campaign in the Atlantic with some skill if no imagination. Now, with mindless devotion to the cause he had slavishly served, he continued to conduct the Navy's affairs as if he was making policy for decades of Nazi hegemony. On 14 April, he volunteered to the Führer the services of 3,000 young naval personnel to operate as guerrillas behind enemy lines in the west, oblivious of the fact that these men were wholly untrained. Four days later, he circulated an order from naval headquarters, applauding the actions of a petty officer of the raiding cruiser *Cormoran*, who languished in a prison camp in Australia. This exemplary figure, said the grand-admiral, had successfully killed every man among his fellow PoWs who displayed communist leanings: "This petty officer is certain of my full recognition for his resolve and his execution. I shall promote him... on his return."

Hitler's ranting against his subordinates had increased in intensity. Guderian described one such session which continued for two hours, "his fists raised, his cheeks flushed with rage, his whole body trembling... After each outburst of rage Hitler would stride up and down the carpet edge, then suddenly stop immediately before me and hurl his next accusation. He was almost screaming, his eyes seemed about to pop out of his head and the veins stood out on his temples." Afterwards Keitel, most despicable of Hitler's military creatures, accosted Guderian and demanded: "How could you contradict the Führer in that way? Didn't you see how excited he was getting? What would happen if as the result of such a scene he were to have a stroke?" After the Allies had seized Remagen, when Hitler demanded reinforcements, he was told that just five tank destroyers were available, under repair at Sennelager. The master of Germany, overlord of armies that once swept Europe, engrossed himself for some minutes in the deployment of five broken-down *Jagdtiger*. To the end, he maintained his determination that the German people should perish, rather than be permitted to save themselves by yielding. "No German town will be declared open," asserted a signal from Berlin to Army Group Centre on 15 April. "Every village and every town will be defended and held by every possible man. Every German who contravenes his obvious natural duty will forfeit his honour and his life."

Desperate shortages caused Hitler to strip weapons and equipment from units which seemed unwilling to fight, to arm and clothe those that would. Boots, uniforms, even underclothes were taken from customs and police departments and naval warehouses for issue to the Wehrmacht. Even among formations which still possessed substantial numbers of tanks and fuel to move them, many were immobilized by mechanical defects or lack of parts. The last available order of battle for the Eastern Front, which is dated 15 March, shows 2nd SS Panzer, for instance, with twenty-seven Panthers of which seventeen were operational, and twenty-six assault guns of which just seven were runners; likewise 9th SS Panzer, with twenty-five assault guns of which eleven were operational, along with twelve out of its thirty-five Panthers. The Grossdeutschland Panzergrenadier Division was reduced to two assault guns, neither operational; five Panthers, of which one was a runner; and six Tigers. This was the sum total of armoured support for a formation with an establishment of 16,000 men.

Hitler exploded when he heard that thousands of small arms were still in the hands of the Indian Legion, formed from prisoners taken while serving with the British. Their unit, he observed, is "a joke. These are Indians who couldn't kill a louse, who'd rather be eaten themselves. They wouldn't kill an Englishman." He expressed similar scepticism about whether much could be expected from the Estonians in Wehrmacht uniform: "What are they still supposed to be fighting for, anyway? They've gone from their homeland." General Wilhelm Burgdorf interjected apologetically: "If there are a lot of fainthearted people even with us, we really can't demand it of those people." It was ironic that amid crisis deficiencies of so many creations of twentieth-century technology for waging war, Germany's generals in 1945 also found themselves protesting the shortage of horses. One of the last signals to OKH from General von Hoffman of 10th Parachute Division, on 16 April, complained that he lacked 60 per cent of the animals essential for his formation: "My parachutists have been obliged to drag their artillery 12 miles, for lack of horses to pull the guns."

Lieutenant Tony Saurma of the Grossdeutschland Division was among those brought back from the beleaguered garrison of Samland on the Baltic by submarine, to train men for the defence of Berlin. He was horrified to be appointed to command a troop of Mark IV tanks dug in near the Larterbahnhof station. "I found myself commanding men of sixty, even seventy. And the Russians were only thirty miles away!" After a few days, Saurma said to the grateful old men: "Go home. We don't need you. And if anybody wants to report me, they can do so." The lieutenant was profoundly relieved when he was reposted to Schleswig-Holstein before the Berlin battle began.

In one of Hitler's rare moments of realism, he dismissed suggestions that he should leave the capital, to maintain his defence of the Reich from the south: "As an inglorious refugee from Berlin, I would have no authority in either northern or southern Germany, and in Berchtesgaden even less." Somewhere in the tortured maze of his consciousness, he knew that the end was at hand. He perceived a dignity in fighting to the last for Berlin, which would be denied to him as a fugitive. His own passing might attain an appropriate grandeur if it also embraced the deaths of sufficient thousands of lesser mortals. "Everyone now has a chance to choose the part which he will play in the film a hundred years hence," Goebbels told his Propaganda Ministry staff in an oration on 17 April. "I can assure you that it will be a fine and elevating picture... Hold out now, so that a hundred years hence the audience does not hoot and whistle when you appear on the screen."

EISENHOWER'S FRANKNESS with Stalin about his lack of ambitions towards Berlin was neither credited nor reciprocated. Stalin did not believe that the Supreme Commander would forgo this great prize when it was plain that the German front was collapsing before the Americans and British. Indeed, Stalin was irked that the enemy had opened to the Western allies so easy a passage. This fed all his paranoia about the collusion natural between bourgeois capitalist societies. Russia's warlord was determined that the Soviet Union should seize Hitler's capital. He shared with his German counterpart an absolute indifference to the human cost of his decisions. The two foremost monsters of twentieth-century history embarked upon their last encounter with matching appetites for a titanic showdown.

At a critical meeting in his study at the Kremlin on 1 April, Stalin told Zhukov and Konev of his belief that the Anglo-Americans were driving for Berlin. Famously, he asked: "Who is going to take Berlin: are we or are the Allies?" Konev instantly gave Stalin the reply he wanted: "It is we who shall take Berlin, and we will take it before the Allies." Stalin smiled thinly: "So that's the sort of man you are." Doubt persists about whether the Russians sincerely feared a Western drive for Berlin, or whether Stalin merely used the threat to goad his marshals. It seems likely that he indeed feared pre-emption.

In Moscow, he observed to Zhukov and Konev that virtually all remaining German military strength was now concentrated on the Oder. Zhukov said that according to his own intelligence reports the Germans had deployed against him some ninety divisions in four armies, together with 1,500 tanks, 3,500 aircraft and 10,000 guns. This was a wildly extravagant estimate. The German divisions were ruins, largely bereft of equipment. It was years since the Luftwaffe had possessed 3,500 operational aircraft. Overall German strength of some 300,000 men facing Zhukov was vastly outweighed by that of the Russian armies. But it was true that Hitler had thrown into his line east of Berlin almost every man capable of holding a weapon, and every fighting vehicle the Wehrmacht and SS could move to the Oder. "I think it's going to be quite a fight," said Stalin. Over the years, Zhukov had become skilled in reading the Soviet warlord's mood by every detail of his behaviour: the tunic he wore, whether he stroked his moustache, whether he lit his Dunhill pipe. Now, he did the latter, usually a good sign. Zhukov and Konev were mighty men at the head of their armies, yet they became no more than useful creatures, utterly at the mercy of his whims, in the presence of their terrible master.

Stalin signalled Eisenhower that he agreed with the Americans that Berlin was no longer important, and that Russia would commit only limited forces. In reality, 2.5 million men and 6,250 tanks were deployed for the assault on Hitler's capital. Zhukov and his 1st Belorussian Front would be granted the dubious honour of launching the assault. Konev's 1st Ukrainian Front would attack from the south. Konev's men would initially drive westwards, south of Berlin, and turn north towards the city only if Zhukov's tank armies failed to smash their way through. "Whoever breaks in first, let him take Berlin," said Stalin, drawing the start line on the Oder bank for his marshals' race for Hitler's capital. Rokossovsky's forces were still mopping up north-east Germany, but would join the attack as soon as they could redeploy. The plan anticipated the capture of the city on 22 April, Lenin's birthday.

It would be foolish to suppose that every man of the Red Army welcomed the opportunity for glory thrust upon him by the Oder crossing and the battle for Berlin. Most had been fighting for a long, long time. Like American and British soldiers, as victory beckoned, they began to cherish the possibility of survival, of going home. "In the last days of the war," wrote Gabriel Temkin, with Twenty-seventh Army near Lake Balaton, "everybody, much more than ever before, was thinking about life and death—his own." "We'd all had enough," said Corporal Nikolai Ponomarev of the 374th Rifle Division. He had been wounded twice, and was now increasingly fearful of being sent to the Far East to fight the Japanese when the German war was over. "In the last month, especially, one felt that one wanted to get home alive," said Vladimir Gormin of 3rd Ukrainian Front. Their loneliness was compounded by the fact that the Red Army was now so far from its homes that its men could no longer pick up Russian stations on their radios.

Zhukov and Konev cleared a zone fifteen miles deep behind their front of all civilians, as they prepared for the battle. They found themselves facing severe difficulties with a flood of new replacements, some of whom reached the armies with only a week's military training. "Many have proved unstable in action, and indeed cowardly," reported 1st Ukrainian Front on 7 April. "There have been cases of self-inflicted wounds. One rifle battalion containing 75% replacements broke and ran. Its officers shot five men on the spot to restore order." Konev's staff reported cases of mutiny which seem astounding given the inevitable fate of those involved. On 6 April, Privates Tarasyuk and Cheburko "categorically refused to take the military oath, asserting that they were Evangelists." Cheburko said: "I follow in the footsteps of Christ. I will not take up arms or kill people." The two men were dispatched immediately to a military tribunal. Another soldier who wounded himself before the battle began was shot in front of his unit. Yet the Political Department continued to record extraordinary instances of dissent. One soldier named Kaleshov, a former captive of the Germans, was rash enough to grumble that Russia's rulers "betrayed us in 1941 and they will betray us again now ... I was better off as a German prisoner." Konev's staff complained that they were desperately short of clothing and equipment for replacements. Sixty-five thousand uniforms ordered in January had still not been delivered, and young soldiers were parading in rotten boots, without tunics or even underclothes: "They don't look like soldiers."

Yet, fortunately for the Red Army, there were some men still eager for glory. Lieutenant Nikolai Dubrovsky's commanding officer of the 136th Independent Artillery Regiment rushed his unit forward to Zhukov's front as soon as he was ordered to move there from East Prussia. The colonel was desperate to qualify for the Berlin campaign medal. Although Dubrovsky himself had been drafted at sixteen in 1942, he had thus far been fortunate enough to see no action. He felt far less emotionally committed to the struggle than many men: "I wanted to fight, because everybody else was fighting, but I felt no hatred for the Germans—I was too young to be embittered." The gunner officer was lucky, first, to come from eastern Russia, which the 1941–42 German onslaught never reached; and second, to serve in a heavy artillery unit, where personal risk was small. From his brigade's Fire Control Centre, Dubrovsky was responsible for calling down 152mm howitzer fire on Hitler's capital from a range of twelve miles.

In this last period of the war, the Soviets' reputation for savagery cost them dearly. In the west, many German soldiers were embracing captivity. All but the most committed Nazi fanatics knew that, if they picked the right moment to surrender, they were likely to survive, and to be humanely treated. On the Eastern Front, by contrast, there was not only a generalized fear about the behaviour of the Russians towards Germany, but a personal one about any man's slender prospects of surviving captivity. "Many Germans seemed to feel that they were going to die anyway, so they might as well die fighting," acknowledged Lieutenant Pavel Nikiforov, a Soviet reconnaissance officer. The Red Army would not have stood at the gates of Berlin in April 1945 but for its ferocious fighting spirit. Yet the dreadful casualties of the last battles might have been greatly diminished had not the Germans fought with the courage of despair. The Stavka seemed belatedly to recognize this, by an order of 20 April calling for "a change of attitude towards prisoners and civilians. We should treat Germans better. Bad treatment of Germans makes them fight more stubbornly and refuse to surrender. This is an unfavourable situation for us." Yet it was far, far too late to alter the mindset of six million men, fostered over four years of merciless struggle.

Zhukov's and Konev's assaults across the Oder began in darkness early on 16 April. Forty-two thousand Russian guns launched a massive bombardment, which they would sustain through days to come. More than seven million shells had been stockpiled. There was little scope for deception when there was no leaf on the trees and the ground was too waterlogged to dig deep. Every German knew full well where the Russians were heading, as Stalin's forces began to close upon Berlin across an arc of advance that extended 235 miles. Soviet aircraft launched the first of 6,500 bombing and strafing sorties against German positions beyond artillery range. As flares of every hue shot into the sky to give the signal, the night crossing of the river began. The Russians switched on huge searchlights to illuminate the assault. The Germans, unsurprisingly, opened furious fire at the lights. "I shall never forgive Zhukov for that folly," said Major Yury Ryakhovsky. "Everyone warned him what would happen, and begged him not to use the lights. But he kept saying stubbornly again and again: 'I have told Stalin that we shall use them.'" The searchlights were manned by women. Ryakhovsky looked in revulsion upon the crews' mangled bodies as they lay around the searchlight mountings.

Only the privileged among the men making the assault crossing possessed boats. The rest were expected to fend for themselves. Most crossed the wintry river, on which great chunks of broken ice still drifted, on primitive rafts. Lieu-tenant Vasily Filimonenko, an artillery forward observation officer, paddled across near Seelow with his five-man signals team clinging to a precarious wooden contraption contrived from doors and fence posts. "I never thought I'd make it," said the gunner. His party was close to foundering when some engi-neers in a boat took them in tow. Intense German fire was whipping over the water. Flares and flames lit up the darkness. The ruins of shattered boats were drifting everywhere. Mortar and artillery rounds were falling among sappers struggling to build a bridge. Filimonenko saw one section of pontoons blasted high into the air by a direct hit. Yet the work went on. The gunner officer was in the water for half an hour before he crawled up the western bank shivering uncontrollably. He had lost one signaller wounded. They had managed to keep their sacred radio dry. They began to report the compass bearings of German muzzle-flashes back to their own guns.

It has been insufficiently recognized in the West that Zhukov's assault across the Oder was a shambles. It was an operation worthy of the worst days of the Red Army, not of its final triumph. The Soviet archives bulge with after-action reports revealing the rage and frustration of many of those who took part, and who witnessed the reckless sacrifice of life. The preparatory bombardment fell largely upon forward positions evacuated by the Germans, and made little impression on their main defences. Many men who had fought at the Vistula crossing compared the effects of the Oder artillery preparation very un-favourably with the devastation achieved four months earlier. The Russian assault met accurate German artillery and mortar fire, especially from batteries at Frankfurt-on-Oder. There were violent complaints from the infantry about tanks lagging behind or becoming snarled in massive traffic jams behind the advance. A Sergeant Safronov reported seeing Soviet armour advancing over their own infantry positions, crushing men under the tracks. Captain Shimkov of the 68th Guards Brigade described how a mass of tanks and self-propelled guns became entangled in a gully, from which they shot blindly towards the enemy "because we had no experience of night firing. We were aiming by instinct." Untrained replacements proved woefully incompetent—one unit reported three machine-guns jammed, because their Moldavian crews had no idea how to clear them. After the battle, political officers compiled an unedify-ing list of officers deemed to have behaved with cowardice or incompetence.

Worst of all, some Soviet minefields had not been properly cleared by the engineers. Hundreds of men died before they had even advanced beyond their own positions. Eight out of the 89th Regiment's twenty-two tanks were wrecked on Russian mines. The 347th Infantry Division alone lost thirty men killed. A subsequent report declared furiously: "The divisional engineer Lieutenant-Colonel Lomov, a Party Member, and a brigade commander, Colonel Lebedev, also a Party Member, were too busy drinking before the attack to do their jobs

properly. Colonel Lomov was too drunk even to report to the divisional commander." It was in the light of behaviour such as this that Zhukov issued an
order on 17 April cancelling the issue of vodka to several formations until further notice.

As daylight grew on the western bank, a pall of dust and smoke hung over
the blasted German defences. Flocks of displaced birds wheeled in the sky. Men
strove to save their eardrums amid the relentless thunder of the bombardment,
now ranging on targets deeper into the German positions. Zhukov's initial optimism at the success of the crossing was replaced by dismay, as his forces battered in vain at the enemy's main line. "The further we got, the tougher the
resistance became," said Vasily Filimonenko. The strongest German defences,
on the Seelow Heights, lay well beyond the reach of the Russians' preliminary
bombardment. Even after Zhukov's men had secured bridgeheads, established
their pontoons and pushed the first tanks forward, they found themselves making little progress. They struggled in the German minefields, for the Red Army
was chronically short of mine detectors. The ground was miserably soft and
treacherous for armoured vehicles, which bogged down in scores. The defenders were resolute. Zhukov found himself engaged in the most bitter fighting his
armies had known since 1943.

ON THE AFTERNOON of 16 April, nineteen-year-old Helga Braunschweig, who
worked in a Berlin telegraph office, was foraging for potatoes in the countryside
east of Berlin with her friend Regina. The S-Bahn proved so badly damaged
that they were obliged to abandon the train and walk. They were soon stopped
at a military police roadblock, where the *Kettenhunden* said: "There's nothing for
you up that way, girls." They wangled a lift in a truck up a side road and found
themselves in Wehrmacht positions on a hill. They lingered to chat and flirt
with the soldiers, even as they listened to the thunder of the guns and watched
the relentless flashes in the distance as the afternoon light faded. The soldiers,
summoned to action, hastily clambered into their trucks, gathering up the girls,
and drove towards the Seelow Heights. Eventually they stopped, pointed the
girls towards a house where they could buy potatoes, and left them in the road.
Helga and her friend filled their bags, then lingered watching the horizon flickering with flame, gripped by a sense of disbelief. Berlin had been awaiting the
Red Army for so long that, now it was coming, they could not grasp what it
meant.

When at last they reached home, a cottage on the north-eastern outskirts of
the city, Helga's mother was almost prostrate with worry about their absence,
but very grateful for the potatoes. The women stayed in the cottage through the
days that followed, as a flood of refugees streamed westwards. Most of their
neighbours left. An SS patrol asked why they were not fleeing: "Don't you know

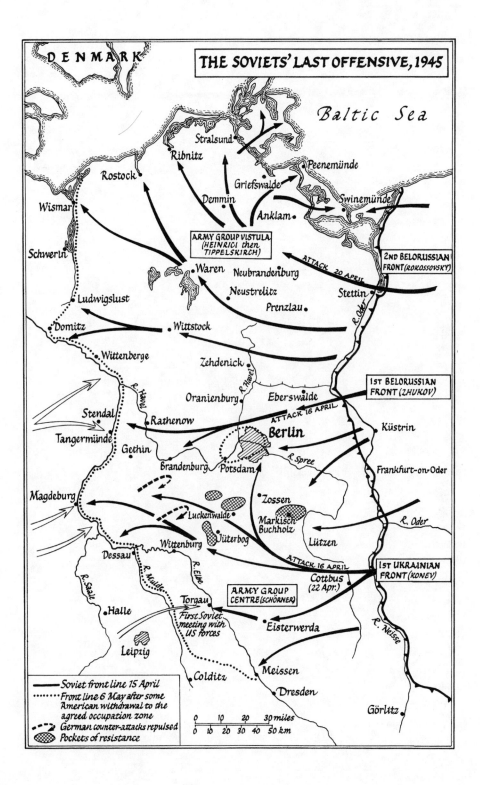

THE SOVIETS' LAST OFFENSIVE, 1945

DENMARK

Baltic Sea

Stralsund
Ribnitz
Rostock
Peenemünde
Griefswalde
Demmin
Swinemünde
Anklam
Wismar
Schwerin

ARMY GROUP VISTULA
(HEINRICI then
TIPPELSKIRCH)

2ND BELORUSSIAN
FRONT (ROKOSSOVSKY)

ATTACK 20 APRIL

Waren
Neubrandenburg
Ludwigslust
Neustrelitz
Domitz
Prenzlau
Stettin
Wittstock
Wittenberge
Zehdenick

1ST BELORUSSIAN
FRONT (ZHUKOV)

Oranienburg
Eberswalde
Küstrin

ATTACK 16 APRIL

Stendal
Rathenow
Berlin

Tangermünde
Gethin
Frankfurt-on-Oder

Brandenburg
Potsdam
R. Spree

Magdeburg
Zossen
Luckenwalde
Markisch
Buchholz
R. Oder

Wittenburg
Jüterbog
Dessau
Lützen

1ST UKRAINIAN
FRONT (KONEV)

ATTACK 16 APRIL
Cottbus
(22 Apr.)

ARMY GROUP
CENTRE (SCHÖRNER)

Torgau
First Soviet
meeting with
US forces
Eisterwerda

Halle
R. Neisse

Leipzig
Meissen

Colditz
Dresden

Görlitz

R. Havel
R. Havel
R. Saale
R. Mulde
R. Elbe

Soviet front line 15 April
Front line 6 May after some
American withdrawal to the
agreed occupation zone
German counter-attacks repulsed
Pockets of resistance

0   10   20   30 miles
0 10 20 30 40 50 km

that the Russians are raping all German women?" Helga's mother shrugged: "That's just Goebbels' propaganda." Her daughter said: "We simply didn't know about what had been happening in the east." Her boyfriend Wolfgang, a Luftwaffe wireless-operator, had contrived his own deft exit from the war by persuading the crew of his aircraft on a sortie one day to divert their course to Sweden, where they were interned, and Wolfgang later married a Swedish girl. Her father was a prisoner of the British. Like every Berliner, she had found the experience of the air raids terrifying and deeply debilitating. Now, perversely and naively, as the Russians advanced she felt: "Thank God they're coming at last. All this will soon be over."

BY THE AFTERNOON of 16 April, Stalin was displaying audible impatience with Zhukov's progress. "So you've underestimated the enemy on the Berlin axis," he said irritably, when the marshal reported by telephone. "Things are going better for Konev." The 1st Ukrainian Front had pushed ahead from its bridgeheads and was now swinging north towards the German capital. Zhukov reacted to Stalin's jibes with characteristic ruthlessness. He ordered formation commanders personally to lead the attacks on the Seelow defences, and warned that further failures would be rewarded with instant dismissal. He took the drastic step of committing armoured divisions even before his infantry had achieved a breakthrough. There was no tactical subtlety here, no signs of a great captain manoeuvring forces with imagination. This was merely a clumsy battering ram, thrusting repeatedly and at fearsome cost against the German defences, as Zhukov vented his own frustrations in the lives of his men. "The worst performances have been those of Sixty-ninth Army, First and Second Guards Tank Armies," he declared furiously, in a circular to all commanders. "These forces possess colossal strength, yet for two days have been fighting unskilfully and indecisively. Army commanders are not watching what is going on—they are skulking six miles behind the front." He ordered that all army commanders should move their command posts to corps headquarters, and likewise that every corps commander should now direct operations from a divisional or brigade HQ. "Any commander who shows himself unable to fulfil his task will be replaced by an abler and braver man," railed the marshal on 18 April. "Tanks and infantry cannot expect the artillery to kill all the Germans! Show no mercy. Keep moving day and night!" The commander of Ninth Guards Tank Army was lacerated for weakness, formally reprimanded and told: "By nightfall on 19 April, you will secure the Freudenberg area at any cost."

The egos of two ferociously ambitious marshals were committed. They were taunted and goaded to a frenzy of rivalry by their master in Moscow, ever willing to exploit any human frailty to achieve his purposes. Whatever is said of Montgomery's vanity, he would never have killed men to satisfy it. On the outskirts of Berlin, however, Russians were dying in their thousands to satisfy an urgency that was not tactical but entirely vainglorious. Zhukov dispatched some patrols not to find Germans but to discover how far Konev's men had got. Konev, in his turn, incited his tank leaders: "Marshal Zhukov's troops are now within six miles of the eastern outskirts of Berlin. I order you to be the first to break into the city tonight!"

Russian dead lay heaped in front of the defences, in a fashion that echoed the worst horrors of the earlier world war. Wounded men were untended for hours on the battlefield, as the scanty Soviet medical services were overwhelmed. The dead lay unburied for days. Zhukov's headquarters ordered prisoners and civilians to be conscripted to remove them, lest epidemic disease be added to the horrors of battle. There were repeated friendly-fire incidents, as Soviet aircraft attacked or shelled their own units in the confusion. This difficulty was soon to worsen, as artillery fire from Konev's and Zhukov's armies began to cross the other's lines. Command and control faltered and even broke down, as Soviet commanders lost sight of their own men.

By sheer weight of fire and numbers, the Red Army ground down the exhausted defenders. German ammunition supplies began to fail. By the evening of 19 April, 1st Belorussian Front had broken through all the German outer defences and was closing on Berlin. Next day, Zhukov's artillery began to fire on the city. The capture of the Seelow Heights had cost the Germans 12,000 dead, the Russians 30,000. In the north, Rokossovsky's armies were pressing the German forces on the lower Oder. Konev reached the Spree and overran OKH headquarters at Zossen. His men found the teleprinters still rattling out messages from the surviving fragments of Hitler's armies. The triumphant Konev begged Moscow to allow him to turn his two tank armies northwards, towards the capital. Stalin acceded.

Zhukov was now seriously alarmed that his rival marshal would defeat him in the race for Berlin. "In the course of three days the infantry have advanced 16 miles," he signalled one of his armoured commanders, "and all this time the tanks have been dragging along behind them." His officers were enraged to learn that the advance of some formations was being held up as men turned aside to loot. Some of the worst offenders in support units were transferred on the spot to rifle companies. Late on 20 April, Zhukov urged the commanders of his two Guards Tank Armies to the fulfilment of "a historic task: to break into Berlin first and to raise the banner of victory." Soviet tank brigades entered the outskirts of Hitler's capital next evening, the 21st. Zhukov urged them on, using the very goad Stalin had applied to himself and Konev: "Due to the slowness of our advance, the Allies are approaching Berlin and will soon take it." Yet in built-up areas Soviet tanks found themselves as vulnerable to teenagers with fausts as their counterparts in Eisenhower's armies. Zhukov pushed forward "fighting reconnaissance groups"—his penal companies, though these had been reduced to strengths of fifteen or twenty men in sacrificial actions at the Oder.

Even when the Russians began to bombard the streets, for many Berliners the need to find food overcame fear. They continued to queue at local shops as shells fell around them. "In Wilmersdorf, the local situation became acute about April 20th, a Friday," wrote a Berlin housewife. "On the weekend, the firing came nearer and the streets grew very empty, except for women doggedly queueing for food, and occasional German tanks seeking or avoiding Russian outposts. On Monday, the ticket collector from our railway station got killed in a cigarette queue. On Tuesday morning, a shell swept over the bridge just as I was crossing it, and destroyed a baker's shop with some of the people in it." Germany's Ministry of Foreign Affairs signalled its foreign missions: "Owing to the gravity of the situation and especially to administrative difficulties, the greater part of the Ministry has been moved to other quarters." Missions were asked to confine their future transmissions to matters of urgent importance.

From the evening of 21 April onwards, Zhukov's tanks were inching forward street by street, paying a price for every intersection. All-arms attack groups composed of tanks, infantry and assault guns worked in tandem, each supported by its own engineer and flamethrower platoons. The guns were responsible for blasting away buildings identified as centres of resistance. Then it was the business of infantry to occupy the debris and mop up. In the streets of Berlin, it was impossible to prevail by firepower alone. German soldiers holding positions in thick rubble were impregnable to anything save a direct hit. Progress could be made only by close-quarters fighting. Casualties on both sides were dreadful. "The first really wounded man I saw," wrote a German housewife manning a Red Cross shelter, "was a boy who came straight from the street running, running, with the whole lower half of his face blown away, a bloody gap, no organ of speech left to scream, and his eyes still fully aware and sick with horror."

Rokossovsky's men of 2nd Belorussian Front were now pushing towards Berlin from the north. In the south, Konev lashed his own men on. "Third Guards Tank Army is conducting itself like a tape worm," he signalled on 20 April: "one brigade is fighting and all the rest are creeping along behind." Its commander was ordered to attack on a broader front. "Your formation has systematically disobeyed orders," he told the leader of XXXVIII Corps on 21 April. "You seem afraid to attack. You overestimate the power of the enemy, and underrate your own. You treat every patch of woodland as a major obstacle. If you cannot do better than this, I shall have you sacked." Zhukov echoed this brutal refrain: "I keep being told that operations are appallingly badly organized, that units are not properly deployed for street fighting," he told his spearhead leaders on 22 April. "Fight around the clock—use searchlights!"

There was now a serious risk that Konev's and Zhukov's men would find themselves killing each other. Tanks of 1st Ukrainian Front were fighting their way into the southern suburbs of Berlin, after advancing more than a hundred miles from the Neisse in six days. To avert a collision, on 22 April Stalin imposed demarcation lines. Konev was ordered to advance towards the Anhalter railway station, halting some 150 yards short of the Reichstag and Hitler's bunker. It would, after all, become Zhukov's privilege, dearly bought by his soldiers, to seize the symbolic bastions of the Third Reich. This was bitterly resented by Konev's officers. When one of them at last met Chuikov, Zhukov's man, he protested that Chuikov was encroaching on 1st Ukrainian Front's patch: "We're advancing here!" Chuikov shrugged indifferently: "Sorry, I've got my own orders." Thus did the cacophony of clashing egos compete with that of gunfire on the streets of Berlin.

The filth, stench and gloom in the shelters grew worse by the hour, as water supplies collapsed. Generators provided power only for a few hours, if at all. One of the largest shelters, the Anhalter Bahnhof next to the main station, housed 12,000 people in conditions so hideously cramped that they were unable to move, even to relieve themselves, for days on end. Even fetching water was a deadly business, when the station was among the principal targets for Soviet guns. At a local street shelter in a residential area, in one corner a woman fortunate enough to possess supplies brewed coffee or "stretched the soup," as she called it. In another, people were urinating or defecating, because it was unthinkable to face the hell in the streets above to address the demands of nature. One of those tending the wounded in a Red Cross shelter was the British wife of a Berliner. On the evening of 27 April, an SS major arrived at the head of several hundred men, demanding to take over the shelter, evict its wretched occupants and create a defensive position. She argued desperately with him, all the time terrified that someone would cry out: "She's English!" At last, he went away. Soon afterwards one of her charges, a Ukrainian girl, went into labour amid the relentless shelling above. The baby was born at five past eight on the morning of 28 April, It was christened Piotr, and laid in an office filing tray. Then an elderly local gardener came in, with six holes in his back, "one as big as your hand." As they strove to dress his wounds, he told his story. He and his wife had sheltered from the barrage in the garden shed on their allotment, until a near-miss blew the entire structure away, tore his clothes to rags and inflicted hideous shrapnel wounds. His wife died on the spot from a heart attack. The man clutched his only undamaged possession, a red and purple bowtie. "I love that tie," he said, gazing wonderingly upon it as the world collapsed. "But I must give it away, now that I am in mourning." Bullets sometimes whipped for thousands of yards across empty air until somewhere in the city, far from immediate fighting, they found a billet in flesh or masonry. A woman sitting up in the bed where she had taken refuge beside her husband, with no sense of imminent peril, was killed by a round fired a mile or more away, which ricocheted off the wall. A pall of dust and smoke shrouded the whole city, as street by street the battle seeped into its remotest recesses.

Hitler raved on 23 April: "The enemy knows I am here. That could provide the best opportunity for us to lead him into a trap here...Everyone must work honestly!" The Army Chief of Staff, Hans Krebs, said: "I believe we still have four days." Hitler said: "In four days, the thing will have been decided." By 25 April, Berlin was entirely encircled. A total of 464,000 Soviet troops, supported by 12,700 guns, 1,500 tanks and 21,000 Katyusha mountings, were deployed for the last act. By 27 April, the German perimeter had shrunk to an area some ten miles long by three wide, from which billowing clouds of smoke rose into the sky. Berliners now called their city the *Reichsscheiterhaufen*—"funeral pyre of the Reich." Zhukov's men achieved an important tactical triumph for their commander by forestalling Konev's tanks to reach the Landwehr Canal, in front of the Tiergarten. The 1st Ukrainian Front swung west, to clear the further side of the city, to the intense disappointment of Konev and his officers. Zhukov was left alone to complete the destruction of the last few acres of ruined streets, monuments and public buildings which remained to Hitler's empire.

Some 45,000 German soldiers maintained the defence, along with 40,000 Volkssturm and 3,000 children of the Hitler Jugend. Foremost among this forlorn hope were men of foreign SS units gathered around the bunker, the government buildings of the Wilhelmstrasse, the Reich Chancellery. Balts, Frenchmen, Scandinavians and Walloons wearing Himmler's runes on their tunics knew that they were a legion of the dead, beyond hope of mercy. Their will to resist was reinforced by SS squads which roamed the streets hanging from the lampposts every man who sought to quit. The defenders of Berlin knew that they must fight and die, or hang and die.

Hitler spent a sleepless night on 26 April, amid the relentless shelling and bombing. He told his military conference next morning: "Today I will lie down a little more at ease, and I only want to be awakened if a Russian tank is standing in front of my room, so I have time to make my preparations." The first of these, of course, was his marriage to Eva Braun. An NKVD team sent to Berlin with the explicit mission of searching for Hitler or his corpse arrived in the city on 29 April with little expectation that they would have work to do. The Russians were convinced that Hitler would flee before the Red Army reached his bunker—indeed, that he had probably already done so. As the Russian team drove in darkness to the Red Army's tactical headquarters through the shattered streets, the first thought of their interpreter Yelena Kogan was that the anti-tank ditches looked exactly like the ones tens of thousands of Russians, including herself, had dug around Moscow three years earlier. "The whole scene was apocalyptic," she said, "relentless gunfire, searchlights probing the sky, burning and collapsing buildings caught in their beams." At Army headquarters, the NKVD group sat down patiently to await the outcome of the battle. The only seat Yelena could find was a petrol can, on which she passed many of the hours that followed.

The first flimsy news of Hitler reached the Russians in unexpected fashion. A prisoner was brought in—a civilian ventilation engineer. He said that he had been called to the bunker to repair a fault in its air-circulation system. The man was sullen, numb, monosyllabic. Patiently, they questioned him. "There was a wedding yesterday," he declared suddenly. "The Führer married Eva Braun." They looked at him as if he was mad. How could there be a wedding, in the heart of Berlin, in these last days? The NKVD team did not believe a word of it.

Even in the midst of this climactic battle alcoholic excess, the curse of the Red Army, provoked grotesque incidents. Zhukov's military prosecutor recorded an episode on 27 April, when the commander of LXXXV Tank Corps became drunk and ordered German women to be brought to him, whom he raped. When Russian soldiers approached his headquarters, he mistook them for Germans and ordered a self-propelled gun to open fire, killing four men and wounding six. The court-martial case against him had to be dropped, allegedly for "lack of proof." From the top, real efforts were being made to stem the manic indiscipline threatening military operations, yet among the fighting formations such matters were still not arousing concern. Zhukov's headquarters reported that "commanders are taking serious steps to stop 'improper behaviour,' but some still delude themselves that the situation is under control." The Red Army's rampage in Berlin began long before the battle was over.

Private Bruno Bochum was one of those German soldiers who possessed no stomach for a hero's death. He was crewing a 105mm gun emplaced in a tank turret by Tegel airfield on the north-west side of Berlin. "It was crazy! There was no real command." Their gun possessed only ten rounds of ammunition. They fired it once, at a low-flying aircraft strafing the runway. On 26 April, a Russian tank clattered past the rear of their position, laden with tommy-gunners. The Germans could have fired at it, but decided that discretion was the better part of survival. The gun crew agreed to scatter and make for a rendezvous in the Grünewald, the woodland west of the city. Bochum set off with one comrade through empty streets, moving in a series of sprints and cautious halts, listening to the artillery fire. They reached the Olympic Stadium, where they found many other stragglers, and lay down exhausted to sleep on its stepped tiers. At first light next day, they set off again. After desultory encounters with Russian patrols, they chanced upon a Wehrmacht headquarters. Bochum was taken before a general, whom he found reading the Roman author Livy amid a mounting artillery barrage. The general questioned him about his personal service; presented him on the spot with the Iron Cross, Second Class; and entrusted him with command of thirty-six men on the south of their modest perimeter.

Bochum thought: "What on earth is the point of this foolishness now?" But, like so many German soldiers for so many years past, he did what he was told. They started digging. Then Bochum fell asleep. When he woke next morning, only two men of his command remained, to defend a frontage of 600 yards. There was small-arms fire on all sides—the Russians were well beyond them. A Katyusha salvo landed close by. A fragment of shrapnel embedded itself in Bochum's purse, and another opened his neck. He found somebody to bandage his wound, then returned to find his two-man command still in their positions. "Throw away your weapons," he told them. "It's over."

The difficulty now was to find someone to whom he might surrender. He met a Russian riding an American Harley-Davidson motorcycle who refused to notice him. He walked cautiously onwards until he rounded a corner and saw a T-34, its crew standing around it, obviously extremely drunk. He took out the white handkerchief he had carried since 6 June 1944 for this very situation, and advanced with his hands high in the air, clutching his symbol of surrender. He was amazed when the first Russian he reached embraced him warmly before taking his watch. "*Wonia kaputt!*" announced the Russian joyously. "The war's over!" This statement was, of course, premature. But it sufficed for these Red soldiers that their own part was done. Bochum was taken into a headquarters where another Russian presented him with a box of cigars, and led him to an officer frying chicken. He was briskly interrogated by a Jewish soldier who spoke perfect German. Then he was pushed into a room full of officer prisoners, where he spent the night. As Bochum joined a long, long column of PoWs being escorted to imprisonment next morning, he merely felt profound relief that his own war was over, that he had survived. "I had my first good rest for weeks, free of fear."

Johannes and Regina Krakowitz seldom left the basement of their apartment building at Gohenstrasse 5, in the eastern part of Berlin, after 20 April, Hitler's birthday. There were perhaps fifty occupants, united in misery and fear. It was their good fortune that there was a butcher's shop on the ground floor. Once during the battle, miraculously the shop had meat. The basement-dwellers risked everything to join the queue. Though one man was injured by shrapnel, they got something to eat, and thought themselves lucky. At moments of desperate need, the Krakowitzes climbed upstairs to their flat to use the lavatory or wash, for as long as water remained available. Otherwise, "we sat in that cellar as if we were paralysed." There were too few chairs, so they took it in turns to sit down. There was Frau Bloch and her son, the Krakowitzes' neighbours. The boy was twenty, and no one could imagine how he had escaped military service. Herr Wendt, who owned a little soap shop, was there—a small man with a comically larger wife. They played gin rummy hour after hour, day after day. Herr Scalimper, a dairy owner, had been drafted unwillingly to join his Volkssturm unit, but his wife and mother were in the cellar, sharing the terrors. When the occupants talked at all, which was seldom, they discussed banal matters, such as what commodities it was possible to buy with ration stamps. The thunder of gunfire and explosions came closer every hour, until someone came down to say that the Russians were at the Prenzlauerallee S-Bahn station, just 200 yards away. That afternoon, 29 April, Hitler and Eva Braun killed themselves in the *Führerbunker*. Their bodies were burned by Otto Günsche, the SS adjutant.

Everywhere across the city, human flotsam was suing for mercy, some less deserving than others. A deputation of diplomats from the Japanese embassy, whose nation was still not at war with Russia, appeared at Soviet headquarters to demand protection, and the return of its looted property, including three cars. A cluster of Ukrainian women saw a Volkssturm man raise a white sheet, only to be killed by his own commander. A Wehrmacht officer emerged from a tunnel to negotiate the safe passage of 1,100 civilians sheltering in the darkness. When he had seen them delivered into the custody of Soviet submachine gunners, he announced that he was returning to his own soldiers, in fulfilment of his military oath. A Soviet officer drew a pistol and shot him down.

On the morning of 30 April, a refugee in the basement of the Krakowitzes' apartment building braved the journey upstairs to listen to a radio. The man returned to declare solemnly, yet in a voice somehow drained of emotion, that the Russians occupied their street. Regina Krakowitz thought simply: "Thank God there will be no more bombing and shelling." Slowly and cautiously, they crept up from their shelter to find that the battle was dying out. Frau Krakowitz was not raped, for which she was forever grateful. "We came through it pretty lucky," she said laconically. Others did not. Margrit Hug was marched by three Russians from the cellar in which she had been cowering for a week and taken to a chemist's cellar: "Was pushed to the ground, some clothes torn off me," she wrote in her diary. "[They] took it in turns to hold the torch. I am not 18."

All that day of 30 April, Russian troops fought yard by yard towards the Reichstag and Kroll Opera House, against a storm of German fire. Smoke and dust rendered it hard to see more than a few hundred yards across the battlefield. So many men fell attempting to cross open ground that the Russians sometimes despaired of making the final breakthrough. More and more tanks and self-propelled guns were brought forward. Perhaps 10,000 German defenders remained within their perimeter. It seemed so hard to kill men dug into positions of masonry and rubble. Late that evening, at desperate risk two men of 756th Regiment, Mikhail Yegorov and Meliton Kantaria, climbed into the dome of the pitted and blasted Reichstag and hoisted the Red victory banner. In the early hours of 1 May, General Krebs, who had succeeded Guderian as Army Chief of Staff, went forward to the Russian lines and attempted to parley with the commander of Eighth Guards Army, the former defender of Stalingrad, about surrender terms. Absurdly, the German appeared to delude himself that, now Hitler was gone, the Allies would be willing to negotiate with a successor regime. After consultations with Stalin and Zhukov, Krebs was brutally informed that only total capitulation was acceptable. He returned to his headquarters. That evening the Russians launched a devastating new barrage against the remaining German perimeter. Next morning, the commander of LVI Panzer Corps requested a ceasefire. At 1500 on the afternoon of 2 May, the Russian guns fell silent. Some 125,000 Berliners had died in the battle. Krebs killed himself.

"The Germans who fought to the last weren't the old men—they were surrendering in their thousands, generals and soldiers together," said Major Yury Ryakhovsky. "It was the young ones who went on and on." In Berlin on 30 April, he was told of a twelve-year-old German boy who had destroyed twelve Soviet tanks with Panzerfausts. "We had never really understood just what the fausts could do. There were piles of them everywhere. Boys were firing at T-34s from a range of two or three metres. You could get nowhere in a straight line—you had to zig-zag everywhere, to and fro across the streets."

"It seemed so strange, when the end was so close, that these young boys were resisting so fiercely," said Lieutenant Vasily Filimonenko. When at last it was all over, he watched enemy soldiers advancing nervously from their positions to surrender, crying *"Hitler kaputt! Hitler kaputt!"*—the Wehrmacht's mantra of renunciation. The Russian officer remembered earlier days, when even in captivity the arrogance of Hitler's soldiers was undimmed. They would tell their captors sneeringly: "You're all for it, you know."

When Yury Ryakhovsky reached the ruins of the Reichstag, he could not bring himself to emulate thousands of Russian soldiers who had already scrawled their names on the walls. "I disliked the idea of behaving like a tourist. We were not there as tourists, I thought." But when Captain Vasily Krylov saw his cousin Nikolai's signature among the mass of graffiti, he wrote beneath it: "I was here, too." Krylov said: "I felt great satisfaction, looking on Berlin. Our vengeance had come. Even when I saw Dresden, I thought: this, also, was right." Filimonenko cherished the end in Hitler's capital as the greatest moment of his life: "Ever since 1941, I had always dreamed of surviving to walk into Berlin." Of a hundred men with whom he had completed his artillery training course in 1940, just three survived to celebrate victory.

Between 16 April and 8 May, the fronts of Zhukov, Konev and Rokossovsky lost 352,425 men, by far the heaviest casualty toll of the battle for Germany.* More than 100,000 of these men were dead. The capture of Berlin displayed outstanding generalship by Konev, not by Zhukov. In his yearning for glory and in his desperation to satisfy Stalin, 1st Belorussian Front's commander battered the enemy into submission through human sacrifice, not manoeuvre. Stalin and the Red Army gained their symbolic triumph, in a fashion and at a cost that no Western ally could envy. Hitler had desired that his own death should be wreathed in the sacrifice of hundreds of thousands of lesser mortals. Zhukov

---

*First Belorussian Front, 179,490 casualties; 2nd Belorussian Front, 59,110; 1st Ukrainian Front, 113,825.

indulged him, making the battle for Berlin a clash of two prehistoric animals, butting and writhing for mastery in a welter of blood, until the lesser beast at last succumbed to its wounds and toppled among the ruins.

A Berlin housewife emerged from her shelter at midday on 2 May, for the first time since 25 April. Firing was still audible in the distance.

> It was raining, and felt very cold. Our legs felt very queer, walking in the street. Berlin as far as the eye could see was a smoking, smouldering ruin. Dead men lay on the ground, and the living clambered over them carrying bedding and household articles. We went back to the shelter to fetch our things, and a mother and child from the Ukraine. Her house had gone, and I was going to nurse her at home. At the entrance was a Russian lieutenant. He said: "Now the war is over." We said: "Thank God."

The mother of Margrit and Karla Hug, both of whom had been repeatedly raped, took a different view. "Mutti decided she did not want any more humiliation and shame for Karla and me," Margrit wrote in her diary for 1 May,

> and took us to the flat where we each drank four cups of Cinzano (after the chemist failed to persuade Mutti that it was not the time to end our lives). I said goodbye to friends and to Franzel, my brother...On the roof, we sat at the edge feet dangling down. Our house has six storeys. Mutti sat behind us, saying, "Jump, girls, jump." I wondered why I did not fall. I wanted to, feeling very drowsy. I saw Vati [her father] standing down below, looking up, shouting: "Don't do it!" The roof of the next house was burning. Bits of burning tar landed on Karla's dress. She cried and moved on to a safer place. A neighbour appeared, and persuaded Mutti not to make us jump.

Yet many, many did kill themselves.

"Nothing is left of Berlin but memories," Lieutenant Gennady Ivanov, one of the more reflective officers in the Red Army, wrote to his parents. "I would never have believed that a great city could be reduced to mere rubble. It seems so strange, after four years of gunfire, now to hear not a single shot around us." It is impossible to dispute the truth of one of Goebbels's last pronouncements before the murder of his children and his own suicide alongside his wife: "The earth will shake as we leave the scene."

CHAPTER SIXTEEN

The Bitter End

RETRIBUTION

"THE GERMANY IN which we found ourselves travelling at the end of April," wrote the correspondent Alan Moorehead, "presented a scene that was almost beyond human comprehension. Around us fifty great cities lay in ruins...Many had no electric light or power or gas or running water, and no coherent system of government. Like ants in an ant-heap the people scurried over the ruins, diving furtively into cellars and doorways in search of loot...Everyone was on the move, and there was a frantic ant-like quality about their activities. Life was sordid, aimless, leading nowhere."

Almost every factory chimney in the greatest industrial society in western Europe stood cold and still. Businesses lay empty, for what business could be done? No trains ran. Refugees huddled in overcrowded ruins, feeding on soup, potatoes and despair. No vessels save Allied warships moved in the ports. The roads were clogged with stony-faced people: soldiers in tattered uniforms or ill-fitting civilian clothes creeping home; families fleeing from the Russians; freed prisoners and slave labourers roaming the landscape in search of freedom, revenge or booty. Thick dust, generated by countless millions of explosive concussions from end to end of Germany, lay upon everything—windows, furniture, vehicles, houses, corpses, living people. The victors observed that a physical pallor of defeat possessed the faces of Germans, a compound of hunger, exhaustion and fear for the future. Among young and old alike, laughter had become a redundant sensation.

The orgy of looting, destruction and rape which followed the Red Army's triumph in Berlin and across the rest of eastern Germany seemed to Stalin a just recompense to his soldiers for their labour, and a fitting chastisement for the German people. The Imperial Japanese Army had been behaving in similar fashion in China since 1937. Napoleon's soldiers likewise shamed the name of France during their campaign in Spain a century and a half before. But nothing on the scale of the Soviet terror had been seen in Europe since the seventeenth century. "It was bitter to learn that Goebbels's propaganda had been factual and accurate," wrote the Danish journalist Paul von Stemann. "It was not that a sex-starved Russian soldier forced himself upon a girl who took his fancy. It was a destructive, hateful and wholesale act of vengeance. Age or looks were irrelevant. The grandmother was no safer than the granddaughter, the ugly and filthy no more than the fresh and attractive." Von Stemann protested to a Soviet officer about the rapes he witnessed all around him. "Keep out of this," the soldier told him sternly. "Just leave it alone. It has nothing to do with you." Most Russians, then and later, excused what took place. Valentin Krulik shrugged: "People had so much hatred to work off."

Ursula Siwik, wife of Hans who was once among Hitler's bodyguard, was raped three times by Russian soldiers in Berlin. Siwik, outraged, said without any hint of irony: "No German soldier would have behaved as they did." Waltraut Ptack, a thirteen-year-old who had escaped with her mother, brother and sister from East Prussia, was huddled with her family in an abandoned seaside villa in Pomerania when the Red Army came. They heard women screaming in nearby houses, then two Russians kicked open their own door. One spoke German. "*Hitler kaputt!*" he said. Then he began to harangue the cringing little group about Germany's crimes in Russia. Waltraut said: "It was so awful having to listen to all this, when we knew that we had done nothing wrong. It wasn't us who had done these things." The Russians raped her mother.

The family lived in unbroken fear through the weeks that followed. They were conscripted to work as forced labourers on a farm. The women never undressed, nor went anywhere alone. Once, they were all herded into a barn, and assumed that they were going to be shot. Instead, as part of a clumsy programme of de-Nazification, they were compelled to watch a Soviet propaganda film with Hitler and his colleagues played by comic actors: "We were meant to laugh, to see how ridiculous they were, but we simply sat frozen with fear."

Nineteen-year-old Helga Braunschweig sat in a cellar with her mother and some twenty other women in a village just outside Berlin through the long, terrifying days of the battle. When at last the shooting died, they emerged thankfully from their refuge, to find Russians outside, eagerly shaking hands and saying: "War finished!" Then soldiers began to set up their cry of "*Uri! Uri!*" The German women were bemused, and at first disbelieving. Then they bowed to the inevitable, and surrendered their watches and jewellery. The Russians' mood became visibly less inhibited and more dangerous. The German woman retreated to their cellar. The older ones urged the younger to dirty their faces and even to smear them with egg yolk. Then a Russian officer entered, and pointed to several Germans in succession: "You! And you! And you!" Helga's mother pleaded with the Russian: "Leave my daughter. Take me." She was ignored. The girl was a virgin, for although she and her boyfriend Wolfgang had often passionately kissed they had never made love. Now, she unwillingly obeyed the Russian's instructions to follow him upstairs, strip and get on the bed. "I thought I had no choice."

The women in their hamlet had supposed that they would be safe if they stuck together. Discovering their mistake, one family killed themselves. By contrast, a committed Nazi among the women now sought favour by offering herself to the conquerors. Helga observed of those days: "What happened in the huge city of Berlin was somehow anonymous. But in our little community, everything seemed somehow so horribly personal." After the first Russian incursion, Helga and her mother hid in the attic of a house for ten days. "Red soldiers during the first weeks of their occupation raped every woman and girl between the ages of twelve and sixty," a British PoW liberated in Pomerania testified. "That sounds exaggerated, but it is the simple truth. The only exceptions were girls who managed to remain in hiding in the woods, or who had the presence of mind to feign ... some infectious disease."

The grotesque comedies precipitated by the Red Army's addiction to alcohol continued even now. On the night of 2 May, the Russian commandant of Lodz became drunk and ordered the city's sirens to be switched on to celebrate the fall of Berlin. This caused panic. Anti-aircraft gunners opened fire, believing there was an air raid, which in turn provoked a flight of civilians. Russian soldiers manning roadblocks saw cars and civilians hastening towards them and supposed themselves under attack. They began shooting, killing and wounding dozens of people. The NKVD arrested the commandant.

Many Russians found in the service of the Wehrmacht were summarily dispatched. "Vlassov's men were kicked to death on the spot," said Gennady Ivanov. "In general, we tried to persuade men not to kill prisoners, but it was very hard. We were living an existence in which people's lives had absolutely no value. All that seemed important was to stay alive and look after oneself." A day or two before the end, Valentin Krulik was ordered to take twenty-five men to accept the surrender of a large body of Germans waiting in their trucks down the road. When he reached the column, he was alarmed to find himself among so many fully armed enemy soldiers. He gestured the German column to follow him into the Russian lines and walked ahead of them until they reached a field headquarters. "What's in the trucks?" an officer demanded. "Germans," answered the lieutenant. "Then get them out of the vehicles, and take them 500 metres into the fields." Krulik never asked what happened to the prisoners, but he guessed.

There were anguished protests from German communists that when they joyfully revealed themselves to their Soviet deliverers they were treated no better than Nazis. Yelena Kogan, the NKVD interpreter in Berlin, saw a man standing with his pregnant wife shouting: "Hooray! The filthy fascists have been smashed by the workers!" His Soviet listeners responded scathingly: "Where

were all you German workers when Germany invaded Russia?" Vasily Filimonenko felt no trace of pity for the Germans. "Let us not kid ourselves—they had
attacked our country. They deserved everything they got." The son of dirt-
poor, illiterate peasants from a village near Novgorod, he had fought for four
long years. His seventeen-year-old sister Evdokia had died as a nurse at Stalingrad. He was outraged, much later, when Germany was allowed to build a war
memorial in Russia, "on land steeped in our blood. It is not a matter of
vengeance, but of justice, the memory of the devastating pain of our country.
For the sake of all our people who died, the war crimes of Germany can never
be forgiven."

Yelena Kogan said: "What the Red Army did in Germany was the darkest
stain on its record in the war." As the first revelations of Russian behaviour, of
the reign of terror sweeping the east, began to seep through to the Western
allies, many American and British soldiers were baffled. Since 1941, they had
been urged to think so warmly of their ally "Uncle Joe." Captain David Fraser
wrote cynically: "The British people were surprised and shocked at that time to
discover that many European peoples regarded the Soviet regime and the Red
Army with a horror and alarm greater than that previously aroused by Nazi
Germany. Any sympathy with the victims of the Bolsheviks...smacked of
incipient leniency to the Germans."

Dorothea Goesse, wife of an Austrian officer of the Wehrmacht's Cossacks,
stood in the middle of the border town of Klagenfurt and watched the British
Army march in. Then, from the opposite direction, she saw approaching a column of Yugoslav communist partisans: "They looked like Ali Baba and his Forty
Thieves." She remembered what her father had said, long ago in September
1939: "A terrible time is coming." Almost six years later, it had arrived. "For us,"
said Dorothea Goesse, whose family had occupied the same castle for 300 years,
"a world was drowning."

HITLER'S DEATH ensured that the end would soon come, but did not itself
terminate the dying. At no single moment did every corner of the German,
Czech, Dutch, Scandinavian, Baltic and Yugoslav battlefields fall silent. Rather,
the struggle stuttered to an end in one corner of Europe after another during the
first two weeks of May, as one by one Hitler's commanders succumbed to the
inevitable. Even as some Russian soldiers, victorious in Berlin, were addressing
themselves to the fruits of victory, elsewhere they were obliged to fight fiercely,
not against an enemy aspiring to victory, but against Germans preferring death
to Soviet captivity. A total of 3,404,950 of Hitler's soldiers were disarmed following the final surrender. Most of these men, it may be assumed, were still offering
at least nominal resistance to the Allies after the fall of Berlin.

On the evening of 1 May, from his headquarters at Plön in north Germany,

Grand-Admiral Karl Dönitz announced on German radio the death of Hitler and his own appointment as the Führer's designated successor:

> German men and women, soldiers of the German armed forces! Our Führer, Adolf Hitler, has fallen. In deepest grief and respect the German people bow. He early recognized the frightful danger of Bolshevism and dedicated his being to this struggle. At the end of this, his struggle, and his unswerving life's path, stands his hero's death in the capital of the German Reich. His life was a unique service for Germany. His mission in the battle against the Bolshevist storm-flood is valid for Europe and the entire civilized world. The Führer has appointed me as his successor. In consciousness of the responsibility, I take over the leadership of the German *Volk* at this fateful hour.

An element of black farce was thus introduced to a tragedy. Instead of seizing the opportunity to offer an immediate capitulation and save thousands of lives, Dönitz's mockery of a government permitted the killing to go on for a further week. The admiral sought negotiations with the Western allies, while striving to sustain resistance to the Russians. Capital sentences for desertion and mutiny continued to be carried out. On the Eastern Front, men fought on, unable to perceive any way to stop.

"I did not mourn Hitler," said Captain Karl Godau of 10th SS Panzer, "but we felt that his death meant the end of everything. We simply could not imagine what might happen next. After all the threats that the Allies had made against Germany, one could not believe that anything good would follow." Maria Brauwers of Jünkerath, however, grieved when she heard of Hitler's passing: "I knew nothing about the Holocaust. But I remembered that the Führer had done many good things before the war, especially for those of us who were young."

Corporal Helmut Fromm, a sixteen-year-old soldier from Heidelberg, shared the agony of the encircled Ninth Army in the fields and forests south of Berlin after the city had fallen and Hitler was dead. In their thousands, some in organized bodies and others alone, they trudged westwards, like some gigantic armed football crowd dispersing after a match, fighting Russians wherever they met them. The roads and surrounding countryside were jammed with fugitives, constantly attacked by Soviet aircraft. Sharing their misery were scores of thousands of civilian refugees of both sexes and all ages, clutching pitiful possessions. The remains of Fromm's unit was commanded by a young Luftwaffe lieutenant, and included two women in army uniform. As they reached a ride in a forest, they suddenly saw two Soviet tanks, which fired at them. "Quick!" said their officer. "Run across while they're reloading!" One of the women stopped dead in the midst of the ride, staring "like a paralysed rabbit" at the T-34 before her. "Run, you silly bitch!" shouted the officer. He raced out and dragged her into the trees. On and on they marched. No one thought of fighting, only of reaching the American lines. Yet when they reached Halle and found Russians, they felt that all hope was gone. Darkness was coming on. Shells were falling all around them. Fromm saw a Russian infantryman shooting down on them from a church tower, and fired a futile burst at the man from his machine-pistol: "It seemed that the world was coming to an end."

He joined several men sheltering behind a slow-moving Tiger. There was a heavy explosion. Stunned, Fromm reached for his Schmeisser and found it plastered with the intestines of his neighbour. He threw away the gun in revulsion. They laid a groaning teenager on the hull of a tank and plunged on into the woods. The Tiger tracks rolled impassively over men lying wounded in its path. Fromm was surprised how unaffected he was by their plight. He felt drained of all sentiment save the urge to survive. He abandoned the sluggish tank to follow an officer whom he saw studying a map by torchlight, because such a man seemed likely to know where he was going. There were soldiers milling everywhere. Suddenly, a shadow loomed ahead in the darkness. A dozen guns were raised. The faceless figure said: "If you start shooting at me, you're all dead, but if you stick to this path, you'll get through."

Early in the morning, however, they found themselves under fire again. Fromm had picked up another weapon, but buried himself as deep as he could behind a log pile. "Don't be so feeble," said an SS man scornfully. "Get up where you've got a field of fire." The boy's gun was jammed with sand. He hurled it aside. At last they moved on, sleep-walking. As night came again, they reached a village. "We'll get through if we run," said an SS man who proved to have a mutual friend with Fromm in Heidelberg. There was a nightmare moment when one German ran into a huge Russian emerging from a cottage. Both men exclaimed in shock and fled in opposite directions. Next morning, as Fromm rested exhausted by the roadside, he saw a VW *Schwimmwagen* race by, bearing a Luftwaffe general adorned with decorations. The boy felt fiercely angry: here was one of the leaders who had brought them all to this, riding in a car while soldiers walked. It was too much. He clambered to his feet and staggered on, almost comatose.

Many Allied soldiers found it confusing to spend the last days of the war fighting children. A British Bren-gunner firing into a house defended by Hitler Jugend trained his weapon on a side door from which it was plain that, sooner or later, the cornered defenders would try to escape. A few minutes later, a figure dashed out. After a burst of Bren fire, the German fell writhing and screaming in the midst of the street. As the British soldier pressed the trigger again, he glimpsed the face of a young boy, who slumped in death. "His features have been printed on my mind ever since," said the infantryman. "I have always asked myself: if I hadn't fired the second burst, might that boy have lived to grow into a decent man?"

"The fourteen-year-olds were very dangerous, because they possessed no sense of adult behaviour," said Major Bill Deedes. "They might produce a grenade they had hidden, and throw it after being taken prisoner." Private Walter Brown and his platoon of the U.S. 90th Division were sickened to find that they had shot ten of a group of fifteen German boys firing on them from a mountainside near the Czech border: "we felt like butchers, and yet those bullets would have killed us as dead as those of any SS soldier." A young captive tossed a "potato masher" grenade at the colonel of the Scots Greys on 2 May. The British officer shot him with his pistol. "The rules of war got very fractured in the last phase—we lost three officers to these child soldiers," said Deedes. "Until then, the courtesies had still obtained. But we ceased to extend them to the Hitler Jugend. I became almost more nervous and jumpy than I had been in Normandy. Here one was facing the odd German who would just stay and pick off a couple of one's men not as part of any military plan or organized defence, but on his own initiative. The war became much less formalized and organized, and in some ways more dangerous as a result."

Teenagers often fought on under circumstances in which adult soldiers would have quit. The British found Wunsdorf airfield near Hanover defended by Hitler Youth manning 40mm flak guns, who shot up the point platoon of 13 Para. Sergeant Scott, one of the battalion medical team, rode forward on a motorcycle prominently displaying a red cross. A German bullet shattered his head. Dr. David Tibbs drove forward. A wounded man said: "Please sir, would you remove Sergeant Scott's brain from my tunic." Tibbs laid the ghastly object reverently on the roadside. A Sherman disposed of the German flak-gunners. When Tibbs soon afterwards found himself trying to treat one of the enemy wounded, the teenager spat at him and rolled away. Here, indeed, was a triumph for Goebbels.

On 6 May, a "frightful thug" appeared at the HQ of the British 13th/18th Hussars, wearing a Red Cross armband and claiming to be a refugee. On being searched, he was found to have a pistol, and admitted to being a German marine. The adjutant wrote: "After a certain amount of argument, we decided he was a proper wrong 'un, and he was duly dispatched by firing squad in the garage." Some soldiers' attitudes to such exercises bemused their comrades. Private Ron Gladman noticed that several men in his company of the Hampshires seemed to enjoy service with firing squads to execute alleged spies and malefactors: "They always put on their best battledress."

Field-Marshal von Manstein, perhaps the most brilliant of all Hitler's commanders, disgraced since 1944, had retired to a house in Schleswig-Holstein to await the end. On 3 May, he invited Field-Marshal von Bock to come to tea. Von

Manstein's adjutant was standing outside his commander's manor-house when he saw British fighters machine-gunning a road nearby. Soon after, von Manstein was summoned to a hospital. The strafing aircraft had hit von Bock's car, killing his wife and daughter and mortally wounding the old field-marshal. Von Bock, swathed in bandages, lived long enough to murmur to his visitor: "Manstein, save Germany!"

As late as 3 May, in Hungary German troops were still fighting fiercely. A moment of black farce took place in Valentin Krulik's unit of Sixth Guards Tank Army. The company commander was frying a pan of eggs for some fellow officers when he glanced through the window and saw men running for their lives in the street outside. He told Krulik to investigate. The lieutenant returned to report that German troops were advancing towards their positions. The company commander threw down the skillet and ran outside to check his fleeing soldiers. He fired a tommy-gun burst in the air, which caused them to halt in their tracks. "Boys!" he shouted. "Don't you know what today is? State Loan Day! Unless you get back to your positions, you won't get a kopek!" They returned to the line. "We went on taking casualties right to the very end," said Krulik. "If we hadn't been willing to take the losses, the war might have gone on much longer. We wanted to get this over. Everyone was now desperate to go home."

In those days, the innocence of childhood seemed to assume a quality of madness. An onlooker in the village of Niemegle, in the path of the Soviet advance, saw grim German soldiers trudging up the main street towards the line, watched by children who chattered and laughed euphorically, their lips caked chocolate brown. A local confectionery factory had thrown open its gates and distributed its entire stocks to the villagers before the Russians could reach them.

Gottfried Selzer, a young artilleryman deployed on the Czech border, thanked God that the Russians were too busy with Prague and Berlin to trouble much with his own area. On 6 May, a rumour swept through the unit, in common with much of the Wehrmacht at this time, that the British and Americans intended to arm the Germans to fight the Russians. Two days later, as dusk fell, their commanding officer summoned them all. "It's over, men," he said. "It's every man for himself now, so get home as best you can." The officers rode away on their horses. The soldiers stripped off their insignia and put on white armbands. Then they started walking, among many thousands of others. Selzer was disconcerted "to watch the mighty Wehrmacht falling to pieces in such a fashion." He and a handful of others crossed the Neisse, were briefly imprisoned by Poles from whom they escaped, then were fortunate enough to be ignored by the Russians as they crossed the Elbe. "We fell happily into the hands of the Americans." He reached home to discover that his only surviving brother Alois had died in the battle for Berlin on 29 April. His parents were distraught with mingled grief for one son and relief that another, at least, had come home. "I simply thanked God for being alive myself."

On the morning of 4 May, a delegation of Breslau churchmen called on the military commandant to urge the surrender of the city. Two days later, the city's commander Hermann von Niehoff went out to meet his Soviet counterpart and offered capitulation in return for assurances about the safety of the garrison. That night, the guns fell silent. About a quarter of the inhabitants of Breslau had been killed or wounded in the siege, 30,000 in all. They had inflicted some 60,000 casualties on the Russians. Little of the great old city survived. Von Niehoff refused the chance of escape in a Storch aircraft, preferring to accept captivity with his men. Gauleiter Hanke, however, eagerly seized the opportunity and fled, never to be heard of again. The Soviet occupying forces embarked upon an orgy of plunder and rape in the ruins of Breslau.

In Czechoslovakia, Field-Marshal Schörner, that dedicated Nazi, maintained the struggle to defend the Reich's last important industrial region, at the head of a million men of Army Group Centre. On his western front, Patton's Third Army was already at the Czech border. Russian armies of 2nd and 4th Ukrainian Fronts pressed on Schörner from the north and east. Yet still the battle continued. On 6 May, as the German perimeter narrowed, Czech partisans rose in revolt in Prague and other cities still held by the Germans. They gained the support of General Vlassov, the most senior Russian officer to have entered Hitler's service, at the head of one of his divisions of mostly Ukrainian soldiers. Vlassov's men, in those last days, made a belated and futile bid to save themselves from Soviet vengeance by turning on the Germans. Czech radio appealed to the nation to rise.

What followed was similar in kind, if not in scale, to earlier events in Warsaw. The Germans, motivated partly by self-preservation and partly by the culture of massacre which now held sway among the doomed fanatics, found means to suppress the revolt with the same energy with which they had addressed previous risings of Poles and Slovaks. A last tragedy, involving the deaths of 3,000 Czechs and terrible damage to their capital, thus took place even after Hitler's death. SS men herded civilians out of their houses into the street, where they were mown down. A senior Wehrmacht officer announced that he cared nothing for armistices, that his men would fight on until they were granted passage westwards. German radio in Prague continued to broadcast signals of defiance and to threaten draconian reprisals against any civilian found in possession of arms. Here was another example of the folly of inciting civilian insurrection against regular troops. The Allies, through the BBC's Czech Service, should surely have sought to deter the insurgents, rather than allow them to immolate themselves. The uprising could not conceivably influence events.

On 8 May, the Russians launched an assault on Prague. They entered the city the next day, too late for a substantial number of its citizens. Churchill suffered a new spasm of dismay when he saw that the Czech capital, too, must fall into communist thraldom. He had raised the issue of Prague with Eisenhower a fortnight before. The Supreme Commander responded that the Czech capital had never played any part in his military plans. "I thought it was too late now to bring the political aspect before him," observed Churchill sadly to the British Chiefs of Staff. In truth, it was never realistic to suppose that the Czechs' political destiny could have altered. The Czech government in exile, profoundly alienated since Czechoslovakia's 1938 betrayal at Munich by Britain and France, had already determined that their nation's future must lie in alliance with the Soviet Union.

But the Czechs might have been spared their immediate misfortunes by a modest military effort. Bradley believed that Patton's formations could have reached Prague in twenty-four hours, in time to save the Czechs from the tragedy in their capital. Twelfth Army Group's commander was probably right. Yet it was Marshall who told Eisenhower to ignore British urging for a push on Prague. "Personally," said the U.S. Chief of Staff, "and aside from all logistic, tactical or strategical implications, I would be loath to hazard American lives for purely political purposes."

On 10 May Schörner surrendered his forces, before himself discarding uniform in favour of Bavarian national costume and escaping westwards in a Storch. He was later captured and imprisoned as a war criminal. Some of his men continued to resist the Russians, even after the formal capitulation. In the fighting around Prague, between 6 and 11 May alone the Russian 1st, 2nd and 4th Ukrainian Fronts reported casualties of 23,383, 14,436 and 11,529 respectively.

Though the struggle persisted in the east for days longer, the formal end of the war between Germany and the Allies came on 8 May 1945. Field-Marshal Wilhelm Keitel, former Chief of Staff of OKW and Hitler's principal military lackey, was brought to a technical school in Karlhorst, one of the few surviving buildings in Russian-occupied Berlin, just before midnight to confirm the surrenders already made to Montgomery at Lüneburg Heath and to Eisenhower at Rheims. Indeed, the ceremony at Karlhorst was rendered necessary by Soviet rage that Keitel had already performed a submission at SHAEF. On 8 May, twenty-four hours later, Allied commanders led by Zhukov were waiting. Tedder, as Eisenhower's deputy, demanded: "Have you received the document of unconditional surrender? Are you ready to execute its provisions?" Keitel fixed his monocle into his left eye and held up the document agreed at Rheims the previous day: "*Ja. In Ordnung.*" In addition to his medals, Hitler's chief soldier still wore his National Socialist Party golden emblem. His aide, Lieutenant-Colonel Karl Brehm, was in tears. Keitel removed a glove, signed the surrender and said drily to Brehm: "You can make your fortune after the war writing a book about this—'With Keitel in the Russian camp.'" The Germans departed back to their cells. The Russians spread the table for one of their prodigious banquets, which lasted until 0400. "When those men left this room," said Andrei Vyshinsky, Soviet deputy commissar for foreign affairs, "Germany was torn from the pages of history. We shall never forgive and never forget." When General Johannes von Blaskowitz surrendered the German forces in Holland to First Canadian Army, an onlooker wrote that the German delegation "looked like men in a dream, dazed, stupefied and unable to realise that their world was utterly finished." As a result of Soviet refusal to recognize the validity of the earlier Rheims surrender, the Russians celebrated "Victory Europe," VE-Day, twenty-four hours after the rest of the world.

SHAEF's Supreme Commander dispatched a wonderfully succinct cable to the Combined Chiefs of Staff: "The mission of this Allied Force was fulfilled at 0241, local time, May 7th 1945//signed//Eisenhower." The leader of the Western allied forces had staked no claims to greatness as a field commander during the campaign in north-west Europe, but he earned the gratitude of history by the forbearance, wisdom and generosity of spirit with which he had managed the march of the Allied armies to victory.

Winston Churchill, to whom more than any other human being the world owed its escape from Nazi domination, broadcast to the British people:

> The German war is therefore at an end...After gallant France had been struck down we, from this island and from our united Empire, maintained the struggle single-handed for a whole year until we were joined by the military might of Soviet Russia, and later by the overwhelming powers and resources of the United States. Finally almost the whole world was combined against the evil-doers, who are now prostrate before us. We may allow ourselves a brief period of rejoicing...

Flight-Lieutenant Richard Hough was reclining on a heap of kitbags in the belly of a Dakota over the Channel, going home on completing his tour as an RAF Typhoon pilot, when a crewman suddenly pulled open the cockpit door and shouted down the fuselage: "It's fucking over!" The passengers went mad, hurling kitbags wildly at each other in an orgy of celebration. An RAF "erk," one of the crew, glanced at the motionless Hough: "Come on, sir, the war's over. Aren't you glad?"

"I shut my eyes, swallowed painfully, and lay very still."

Lieutenant Vasily Kudryashov heard the news in the tiny apartment in Leningrad to which he had returned after losing a foot in his T-34 a few months earlier. "I felt a great sadness not to be with my unit," he said. "I thought of all the things I might have accomplished that I hadn't. I could have done so much more." His father had been killed as a supply officer on the Baltic Front in 1944. He himself had lost four crews in action. His family's home had been destroyed in the siege of Leningrad. "I still felt a terrible anger towards the Germans," he said.

"It's over! Europe is at peace!" shouted a signaller at 0200, after picking up a plain-language transmission at the headquarters near Berlin where Yulia Pozdnyakova was serving. She celebrated by drinking some condensed milk, because her corporal would not allow a seventeen-year-old to drink alcohol. "For me, the whole war had been like some terrible fairytale. Now, we laughed and we cried and we wrote letters about how wonderful it was to be alive."

"We didn't celebrate the end of the war," said Private Ron Gladman of the 1st Hampshires. "It was reward enough to have survived." On 8 May, "three beautiful Red Army reconnaissance men" appeared at the Latvian farm where ten-year-old Gennady Trofimov, together with his mother, grandmother and sister, had spent the last icy, starving months of the war in slavery. The soldiers asked suspiciously: "Who are you?" Every Russian had been conditioned to treat every citizen of the motherland whom he met in German hands as an actual or potential traitor. The Germans in their area had fought to the very last day. The liberated family walked to the local Soviet headquarters and asked how they might get home. An officer said: "Well, mother—you see this horse and cart? You take it, and drive yourselves back to Novgorod." And so they did, performing a journey of a thousand miles. They returned to find themselves outcasts, the children tormented as "fritzies" because they had lived among the Germans. Not only was Gennady's father lost, but two uncles were dead. His aunt and her fifteen-year-old daughter had been hanged by the Germans in Latvia in April 1945. They later found one seven-year-old cousin alive in an orphanage, unaware of her own age or identity. The city of Novgorod was a ruin. Yet these indomitable people survived.

Lieutenant Gennady Ivanov was in Rostock with his tank battalion when the radio operators picked up news of the German surrender. He emptied his captured Mauser into the air. Many crews leaped into the tanks, started up and drove the few hundred yards to the sea to fire a triumphant salvo from their guns. Ivanov's crew carried 100 per cent alcohol diluted with water in one of their external fuel tanks, and broached this stock at once. His friend Kazak dressed himself in a top hat and dress suit, and careered through the lines on a motorbike. "We got so drunk that if the Germans had any fight left in them, they could have wiped out the whole brigade," said Ivanov happily. His men noted with contempt the terrified servility of the local civilians, who bowed even to private soldiers. Now, Germans seemed to possess only two words in their vocabulary—"*Kamerad!*" and "*Gut!*" Civilians of all ages and both sexes raised their hands in the air reflexively at the very sight of a Russian soldier.

Inge Stolten, a Düsseldorf housewife evacuated to Thuringia, smashed the family radio in despair when she heard the news of Germany's surrender. She had been an ardent Nazi all her adult life. She saw this moment as the end of all her dreams. She was an educated woman who spoke good English and French. Yet she sincerely believed that the Americans would kill all Germans when they arrived.

At the farm in Saxony where eleven-year-old Jutta Dietze was an evacuee, the child burst into tears when she heard that Germany had surrendered. "We were so indoctrinated that we had never considered any possible ending of the war except victory. I thought: this is the end of Germany. We'll never be allowed to sing our German folk songs again. We shall never again be allowed to be proud of being Germans." In a cell in Moscow's Butykri prison, Major Karl-Günther von Hase heard the fireworks exploding outside. "*Hitler kaputt!*" said his guards tersely. He sat down on his palliasse, put his head in his hands and sobbed: "I thought of all the comrades I had lost in the war. I felt only an over-whelming sadness about what had happened to Germany." He spent three years in Russian captivity before he was able to return to formalize the marriage cer-emony to his fiancée Renate which had been solemnized by proxy during the siege of Schneidemühl in February 1945.

Eleonore von Joest, who had escaped from East Prussia, exulted: "Now life begins!" she thought. Then she and her family began to ask each other: "Who else is left alive?" Lieutenant Vladimir Gormin, with 3rd Ukrainian Front, saluted his commanding officer and reported solemnly: "Colonel, the war is over." The colonel, a much older man whose son had died in the war, leaned for-ward and kissed the lieutenant three times. By evening, their soldiers were toss-ing officers skywards in blankets, beginning an orgy of drinking that left no man sober for three days.

In Pomerania, Waltraut Ptack and her family were ordered by Russian sol-diers, most of them very drunk, to ring the local church bells, and indeed to keep ringing them for many hours: "We did not mind doing this, because for us, too, it was a happy day. But it did not prove a happy day for many of the German women there."

"I suppose I should feel elated," Lieutenant Christopher Cross of 2nd Ox & Bucks wrote to his parents, "but I feel tired and disgusted, and I can't get the smell of Germans out of my mouth and nose, no matter how much I clean my teeth. Disgust, contempt and a little pity mix ill. What now, I wonder?"

Lieutenant Hans-Otto Polluhmer, former signals officer of 10th SS Panzer, heard the news with his comrades in a prison camp in Oklahoma. Some men expressed delirious joy. Others succumbed to despondency: "Everything we had fought for seemed to have been in vain." Several prisoners killed them-selves. Polluhmer had heard the news of Hitler's accession to power in 1933, as the family listened to the radio on his tenth birthday. His father had said: "My boy, this is the finest birthday present you could have." Now, Polluhmer learned that his parents had been found dead in their flat near Potsdam. He never knew whether they died at the hands of the Russians or destroyed themselves.

Those who had most cause to rejoice were the liberated peoples of Europe. "Every day seemed a festival day to us," said Theodore Wempe, a Dutch Resistance worker in Apeldoorn. In a little town outside Amsterdam, twenty-year-old Bob Stompas saw a Jew burst from the hiding place he had occupied for four years, and stand in the midst of the street crying to the sky: "I'm alive! I'm alive!"

IN THE ENTIRE north-west Europe campaign since June 1944, American forces had lost 109,820 men killed and 356,660 wounded. Eisenhower's British, Canadian and Polish formations reported total casualties of 42,180 men killed, 131,420 wounded. These figures contrasted with the Red Army's losses on the Eastern Front between October 1944 and May 1945 alone of 319,000 killed, well over half a million dead since D-Day in June 1944. Field-Marshal Keitel observed ingratiatingly to his Soviet captors: "Germany and Russia have suffered the greatest losses in the war, while the Western allies have suffered very little." Yet the "big picture" masks the extraordinary weight of casualties that fell upon the footsoldiers. At the end of the campaign, the U.S. 2nd Infantry Regiment, with an established strength of 3,000 men, calculated that since D-Day it had sustained 3,745 battle and 3,677 non-battle casualties. Some 714 of its men had been killed, 2,736 wounded, 215 missing, and eighty were known to be prisoners. The U.S. 4th Infantry Division lost a total of 4,834 men killed between June 1944 and May 1945, more than 100 per cent of its rifle strength. Private Len Stokes of the 7th Somersets found that just five men of the 120-strong infantry company with which he had landed in Normandy in June 1944 remained in its ranks on VE-Day. The company had lost 105 men killed or wounded in Normandy; twenty-four in Belgium and Holland; eighty-seven in Germany—about 180 per cent of its strength.

IT IS UNREMARKABLE that Hitler and other senior Nazis chose suicide in the face of defeat. It seems more noteworthy that so many senior officers and ordinary Germans also killed themselves. There is no German cultural tradition of suicide as a response to military failure, of the kind familiar in Japan. No significant number of Germans took their own lives in the face of their nation's earlier defeat in 1918. In the whole of the First World War, sixty-three German generals died on active service, while 103 died of other causes. In the Second World War, twenty-two generals were executed by Hitler. Another 963 died or were posted missing on active service. An astonishing 110 killed themselves. Model, we know, took the view that "it is unthinkable for a field-marshal to allow himself to be captured." Rommel felt obliged to accept poison to spare his family from the consequences of Hitler's belief in his treachery. British troops of 13 Para briefly occupied an elderly German general's magnificent castle. They confiscated all his personal weapons except a pistol. When the Russians took over, they smashed everything—family paintings, heirlooms, furniture. The general used his remaining weapon to shoot himself. The burgomaster of Leipzig, together with his wife and daughter, the city treasurer, his wife and daughter and four Volkssturm men all killed themselves in various offices of the city hall, with poison or pistols. The burgomaster's body was found slumped, his glazed and empty eyes staring upwards at a portrait of Hitler on the wall. Major-General Georg Majewiski, commanding the German garrison in Pilsen, surrendered to the U.S. Third Army in a brief ceremony, which he concluded by shooting himself in front of his staff and an American officer of 16th Armored Division.

The most common cause of self-destruction appears to have been despair, an unheroic desire to escape from acknowledgement of Germany's defeat and its consequences. The young mayor of Barth appeared at the gates of a local PoW camp. He sought the assistance of its American and British prisoners to have Barth declared an open town and spare it from destruction. When they protested their impotence, the mayor returned home and hanged himself alongside his wife. There were many cases such as that of General von Bothmer, who shot himself after being stripped of his rank and sentenced to five years' imprisonment for failing to hold Bonn. Some officials chose to die because they anticipated retribution for their crimes in the name of the Nazis. A significant number of people decided that the passing of Hitler's Reich signalled the end of life as they knew it, or wished to know it. Thousands of civilians killed themselves in fear of the Red Army, or after suffering early experience of its behaviour.

A schoolteacher told the girls of her class two days before the fall of Berlin: "If a Russian soldier violates you, then remains nothing but death." Ruth Andreas-Friedrich commented in her diary on 6 May that more than half of this woman's students had taken their teacher at her word, often by drowning themselves in the nearest body of water. "They kill themselves by the hundreds. The phrase 'honour lost, everything lost' had been the words of a distraught father who presses a rope into the hand of his daughter who has been violated twelve times. Obediently she goes and hangs herself at the nearest window transom." Sexual violation was, perhaps, the most comprehensible reason for self-destruction. No one has ever reliably quantified the suicides in Germany in 1945, but these certainly ran into many tens of thousands. In every city occupied by the victors, corpses hung from the rafters, or lay slumped where poison had done its business with them.

Everywhere, surviving servants of the Third Reich were striving to rid themselves of the trappings of allegiance, which now placed them in mortal peril. An SS general arrived at a *Schloss* which harboured two Englishwomen married to Germans. "My dears," he said apologetically, "excuse this dreadful uniform," and hastened to discard it. The leader of the Belgian SS, Léon Degrelle, demanded a U-boat to escape to Spain or Japan. Degrelle did not get his submarine, but he was successful in escaping vengeance. Dönitz, at Kriegs-marine headquarters in Flensburg, provided SS men with naval uniforms, in accordance with Heinrich Himmler's last advice to his personal followers, "to dive for cover in the Wehrmacht." Rudolf Hoess, commandant of Auschwitz, was given an order on 6 May posting him to Naval Headquarters on the island of Sylt, disguised and equipped with the papers of boatswain's mate Franz Lang. Dönitz's behaviour during his brief, grotesque masquerade as the last Führer makes a mockery of delusions that he was a mere naval officer who fell into bad company. He was fortunate to escape the gallows at Nuremberg.

In some cases, Germans themselves exposed senior Nazi officials. Martin Mutschmann, gauleiter of Saxony, was brought forth from the house in Annebourg where he had been hiding, after an informer denounced him. The local burgomaster marched the Nazi official through the streets in his under-pants, then displayed his captive before the war memorial in the town square, before surrendering him to the Russians. The gauleiter survived a half-hearted attempt to slash his own wrists.

On 7 May, in the ruins of Dresden, the inhabitants heard firing to the north-west. A deputation from the local hospital called upon Emil Bergander. They begged him to destroy the alcohol stocks at his distillery: "If the Russians get at them, they'll do vile things." Bergander said: "They'll do even more vile things if they find we've deliberately got rid of it." He compromised, by selling off stock at the gates at rock-bottom prices. He said with passionate determination to his son: "We and the factory have survived the bombing. Now we are going to survive the Russians." That night, the two stood on the roof of the building, watching the few remaining houses of Neustadt, on the opposite side of the river, burning fiercely. There was a series of thunderous explosions as the Wehrmacht demolished the bridges. "The Russians will be here tomorrow," said his father resignedly.

The eighth of May was a beautiful day, which began with a flight of Stor-moviks making low passes over the city. The Berganders went to the distillery with Anna, their Russian maid, in readiness to act as interpreter. They heard engines, and expected tanks. Instead, anticlimactically, a single Russian soldier plodded up the road. When he reached them, he levelled his sub-machine-gun. Anna, who was from Smolensk, started explaining to him what the distillery was. "Have a drink," she said encouragingly. Soon afterwards, another truckload of Russians arriving, firing their weapons exuberantly in the air. They all packed into the distillery office, exchanging toasts. The courtyard became crowded with Italian prisoners and Russian slave labourers who had heard of the arrival of Soviet troops. Soon the Russians were very drunk. The Germans remained uneasily sober. A Russian crashed his truck into a wall after indulging in their hospitality, whence the vehicle had to be rescued by a T-34. Finally, a young lieutenant arrived in a jeep to take formal possession of the distillery. The

Berganders' alcoholic diplomacy had achieved its objective. While there were many Soviet atrocities elsewhere in Dresden, there were none in their corner of the city. For a brief time at least, a strange harmony reigned, uncharacteristic of eastern Germany under the Red Army.

If conditions in western Germany and Austria were nothing like as unhappy as those in the east, the chaos seemed desperate enough to those in its midst. Millions of people were clogging every road: Allied soldiers doing their business; liberated prisoners seeking refuge or vengeance; German soldiers struggling to get to their homes; refugees fleeing the Russians. Daily scenes of horror were enacted in the American and British zones, even if these lacked the formal sanction granted to mayhem by the Red Army. The rampage of east European ex-prisoners dismayed many Allied soldiers. "I don't think there is a girl left over 14 who hasn't been raped on some of the farms round here," a British officer, a Jew born in Germany, wrote to his wife. "One surely has not too much sympathy with the German people; but *this* sort of punishment—well, as Colonel Bird expressed it, is so *untidy.*" Ron Graydon and some of his fellow PoWs liberated by the Red Army from a camp at Mühlberg were bewildered to find German women beseeching them to accept their sexual services, simply to save themselves from their Russian occupiers.

The Germans, wrote Alan Moorehead,

> expected to be ill-treated. They had an immense sense, not of guilt, but of defeat. If a man's shop was entered and looted by allied soldiers, he never dreamed of protesting. He expected it. And the reason for this was that he was afraid. Mortally and utterly afraid. One saw few tears. For the Germans the catastrophe had gone far beyond that point. Tears were a useless protest in front of the enormity of the shelling and the bombing. And so one was always surrounded by those set wooden faces. Sometimes our car got stuck in the mud. At a word, the Germans ran to push it out. Once a German came up to my driver and said: "The Russian prisoners of war are looting my shop. Will the English soldiers please come and see they do it in an orderly manner?"

An ashen-faced German officer at one PoW camp told the British that he and his men were getting out ahead of the Russians. He advised the prisoners to join them. The British refused, saying that the Russians were their allies. The German said: "You do not understand how brutal the Russians can be." But only the small Polish contingent, fearing the Russians above all else, departed with the guards. Next morning, a group of wild horsemen on shaggy ponies appeared, followed by an equally disorderly mob of infantrymen. The French PoWs attacked the carefully hoarded clamps of potatoes. The British felt too stupefied by the speed of what was happening to do anything at all. Russian

prisoners in the next compound broke out, slaughtered the cattle at a neighbouring farmhouse and began an orgy of looting and gorging their starved bodies. The British prisoners sent out a few patrols, and were so disturbed by the
tales of chaos in the countryside that they decided it would be safer to stay
where they were. Under Russian escort, almost as much captives as they had
been a few days earlier, they were marched thirteen miles to a nearby town,
where they were held for long, dreary, hungry weeks before being grudgingly
repatriated.

When Corporal Harry Trinder was freed from his PoW camp by the Americans, he found himself pushed into a truck heading for the rear, carrying fifty
German prisoners. This felt very strange, all the more so when the GI driver
gave him brief instruction on the workings of the .30 calibre machine-gun
mounted on the roof. He explained that Trinder must act as guard. "After about
an hour, we had to stop because of an obstruction on the road. A large number
of the Germans on the truck jumped down and started racing across the fields. I
don't know what I was thinking of, but I swung the cannon round and let off a
continuous burst of fire until I was pulled off the gun by the Germans still on
the truck. Then an American officer arrived...and said that I had killed or
injured 15 Germans, and I was put in an escorting jeep under arrest. I explained
my own history, and was released." By contrast, Private Bill Bampton and some
other liberated British prisoners were offered weapons "to take a bit of revenge
if we felt like it, but we were too dazed and happy to think of that."

Many Poles harboured implacable grudges against the Germans. Those who
found themselves in Germany when peace came, as prisoners or forced labourers, possessed exceptional opportunities to avenge themselves. At Piotr
Tareczynski's PoW camp, "we were unofficially told that anyone who had any
personal grievance to settle with any German could do so within a fortnight of
the announcement, and would be immune from prosecution, regardless of what
form his revenge took. Personally, I had no personal accounts to settle with anyone, and just wanted to be left alone." The wife of a large estate-owner implored
a British sergeant to stop the looting of cherished family possessions. The NCO
replied that he could do nothing, because he was not allowed to interfere with
the Poles.

Soon after Texan GI Bud Lindsey was liberated from PoW camp, he
received a touching letter from an Indian soldier who had been his friend
behind the wire. "The only thing which I will miss when I am away from here
will be 'my sweet American,'" wrote Armin Ghafur Dist, who hailed from
Campbellpore in the Punjab. "When I reach my own home I will tell The Old
Girl (my mother) that the American tanks brought the happiest day of my life
on 29 April. Freedom! Freedom! After hard long starving nights...good on you
America. The Gerry is *kaputt* now!" Six-year-old Klaus Fischer's chief impres-

sion of American occupation was that everything seemed scented—the fresh coffee, even the chewing gum: "We had not *smelt* sensation for years."

GOING HOME

SIXTEEN-YEAR-OLD Corporal Helmut Fromm's odyssey westwards from Ninth Army's Berlin encirclement continued on foot and by bicycle through the early days of May. Sometimes he travelled alone, sometimes with one of the innumerable small groups of desperate men thronging the countryside. He was among a cluster of fugitives who eventually reached the Elbe at Magdeburg to find the bridge blown and the Americans on the far side. He rode a bicycle upstream to a dam, searching for a crossing. A German military police party stopped him and demanded his medical discharge certificate. He was fortunate enough to be able to talk his way through. There was a great crowd of men at the Elbe bank. Fromm threw his bike and machine-pistol into the water. A gunner officer rowed alone in a small boat to the far bank and smartly saluted the American officer on the far side. After a few moments' conversation, the officer shouted across: "Men! They'll let us come over if we don't give the Hitler salute!" Somebody said: "If the *Amis* want us to stick our fingers up our arses, we'll do it." On the far bank, Fromm met his first gum-chewing American. "What will happen to us?" he asked. "You'll be going home," said this amiable enemy. "Now quick march, friends!" They were placed in a cage guarded by black Americans, who jovially referred to the Germans as "white negroes." The only indignity they suffered was to be pelted with stones by newly liberated Allied prisoners. Fromm made the last entry of the war in his diary: "Lord, your mercy is endless."

The family of sixteen-year-old Hans Moser, a former Luftwaffe flak gunner, possessed the luxury of a small country home in the hills a few miles above Neumarkt in Bavaria. Late in April, they had taken refuge there, to await the end. A group of SS defended the town ferociously against the advancing Americans. Neumarkt changed hands several times, and paid the price. From the hills, the Mosers could see flames rising from the ruins. At last, the shooting stopped. Moser's uncle Hans, the burgomaster, put on a top hat and tailcoat and went out formally to receive the Americans. The first soldiers pushed him brusquely aside. The teenage Hans had outgrown his civilian clothes. His Luftwaffe uniform was the only outfit he possessed. On the strength of it, he was thrown into a barn under guard for some days, along with a host of other uniformed stragglers and local officials. The boy proudly rejected the offer of candy from a GI: "They were the enemy. I didn't see this as a liberation. I hated our helplessness—the fact that now these Americans could do absolutely anything they liked with us." His mother, a committed Nazi, was deeply distressed by Germany's defeat, but when she heard of Hitler's death, like tens of millions of former believers, she was past caring about his fate. She asked simply: "What happens to our family now?" His father, a devout Catholic who had been badly wounded in the First World War, was merely grateful that it was over.

Captain Leopold Goesse watched his thousand-strong Cossack unit of the Wehrmacht parade near the Austrian border and proudly advance their blue-and-black Cossack standard. They swore a new oath of allegiance, in place of that which had died with Hitler, to their flag. Goesse, a young Austrian aristocrat, had never felt entirely comfortable with the Cossacks. Despite some historians' idealization of those who were ruthlessly returned to Stalin, the murderous record of Cossacks who served the Wehrmacht in northern Italy and Yugoslavia deserves more attention than it has received. Goesse was troubled by the incidence of rape and looting in his own unit: "There were severe disciplinary problems...I didn't feel like a Cossack, as some German officers did." The knowledge of the Cossacks' assured fate if they remained in Yugoslavia caused them to march hastily across the Austrian border in the first days of May, among a host of retreating German soldiers abandoning their weapons. They forded the river into Carinthia to escape the attentions of Bulgarian troops guarding the bridges. The Cossacks' German officers sought out the nearest British unit and offered their surrender.

A British officer urged them to throw down their weapons and surrender to the Bulgarians—"They are our allies." Goesse said, in the excellent English he had learned among British friends before the war—his father had attended an English public school—"I'm sorry, sir, but we know the Bulgarians better than you do." The British officer went to talk to the Bulgarians. He returned to say: "You're right. They're not gentlemen. They want to shoot you all." The Cossacks established themselves amid a ring of British tanks and military police. In the days that followed, apprehension grew among the Germans as well as the Cossacks about their likely fate. Goesse was able to exploit his position as an English-speaking liaison officer to effect an escape to his family schloss, a few hours away. He hid in its attic for some weeks, until he adopted a new role as sporting guide for British officers of the army of occupation, clad in British battledress and the protective social armour common to the European upper classes. His aide even brought home his horse Bitomka, on which his wife later learned to ride. The Goesses were able to save a few Cossacks, who escaped to their schloss and were helped to disappear, having been provided with civilian clothes: "We burned their uniforms and those beautiful Cossack hats." The remainder of those in British hands were handed over to the Russians, and shot. Their German officers remained in Soviet captivity for a decade.

"What extraordinary people the Germans are," mused Bill Deedes. The British officer found himself being addressed by a German colonel in a PoW cage almost as if he was a subordinate. "It seemed that the concept of defeat was right outside his reckoning." Even now, many Germans seemed to regret only that they had lost the war. The last order of the day on 6 May from the general commanding 17th SS Panzergrenadier Division declared defiantly: "Every man of the division should look to the future with pride. If our soldiers do as much towards building a new Germany as they have done towards fighting for the old one, our nation will rise again."

Field-Marshal Schörner, who had driven his men to resist fiercely to the end, said wistfully in captivity: "It might have been different if we had only had to deal with Britain..." He added, not without satisfaction: "Britain has lost its leading role in Europe. Russia now dominates Germany. Soon, she will be able to take the next step—to the Channel." Another German officer in Soviet captivity spoke with scorn of Russian demands for reparations: "Russians tend to forget that Germany has also suffered huge damage, mostly from the British and Americans. We never took plant or material from Russia. This is simply an attempt by Russia to enrich herself at our expense." A German general said: "Think how many roads and railways we built in the territory we occupied in Russia." A Wehrmacht doctor suggested that Russians should reflect that "some of the destruction was the consequence of their own actions... the figures are meaningless—we can never pay anyway. Poor Russians! They talk as if we were living in castles in their country. Russians don't even know what a castle looks like!" A lieutenant said: "The only damage I ever did to Russia was to slaughter a couple of pigs. I wish I had killed the whole herd!" Some captives made pitiful efforts to divide the Allies. Göring, interviewed by a Russian officer in his American prison, "whispered to his interpreter that he had something important to say, when no British or Americans were present." They never discovered what this was.

Von Rundstedt, being driven as a captive through the ruins of Kassel, angrily reproached his escorting officer: was not he, as an American, shocked by the devastation caused by Allied bombing? Several times during their journey, reported von Rundstedt's guardian, the rugged old veteran "broke down in tears of self-pity and rage" about the humiliations of defeat and imprisonment. The Russians reported that those members of the German high command who fell into their hands behaved in a "most defiant" manner:

> They professed to be outraged that they were being isolated from the Americans and British. F-M Keitel and other generals under interrogation answered questions only briefly... Negotiations between General Zhukov and the Allies went well, except for the 2–3 hours delay in signing the capitulation, which was attributable to the negligence of a Foreign Ministry official, Ambassador Svirnov, who had omitted four lines from the text of the document. This was noticed by the Allies, who refused to sign

the draft... During dinner, Keitel said that the present German government had learned its lesson from this war, and hoped that in future the
German nation would display the same unity as the Soviet Union had
done. He had no doubt that Germany would assume its place in the world
again, and would enjoy normal relations with Russia.

General Erich von Straube, after signing the surrender of his forces in Holland to First Canadian Army, was being escorted back to the German lines by
Brigadier James Roberts. After driving for some twenty minutes in silence, von
Straube's aide tapped Roberts on the shoulder and said that his commander
wished to know what the brigadier had done before the war: "Were you a professional soldier?" Roberts was momentarily bemused by the question. He had
indeed been a soldier for so long that his other life seemed impossibly remote.
Then he realized that the German was seeking some crumb of solace for his
defeat. He answered von Straube: "No, I wasn't a regular soldier. Very few
Canadians were. In civilian life I made ice cream."

The victors embarked upon the colossal task of sorting millions of people
displaced from their homes and their lives, which would continue for a decade
to come. Every Allied soldier who served in Germany was awed by the tide of
humanity surging among the armies now at rest. "There were thousands of
men," wrote Carl Basham, a GI from Ohio, stationed at Marburg rail station,

> clinging precariously to the boxcars of the slow-moving trains, a bag of
> personal effects in their spare hands. Where were they going? Where were
> their families? Where was their home? Most were quiet, grim, sullen, in
> shock. Many had been wounded in some manner, and had staggered from
> hospital beds in fear of the Russians. Despite their civilian clothes, it was
> plain that most were former soldiers, in fear for their lives. Others
> appeared to have been allied or Axis civilians forced into service with the
> German army. Others again were merely German civilians, moving west-
> wards as fast as possible.

The Soviets supervised these vast migrations of population in predictably
pitiless fashion. An NKVD report described thousands of Germans leaving
Czechoslovakia every day after the war's end. German nationals were evicted
from their houses at fifteen minutes' notice, permitted to take with them only
five marks and none of their household possessions, in pursuit of the policy
agreed between the Allies, of relocating minorities to their "natural national
homes." The commanding officer of the Red Army's 28th Czech Rifle Regiment
evicted every ethnic German in his area on his own initiative. "I hate them all,"
he said laconically. The NKVD complained that such unilateral action was
compounding the administrative problems of occupation: "As a result, we have

tens of thousands of starving and begging Germans on the move. Typhoid and other infectious diseases are rife. There are many cases of suicide." One local commandant registered seventy-one suicides in a single day. Colonel-General Hesleni, commanding the Third Hungarian Army, which fought against the Russians to the end, slashed his wrists with a fragment of glass from the window pane of his cell, leaving a terse note: "I have killed myself because of my health. With a stomach like mine, I could never survive imprisonment."

Throughout their advance across Germany, the Americans and British were relieved to encounter negligible resistance from "werewolf" units, which had been so prominent a feature of Nazi propaganda since the winter of 1944. Beyond the assassination of the Allied-appointed burgomaster of Aachen, there was no significant hostile activity behind the Western Front. In the east, however, it was another story. For weeks after the German surrender, the NKVD continued to report incidents of sniping at Red soldiers, mostly by boys of sixteen and seventeen. This plainly reflected their greater hatred of the Russians, however futile.

Some SS fanatics believed, probably rightly, that only death awaited them in the hands of the Red Army. They fought on for weeks after VE-Day. Men of Gennady Klimenko's division were attacked by SS troops while driving through a Hungarian forest as late as 20 May. "Our men had dropped their guard," said Klimenko. "Quite a lot of people were killed like that, after it was all supposed to be over."

And then there were the camps. Polish officer Piotr Tareczynski finished the war with his PoW contingent alongside concentration-camp prisoners at Sandbostel.

> At first they mobbed us, hoping for food. Finding that we had none, they drifted away. Most sat in the sun and seemed to doze. Several toppled to one side, and were obviously dead. We had to remove several hundred of their corpses. We were surprised, not shocked. One's mind only registered whatever we saw without much emotion or even horror. By that time we had heard of concentration camps, and had some vague idea they were extermination centres. On seeing one in real life, one's reaction was: "So—this is what it looks like."

Tareczynski spoke with the detachment of a man whose sensibilities had been dulled by six years of his own sufferings. The soldiers of liberating armies were shocked beyond reason by the Nazis' vast monuments to human savagery and tragedy, which scarred Germany from end to end.

When Zinaida Mikhailova saw the first Soviet soldiers walk into her compound at Ravensbrück, she and some of the other Russian women burst into tears and tried to embrace them. The Red Army men pushed away the ragged skeletons in revulsion. Zinaida had been in the camp for three years. Some of her fellow inmates were catatonic. "Quite a few simply could not understand the meaning of liberation at all," she said. "Our minds were not very well." Twenty-three thousand women survived. At Ravensbrück alone, some 115,000 prisoners had died during the previous two years, including Anne Frank and the British agent Violette Szabo.

When Veta Kogakevich was liberated by the Red Army from her camp in Poland, she believed herself to be about seven years old. She was sent to an orphanage in Novgorod, where she was presented with a birthday, arbitrarily selected as 28 October. It was twenty years before she was able to discover any clues about her own background, since all documentation about her origins in Belorussia had been destroyed. She was the youngest survivor of her camp.

The U.S. 82nd Airborne Division liberated Jerzy Herszburg's concentration camp at Wöbbelin on 2 May. "We felt too exhausted to celebrate in any jubilant way," he observed, but one of his friends fulfilled an old, old promise, to kiss the feet of the first Allied soldier he saw. Afterwards, said Herszburg, as they strove to come to terms with the miracle of their own survival and the nightmare they had experienced, "I believed that we were fortunate that there were no psychologists or social workers with us, to help sort out our problems."

Lieutenant Dorothy Beavers was one of a U.S. Army medical team dispatched to Ebensee. "Nothing had prepared us for the camps," she said. To their amazement, many of the inmates spoke English. These were highly educated Hungarian Jewish girls, reduced by lice and starvation to the last waystation before death. When a photographer from *Life* magazine appeared, one of them ran away into a field. "Look at me," she sobbed to Dorothy. "I'm twenty years old, and no man will ever want me now." It was Edith Gabor. Many of her fellow prisoners were suffering from tuberculosis, and all had ulcers. As the nurses gently bathed them and treated their hurts, Dorothy Beavers was astonished to hear them describing pre-war trips to London, visits to the British Museum. "We discussed Shakespeare, Dante, Beethoven—and the food we'd prepare for the Jewish holidays." The nurse spent six weeks at Ebensee, administering plasma to men and women at the last extremities of life, carefully weaning them on to a liquid diet. "It was the greatest shock of my life, to see hay ladders jammed with bodies. It got to us all. After two weeks, we were just sitting around staring into space." Medical teams began to arrive at the camp, to take away their own nationals. An Italian doctor turned up one day and asked: "Any Italians here?" "Yeah, one guy," came back the answer, "but he's dying." "If he is going to die," said the doctor passionately, "he is going to die with us."

Edith Gabor was photographed at Ebensee by *Life*. She met Clark Gable, though she was made to promise that she would not say who he was, for fear of causing a riot among the other prisoners. Many months later, she went home to Budapest. She found her family's apartment in the hands of hostile strangers who demanded, "Who are you?," then closed the door on her for ever. The Gabors had lost everything, including the lives of most of the family. By a miracle, Edith discovered her eight-year-old brother Georg living as a scavenger on the streets nearby. She learned that their mother had been shot soon after Edith was deported to Ravensbrück.

As Staff-Sergeant Henry Kissinger, serving with the U.S. Counter-Intelligence Corps, processed concentration-camp prisoners, he was taken aback to find a Pole spitting in his face: "Why do you care for the Jews first?" the man demanded savagely. When the Germans ran the camp, this man said, the place of Jews—at the bottom of a hierarchy in which professional criminals commanded the summit—had been properly recognized.

Most Germans, of course, declared passionately that they had known nothing of the existence of the camps. Yet even when the revelation was forced upon them, Allied soldiers noted the local civilians' apparent indifference. A British supervising officer expressed disgust that German civilians conscripted to bury the dead "displayed no emotion at all—the denial, the absence of any sense of collective responsibility, shocked us all." This young man, Cliff Pettit, wrote home to his parents about the German burial parties for their victims: "They do it with as little concern as if they were sweeping up their own homes and burying old tins."

Nikolai Maslennikov was unable to grasp the fact of liberation when Soviet tanks rolled into Sachsenhausen concentration camp on 19 April. "For the last six weeks, I was scarcely able to walk, or even to move. In the final days, I simply felt a huge indifference. I was waiting to die. Nothing seemed to matter any more." He spent six months in hospital before returning to Leningrad, where he found that his parents were dead, as was his girlfriend Lena.

"Sometimes we despaired for these men," wrote Brenda McBryde, one of the nurses who cared for liberated prisoners. "What future was there for them? No one knew where their families were, and they themselves seemed to have forgotten that they ever had wives or children. They only cared for the food trolley. Every other instinct or emotion had been suppressed except the will to survive."

Among the Germans, children found it as hard as adults to adjust to their new circumstances. One night the farmer with whom Jutta Dietze and her family lodged as evacuees invited some American soldiers to share their supper. A local boy came in, to collect the children for labour duty. "*Heil Hitler!*" he said mechanically as he came through the door. The Americans laughed indulgently. Yet a few weeks later the Americans departed, and the Russians came. Some Mongolian soldiers strode into the kitchen and observed a photograph of Jutta's father in Wehrmacht uniform, which they had been careless enough to keep on the dresser. "Nazi! Nazi!" the Russians shouted angrily at the frightened children. The family sought to mollify the occupiers by assuring them that their father was nobody important. In justice to their new masters, though the Germans found the Russians very dirty, they behaved much less badly than everyone had feared. Brutality was not universal, once the heat of battle had cooled.

At last, soldiers' minds began to turn from fighting to the fulfilment of desires which had been in abeyance. Twenty-two-year-old Private Harold Lindstrom from Alexandria, Minnesota, decided to deal with a matter that had played on his mind for many months. He was a virgin. Deeply fearful of disease, he walked to a park, where he met a girl walking a dachshund: "She was a slim brunette, kind of pretty and neatly dressed, wearing a plain dress and knee-high white stockings." He said hello, and she gave him a big smile. He asked nervously: "Zig zig?" She took his hand, led him confidently into a park shelter, and unzipped his trousers. The process was quickly over. He pulled out an almost full packet of Lucky Strikes and was on the point of handing them over when he changed his mind. "Somehow, I just couldn't be too nice to her as she was a German, our enemy." He gave her only the three cigarettes which he had been told was the correct tariff. She said "Zank you" and disappeared.

Private Henry Williams, a New Yorker with the 273rd Field Artillery, learned that near his billet was living a local celebrity, Frau Winifried Wagner, granddaughter of the composer. Off-duty one afternoon, Williams knocked on the door of her little chalet at Oberwarmensteinach. A robust forty-year-old welcomed him in perfect English, and solicited his assistance in preventing the requisitioning of her home and car. The GI explained that he was merely sightseeing. Without embarrassment, Frau Wagner indulged him in some reminiscences: "You know, Mr. Williams, the Führer used to come every year to our festival. He did love Wagner's music so much. Poor dear Führer. It soothed him just to be with us. The children adored him. By the way, how is my dear friend Henry Ford?" While Private Williams was indulging one bizarre cultural pilgrimage, Soviet Lieutenant Gennady Klimenko was engaged upon another. He strolled through the great city cemetery of Vienna, marvelling at the famous names on the tombstones. At the devastated opera house, he was solemnly shown to the door of Goebbels's box, which he opened to gaze upon a bomb-blasted void.

Victor Klemperer, for whom the end of the war signalled deliverance after twelve years of mortal danger among the Nazis, was surprised by how soon the miseries of peace began to cause him almost as much distress as those of war. "What good is all awareness of the peril we have come through?" he pondered on 13 May.

> You may put on the light, you may watch the never-ending fly-past without a care, there is no Gestapo for you to fear, you once again have the same rights—no, probably more rights than those around you—what good is it all? Unpleasantnesses are more bothersome than the nearness of

death, and the unpleasantnesses are piling up now and our powers of resistance and patience are very much shaken. The terrible heat, the great plague of mosquitoes on top of that. The lack of anything to drink—now even the inn has run out of coffee. The lack of underwear, the unspeakable primitiveness of everything that has to do with eating: plate, bowl, cup, spoon, knife, partly (or mostly) completely absent... I know it all sounds funny, one could also say presumptuous, after everything we had to put up with before; these are no more than everyday calamities. But as such they simply do torment one very greatly.

Ten million German soldiers had become prisoners in the hands of the Allies. In mid-May 1945, the NKVD reported that they were holding 1,464,803 Germans, including ninety-three generals, in camps within Germany alone, in addition to millions more who had already been shipped east. The Allies were spared one difficulty: there was no lack of available prison accommodation ready to house those who had built it. At one of the host of camps throughout Russia to which Stalin was dispatching his captives, the commandant invited his 150 guards to take turns hitting Germans. Russian civilians who passed the compounds retained sufficient hot anger to shout abuse at the prisoners for many months. Ibragim Dominov, a guard from Kazan in Tartary, sometimes talked to the Germans. When they told him about their homes, their cattle, their pigs, he said: "You must have been fascists, to have owned so much." The most wretched, hopeless, despairing inmates were Cossacks, denied even the privilege of being permitted to sing on the way to labour in the coal mines. Each year that followed, the prisoners were told: "You could be released next year." They never were.

Lieutenant Tony Saurma of the Grossdeutschland Division contrived to get himself swiftly liberated from British captivity, on the ground that he was an agricultural worker. This was a loose interpretation of his family's possession of immense Silesian estates which were now lost for ever. Saurma hiked for days to reach his family at a country house near Augsburg. One morning, as he walked tired and dusty up a long avenue of apple trees, he saw a pony and trap coming the other way, containing two women. They were his mother and sister Dolly. "It's Tony!" they shouted, overjoyed. Saurma's elder brother Karl-Georg, a twenty-two-year-old officer of 6th Panzer, had been incinerated in his tank on the Moselle, leaving too few remains even to bury. Yet now one son, at least, had come home.

When Ursula Salzer escaped from Pillau on a hospital ship in March 1945, her fifty-seven-year-old father remained to serve with his Volkssturm unit. He shrugged indifferently: "It can't be that bad. The Russians are only human beings." When he returned from Soviet captivity three years later, Herr Salzer was unrecognizable. His teeth had been smashed with a rifle butt when he was found scavenging in the camp rubbish dump. He was suffering acute malnutrition. He said simply to his daughter: "Thank God you weren't there. You would never have survived."

There has been bitter criticism of the manner in which the Allies permitted many Nazis to escape justice in 1945. It is undoubtedly true that all manner of evil men were allowed to disappear into the undergrowth of post-war Europe, South America or even the United States, by neglect or wilful indulgence. But consider the circumstances: by the war's end, most of those who had taken part were suffering from a profound moral, as well as physical and mental, exhaustion. Those who had fought in the American and British armies suffered no doubts about the virtue of their cause, yet most felt compromised by their experiences. That is the fate of all thoughtful men who take part in all wars. "Is there any place that is free from evil?" the novelist Evelyn Waugh reflected, expressing a British officer's view of Europe in 1945. "It is too simple to say that only the Nazis wanted war...Even good men thought that their private honour would be satisfied by war. They could assert their manhood by killing and being killed. They would accept hardship in recompense for having been selfish and lazy. Danger justified privilege."

Waugh's was an elitist vision, shared by only the most thoughtful Allied soldiers. Most American and British soldiers had simply seen a job to be done, which they were profoundly grateful now to have completed. Yet, in the course of the war, many had also come to share the novelist's disbelief in moral absolutes. Few, if any, of Eisenhower's soldiers were responsible for acts of wickedness remotely comparable to those of Hitler's armies. But most had seen prisoners casually killed, towns levelled, civilians reduced to destitution in a manner which made them instinctively reluctant to pass judgement upon others, even if these wore German uniforms. The Western allies reserved their anger, and commitment to retribution, for those Germans who had been concerned in the most monstrous evils of all, the concentration-camp system and the destruction of the Jews.

Only the Russians, driven by personal suffering and Stalin's insatiable appetite for vengeance against enemies real and imagined, sustained policies of absolute ruthlessness in all the regions of Europe which they occupied. Ironically, the NKVD showed its willingness selectively to indulge former Nazis if these were willing to assist in the subjection of their country to its new masters. Beria's men reserved the most savage rewards for their own countrymen who had allowed themselves to be captured by the Germans, irrespective of the degree of culpability involved. Heroes who had been shot down in flames in 1944 were subjected to the same humiliations and lasting disgrace as those who had surrendered in 1941 because they lacked rifles with which to defend the motherland.

Around 1.68 million Russian prisoners were returned to the Soviet Union in

1945, out of the 4,059,000 captured by the Germans. Of these, 930,287 were liberated from camps, while the remaining 740,000 were found elsewhere, acting as slave labourers. These totals do not include men captured while serving in Hitler's forces, many of whom were shot out of hand. By 1953, some 5,457,856 Soviet citizens had been returned to their grateful motherland—this figure includes great numbers of people who had fled west, rather than be captured in arms by the Germans. Russian historians estimate that 20 per cent of all those repatriated were either executed or given a maximum twenty-five-year sentence in the Gulag. Some three million other former prisoners served shorter sentences. An NKVD report of 26 May detailed 40,000 "Vlassov men" returned by the British, including 9,000 family members and 1,000 German personnel. Twenty-nine thousand were dispatched to work in coal mines at Prokopiezki and Kenerova, the remainder to Camp 535 for "dangerous prisoners." None is thought to have survived.

Some of the Western sympathy extended to repatriated Russians who fought in Wehrmacht uniform seems misplaced. Appalling atrocities were carried out by Russians, Ukrainians, Cossacks and men from the Baltic states under German command in northern Italy, Yugoslavia, Poland, not to mention the Soviet Union. Thousands of Ukrainians and citizens of the Baltic states who served as concentration-camp guards, and were eventually returned to Stalin, must rank low on the roster of those deserving of pity. This should be reserved for millions of other Russians, hapless captives of the Germans, often victims of the concentration camps, on their return to Soviet jurisdiction. They were subjected to the same repatriation procedures as Russians who had actively served the Nazis. Only some 20 per cent were allowed to return home. All Stalin's citizens who survived captivity were marked for the rest of their lives as suspect persons—"socially dangerous." Few were permitted to rise or prosper in the post-war Soviet Union.

Genrikh Naumovich survived Mauthausen concentration camp after refusing to join the Vlassov Army fighting with the Germans. He was liberated by the Americans on 5 May, his twenty-second birthday, one of 68,268 inmates who lived. Another 195,000 prisoners had died there. Naumovich spent some weeks at the end of the war driving for a Red Army division's medical team. Remarkably, he harboured no animosity towards the German people. "The SS and Gestapo were animals. But ordinary German soldiers suffered as much as we did." When at last Naumovich returned home, his mother fainted. She had always waited for him, but knew nothing of his fate. He was not held in an NKVD screening camp when he returned, but his papers bore the indelible mark of an ex-prisoner. He could find no work. Finally, in despair, he went to the local police chief and demanded to know how he might support himself. The man replied with a sneer: "As a prisoner of the facists, you're lucky to be allowed to live in this city at all. You can clean shoes on the Nevsky Prospect!"

Naumovich finally found work as a mechanic. "I hated Stalin. The very word made me feel sick. The Germans used to say to us: 'We can do exactly what we like with you, because Stalin has washed his hands of you!' Now, I believed them. All the prisoners who came home were unjustly treated. Was it their fault that in 1941 they were asked to fight without rifles? Was it their fault that the artillery ran out of shells?"

Eighteen-year-old Viktor Mamontov returned from Belsen to find that among his entire extended family only his mother, a seamstress, survived. He himself was "detained" in Belorussia for many months, constantly interrogated by the NKVD. When finally released in February 1946, he was refused a passport and could get work only on a construction site. His health never fully recovered. Many people who had endured his experience, he said, "started to hate not only the Germans, but each other. Many ex-prisoners drank themselves to death. After the war, it was very hard to live."

Liberated in Germany by the Americans, seven-year-old Valya Brekeleva and her family of slave labourers went home to Novgorod as non-persons. "Most of the people from our village who went to Latvia survived. But most of those who were sent to Germany had died. For those of us who remained, the suspicion was always there." Most of her family were killed by one side or the other in the course of the war. Her mother died in 1947, worn out by the struggle to keep her daughters alive. She was thirty-six. Her father completed his sentence for "political crimes" and came home from the Urals in 1951, an old man. Even after Valya had completed university and applied for work at a Kazan shipbuilders in the 1960s, when the manager saw that her papers showed her to be an ex-Nazi prisoner he said grimly: "Before we consider anything else, we have got to establish whether you have done damage to the state."

Georgi Semenyak, who survived the ordeal on the concentration-camp barges in the Baltic, finally returned home on 5 December 1945. His parents had heard no word of him since 1941. He would have relished an opportunity to serve some time guarding German prisoners, but was discharged as unfit for further military duty. He was dismayed to learn that, as an ex-prisoner of the fascists, he was ineligible to go to university. After experiencing great difficulties, he found work as an electrician, but was discharged when his employers discovered that he was an ex-PoW. For the next forty-five years, he performed menial jobs in an industrial plant, all that were available to him, as a "person of the second sort."

Captain Vasily Legun, a Soviet bomber pilot held prisoner by the Germans for two years, woke one morning at the work camp in Czechoslovakia where he spent his last weeks as a prisoner and found the German guards gone. He and others broke into the camp armoury, seized weapons and took over the local town, some twelve miles from Prague. When they met the Red Army, they were enlisted to round up German stragglers, which involved them in some firefights which continued until 17 May. Then he and the other prisoners were flown to join some 30,000 other former PoWs at an NKVD screening camp in the Ukraine. They endured weeks of brutal interrogation about their captivity, sometimes by day and sometimes by night, once stripped naked. "It was worse than the German camps, because we had no idea what would happen to us. We were now prisoners of the country we had fought to defend. We were all treated as traitors. The experience killed our spirit." NKVD agents visited Legun's apartment in Moscow. His wife had been told that he was dead, and now all his personal property and papers were removed. After four months, he was released from captivity, but his papers too contained the fatal words about his former PoW status. For many years he was unable to gain proper employment. He became a gold prospector, eking out a living in the remote northern wastelands of Russia. His Party membership was not restored until 1957.

SIXTY YEARS ONWARDS, any civilized person must react with horror to the human consequences of the catastrophe that befell the German people in the last months of the war. The battle for the Third Reich cost the lives of something like 400,000 Germans killed in ground fighting and by aerial bombardment in 1945 alone, together with anything up to two million who died in the flight from the east. Eight million became homeless refugees. Yet it is hard to conceive any less dreadful conclusion to the nightmare Hitler and his nation had precipitated. When the German people failed to depose their leader, when they made the choice, conscious or otherwise, to fight to the end, they condemned Germany to the fate which it suffered in the closing months of the Second World War. Japan's surrender in August 1945, before the Allies were obliged to invade its mainland, undoubtedly spared it from death and destruction on a scale to match that which took place in Germany. It is relevant to observe that Japanese casualties from the dropping of atomic bombs at Hiroshima and Nagasaki, which precipitated that surrender, were vastly smaller than those suffered by the Germans in the struggle to defend their country, and in the flight from the invaders.

In 1918, the German government had surrendered while its armies were still fighting exclusively upon foreign soil. Ordinary Germans suffered severely from famine, and two million of the Kaiser's soldiers had died upon the battlefield. But the physical fabric of their country remained almost untouched. The foundations of National Socialism were built upon the myth that the German Army had never been defeated, that the German people were the victims of the notorious "stab in the back" by politicians and leftist revolutionaries. To this day, many Germans decline to accept any responsibility for the horrors the First World War brought upon Europe, and blame subsequent events upon the "great injustice" done to them by the 1919 Versailles Treaty.

In 1945, by contrast, every man, woman and child in Germany was brought face-to-face with the price of Hitler, the consequences of the dreadful lunge for greatness upon which he had led his people, and which so many supported until its failure was manifest. A few noble souls, of the stamp of Adam von Trott, recognized Hitler from the outset as an absolute evil. Yet most of the July 1944 bomb plotters turned against the Nazis only when it became plain that they were leading Germany to defeat. The German officer corps bore almost as great a responsibility for Germany's fate as their Führer. The scope of Hitler's ambitions for world domination was matched in May 1945 by the depth of Germany's abasement. In Russian eyes, justice was thus done. For the Western allies, who had suffered much less at the hands of the Nazis, and for whom humanity ranked higher in the scale of virtues, the spectacle of Germany's devastation gave rise to more complex emotions. In the midst of the revelations about the concentration camps, the evidence accumulating from every corner of occupied Europe about the bestiality of the Nazi record, it seemed possible to find pity for some Germans as individuals, but very little for their society as an entity.

The nation's fate prompted a revulsion among its people against Germany's historic militarism which persists to this day. "I grew up in a world in which the only thing that all of us cared about was that there should be no more war," said Anita Barsch, who as a child endured the flight from East Prussia. "I wasn't angry—just sad. It was Germans, after all, who refused to allow us to flee in time to save ourselves." It is possible to be appalled by the behaviour of the Soviet Union in eastern Europe, and by the excesses of the Anglo-American air bombardment, without seeing reason to transfer blame for these horrors from Hitler and those who made his European rampage possible.

Insofar as any conflict in history has been waged between the forces of virtue and those of evil, it was the Second World War. Dwight Eisenhower could justly entitle his memoirs *Crusade in Europe*. Yet Soviet involvement in the Grand Alliance posed greater moral issues than the Western allies found it convenient to recognize at the time, and than some historians have acknowledged since. Degrees of evil are never easily measured, yet Stalin seems at least as great a monster of the twentieth century as Hitler. The Soviet dictator's crimes have incurred less popular censure only because most people in the West know less about them, and have never seen films and photographs of Soviet mass murders, of the kind hideously familiar in the case of Nazi crimes. Allied victory in 1945 was deeply compromised by Anglo-American dependence upon one tyranny to encompass the destruction of another. This was not merely a political and moral issue, but a military one also. The democracies found it convenient, perhaps essential, to allow Stalin's citizens to bear a scale of human sacrifice which was necessary to destroy the Nazi armies, but which their own nations' sensibilities rendered them unwilling to accept. Marshall's note to Stimson in May 1944, cited above, almost explicitly acknowledges as much.

The Western allies indulged the Soviet Union from 1941 onwards because they perceived its indispensability. Washington's deference to Stalin in the last months of the war reflected a delusion, understandable at the time, that Soviet military assistance would be needed in the Far East after Germany was defeated, to encompass the swift defeat of Japan. Even given the demands of statesmanship, it is chilling to read the words of Truman's 1945 testament to Stalin, in the hour of victory. Stalin, said the new president of the world's greatest democracy, "had demonstrated the ability of a peace-loving people, with the highest degree of courage, to destroy the evil forces of barbarism." Churchill was at least as fulsome. In the bitter words of a modern Russian historian, General Dmitry Volkogonov, Stalin had "translated the nation's tragedy into his personal triumph."

Even after the Second World War ended and the Cold War began, many thoughtful British and Americans restrained their strictures upon Soviet wartime behaviour because they recognized that Russian sacrifices had made it possible to defeat Hitler at relatively small cost in American and British lives. To this day, some people are surprised to be reminded that the U.S. and British armed forces each suffered fewer than 300,000 fatal casualties as a direct result of enemy action, about the same as the forces of Yugoslavia, and approximately half America's 600,000 battle deaths in its Civil War. For every British and American citizen who died, more than thirty of Stalin's people—many of them from his subject republics—perished.

No American or British commander in north-west Europe revealed the highest gifts of generalship, because a combination of cautious grand strategy and the limitations of Allied troops denied the few plausible candidates for greatness scope to demonstrate it. Had Patton, for instance, been leading Waffen SS formations, he possessed the energy and grasp of war to have performed spectacular feats. As it was, constrained by the nature of American citizen soldiers, he showed flashes of inspiration, but his army experienced as much hard plodding as any on the Western Front. Montgomery was a meticulous planner of operations, Market Garden excepted, but his soldiers rarely displayed the tactical energy to deliver grand coups. They were deeply grateful that their commander did not demand from them the sacrifices required by Soviet battlefield triumphs. This helps to explain the lasting affection in which Monty is held by those whom he led. Conversely, had von Manstein or Zhukov commanded troops burdened by the decencies of the democracies, these formidable commanders might have emerged from the war as apparently pedestrian fellows. Over the course of history, many ruthless generals have been able to forge armies after their own image, in the manner of Genghiz Khan. But by the mid-twentieth century civilized societies imposed upon their military leaders parameters of humanity and respect for life. Thus it was that the least civilized combatants of the Second World War performed the most notable military feats achieved by flesh and blood. It was left to the Western allies to amaze the world by the deeds that could be accomplished through the brilliant application of technology and industrial might.

I remarked in *Overlord* that no military plan is in isolation good or bad. It must be judged according to the capabilities of those available to carry it out. Eisenhower's armies possessed insufficient mass and combat power to defeat Germany in the autumn of 1944 until months more bombing, shelling and above all Soviet assault had ground down Hitler's forces to the point of collapse. If Allied soldiers had possessed the energy, commitment and will for sacrifice of either the German or Russian armies, they might have achieved a decisive breakthrough. But American and British soldiers were not panzergrenadiers. Socially and morally, we should be profoundly grateful that it was so. If this view is accepted, then it becomes no more relevant to suggest that the Allies could have won the war in 1944 than to debate how history might have turned out if the ancient Britons had learned to fight like Roman legionaries. To have achieved a swift victory, Eisenhower's soldiers would have needed to be different people. If American and British soldiers of 1944–45 had matched the military prowess and become imbued with the warrior ethos of Hitler's armies, it is unlikely that we should today hold the veterans of the Second World War in the just regard that we do. They fought as bravely and as well as any democracy could ask, if the values of civilization were to be retained in their ranks.

Yet the consequence of the Western allies' measured approach to fighting their war against Germany, coupled with the delusion of many German soldiers that "duty" and "honour" required them to fight to the last, was that eastern Europe became Soviet booty, exchanging the tyranny of Hitler for that of Stalin in 1945. America's Chiefs of Staff recognized, as Churchill was unwilling to do, that the Soviets could be denied their new empire only by fighting a war with them, which was unthinkable militarily as well as politically. "After the defeat of Japan," they recorded, "the United States and the Soviet Union will be the only military powers of the first magnitude ... While the United States can project its military power into many areas overseas, it is nevertheless true that the relative strength and geographic positions of these two powers preclude the military defeat of one ... by the other, even if that power were allied with the British Empire."

At one of the first big fashionable weddings in London after peace came, the MP and society diarist "Chips" Channon stood gazing complacently upon the jewelled throng. He observed to Emerald Cunard: "This is what we have been fighting for." With blinding penetration, Lady Cunard demanded: "What? Are they all Poles?" Long after the din of battle had died elsewhere in Europe, it persisted in Poland. Almost unreported in the West, a guerrilla war continued for many months between the communist regime and the survivors of the "London Poles," whose only crime was their yearning for freedom. Casualties were substantial, for the anti-communists fought with the despair of men and women who knew that capture meant death. "Bands of Army Krajowa bandits are continuing fighting in many parts of Poland," Beria reported to Stalin on 17 May 1945, "attacking prisons, militia headquarters, state security departments, banks, businesses and democratic organizations." He claimed that twenty-eight AK groups, comprising 6,000 men and women, together with 4,000 men of the Ukrainian Patriotic Army were still active in Poland. Beria concluded that it was impossible to use communist Polish troops against the AK, since these were unreliable. Instead, he had committed five NKVD regiments and a motorized infantry battalion. The communist Polish government had also requested the deployment of the two best available infantry divisions for internal security, and Beria proposed to deploy an additional three regiments of NKVD Frontier Guards. All this was designed to complete the "liberation" of the people for whose freedom the Western democracies had gone to war with Hitler in 1939.

One important social and historical consequence of the behaviour of the Red Army in eastern Europe and Germany in 1945 deserves attention here. It caused many German soldiers to feel justified in having prolonged their resistance. They cherished through the balance of their lives a conviction that they had acted rightly and honourably in seeking to preserve their kin from Soviet barbarism. Most forgot to consider why the Soviets acted as they did. They failed to reflect that it was German savagery which provoked Russian savagery, which indeed had obliged Stalin's tyranny to enter the war at all. They erased from their consciousnesses the memory of Germany's bloody deeds in the east, which far outstripped anything done in the Reich by the Red Army. Turning reality on its head, many Germans chose to see the ravaging of their own country as a unique phenomenon, and to regard a determination to escape vengeance for their own nation's crimes as sufficient justification for fighting on under Hitler's banner. Their logic was not dissimilar from that of the convicted murderer who hopes to be applauded for his courage because he struggles with the hangman to the trapdoor of the gallows. It would have been incomparably harder for Stalin to allow, far less to justify, the Red Army's barbarism in Germany in 1945 had Germans not resisted to the end. Far from serving their society's interests by maintaining the struggle, Germany's soldiers ensured that its eventual fate was very much worse than it might otherwise have been. It could have become rational to defend the east to the last only if the Western allies were meanwhile granted an easy passage into Germany.

Those who fulfil law-abiding and peaceful lives find it hard to grasp what it must be like for men who have committed unspeakable crimes against their fellow humans to return to an after-life in civilization. All men who participate in wars find themselves obliged to do things which, if they are decent people, they afterwards regret. That was the case with many American and British soldiers, and some German and Russian ones, after the Second World War. More than a few were traumatized for years by events in which they had participated. Other Germans and Russians, however, including those who must be categorized as war criminals, suffered no guilts or doubts. They developed a mechanism for justifying their actions, and for expunging memories, which has served them well. How else could the mass-killers, so many of whom went unpunished, have continued to go to work, visit the local café, shop at the supermarket, watch television, kiss their children and grandchildren goodnight until death claimed them in their beds? It is necessary for mankind to be capable of forgetting, and for societies to know how to forgive. But it must be a matter for regret that many individuals who bore responsibility for terrible deeds escaped a reckoning.

The Western allies were obliged to conclude the Second World War having freed western Europe from the tyranny of Hitler while acquiescing in the subjection of eastern Europe to that of Stalin. He had got there first. More than any other combatant, the United States chose to focus overwhelmingly upon its military objective, the destruction of Hitler, with limited regard for the political future, save a general commitment to self-determination for all nations. This was intended to be altruistic, but it also proved naive. The British were wrong after the war to seek to blame the United States for the Soviet Union's seizure of eastern Europe. It is hard to see how this could have been prevented, given the Western allies' sluggish conduct of the war, for which the British bore at least as much responsibility as the United States. But despite all the efforts of Roosevelt's apologists to argue that his conduct towards Stalin reflected merely a pragmatic view of strategic realities, the balance of evidence suggests that the U.S. president was indeed slow to perceive the depth of horror and cruelty which Stalin represented. Roosevelt treated Churchill and his fears about eastern Europe with a condescension merited only by American might, not by superior judgement. The president fully recognized Soviet perfidy only in the last weeks of his life, as Moscow systematically breached all its Yalta undertakings to support pluralism in the governance of the "liberated" countries of eastern Europe.

Churchill could have attended Roosevelt's funeral in April 1945. The logistical difficulties were surmountable, as Roy Jenkins has observed. Yet he chose not to do so. It is difficult not to regard the prime minister's absence as a reflection of the alienation between himself and the president, which grew grave indeed in the last months of Roosevelt's life. By 1945, the Russians cared little for British remonstrances, but they respected the power of the Americans. Stalin's recognition that the United States would do little to frustrate his designs upon eastern Europe confirmed his belief that he possessed freedom of action there.

So much public sentiment was lavished upon the partnership between Britain and the United States during the war years, above all through the rhetoric of Churchill, that it is important to emphasize that affection played no part in the decisions or actions of either ally. At all times, tough negotiation and hard-headed calculation determined American and British behaviour. It remains highly doubtful that the United States would have entered the war against Germany within a useful time frame had not the Japanese attacked Pearl Harbor, and had not Hitler thereafter declared war upon America. By 1945 relations between Britain and America had become profoundly strained. While Britain had bankrupted itself to play its part in the defeat of Hitler, the United States emerged from the war richer than it had ever been. There was deep resentment among Churchill's people of American wealth and British poverty, matched by American exasperation about Britain's residual pretensions to influence, and to empire. All those holding power in the United States and its armies recognized that only two powers would count in the post-war world, and Britain would not be one of them. It is against this background that Eisenhower's great achievement should be measured. He sustained the military partnership between allies who were weary to death of each other, and led them to share in victory with the façade of unity unbroken.

The battle for Germany began as the largest single military event of the twentieth century, and ended as its greatest human tragedy. More than half a century later, we may be profoundly grateful that its worst consequences have been undone without another war. The men who fought and died for the freedom of Europe received their final reward with the collapse of the Soviet tyranny, two generations after the destruction of its Nazi counterpart.

ACKNOWLEDGEMENTS

My first debts for this book must be to Ash Green of Knopf in New York and Jeremy Trevathan of Macmillan in London. Back in the spring of 2001, they offered me the financial backing to make the project possible. This required a leap of faith, since it was more than fifteen years since I had last written a major work of history. During the interval, I had enjoyed a sabbatical masquerading as a newspaper editor. My long-suffering agents in New York and London, Peter Matson and Michael Sissons, deserve the credit for convincing my publishers that I remained capable of putting pen to paper. Michael Sissons also read and made very helpful criticisms of an early draft of my manuscript. Peter James has achieved an enviable reputation as one of the foremost editors in British publishing. My own experience with him leads me to pay homage to his brilliant skills as a shaper of prose, pruner of excesses, arbiter of grammar and logic. If this book is comprehensible to the general reader, as distinct from the military-history buff, then Peter deserves the credit. My text is vastly improved by his contribution.

In 2002, I travelled extensively in the countries whose experiences form the book's theme. I owe a great deal to the people of five nations who endured my questioning, often for several hours. I am especially grateful to those such as Elfride Kowitz, now Johnson, who also passed me on to their friends and contemporaries—in her case to other witnesses who experienced the horrors of East Prussia in 1945.

Antony Beevor, who has written wonderfully well about Russia in the Second World War, introduced me to his enchanting researcher and translator, Dr. Luba Vinogradova, whose assistance and companionship has been one of the pleasures of preparing my own work. Luba's charm, together with her obvious affection and admiration for the veterans of the Great Patriotic War, again and again made it possible to overcome the instinctive suspicions of elderly Russians in remote places about a foreign writer investigating their experience. At the outset Luba begged me not to follow the line of questioning pursued by a BBC interviewer, who established his agenda by asking every veteran: "Did you rape anybody?" I had no trouble acceding to her wishes. Interviewing veterans of the Red Army and Russians of both sexes who lived through the war has been among the most fascinating and emotional experiences of my professional life.

In Germany, Nathalie Hillsmann was responsible for locating veterans for me, and organizing my travels. Georgia Wimhöfer, Ingo Stinnes and Angelica von Hase shared the burden of interpreting on my various research trips. Angelica was also responsible for researching and translating extracts from documents in the German military archive in Freiburg. Major John Zimmermann, who is writing the volume covering the last phase of the Second World War in the Potsdam Military History Institute's magnificent history of the period, gave me some important pointers when we met at the beginning of my project. He was afterwards generous enough to read and make significant comments on my manuscript.

I am indebted to my old journalistic friend Henri van der Zee both for his superb book *The Hunger Winter*, describing Holland's experience in the last year of the war, and for his assistance in making connections in his country. My own account draws heavily upon his narrative. His former newspaper, *De Telegraaf*, published my appeal for Dutch memories of the period, which produced a deluge of letters and personal memoirs, and enabled me to meet and interview some important witnesses.

In Britain, I researched extensively in the wonderful manuscript collection of the Liddell Hart Archive at King's College, London, of which I am privileged to be a trustee. Thanks are due to Patricia Methven, its director, and to her staff. Likewise to Stephen Walton and his colleagues at the Imperial War Museum, whose manuscript collection becomes more important to historians every year, with the passing of those who lived through the war. The Public Record Office remains a delightful place to work, as well as a peerless source of information. I am grateful to its military specialist, William Spencer, for his advice and assistance. The staff of the Tank Museum at Bovington provided much useful guidance and advice. I clambered about inside their remarkable collection of German and Soviet vehicles, and rode their working Sherman and Comet tanks. I always find such experience invaluable, in helping to understand what it was like to fight in an armoured vehicle sixty years ago. The London Library and the RUSI Library in Whitehall are peerless sources of relevant published works. I enjoyed the benefits of an exchange of material with Professor Norman Davies, from which he gained little and I learned much. He borrowed a collection of documents I had secured from the Russian State Archive to add to his own huge researches, and I was able to read before publication the manuscript of his authoritative new book on the Warsaw Rising. Roger Moorhouse, who assisted Professor Davies on his own work, also helped me with some German translations. Among the veterans whom I interviewed, I must single out Field-Marshal Lord Carver, who commanded a brigade in north-west Europe, and was a friend to me for many years before his death. I greatly respected his judgement as an historian as well as his record as a distinguished soldier. The same is true of General Sir David Fraser and Field-Marshal Lord Bramall, whose views have significantly influenced my own conclusions.

In the United States, beyond interviewing veterans, for the first time I had the pleasure of working at the United States Army's Military History Institute at Carlisle Barracks, Pennsylvania. Its staff were immensely helpful. Its collection is, of course, a treasure trove of books, documents and recorded interviews. Most of its Oral History collection is available in transcript, and its holding of diaries and personal papers of key figures in the wartime U.S. Army is without equal. I owe a debt also to Tim Nenninger at the National Archives in Washington, D.C. Its magnificent new building is a revelation after the miseries of researching a generation ago at the NA's old premises in Suitland, Maryland. The late Dr. Stephen Ambrose became, sadly, a controversial figure in the last year or two of his life. I can only express gratitude that I was able to borrow material from his large collection of unpublished manuscripts written by veterans of the Second World War, together with copies of some privately published memoirs. Such works have become an important source for historians of the period. I am also grateful to Dr. Williamson "Wick" Murray, an historian whom I much admire, for drafting a reading list for me at the outset of this project, of important works on American battlefield performance. I pursued almost all of Wick's suggestions.

Friends and specialists in three countries were kind enough to read and comment upon my draft manuscript: in Britain, the doyen of military historians Professor Sir Michael Howard, CH, MC, and Don Berry, my former colleague at the *Daily Telegraph*, whose editorial judgement I have always respected so much; in Germany, Gotz Bergander and Major John Zimmermann; in the United States, Wick Murray and a fellow military historian whom I have admired for thirty years, Professor Russell Weigley. The latter's books, especially his huge work *Eisenhower's Lieutenants*, remain for me among the most important studies of the American campaign in north-west Europe. None of those above bears the smallest responsibility for what I have written, and least of all for my mistakes. They were invited to offer general comments, before this manuscript was sent to its publishers.

I must thank my secretary, Rachel Turner, who worked for me in the editor's office of the *Daily Telegraph* for so long, and is once more doing many things for me without which this book could not have been written. It is a cliché for authors to conclude by paying tribute to their wives, yet only writers' families know how painful it is to live in a house in which a book is taking shape. The proverbial wife's plea "For richer, for poorer, but please God not for lunch" is set at naught when an author is scribbling day and night about issues which perforce become obsessions. When I tell Penny that my debt to her is beyond payment, she is inclined to murmur: "I'm just glad you know it."

SOURCES AND REFERENCES

With a book of this kind, a bibliography would represent a mere virility parade. The published literature is vast, and I have been reading about this period for forty years. Such a list would become a catalogue of hundreds of books on my own shelves, and many more besides. Instead, it seems more useful and relevant to detail books as sources for specific passages of text, and of course for quotations, where appropriate.

Major sources of documents are abbreviated as follows: works from the Public Record Office in London—PRO; the Imperial War Museum—IWM; the Liddell Hart Archive—LHA; the German Bundesarchiv—BA; the U.S. National Archive—NA; the United States Army's Military History Institute at Carlisle Barracks, Pennsylvania—USAMHI; the Stephen Ambrose manuscript collection at the U.S. National D-Day Museum in New Orleans, Louisiana—SA; material quoted from the British Second Army's daily Intelligence Reports, of which a full set is held in the papers of General Sir Miles Dempsey in the Liddell Hart Archive at King's College, London—Second Army MD; Russian Ministry of Defence Archives—RMDA; Russian State Archives—RSA. A special difficulty exists in the latter case. A foreign researcher is overwhelmingly dependent upon requesting specified material of which photocopies are supplied by RSA staff. Luba Vinogradova has translated aloud for me many hundreds of pages of such material. Some of these documents bear file numbers. Others do not, for which I apologize to students who wish to follow in my wake.

Several German documents quoted in my text were captured by the Russians, and are today held in Moscow archives in Russian translation. No doubt there are linguistic oddities about some of this material, which appears here after yet another transition, into English. I have quoted from several Russian and German published works which I have not myself read, and which are reproduced in other works. I have given references to the original texts, which seems most helpful to students.

A note is due about the source of some German civilian letters from which I have used extracts. Especially in the last months of the war, advancing Allied troops captured large quantities of mail destined for the Wehrmacht or removed from the bodies of German soldiers. The most interesting and vivid of these were translated and circulated among the intelligence reports of the American and British armies. Many of the German letters from which I quote are derived from this source. There is no reason to doubt their authenticity, but names and addresses are sometimes incomplete or inaccurate.

I should draw special attention to the manuscript of the Danish journalist Paul von Stemann. Von Stemann after the war made his home in Britain, and married an Englishwoman. To his deep sadness, he never found a publisher for the memoir of his wartime experiences, which now reposes in the Imperial War Museum. I have written relatively little about the battle for Berlin in my own text, because the story is so well known. But I have quoted extensively from von Stemann's remarkable description of life in Hitler's capital, which as far as I know has never been exploited by an historian. I am most grateful to his widow for permission to do so.

Much of the quoted material in this book is derived from personal interviews with the individuals concerned. This raises an issue which is hotly debated among modern historians: how far is oral testimony to be relied upon, especially when it is taken from very elderly men and women? My own answer is that it forms a fascinating, almost indispensable part of the jigsaw, so long as one recognizes its limitations. It would be absurd to rely upon oral evidence for facts and dates. The remarks of many Russian veterans are still deeply coloured by national pride. A reluctance persists to discuss issues which are perceived as national embarrassments. For instance, I asked every Russian Jewish veteran I met about their experience of anti-semitism in the Red Army. All denied its existence, which defies credibility. Likewise, I would not care to offer on oath in a court of law the evidence of some German veterans with heavy consciences.

What personal recollection does for me, as a writer, is to clothe with the flesh and blood of humanity the dry detail of official records and written narratives. At their best, personal memories give a sense of how people thought and behaved, and marginal details of experience which are unrecorded in any official file—the discomforts of a certain tank, what men did in off-duty hours, how they felt about their allies and their enemies, vivid snapshots of personal recollection. Some witnesses, of course, weave fantasies. Others are highly selective about what they choose to remember or to recount. Any experienced researcher develops some instinct about these things, but it would be naive not to acknowledge that a few witnesses' untruths probably survive into my published narrative. If this is so, I do not believe that they are of a character to significantly distort the text. I never rely upon unsupported oral testimony to make a case on a matter of substance.

A key point, it seems to me, is that it is wrong to suppose that written evidence possesses an intrinsic reliability absent in oral testimony. The scientist Solly Zuckerman once told me that when he wrote his memoirs he researched the minutes of important wartime meetings he had attended in the British Public Record Office. These documents, he said, bore scant relationship to his own recollection of what took place. They merely reflected the personal prejudices of whoever was responsible for keeping the record. It does not matter here whether Zuckerman's memory was correct or the minutes of which he was so sceptical. The point is that written "evidence" about matters of life and death, which all documentation about the Second World War is, should be treated with at least as much caution and scepticism as interviews with witnesses. Over the years, I have encountered extraordinary deceits in official war diaries and suchlike, often designed to achieve post-facto rationalization of what was, to those who took part, merely a "cock-up" which cost lives. Many wartime military commanders exercised a baleful influence upon the writing of their country's official histories after 1945. I am an unstinting admirer of Winston Churchill, but his history of the Second World War is wildly unreliable. The essence of all these things is, of course, to strive for a balance of evidence.

This book's sources reflect a mingling of official records, published accounts, unpublished narratives and oral testimony, as detailed below. I have given references for all original or unpublished material, and for direct quotations from published authors. I have not given sources for oft-published and familiar quotations from leading figures and material in the public domain, which seem redundant.

INTRODUCTION

xiv "Some twenty-seven million": Antony Beevor, *The Fall of Berlin* (Viking: 2002).

xvi "Perhaps the annihilation": Victor Klemperer, *To the Bitter End* (Phoenix: 2000), p. 443.

CHAPTER ONE: TIME OF HOPE

3 "Allies of a Kind": I have borrowed this heading from the title of my friend the late Christopher Thorne's magnificent work on wartime Anglo-American relations, which should be compulsory reading for anyone studying this theme: *Allies of a Kind* (Hamish Hamilton: 1978).

3 "he considered the Russians 'so foul' ": Quoted Sir John Kennedy, *The Business of War* (Hutchinson: 1957), p. 147.

4 "So we had won after all!": Winston S. Churchill, *The Second World War*, vol. iii, *The Grand Alliance* (Cassell: 1951), p. 539.

4 "I didn't work up a great hate": AI Nicholas Kafkalas.

4 "Unfortunately [for the British]": Forrest C. Pogue, *Pogue's War* (University of Kentucky Press: 2001), pp. 189–90.

5 "Up till Overlord": John Colville, *The Fringes of Power* (Hodder & Stoughton: 1985), 3.20.45.

5 "Up to July 1944": Lord Moran, *Churchill: The Struggle for Survival 1940–65* (Constable: 1966), 7.5.54.

5 "Roosevelt envied Churchill's genius": John Grigg reviewing Roy Jenkins's *Churchill* in *The Times*, 10.3.01.

5 "a more perceptive and less romantic": Conrad Black, *Roosevelt* (Weidenfeld & Nicolson: 2003), p. 996.

6 "As [Roosevelt's] grip slackened": Thorne, op. cit., p. 395.

6 "American opinion on the landing": Kennedy, op. cit., p. 299.

6 "One got the impression": AI Lord Carrington.

7   "Once he and his platoon": AI Vitold Kubashevsky.

7   "When correspondents reported": Quoted Alexander Werth, *Russia at War* (Barrie & Rockcliffe: 1964), p. 898.

7   "A watching six-year-old": AI Dr. Galya Vinogradova.

7   "Yet a Western correspondent": Werth, op. cit., p. 863.

8   "A recent American study": Williamson Murray and Allan R. Millett, *A War to Be Won* (Harvard University Press: 2000), p. 451.

8   "What were you looking for": Michel Sebastian, *Journals 1935–44* (Heinemann: 2001), p. 618.

8   "In Bucharest, the Rumanian": Ibid., p. 611.

9   "*Ils ne payent pas*": Ibid., p. 610.

9   "Russians had a stereotype": Yelena Senyavshaya, *Journal Voenno-Istorichesky Archiv*, no. 2 (26), 2000, p. 116.

9   "I can't say we liked": Ibid.

9   "Come on, we said": Ibid., p. 119.

9   "Lieutenant Valentin Krulik": AI Valentin Krulik.

9   "As Major Dmitry Kalafati": AI Dmitry Kalafati.

10 "Lieutenant Vladimir Gormin": AI Vladimir Gormin.

10 "I was indignant that": AI Yulia Pozdnyakova.

10 "Three of our agents": 1.14.45, RSA Stalin files.

10 "I do not believe that": Quoted Walter Isaacson and Evan Thomas, *The Wise Men* (Faber: 1986), p. 244.

11 "The British would take": FDR to Stettinius, 3.17.45.

11 "We spoke very little": AI Yury Ryakhovsky.

11 "It was a pity": AI Pavel Nikiforov.

11 "Complex feelings of insecurity": Orlando Figes, *Natasha's Dance* (Weidenfeld & Nicolson: 2002), p. 63.

11 "They are aware": Sebastian, op. cit., p. 618.

11 "I was filled with": Milovan Djilas, *Wartime* (Secker & Warburg: 1980), p. 391.

11 "John Erickson, British": John Erickson, *The Road to Berlin* (Weidenfeld & Nicolson: 1983), p. 314.

12 "In those days": AI W. F. Deedes.

13 "Normandy had been": AI Captain "Dim" Robbins.

13 "We thought: that's it": Jackson letter to the author, 8.10.2001.

14 "we were told that": AI Captain "Dim" Robbins.

14 "Everything is going": George Turner-Cain Diary, LHA.

14 "A Jerry gives himself": John M. Thorpe, unpublished MS "A Soldier's Tale," G. P. B. Roberts Papers, LHA.

14 "Dear Mum": Gow Papers, IWM, Cons. shelf.

14 "We could not believe our eyes": Rudolf Lehmann and Ralf Tiemann, *The Leibstandarte, Parts iv/1 and iv/2* (J. J. Fedorowicz Publishing: 1993), p. 237.

15 "Well, that's it then": AI Fritz van den Broek.

15 "It was a glorious feeling": AI Theodore Wempe.

15 "This period was made up": Brigadier J. S. W. Stone, MS, LHA.

15 "As we went across France": Hansen Papers, box 39a, USAMHI.

15 "Early victory in": H. G. Nicholas ed., *Washington Despatches 1941–45* (Weidenfeld & Nicolson: 1981), p. 418.

15 "The Allied Control Commission": F. S. V. Donnison, *Civil Affairs and Military Government: North-West Europe 1944–46* (HMSO: 1961), p. 72.

15 "Until mid-September": Pogue, op. cit., p. 189.

15 "It is at least as likely": Quoted F. H. Hinsley and others, *British Intelligence in the Second World War,* vol. iii, part 2 (HMSO: 1988), p. 179.

16 "[It] is tolerably certain": Ibid.

16 "Brad believes the Germans": Hansen Diary, USAMHI.

16 "The Allies should be": Second Army, MD.

16 "Our only hope": Ibid.

17 "We were amazed that": AI Helmut Günther.

17 "For the thousands locked up": Von Stemann, unpublished MS, IWM, p. 182.

17 "and then the war will be over": Ibid., p. 185.

17 "It is dreadful to read": Second Army MD.

17 "My nerves are bad": Ibid.

17 "Today is Sunday": Ibid.

18 "Asked whether they still believed": Ibid.

18 "a belief that I had": AI Hans-Otto Polluhmer.

18 "Eugen Ernst": AI Stolten.

18 "An American survey of": Quoted Omer Bartov, *Hitler's Army* (Oxford University Press: 1991), p. 144.

18 "We reached a point where": Quoted Michael Reynolds, *Men of Steel* (Spellmount: 1999), p. 39.

19 "We recognized that": AI Bruno Bochum.

19 "Throughout August": Charles Richardson, *Send for Freddie* (Kimber: 1987), p. 164.

19 "Both Antwerp and Rotterdam": L. F. Ellis, *Victory in the West,* vol. ii (HMSO: 1968), p. 5.

20 "Had any indication been given": G. P. B. Roberts, *From the Desert to the Baltic* (Kimber: 1987), p. 212.

21 "quite unfit to command troops": BLM to Commodore William Hayes, quoted Jeffrey Williams, *The Long Left Flank* (Leo Cooper: 1985), p. 22.

21 "The C-in-C intimated": Crerar Papers, quoted ibid., p. 35.

21 "Crerar refused to raise the issue": Ibid., p. 38.

21 "a bad mistake—I underestimated": Field-Marshal the Viscount Montgomery, *Memoirs* (Collins: 1958), p. 297.

22 "blamed himself specifically": Richardson, op. cit., p. 161.

22 "grew steadily more": Ibid., p. 166.

22 "Transport, signals and heavy": Second Army MD.

22 "My men can eat their belts": Murray and Millett, op. cit., p. 433.

23 "In September, 1,400": David Fletcher, *British Military Transport* (HMSO: 1956), p. 109.

23 "utter disregard of property": 1.23.45, NA, RG492–332, box 12.

24   "In the ten days ending": PRO, WO106/4348.

24   "I am being attacked": Quoted Carlo d'Este, *Patton: A Genius for War* (Harper-Collins: 1995), p. 662.

25   "The movement naturally produced": Ronald Ruppenthal, *The Logistical Support of the Armies*, vol. ii (Department of the Army: 1959), p. 31.

25   "lethargy and smugness": Ibid., p. 349.

25   "Lee…never ceased": Ibid., p. 362.

26   "an efficient little shit": C. P. Stacey, *A Date with History* (Deneau: 1984), p. 135.

26   "The difference between him": Goronwy Rees, *A Bundle of Sensations* (London: 1960), p. 174.

26   "We had total faith": AI Roy Dixon.

27   "I've just been sacked": O'Connor MSS 11/14, LHA.

27   "A member of Montgomery's staff": T. E. B. Howarth private communication to the author. Howarth, one of Montgomery's liaison officers, edited a collection of personal reminiscences about the field-marshal, *Monty at Close Quarters* (Leo Cooper: 1985). He told me the above story, expressing regret that he had felt obliged to exclude it from the anthology, "because I don't think the world's quite ready for it yet." I am happy to remedy the omission.

27   "was sowing the seeds": Lord Tedder, *With Prejudice* (Cassell: 1966), p. 586.

28   "There was a confusion of": Richardson, op. cit., p. 163.

28   "to hustle all": Harry Butcher, *My Three Years with Eisenhower* (Simon & Schuster: 1946), p. 551.

29   "Have you not got": Field-Marshal Lord Alanbrooke, *War Diaries 1939–1945* (Weidenfeld & Nicolson: 2001), p. 226.

29   "Whatever balls-ups": AI Field-Marshal Lord Bramall.

30   "almost with a physical pain": Ladislas Farago, *Patton: Ordeal and Triumph* (Dell Books: 1979), p. 647.

30   "I am no Montgomery-lover": WBS to DDE, 4.1.48, Smith Papers quoted Carlo d'Este, *Eisenhower* (HarperCollins: 2003), p. 581.

31   "Brad and Patton agree": Hansen Diary, op. cit.

33   "The national press is": Turner-Cain Diary, op. cit.

33   "My own choice of": DDE to BLM, 9.20.44, Papers of Field-Marshal Viscount Montgomery.

CHAPTER TWO: THE BRIDGES TO ARNHEM

34   "No wife or mother": Winston S. Churchill, *The Second World War*, vol. v, *Closing The Ring* (Cassell: 1952), p. 583.

35   "Brereton": Hansen Diary, op. cit.

35   "I am for the latter": General James Gavin Diary, box 8, USAMHI.

35   "This is the end": AI W. F. Deedes.

35   "Yet when Bedell-Smith": Charles B. MacDonald, *The Siegfried Line Campaign* (Office of the Chief of Military History: 1963), p. 122.

36   "[Browning] unquestionably lacks": Gavin Diary, op. cit.

36 "We called it Operation KCB": AI John Killick.

36 "It looks very rough": Gavin Diary, op. cit., 9.12.44.

37 "De Guingand telephoned": Richardson, op. cit., p. 164.

37 "Montgomery's jealousy of": AI General Sir David Fraser.

37 "We feared we'd never": AI Bob Peatling.

38 "the biggest and thickest men": AI Jack Reynolds.

38 "There is no doubt": Julius Neave Diary, IWM, 98/23/1.

38 "we were young": AI John Killick.

39 "More than life itself": Jack Curtis Goldman, *Tales of a Combat Glider Pilot* (privately published: 2000), p. 94.

39 "We were really happy": Ibid., p. 97.

40 "those whom the MO thought": Trinder MS, IWM, 85/8/1.

41 "These soldiers were thinking": I should acknowledge a debt to Robert Kershaw's excellent study of the German experience at Arnhem, *It Never Snows in September* (Crowood: 1990), for much eyewitness testimony and significant insights into the German tactical conduct of the battle.

44 " 'Idiots!' we thought": AI Wolfgang Dombrowski.

44 "Head for the sound of gunfire!": AI Erwin Heck.

44 "They were so beaten": Quoted Kershaw, op. cit., p. 105.

45 "Take that fucking": AI John Killick.

45 "Peatling returned after an hour": AI Bob Peatling.

47 "On Monday morning": AI Jack Reynolds.

48 "In some ways": AI John Killick.

48 "A tall, lithe figure": Chester Wilmot, *The Struggle for Europe* (Collins: 1952), p. 470.

48 "At the time": AI General Sir David Fraser.

49 "Captain Karl Godau": AI Karl Godau.

50 "Jack Reynolds and his unit": AI Jack Reynolds.

51 "There was a lot of toing": AI Ron Graydon.

51 "In his lonely attic": AI Bob Peatling.

51 "I was amazed by their stupidity": James Gavin MS, "Beyond the Stars," p. 91, Gavin Papers, USAMHI.

54 "Ridgway himself, that very": Clay Blair, *Ridgway's Paratroopers* (Dial Press: 1985), p. 341.

54 "A British tank commander": Andy Cropper, *Dad's War* (Anmas Publications: 1995).

55 "One of the worst sights": Thorpe MS, op. cit., LHA.

55 "Very bitter fighting": Turner-Cain Diary, op. cit., LHA.

56 "*Intention:* 12 KRRC": Operation order in possession of Major W. F. Deedes.

56 "Keep up lads": N. L. Francis MS, IWM, 88/58/1.

56 "Brigadier arrived in the p.m.": Neave Diary, op. cit., 9.25.44, IWM.

57 "In the years to come": Quoted *The Brereton Diaries* (William Morrow: 1946), p. 371.

57 "The soldiers who beat back": Second Army MD, 12.8.44.

57 "Private Bob Peatling": AI Bob Peatling.

58 "There was considerable": Wilmot, op. cit., p. 519.

59 "it is arguable that Eisenhower": Geoffrey Powell, *The Devil's Birthday* (Buchan & Enright: 1984), p. 252.

59 "Sergeant Erwin Heck": AI Erwin Heck.

60 "It was pretty dismaying": AI John Killick.

60 "Lieutenant Jack Reynolds": AI Jack Reynolds.

60 "When Corporal Denis Thomas": AI Denis Thomas.

60 "Gavin of the U.S. 82nd": James Gavin, *On to Berlin* (Viking: 1978), p. 232.

60 "Air Chief Marshal Sir Arthur Harris": To the author, 8.4.77.

61 "The enemy has gained": British Second Army Intelligence Report.

61 "the Germans would have": Freddie de Guingand MS, "Arnhem—A Note for Posterity," quoted Richardson, op. cit., p. 166.

CHAPTER THREE: THE FRONTIERS OF GERMANY

65 "The Allied drive lost": Report of General Board of U.S. Forces in ETO, "Strategy of Campaign in North-West Europe 1944–45," USAMHI.

66 "In one of the Moselle bridgeheads at Comy": NA, RG492–332, box 11.

67 "We lost time because": Ibid.

67 "Every day seems like the day": Reimers Papers, USAMHI.

67 "Von Rundstedt's deployments": Wilmot, op. cit., p. 482.

68 "I took a dim view": NA, RG492–332, box 11.

69 "Bradley argued that": Hansen Papers, box 39a, USAMHI.

69 "We were still pretty good": AI Max Wind.

70 "They're coming out!": NA, RG492–332, box 2.

71 "I think that the": NA, RG492–332, box 6.

71 "If one gets hit": Ibid.

73 "I wonder if it would": AIs Field-Marshal Lord Bramall, General Sir David Fraser, Field-Marshal Lord Carver.

74 "Major-General Gerald Templer": Norman Craig, *The Broken Plume: A Platoon Commander's Story* (IWM: 1982), p. 33.

75 "A few guys carry your": Captain Willie Knowlton, 12.31.44, quoted Dan Bied, *Hell on Earth* (privately published: 1979).

75 "The average man": William E. DuPuy oral history interview, USAMHI.

76 "Too much cannot be said": USAMHI, D769AZ, no. 15, c.4.

76 "The colonel's the only real soldier": Charles Felix, *Crossing the Sauer* (Burford Books: 2000), p. 138.

76 "An infantry assault": William L. Devitt, *Shavetail* (Northstar Press: 2001), p. 125.

76 "The first advice": AI "Red" Thompson.

77 "Lieutenant William Devitt": Devitt, op. cit., p. 126.

77 "Nobody had time to": AI "Red" Thompson.

77 "If the men can be": NA, RG492–332, box 12, report of 4.11.45.

77 "A U.S. officer described an action": USAMHI, oral history interviews quoted Robert Sterling Rush, *Hell in Huertgen Forest* (Kansas University Press: 2001), p. 323.

77 "Two British divisions": PRO, WO106/4348.

77 "I never failed to be": "Report of U.S. Board on Organization Equipment & Tactical Employment of Infantry Divisions," USAMHI, D769AZ, no. 15, c.4.

78 "Enlisted personnel": NA, RG492–332, box 12.

78 "Riflemen, Patton told": USAMHI, D769AZ no. 15 c.4—Patton at Bad Nauheim, 11.20.45.

78 "Many Allied commanders": Pogue, op. cit., pp. 328, 333.

78 "Reliance on fire superiority": NA, RG492–332 box 3, report of 9.13.44.

78 "Von Rundstedt asserted": PRO, WO205/1020, vol. i.

78 "That [British] infantry": Timothy Harrison Place, *Military Training in the British Army, 1940–44* (Frank Cass: 1997), p. 170.

78 "artillery-dominated tactics": Ibid.

79 "The director of military": PRO, WO231/8, 12.18.43.

79 "The American soldier": NA, RG492–332 box 10, report of 5.7.45.

79 "There has been considerable": Ibid.

79 "The British army's reliance": David French, *Raising Churchill's Army* (Oxford University Press: 2000), p. 285.

80 "As an infantryman": DuPuy Papers, op. cit.

80 "We walked over the hill": Trotter unpublished MS, quoted Sterling Rush, op. cit., p. 80.

80 "We seldom knew what": AI Wally Aux.

81 "The great story used to be": AI Roy Dixon.

81 "I thought our tactics": AI Field-Marshal Lord Bramall.

81 "The British Army was": AI General Sir David Fraser.

81 "men walk when they should": PRO, WO208/3111.

81 "The Americans seemed to us": AI Walter Schaefer-Kuhnert.

81 "With the Allies it was always": AI Rolf-Helmut Schröder.

82 "Yet Sergeant Helmut": AI Helmut Günther.

82 "The tank's inherent": Harrison Place, op. cit., p. 130.

82 "Teach the men to work": NA, RG492–332 box 12.

83 "If you won't get in front": AI Patrick Hennessy.

83 "During the advance to Metz": NA, RG492–322 box 12, report of 2.22.45.

83 "The infantry always thought": AI Major-General Roy Dixon.

83 "One always felt that": AI Captain "Dim" Robbins.

83 "The infantry commander sees": Quoted *Panzertruppen*, vol. ii, ed. Thomas L. Jentz (Schiffer: 1996).

84 "In defence, they took pieces": DuPuy Papers, op. cit.

85 "The qualitative superiority": For a full discussion of this issue see the author's *Overlord*.

86 "Before we went into Normandy": Belton Cooper, *Death Traps* (Presidio: 1998), p. viii.

86 "The Sherman was a very": AI David Fraser.

86 "I thought: 'To hell' ": AI Patrick Hennessy.

86 "A deluge of field reports": NA, RG492–322 box 6.

87 "Had they been Russians": Henry Metelmann, *Through Hell for Hitler* (Spellmount: 2001), p. 285.

87   "I'll take him behind": AI Captain "Dim" Robbins.

87   "Wehrmacht Sergeant Otto Cranz's": AI Otto Cranz.

87   "considered it bad psychology": NA, RG492–322 box 12, report of 2.16.45.

87   "Front line troops deplore": Second Army MD.

87   "finally we said 'to hell' ": NA, RG492–322 box 11.

88   "some unfortunate incidents in": d'Este, *Patton,* op. cit., p. 700.

88   "because they think they will": NA, RG 492–322 box 12, report of 1.21.45.

88   "the Germans had a pretty good record": AI David Tibbs, 13 Para war diary in possession of Dr. David Tibbs, cited in manuscript memoir loaned to author.

88   "There were body parts": AI Tony Carullo.

89   "You were not afraid of being": AI Helmut Schmidt.

89   "The whole experience": AI Iolo Lewis.

89   "I cannot say that": AI Henry Kissinger.

89   "For my generation": Arthur Schlesinger, *A Life in the Twentieth Century* (Houghton Mifflin: 2000), p. 353.

89   "Gee, I'll have something": AI Rueben Cohen.

89   "Very few of us were": AI Roy Ferlazzo.

90   "in indescribably cold": Hansen Diary, op. cit., 1.22.45.

90   "I remember wondering what": Michael Carver, *Out of Step* (Hutchinson: 1989), p. 196.

90   "We were absolutely certain": AI Lord Carrington.

90   "Hate them?": AI Tony Carullo.

91   "The Germans were just": AI Roy Ferlazzo.

91   "I never hated the Germans": AI Captain "Dim" Robbins.

91   "I let him go": Sergeant Reg Romain MS, IWM.

92   " 'General,' said the hapless": James K. Woolnough Oral History Interview, 1971, Woolnough Papers box 1, USAMHI.

CHAPTER FOUR: THE RUSSIANS AT THE VISTULA

95   "Is there still a Tsar?": WSC, "The Dream" published in the *Sunday Telegraph,* 12.30.66.

95   "Don't worry, we'll find you": She was finally shot in 1941. Simon Sebag Montefiore, *Stalin* (Weidenfeld & Nicolson: 2003), p. 283.

95   "He was of small stature": Djilas, op. cit., p. 386.

96   "Our benefactor thinks": Quoted Figes, op. cit., p. 496.

96   "Stalin loses": Sebag Montefiore, op. cit., p. 476.

97   "They died in the hundreds": The former figure is a reliable minimum, but even the best modern researchers agree that all estimates are wildly speculative; see Anne Applebaum, *Gulag* (Penguin: 2003), passim.

97   "Who but us could have": Quoted Senyavshaya, op. cit., p. 20.

98   "A quarter of all deportees": Applebaum, op. cit., p. 525.

98   "Beria reported to Stalin": RSA, 9401 om.2 g.66 1–1 430, 1–1 427.

98   "It was nauseating": *The Memoirs of General the Lord Ismay* (Heinemann: 1960), p. 233.

100   "Three months earlier": F. H. Hinsley and others, *British Intelligence in the Second World War*, vol. iii, part 2 (HMSO, 1988), p. 283.

100   "On 31 July": Ibid.

101   "Lieutenant-General Wladyslaw Anders": Letter to Lieutenant-Colonel Marian Dortycz-Malewicz, 8.31.44, quoted Norman Davies, *Rising '44* (Macmillan: 2003), pp. 348–50.

101   "Army Krajowa considers": RMDA, vol. xv 3(1), pp. 433, 436–7.

101   "Sceptical civilians": Ibid.

101   "A Western correspondent quizzed": Werth, op. cit., p. 877.

102   "In November, Alexander felt": See British official history *The Mediterranean and the Middle East*, vol. vi, part III (HMSO: 1988), passim and appendix 7, and private information Professor Sir Michael Howard, MC.

102   "We don't want British": Werth, op. cit., p. 878.

103   "Why die for Stalin": Leaflet found by the Algonquin Regiment 10.27.44, quoted Denis Whitaker and Shelagh Whitaker, *The Battle of the Scheldt* (Souvenir Press: 1984), pp. 208–9.

103   "Within a very short space": Senyavshaya, op. cit., p. 115.

103   "Even the most distinguished": Norman Davies, *Rising 44* (Macmillan: 2003), passim. I am much indebted to Professor Davies for the opportunity to read his book in manuscript.

103   "George Orwell, almost alone": *Tribune*, 9.1.44.

104   "I am informed by my officers": Werth, op. cit., p. 878.

104   "the clown in the circus": Konstantin Rokossovsky, *A Soldier's Duty* (Moscow: Progress, 1968).

104   "He also cherished": The absence of such sentiment fuelled his animosity towards the Poles, and did not prevent the Soviet Union from asserting in its standard school history text on the Second World War which continued to be used as late as 1985 that "The Polish people, who had groaned for five years under the Fascist yoke, joyfully greeted their liberators. The Polish patriots set up a Polish National Liberation Committee. The forces of internal reaction, in order to prevent the patriotic NLC from being established, decided to mount an uprising in Warsaw" (I. V. Bekhin and others, *Istoriya SSSR*, trans. and ed. Graham Lyons [Leo Cooper: 1976], p. 71).

105   "The British and Americans are": RMDA, vol. xv 5/4, p. 269.

105   "The interview was not": Ibid., p. 283.

106   "An officer of the Army Krajowa": AI Major Kazimierz Sztermal.

106   "We have been treated": Quoted Davies, op. cit., p. 383.

106   "These people [the Home Army]": Quoted in Churchill telegram to Roosevelt, 8.22.44, quoted Martin Gilbert, *Road to Victory* (Heinemann: 1986), p. 925.

106   "Nazi and Soviet repressions": Davies, op. cit., p. 420.

107   "Is this the road": Djilas, op. cit., p. 416.

107   "We knew that Warsaw": AI Alexandr Markov.

107   "I felt terrible about": AI Yelena Kogan.

107   "When you look at them": Quoted Senyavshaya, op. cit., p. 121.

107   "It never looked easy": AI Anna Nikyunas.

107 "It was a great thing": AI Yury Ryakhovsky.
107 "It was a wonderful life": AI Pavel Nikiforov.
108 "It was good to be out": AI Anatoly Osminov.
108 "We were different people": AI Nikolai Timoshenko.
108 "Where are we": AI Gennady Klimenko.
108 "We were so used to living": AI Nikolai Timoshenko.
108 "Higher commands were": See RMDA, vol. xv 5/4, passim and documents collected in *The Great Patriotic War,* Book 3: *Liberation* (Nauka: 1999), Report of the State Defence Committee, Moscow.
108 "I've been waiting four": AI Vasily Kudryashov.
109 "Here in the east": Quoted Bartov, op. cit., pp. 130–1.
109 "Increasingly during the last two": Ibid., p. 168.
109 "The rule of war is": AI Nikolai Timoshenko.
109 "We killed prisoners just": AI Vasily Krylov.
109 "There was no serious": AI Pavel Nikiforov.
109 "Vitold Kubashevsky hated": AI Vitold Kubashevsky.
110 "They are completely shameless": Quoted Senyavshaya, op. cit., p. 22.
110 "Political officers held": Ibid., p. 28.
110 "Lieutenant Vasily Kudryashov's orderly": AI Vasily Kudryashov.
110 "long periods of humility": Figes, op. cit., p. 167.
110 "A German doctor": Hans von Lehndorff, *East Prussian Diary* (Oswald Woolf: 1963), pp. 114–15.
111 "I always felt that I knew": Report of 1/24 Panzer Regiment, quoted Jentz, *Panzertruppen,* op. cit., p. 223.
112 "this incredible wall of fire": AI Valentin Krulik.
112 "Of course the Red Army": AI Vladimir Gormin.
113 "The Russians didn't think": AI Tony Saurma.
113 "The Russians were not good soldiers": AI Rolf-Helmut Schröder.
113 "The Russian—that pig—has": Helmut Heiber and David M. Glantz eds., *Hitler and His Generals* (military conference records), (Greenhill: 2002), military conference, 1.9.45, p. 590.
114 "Private Vitold Kubashevsky": AI Vitold Kubashevsky.
115 "I was not surprised the Germans": AI Yury Ryakhovsky.
115 "They were wonderful": AI Nikolai Timoshenko.
116 "a land so flat": AI Valentin Krulik.
116 "The NKVD claimed that": RSA, Stalin files shelf 1–1 box 16.
116 "[Russian] soldiers' conduct": Gabriel Temkin, *My Just War* (Presidio: 1998), pp. 200–1.
116 "Oelmer violently protested": Quoted Jentz, *Panzertruppen,* op. cit., p. 221.
117 "Major Dmitry Kalafati": AI Dmitry Kalafati.
118 "Because of the mountainous terrain": RMDA, vol. xv 3(1), p. 463.
118 "Between 8 September and": Colonel-General G. F. Krivosheev ed., *Grif Setretnosti Snyat* (Moscow: 1993).
118 "This war is not as in": Djilas, op. cit., p. 398.
119 "For some reason": RSA, Stalin files.

119 "On 31 December, he declared": RSA, Stalin files, box 14/3.
119 "Suddenly the Major raised": Alexander Klein, *Ulikbi Nevoli*, p. 396, quoted Applebaum, op. cit., p. 400.
120 "Stalin issued an order": Stalin order of 1.11.45, RSA Stalin files, shelf 1–1 file 28.
122 "Captain Vasily Krylov": AI Vasily Krylov.
122 "Twenty-one-year-old": AI Yury Ryakhovsky.
122 "The men of the Red Army": I should acknowledge a debt to Orlando Figes, op. cit., for many observations about Russian culture and thought.
123 "It is when they sing": Von Lehndorff, op. cit., p. 134.
123 "Vitold Kubashevsky remarked": AI Vitold Kubashevsky.
123 "One night in Yugoslavia": AI Leopold Goesse.
124 "One has to work and work": RMDA, vol. xv 3(1), p. 241.
124 "But you got used to it": AI Anatoly Osminov.
124 "My corporal often saved me": AI Vladimir Gormin.
124 "If you got the wrong": AI Pavel Nikiforov.
124 "The T-34 was not": AI Vasily Kudryashov.
125 "Vasily Kudryashov's T-34": Ibid.
125 "and all sorts of other things": AI Vladimir Gormin.
125 "Orders were never": AI Alexandr Sergeev.
126 "Ninety per cent": AI Gennady Klimenko.
126 "The statistics were": AI Vladimir Gormin.
126 "You should know that": Senyavshaya, op. cit., p. 18.
126 "I had so much hatred": Ibid., p. 37.
127 "War and women in trenches": Temkin, op. cit., p. 202.
127 "Abortions at the front": AI Nikolai Senkevich.
127 "Whole trainloads of": AI Gennady Klimenko.
127 "Every senior officer": AI Vasily Krylov.
127 "Corporal Anna Nikyunas": AI Anna Nikyunas.
128 "Vasily Krylov was manning": AI Vasily Krylov.
128 "At first, it all seemed": AI Natalia Ivanova.
130 "A soldier who distinguishes": *Orders of the State Defence Committee of the USSR*, published Moscow, 1997.
130 "I once watched a penal": AI Yury Ryakhovsky.
130 "The commander of Anatoly": AI Anatoly Osminov.
130 "One felt no pity": AI Vitold Kubashevsky.
130 "I saw him crouching": Temkin, op. cit., p. 182.
131 "I went away a boy": AI Vasily Kudryashov.
131 "It was a question of making": AIs Nikolai Timoshenko, Nikolai Senkevich.

CHAPTER FIVE: WINTER QUARTERS

134 "I was never able to convince": Tedder, op. cit., p. 600.
135 "We had five divisions": Whitaker and Whitaker, op. cit., p. 217.

135 " 'Unfortunately,' wrote the colonel later": Ibid., p. 194.

135 " 'Battle morale' is definitely not": Quoted Williams, op. cit., p. 135.

136 "Living conditions at the front": Will R. Bird, *North Shore Regiment* (Brunswick Press: 1963), p. 446.

136 "Among the British formations": AI Kenneth Pollitt.

137 "Wilhelmina Helder, a twenty-year-old": AI Wilhelmina Helder.

138 "The regiment had seldom been": A. R. Leakey, unpublished MS, "Nine Lives," LHA.

138 "hard fighting and heavy casualties": Turner-Cain MS, op. cit.

138 "Major-General 'Pip' Roberts": Roberts, op. cit., p. 214.

139 "It was you, Prime Minister": W. F. Deedes, private information to the author, based on a conversation with Montgomery c. 1965.

139 "The *Sketch* had a big write-up": Turner-Cain MS, op. cit.

139 "When you analyse how difficult": Hansen Papers, box 391, USAMHI.

139 "The British have had tough": Hansen Diary, 10.31.44, USAMHI.

139 "what was at this stage": Wilmot, op. cit., p. 527.

140 "rather depressed at the state": PRO, CAB106/1124, Ramsay Diary.

140 "Some people begin to believe": Quoted Henri van der Zee, *The Hunger Winter* (Norman & Hobhouse: 1982), p. 68.

141 "There was a change of mood": AI Captain "Dim" Robbins.

141 "We don't want any Victoria": AI Roy Dixon.

141 "I'd simply got into a state": AI Captain "Dim" Robbins.

141 "Two mornings in succession": AI Denis Thomas.

142 "After the airborne operation": AI W. F. Deedes.

143 "I was terribly impressed by": AI Roy Dixon.

143 "There was something happening all": AI Field-Marshal Lord Bramall.

143 "A British sniper watched": Lieutenant Peter Downward, unpublished narrative lent to the author, p. 102.

143 "It is believed that certain": "Combat Fatigue," USAMHI, D769AZ no. 91 c.4.

144 "I had his head spot": Downward MS, op. cit., p. 116.

144 "Corporal Stan Proctor was proudly": Stan Proctor, *A Quiet Little Boy Goes to War* (Dragon Print Centre: 1996), p. 149.

144 "Dr. David Tibbs was driving": AI David Tibbs.

144 "I could worry every minute": Harold Fennema, unpublished MS, "What did you do in the war, Daddy?," SA.

145 "Corporal Iolo Lewis put his hand": AI Iolo Lewis.

145 "I saw a line of soldiers": Cropper, op. cit., p. 52.

145 "During the Scheldt battle": Carl Shilleto, *The Fighting 52nd Recce* (Eskdale Publishing: 2001), p. 45.

146 "I figured somebody had to do it": Cooper, op. cit., p. 243.

146 "All the ones who said before": AI Roy Dixon.

146 "A squadron commander of 2nd Fife": Steel-Brownlie MS, IWM, 92/37/1.

147 "The British soldier is a little slow": PRO, WO208/3111.

147 "Propaganda loudspeakers were": PRO, WO106/43480.

147 "Few thought that Germany": PRO, WO218/311, 1.17.45.

147 "We felt they were more": AI Patrick Hennessy.

147 "always felt conscious that": AI Captain "Dim" Robbins.

147 "Until a very late stage": *Times Literary Supplement,* 4.21.78.

148 "Operation Clipper on 18 November": PRO, WO106/4348.

149 "The Allies burdened themselves": Ruppenthal, op. cit., passim.

149 "They seemed to be much more": Gavin MS, op. cit., p. 91.

149 "I just accepted how long": AI Field-Marshal Lord Carver.

150 "Every day I feel older": Alanbrooke, op. cit., p. 646, 1.18.45.

151 "The outside world didn't": AI W. F. Deedes.

151 "There was always someone": AI Captain "Dim" Robbins.

151 "[Tom] Driberg—Austrian": Letter in Montgomery Papers, quoted Nigel Hamilton, *Monty: The Field Marshal* (Hamish Hamilton: 1986), p. 278.

151 "The contrast with our own": AI John Denison.

151 "A private of the Duke of Cornwall's": George Taylor, *Infantry Colonel* (privately published: 1990), p. 61.

151 "The Americans seemed": AI Lord Carrington.

151 "We thought of the Americans": AI General Sir David Fraser.

152 "Funny lot the Americans": AI Patrick Hennessy.

152 "The Americans are least good": AI Field-Marshal Lord Bramall.

152 "a general feeling that": Berlitz MS, author's collection.

152 "Many men are weak": PRO, WO208/3111.

152 "It is very difficult": PRO, CAB106/1069.

152 "Deficiencies in infantry": PRO, WO205/152.

152 "I don't think this outfit": Fennema MS, op. cit., SA.

153 "A very pleasant day": Proctor, op. cit., p. 110.

153 "A British officer described": AI John Denison.

153 "We thought about girls": AI Field-Marshal Lord Bramall.

153 "There is a feeling of optimism": PRO, CAB106/1068.

154 "This is a larger total": Arch Dempsey Papers, LHA.

CHAPTER SIX: GERMANY BESIEGED

155 "Lieutenant Leopold Goesse": AI Leopold Goesse.

155 "Heinz Knoke, a Luftwaffe": Heinz Knoke, *I Flew for the Führer* (Evans: 1979), p. 44.

155 "Eleonore Burgsdorf and her family": AI Eleonore Burgsdorf.

155 "Katharina Minniger, a twenty-two": AI Katharina Minniger.

155 "Lieutenant Helmut Schmidt": AI Helmut Schmidt.

156 "Why are you looking": Letter lent to the author by Ursula Salzer.

156 "The vain hope that": Von Stemann MS, op. cit.

156 "*In meiner Jugend*": *The Berlin Diaries of Missie Vassiltchikov* (Chatto & Windus: 1981), p. 239.

156 "Maria Hustreiter was": AI Maria Hustreiter.

157 "Ten-year-old Jutta": AI Jutta Dietze.

157 "This is now a dead town": Second Army MD.

158 "Fourteen-year-old Eggert": AI Eggert Stolten.

158 "Regina Krakowick lost everything": AI Regina Krakowick.

159 "We are getting more and more": This report was evidently captured by the Soviets, and appears in RSA, 9401 om.2 g.97.

160 "I have never before seen": Klemperer, op. cit., p. 455.

160 "When the enemy reaches": Aachen, 9.15.44, Second Army MD.

161 "Helmut Fromm, who was serving": AI Helmut Fromm.

161 "For the average German family": *Statistiches Fahrbuch, 1957,* pp. 470–1.

161 "Well, my dear Hans": Second Army MD.

161 "Albert Speer, as armaments": Albert Speer, *Inside the Third Reich* (Weidenfeld & Nicolson: 1970), p. 378.

162 "Some of the foreign workers": See Alan Milward, *The German Economy at War* (Athlone Press: 1965), passim.

162 "In addition, German industry": Mark Harrison ed., *The Economics of World War II* (Cambridge University Press: 1998), p. 158.

162 "A statistical breakdown of": *U.S. Strategic Bombing Survey,* U.S. Department of Defense, 1946.

162 "The RAF's legendary": 12.16.43, quoted Alexandra Richie, *Faust's Metropolis* (HarperCollins: 1998), p. 530.

163 "It was fantastic how": AI Rolf-Helmut Schröder.

163 "Since last night, our": Second Army MD.

164 "There was no guilt about": AI Gotz Bergander.

164 "Most Germans realized": AI John Zimmermann.

165 "After 20 July": AI Karl-Ludwig Mahlo.

165 "There were some serious Nazis": AI Tony Saurma.

165 "We retained some illusions": AI Rolf-Helmut Schröder.

165 "The ordinary German fighting": Knoke, op. cit., p. 162.

165 "believing that I could": AI Karl-Günther von Hase.

166 "Wilhelm Pritz, an infantry": AI Wilhelm Pritz.

167 "An order of 20 November": Second Army MD.

167 "The contents of this letter": U.S. Third Army Intelligence Report, MD.

167 "A PW of 353rd Division": Second Army MD.

168 "A total of 44,955 men": The scale of the problem has been underestimated by many historians, believes one modern German researcher, Major John Zimmermann.

168 "You silly sods": AI Tony Saurma.

168 "We knew we were still pretty": AI Max Wind.

168 "Twenty-six-year-old Captain Walter": AI Walter Schaefer-Kuhnert.

169 "I knew that I was against": AI Helmut Schmidt.

169 "I get so angry when": AI Otto Cranz.

169 "I wonder what Hitler's": RSA, Stalin files, shelf 1–1 file 72.

169 "Beria reported to Stalin": RSA, 9401 om.2 g.66 1–1 318.

171 "That would finally be": Heiber and Glantz, op. cit., p. 587.

174   "Even officers with little": Bartov, op. cit., p. 126.

174   "The Potsdam Military History": *Germany and the Second World War*, vol. iv (Oxford: 1998), passim.

175   "A remarkable year is drawing": Helmuth von Moltke, *Letters to Freya* (Collins Harvill: 1991), pp. 394 and 412.

CHAPTER SEVEN: HELL IN THE HÜRTGEN

176   "It was a relief to see": Alanbrooke, op. cit., p. 668, 3.3.45.

176   "Near Hürtgen, the U.S. 30th": AI Werner Kleeman.

176   "It is a mistake to try to": Personal minutes, 1.4.45, quoted Gilbert, op. cit., p. 1140.

177   "One advantage of being in Germany": Fennema MS, op. cit.

177   "Most NCOs were hill-billies": AI Werner Kleeman.

178   "The stagnation of the war": Klemperer, op. cit., p. 456.

178   "I do not like the layout": Alanbrooke, op. cit., p. 619, 11.8.44.

178   "[who] is detached and by": Ibid., p. 628, 11.24.44.

178   "[Eisenhower] *quite* incapable": Ibid., pp. 634–5, 12.12.44.

178   "The most likely way to make": Russell F. Weigley, *Eisenhower's Lieutenants* (Sidgwick & Jackson: 1981), p. 365.

179   "We're still a first-class": NA, RG492–322 box 3.

179   "We are taking three trees": Pogue, op. cit., p. 289.

179   "The trees were so dense": Devitt, op. cit., p. 75.

179   "Until that time": Ibid., p. 71.

179   "They looked like a collection": Ibid., p. 75.

180   "Look, Haney, that's": Ibid., pp. 76–84.

181   "It was a beautiful sight": Ibid.

181   "Private Robert McCall": Unpublished MS, IWM, 81/15/1.

182   "Attacking forces were interfered with": Pogue, op. cit., p. 273.

182   "It was very cold and very wet": AI Tony Moody.

183   "Telephone wiremen were": AI Karl Godau.

183   "It was so dark that": Ralph Gordon, *Infantryman* (privately published: 2000), p. 79.

183   "We were thankful we were still": Ibid., p. 86.

184   "Battle exhaustion cases occurred": PRO, WO218/3111, 5.23.45.

184   "Comparable American ETO": U.S. Army Medical Department, *Medical Statistics in World War II* (Washington, D.C.: 1975), p. 43.

184   "enormous number of psychiatric": Van Crefeld study for the U.S. Department of Defense, *Fighting Power*, 1980, p. 114.

184   "Combat fatigue was one": "Combat Fatigue," USAMHI, D769AZ no. 91 c.4.

184   "The strain of battle": Chesarek Papers, box 3, USAMHI.

185   "There were increasing signs": d'Este, *Eisenhower,* op. cit., p. 629.

185   "several hundred thousand": Van Crefeld, op. cit., p. 116.

185   "Available statistics show that": R. A. Gabriel and P. L. Savage, *Crisis in Command: Mismanagement in the Army* (New York: 1978), table 1.

185 "On 1 January 1945": Donald Thomas, *An Underworld at War* (John Murray: 2003), p. 220.

185 "A further 10,000 British": S. F. Crozier, *History of the Royal Corps of Military Police* (Gale & Polden: 1951), p. 121.

185 "A sample of British offenders": John Ellis, *The Sharp End* (Pimlico: 1993), p. 244.

185 "In Brussels in December 1944": Quoted ibid., p. 233.

185 "In the British Army, concern": W. J. F. Eassic Papers, IWM, 75/55/1.

185 "Eisenhower was driven": d'Este, *Eisenhower,* op. cit., p. 629.

185 "The U.S. Army suffered": This issue has been exhaustively discussed by several writers, including the author in *Overlord.*

185 "We are about to invade": K. R. Greenfield, V. D. Wiley, and Palmer, *The Organization of Ground Combat Troops* (Department of the Army: 1947), p. 323.

186 "Only 27.4 per cent of American": R. R. Palmer, *The Procurement and Training of Ground Combat Forces* (Department of the Army, 1948), p. 17.

186 "Charles Felix's unit was": Felix, op. cit., p. 157.

186 "Replacements...are not": NA, RG492–322 box 3.

186 "saw in the emergency retraining": Ruppenthal, op. cit., p. 468.

186 "as a legitimate dumping ground": Major-General J. E. Utterson-Kelson, PRO, WO199/725.

187 "Yet the root cause of Eisenhower's": For a wider discussion of the fascinating statistical issues of combat availability see, for instance, Ellis, op. cit., passim.

187 "It's Sunday, my God": U.S. 4th Division Intelligence Report, in possession Werner Kleeman.

188 "The forest was a very brutal": AI Willi Pusch.

189 "The soldiers of the regiment": Rush, op. cit., p. 284.

190 "The German Army almost": Weigley, op. cit., p. 372.

190 "Do you have a good prayer": d'Este, *Patton,* op. cit., p. 685.

190 "There he sat, big as life": Bill Mauldin, *The Brass Ring* (W. W. Norton: 1971), chapter 15.

191 "I always admired Patton": Quoted d'Este, *Patton,* op. cit., p. 694.

191 "would surrender not to fighting": General Hobart Gay Diary, USAMHI.

191 "The combat efficiency of the troops": Ibid.

192 "Staff-Sergeant Bill Getman": Unpublished Bill Getman MS, SA.

192 "Many people here are resigned": Hansen Diary, op. cit.

192 "The average infantryman was nearly": Pogue, op. cit., pp. 221, 266.

193 "A Company of the 4th Division's": Quoted Rush, op. cit., pp. 41, 328.

193 "the most ineptly fought": d'Este, *Eisenhower,* op. cit., p. 627.

193 "We never do anything bold": D. K. R. Crosswell, *The Chief of Staff* (Greenwood Press: 1991), p. 135.

193 "If we were fighting": Hansen Diary, op. cit.

195 "a very, very, small man": Alanbrooke, op. cit., p. 473, 11.18.43.

196 "Yet, 'to put it candidly' ": Omar Bradley, *A General's Life* (Simon & Schuster: 1983), p. 343.

CHAPTER EIGHT: THE BULGE: AN AMERICAN EPIC

198 "He [Hitler] was incapable of ": *The Fatal Decisions,* ed. William Richardson and Seymour Friedlin (Michael Joseph: 1956), p. 225.

198 "Once, in a battle on the Eastern": AI Tony Saurma.

199 "some were very inexperienced": AI Rolf-Helmut Schröder.

199 "a stooped figure with a pale": Richardson and Friedlin, op. cit., pp. 231–2.

199 "Our soldiers still believed": Ibid., p. 228.

199 "My comrades and I entered": Lemcke quoted *The Battle of the Bulge,* compiled by Hans J. Wijers (Brunnen: 2001), p. 54.

199 "how long Sixth [SS] Panzer Army": Second Army MD.

200 "Hobart Gay, Patton's Chief ": Gay Diary, op. cit.

200 " 'Madness,' wrote Winston Churchill": Churchill, *The Grand Alliance,* op. cit., p. 536.

201 "Neither the 99th nor 106th": Pogue, op. cit.

201 "A buddy of Private Eugene Gagliardi": Quoted Wijers, op. cit., p. 65.

201 "Private 'Red' Thompson desperately": AI "Red" Thompson.

201 "a feast for us": Quoted Wijers, op. cit., p. 58.

202 "I never took part in an attack": Ibid., p. 93.

203 "Watch for every opportunity": Sixth SS Panzer, 11.30.44, Second Army MD.

203 "Private Donald Doubek's platoon": Donald Doubek MS, SA.

204 "Private Murray Mendelsohn, a combat": AI Murray Mendelsohn.

204 "On 28th Division's battlefield": Charles B. MacDonald, *The Battle of the Bulge* (Weidenfeld & Nicolson: 1984), p. 151.

205 "I had the disgusted impression": Quoted Wijers, op. cit., p. 169.

205 "An officer who called on his": Tom Bigland, *Bigland's War* (privately published: 1990), p. 81.

206 "it was evident that the": Carol Mather, *When the Grass Stops Growing* (Leo Cooper: 1997), p. 287.

206 "Until more is known of this new": Second Army MD.

206 "Well, Brad, you've been": Hansen Papers, box 42a, USAMHI.

206 "Big issues are involved": Second Army MD.

207 "It looks as if we may now": PRO, CAB106/1071, BLM to AB, 12.17.44 and 12.19.44.

207 "General, there's some rumor": William K. Harrison oral history interview, USAMHI.

207 "What shall I do?": Ibid.

207 "the most frightening thing": James Woolnough oral history interview, USAMHI.

208 "The enemy was in total confusion": AI Werner Sternebecke.

208 "They seemed as protective about": MacDonald, op. cit., p. 369.

208 "I hated to give up like that": Wijers, op. cit., p. 190.

209 "lots of equipment and matériel": NA, RG492–322 box 12.

209 "a quivering hulk": Major Ben Legare quoted MacDonald, op. cit., p. 387.

209   "The 90th Division had a joke": Reimers Papers, USAMHI.

209   "We needed a few samples": Hansen Diary, op. cit.

209   "If you try to take them back": Interview Morris L. Harvey quoted Rush, op. cit., p. 317.

209   "Private Bill True of the 101st": Bill True unpublished MS, "The Cow Spoke French," SA.

210   "The whole matter of killing": Pogue, op. cit., p. 297.

210   "This was the only time": Donald Shoo MS, SA.

210   "We were in a state of confusion": Quoted Wijers, op. cit., p. 38.

210   "We had no idea what was going on": AI Murray Mendelsohn.

210   "If this is the way it is": Melvin Zais MS, USAMHI.

211   "remarkable how little we know": Pogue, op. cit., p. 295.

211   "Very stupid": Tedder, op. cit., p. 648.

211   "Enemy morale was higher": Report of General Board of U.S. Forces, "Strategy in North-West Europe," USAMHI.

211   "For once, we find ourselves": Second Army MD.

211   "For English soldiers": Ibid.

212   "The roads are littered with": U.S. 7th Armored Division Intelligence Report quoted ibid.

212   "A belief would long persist": MacDonald, op. cit., p. 618.

213   "a very grave disappointment": Richardson and Friedlin, op. cit., p. 241.

213   "incapable of carrying out": Ibid., p. 236.

214   "Whenever you attack the enemy": AI "Pip" Roberts, 1983.

215   "If U.S. forces had not held": Rush, op. cit., p. 345.

215   "I spotted our battalion commander": Hubert Meyer, *History of the 12th SS Division Hitlerjugend* (J. J. Fedorwicz Publishing: 1994), p. 252.

215   "When I reached the vicinity": Ibid.

216   "Everywhere there is a feeling of": Hansen Diary, op. cit., 1.1.45.

216   "The whole action was an example": Pogue, op. cit., p. 322.

216   "Headquarters continues to be a madhouse": Hansen Diary, op. cit.

217   "My eyes were red, swollen": William B. Folkestad, *The View from the Turret* (Burd Street Press: 2000), p. 69.

217   "Major William Desobry": William Desobry oral history interview, USAMHI.

219   "absolute chaos": Charles Skelnar, unpublished MS, "My Days of Honor in World War II," SA.

219   "As soon as you lifted up": Henry Hills MS, SA.

221   "Here is a guy who really": Harrison oral history interview, op. cit.

221   "Von Manteuffel asserted afterwards": Richardson and Friedlin, op. cit., p. 249.

221   "What's the form?": Mather, op. cit., p. 288.

221   "He humiliated the shyest": Hamilton, op. cit., p. 250.

222   "I would like to give you a word of warning": PRO, CAB106/1069.

222   "There was ferocious U.S. criticism": H. G. Nicholas ed., *Washington Dispatches 1941–45* (Weidenfeld & Nicolson: 1981), p. 481.

222   "I think I see daylight now": PRO, CAB106/1071.

223 "I said he would probably find it": Ibid.

223 "Our outfit broke": AI John Capano.

223 "My first reaction was fear": Devitt, op. cit., p. 181.

224 "The Germans' morale": AI Hal McCown.

224 "There was an other-worldly": Alan Moorehead, *Eclipse* (Granta: 2000), p. 217.

225 "This is not going to be easy": AI Rolf-Helmut Schröder.

225 "The fact that the Hun": Quoted Tedder, op. cit., p. 629.

225 "The situation is normal": Ridgway Papers, box 5A, USAMHI.

225 "I want every man imbued": Ibid.

226 "At least one man of the 75th": Harold Lindstrom MS, SA.

227 "When the U.S. 743rd Tank": Folkestad, op. cit., p. 75.

228 "Felix had been relieved to see": Felix, op. cit.

228 "I don't represent any general": Hansen Diary, op. cit.

228 "As the sun came out": AI Iolo Lewis.

228 "Since 24 December Guderian": Heinz Guderian, *Panzer Leader* (Michael Joseph: 1952), p. 383.

229 "Provided the two 'gateposts' ": Alanbrooke, op. cit., p. 637, 12.21.44.

229 "It's a fickle world": Gay Diary, op. cit.

230 "I'm sure that, 50 years": Ibid., p. 161.

231 "Their [the British] press": Hansen Diary, op. cit.

231 "Without haste and without any trace": Second Army MD.

231 "Monty did a good job": Bigland, op. cit., pp. 82–3.

231 "The Arnold–King–Marshall": PM's personal minute, D.218/4, 7.6.44, Churchill Papers 20/153, quoted Gilbert, op. cit., p. 843.

232 "You pay him too high": Colville, op. cit., 2.23.45.

232 "Hobbs said apologetically that": Ridgway Papers, box 5A, XVIII Corps conference, 1.13.45, USAMHI.

232 "We are training": Gavin Diary, op. cit.

233 "If only this idiotic war": Second Army MD, 1.17.45.

233 "mostly Ukrainians who do not even": Ibid.

233 "didn't so much lose heart": DuPuy Papers, op. cit.

233 "That's it—we've lost the war": AI Rolf-Helmut Schröder.

233 "The enemy can claim to have wrested": Second Army MD.

234 "This was the coldest night": Folkestad, op. cit., p. 84.

234 "Sergeant Clifford Laski": NA, RG492–322 box 6.

234 "Staff-Sergeant Charles Skelnar's": Skelnar MS, op. cit., SA.

234 "I felt proud": AI George Sheppard.

234 "Interestingly, a British expert": Reynolds, op. cit., p. 135.

235 "There was a serious discussion": Hansen Papers, box 40B, USAMHI.

235 "During the half-hearted": Tedder, op. cit., p. 633.

235 "considerably retarded the": Alanbrooke, op. cit., p. 677, 3.25.45.

235 "Upon the conclusion of": "Strategy in North-West Europe," op. cit., USAMHI.

235 "strong defensive positions": Report of the General Board of U.S. Forces in ETO, "Strategy of the Campaign in Western Europe 1944–45," USAMHI.

CHAPTER NINE: STALIN'S OFFENSIVE

239   "Zhukov was very popular": AI Anatoly Osminov.
239   "Lieutenant Vasily Filimonenko": AI Vasily Filimonenko.
239   "Everyone was terrified": AI Evsei Igolnik.
240   "Stalin won the war": AI Nikolai Ponomarev.
240   "He saved the Soviet state": AI Fyodor Romanovsky.
240   "Is there no one to rid": AI Nikolai Senkevich.
240   "We were fighting for our": AI Anna Nikyunas.
240   "You should obey Stalin": AI Yury Ryakhovsky.
240   "I often prayed to God": AI Nikolai Ponomarev.
240   "but many men crossed": AI Anatoly Osminov.
240   "We all stand together": AI Alexander Sergeev.
240   "Seventeen-year-old Yulia": AI Yulia Pozdnyakova.
241   "saying that he refused": Guderian, op. cit., p. 377.
241   "If something happens down there": Helmut Heiber and David M. Glantz, *Hitler and his Generals* (Greenhill: 2002), p. 651.
241   "A very stupid disposition": Tedder, op. cit., p. 647.
241   "Sergeant Nikolai Timoshenko": AI Nikolai Timoshenko.
242   "A deserter from 118th": BA, RH2/319.
242   "Yulia Pozdnyakova, a signaller": AI Yulia Pozdnyakova.
242   "In January 1945 we could see": AI Nikolai Ponomarev.
243   "Lieutenant Valentin Krulik's unit": AI Valentin Krulik.
243   "On 11 January, an OKW report": BA, RH2/331B.
243   "When you haven't had": Letter lent to the author by Ursula Salzer.
243   "The Eastern Front is": Guderian, op. cit., p. 387.
243   "On 12 January": PRO, WO106/5924.
244   "May all good fortune": 1.9.45, quoted Gilbert, op. cit., p. 1143.
244   "We now had to pay for": Richardson and Friedlin, op. cit., p. 251.
245   "In the trenches, we all knew": AI Alexandr Sergeev.
245   "Morale was very high": AI Gennady Klimenko.
245   "As early as 15 January": BA, RH2/319.
245   "The battle in the Vistula": BA, RH2/320.
246   "Thousands of soldiers": BA, RH2/331A.
247   "Lieutenant Vasily Kudryashov was": AI Vasily Kudryashov.
247   "Captain Abram Skuratovsky": AI Abram Skuratovsky.
247   "*O blad! Generals*": Temkin, op. cit., p. 216.
247   "If we could have made good": AI Yury Ryakhovsky.
248   "Red Army signaller Yulia": AI Yulia Pozdnyakova.
248   "Used in isolation": BA, RH2/331A.
249   "The VS consists of men": BA, RH2/331B.
249   "There are still a lot of Germans": RSA, 9401 om.2 g.93.
250   "For everyone else, a German": AI Yelena Kogan.
250   "we wanted to go out": AI Alexandr Markov.

252 "As early as December 1944": RSA, 9401 om.2 g.68 449.

252 "In order to re-establish order": RSA, Stalin files.

252 "A report to Stalin from Beria": RSA, Stalin files, box 14/3.

253 "On 24 January, Beria": RSA, 9401 om.2 g.68 448.

253 "One had to be very": AI Fyodor Romanovsky.

253 "The prospect of the end": Colville, op. cit., 1.8.45.

253 "Make no mistake": Ibid., 1.23.45.

253 "Great Britain and the British Commonwealth": WSC, telegram to Peter Fraser, 2.24.45, quoted Gilbert, op. cit., p. 1231.

254 "It is incredible to view": Hansen Diary, op. cit., 1.23.45.

254 "A British SOE mission": Peter Kemp, *The Thorns of Memory* (Sinclair-Stevenson: 1990), p. 265.

255 "I'll never forget those Russian": Ferdinand Chesarek oral history interview, USAMHI.

255 "What a disorderly rabble": Dr. Richard Feltham quoted Patricia Sewell, *Healers in World War II* (McFarland: 2001), p. 176.

255 "There seemed to be little": Kemp, op. cit., p. 261.

256 "You traitor!": AI Vasily Kudryashov.

256 "For fun, a soldier": AI Valentin Krulik.

256 "From the enemy's behaviour": BA, RH2/328.

257 "The Front commander took": RMDA, vol. xv 5/4, p. 110, report of 4.27.45.

258 "On the night of 19 February": RSA, 9410 om.2 g.93.

259 "This ban was soon": RSA, 9401 om.2 g.95 252.

259 "It seems remarkable that": RSA, 9410 om.2 g.93.

260 "Amid all the stresses": BA, RH2/323.

260 "Between 12 January": BA, RH2/8496.

CHAPTER TEN: BLOOD AND ICE: EAST PRUSSIA

261 "East Prussia was a province": AI Helmut Schmidt.

262 "mysterious splendour. Whoever": Von Lehndorff, op. cit., p. 1.

262 "It was incredibly quiet": AI Ursula Salzer.

262 "I hope you're satisfied": AI Elfride Kowitz.

263 "I was not so critical of bombing": AI Michael Wieck.

263 "It seemed crazy that": AI Hans Siwik.

263 "Yes, *you're* flying": Von Lehndorff, op. cit., p. 2.

263 "We are a master race": Koch speech in Kiev, 1943.

264 "The President said he thought": Robert Sherwood, *Roosevelt and Hopkins* (Harper: 1948), p. 710.

264 "They want to take": RSA, Stalin files, shelf 1–1 file 72.

264 "In the farmyard stood a cart": Quoted Alfred M. de Zayas, *Nemesis at Potsdam* (Routledge & Kegan Paul: 1977), p. 63.

265 "I was so young": AI Lise-Lotte Kussner.

266 "For us Prussians": Guderian, op. cit., p. 388.

266   "A Wehrmacht report from": BA, RH2/331B.

267   "It sounded as if a lot of heavy": Von Lehndorff, op. cit., p. 3.

267   "Comrades! You have now": Quoted Christopher Duffy, *Red Storm Over the Reich* (Routledge: 1991), p. 285.

268   "How shall I avenge myself": Senyavshaya, op. cit., p. 28.

268   "Hatred for the enemy": Ibid., p. 25.

268   "German villages looked": AI Gennady Klimenko.

268   "Great country!": AI Vladimir Gormin.

268   "In the view of some Russians": Senyavshaya, op. cit., p. 29.

268   "Mugs and wooden spoons": RSA, Stalin files.

268   "my soldiers promptly spitted": AI the officer concerned, who said to the author's interpreter in Russian, "But don't mention that to the *anglichane*."

269   "Nikolai Dubrovsky was an": AI Nikolai Dubrovsky.

269   "Major Yury Ryakhovsky never doubted": AI Yury Ryakhovsky.

269   "Corporal Anatoly Osminov spotted": AI Anatoly Osminov.

269   "When Captain Vasily Krylov gazed": AI Vasily Krylov.

270   "Soldiers didn't understand": quoted Senyavshaya, op. cit., p. 29.

270   "We don't have time to start": AI Vasily Krylov.

270   "Russian soldiers wandered": RSA, report Beria to Stalin, 1.27.45.

270   "Lieutenant Alexandr Sergeev's": AI Alexandr Sergeev.

270   "Our boys would open": AI Alexandr Markov.

271   "When seventeen-year-old Joseph": Joe Volmar, *I Learned to Fly for Hitler* (Kron Publications: 1999), p. 179.

272   "He warmed to the memory of": AI Hans Siwik.

273   "The oldest boys": Guy Sajer, *The Forgotten Soldier* (Sphere: 1977), pp. 475–6.

275   "Any further losses would": BA, RH2/329.

277   "Waltraut Ptack was only thirteen": AI Waltraut Ptack.

278   "Twenty-year-old Eleonore": AI Eleonore Burgsdorff.

279   "You must go—quickly": AI Lise-Lotte Kussner.

280   "The first shattering reports": Von Stemann MS, op. cit., p. 192.

281   "In the last days of January": Volmar, op. cit., p. 191.

282   "Twenty-year-old Elfride": AI Elfride Kowitz.

283   "The highway along the Frisches Haff": RSA, Stalin files.

283   "would be home in time": Von Lehndorff, op. cit., pp. 32–3.

284   "I tramped through the powdery": Ibid., p. 20.

284   "Among the very few people": AI Michael Wieck.

288   "But, by a dreadful irony": Christopher Dobson, John Miller and Ronald Payne, *The Cruellest Night* (Hodder & Stoughton: 1979), passim.

288   "Now that the evacuation": RSA, 9401 om.2 g.83.

289   "The Königsberg battle was very": AI Anatoly Osminov.

289   "Lieutenant Alexandr Sergeev of the 297th": AI Alexandr Sergeev.

290   "The further side of the pond": Von Lehndorff, op. cit., p. 49.

291   "The reasons for the fall of Königsberg": BA, RH2/336.

291   "Beria reported that there were 32,573": RSA, 9401 om.2 g.95 237a.

291   "Dr. Karl Ludwig Mahlo": AI Karl Ludwig Mahlo.

292 "We were in tearing spirits": AI Abram Skuratovsky.

292 "Corporal Anatoly Osminov's unit": AI Anatoly Osminov.

292 "We stood close together": Von Lehndorff, op. cit., p. 59.

292 "Through the siege of Königsberg": AI Michael Wieck.

294 "The bulk of those who fled": AI Helmut Schmidt.

294 "It was our holocaust": AI a survivor of East Prussia, whose name I think it is tactful to leave anonymous.

295 "You have, of course, read": Djilas, op. cit., p. 435.

296 "In his generous instincts": Dwight Eisenhower, *Crusade in Europe* (Doubleday: 1948), pp. 473–4.

296 "Private Vitold Kubashevsky, for instance": AI Vitold Kubashevsky.

296 "All of us knew very well": Alexandr Solzhenitsyn, *Gulag Archipelago*, vol. i (Harper & Row [paperback]: 1974), p. 21.

296 "Speed, frenzy and savagery": Erickson, op. cit., pp. 466–7.

296 "We were forced to leave a land": *Documents on the Expulsions of the German People East of the Oder-Neisse Rivers,* Federal Ministry for Expellees, Refugees and War Victims, 1953.

297 "At his post on the shore": AI Vitold Kubashevsky.

297 "I do not suppose that at any moment": Quoted Gilbert, op. cit., p. 1182.

CHAPTER ELEVEN: FIRESTORMS: WAR IN THE SKY

298 "Meanwhile—still during the night": Martin Middlebrook and Chris Everitt, *Bomber Command War Diaries* (Viking: 1985), pp. 601–3.

299 "The bombing of Germany": Statistics for fatal casualties from bombing vary immensely, because so much documentation was lost in the last months of the war: reputable recent authorities offer estimates which range between a low of 305,000 and a high of 700,000. It is unlikely that this issue will ever be conclusively resolved.

302 "During the armies' advance": Weigley, op. cit., p. 668.

302 "The gross claims of our airmen": Hansen Diary, op. cit.

304 "During the past few weeks": Quoted Tedder, op. cit., p. 613.

305 "a considerable commander": Anthony Montague-Brown, *Long Sunset* (Cassell: 1995), p. 201.

306 "We should never allow": Eaker to Spaatz quoted Wesley Frank Craven and James Lee Cate, *The Army Air Forces in World War II* (University of Chicago Press: 7 vols. 1948–58), vol. iii, p. 733.

306 "after September 1944, no one": Michael Sherry, *The Rise of American Air Power* (Yale University Press: 1987), pp. 221, 250.

307 "Richard Overy, among others": See Richard Overy, *War and Economy in the Third Reich* (Oxford University Press: 1994), *Why the Allies Won* (Cape: 1995), passim. Overy's analysis has caused me to modify some of the views I adopted in my earlier book *Bomber Command* about the scale of damage inflicted on the German war economy by bombing between 1942 and 1944.

307 "[it] actually works in our favour": David Irving, *Hitler's War* (Viking: 1977), pp. 574–5.

308 "I felt that again our efforts": Tedder, op. cit., p. 607.

310 "In bright sunlight, even with": Carl Fyler, *Staying Alive* (J. H. Johnson: 1995).

310 "Each time I close": Knoke, op. cit., p. 164.

310 "Returning from bombing oil refineries": Arthur M. Miller, unpublished MS, SA.

311 "Staff-Sergeant Delbert Lambson": Delbert D. Lambson, *When I Return in Spring* (Delzona Press: 1995).

312 "I can go out on a mission": Robert Burger, unpublished MS, SA.

312 "Major Jack Ilfrey said": AI Jack Ilfrey.

312 "Nice day, but nothing for us": Unpublished MS, IWM, 92/26/1.

313 "Dear Mom": Harry Conley and Stuart G. Whittelsey, unpublished MS, "No Foxholes in the Sky," SA.

313 "We had to hang around the Halifax": Unpublished David Sokoloff MS, SA.

315 "Eddie Lovejoy, a navigator with": Eddie Lovejoy, *Better Born Lucky Than Rich* (Media: 1986), pp. 85–6.

315 "Other people in the squadron": AI Bill Winter.

316 "made you feel as if they had cleaned": Unpublished Richard Burt MS, SA.

316 "I thought a lot about our guys": AI Ira Wells.

316 "We were the Lindbergh generation": AI Harold Dorfman.

317 "We never thought about what": AI Bill Winter.

317 "Sergeant Jack Brennan": AI Jack Brennan.

318 "Our gunners never fired": AI Bill Winter.

319 "There would be seconds": Lloyd O. Kreuger, *Trials and Tribulations of a Lady* (Canyon Lake: 2001), p. 37.

319 "The flak was brutal": AI William Leek.

320 "Ammunition began to explode": Unpublished Teresa K. Flatley MS, SA.

321 "We just wanted to get it over": AI Ira Wells.

321 "Bledisloe had spent almost two": Marvin Bledisloe, *Thunderbolt!* (Van Nostrand Reinhold: 1982).

322 "Yet Major Jack Ilfrey": Jack Ilfrey, *Happy Jack's Go Buggy* (Schiffer Military: 1946).

322 "The landscape looked just like": Richard Hough, *One Boy's War* (Heinemann: 1975), p. 137.

323 "You sometimes saw too much": Ibid., p. 146.

323 "They *are* shits": Paul Richey, *Fighter Pilot* (Guild Publishing: 1990), p. 108.

323 "that we are the barbarians": Eaker to Spaatz 1.1.45 quoted Ronald Schaffer, "American Military Ethics in World War II," *Journal of American History* 67, September 1980, p. 328.

324 "CLARION hit people": AI John Zimmermann.

324 "I could see the cannon strikes": Hough, op. cit., p. 147.

324 "We sometimes thought the Allied": AI Helmut Lott.

324 "you feel as if you are flying": Jack Pitts, *P-47 Pilot* (Pitts Enterprise: 1997), pp. 74, 86.

325 "I felt sorry for the German": AI Tony Mann.

325 "There were four men unloading": Pitts, op. cit., p. 88.

325 "that it would be good to fight": Hansen Diary, op. cit., 9.21.44.

326 "an appeal to the chivalry": Guderian, op. cit., p. 418, 3.6.45.

326 "The sky became black": AI Helmut Schmidt.

326 "It was a war of despair": Von Stemann MS, op. cit., p. 153.

326 "I'll describe to you today": Second Army MD.

327 "We spend most of our lives": Ibid.

327 "At 4 o'clock, I arrived": Ibid.

327 "Everyone is convinced that no opposition": PRO, WO106/5922.

328 "We discussed why the Germans carried": Von Stemann MS, op. cit., p. 154.

328 "The Berlin diarist 'Missie' ": Vassiltchikov, op. cit., pp. 120, 148.

328 "We lived in a dark world": AI Klaus Fischer.

328 "during this period of vast": Mathilde Wolff-Monckeberg, *On the Other Side* (Pan: 1982), p. 119.

329 "I came to live in a fantasy": AI Vilda Geertz.

329 "The streetcars don't run": Second Army MD.

329 "When Joyce Kuhns fled": AI Joyce Kuhns.

329 "Hans Moser was the sixteen-year-old": AI Hans Moser.

330 "Lieutenant Henry Docherty": PRO, WO309/1621, WO309/291.

330 "On 28 February 1945": PRO, WO309/106.

331 "Bud Lindsey, a nineteen-year-old": Al Lindsey, *A Soda Jerk Goes to War* (privately published: 2001).

332 "That everything was dissolving": Von Stemann MS, op. cit.

332 "all around us was the manmade": Ibid., p. 150.

332 "I had a lot of imagination": AI Gotz Bergander.

334 "We walked slowly, for I was now": Klemperer, op. cit., pp. xvi, 500–10.

334 "It was terrible, the bodies": Ibid., p. 502.

335 "The bombing of Dresden": AI Gotz Bergander.

337 "Yet when a nation had tolerated": AI Henry Kissinger.

337 "The smell is nauseating and clings": Vassiltchikov, op. cit., p. 260.

CHAPTER TWELVE: MARCHING ON THE RHINE

338 "friendly and intimate co-operation": Tedder, op. cit., p. 638.

338 "If the field-marshal had not been": Weigley, op. cit., p. 575.

339 "So far as I can see": PRO, CAB106/1070.

339 "lit out so vigorously that he carried": Quoted Forrest Pogue, *Marshal: Organizer of Victory*, vol. iii (Viking: 1973), p. 516.

339 "to express his full dislike": Alanbrooke, op. cit., p. 653, 2.1.45.

339 "An unsatisfactory meeting with": Ibid.

340 "We must make certain": Alfred D. Chandler, *Papers of Eisenhower*, vol. iv (Johns Hopkins University Press: 1970), p. 2438.

341 "The Germans appear to be beaten": Gavin Diary, op. cit.

341 "Poor discipline was reflected": "Trench Foot," USAMHI, D769AZ no. 94 c.3.

341 "On 6 February, the Wehrmacht": BA, RH2/8496.

342 "Our battery was still fully equipped": AI Karl Godau.

342 "Panzer Lehr Division found": Helmut Ritgen, *Die Geschilhte der Panzer Lehr Division im Western 1944–45* (Stuttgart: Motorbuch Verlag, 1979), p. 276.

342 "We had to blow them up": Helmut Günther, *Von der Hitler-Jugend zur Waffen SS* (Coburg: Nation Europa Verlag, 2001), p. 252.

342 "It was 'subsistence warfare' ": AI George Schwemmer.

343 "It is essential that the change": BA, RH2/328.

343 "When I reported back to my commander": Helmut Schmidt, *Kindheit und Jugend unter Hitler* (Berlin: Siedler, 1992), p. 233.

344 "My flashlight revealed his greatly": Howard M. Randall, *War Chronicle* (Sunbelt Media: 1999), p. 7.

344 "Yet Lieutenant Tony Moody": AI Tony Moody.

344 "The casualties themselves": Brenda McBryde, *A Nurse's War* (Chatto & Windus: 1979), pp. 149–50.

345 "Tell them to go to hell": Martin Blumenson, *The Patton Papers,* vol. ii (Houghton Mifflin: 1974), p. 629.

345 "Private Charles Felix was at a battalion": Felix, op. cit., p. 65.

346 "He overdid it": Gay Diary, op. cit., 2.1.45.

346 "A few of the men we had to put": DuPuy, op. cit.

346 "Lieutenant William Devitt of the 330th": Devitt, op. cit., p. 128.

346 "Sergeant Tony Carullo's": AI Tony Carullo.

347 "When the U.S. 90th Division": NA, RG492–332, box 10.

348 "There was something a bit scary": Interview with John S. D. Eisenhower, *World War II,* May 1994.

348 "For a victorious army": NA, RG492–332, box 10.

348 "Everybody hated Veritable": AI Field-Marshal Lord Carver.

348 "Private David Williams of the 104th": David Williams MS, IWM, 98/3/1.

349 "It has been quite bloody": Turner-Cain MS, op. cit.

349 "Private Frank Rumph dashed": Frank Rumph, unpublished MS, SA.

349 "The Reichswald was the nastiest": AI Field-Marshal Lord Bramall.

350 "at the last stage before frostbite": Len Stokes, MS Diary, IWM.

350 "What's up, Frank?": Dai Evans, MS, IWM, 92/37/1.

351 "It is tough going": PRO, CAB106/1071.

351 "It was the bravest thing": AI Cliff Pettit.

351 "Every night, we kept wondering": AI John Langdon.

351 "Bomb craters and fallen trees": Captain J. L. J. Meredith, *The Story of the Seventh Battalion, the Somerset Light Infantry* (no publisher: 1945), p. 132.

352 "any action deserving of the VC": Sir Arthur Harris to the author, 8.7.77.

353 "As usual, the rough plan": Peter White, *With the Focks* (Sutton: 2001), p. 199.

353 "one young German still firing": *War History of the 4th Battalion, King's Own Scottish Borderers* (Halle: 1946), p. 143.

354 "of nuisance value only": White, op. cit., p. 219.

354 "There was never an easy way": AI Cliff Pettit and *The Regimental Journal of the Cameronians,* 1997.

355 "I do loathe all this destruction": General Sir David Fraser, *Wars and Shadows* (Penguin: 2002), p. 250.

356 "The reputation of the Waffen SS": NA, RG492–332, box 4.

357 "Twenty-two-year-old Katharina Minniger": AI Katharina Minniger.

357 "They were in a terrible state": AI Hildegarde Platten.

358 "the farmer went into a spiel": Evans MS, op. cit.

359 "undue acceptance of parental authority": PRO, WO106/5924, CI, Newssheet no. 17.

359 "this was the one period of my life": AI Henry Kissinger.

359 "Helmut Lott, a fifteen-year-old": AI Helmut Lott.

360 "on 16 March Dr. Alfred Meyer": PRO, WO106/5924.

360 "I was dismayed to look out": AI Lord Carrington.

360 "I'm going to end up defending": AI Karl Godau.

360 "Those who weaken must be": AI Rolf-Helmut Schröder.

360 "Lieutenant Tony Saurma's loader": AI Tony Saurma.

361 "Most German soldiers realize": RMDA, vol. xv 4/5, p. 28.

361 "I have four divisions, facing 22 Soviet": BA, RH2/333.

362 "On 13 March, the Luftwaffe's": Ibid.

362 "The whole cavalcade looked like": Henry Metelmann, *Through Hell for Hitler* (Spellmount: 2001), pp. 185–6.

362 "Since the issue": Second Army MD.

363 "Likewise Lieutenant Hummel": RMDA, vol. xv 4/5, p. 64.

363 "It fills me with utter gloom": Fraser, op. cit., pp. 248–9.

363 "I am here to represent": Speer, op. cit., p. 434.

363 "Most people are still": Von Lehndorff, op. cit., p. 38.

364 " 'Mind you,' said the gunner amiably": Colin McInnes, *To the Victors the Spoils* (Penguin: 1966), p. 176.

366 "It just means moving the catastrophe": Heiber and Glantz, op. cit., p. 681.

367 "what we were doing was no longer": AI Walter Schaefer-Kuhnert.

369 "The casualties to glider pilots": PRO, WO106/4348.

370 "wonderful spirit of the men": AI David Tibbs.

370 "Also, that as a young man": Downward MS, op. cit., p. 107.

371 "but then as we were about six or eight feet": Goldman, op. cit., p. 124.

372 "It was chaos": Quoted Denis Edwards, *The Devil's Own Luck* (Leo Cooper: 2001), p. 221.

373 "Peter Downward was overwhelmed": Downward MS, op. cit., pp. 109–10.

374 "One of the stranger cargoes": IWM, HS6/704.

375 "I honestly believe that he would": Alanbrooke, op. cit., p. 678, 3.26.45.

375 " 'With hindsight,' observed Kurt": Kurt von Tippelskirch, *Geschichte des Zweiten Weltkriegs* (Bonn: Athenäum-Verlag, 1951), p. 558.

375 "My only experience of war": AI John Langdon.

375 "There was an impatience, even desperation": AI John Denison.

375 "The liberation of Germany": Turner-Cain Diary, op. cit.

376 "Wilhelm Pritz had endured": AI Wilhelm Pritz.

377 "In Normandy, these had accounted": PRO, WO205/1164, ORC report no. 6, appendix A.

377 "They would grab at any straws": Cooper, op. cit., p. 211.

377 "Observers said it looked more like": Ibid., p. 240.

377 "The men as a whole are not well trained": NA, RG492–332, box 12.

378 "Under stress, not infrequently": AI David Tibbs.

378 "There was a certain reluctance": AI Roy Dixon.

378 "The willpower to keep going": AI W. F. Deedes.

378 "they are performing very well": NA, RG492–332, box 12.

379 "An officer of the Highland Light Infantry": Tom Flanagan, unpublished MS, IWM, 87/1911.

379 "He looked for places where the enemy": Andrew Wilson, *Flamethrower* (Kimber: 1984), pp. 194–5.

380 "by April 1945, one in 165": PRO, CAB106/1069.

380 "The sense that, with luck": AI General Sir David Fraser.

CHAPTER THIRTEEN: PRISONERS OF THE REICH

382 "The SS directly employed some 300,000": See Milward, op. cit., passim.

383 "They could have been quicker": AI Nikolai Maslennikov.

383 "You just accepted it": AI Ron Graydon.

383 "Tom Barker, from Eastbourne": I am indebted to Tom Barker for the opportunity to read and make use of the fascinating MS memoir of his experiences as a prisoner.

384 "Stanislas Domoradzki, a Pole": Stanislas Domoradzki, MS memoir, SA.

384 "As an officer, Captain John Killick": AI John Killick.

385 "we were told by the guards": Burt MS, op. cit.

385 "their morale was at rock bottom": Robert Harding, *Copper Wire* (Chess Mail: 2001).

385 "A twenty-year-old Liberator gunner": AI Charles Becker.

385 "I have seen men degrade themselves": Harding, op. cit.

385 "Oh, you were only inside": AI Denis Thomas.

386 "Richard Feltham was amazed": Feltham quoted Sewell, op. cit.

386 "When news of D-Day reached": Barker MS, op. cit.

386 "We were never satisfied": Peter Campbell MS, IWM, 86/35/1.

386 "Escape starts as a madness": Ibid.

386 "John Killick suffered a special difficulty": AI John Killick.

387 "The only thing that would end": George Millar, *Horned Pigeon* (Doubleday: 1946), p. 434.

387 "Their demeanour was aloof": Lindsey, op. cit.

387 "the fault of that stupid Geneva Convention": Guderian, op. cit., p. 427.

388 "Göring pointed out to Hitler": Heiber and Glantz, op. cit., p. 634.

388 "The young British soldier walked": Barker MS, op. cit.

389 "American airman Richard Burt": Burt MS, op. cit.

389 "Bill Bampton, a private of the East Surreys": Bill Bampton MS, IWM.

390 "Dr. Helmut Hugel, a German": Hugel Diary, IWM.

392 "Jerome Alexis rode on the hull": Jerome Alexis, unpublished MS, SA.

392 "I feel terrible": d'Este, *Patton*, op. cit., pp. 714–19.

393 "Every day a sort of ": Sewell, op. cit., p. 168.

393 "In Stalag XIB": AI Denis Thomas.

393 "The saga of one of these men": AI Mikhail Devyataev.

396 "Boredom is usually associated": Jerzy Herszburg, unpublished MS, IWM, 86/89/1.

398 "We have taken steps to improve": RSA, Stalin files 1135/5, Beria memorandum of 10.24.44.

398 "In the camps, many people died": AI Nikolai Maslennikov.

400 "Zinaida Mikhailova spent three years": AI Zinaida Mikhailova.

401 "Edith Gabor shared with": AI Edith Gabor.

404 "In my opinion, a disproportionate": PRO, FO371/42817 WR993.

404 "Gennady Trofimov was eight when he": AI Gennady Trofimov.

405 "Viktor Mamontov was sixteen when he": AI Viktor Mamontov.

408 "People soon realized that resistance": AI Ted Van Meurs.

408 "At first when they took Jews": AI Bert Egbertus.

408 "For most of the population": AI Hans Cramer.

408 "His attitude is typical": Second Army MD.

408 "There is considerable indifference": Turner-Cain Diary, op. cit.

409 "security doubts on the reliability": PRO, WO219/3738.

409 "The discovery that liberation": PRO, WO219/11.

409 "There were some nice German officers": AI Cas Tromp.

409 "It was not so bad for Dutch people": AI Bert Egbertus.

409 "Ted Van Meurs, a medical student": AI Ted Van Meurs.

410 "Not a person was to be seen": Quoted van der Zee, op. cit., p. 46.

410 "It is unacceptable that bad": Second Army MD.

410 "Eight-year-old Roelof Olderman": AI Roelof Olderman.

411 "Cas Tromp was sent almost daily": AI Cas Tromp.

411 "One day, Bert Egbertus's mother": AI Bert Egbertus.

411 "So too were Jan and Tom Wempe": AI Theodore Wempe.

411 "Willem van den Broek's mother": AI Willem van den Broek.

412 "My mother was crying all the time": AI Hans Cramer.

413 "Theodore Wempe thrilled each time": AI Theodore Wempe.

414 "Take a litre of water": van der Zee, op. cit., p. 150.

414 "Jan de Boer, one of nine children": Jan de Boer letter to the author, 11.9.02.

414 "A Dutchman said he learned that winter": van der Zee, op. cit., p. 65.

414 "Twelve-year-old Willem van": AI Willem van den Broek.

415 "the shrunken bodies were lying": van der Zee, op. cit., p. 158.

415 "The expression": Ibid., p. 190.

415 "Bertha Schonfeld felt irrationally safe": AI Bertha Schonfeld.

415 "The British Foreign Office told the Dutch": Norman Longmate, *Hitler's Rockets* (Hutchinson: 1985), p. 320.

415 "Antoinette Hamminga, a teenager": Antoinette Hamminga letter to the author, 1.10.03.

416 "an example should be made": PRO, HW/1 3709.

417 "Extremely fierce fighting": Ibid.

417 "Surely you must know the war": Elsa Caspers, *To Save a Life* (Macdonald: 1995), p. 134.

417 "We did it just for fun": Annie van Beek letter to the author, 11.18.02.

CHAPTER FOURTEEN: COLLAPSE IN THE WEST

418 "whose strategic significance was": Weigley, op. cit., p. 678.

419 "Ridgway told the German colonel": Gerald Devlin, *Paratrooper!* (Robson: 1979), p. 633.

419 "Lieutenant Rolf-Helmut Schröder": AI Rolf-Helmut Schröder.

419 "what looked like a dark": Robert Burger, unpublished MS, SA.

420 "When Ike's son John": Bradley, op. cit., p. 397.

421 "The PM is increasingly": Alanbrooke, op. cit., p. 680, 4.1.45.

421 "there would definitely be a race": Quoted d'Este, *Eisenhower*, op. cit., p. 691.

422 "More than one major historian": Weigley, op. cit., p. 687.

422 "efforts to make sure that the Americans": Cornelius Ryan, *The Last Battle* (Collins: 1966), p. 185.

422 "Eisenhower might well have sent": Stephen Ambrose, *Eisenhower: The Soldier* (Allen & Unwin: 1984), p. 392.

423 " 'I decided,' he wrote in his": Eisenhower, op. cit., p. 433.

423 " 'Apparently,' Murphy wrote": *Foreign Relations of the U.S.*, vol. iii (U.S. Government Printing Office: 1965), p. 229.

423 "If you look at the world geopolitically": AI Henry Kissinger.

425 "Staff-Sergeant Henry Kissinger": Ibid.

426 "There was little that was cheerful": Tedder, op. cit., p. 688.

427 "Allied officers often enlisted": NA, RG492–332, box 12.

427 "The leading vehicle got knocked": Leakey MS, op. cit.

427 "It seemed a stupid time to die": Hough, op. cit., p. 169.

427 "On the Elbe front a weakish": PRO, HW1/3715, Ultra.

428 "a deficiency of leadership": Ibid.

428 "Private Ralph Gordon of First Army's": Gordon, op. cit., p. 87.

428 "In Lieutenant Howard Randall's": Randall, op. cit., p. 134.

428 "Consideration was not given to sick": Major G. Gatling, copy report held by Werner Kleeman.

428 "A German woman handed": AI Werner Kleeman.

428 "As men of the British 7th Somersets": Stokes MS Diary.

429 "Lieutenant-Colonel Ferdinand Chesarek": Chesarek oral history interview, op. cit.

429 "One night a British sentry woke": Wilson, op. cit., p. 199.

429 "A contemporary British report": PRO, WO106/4348, report no. 32.

429 "Did he have a Luger?": Felix, op. cit., p. 143.

429 "Lieutenant Howard Randall's": Randall, op. cit., p. 128.

429 "Please do not let your men rape": AI David Tibbs.

430 "During street fighting in Bremen": White, op. cit., p. 434.

430 "The Germans were very hungry": AI W. F. Deedes.

430 "Rape became a large problem": "Military Offenders," USAMHI, D769AZ no. 84.

430 "Sergeant Colin McInnes gazed": McInnes, op. cit., p. 161.

430 "A British war correspondent": Macdonald Hastings of *Picture Post*, private communication to the author.

430 "In 'Red' Thompson's platoon": AI "Red" Thompson.

431 "Lieutenant Tom Flanagan of the British": Flanagan MS, op. cit.

431 "Pitiable middle-aged lady": Proctor, op. cit., p. 128.

432 "In 21st Army Group throughout": *Report of the Army and Air Force Court Martial Committee,* Cmd 7608, 1949.

432 "The countryfolk and their houses and farms": Turner-Cain Diary, op. cit.

432 "An escaped Canadian pilot": Steel-Brownlie MS, op. cit.

432 "Outside the town of Büdingen": AI Helmut Lott.

432 "The attitude of civilians was really": PRO, WO205/622.

432 "It sure makes you feel silly": Quoted Robert Kee, *1945: The World We Fought For* (Hamish Hamilton: 1985), p. 210.

433 "Private Denis Christian": AI Denis Christian.

433 "With hindsight, it seemed": Downward MS, op. cit.

433 "*Es ist alles*": IWM, H56/704.

433 "Sergeant Robert Brookshire": Robert Brookshire, unpublished MS, SA.

434 "There was some of the hardest fighting": Hansen Papers, box 45B, USAMHI.

434 "Fanaticism is nasty": AI Captain "Dim" Robbins.

434 "They were absolute sods": AI Patrick Hennessy.

434 "A comrade noticed Fuller's body": Steel-Brownlie MS, op. cit.

434 "Clothing and underwear were caught": Ibid.

435 "Once we got into Germany": AI General Sir David Fraser.

435 "Germans are becoming increasingly bitter": PRO, WO106/5924.

435 "Charles Farrell, a Scots Guards": Charles Farrell, *Reflections* (Pentland Press: 2000), p. 131.

435 "A British tank officer glimpsed": Steel-Brownlie MS, op. cit.

436 "In Germany it was a swan": AI Roy Dixon.

436 "War is a very fatiguing experience": AI W. F. Deedes.

436 "Until the very last moment": AI Viktor Mamontov.

436 "The phrase 'that's what we are fighting for' ": Dr. A. R. Horwell MS, IWM, 91/21/3.

437 "At Belsen, I felt a curious elation": AI David Tibbs.

437 "Take no initiative in organizing": RMDA, vol. xv 5/4, p. 337, order of 4.24.45.

437 "A British officer complained to the Russians": Ibid., pp. 353–4, Moscow correspondence with Admiral Archer, 5.15.45.

437 "After long journeys": PRO, PREM 3/398/4 f. 276, quoted Gilbert, op. cit., p. 1312.

437 "If the British and Americans had not": RSA, 9401 om.2 g.97.

438 "Berlin never seemed so peaceful": von Stemann MS, op. cit.

438 "We pretended that, having been through": Ibid.

439 "The participants appeared to take it all": Ibid.

440 "Ilse Bayer, twenty-five-year-old": Unpublished MS, "My Life in Germany," IWM, 95/13/1.

440 "Eleonore von Joest, who had trekked": AI Eleonore von Joest.

441 "Henner Pflug fell into conversation": AI Henner Pflug.

441 "Lieutenant Rolf-Helmut Schröder served": AI Rolf-Helmut Schröder.

441 "Late in March after his unit": AI Helmut Schmidt.

442 "When Sergeant George Schwemmer": AI George Schwemmer.

442 "In the path of Konev's armies": AI Helmut Fromm.

442 "On 5 April, Victor Klemperer sat": Klemperer, op. cit., pp. 541–2.

443 "A delegation of diplomats from the Japanese": PRO, HW/1 3715.

443 "Captain Walter Schaefer-Kuhnert": AI Walter Schaefer-Kuhnert.

443 "Moser and his young comrades": AI Hans Moser.

444 "Captain Mackert, one of its battalion": H. Spaeter and W. Schramm, *Die Geschichte des Panzerkorps Grossdeutschland* (Bielefeld: 1958), p. 665.

444 "The atmosphere was truly hopeless": Tiemann, op. cit., pp. 277–8.

444 "At the makeshift hospital in the school": AI Melany Borck.

445 "The flares being dropped by aircraft": Fleming MS, IWM.

445 "Lieutenant Philip Dark": Philip Dark MS, IWM.

CHAPTER FIFTEEN: "THE EARTH WILL SHAKE AS WE LEAVE THE SCENE"

448 "I was a professional—I had to do my duty": AI Karl-Günther von Hase.

449 "Suddenly, Krulik saw an 85mm anti-tank": AI Valentin Krulik.

449 "We were at the end of our physical strength": Meyer, op. cit., p. 302.

450 "The situation is hopeless": BA, RH2/336.

450 "Our problem in 1945": AI Valentin Krulik.

451 "The garrison of Vienna": BA, RH2/336.

451 "He was a son of East Prussia": K. Dieckert and H. Grossman, *Der Kampf um Ostpreussen* (Munich: Gräfe und Unzer, 1960), p. 165.

451 "I still believe in some kind of miracle": Quoted J. Thorwald, *Es begann an der Weichsel* (Stuttgart: Steingrüber: 1950), p. 262.

451 "On 12 March, Russians found sixteen members": RMDA, vol. xv 4/5, pp. 211–12, 2nd Belorussian Front report of 3.12.45.

451 "Many Germans in areas we have occupied": Ibid., report of 4.4.45, p. 213.

452 "A gun would fire": M. E. Katukov, *Na Ostrie Glavnovo Udara*, 2nd edn. (Moscow: Voenizdat, 1976), p. 386.

452 "Lieutenant Gennady Ivanov": AI Gennady Ivanov.

454 "The colonel looked about inquisitively": H. Schaufler, *1945... Panzer an der Weichsel* (Stuttgart: Motorbuch-Verlag, 1979), p. 102.

454 "Fourteen-year-old Erich Pusch": AI Erich Pusch.

455 "Twenty-five-year-old Frieda Engler": AI Elfi Kowitz.

455   "The Russians swept into the air-raid shelter": AI Anita Bartsch.

456   "The whole place stank of corpses": AI Vasily Krylov.

456   "It was very difficult to maintain order": AI Fyodor Romanovsky.

456   "Yelena Kogan's commanding officer": AI Yelena Kogan.

457   "preposterous…I used such argumentative": Guderian, op. cit., p. 402.

458   "If all our gauleiters in the east": Heiber and Glantz, op. cit., p. 672.

459   "we saw it as our death sentence": AI Karl Godau.

460   "This petty officer is certain of my full": *Ostseebefehl*, Nr. 19, 4.19.45, IWM.

460   "his fists raised, his cheeks flushed": Guderian, op. cit., pp. 414–15.

460   "No German town will be declared": BA, RH2/336.

460   "a joke. These are Indians who": Heiber and Glantz, op. cit., pp. 711–12.

461   "One of the last signals to OKH": BA, RH2/336.

461   "I found myself commanding men of sixty": AI Tony Saurma.

461   "As an inglorious refugee from Berlin": Heiber and Glantz, op. cit., p. 722.

461   "Everyone now has a chance to choose": Rudolf Semmler, *Goebbels: The Man Next to Hitler* (Westhouse: 1947), p. 194.

463   "In the last days of the war": Temkin, op. cit., p. 215.

463   "We'd all had enough": AI Nikolai Ponomarev.

463   "In the last month, especially": AI Vladimir Gormin.

463   "Many have proved unstable in action": Ministry of Defence Archives, *The Great Patriotic War*, ed. Major-General V. A. Zolotarev (Terra: 1995), vol. xv 4/5, p. 152.

463   "betrayed us in 1941 and they will betray": Ibid., p. 153.

463   "They don't look like soldiers": Ibid.

463   "I wanted to fight, because everybody else": AI Nikolai Dubrovsky.

464   "Many Germans seemed to feel that": AI Pavel Nikiforov.

464   "a change of attitude towards prisoners": RMDA, vol. xv 4/5, p. 120.

464   "I shall never forgive Zhukov for that folly": AI Yury Ryakhovsky.

465   "I never thought I'd make it": AI Vasily Filimonenko.

465   "A Sergeant Safronov reported seeing": RMDA, vol. xv 4/5, p. 95.

465   "The divisional engineer Lieutenant-Colonel Lomov": Ibid., p. 89, Political Department Report of 4.18.45.

466   "The further we got": AI Vasily Filimonenko.

466   "nineteen-year-old Helga Braunschweig": While all other names given in the text of this book are authentic, this woman asked for her identity to be protected by a pseudonym, because of embarrassment about her account of rape by the Russians.

467   "Any commander who shows himself": Quoted RMDA, vol. xv 4/5, p. 95.

468   "Marshal Zhukov's troops are now within": Ibid., p. 160, 4.20.45.

468   "In the course of three days the infantry": Ibid., p. 96.

468   "Due to the slowness of our advance": Ibid., p. 515.

469   "In Wilmersdorf, the local situation": Brigadier J. S. W. Stone Papers, LHA.

469   "Owing to the gravity": PRO, HW/13715, Ultra.

469   "The first really wounded man": Stone Papers, LHA.

469   "Third Guards Tank Army is conducting": RMDA, vol. xv 5/4, p. 160.

469   "I keep being told that operations": Ibid., p. 101.

470 "She's English!": Stone Papers, LHA.

471 "The enemy knows I am here": Heiber and Glantz, op. cit., pp. 718–19.

471 "Today I will lie down a little more": Ibid., p. 730.

471 "The whole scene was apocalyptic": AI Yelena Kogan.

472 "commanders are taking serious steps": RMDA, vol. xv 5/4, pp. 245–6, report of 5.2.45.

472 "It was crazy!": AI Bruno Bochum.

473 "Johannes and Regina Krakowitz seldom": AI Regina Krakowitz.

474 "A deputation of diplomats from the Japanese": RSA, 9401 om.2 g.95 1–1 283.

474 "A Wehrmacht officer emerged": RMDA, vol. xv 5/4, p. 223, report of 4.24.45.

474 "Thank God there will be no more bombing": AI Regina Krakowitz.

474 "Was pushed to the ground": Margrit Hug diary loaned to the author.

475 "The Germans who fought to the last": AI Yury Ryakhovsky.

475 "It seemed so strange, when the end": AI Vasily Filimonenko.

475 "I disliked the idea of behaving": AI Yury Ryakhovsky.

475 "I was here, too": AI Vasily Krylov.

476 "Mutti decided she did not want": Stone Papers, LHA, anon. narrative.

476 "Nothing is left of Berlin but memories": Jeremy Noakes and Geoffrey Pridham eds., *Nazism 1919–45* (Exeter University Press: 1974), 4 doc. 1397, p. 667.

CHAPTER SIXTEEN: THE BITTER END

477 "The Germany in which we found ourselves": Moorehead, op. cit., p. 260.

478 "It was bitter to learn that Goebbels's": von Stemann MS, op. cit.

478 "People had so much hatred": AI Valentin Krulik.

478 "No German soldier would have behaved": AI Hans Siwik.

479 "Red soldiers during the first weeks": *Congressional Record*, U.S. Senate, 12.4.45, p. 11,374.

479 "On the night of 2 May": RSA, 9401 om.2 g.95 1–1 294.

479 "Vlassov's men were kicked to death": AI Gennady Ivanov.

479 "A day or two before the end": AI Valentin Krulik.

479 "Yelena Kogan, the NKVD interpreter": AI Yelena Kogan.

480 "Let us not kid ourselves": AI Vasily Filimonenko.

480 "What the Red Army did in Germany": AI Yelena Kogan.

480 "The British people were surprised": Fraser, op. cit., p. 257.

480 "Dorothea Goesse, wife of an Austrian": AI Leopold Goesse.

481 "I did not mourn Hitler": AI Karl Godau.

481 "I knew nothing about the Holocaust": AI Maria Brauwers.

481 "Corporal Helmut Fromm": AI Helmut Fromm.

483 "The fourteen-year-olds were very dangerous": AI W. F. Deedes.

483 "we felt like butchers": Walter L. Brown, *Up Front with US* (privately published: 1979), p. 490.

483 "The rules of war got very fractured": AI W. F. Deedes.

483 "After a certain amount of argument": Neave Diary, op. cit.

483   "They always put on their best": Ron Gladman, *Citizen Soldier* (West Somerset Free Press: 1995), p. 63.

483   "Field-Marshal von Manstein": Alexandr Stahlberg, *Bounden Duty* (Brassey's: 1990), p. 400.

484   "He told Krulik to investigate": AI Valentin Krulik.

484   "An onlooker in the village of Niemegle": von Stemann MS, op. cit.

484   "It's over, men": AI Gottfried Selzer.

486   "I thought it was too late now": PM's minute, D.121/5 4.24.45, quoted Gilbert, op. cit., p. 1310.

487   "looked like men in a dream": War Diary, GSHO, 1 Cdn Corps, appendix 43.

487   "Flight-Lieutenant Richard Hough": Hough, op. cit., p. 150.

487   "I felt a great sadness": AI Vasily Kudryashov.

488   "We didn't celebrate the end of the war": Gladman, op. cit., p. 86.

488   "three beautiful Red Army reconnaissance": AI Gennady Trofimov.

488   "Lieutenant Gennady Ivanov was in Rostock": AI Gennady Ivanov.

488   "Inge Stolten, a Düsseldorf housewife": AI Eggert Stolten.

489   "We were so indoctrinated that we had never": AI Jutta Dietze.

489   "In a cell in Moscow's Butykri prison": AI Karl-Günther von Hase.

489   "Now life begins!": AI Eleonor von Joest.

489   "Colonel, the war is over": AI Vladimir Gormin.

489   "We did not mind doing this": AI Waltraut Ptack.

489   "I suppose I should feel elated": Cross Papers, IWM, 91/8/1.

489   "Everything we had fought for": AI Hans-Otto Polluhmer.

490   "Every day seemed a festival": AI Theodore Wempe.

490   "In a little town outside Amsterdam": AI Bob Stompas.

490   "Germany and Russia have suffered": RSA, 9401 om.2 g.96.

491   "If a Russian soldier violates you": Ruth Andreas-Friedrich, *Shauplatz Berlin*, (Frankfurt am Main: Suhrkamp, 1984), pp. 37–40.

491   " 'My dears,' he said apologetically": Mrs. A. S. C. McVean MS, IWM.

492   "to dive for cover in the Wehrmacht": Peter Padfield, *Dönitz* (Cassell: 2001), p. 423.

492   "Martin Mutschmann, gauleiter of Saxony": RSA, 9401 om.2 g.96.

492   "If the Russians get at them": AI Gotz Bergander.

493   "I don't think": Horwell MS, op. cit.

493   "expected to be ill-treated": Moorehead, op. cit., p. 221.

493   "You do not understand how brutal": Harding, op. cit.

494   "When Corporal Harry Trinder was freed": Harry Trinder MS, IWM, 85/8/1.

494   "The wife of a large estate-owner": Ann Villiers MS, IWM.

494   "Soon after Texan GI Bud Lindsey": Lindsey, op. cit.

495   "We had not *smelt*": AI Klaus Fischer.

495   "Sixteen-year-old Corporal Helmut Fromm's": AI Helmut Fromm.

495   "The family of sixteen-year-old Hans Moser": AI Hans Moser.

496   "Captain Leopold Goesse watched": AI Leopold Goesse.

496   "What extraordinary people the Germans are": AI W. F. Deedes.

497   "Think how many roads and railways": RSA, 9401 om.2 g.99.

497   "whispered to his interpreter that he had something": Ibid., g.97.

497   "Von Rundstedt, being driven as a captive": NA, RG492–332, box 12.

497   "They professed to be outraged": RSA, 9401 om.2 g.96.

498   "Were you a professional soldier?": Williams, op. cit., p. 300.

498   "There were thousands of men": Carl Basham MS, SA.

498   "The NKVD complained that such unilateral": RSA, 9401 om.2 g.96.

499   "Colonel-General Hesleni": Ibid.

499   "In the east, however, it was another": RSA, 9401 om.2 g.97.

499   "Our men had dropped their guard": AI Gennady Klimenko.

499   "At first they mobbed us": Piotr Tareczynski MS, IWM.

499   "When Zinaida Mikhailova saw the first": AI Zinaida Mikhailova.

500   "When Veta Kogakevich was liberated": AI Veta Kogakevich.

500   "We felt too exhausted to celebrate": Herszburg MS, op. cit.

500   "Nothing had prepared us for the camps": AI Dorothy Beavers.

500   "Any Italians here?": AI David Pecora.

501   "Why do you care for the Jews first?": AI Henry Kissinger.

501   "displayed no emotion at all": AI Cliff Pettit.

501   "For the last six weeks": AI Nikolai Maslennikov.

501   "Sometimes we despaired for these men": McBryde, op. cit., p. 169.

501   "One night the farmer with whom": AI Jutta Dietze.

502   "Twenty-two-year-old Private Harold Lindstrom": Lindstrom MS, op. cit.

502   "Private Henry Williams, a New Yorker": Donald T. Peak, *Fire Mission* (Sunflower University Press: 2001), p. 189.

502   "What good is all awareness of the peril": Klemperer, op. cit., pp. 584–5.

503   "You must have been fascists": AI Ibragim Dominov.

503   "Lieutenant Tony Saurma of the Grossdeutschland": AI Tony Saurma.

503   "When Ursula Salzer escaped": AI Ursula Salzer.

504   "Is there any place that is free from evil?": Evelyn Waugh, *Unconditional Surrender* (Chapman & Hall: 1961).

505   "An NKVD report of 26 May": RSA, 9401 om.2 g.96.

505   "Genrikh Naumovich survived Mauthausen": AI Genrikh Naumovich.

506   "Eighteen-year-old Viktor Mamontov": AI Viktor Mamontov.

506   "Most of the people from our village": AI Valya Brekeleva.

506   "Georgi Semenyak, who survived": AI Georgi Semenyak.

506   "Captain Vasily Legun, a Soviet bomber": AI Vasily Legun.

508   "I grew up in a world in which": AI Anita Barsch.

509   "translated the nation's tragedy": D. Volkogonov, *Stalin, Triumph and Tragedy* (Weidenfeld & Nicolson: 1991), p. 509.

510   "After the defeat of Japan": Quoted Maurice Matloff, *Strategic Planning for Coalition Warfare 1943–44* (Department of the Army: 1959), pp. 533–4.

510   "This is what we have been fighting for": Robert Rhodes James ed., *"Chips": The Diaries of Sir Henry Channon* (Weidenfeld & Nicolson: 1967), p. 414.

511   "Bands of Army Krajowa bandits": RSA, 9401 om.2 g.96.

512   "The logistical difficulties were surmountable": Roy Jenkins, *Churchill* (Macmillan: 2001), pp. 783–6.

INDEX

GRATEFUL ACKNOWLEDGMENT IS MADE FOR PERMISSION
TO REPRODUCE THE FOLLOWING ILLUSTRATIONS:

PHOTO INSERT 1

Maria Brauwers: page 9, bottom left.

Camera Press: page 4, top right.

Peter Carrington; page 15, bottom left.

Sergeant Otto Crantz: page 8, bottom right.

William Devitt: page 14, bottom right.

Mikhail Devyataev: page 10, bottom right.

Helmut Fromm: page 9, top left.

Karl Godau: page 8, center right.

J. Curtis Goldman: page 14, bottom left.

Vladimir Gormin: page 11, bottom left.

Hulton Archive/Getty Images: page 2, bottom; page 4, top left, bottom left, and center right; page 5, bottom left and top right; page 7, top and bottom; page 12, bottom; page 13, bottom left; page 15, top right; page 16, bottom left and bottom right.

Evsei Igolnik: page 11, top.

Imperial War Museum: page 1, top; page 2, top; page 3, top and bottom; page 6, top and bottom; page 12, top left and top right; page 13, top and bottom right; page 16, top.

Gennady Ivanov: page 10, top right.

Dr. Henry Kissinger: page 15, bottom right.

Vasily Kudrashov: page 10, top left.

Zinaida Mikhailova: page 11, bottom right.

Tony Moody: page 14, top left.

Hans Moser: page 8, bottom left.

Polish Underground Movement Study Trust: page 1, bottom.

Popperfoto: page 4, bottom right.

Jack Reynolds: page 3, bottom.

Klaus Salzer: page 9, top right.

Alexandr Sergeev: page 10, bottom left.

Paul von Stemann: page 8, top right.

Dr. David Tibbs: page 14, top right.

TRH Pictures: page 15, top left.

Michael Wieck; page 9, bottom right.

Joe Volmar: page 8, center left.

Ullstein Bild: page 5, top left, center right, and bottom right; page 8, top left.

PHOTO INSERT 2

akg-images: page 15, top left.

Harold Dorfman: page 6, top and center.

Hulton Archive/Getty Images: page 9, bottom left and right; page 10, top and bottom; page 12, top and center; page 14, center and bottom left; page 15, bottom; page 16, top, center, and bottom.

Imperial War Museum: page 3, bottom; page 4, top and bottom; page 5, top and bottom; page 7, top; page 8, top and bottom; page 9, top; page 12, bottom; page 13, top; page 14, top and bottom right.

Lee Miller Archives: page 13, bottom.

Popperfoto: page 6, bottom; page 15, top right.

Time Life Pictures/Getty Images: page 7, bottom.

Sir Max Hastings was a foreign correspondent for many years, reporting from more than sixty countries for BBC TV and the *Evening Standard*. He has reported on conflicts in the Middle East, Indochina, Angola, India, Zimbabwe, and finally, in the 1982 Falklands War. He has presented historical documentaries for television, including a series on the Korean War. In 2003 he presented a documentary on Churchill and his generals. Hastings is the recipient of numerous awards from the United Kingdom for his books and journalism, including Journalist of the Year in 1982, and Editor of the Year in 1988. He has written eighteen books on military history and current events. *Bomber Command* earned the Somerset Maugham Prize for nonfiction; *The Battle for the Falklands* and *Overlord: D-Day and the Battle for Normandy* also received awards. For sixteen years, he was successively editor in chief of the *Daily Telegraph* and the *Evening Standard,* from which he retired in 2002. Hastings has published two memoirs, *Going to the Wars* (2000) about his experiences as a war correspondent, and *Editor* (2003) about his time running newspapers. He makes his home outside London and continues to contribute to newspapers on political and defense issues, as well as writing books.

A NOTE ON THE TYPE

This book was set in Janson, a typeface long thought to have been made by the Dutchman Anton Janson, who was a practicing typefounder in Leipzig during the years 1668–1687. However, it has been conclusively demonstrated that these types are actually the work of Nicholas Kis (1650–1702), a Hungarian, who most probably learned his trade from the master Dutch typefounder Dirk Voskens. The type is an excellent example of the influential and sturdy Dutch types that prevailed in England up to the time William Caslon (1692–1766) developed his own incomparable designs from them.

COMPOSED BY NORTH MARKET STREET GRAPHICS, LANCASTER, PENNSYLVANIA

PRINTED AND BOUND BY BERRYVILLE GRAPHICS, BERRYVILLE, VIRGINIA

DESIGNED BY ROBERT C. OLSSON